A FRAMEWORK FOR MARKETING MANAGEMENT

Second Edition

Philip Kotler

Northwestern University

Prentice
Hall

Pearson Education International

Acquisitions Editor: Wendy Craven
Editor-in-Chief: Jeff Shelstad
Assistant Editor: Melissa Pellerano
Editorial Assistant: Danielle Rose Serra
Media Project Manager: Anthony Palmiotto
Marketing Manager: Michelle O'Brien
Marketing Assistant: Amanda Fisher
Managing Editor (Production): Judy Leale
Production Editor: Keri Jean Miksza
Production Assistant: Joe DeProspero
Permissions Supervisor: Suzanne Grappi
Associate Director, Manufacturing: Vinnie Scelta
Production Manager: Arnold Vila
Manufacturing Buyer: Diane Peirano
Design Manager: Maria Lange
Designer: Blair Brown
Interior Design: Janet Slowik/Blair Brown
Cover Design: Blair Brown
Cover Illustration/Photo: Omni-Photo Communications, Inc./Grace Davies
Interior Chapter-Opening Image: Digital Vision Ltd.
Manager, Print Production: Christy Mahon
Composition: UG / GGS Information Services, Inc.
Full-Service Project Management: Heidi Straight
Printer/Binder: Courier-Westford

Credits and acknowledgments borrowed from other sources and reproduced, with permission, in this textbook appear on appropriate page within text.

This book may be sold only in those countries to which it is consigned by Pearson Education International. It is not to be re-exported and it is not for sale in the U.S.A., Mexico, or Canada.

Pearson Education LTD.
Pearson Education Australia PTY, Limited
Pearson Education Singapore, Pte. Ltd
Pearson Education North Asia Ltd
Pearson Education, Canada, Ltd
Pearson Educación de Mexico, S.A. de C.V.
Pearson Education–Japan
Pearson Education Malaysia, Pte. Ltd
Pearson Education Upper Saddle River, New Jersey

10 9 8 7 6 5 4
ISBN 0-13-120427-0

Brief Contents

Preface xvi

Part I   UNDERSTANDING MARKETING MANAGEMENT 1

1. Defining Marketing for the Twenty-First Century 1
2. Adapting Marketing to the New Economy 23
3. Building Customer Satisfaction, Value, and Retention 37

Part II   ANALYZING MARKETING OPPORTUNITIES 57

4. Winning Markets Through Strategic Planning, Implementation, and Control 57
5. Understanding Markets, Market Demand, and the Marketing Environment 85
6. Analyzing Consumer Markets and Buyer Behavior 111
7. Analyzing Business Markets and Buyer Behavior 131
8. Dealing with the Competition 148
9. Identifying Market Segments and Selecting Target Markets 170

Part III   MAKING MARKETING DECISIONS 188

10. Developing, Positioning, and Differentiating Products Through the Life Cycle 188
11. Setting Product and Brand Strategy 211
12. Designing and Managing Services 228
13. Designing Pricing Strategies and Programs 244

Part IV   MANAGING AND DELIVERING MARKETING PROGRAMS 266

14. Designing and Managing Value Networks and Marketing Channels 266
15. Managing Retailing, Wholesaling, and Market Logistics 284
16. Designing and Managing Integrated Marketing Communications 302
17. Managing the Sales Force 332

Glossary 349

Index 353

Contents

Preface   xvi

Part I   **UNDERSTANDING MARKETING MANAGEMENT**   **1**

1.   **Defining Marketing for the Twenty-First Century**   **1**
Marketing Management at eBAY   1
The New Economy   2
Marketing Tasks   4
The Scope of Marketing   *4*
The Decisions That Marketers Make   *5*
Marketing Concepts and Tools   *6*
Defining Marketing   *6*
Core Marketing Concepts   *6*
Company Orientations Toward the Marketplace   12
The Production Concept   *12*
The Product Concept   *13*
The Selling Concept   *13*
The Marketing Concept   *13*
Integrated Marketing   *15*
Profitability   *15*
Marketing Skills: Internal Marketing   *16*
The Customer Concept   *16*
The Societal Marketing Concept   *17*
How Business and Marketing Are Changing   18
Company Responses and Adjustments   *18*
Marketer Responses and Adjustments   *19*
Executive Summary   19
Notes   20

2.   **Adapting Marketing to the New Economy**   **23**
Marketing Management at NTT DoCoMo   23
The Major Drivers of the New Economy   24
Digitalization and Connectivity   *24*
Disintermediation and Reintermediation   *24*

Customization and Customerization   25

Industry Convergence   25

How Business Practices Are Changing   25

How Marketing Practices Are Changing: E-Business   26

Internet Domains: B2C (Business-to-Customer)   27

Internet Domains: B2B (Business-to-Business)   27

Internet Domains: C2C (Consumer-to-Consumer)   27

Internet Domains: C2B (Consumer-to-Business)   28

Pure-Click versus Brick-and-Click Companies   29

How Marketing Practices Are Changing: Setting Up
Web Sites   30

Designing an Attractive Web Site   30

Marketing Skills: Web Site Design   31

Placing Ads and Promotion Online   31

Building a Revenue and Profit Model   32

How Marketing Practices Are Changing: Customer Relationship
Marketing   33

Customer Databases and Database Marketing   34

Data Warehouse and Datamining   34

Executive Summary   35

Notes   36

3.   **Building Customer Satisfaction, Value,
and Retention   37**

Marketing Management at Caterpillar   37

Defining Customer Value and Satisfaction   38

Customer Perceive Value   38

Total Customer Satisfaction   40

The Nature of High-Performance Businesses   41

Stakeholders   41

Processes   41

Resources   42

Organization and Organizational Culture   42

Delivering Customer Value and Satisfaction   43

Value Chain   43

The Value Delivery Network   44

Attracting and Retaining Customers   44

Attracting Customers   44

Lost Customers and Customer Lifetime Value   45

The Need for Customer Retention   45

Customer Relationship Marketing: The Key   47

Marketing Skills: Winning Back Lost Customers 48
Forming Strong Customer Bonds 49
Customer Profitability: The Ultimate Test 50
Implementing Total Quality Management 52
Executive Summary 53
Notes 54

Part II   ANALYZING MARKETING OPPORTUNITIES 57

4. Winning Markets Through Strategic Planning, Implementation, and Control 57
Marketing Management at Starbucks 57
Strategic Planning: Three Key Areas and Four Organizational Levels 58
Corporate and Division Strategic Planning 59
Defining the Corporate Mission 59
Establishing Strategic Business Units (SBUs) 60
The Boston Consulting Group Approach 61
The General Electric Model 62
Critique of Portfolio Models 64
Planning New Businesses, Downsizing Older Businesses 64
Business Strategic Planning 65
Business Mission 65
SWOT Analysis 65
Goal Formulation 66
Strategy Formulation 67
Program Formulation and Implementation 67
Marketing Skills: Managing Implementation 68
Feedback and Control 69
The Marketing Process 69
The Value-Delivery Sequence 69
Steps in the Marketing Process 70
Product Planning: The Nature and Contents of a Marketing Plan 71
Managing the Marketing Process 72
Organization of the Marketing Department 72
Building a Companywide Marketing Orientation 75
Injecting More Creativity into the Organization 76
Marketing Implementation 76
Evaluation and Control 76
Annual-Plan Control 77
Profitability Control 79

Efficiency Control   79

Strategic Control   80

Executive Summary   80

Case Pilot   81

Notes   82

5.   **Understanding Markets, Market Demand, and the Marketing Environment   85**

Marketing Management at Tesco   85

Supporting Marketing Decisions with Information, Intelligence, and Research   86

Internal Records System   87

Marketing Intelligence System   87

Marketing Research   89

Marketing Decision Support System   94

Forecasting and Demand Measurement   94

Which Market to Measure?   94

Demand Measurement   95

Company Demand and Sales Forecast   96

Estimating Current Demand   97

Estimating Future Demand   98

Macroenvironmental Trends and Forces   99

Marketing Skills: Spotting Trends   99

Demographic Environment   100

Economic Environment   102

Natural Environment   103

Technological Environment   103

Political-Legal Environment   104

Social-Cultural Environment   105

Shifts of Secondary Cultural Values Through Time   106

Executive Summary   106

Case Pilot   107

Notes   108

6.   **Analyzing Consumer Markets and Buyer Behavior   111**

Marketing Management at Whirlpool   111

How and Why Consumers Buy   112

Cultural Factors   113

Social Factors   113

Personal Factors   115
Psychological Factors   117
The Consumer Buying Decision Process   120
Buying Roles   120
Buying Behavior   120
The Stages of the Buying Decision Process   121
Marketing Skills: Gauging Customer Satisfaction   125
Executive Summary   127
Notes   127

7.   Analyzing Business Markets and Buyer Behavior   131
Marketing Management at Covisint   131
What Is Organizational Buying?   132
The Business Market Versus the Consumer Market   132
Socialized Organizational Markets   133
Business Buying Situations   136
Participants in the Business Buying Process   137
Major Influences on Business Buying   138
Marketing Skills: Marketing Across Cultures   141
The Purchasing/Procurement Process   141
Problem Recognition   141
General Need Description and Product Specification   142
Supplier Search   143
Proposal Solicitation   143
Supplier Selection   143
Order-Routine Specification   144
Performance Review   144
Executive Summary   144
Case Pilot   145
Notes   145

8.   Dealing with the Competition   148
Marketing Management at Procter & Gamble   148
Competitive Markets and Competitors   149
Market Attractiveness   149
Identifying Competitors   151
Industry Concept of Competition   151
Market Concept of Competition   153
Competitor Analysis   154
Strategies   154
Objectives   154
Strengths and Weaknesses   155
Reaction Patterns   155

The Competitive Intelligence System   156
 Designing the Competitive Intelligence System   156
 Selecting Competitors to Attack and to Avoid   157
Designing Competitive Strategies   158
 Market-Leader Strategies   158
 Market-Challenger Strategies   161
 Market-Follower Strategies   164
 Marketing Skills: Guerrilla Marketing   164
 Market-Nicher Strategies   165
 Balancing Customer and Competitor Orientations   166
Executive Summary   167
Notes   167

9. Identifying Market Segments and Selecting Target Markets   170

Marketing Management at Hallmark Cards   170
Using Market Segmentation   171
 Segment Marketing   171
 Niche Marketing   172
 Local Marketing   172
 Individual Marketing   173
 Patterns of Market Segmentation   173
 Market-Segmentation Process   174
 Effective Segmentation   174
Segmenting Consumer and Business Markets   175
 Bases for Segmenting Consumer Markets   175
 Bases for Segmenting Business Markets   180
Market Targeting Strategies   181
 Evaluating and Selecting Market Segments   181
 Marketing Skills: Evaluating Segments   182
 Targeting Multiple Segments and Supersegments   184
 Ethical Choice of Market Targets   184
Executive Summary   185
Notes   185

PART III MAKING MARKETING DECISIONS   188

10. Developing, Positioning, and Differentiating Products Through the Life Cycle   188

Marketing Management at Red Bull   188
Challenges in New Product Development   189
 Types of New Products   189
 Why New Products Fail—and Succeed   190

Managing New Products: Ideas to Strategy   190
   Idea Generation   191
   Idea Screening   191
   Concept Development   192
   Concept Testing   192
   Marketing Strategy Development   193
   Business Analysis   193
Managing New Products: Development to Commercialization   194
   Product Development   194
   Market Testing   195
   Commercialization   196
The Consumer Adoption Process   197
   Stages in the Adoption Process   197
   Factors Influencing the Adoption Process   197
Marketing Through the Product Life Cycle   198
   Product Life Cycles   198
   Marketing Strategies: Introduction Stage   200
   Marketing Strategies: Growth Stage   200
   Marketing Strategies: Maturity Stage   201
   Marketing Strategies: Decline Stage   201
   Critique of the Product Life Cycle Concept   202
Positioning and Differentiating Strategy   202
   Two Views of Positioning   202
   How Many Ideas to Promote in Positioning?   203
   Marketing Skills: Managing Positioning   203
   Communicating the Positioning   204
   Adding Further Differentiation   204
   Differentiation Tools   204
Executive Summary   207
Notes   208

11.   Setting Product and Brand Strategy   211
Marketing Management at Arts & Entertainment
(A&E) Network   211
The Product and the Product Mix   212
   Product Levels   212
   Product Classifications   213
   Product Mix   214
Product-Line Decisions   215
   Product-Line Analysis   215
   Product-Line Length   215
   Line Modernization, Featuring, and Pruning   216

Brand Decisions 216
> What Is a Brand? 216
> Building Brand Identity 216
> Brand Equity 217
> Branding Challenges 218
> Marketing Skills: Building a Cult Brand   219

Packaging and Labeling 224
> Packaging 224
> Labeling 225

Executive Summary 225

Notes 226

12. **Designing and Managing Services 228**

Marketing Management at E*Trade 228

The Nature of Services 229
> Categories of Service Mix 229
> Characteristics of Services and Their Marketing
>   Implications 229

Marketing Strategies for Service Firms 231
> Managing Differentiation 234
> Managing Service Quality 234
> Marketing Skills: Service Recovery   238
> Managing Productivity   238

Managing Product Support Services 239
> Presale Service Strategy 239
> Postsale Service Strategy 240
> Major Trends in Customer Service 240

Executive Summary 241

Notes 241

13. **Designing Pricing Strategies and Programs 244**

Marketing Management at Intel 244

Setting the Price 245
> Step 1: Selecting the Pricing Objective 245
> Step 2: Determining Demand 247
> Step 3: Estimating Costs 248
> Step 4: Analyzing Competitors' Costs, Prices,
>   and Offers 250
> Step 5: Selecting a Pricing Method 250
> Marketing Skills: Online Auctions   254
> Step 6: Selecting the Final Price 255

Adapting the Price   256
    Geographical Pricing   257
    Price Discounts and Allowances   257
    Promotional Pricing   257
    Discriminatory Pricing   257
    Product-Mix Pricing   259
Initiating and Responding to Price Changes   260
    Initiating Price Cuts   260
    Initiating Price Increases   261
    Reactions to Price Changes   262
    Responding to Competitors' Price Changes   262
Executive Summary   263
Notes   264

Part IV   **MANAGING AND DELIVERING MARKETING
               PROGRAMS   266**

14.   **Designing and Managing Value Networks and Marketing
        Channels   266**

Marketing Management at Carmax   267
What Is a Value Network and Marketing Channel System?   267
What Work Is Performed by Marketing Channels?   268
    Channel Functions and Flows   269
    Channel Levels   270
    Service Sector Channels   271
Channel-Design Decisions   271
    *Analyzing Customers' Desired Service Output
       Levels   272*
    Establishing Objectives and Constraints   272
    Identifying Major Channel Alternatives   273
    Evaluating the Major Alternatives   274
Channel-Management Decisions   275
    Selecting Channel Members   275
    Training Channel Members   275
    Motivating Channel Members   276
    Evaluating Channel Members   276
    Modifying Channel Arrangements   276
    Marketing Skills: Evaluating Intermediaries   277
Channel Dynamics   278
    Vertical Marketing Systems   278
    Horizontal Marketing Systems   279
    Multichannel Marketing Systems   279

Conflict, Cooperation, and Competition 280

Legal and Ethical Issues in Channel Relations 281

Executive Summary 282

Notes 282

15. **Managing Retailing, Wholesaling, and Market Logistics 284**

Marketing Management at Mall of America 284

Retailing 285

Types of Retailers 285

Retailer Marketing Decisions 287

Trends in Retailing 290

Wholesaling 290

Marketing Skills: Experience Marketing 291

The Growth and Types of Wholesaling 292

Wholesaler Marketing Decisions 293

Trends in Wholesaling 294

Market Logistics 294

Market-Logistics Objectives 295

Market-Logistics Decisions 296

Market-Logistics Lessons 299

Executive Summary 299

Notes 300

16. **Designing and Managing Integrated Marketing Communications 302**

Marketing Management at Yahoo! 302

Developing Effective Marketing Communications 303

Step 1: Identify the Target Audience 303

Step 2: Determine the Communication Objectives 304

Step 3: Design the Message 305

Step 4: Select the Communication Channels 307

Step 5: Establish the Marketing Communications Budget 308

Step 6: Decide on the Marketing Communications Mix 309

Step 7: Measure Results 311

Step 8: Manage the Integrated Marketing Communications Process 311

Developing and Managing the Advertising Campaign 312

Setting Advertising Objectives 312

Deciding on the Advertising Budget 313

Choosing the Advertising Message 313
Developing Media Strategies 315
Evaluating Advertising Effectiveness 318
Sales Promotion 318
Purpose of Sales Promotion 319
Major Decisions in Sales Promotion 319
Public Relations 322
Marketing Public Relations 322
Major Decisions in Marketing PR 322
Direct Marketing 323
The Growth of Direct Marketing 324
The Benefits of Direct Marketing 324
Integrated Direct Marketing 324
Major Channels for Direct Marketing 325
Marketing Skills: Permission Marketing   328
Executive Summary 328
Notes 329

17.   **Managing the Sales Force 332**
Marketing Management at Tiffany 332
Designing the Sales Force 333
Sales Force Objectives and Strategy 333
Sales Force Structure 334
Marketing Skills: Major Account Management   335
Sales Force Size 336
Sales Force Compensation 336
Managing the Sales Force 337
Recruiting and Selecting Sales Representatives 337
Training Sales Representatives 338
Supervising Sales Representatives 338
Motivating Sales Representatives 339
Evaluating Sales Representatives 340
Principles of Personal Selling 341
Sales Professionalism 342
Negotiation 343
Relationship Marketing 344
Executive Summary 345
Notes 345

Glossary 349

Index 353

Framework for Marketing Management—Suggested Cases

Case Number	Case Name	All Authors	Key Concept	Source
9-594-074	Planet Reebok (A)	Quelch, John A.; Harper, Jamie	Advertising	Harvard Business School Publishing
9-596-076	Dewar's (A): Brand Repositioning in the 1990s	Silk, Alvin J.; Klein, Lisa R.	Brands	Harvard Business School Publishing
9-500-041	VerticalNet (www.verticalnet.com)	Narayandas, Das	Business-to-Business Marketing	Harvard Business School Publishing
9-500-052	Webvan: Groceries on the Internet	Deighton, John; Bakshi, Kayla	Consumer Marketing	Harvard Business School Publishing
9-595-035	Nestle Refrigerated Foods: Contadina Pasta & Pizza (A)	Rangan, V. Kasturi; Bell, Marie	Consumer Marketing	Harvard Business School Publishing
9-501-050	Customer Value Measurement at Nortel Networks—Optical Networks Division	Narayandas, Das	Customer Retention	Harvard Business School Publishing
9-500-092	yesmail.com	Wathieu, Luc	Direct Marketing	Harvard Business School Publishing
9-500-048	Alloy.com: Marketing to Generation Y	Deighton, John; McWilliams, Gil	Direct Marketing	Harvard Business School Publishing
9-599-093	Egghead to Egghead.com (A)	Rangan, V. Kasturi; Bell, Marie	Distribution Channels	Harvard Business School Publishing
9-500-015	Autobytel.com	Moon, Youngme	Distribution Channels	Harvard Business School Publishing
9-800-305	Staples.com	Jacobson, Joanna; Eisenmann, Thomas; Morris, Gillian	Electronic Commerce	Harvard Business School Publishing
SAW001	Rand McNally: Navigating the Wireless Landscape	Sawhney, Mohanbir	Electronic Commerce	Kellogg
SAW002	Wingcast: Creating and Capturing Value in Telematics	Sawhney, Mohanbir	Electronic Commerce	Kellogg
SAW003	Asera: Strategic Positioning for Success	Sawhney, Mohanbir	Electronic Commerce	Kellogg
SAW004	Illinois Superconductor Corporation: Forecasting Demand for Superconducting Filters	Sawhney, Mohanbir	Electronic Commerce	Kellogg
SAW005	Sun Microsystems and Jini: The Battle for Mind Share	Sawhney, Mohanbir	Electronic Commerce	Kellogg
SAW006	Rockwell Automation: The Channel Challenge in the MRO Market	Sawhney, Mohanbir	Electronic Commerce	Kellogg
SAW007	TiVo: Changing the Face of Television	Sawhney, Mohanbir	Electronic Commerce	Kellogg
9-594-023	Mary Kay Cosmetics: Asian Market Entry	Quelch, John A.; Laidler, Nathalie	Market Entry	Harvard Business School Publishing
9-591-025	Zenith: Marketing Research for High Definition Television (HDTV)	Sultan, Fareena	Market Research	Harvard Business School Publishing
9-596-059	Marketing the National Hockey League	Rangan, V. Kasturi; Bell, Marie	Market Research	Harvard Business School Publishing
9-594-001	American Airlines' Value Pricing (A)	Silk, Alvin J.; Michael, Steven C.	Market Segmentation	Harvard Business School Publishing
9-594-106	Goodyear: The Aquatred Launch	Quelch, John A.; Isaacson, Bruce	Marketing Implementation	Harvard Business School Publishing
9-500-008	CVS: The Web Strategy	Deighton, John; Shah, Anjali	Marketing Management	Harvard Business School Publishing
9-501-038	TiVo	Wathieu, Luc; Zoglio, Michael	Marketing Planning	Harvard Business School Publishing
9A94A012	Evergreen Trust	Pearce, M.R.	Marketing Planning	Ivey
9-500-090	Merrill Lynch: Integrated Choice	Rangan, V. Kasturi; Bell, Marie	Marketing Strategy	Harvard Business School Publishing
9-597-028	Tweeter etc.	Gourville, John; Wu, George	Marketing Strategy	Harvard Business School Publishing
9-597-032	Sony Corp.: Car Navigation Systems	Quelch, John A.; Fujikawa, Yoshinori	Marketing Strategy	Harvard Business School Publishing
9-595-057	The Black & Decker Corp. (A): Power Tools Division	Dolan, Robert J.	Marketing Strategy	Harvard Business School Publishing
9-575-072	Optical Distortion, Inc. (A)	Clarke, Darrel G.; Wise, Randall E.	Marketing Strategy	Harvard Business School Publishing
9-575-060	Southwest Airlines (A)	Lovelock, Christopher H.	Pricing Strategy	Harvard Business School Publishing
9-591-133	Barco Projection Systems (A): Worldwide Niche Marketing	Moriarty, Rowland T., Jr.; McQuade, Krista	Product Lines	Harvard Business School Publishing
9-500-070	Priceline.com: Name Your Own Price	Dolan, Robert J.	Product Planning	Harvard Business School Publishing
9-799-158	Matching Dell	Rivkin, Jan W.; Porter, Michael E.	Strategic Planning	Harvard Business School Publishing

Preface

A *Framework for Marketing Management* is a concise paperback adapted from Philip Kotler's number-one selling textbook, *Marketing Management, Eleventh Edition*. This book focuses on key points such as how to analyze the market and competitors, how to develop strategies, and how to deliver and manage effective marketing programs. Its streamlined approach will appeal to those professors who want an authoritative account of what is going on in the field of marketing management plus a text that is short enough to let them incorporate outside cases, simulations, and projects.

THIS EDITION

Marketing is of interest to everyone, whether they are marketing goods, services, properties, persons, places, events, information, ideas, or organizations. Like the eleventh edition, *A Framework for Marketing Management, Second Edition* is dedicated to helping companies, groups, and individuals adapt their marketing strategies and management to the new technological and global realities.

   A Framework for Marketing Management retains all the strengths of the larger book. This edition emphasizes the following:

- ■ The Internet and its uses and effects
- ■ Demand chain and supply management
- ■ Customer relationship management and partner relationship management
- ■ Alternative go-to-market channels
- ■ Brand building and brand asset management

   At the same time, it builds upon the fundamental strengths of past editions.

- ■ Managerial orientation
- ■ Analytical approach
- ■ Multidisciplinary perspective
- ■ Universal applications
- ■ Comprehensive and balanced coverage

FEATURES OF THE SECOND EDITION

Four-Part Organization

Part I features understanding marketing management. Part II covers analyzing marketing opportunities. Part III describes how to make marketing decisions. Part IV discusses managing and delivering marketing programs.

New Chapter

In Chapter 2, *Adapting Marketing to the New Economy*—coverage exploring the impact of the Internet and new technologies and customer relationship management has been fully updated, expanded, and now appears much earlier. This chapter provides a framework for understanding how business and marketing practices are changing as a result of the Internet and new technologies, including the need for revenue and profit planning.

New Chapter Opening Vignettes

Marketing Management at . . . feature opens each chapter. These vignettes give students a chance to see how marketing managers have applied key principles in actual company situations, making explicit the connection between theory and implementation at leading firms such as eBay, NTT DoCoMo, Caterpillar, and Starbucks.

New Analysis with a Twist of Skills

A Marketing Skills feature appears in each chapter. Each example includes an explanation of what the marketing skill is, *why it's important, how to develop it,* and *how to apply it.* Among the skills covered are managing implementation, internal marketing, spotting trends, and winning back lost customers.

New Interactive Case Analysis Tool Assignments

Case Pilot interactive case analysis tool assignments. Case analysis is an essential skill for any business student, so why not give your students a chance to enhance their skills? End of chapter case analysis assignments in Chapters 4, 5, and 7 send students to Case Pilot, a new, *free,* interactive case tool now available on *www.prenhall.com/kotler*. This one of a kind tool helps your students develop the fundamentals of case study analysis. Three sample cases from the high-technology, service, and consumer product sectors enable students to write problem statements, identify key marketing issues, perform SWOT analysis, and develop solutions. Students even have the ability to self-score all their work.

COURSECOMPLETE—CASEBOOKS AND COURSEPACKS TO SUPPLEMENT THIS BOOK

Prentice Hall Custom Business Resources can provide you and your students with all of the texts, cases, and articles needed to enhance and maximize the learning in your unique marketing course. Prentice Hall has access to thousands of readings, articles, and cases specific to marketing. We've partnered with today's leading case institutions such as Harvard Business School Publishing and coursepack providers like Xanadu, so we can bring you the *MOST* choices yet the *EASIEST* access and ordering process.

Easy as 1-2-3

You can create your unique CoursePack in minutes using our online database at *www.prenhall.com/custombusiness*, or simply tell our dedicated specialist what you'd like over the phone and we'll handle the rest.

Value-Priced Packages

Let us package your custom CoursePack or Case Book with this textbook and your students will receive a package discount. Ask your local Prentice Hall representative or visit and bookmark the Prentice Hall Custom Business Resources Web site at *www.prenhall.com/custombusiness* for one stop shopping.

MARKETING PLAN PRO AND NEW MARKETING PLAN: A HANDBOOK

Marketing Plan Pro is a highly rated commercial software package that guides students through the entire marketing plan process. The software is totally interactive and features 10 sample marketing plans, step-by-step guides, and customizable charts. Customize your marketing plans to fit your marketing needs by following easy-to-use plan wizards. The new *Marketing Plan: A Handbook*, by Marian Burk Wood, supplements the in-text marketing plan material with an in-depth guide to what student marketers really need to know. The software and handbook are available as value-pack items with this text. Contact your local Prentice Hall representative for more information.

A COMPREHENSIVE SUPPLEMENTS PACKAGE

- *Instructor's Manual:* Contains chapter overviews and teaching objectives, plus suggested lecture outlines—providing structure for class discussions around key issues. A listing of key contemporary articles is included, along with synopses and ideas for class/course utilization of the materials, and an overall framework tying together the suggested support materials. Harvard case analyses are also provided, integrating the current topic areas. In addition, there are references to the Marketing Plan Pro software.

- *Test Item File:* Brand new, completely revamped since the last edition! Includes more than 70 questions per chapter, consisting of multiple-choice, true/false, essay, and mini-cases with questions. Page references are provided for each question.

- *Prentice Hall Electronic Test Manager:* Windows-based Test Manager creates exams and allows you to evaluate and track students' results. It is easily customizable for individual needs.

- *PowerPoint Express:* Easily customizable for even the most novice user, this presentation includes basic chapter outlines and key points from each chapter. The best option if you want to incorporate your own material!

- *PowerPoint Expanded:* Includes the basics found in the Express version but also art from the text. The best option if you want a complete presentation solution! Both Powerpoint presentations are available from the Prentice Hall Web site at *www.prenhall.com/kotler.*

- *Prentice Hall Video Gallery: Marketing Management, Volumes I and II:* Make your classroom "newsworthy." PH and BusinessNOW have partnered to create a completely new Marketing Management video library. Using today's popular newsmagazine format, students are taken on location and behind closed doors. Each news story profiles a well-known or up-and-coming company leading the way in its industry. Highlighting more than 20 companies, including Starbucks, Intel, Accenture, DoubleClick, P&O Ned Lloyd, and more, the issue-focused footage includes interviews with top executives, objective reporting by real news anchors, industry research analysts, and marketing and advertising campaign excerpts. Extensive teaching materials are available to accompany the video library.

■ *Expanded Companion Website with Case Pilot. www.prenhall.com/kotler:* Go beyond the text. Our acclaimed Web resource provides professors and students with a customized course Website that features a complete array of teaching and learning material. **For instructors:** downloadable versions of the Instructor's Resource Manual and Powerpoint slides, plus additional resources such as current events and Internet exercises. Or, try the Syllabus Builder to plan your own course! **New for students:** Case analysis is an essential skill for any business student, so why not give your students a chance to enhance their skills? End-of-chapter case analysis assignments in Chapters 4, 5, and 7 send students to Case Pilot, a new, free, interactive case tool now available on *www.prenhall.com/kotler*. This one of a kind tool helps your students develop the fundamentals of case study analysis. Three sample cases from the high-technology, service and consumer product sectors enable students to write problem statements, identify key marketing issues, perform SWOT analysis, and develop solutions. Students even have the ability to self-score all their work.

■ *Innovative Online Courses: Standard Online Courses in Blackboard, WebCT, and CourseCompass:* No technical expertise needed. Teach a complete online course or a Web-enhanced course. Add your own materials, take advantage of online testing and gradebook opportunities, utilize the bulletin board, and discussion board functions. All courses are free to your students with purchase of the text.

Acknowledgments

This edition of *Framework for Marketing Management* bears the imprint of many people who have contributed to the previous edition of this text and to *Marketing Management, Eleventh Edition*. A special note of gratitude is owed to Marian Wood for her editorial and developmental assistance. Many thanks also to both the dedicated editorial and production teams at Prentice Hall who consistently provide me with professional support. I gratefully acknowledge the many reviewers at other universities who helped shape this new edition.

Vernon Stauble, California State Polytechnic
Gopal Iyer, Florida Atlantic University
Robert Kuchta, Lehigh University
Steven Lysonski, Marquette University
Brian Engelland, Mississippi State University
Bill Archer, Northern Arizona University
William Robinson, Purdue University
Jeff Conant, Texas A&M University
John Antil, University of Delaware
Thomas Gruca, University of Iowa
Robert Spekman, University of Virginia
Ron Michaels, University of Central Florida
Susan Keaveney, University of Colorado, Denver
K. Padmanabhan, University of Michigan, Dearborn
Jack Kasulis, University of Oklahoma
Mike Dailey, University of Texas, Arlington
Edwin Stafford, Utah State University
Mike Swenson, Brigham Young University
Brian Gibbs, Vanderbilt University
Carol A. Scott, University of California at Los Angeles
Prof. Jack K.H. Lee, City University of New York Baruch College
James McCullough, Washington State University
Kimberly A. Taylor, Florida International University
Louis Nzegwu, University of Wisconsin, Platteville
Mark Houston, University of Missouri, Columbia
Marian Chapman Moore, Duke University
Nicole Howatt, University of Central Florida
Naomi Mandel, Arizona State University
Ruth Clottey, Barry University

Philip Kotler
S.C. Johnson Distinguished Professor of International Marketing
J.L. Kellogg Graduate School of Management
Northwestern University
Evanston, Illinois
November 2002

CHAPTER 1

Defining Marketing for the Twenty-First Century

In this chapter, we will address the following questions:

1. What is the new economy like?
2. What are the tasks of marketing?
3. What are the major concepts and tools of marketing?
4. What orientations do companies exhibit in the marketplace?
5. How are companies and marketers responding to the new challenges?

MARKETING MANAGEMENT AT EBAY

One of the shining stars of the new economy is eBay (*www.ebay.com*), the world's largest online auction site. Through eBay's efficient one-to-one exchange format, 37 million members buy and sell all kinds of goods and services, from cars, collectibles, and computers to paintings, pearls, and Pez dispensers. Although most exchanges occur between individuals, even corporations like Sears, Sun, IBM, Home Depot, and KitchenAid use eBay to sell excess inventory, outdated merchandise, or damaged items to bargain-hunters.

Inside eBay's operation, each category manager functions like a brand manager, collecting data on transactions and customers to better understand the market and offer improvements that will reinforce customer loyalty and satisfaction. The head of marketing and merchandising constantly analyzes customer behavior to determine the effectiveness of different promotional efforts and determine which items sell best and at what prices. This is how management knows that eBay auctions a Corvette every three hours and puts diamond jewelry up for sale every six minutes. In this fast-growing online community, buyers rate sellers so prospective bidders can learn from the experiences of others who were pleased or had problems with their purchases. Not only is eBay the most popular auction Web site, its operating margin makes it one of the most profitable of the new economy businesses.[1]

The new economy has brought success to eBay and other organizations that use technology to apply marketing concepts like customer focus, good value, quality service, and efficient exchange mechanisms for satisfying customer needs and wants. In contrast, the old economy was based on the Industrial Revolution and on managing manufacturing industries. Manufacturers standardized products to bring down costs and aimed to continually expand their market shares and achieve economies of scale. Seeking efficiency, they replicated their procedures and policies in every geographic market and managed operations hierarchically, with a top boss issuing orders to middle managers, who in turn guided the workers.

Unlike the old economy, the new economy is based on the digital revolution and the management of information about customers, products, prices, competitors, and every other aspect of the marketing environment. Information can be infinitely differentiated, analyzed, personalized, and electronically dispatched to many people in a short period. With public and accessible information—such as eBay's bid notifications and its seller feedback system—consumers and business buyers can be better informed and make better choices.

THE NEW ECONOMY

The digital revolution has placed a whole new set of capabilities in the hands of consumers and businesses. Consider what consumers have today that they didn't have yesterday:

- *A substantial increase in buying power.* Consumers and business buyers are only a click away from comparing competitor prices and product attributes, getting answers, making purchases, even naming the price they want to pay for a product.
- *A greater variety of available goods and services.* People can order almost anything over the Internet: furniture (Ethan Allen), washing machines (Sears), management consulting ("Ernie"), even medical advice (cyberdocs). Furthermore, buyers can order virtually anything from anywhere in the world.
- *A great amount of information about practically anything.* Online, people can read almost any newspaper in any language from any nation and access encyclopedias, dictionaries, medical information, movie ratings, consumer reports, and other information sources.
- *A greater ease in interacting and placing and receiving orders.* Buyers can place orders from home, office, or mobile phone 24 hours a day, 7 days a week, for convenient delivery to home or office.
- *An ability to compare notes on products and services.* Customers can enter chat rooms and log onto specialized sites to exchange information and opinions on areas of common interest.

The new economy has also brought companies a new set of capabilities. First, they can operate a powerful new information and promotional channel with augmented geographical reach. Using one or more Web sites, a company can explain its products and services, its history, its business philosophy, its job opportunities, and other information of interest to stakeholders. Companies such as Grainger are posting huge catalogs on their sites so customers from around the world can search for and order products.

Second, companies can collect fuller and richer information about markets, customers, prospects and competitors. Conducting marketing research using the Internet, marketers can arrange for focus groups, distribute questionnaires, and gather primary data in other ways.

Third, companies can use intranets to facilitate and speed up internal communication, allowing employees to query one another, seek advice, obtain training, keep internal manuals and policies updated, and access needed information from internal sources. Going further, companies can use the Internet for two-way communication with customers and prospects, for recruiting, and for making transactions more efficient. Extranets allow companies to link suppliers and distributors for sending and receiving information, placing orders, and making payments more efficiently.

Fourth, marketers can efficiently send ads, coupons, samples, and information to customers on request. They can also customize offerings, services, and messages to individual customers, based on information from internal databases and supplemental information. Because all companies are buyers as well as sellers, they can achieve substantial savings by using the Internet to compare sellers' prices and purchasing materials through online auctions or by posting their own terms. Finally, companies can significantly improve logistics and cost-efficiency while improving accuracy and service quality through the online exchange of information, orders, transactions, and payments between companies, their business partners, and their customers.

Whereas the Industrial Age was characterized by mass production and mass consumption, stores overstuffed with inventory, ads everywhere, and rampant discounting, the Information Age is leading to more accurate levels of production, more targeted communications, and more relevant pricing. This book will consider how marketing is changing under the impact of these new forces.

Marketing deals with identifying and meeting human and social needs. One of the shortest definitions of marketing is "meeting needs profitably." Whether the marketer is Procter & Gamble, which created Crest Whitestrips in response to people's desire for whiter teeth; or Monster.com, which developed an online résumé databank so job-hunters and employers can find each other more efficiently; or CarMax, which invented a new way to sell used cars because people want more certainty when buying such vehicles—all illustrate a drive to turn a private or social need into a profitable business opportunity.[2] However, seemingly invincible businesses such as Sears, Levi Strauss, General Motors, Kodak, and Xerox have had to rethink their business models when confronted with newly empowered customers and new competitors. Companies must carefully monitor their customers and competitors, continuously improve their value offerings, carefully define the target market and value proposition, and take a long-term view to satisfying customers, stockholders, employees, suppliers, and channel partners.

MARKETING TASKS

The book *Radical Marketing* praises companies such as Harley-Davidson for succeeding by breaking all of the rules of marketing.[3] Instead of commissioning expensive marketing research, spending huge sums on advertising, and operating large marketing departments, these companies stretch their limited resources, stay close to their customers, and create more satisfying solutions to customers' needs. They form buyers clubs, use creative public relations, and deliver quality products to win long-term customer loyalty.

We can distinguish three stages through which marketing practice might pass. *Entrepreneurial marketing* is practiced by individuals who start a company because they see an opportunity. Jim Koch, founder of Boston Beer Company, started out carrying bottles of Samuel Adams from bar to bar to persuade bartenders to carry it. For 10 years, he sold his beer through direct selling and grassroots public relations. Today this business leads the U.S. craft beer market.[4]

As small companies achieve success, they move toward more *formulated marketing*. For example, Boston Beer now spends millions on television advertising, employs more than 175 salespeople, and has a marketing department to conduct research and handle many of the other tasks of a professionally run marketing company.

The final stage is *intrepreneurial marketing*. Many large companies get stuck in formulated marketing, poring over the latest ratings, scanning research, trying to fine-tune promotions. These companies lack the creativity and passion of the guerrilla marketers in the entrepreneurial stage.[5] Their brand and product managers need to start living with their customers and visualizing new ways to add value to their customers' lives.

The bottom line is that effective marketing can take many forms. There will be a constant tension between the formulated side of marketing and the creative side. It is easier to learn the formulated side, which will occupy most of our attention in this book; but we will also describe how creativity and passion operate in many companies.

The Scope of Marketing

Marketing people are involved in marketing 10 types of entities: goods, services, experiences, events, persons, places, properties, organizations, information, and ideas.

Goods. Physical goods constitute the bulk of most countries' production and marketing effort. Each year U.S. companies alone market billions of canned and frozen food products, millions of tons of steel, and other mainstays of a modern economy. Thanks to the Internet, even individuals can market goods.

Services. As economies advance, a growing proportion of their activities are focused on the production of services. The U.S. economy today consists of a 70–30 services-to-goods mix. Services include the work of airlines, hotels, and maintenance and repair people, as well as professionals working within or for companies, such as accountants, lawyers, programmers, and doctors. Many market offerings consist of a variable mix of goods and services.

Experiences. By orchestrating several services and goods, one can create, stage, and market experiences. Walt Disney World's Magic Kingdom is an experience; so is the Hard Rock Cafe.

Events. Marketers promote time-based events, such as the Olympics, trade shows, sports events, and artistic performances.

Persons. Celebrity marketing has become a major business. Artists, musicians, CEOs, physicians, high-profile lawyers and financiers, and other professionals draw help from celebrity marketers.[6]

Places. Cities, states, regions, and nations compete to attract tourists, factories, company headquarters, and new residents.[7] Place marketers include economic development specialists, real estate agents, commercial banks, local business associations, and advertising and public relations agencies.

Properties. Properties are intangible rights of ownership of either real property (real estate) or financial property (stocks and bonds). Properties are bought and sold through the marketing efforts of real estate agents (for real estate) and investment companies and banks (for securities).

Organizations. Organizations actively work to build a strong, favorable image in the mind of their publics. Philips, the Dutch electronics company, advertises with the tag line, "Let's Make Things Better." The Body Shop and Ben & Jerry's gain attention by promoting social causes. Universities, museums, and performing arts organizations boost their public images to compete more successfully for audiences and funds.

Information. Among the marketers of information are schools and universities; publishers of encyclopedias, nonfiction books, and specialized magazines; makers of CDs; and Internet Web sites. The production, packaging, and distribution of information is one of society's major industries.[8]

Ideas. Every market offering includes a basic idea. In essence, products and services are platforms for delivering some idea or benefit to satisfy a core need.

Marketers are skilled in stimulating demand for these 10 types of entities. However, this is too limited a view of the tasks that marketers perform. Just as production and logistics professionals are responsible for supply management, marketers are responsible for demand management. They may have to manage negative demand (avoidance of a product), no demand (lack of awareness or interest in a product), latent demand (a strong need that cannot be satisfied by existing products), declining demand (lower demand), irregular demand (demand varying by season, day, or hour), full demand (a satisfying level of demand), overfull demand (more demand than can be handled), or unwholesome demand (demand for unhealthy or dangerous products). To meet the organization's objectives, marketing managers seek to influence the level, timing, and composition of these various demand states.

The Decisions That Marketers Make

Marketing managers face a host of decisions, from major ones such as what features to design into a new product, how many salespeople to hire, or how much to spend on advertising, to minor decisions such as the wording or color for new packaging. These questions vary in importance depending on the marketplace in which the organization is active. The four major categories of markets are: consumer markets, business markets, global markets, and nonprofit and governmental markets.

Marketing Concepts and Tools

Marketing boasts a rich array of concepts and tools to help marketers address the decisions they must make. We will first define marketing and then describe its major concepts and tools.

Defining Marketing

We can distinguish between a social and a managerial definition for marketing. According to a social definition, **marketing** is a societal process by which individuals and groups obtain what they need and want through creating, offering, and exchanging products and services of value freely with others.

As a managerial definition, marketing has often been described as "the art of selling products." But Peter Drucker, a leading management theorist, says that "the aim of marketing is to make selling superfluous. The aim of marketing is to know and understand the customer so well that the product or service fits him and sells itself. Ideally, marketing should result in a customer who is ready to buy."[9]

The American Marketing Association offers this managerial definition: Marketing (management) is the process of planning and executing the conception, pricing, promotion, and distribution of ideas, goods, and services to create exchanges that satisfy individual and organizational goals.[10] Coping with exchange processes—part of this definition—calls for a considerable amount of work and skill. We see **marketing management** as the art and science of choosing target markets and getting, keeping, and growing customers through creating, delivering, and communicating superior customer value.

Core Marketing Concepts

Marketing can be further understood by defining several of its core concepts.

Target Markets and Segmentation A marketer can rarely satisfy everyone in a market. Not everyone likes the same soft drink, automobile, college, and movie. Therefore, marketers identify and profile distinct groups of buyers who might prefer or require varying products and marketing mixes. These *market segments* can be identified by examining demographic, psychographic, and behavioral differences among buyers. The firm then decides which segments present the greatest opportunity—which are its **target markets.** For each chosen target market, the firm develops a *market offering*. The offering is positioned in the minds of the target buyers as delivering some central benefit(s). For example, Volvo develops its cars for the target market of buyers for whom automobile safety is a major concern. Volvo, therefore, positions its car as the safest a customer can buy.

Traditionally, a "market" was a physical place where buyers and sellers gathered to exchange goods. Economists now describe a market as a collection of buyers and sellers who transact over a particular product or product class (the housing market or grain market); but marketers view the sellers as the industry and the buyers as the market. As Figure 1.1 shows, sellers send goods, services, and communications to the market; in return they receive money and information. The inner loop shows an exchange of money for goods and services; the outer loop shows an exchange of information.

FIGURE 1.1   A Simple Marketing System

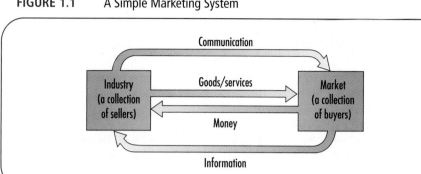

Marketplace, Marketspace, and Metamarket   Today we can distinguish between a marketplace and a marketspace. The **marketplace** is physical, as when one goes shopping in a store; **marketspace** is digital, as when one goes shopping on the Internet. Many observers believe that an increasing amount of purchasing will shift into marketspace.[11]

The **metamarket,** a concept proposed by Mohan Sawhney, describes a cluster of complementary goods and services that are closely related in the minds of consumers but are spread across a diverse set of industries. The automobile metamarket consists of automobile manufacturers, car dealers, financing companies, insurance companies, mechanics, parts dealers, service shops, auto magazines, classified auto ads in newspapers, and auto Web sites. Car buyers can get involved in many parts of this metamarket. This has created an opportunity for *metamediaries* to assist buyers to move seamlessly through these groups, although they are disconnected in physical space. One example is Edmund's (*www.edmunds.com*), where buyers can find car prices and search for dealers, financing, and accessories. Metamediaries can serve various metamarkets, such as the home ownership market, the parenting and baby care market, and the wedding market.[12]

Marketers and Prospects   A **marketer** is someone who is seeking a response (attention, a purchase, a vote, a donation) from another party, called the **prospect**. If two parties are seeking to sell something to each other, both are marketers.

Needs, Wants, and Demands   The marketer must try to understand the target market's needs, wants, and demands. **Needs** describe basic human requirements such as food, air, water, clothing, and shelter. People also have strong needs for recreation, education, and entertainment. These needs become **wants** when they are directed to specific objects that might satisfy the need. An American needs food but wants a hamburger, French fries, and a soft drink. A person in Mauritius needs food but wants a mango, rice, lentils, and beans. Wants are shaped by one's society. **Demands** are wants for specific products backed by an ability to pay. Many people want a Mercedes; only a few are able and willing to buy one. Companies must measure not only how many people want their product, but also how many would actually be willing and able to buy it.

These distinctions shed light on the criticism that "marketers create needs." Needs preexist marketers. Marketers, along with other societal factors, influence wants. Marketers might promote the idea that a Mercedes would satisfy a person's need for social status. They do not, however, create the need for social status.

Product, Offering, and Brand   Companies address needs by putting forth a **value proposition**, a set of benefits they offer to customers to satisfy their needs. The intangible value proposition is made physical by an **offering**, which can be a combination of products, services, information, and experiences. A **brand** is an offering from a known source. A brand name such as McDonald's carries many associations in the minds of people: hamburgers, fun, children, fast food, golden arches. These associations make up the **brand image**. All companies strive to build brand strength—that is, a strong, favorable brand image.

Value and Satisfaction   The offering will be successful if it delivers value and satisfaction to the target buyer. The buyer chooses between different offerings on the basis of which is perceived to deliver the most value. Value can be seen as primarily a combination of quality, service, and price (QSP), called the **customer value triad**. Value increases with quality and service and decreases with price.

More specifically, **value** is a ratio between what the customer gets (both functional and emotional benefits) and what he gives (monetary costs, time costs, energy costs, and psychic costs). Thus value is given by:

$$\text{Value} \;=\; \frac{\text{Benefits}}{\text{Costs}} \;=\; \frac{\text{Functional benefits} + \text{emotional benefits}}{\text{Monetary costs} + \text{time costs} + \text{energy costs} + \text{psychic costs}}$$

Based on this equation, the marketer can increase the value of the customer offering by (1) raising benefits, (2) reducing costs, (3) raising benefits and reducing costs, (4) raising benefits by more than the increase in costs, or (5) lowering benefits by less than the reduction in costs. Customers choosing between two value offerings, V_1 and V_2, will examine the ratio V_1/V_2. They will favor V_1 if the ratio is larger than one; they will favor V_2 if the ratio is smaller than one; and they will be indifferent if the ratio equals one.

Exchange and Transactions   **Exchange**, the core concept of marketing, is the process of obtaining a desired product from someone by offering something in return. For exchange potential to exist, five conditions must be satisfied:

1. There are at least two parties.
2. Each party has something that might be of value to the other party.
3. Each party is capable of communication and delivery.
4. Each party is free to accept or reject the exchange offer.
5. Each party believes it is appropriate or desirable to deal with the other party.

Whether exchange actually takes place depends upon whether the two parties can agree on terms that will leave them both better off (or at least not worse off) than before. Exchange is a value-creating process because it normally leaves both parties better off.

Two parties are engaged in exchange if they are negotiating—trying to arrive at mutually agreeable terms. When they reach agreement, a transaction takes place. A **transaction** is a trade of values between two or more parties, involving at least two things of value, agreed-upon conditions, a time of agreement, and a place of agreement. Usually a legal system exists to support and enforce compliance among transactors.

A transaction differs from a transfer. In a **transfer**, A gives a gift, a subsidy, or a charitable contribution to B but receives nothing tangible in return. Transfer behavior can also be understood through the concept of exchange. Typically, the transferer expects something in exchange for his or her gift—for example, gratitude or seeing changed behavior in the recipient. Professional fund-raisers provide benefits to donors, such as thank-you notes. Contemporary marketers have broadened the concept of marketing to include the study of transfer behavior as well as transaction behavior.

Marketing consists of actions undertaken to elicit desired responses—including **behavioral responses**, such as a vote or support—from a target audience. To effect successful exchanges, marketers analyze what each party expects from the transaction. Suppose Caterpillar, the world's largest manufacturer of earth-moving equipment, researches the benefits that a typical construction company wants when it buys such equipment. The items shown on the prospect's want list in Figure 1.2 are not equally important and may vary from buyer to buyer. One of Caterpillar's tasks is to discover the relative importance of these different wants to the buyer.

Caterpillar also has a want list. If there is a sufficient match or overlap in the want lists, a basis for a transaction exists. Caterpillar's task is to formulate an offer that motivates the construction company to buy Caterpillar equipment. The construction company might, in turn, make a counteroffer. This process of negotiation leads to mutually acceptable terms or a decision not to transact.

Relationships and Networks   Transaction marketing is part of a larger idea called relationship marketing. **Relationship marketing** aims to build long-term mutually satisfying relations with key parties—customers, suppliers, distributors—in order to earn and retain their long-term preference and business.[13] Marketers accomplish this by promising and delivering high-quality products and services at fair prices to the other parties over time. Relationship marketing builds strong economic, technical, and social ties among the parties. It cuts down on transaction costs and time. In the most successful cases, transactions move from being negotiated each time to being a matter of routine.

FIGURE 1.2   Two-Party Exchange Map Showing Want Lists of Both Parties

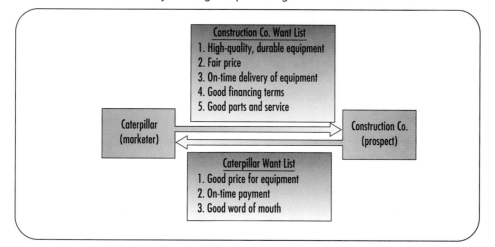

The ultimate outcome of relationship marketing is the building of a unique company asset called a marketing network.[14] A **marketing network** consists of the company and its supporting stakeholders (customers, employees, suppliers, distributors, university scientists, and others) with whom it has built mutually profitable business relationships. Increasingly, competition is not between companies but rather between marketing networks, with the profits going to the company that has the better network.

Marketing Channels   To reach a target market, the marketer uses three kinds of marketing channels. *Communication channels* deliver messages to and receive messages from target buyers. They include newspapers, magazines, radio, television, mail, telephone, billboards, posters, fliers, CDs, audiotapes, and the Internet. Beyond these, communications are conveyed by facial expressions and clothing, the look of retail stores, and many other media. Marketers are increasingly adding dialogue channels (e-mail and toll-free numbers) to counterbalance monologue channels (such as ads).

The marketer uses *distribution channels* to display or deliver the physical product or service(s) to the buyer or user. There are physical distribution channels and service distribution channels, which include warehouses, transportation vehicles, and various trade channels such as distributors, wholesalers, and retailers. The marketer also uses *service channels* to carry out transactions with potential buyers. Service channels include warehouses, transportation companies, banks, and insurance companies that facilitate transactions. Marketers clearly face a design problem in choosing the best mix of communication, distribution, and service channels for their offerings.

Supply Chain   Whereas marketing channels connect the marketer to the target buyers, the **supply chain** describes a longer channel stretching from raw materials to components to final products that are carried to final buyers. The supply chain for women's purses starts with hides and moves through tanning operations, cutting operations, manufacturing, and the marketing channels that bring products to customers. This supply chain represents a value delivery system. Each company captures only a certain percentage of the total value generated by the supply chain. When a company acquires competitors or moves upstream or downstream, its aim is to capture a higher percentage of supply chain value.

Competition   **Competition** includes all of the actual and potential rival offerings and substitutes that a buyer might consider. Suppose an automobile company is planning to buy steel for its cars. The car manufacturer can buy from U.S. Steel or other U.S. or foreign integrated steel mills; save money by buying from a minimill such as Nucor; buy aluminum for certain parts of the car to lighten the car's weight; or buy engineered plastics for bumpers instead of steel. U.S. Steel would be thinking too narrowly of competition if it thought only of other integrated steel companies. In fact, U.S. Steel is more likely to be hurt in the long run by substitute products than by its immediate steel company rivals. U.S. Steel also must consider whether to make substitute materials or stick only to those applications where steel offers superior performance.

We can distinguish four levels of competition, based on degree of product substitutability. In *brand competition*, a company sees its competitors as other companies that offer similar products and services to the same customers at similar prices. Volkswagen might see its major competitors as Toyota and other manufacturers of medium-price automobiles, rather than Mercedes or Hyundai. In *industry competition*, a company sees its competitors as all companies that make the same product or class of products. Thus, Volkswagen would be competing against all other car manufacturers.

In *form competition*, a company sees its competitors as all companies that manufacture products that supply the same service. Volkswagen would see itself competing against manufacturers of all vehicles, such as motorcycles, bicycles, and trucks. Finally, in *generic competition*, a company sees its competitors as all companies that compete for the same consumer dollars. Volkswagen would see itself competing with companies that sell major consumer durables, foreign vacations, and new homes.

Marketing Environment   Competition represents only one force in the environment in which all marketers operate. The overall marketing environment consists of the task environment and the broad environment.

The **task environment** includes the immediate actors involved in producing, distributing, and promoting the offering, including the company, suppliers, distributors, dealers, and the target customers. Material suppliers and service suppliers such as marketing research agencies, advertising agencies, Web site designers, banking and insurance companies, and transportation and telecommunications companies are included in the supplier group. Agents, brokers, manufacturer representatives, and others who facilitate finding and selling to customers are included with distributors and dealers.

The **broad environment** consists of six components: demographic environment, economic environment, natural environment, technological environment, political-legal environment, and social-cultural environment. These environments contain forces that can have a major impact on the actors in the task environment, which is why smart marketers track environmental trends and changes closely.

Marketing Program   The marketer's task is to build a marketing program or plan to achieve the company's desired objectives. The **marketing mix** is the set of marketing tools that the firm uses to pursue its marketing objectives in the target market.[15] McCarthy classified these tools into four broad groups that he called the four Ps of marketing: product, price, place, and promotion.[16] Figure 1.3 shows the particular marketing variables under each P of the marketing mix.

Marketing-mix decisions influence trade channels as well as final consumers. Typically, the firm can change its price, sales-force size, and advertising expenditures in the short run, although it can develop new products and modify its distribution only in the long run. Thus, the firm tends to make fewer marketing-mix changes in the short run than the number of marketing-mix decision variables might suggest.

Robert Lauterborn suggested that the sellers' four Ps correspond to the customers' four Cs.[17]

Four Ps	Four Cs
Product	Customer solution
Price	Customer cost
Place	Convenience
Promotion	Communication

Winning companies are those that meet customer needs economically and conveniently and with effective communication.

FIGURE 1.3   The Four P Components of the Marketing Mix

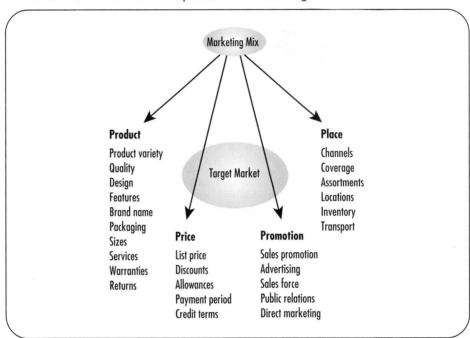

COMPANY ORIENTATIONS TOWARD THE MARKETPLACE

Marketing management is the conscious effort to achieve desired exchange outcomes with target markets. But what philosophy should guide a company's marketing efforts? What relative weights should be given to the often-conflicting interests of the organization, customers, and society? Dexter Corporation faced this conflict with one of its most popular products, a profitable grade of paper used in tea bags. Unfortunately, the materials in this paper accounted for 98 percent of Dexter's hazardous wastes. So while Dexter's product was popular with customers, it was also detrimental to the environment. Dexter assigned an employee task force to tackle this problem. The task force succeeded, and the company increased its market share while virtually eliminating hazardous waste.[18]

Clearly, marketing activities should be carried out under a well-thought-out philosophy of efficient, effective, and socially responsible marketing. However, there are six competing concepts under which organizations conduct marketing: production concept, product concept, selling concept, marketing concept, customer concept, and societal marketing concept.

The Production Concept

The **production concept**, one of the oldest in business, holds that consumers prefer products that are widely available and inexpensive. Managers of production-oriented businesses concentrate on achieving high production efficiency, low costs, and mass distribution. Managers of production-oriented businesses concentrate on achieving high production efficiency, low costs, and mass distribution, assuming that consumers want product availability and low prices. This orientation is also used when a company wants to expand the market.

The Product Concept

Other businesses are guided by the **product concept**, which holds that consumers favor those products that offer the most quality, performance, or innovative features. Managers in these organizations focus on making superior products and improving them over time, assuming that buyers can appraise quality and performance. Product-oriented companies often design their products with little or no customer input, trusting that their engineers can design exceptional products. A General Motors (GM) executive said years ago: "How can the public know what kind of car they want until they see what is available?" GM today asks customers what they value in a vehicle and includes marketing people in the very beginning stages of design.[19]

However, the product concept can lead to marketing myopia.[20] Railroad management thought that travelers wanted trains rather than transportation and overlooked the growing competition from airlines, buses, trucks, and automobiles. Coca-Cola, focused on its soft drinks, missed seeing the market for coffee bars and fresh-fruit juice bars that eventually impinged on soft drink sales. These organizations are looking into a mirror when they should be looking out of the window.

The Selling Concept

The **selling concept**, another common business orientation, holds that consumers and businesses, if left alone, will ordinarily not buy enough of the organization's products. The organization must, therefore, undertake an aggressive selling and promotion effort. This concept assumes that consumers must be coaxed into buying, so the company has a battery of selling and promotion tools to stimulate buying.

The selling concept is practiced most aggressively with unsought goods—goods that buyers normally do not think of buying, such as insurance and funeral plots. The selling concept is also practiced in the nonprofit area by fund-raisers, college admissions offices, and political parties. Most firms practice the selling concept when they have overcapacity. Their aim is to sell what they make rather than make what the market wants. In modern industrial economies, productive capacity has been built up to a point where most markets are buyer markets (the buyers are dominant) and sellers have to scramble for customers. Prospects are bombarded with sales messages. As a result, the public often identifies marketing with hard selling and advertising.

However, marketing based on hard selling carries high risks. It assumes that customers who are coaxed into buying a product will like it; and if they don't, that they won't bad-mouth it or complain to consumer organizations and will forget their disappointment and buy it again. These are indefensible assumptions. One study showed that dissatisfied customers may bad-mouth the product to 10 or more acquaintances; today bad news travels even faster and farther with the Internet.[21]

The Marketing Concept

The marketing concept, based on central tenets crystallized in the mid-1950s, challenges the three business orientations just discussed.[22] The **marketing concept** holds that the key to achieving organizational goals consists of the company being more effective than competitors in creating, delivering, and communicating customer value to its chosen target markets.

Theodore Levitt of Harvard drew a perceptive contrast between the selling and marketing concepts: "Selling focuses on the needs of the seller; marketing, on the needs of the buyer. Selling is preoccupied with the seller's need to convert his product into cash; marketing, with the idea of satisfying the needs of the customer by means of the product and the whole cluster of things associated with creating, delivering, and finally consuming it."[23]

The marketing concept rests on four pillars: target market, customer needs, integrated marketing, and profitability. The selling concept takes an inside-out perspective. It starts with the factory, focuses on existing products, and calls for heavy selling and promoting to produce profitable sales. The marketing concept takes an outside-in perspective. It starts with a well-defined market, focuses on customer needs, coordinates activities that affect customers, and produces profits by satisfying customers.

Target Market   Companies do best when they choose their target market(s) carefully and prepare tailored marketing programs. For example, Madrid-based Terra Lycos became a top Internet service provider by developing tailored marketing programs targeting the most prosperous one-fifth of Hispanics across eight different markets.[24]

Customer Needs   A company can carefully define its target market yet fail to correctly understand the customers' needs. Understanding customer needs and wants is not always simple. Some customers have needs of which they are not fully conscious; some cannot articulate these needs or use words that require some interpretation. We can distinguish among five types of needs: stated needs, real needs, unstated needs, delight needs, and secret needs.

Responding only to the stated need may shortchange the customer. For example, if a customer enters a hardware store and asks for a sealant to seal glass windowpanes, she is stating a solution, not a need. If the salesperson suggests that tape would provide a better solution, the customer may appreciate that the salesperson met her need and not her stated solution.

A distinction needs to be drawn between responsive marketing, anticipative marketing, and creative marketing. A *responsive* marketer finds a stated need and fills it, while an *anticipative* marketer looks ahead to the needs that customers may have in the near future. A *creative* marketer discovers and produces solutions that customers did not ask for, but to which they enthusiastically respond. Sony is a creative marketer: it has introduced many successful new products that customers never asked for or even thought were possible, including Walkmans and videocameras. Thus, Sony is a market-driving firm, not just a market-driven firm. Akio Morita, its founder, proclaimed that he doesn't serve markets; he creates markets.[25]

Why is it supremely important to satisfy the needs of target customers? Because a company's sales come from two groups: new customers and repeat customers. One estimate is that attracting a new customer can cost five times as much as pleasing an existing one.[26] Also, it might cost 16 times as much to bring the new customer to the same level of profitability as that of the lost customer. Customer retention is, therefore, more important than customer attraction.

Integrated Marketing

When all of the company's departments work together to serve the customers' interests, the result is **integrated marketing**. Integrated marketing takes place on two levels. First, the various marketing functions—sales force, advertising, customer service, product management, marketing research—must work together. All of these functions must be coordinated from the customer's point of view.

Second, marketing must be embraced by the other departments. According to David Packard of Hewlett-Packard: "Marketing is far too important to be left only to the marketing department!" Marketing is not a department so much as a company-wide orientation requiring good internal teamwork. To foster teamwork, the company must carry out internal marketing as well as external marketing. **External marketing** is marketing directed at people outside the company. **Internal marketing** is the task of hiring, training, and motivating able employees who want to serve customers well. Internal marketing must precede external marketing. It makes no sense to promise excellent service before the company's staff is ready to provide it. (See "Marketing Skills: Internal Marketing.")

Managers who see the customer as the company's real "profit center" consider the traditional organization chart—a pyramid with the CEO at the top, management in the middle, and front-line people and customers at the bottom—obsolete. Master marketing companies invert the chart, putting customers at the top and getting all managers personally involved with customers. Next in importance are the front-line people who meet, serve, and satisfy the customers; under them are the middle managers, who support the front-line people so they can serve the customers; and at the base is top management, whose job is to hire and support good middle managers.

Profitability

The ultimate purpose of the marketing concept is to help organizations achieve their objectives. In the case of private firms, the major objective is profit; in the case of non-profit and public organizations, it is surviving and attracting enough funds to perform useful work. Private firms should aim to achieve profits as a consequence of creating superior customer value, by satisfying customer needs better than competitors. For example, Perdue Farms has achieved above-average margins marketing chicken—a commodity if ever there was one! The company has always aimed to control breeding and other factors in order to produce tender-tasting chickens for which discriminating customers will pay more.[28]

Only a handful of companies stand out as master marketers: Procter & Gamble, Disney, Nordstrom, Wal-Mart, Milliken & Company, McDonald's, Marriott Hotels, and several Japanese (Sony, Toyota, Canon) and European companies (IKEA, Club Med, Nokia, ABB). These companies focus on the customer and are organized to respond effectively to changing customer needs. They all have well-staffed marketing departments, and all of their other departments—manufacturing, finance, research and development, personnel, purchasing—accept the customer as king. Several scholars have found that by embracing the marketing concept, companies can achieve superior performance.[29]

Despite the benefits, firms face three hurdles in converting to a marketing orientation: organized resistance, slow learning, and fast forgetting. Some company departments (often manufacturing, finance, and research and development) believe a

MARKETING SKILLS: INTERNAL MARKETING

One of the most valuable skills marketers can have is the ability to select, educate, and rally people inside the organization so all employees enthusiastically participate in external marketing to build satisfying and profitable long-term relationships with customers. Internal marketing starts with the selection of managers and employees who have a positive attitude toward the company, its products, and its customers. The next step is to train, motivate, and empower the entire staff so they have the knowledge, tools, and authority to play their roles in delivering value to the customer base. After establishing standards for employee performance, the final step is to monitor employee actions and reward good performance—then continue the cycle of internal marketing through ongoing communication, motivation, and feedback.

Developing internal marketing skills takes planning, time, and perseverance. Not every communication or motivation attempt will successfully influence every employee, just as not every advertisement or sales call will successfully influence every customer. Nor is internal marketing going to be effective if it is treated as a slogan or passing fad. When internal marketing really works, however, it can help propel a company to the top of its industry.

For example, internal marketing is a key strength at Southwest Airlines, where top management pays close attention to recruitment and training, internal communication, and workforce motivation. The CEO and president constantly visit different Southwest facilities, send birthday cards to employees, and share customer comments with employees. Southwest's employees deliver superior service with a smile, and they are so dedicated that some have worked without pay to keep the airline's costs down during difficult periods. Clearly, Southwest's managers are good role models for learning how to apply the critical skill of internal marketing.[27]

stronger marketing function threatens their power in the organization. Resistance is especially strong in industries where marketing is being introduced for the first time—for instance, in law offices, colleges, deregulated industries, and government agencies. In spite of the resistance, many companies manage to introduce some marketing thinking into their organization. Ultimately, marketing emerges as the integrative function within the organization.

The Customer Concept

Today many companies are moving beyond the marketing concept, which works at the level of customer segments, to apply the customer concept by shaping offers, services, and messages for individual customers (see Figure 1.4). These companies hope to achieve profitable growth through capturing a larger share of each customer's expenditures, building high customer loyalty, and focusing on customer lifetime value. This approach has become practical as a result of advances in factory customization, computers, the Internet, and database marketing software. It works best for companies that normally collect a great deal of individual customer information, carry many

FIGURE 1.4   The Customer Concept

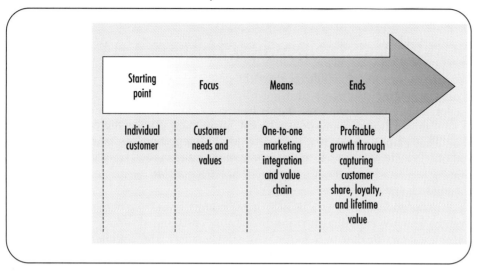

Starting point	Focus	Means	Ends
Individual customer	Customer needs and values	One-to-one marketing integration and value chain	Profitable growth through capturing customer share, loyalty, and lifetime value

products that can be cross-sold or that need periodic replacement or upgrading, and/or sell products of high value.

The Societal Marketing Concept

Some have questioned whether the marketing concept is an appropriate philosophy in an age of environmental deterioration, resource shortages, explosive population growth, world hunger and poverty, and neglected social services. Are companies that successfully satisfy consumer wants necessarily acting in the best, long-term interests of consumers and society? The marketing concept sidesteps the potential conflicts among consumer wants, consumer interests, and long-term societal welfare.

Situations in which firms are criticized for satisfying consumer wants at society's expense call for a new term that enlarges the marketing concept. We propose calling it the **societal marketing concept**, which holds that the organization's task is to determine the needs, wants, and interests of target markets and to deliver the desired satisfactions more effectively and efficiently than competitors in a way that preserves or enhances the consumer's and the society's well-being.

The societal marketing concept calls upon marketers to build social and ethical considerations into their marketing practices. They must balance and juggle the often-conflicting criteria of company profits, consumer wants, and public interest. Yet a number of companies—including Patagonia—have achieved notable sales and profit gains by adopting and practicing the societal marketing concept.

Patagonia, which sells outdoor apparel and gear, practices a form of the societal marketing concept called **cause-related marketing**. Pringle and Thompson define this as "activity by which a company with an image, product, or service to market builds a relationship or partnership with a 'cause,' or a number of 'causes,' for mutual benefit."[30] Companies see cause-related marketing as an opportunity to enhance their corporate reputation, raise brand awareness, increase customer loyalty, build sales, and increase press coverage. They believe that customers will increasingly look for demonstrations of good corporate citizenship that go beyond supplying rational and emotional benefits.

HOW BUSINESS AND MARKETING ARE CHANGING

We can say with some confidence that "the marketplace isn't what it used to be." It is changing radically as a result of major forces such as technological advances, globalization, and deregulation. These forces have created new behaviors and challenges.

Customers increasingly expect higher quality and service and some customization. They perceive fewer real product differences and show less brand loyalty. They can obtain extensive product information from the Internet and other sources, permitting them to shop more intelligently. They are showing greater price sensitivity in their search for value.

Brand manufacturers are facing intense competition from domestic and foreign brands, which is resulting in rising promotion costs and shrinking profit margins. They are being further buffeted by powerful retailers who command limited shelf space and are putting out their own store brands in competition with national brands.

Store-based retailers are suffering. Small retailers are succumbing to the growing power of giant retailers and "category killers." Store-based retailers are seeing margins shrink as they face growing competition from catalog houses; direct-mail firms; newspaper, magazine, and TV direct-to-customer ads; home shopping TV; and Internet-based retailers. In response, entrepreneurial retailers are enhancing entertainment with coffee bars, lectures, demonstrations, and performances, marketing an "experience" rather than a product assortment.

Company Responses and Adjustments

Given these changes, companies are doing a lot of soul-searching, and many highly respected firms are adjusting in a number of ways. One trend is *reengineering*, moving from a focus on functional departments to reorganizing by key processes, each managed by multidiscipline teams. A second is *outsourcing*, switching from making everything inside the company to buying more products from outside if this is cheaper and better. Virtual companies outsource everything, own very few assets and, therefore, earn extraordinary rates of return. A trend toward *e-commerce* is also occurring, with companies moving from attracting customers to stores and selling through salespeople to making virtually all products available on the Internet. Business-to-business purchasing is growing fast on the Internet, and personal selling can increasingly be conducted electronically.

Another reaction is the trend toward *benchmarking*, in which firms stop relying on self-improvement and start studying world-class performers to adopt best practices. Also, more companies are forming *alliances* with networks of partner firms rather than trying to win alone.[31] In addition, companies are buying from fewer but more reliable suppliers who work closely in a *supplier-partnership* relationship with the company. They are becoming *market-centered*, organizing by market segment rather than by products. And they are becoming both *global and local*. Finally, companies are becoming *decentralized*. Instead of being managed from the top, more are encouraging initiative and "intrepreneurship" at the local level.

Marketer Responses and Adjustments

Marketers also are rethinking their philosophies, concepts, and tools for the new economy. Many are using *customer relationship marketing*. Rather than focus on transactions, they want to build long-term, profitable customer relationships by focusing on their most profitable customers, products, and channels. Companies are also shifting from making a profit on each sale to making profits by managing *customer lifetime value*. Some companies offer to deliver a constantly needed product on a regular basis at a lower price per unit because they will capture the customer's business for a longer period. From a focus on gaining market share, companies are moving toward a focus on building *customer share* by offering a larger variety of goods to their existing customers and by training employees in cross-selling and up-selling.

Using *target marketing*, companies are not selling to everyone but trying to be the best firm serving well-defined target markets. Target marketing is being facilitated by the proliferation of special-interest magazines, TV channels, and Internet newsgroups. Companies are also moving away from selling the same offer in the same way to everyone in the target market and, instead, are individualizing and customizing messages and offerings. To do this, they are going beyond collecting sales data to build a *customer database* with information about individual customers' purchases, preferences, demographics, and profitability. Companies can then apply datamining techniques to discover new segments and trends in this data warehouse.

Using *integrated marketing communications*, marketers are no longer relying on one communication tool such as advertising, but rather blending several tools to deliver a consistent brand image to customers at every brand contact. They are also thinking of intermediaries not as customers but as *channel partners* in delivering value to final customers. Moreover, companies are changing from the mindset that marketing is done only by marketing, sales, and customer support personnel to recognizing that *every employee is a marketer* and must be customer-focused. Finally, model-based decision making is emerging. Rather than making decisions on intuition or slim data, marketers are basing decisions on models and marketplace facts.

These major themes will be examined throughout this book to help marketers and companies sail safely through the rough but promising waters ahead and adapt their marketing actions in line with changes in their marketplaces and marketspaces.

EXECUTIVE SUMMARY

The digital revolution has given consumers and companies new capabilities. Whereas the Industrial Age was characterized by mass production and mass consumption, high inventory levels, ubiquitous ads, and discounting, the Information Age allows more accurate levels of production, more targeted communications, and more relevant pricing.

Marketers can be involved with 10 types of entities (goods, services, experiences, events, persons, places, properties, organizations, information, and ideas). They can operate in consumer, markets, global, or nonprofit and governmental markets. Marketing is a societal process by which individuals and groups obtain what they need and want through creating, offering, and exchanging products and services of value freely with others. Marketing management is the art and science of choosing target markets and getting, keeping, and growing customers through creating, delivering, and communicating superior customer value.

Rather than try to satisfy everyone, marketers segment their markets and develop an offering that is positioned in the minds of the target market. Needs—basic human requirements—become wants when they are directed to specific objects that might satisfy the need. Companies address needs with an offering that represents a value proposition. Successful offerings deliver value and satisfaction to customers.

Every marketing exchange requires at least two parties—both with something valued by the other party, both capable of communication and delivery, both free to accept or reject the offer, and both finding it appropriate or desirable to deal with the other. An agreement to exchange constitutes a transaction, part of the larger idea of relationship marketing. Through customer relationship marketing, organizations aim to build enduring, mutually satisfying bonds with customers to earn and retain their long-term business. Reaching out to a target market entails communication channels, distribution channels, and service channels. The supply chain, which stretches from raw materials to the final products for final buyers, represents a value delivery system.

Marketers face brand, industry, form, and generic competition. The marketing environment can be divided into the task environment (the immediate actors in producing, distributing, and promoting the offering) and the broad environment (forces in the demographic, economic, natural, technological, political-legal, and social-cultural environment). Within these environments, marketers create a marketing program through the marketing mix—the set of marketing tools used to pursue marketing objectives in the target market. The marketing mix consists of the four Ps: product, price, place, and promotion.

Companies can adopt one of six orientations toward the marketplace. The production concept assumes that consumers want widely available, affordable products. The product concept assumes that consumers want products with the most quality, performance, or innovative features. The selling concept assumes that customers will not buy enough products without an aggressive selling and promotion effort. The marketing concept assumes the firm must be better than competitors in creating, delivering, and communicating customer value to its chosen target markets. The customer concept assumes that the company will achieve profitable growth and capture long-term share and loyalty by shaping offers and activities to individual customers. The societal marketing concept assumes that the firm must satisfy customers more effectively and efficiently than competitors while still preserving the consumer's and the society's well-being.

The combination of technology, globalization, and deregulation is influencing marketers and customers in a variety of ways. Companies have made adjustments in response to the changes brought on by these forces. In turn, savvy marketers must alter their marketing to keep pace with changes in the marketplace and the marketspace.

NOTES

1. Eryn Brown, "How Can a Dot-Com Be This Hot?" *Fortune*, January 21, 2002, pp. 87+; Mary Anne Ostrom, "Big Retailers Turn to Using EBay," *Mercury News*, January 21, 2002, (*www.mercurycenter.com*).

2. See Saul Hansell, "The Monster That's Feasting on Newspapers," *New York Times*, March 24, 2002, sec. 3, pp. 1, 13; and James R. Healey, "Circuit City Plans to Push CarMax Out

of the Nest," *USA Today*, February 25, 2002, (*www.usatoday.com/money/warn/2002-02-22-circuit-city.htm*).

3. Sam Hill and Glenn Rifkin, *Radical Marketing* (New York: HarperBusiness, 1999).

4. "Boston Beer Reports Barrelage Down, But Net Sales Stable," *Modern Brewery Age*, March 1, 1999, (*www.hoovers.com*).

5. Jay Conrad Levinson and Seth Grodin, *The Guerrilla Marketing Handbook* (Boston: Houghton Mifflin, 1994).

6. See Irving J. Rein, Philip Kotler, and Martin Stoller, *High Visibility* (Chicago: NTC Publishers, 1998).

7. See Philip Kotler, Irving J. Rein, and Donald Haider, *Marketing Places: Attracting Investment, Industry, and Tourism to Cities, States, and Nations* (New York: Free Press, 1993).

8. See Carl Shapiro and Hal R. Varian, "Versioning: The Smart Way to Sell Information," *Harvard Business Review* (November–December 1998): 106–14.

9. Peter Drucker, *Management: Tasks, Responsibilities, Practices* (New York: Harper & Row, 1973), pp. 64–65.

10. Peter D. Bennett, ed., *Dictionary of Marketing Terms*, 2d ed. (Chicago: American Marketing Association, 1995).

11. See Jeffrey Rayport and John Sviokla, "Managing in the Marketspace," *Harvard Business Review* (November–December 1994): 141–50. Also see their "Exploring the Virtual Value Chain," *Harvard Business Review* (November–December 1995): 75–85.

12. From a lecture by Mohan Sawhney, faculty member at Kellogg Graduate School of Management, Northwestern University, June 4, 1998.

13. See Regis McKenna, *Relationship Marketing* (Reading, MA: Addison-Wesley, 1991); Martin Christopher, Adrian Payne, and David Ballantyne, *Relationship Marketing: Bringing Quality, Customer Service, and Marketing Together* (Oxford, UK: Butterworth-Heinemann, 1991); and Jagdish N. Sheth and Atul Parvatiyar, eds., *Relationship Marketing: Theory, Methods, and Applications*, 1994 Research Conference Proceedings, Center for Relationship Marketing, Roberto C. Goizueta Business School, Emory University, Atlanta, GA.

14. See James C. Anderson, Hakan Hakansson, and Jan Johanson, "Dyadic Business Relationships Within a Business Network Context," *Journal of Marketing* (October 15, 1994): 1–15.

15. See Neil H. Borden, "The Concept of the Marketing Mix," *Journal of Advertising Research*, 4 (June): 2–7. For another framework, see George S. Day, "The Capabilities of Market-Driven Organizations," *Journal of Marketing* 58, no. 4 (October 1994): 37–52.

16. E. Jerome McCarthy, Basic Marketing: *A Managerial Approach*, 13th ed. (Homewood, IL: Irwin, 1999). Two alternative classifications are worth noting. Frey proposed that all marketing decision variables could be categorized into two factors: the offering (product, packaging, brand, price, and service) and methods and tools (distribution channels, personal selling, advertising, sales promotion, and publicity).

17. Robert Lauterborn, "New Marketing Litany: 4 Ps Passe; C-Words Take Over," *Advertising Age*, October 1, 1990, p. 26. Also see Frederick E. Webster Jr., "Defining the New Marketing Concept," *Marketing Management* 2, no. 4 (1994): 22–31; and Frederick E. Webster Jr., "Executing the New Marketing Concept," *Marketing Management* 3, no. 1 (1994): 8–16. See also Ajay Menon and Anil Menon, "Enviropreneurial Marketing Strategy: The Emergence of Corporate Environmentalism as Marketing Strategy," *Journal of Marketing* 61, no. 1 (January 1997): 51–67.

18. Kathleen Dechant and Barbara Altman, "Environmental Leadership: From Compliance to Competitive Advantage," *Academy of Management Executive* 8, no. 3 (1994): 7–19. Also see Gregory R. Elliott, "The Marketing Concept: Necessary, but Sufficient? An Environmental View," *European Journal of Marketing* 24, no. 8 (1990): 20–30.

19. David Welch and Gerry Khermouch, "Can GM Save an Icon?" *BusinessWeek*, April 8, 2002, pp. 60-67.

20. See Theodore Levitt's classic article, "Marketing Myopia," *Harvard Business Review* (July–August 1960): 45–56.
21. See Karl Albrecht and Ron Zemke, *Service America!* (Homewood, IL: Dow Jones-Irwin, 1985), pp. 6–7.
22. See John B. McKitterick, "What Is the Marketing Management Concept?" *The Frontiers of Marketing Thought and Action* (Chicago: American Marketing Association, 1957), pp. 71–82; Fred J. Borch, "The Marketing Philosophy as a Way of Business Life," *The Marketing Concept: Its Meaning to Management*, Marketing series, no. 99 (New York: American Management Association, 1957), pp. 3–5; and Robert J. Keith, "The Marketing Revolution," *Journal of Marketing* (January 1960): 35–38.
23. Levitt, "Marketing Myopia," p. 50.
24. David J. Lynch, "Net Company Terra Aims for Hispanic Connection," *USA Today*, January 20, 2000, pp. B1-2; Terra Lycos home page.
25. Akio Morita, *Made in Japan* (New York: Dutton, 1986), ch. 1.
26. See Patricia Sellers, "Getting Customers to Love You," *Fortune*, March 13, 1989, pp. 38–49.
27. Jane Lewis, "The Leaders Who Changed HR," *Personnel Today*, January 22, 2002, pp. 2+; Kim Clark, "Nothing But the Plane Truth," *U.S. News & World Report*, December 31, 2001, p. 58; Beth Zacharias, "Southwest Wins a Flying Fan," *Business Review*, October 29, 2001, p. 12.
28. Suzanne L. MacLachlan, "Son Now Beats Perdue Drumstick," *Christian Science Monitor*, March 9, 1995, p. 9; Sharon Nelton, "Crowing Over Leadership Succession," *Nation's Business*, May 1995, p. 52.
29. See Ajay K. Kohli and Bernard J. Jaworski, "Market Orientation: The Construct, Research Propositions, and Managerial Implications," *Journal of Marketing*, April 1990, pp. 1–18; John C. Narver and Stanley F. Slater, "The Effect of a Market Orientation on Business Profitability," *Journal of Marketing*, October 1990, pp. 20-35; Stanley F. Slater and John C. Narver, "Market Orientation, Customer Value, and Superior Performance," *Business Horizons*, March–April 1994, pp. 22–28; A. Pelham and D. Wilson, "A Longitudinal Study of the Impact of Market Structure, Firm Structure, Strategy and Market Orientation Culture on Dimensions of Business Performance," *Journal of the Academy of Marketing Science* 24, no. 1 (1996): 27–43; Rohit Deshpande and John U. Farley, "Measuring Market Orientation: Generalization and Synthesis," *Journal of Market-Focused Management* 2 (1998): 213–32.
30. See Hanish Pringle and Marjorie Thompson, *Brand Soul: How Cause-Related Marketing Builds Brands* (New York: John Wiley & Sons, 1999). Also see Marilyn Collins, "Global Corporate Philanthropy—Marketing Beyond the Call of Duty?" *European Journal of Marketing* 27, no. 2 (1993): 46–58.
31. See Leonard L. Berry, *Discovering the Soul of Service* (New York: Free Press, 1999), especially ch. 7.

CHAPTER 2

Adapting Marketing to the New Economy

In this chapter, we will address the following questions:

1. What are the major forces driving the new economy?
2. How are business and marketing practices changing as a result of the new economy?
3. How has the Internet changed the way marketers use customer databases and practice customer relationship management?

MARKETING MANAGEMENT AT NTT DOCOMO

All over Japan, NTT (Nippon Telephone and Telegraph) DoCoMo makes money when mobile phones ring. Loosely translated, *docomo* means "everywhere"—an apt description of the service's pervasive reach. More than 31 million customers use the DoCoMo phone service for Internet access as well as telephone calls. On the Web, they can subscribe to the latest installment of a *manga* graphic story, send and receive instant messages from friends and relatives, subscribe to weather reports, and even order goods. Rather than browse in a store, a customer can use the phone's compact Web viewing screen to look for a particular item (such as running shoes), choose a brand from among thousands listed, select a particular style and size, and place an order. Because the customer's address is already in the system's memory, the order will be sent automatically to a nearby 7-11 store for pickup or, for an extra fee, delivery.

DoCoMo uses its technology and networks to track the goods and services accessed by each customer and summarize all transactions into a single monthly bill listing subscriber fees, usage fees, and all purchases. Content providers charge the equivalent of a few dollars for monthly subscriptions; DoCoMo profits by collecting these fees from customers and subtracting a 9 percent commission before sending the remainder to the providers. These commissions add up, given that the average mobile phone user in Japan spends about $63 per month, compared with $53 per month for the average user in the United States. Customers can even pay their DoCoMo bills at the nearest 7-11 store. Based on DoCoMo's huge popularity in Japan—and its enviable earnings record of $3 billion yearly—NTT has launched a similar system in Germany, the Netherlands, and Belgium.[1]

Today's companies need fresh thinking about how to operate and compete in the new economy, a hybrid economy made up of old and new elements. NTT DoCoMo is quickly gaining experience in this hybrid economy by blending advanced technology to provide superior service, customer by customer. Many standard marketing practices of the old economy, such as mass media advertising, sales promotion, and sales force calls, will continue to be important. However, now businesses also have to quickly anticipate and respond to emerging customer needs and expectations driven, in part, by the Internet and other technologies—or risk having competitors satisfy those needs first.

In this chapter, we will first describe the key drivers of the New Economy and examine how business and marketing practices are changing.[2] Then we will look at how companies are using the Internet, customer databases and datamining, and customer relationship management (CRM) to improve their marketing performance.

THE MAJOR DRIVERS OF THE NEW ECONOMY

Many forces play a major role in reshaping the world economy, among them technology, globalization, and market deregulation. Here we will describe four specific drivers that underpin the new economy: (1) digitalization and connectivity; (2) disintermediation and reintermediation; (3) customization and customerization; and (4) industry convergence.

Digitalization and Connectivity

Much of the world's business is now carried over networks connecting people and companies. These networks are intranets when they connect people within a company to one another and to the company mainframe; extranets when they connect a company with its suppliers and distributors; and the Internet when they connect users to the worldwide "information repository." Companies also interact with suppliers and customers to buy and sell over the Internet.

Global connectivity is being further enhanced by wireless communication. Consumers and businesses in Europe and Japan are already deeply involved in *m-commerce* (*m* for mobile) using systems such as NTT DoCoMo; the U.S. market for m-commerce is much less developed.

Disintermediation and Reintermediation

The amazing success of early online dot-coms such as AOL, Amazon, eBay, Yahoo! and others struck terror in the hearts of many established manufacturers and retailers. Compaq had its hands tied because it sold its computers through retailers, whereas Dell Computer, which sold directly to customers, was able to grow faster by harnessing the Internet to sell online. Many established intermediaries—notably bookstores, music stores, travel agents, and stockbrokers—felt intense pressure as online competitors emerged. They feared, and rightly so, being *disintermediated* by the new e-tailers. Although some established middlemen lost their businesses, new Web-based middlemen such as Priceline.com sprang up to serve businesses and consumers, bringing *reintermediation* on a grand scale.

Traditional "brick-only" firms—such as Compaq, Barnes & Noble, and Merrill Lynch—dragged their feet, hoping that the assault of online-only firms would falter or disappear. They finally created their own Internet sales channels, offering a careful blend of off-line and online operations to retain the loyalty of retailers, brokers, and agents. Ironically, some competitors with off-line and online channels became stronger than pure dot-coms because they had a larger pool of resources and well-established brand names. Meanwhile, many Web-based businesses have had financial woes, downsized to cut costs, and eventually declared bankruptcy—even as other pure dot-coms continue to prosper.

Customization and Customerization

Customization means that the company is able to provide individually differentiated products, services, prices, and delivery channels for each customer. By going online, companies enable consumers to become *prosumers*, self-producing consumers who can essentially design their own goods. Companies have also acquired the capacity to interact individually with each customer by *personalizing* messages, products, and services. The combination of operational customization and marketing customization has been called **customerization**.[3]

Customization may be very difficult to implement for complex products such as automobiles, and it can raise costs beyond what customers are willing to pay. Another potential problem is that some customers don't know what they want until they see actual products, and companies do not want to allow customers to cancel orders once production begins. In addition, customized products may be hard to repair. On the other hand, customization has worked well for some products—laptop computers and skincare products—and is an opportunity worth investigating.

Industry Convergence

Industry boundaries are blurring at an incredible rate. Pharmaceutical companies, at one time essentially chemical companies, are now adding biogenetic research capacities in order to formulate new drugs, new cosmetics (cosmoneuticals), and new foods (nutriceuticals). Film companies such as Kodak were also chemical companies but now are moving into electronics to digitize their image-making capabilities. All these companies are recognizing that many new opportunities lie at the intersection of two or more industries.

HOW BUSINESS PRACTICES ARE CHANGING

The changes in technology and economy are eliciting a new set of beliefs and practices on the part of business firms. Table 2.1 shows the major business beliefs in the old economy and how these beliefs have shifted in the new economy.

Today's economy and most companies are a hybrid of the old and the new economy. Companies need to retain skills and competencies that have worked in the past, but they also need to add new knowledge and competencies if they hope to grow and prosper.

TABLE 2.1   Old Economy versus New Economy

Old Economy	New Economy
Organize by product units	Organize by customer segments
Focus on profitable transactions	Focus on customer lifetime value
Look primarily at financial scorecard	Look also at marketing scorecard
Focus on shareholders	Focus on stakeholders
Marketing does the marketing	Everyone does the marketing
Build brands through advertising	Build brands through performance
Focus on customer acquisition	Focus on customer retention
No customer satisfaction measurement	Measure customer satisfaction and retention rate
Overpromise, underdeliver	Underpromise, overdeliver

Similarly, today's marketplace is made up of traditional consumers (who don't buy online), cyberconsumers (who mostly buy online), and hybrid consumers (who do both).[4]

Most consumers are hybrid: they shop in grocery stores but occasionally order online from Peapod; they buy books in Barnes & Noble bookstores and sometimes order books from bn.com. Thus, most companies will need a presence both off-line and online to cater to these hybrid consumers. Companies are already adjusting their marketing practices to meet these new conditions. We will examine three marketing practices in which companies and their marketers are getting involved: e-business, Web sites, and customer relationship management.

HOW MARKETING PRACTICES ARE CHANGING: E-BUSINESS

E-business describes the use of electronic means and platforms to conduct a company's business. The Internet helps companies conduct business faster, more accurately, over a wider range of time and space, at less cost, and with the ability to customize and personalize customer offerings. Organizations have set up Web sites to distribute information and promote goods and services. They use Intranets to facilitate internal communication among employees and Extranets to facilitate the exchange of data, orders, and payments with suppliers and distributors. Bill Gates of Microsoft claims that his company is almost entirely run electronically; hardly any paper flows because everything is on the computer screen.[5]

E-commerce is more specific than e-business; it means that in addition to providing information about the company's history, policies, products, and job opportunities, the Web site allows transactions or facilitates the online sale of products and services. In turn, e-commerce has given rise to e-purchasing and e-marketing. With **e-purchasing**, companies use the Internet to efficiently purchase goods, services, and information from online suppliers. **E-marketing** describes a company's efforts to inform, communicate, promote, and sell its products and services over the Internet.

E-business and e-commerce take place mainly over four major Internet domains: B2C (business-to-consumer), B2B (business-to-business), C2C (consumer-to-consumer), and C2B (consumer-to-business). In addition, e-businesses can take the form of pure-click or brick-and-click companies.

Internet Domains: B2C (Business-to-Consumer)

More than 100 million Americans go online to look for information, research a product or service before buying, find travel information, and find out about movies, books, and leisure activities.[6] The most frequent online consumer purchases (in terms of the percentage of online buyers saying they have purchased in the category) have been books (58 percent), music (50 percent), software (44 percent), air tickets (29 percent), PC peripherals (28 percent), clothing (26 percent), videos (24 percent), hotel reservations (20 percent), toys (20 percent), flowers (17 percent), and consumer electronics (12 percent).

The Internet is most useful for B2C products and services when the consumer seeks greater ordering convenience (e.g., books and music), lower cost (e.g., stock trading or news reading), or information about product features and prices (e.g., automobiles or computers). It is less useful for products that must be touched or examined in advance, although consumers can and do order major appliances, computers, even flowers or wine without seeing or trying these products in advance. With B2C, the exchange process has become customer-initiated and customer-controlled; often marketers must wait until customers invite them to participate in the exchange. Even after marketers enter the exchange process, customers insulate themselves with the help of agents and intermediaries and define what information they need, what offerings they are interested in, and what prices they are willing to pay.

Internet Domains: B2B (Business-to-Business)

More activity is conducted on B2B sites than on B2C sites. B2B sites are making markets more efficient and changing the supplier-customer relationship in profound ways (see Figure 2.1). Major research firms estimate that B2B commerce is ten to fifteen times greater than B2C commerce. Business buyers often get better prices by using B2B auction sites, spot exchanges, online product catalogues, barter sites, and other online resources. Many major enterprises, including Ford, General Electric, and Merck, have invested millions in Web-based procurement systems. The result: Invoices that used to cost $100 to process now cost as little as $20. Companies are also forming online *buying alliances* to secure even deeper volume discounts from suppliers. GM, Ford, and DaimlerChrysler formed Covisint and believe they can save as much as $1,200 a car by combining their purchases on this electronic marketplace.

In addition, business buyers have access to more information from (1) supplier Web sites; (2) *infomediaries*, third parties that add value by aggregating information about alternatives; (3) *market makers*, third parties that create markets linking buyers and sellers; and (4) *customer communities*, online groups in which customers swap stories about suppliers' products and services.[7] As a result, pricing is more transparent. Price pressure on undifferentiated products will increase, whereas buyers will gain a better picture of the true value of highly differentiated products. Suppliers of superior products will be able to offset price transparency with value transparency; suppliers of undifferentiated products will have to drive down costs to compete.

Internet Domains: C2C (Consumer-to-Consumer)

With C2C, consumers are increasingly creating online product information, not just consuming it. They join Internet interest groups and chat rooms to share information, so that "word of Web" is joining "word of mouth" as an important buying influence.

FIGURE 2.1   The Supplier-Customer Relationship, Traditional versus New Economy

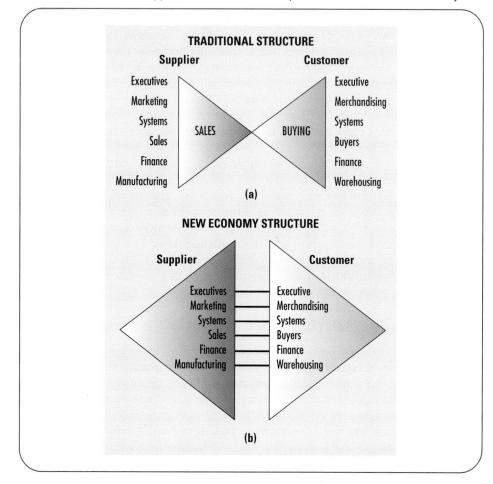

Information about good companies and products travels fast, and information about bad companies and products travels even faster. As noted in Chapter 1, eBay is a one-to-one online trading community with millions of registered users, mainly consumers who want to either buy or sell offerings in more than 1,000 categories.

Internet Domains: C2B (Consumer-to-Business)

Consumers are also finding it easier to communicate with companies on the Web. Companies invite prospects and customers to e-mail questions, suggestions, and even complaints. Some sites even include a "call-me" button—when a customer clicks it, his or her phone rings with a company representative ready to answer questions. Although many online merchants respond slowly to consumer inquiries, smart on-line marketers answer quickly and send out newsletters, special offers based on purchasing histories, reminders of service requirements or warranty renewals, or announcements of special events. Frustrated consumers have the option of using sites such as eComplaints and PlanetFeedback.com to communicate their dissatisfaction with businesses and products.[8]

Pure-Click versus Brick-and-Click Companies

Among e-businesses, we can distinguish between **pure-click** companies, those that launched a Web site without any previous existence as a firm, and **brick-and-click** companies, established companies that added an online site for information or e-commerce.

Pure-Click Companies   Pure-click companies can be search engines, Internet Service Providers, commerce sites, transaction sites, content sites, and enabler sites. Search engines and portals such as Yahoo! started as search engines and later added services such as news, weather, and storefronts, hoping to become the user's point of entry on the Internet. Internet Service Providers (ISPs) such as AOL provide Internet and e-mail connections for a fee. Commerce sites such as Amazon.com sell books, music, and so on. Transaction sites such as eBay take a commission for transactions conducted on their sites. Content sites such as WSJ.com (operated by the *Wall Street Journal*) offer financial news and other information. Enabler sites provide the hardware and software that enable Internet communication and commerce.

Pure-click firms have failed for a variety of reasons: Many rushed into the market without proper research or planning; had poorly designed Web sites; or lacked adequate infrastructures for on-time shipping and customer service. To acquire customers, pure-clicks often spent lavishly on mass marketing and off-line advertising, relied on buzz instead of using target marketing, and focused mainly on customer acquisition instead of building relationships to form a loyal base of frequent users. Finally, many pure-clicks failed to build a sound business model that would deliver eventual profits. Webvan, an online grocery retailer, overexpanded and opened automated warehouses that operated far below the break-even point. Unable to attract frequent users, the company filed for bankruptcy after operating less than three years.

Still, many pure-click dot-coms are surviving and even prospering, and others have fundamentally sound business plans even though they are showing losses today. The ISP Earthlink, for example, enjoys a monthly contribution margin of at least $9 from each subscriber to its Internet and e-mail services. Subscribers become profitable for Earthlink after their fees cover the $100 average cost of acquiring a new customer, which takes about 11 months.

Brick-and-Click Companies   Many established companies moved quickly to open Web sites describing their business but resisted adding e-commerce out of concern that they would be seen as competing with their off-line retailers and agents. For example, Merrill Lynch hesitated to introduce online stock trading to compete with E*TRADE, Schwab, and other online brokerages, fearing that its own brokers would rebel. Even the store-based bookseller Barnes & Noble delayed opening an online site to challenge Amazon.com because it was concerned about the effect on store sales.

Liberty Mutual solved this problem by asking its online customers to indicate whether they prefer to buy directly or through a financial advisor. When customers choose the advisor, Liberty Mutual relays information about their needs to an advisor for personal follow-up. As another example, Avon conducted research and found little overlap between existing customers and potential online customers, so the company initiated e-commerce, and offered to help its reps set up their own Web sites, as well.[9]

Although brick-and-click firms face channel conflict issues, many are likely to have more success online than pure-click competitors. First, companies such as Merrill Lynch and Wal-Mart have better known brand names; their cost of acquiring a new customer is $12 compared to the $82 that pure click e-tailers spend to acquire a new customer.[10] Second, they have greater financial resources and access to funds. Third, they have deeper industry knowledge and experience, good supplier relationships, and a large customer base. Fourth, they can be reached 24 hours a day, 7 days a week, and the retailers accept merchandise returns in their stores. And fifth, the Internet allows them to serve many customers far from their store locations.

HOW MARKETING PRACTICES ARE CHANGING: SETTING UP WEB SITES

Clearly all companies need to move into e-marketing and e-purchasing. In deciding to operate a Web site, companies must answer many questions about attracting and retaining visitors, advertising online, dealing with channel partners, putting the site together, and making it profitable. Many of these questions will be addressed throughout the book. Here we address only three: designing a Web site; promoting online; and building a revenue and profit model.

Designing an Attractive Web Site

A key challenge is to design a site that is attractive on first viewing, interesting enough to encourage repeat visits, and achieves the company's objectives. Early text-based Web sites have increasingly been replaced by sophisticated sites that provide text, sound, and animation (see *www.gap.com* or *www.1800flowers.com*). Rayport and Jaworski have proposed that effective sites feature specific design elements that they call the 7Cs:[11]

- *Context*. Layout and design.
- *Content*. Text, pictures, sound, and video on the site.
- *Community*. How the site enables user-to-user communication.
- *Customization*. Site's ability to tailor itself to different users or to allow users to personalize the site.
- *Communication*. How the site enables site-to-user, user-to-site, or two-way communication.
- *Connection*. Degree to which the site is linked to other sites.
- *Commerce*. Site's capabilities to enable commercial transactions.

Designing an attractive Web site is an important skill for marketers. Even marketers who outsource this task should be knowledgeable about good site design principles (see "Marketing Skills: Web Site Design"). Once a site is built, to encourage repeat visits, the company needs to pay particular attention to context and content factors.

Context Factors   Visitors judge a site's performance on its ease of use and its physical attractiveness. Ease of use covers three key attributes: whether the site loads quickly; whether the home page is easy to understand; and whether the visitor can easily navigate to other pages that open quickly. The site's physical attractiveness is determined by the following factors: (1) the individual pages look clean and not overly crammed with content; (2) the type faces and font sizes are very readable; and (3) the site makes good use of color and sound.

Content Factors   Context factors facilitate repeat visits, but they do not ensure that this happens. Content that is interesting, useful, and continuously changing will draw

MARKETING SKILLS: WEB SITE DESIGN

What if a Web site opened—and nobody visited? Considering the time, money, and effort companies must invest in a Web site, marketers must be familiar with the fundamentals of design, starting with an understanding of how Internet surfers behave. On the Web, visitors control what they see and for how long— and many are impatient. Therefore, designers should keep things simple, choosing graphics that will load quickly and grab attention. In addition, they need to show what the site will do for users through an informative home page, clearly labeled links, and search capabilities. Because reading words on a screen is not as easy as reading words in print, a well-designed site will use headlines, bullet points, and short bursts of text to convey key ideas. In addition, designers must think about how visitors are likely to move through the site and prominently position links so visitors can easily find different types of information.

When a company wants to reach a global audience, the Web site should accommodate different languages, customs, and content. Another important task is to plan out a logical navigation path for visitors by coordinating the graphics, words, and links. Remember that some visitors may click past introductory pages to view specific details. As a result, a good site design will help visitors determine where they are on the site, what else is available, and how they can get to the exact information they want. Finally, Web designers should test and retest to be sure prospective visitors will not get lost or frustrated in accessing the site—and to determine whether the site is set up to accomplish its purpose.

Web design is a valued skill at Yahoo! This well-trafficked portal looks exciting, organizes links so visitors can find what they need, and even allows visitors to customize the site to their personal specifications. The company carefully localizes the site's content and functionality for each country. As one example, U.S. users sort names in online address books alphabetically. However, users in some Asian nations sort names according to the number of strokes in each character. Incorporating these nuances into the design of local Yahoo! sites helps the company appeal to its target audiences and encourage long-term loyalty.[12]

repeat visits. Certain types of content are effective in attracting first-time visitors and bringing them back again: (1) deep information with links to related sites, (2) changing news of interest, (3) changing free offers, (4) contests and sweepstakes, (5) humor and jokes, and (6) games.

Getting Feedback   From time to time, a company needs to reassess its site's attractiveness and usefulness. One way to do this is to ask site design experts. But the more important source of feedback is users, who can explain what they like and dislike about the site and offer suggestions for improvement. Hallmark, General Electric, and other firms have users test and critique company sites, then retest over time as the sites change.[13]

Placing Ads and Promotion Online

Although Internet users generally do not welcome advertising, advertising does appear on the Internet. A company has to decide which forms will be most cost-effective in achieving specific advertising objectives.

Banner ads, small boxes containing text and perhaps a picture, are the most extensively used Internet advertising tools. Companies placing banner ads on relevant Web sites generally pay according to the size of the audience reached. Sometimes companies barter for banner placement rather than paying. Response is not very large: viewers are clicking on less than 1/2 of 1 percent of banner ads. Companies placing banner ads should ideally arrange to pay only when sales actually result from the click-throughs on these ads.

Many companies gain online exposure by sponsoring special content on Web sites that carry news, financial information, and so on. *Sponsorships* are best placed in well-targeted sites offering information or services related to the company and its customer base. The sponsor pays for posting the content and is publicly acknowledged as the sponsor of that page or site.

A **microsite** is a limited area on the Web managed and paid for by an external advertiser. Microsites are particularly relevant for companies selling low-interest products such as insurance. For example, an insurance company can create a microsite within a used-car site, offering advice for buyers of used cars and at the same time offering a good insurance deal.

Interstitials are advertisements that 'pop-up' between changes on a Web site. Ads for Johnson & Johnson's Tylenol headache reliever pop up on brokers' Web sites whenever the stock market falls by 100 points or more. **Browser ads** pay viewers to watch. Companies can also set up **alliances** and **affiliate (or associate) programs**. When one Internet company works with another, they end up "advertising" each other. Amazon has more than 500,000 associates that post Amazon banners on their Web sites.

Companies can also undertake guerrilla marketing actions for publicity and to generate word-of-mouth. When Yahoo! started its Denmark site, it distributed apples in the country's busiest train station with the message that a trip to New York was being given away on the Yahoo! site within a few hours; it also got publicity in Danish newspapers.

Building a Revenue and Profit Model

Dot-com companies need a viable **revenue and profit model**, a business model that specifies the main revenue sources, and the projected revenue, costs, and income the firm expects to achieve. Revenues may come from several sources:

- *Advertising income.* Sales of banner ads are one source of revenue.

- *Sponsorship income.* A dot-com can solicit sponsors for some of its content and collect sponsor fees.

- *Alliance income.* A company can invite business partners to share costs in setting up the Web site in exchange for free advertising.

- *Membership and subscription income.* Some Web sites charge a subscription fee to use the site. The *Wall Street Journal* site successfully collects subscription fees for accessing its online edition; Economy.com, a research firm, broke even only a few weeks after it started charging corporate subscribers $17 per month.[14]

- *Profile income.* Sites that have accumulated the profiles of a particular target group may be able to sell these profiles if they get permission. At the same time, there is a code of ethics that warns against the wrongful sale or misuse of customer information, and legal moves may soon limit this option.

- *Product and service sales income.* E-commerce sites draw a good portion of their revenue from marking up the prices of their goods and services.
- *Transaction commissions and fees.* Dot-coms can charge commission fees on transactions between other parties. For example, eBay puts buyers in touch with sellers and takes a commission of up to 5 percent on each transaction.
- *Market research/information.* Companies can charge for special market information or intelligence. NewsLibrary charges a dollar or two to download copies of archived news stories. LifeQuote provides price comparisons from different life insurance companies and gets a commission of 50 percent of the first year's premium from the company chosen by the consumer.
- *Referral income.* Companies can collect revenue by referring customers to other sites. Edmund's receives a "finder's fee" every time a customer fills out an Auto-By-Tel form at Edmund's site, regardless of whether a deal is consummated.

How many dot-coms are profitable today? McKinsey & Company studied more than 200 B2C e-businesses and found that 20 percent were making an operating profit. The best performers were transaction sites, with media and content sites lagging behind.[15]

HOW MARKETING PRACTICES ARE CHANGING: CUSTOMER RELATIONSHIP MARKETING

In addition to e-marketing, companies are becoming more skillful in customer relationship marketing and database marketing. **Customer relationship marketing (CRM)** enables companies to provide excellent real time customer service by developing a relationship with each valued customer through the effective use of individual account information. Based on what they know about each customer, companies can customize market offerings, services, programs, messages, and media.

Customer relationship marketing holds that a major driver of company profitability is the aggregate value of the company's customer base.[16] Winning companies are more productive in acquiring, keeping, and growing customers. These companies improve the value of their customer base by excelling at reducing customer defection rates; increasing the life of each customer relationship; enhancing customer sales and profit potential; making low-profit customers more profitable—or terminating them; and focusing on high value customers. As Table 2.2 shows, marketing to individual consumers is not the same as marketing to the masses.

Peppers and Rogers suggest a four-step framework for one-to-one marketing:[17]

- Identify your prospects and customers. Do not go after everyone.
- Differentiate customers in terms of their needs and their value to your company, then lavish more effort on the most valuable customers (estimate customer value by the net present value of all future profits coming from purchases, margin levels, and referrals, less customer-specific servicing costs).
- Interact with individual customers to learn more about their individual needs and to build stronger relationships.
- Customize products, services, and messages to each customer.

TABLE 2.2   Mass Marketing versus One-to-One Marketing

Mass Marketing	One-to-One Marketing
Average customer	Individual customer
Customer anonymity	Customer profile
Standard product	Customized market offering
Mass production	Customized production
Mass distribution	Individualized distribution
Mass advertising	Individualized message
Mass promotion	Individualized incentives
One-way message	Two-way messages
Economies of scale	Economies of scope
Share of market	Share of customer
All customers	Profitable customers
Customer attraction	Customer retention

Source: Adapted from Don Peppers and Martha Rogers, The One-to-One Future (New York: Doubleday/Currency, 1993). See their Web site *www.1to1.com.*

Customer Databases and Database Marketing

Successful companies know their customers: They collect information, and store it in a customer database, and apply database marketing. A **customer database** is an organized collection of comprehensive information about individual customers or prospects that is current, accessible, and actionable for such marketing purposes as lead generation, lead qualification, sale of a product or service, or maintenance of customer relationships. **Database marketing** is the process of building, maintaining, and using customer databases and other databases (products, suppliers, resellers) for the purpose of contacting, transacting, and building relationships.

A customer database contains much more information than a **customer mailing list**, which is simply a set of names, addresses, and telephone numbers. Ideally, a customer database would contain the consumer's past purchases, demographics (age, income, family members, birthdays), psychographics (activities, interests, and opinions), mediagraphics (preferred media), and other useful information. A **business database** should contain past purchases of business customers; past volumes, prices, and profits; buyer team member names (and their ages, birthdays, hobbies, and favorite foods); status of current contracts; an estimate of the supplier's share of the customer's business; competitive suppliers; assessment of competitive strengths and weaknesses in selling and servicing the account; and buying practices, patterns, and policies.

Data Warehouses and Datamining

Savvy companies capture information every time a customer comes into contact with any of its departments by making a purchase, requesting a service call, sending an online query, or returning a mail-in rebate card. They store this information in a **data warehouse** and analyze it to draw inferences about each individual customer's needs and responses. This allows the company's customer service reps or telemarketers to respond knowledgeably to customer inquiries based on a total picture of the customer relationship. Through **datamining**, marketing statisticians can extract useful information about individuals, trends, and segments from a massive data warehouse. Datamining involves the use of sophisticated statistical and mathematical techniques such as cluster analysis, automatic interaction detection, predictive modeling, and neural networking.

In general, companies can use their databases to (1) identify the best prospects by sorting through a mass of responses; (2) match a specific offer with a specific customer as a way to sell, cross-sell, and up-sell; (3) deepen customer loyalty by remembering customer preferences and offering relevant incentives and information; (4) reactivate customer purchasing through reminders or timely promotions; and (5) avoid serious mistakes such as sending a customer two offers for the same product but at different prices.

However, a variety of problems can deter a firm from effectively using database marketing for CRM. The first is the large investment in computer hardware, database software, analytical programs, communication links, and skilled personnel as well as the difficulty in collecting the right data on all the occasions of company interaction with individual customers. Thus, building a customer database would not be worthwhile where the product is a once-in-a-lifetime purchase (e.g., a grand piano); where customers show little brand loyalty; where the unit sale is very small (e.g., a candy bar); and where the cost of gathering data is prohibitively high.

The second problem is the difficulty of getting everyone in the company to be customer-oriented and to use the available information for CRM rather than carrying on traditional transaction marketing. The third problem is that not all customers want an ongoing relationship with a company and may resent having their personal data collected and stored. Marketers must be concerned about customer attitudes toward privacy and security. For example, America Online, under fire from privacy advocates, junked a plan to sell subscribers' telephone numbers. Online companies would be smart to explain their privacy policies, and allow consumers to avoid having their information stored in a database. A fourth problem is that information must be updated continuously because people move, drop out, or change their interests.

One consulting firm reported that 70 percent of firms found little or no improvement from implementing a CRM system. The reasons are many: the system was poorly designed, it became too expensive, users didn't make much use of it or report much benefit, collaborators ignored the system, and so on. All this points to the need for each company to determine how much to invest in building and using database marketing to manage its customer relationships.

EXECUTIVE SUMMARY

Four major drivers of the new economy are digitalization and connectivity, disintermediation and reintermediation, customization and customerization, and industry convergence. The new economy is shifting old economy business practices toward organizing by customer segments (instead of only byproducts), focusing on customer lifetime value (instead of only transactions), focusing on stakeholders (not only shareholders), getting everyone involved in marketing (instead of only the marketing department), building brands through behavior (not just advertising), focusing on customer retention (as much as customer acquisition), measuring customer satisfaction, and underpromising and overdelivering.

E-business, using electronic means and platforms to conduct business, is broader than e-commerce, selling goods and services online. Many companies are starting to use e-purchasing and e-marketing. E-business and e-commerce occurs mainly over four major Internet domains: B2C (business-to-consumer), B2B (business-to-business), C2C (consumer-to-consumer), and C2B (consumer-to-business). In addition, e-businesses can be either pure-click or brick-and-click companies.

Companies face many questions in adopting e-marketing, including how to design an attractive Web site, how to advertise online, and how to build a sound revenue and profit model for dot-com businesses. Companies are also becoming skilled in customer relationship management (CRM), which focuses on meeting the individual needs of valued customers. This requires building a customer database and using data-mining to detect trends, segments, and individual needs to guide marketing activities.

NOTES

1. "A La I-Mode: Mobile Telecoms," *The Economist*, March 30, 2002; Lisa Takeuchi Cullen, "Deflating DoCoMo," *Time International*, February 25, 2002, pp. 10+.
2. Donna L. Hoffman, "The Revolution Will Not Be Televised," *Marketing Science* (Winter 2000): 1–3; George S. Day and David B. Montgomery, "Charting New Directions for Marketing," *Journal of Marketing*, Special Issue (1999): 3–13.
3. See Yoram J. Wind and Vijay Mahajan with Robert E. Gunther, *Convergence Marketing: Strategies for Reaching the New Hybrid Consumer* (Upper Saddle River, NJ: Prentice Hall PTR, 2002).
4. Wind, op. cit.
5. Bill Gates with Collins Hemingway, *Business @ the Speed of Thought: Using a Digital Nervous System* (New York: Warner Books, 1999).
6. *Pew Internet & American Life Project Survey*, November–December 2000.
7. See Ralph A. Oliva, "Nowhere to Hide," *Marketing Management* (July/August 2001): 44–46.
8. Gary M. Stern, "You Got a Complaint?" *Link-Up*, September 2001, p. 28.
9. Chuck Martin, *Net Future* (New York: McGraw-Hill, 1999).
10. J. Timothy Hunt, "Beyond Point and Click," *Financial Post—Canada*, May 1, 2001.
11. Jeffrey F. Rayport and Bernard J. Jaworski, *e-commerce* (New York: McGraw-Hill, 2001), p. 116.
12. Kate O'Sullivan, "Duh-Sign of the Times" *Inc*, November 1, 2001, *www.inc.com*; Joan Hamilton, "Diss My Web Site, Please," *BusinessWeek*, November 20, 2000, pp. EB-128, EB-130; Courtland L. Bovée and John V. Thill, *Business Communication Today* 7th ed. (Upper Saddle River, NJ: Prentice Hall, 2003), Component Chapter A.
13. Hamilton, "Diss My Web Site, Please."
14. Kimberly Weisul, "Yes, They Really Pay To See These Sites," *BusinessWeek*, January 21, 2002, p. 8.
15. Tilman Kemmler, Monika Kubicová, Robert Musslewhite, and Rodney Prezeau, "E-Performance II–The Good, the Bad, and the Merely Average," *The McKinsey Quarterly* (2001): *www.mckinseyquarterly.com*.
16. See George S. Day, "Capabilities for Forging Customer Relationships," *Working Paper Series, Marketing Science Institute*, Report No. 00-118, 2000.
17. Don Peppers and Martha Rogers, *The One-to-One Future* (New York: Doubleday/Currency, 1993).

CHAPTER 3

Building Customer Satisfaction, Value, and Retention

In this chapter, we will address the following questions:

1. What are customer value and satisfaction, and how can companies deliver them?
2. What makes a high-performance business?
3. How can companies both attract and retain customers?
4. How can companies improve both customer and company profitability?
5. How can companies deliver total quality?

MARKETING MANAGEMENT AT CATERPILLAR

One of the world's largest manufacturers is also one of the most customer-centered companies around. Caterpillar, with more than $20 billion in annual sales, has a long history of listening to customers. From infrastructure work such as highway construction to agricultural applications for large and small farmers alike, Caterpillar offers a range of heavy equipment (such as tractors) and related services for business and government buyers on every continent.

When Caterpillar was developing a new tractor line not long ago, it surveyed and interviewed hundreds of growers in North America, Europe, and Australia to identify needs, buying criteria, and desirable benefits. It also gathered feedback from customers who had visited its main factory and polled its grower and dealer advisory panels. After designing prototypes, the company field-tested them under various conditions and studied how the features helped customers achieve their goals of higher efficiency and productivity. Caterpillar's marketers communicated the value of "farmer-driven design" when advertising this line to dealers and customers. Another customer-centered feature in many Caterpillar tractors is an onboard satellite system to signal the dealer when a customer's equipment requires servicing. Finally, the company has developed a Value Chain Accelerator Program to coordinate the flow of raw materials and parts from suppliers to factories for better production and resource planning—thus allowing Caterpillar to meet customer expectations for timely and cost-effective offerings.[1]

How can companies go about winning customers and outperforming competitors? The answer, as Caterpillar well knows, lies in doing a better job of meeting or exceeding customer expectations. Customer-centered companies are adept at building customers, not just products; they are skilled in market engineering, not just product engineering.

Too many companies think that it is the marketing or sales department's job to acquire and manage customers. In fact, marketing is only one factor in attracting and keeping customers. The best marketing department in the world cannot sell products that are poorly made or fail to meet a need. The marketing department can be effective only in companies whose departments and employees have designed and implemented a competitively superior customer value-delivery system. This chapter describes and illustrates the philosophy of the customer-focused firm and value marketing.

DEFINING CUSTOMER VALUE AND SATISFACTION

Customers today face a vast array of product and brand choices, prices, and suppliers. How do they make their choices? We believe that customers estimate which offer will deliver the most value. Customers are value-maximizers, within the bounds of search costs and limited knowledge, mobility, and income. They form an expectation of value and act on it. Whether the offer lives up to the value expectation affects both satisfaction and repurchase probability.

Customer Perceived Value

Our premise is that customers will buy from the firm that they perceive offers the highest customer delivered value (see Figure 3.1). **Customer perceived value (CPV)** is the difference between the prospective customer's evaluation of all the benefits and all the costs of an offering and the perceived alternatives. **Total customer value** is the perceived monetary value of the bundle of economic, functional, and psychological benefits customers expect from a given market offering. **Total customer cost** is the bundle of costs that customers expect to incur in evaluating, obtaining, using, and disposing of the given market offering.

As an example, suppose the buyer for a residential construction company wants to buy a tractor from either Caterpillar or Komatsu. After evaluating the two tractors, he decides that Caterpillar has a higher product value, based on perceived reliability, durability, performance, and resale value. He also decides that Caterpillar's personnel are more knowledgeable, and perceives that the company will provide better services, such as maintenance. Finally, he places higher value on Caterpillar's corporate image.

FIGURE 3.1   Determinants of Customer Delivered Value

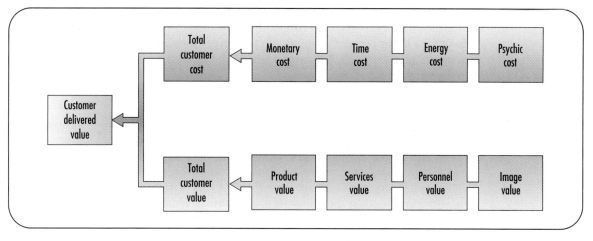

He adds up all of the values from these four sources—product, services, personnel, and image—and perceives Caterpillar as delivering greater customer value.

The buyer also examines his total cost of transacting with Caterpillar versus Komatsu. In addition to the monetary cost, the total customer cost includes the buyer's time, energy, and psychic costs. Then the buyer compares Caterpillar's total customer cost to its total customer value and compares Komatsu's total customer cost to its total customer value. In the end, the buyer will buy from the company that he perceives is offering the highest delivered value.

According to this theory of buyer decision making, Caterpillar can succeed in selling to this buyer by improving its offer in three ways. First, it can increase total customer value by improving product, services, personnel, and/or image benefits. Second, it can reduce the buyer's nonmonetary costs by lessening the time, energy, and psychic costs. Third, it can reduce its product's monetary cost to the buyer. If Caterpillar wants to win the sale, it must offer more delivered value than Komatsu does.[2]

Some marketers might argue that this process is too rational, because buyers do not always choose the offer with the highest delivered value. Suppose the customer chose the Komatsu tractor. How can we explain this choice? Here are three possibilities:

1. The buyer might be under orders to buy at the lowest price, regardless of delivered value. To win this sale, Caterpillar must convince the buyer's manager that buying only on price will result in lower long-term profits.
2. The buyer will retire before the company realizes that the Komatsu tractor is more expensive to operate than the Caterpillar tractor. To win this sale, Caterpillar must convince other people in the buyer's company that its offer delivers greater long-term value.
3. The buyer enjoys a long-term friendship with the Komatsu salesperson. Here, Caterpillar must show the buyer that the Komatsu tractor will draw complaints from the tractor operators when they discover its high fuel cost and need for frequent repairs.

Still, customer perceived value is a useful framework that applies to many situations and yields rich insights. Here are its implications: First, the seller must assess the total customer value and total customer cost associated with each competitor's offer to know how his or her own offer rates in the buyer's mind. Second, the seller who is at a customer perceived value disadvantage can try to increase total customer value or try to decrease total customer cost.[3]

Total Customer Satisfaction

Whether the buyer is satisfied after making a purchase depends on the offer's performance in relation to the buyer's expectations. **Satisfaction** is a person's feelings of pleasure or disappointment resulting from comparing a product's perceived performance (or outcome) in relation to his or her expectations. If the performance falls short of expectations, the customer is dissatisfied. If performance matches expectations, the customer is satisfied; if it exceeds expectations, the customer is highly satisfied or delighted.[4]

High customer satisfaction or delight creates an emotional bond with the brand or company, not just a rational preference. Xerox's senior management found out that its "completely satisfied" customers are six times more likely to repurchase Xerox products over the following 18 months than its "very satisfied" customers.[5]

How do buyers form their expectations? From past buying experience, friends' and associates' advice, and marketers' and competitors' information and promises. If marketers raise expectations too high, the buyer is likely to be disappointed. However, if the company sets expectations too low, it won't attract enough buyers (although it will satisfy those who do buy).

Clearly, the key to generating high customer loyalty is to deliver high customer value. Michael Lanning, in *Delivering Profitable Value*, says a firm must develop a competitively superior value proposition aimed at a specific market segment, backed by a superior value-delivery system.[6] The **value proposition** consists of the whole cluster of benefits the company promises to deliver; it is much more than the core positioning of the offering. Basically, it is a statement about the resulting experience customers will gain from the offering and their relationship with the supplier. The brand must represent a promise about the total resulting experience that customers can expect. Whether the promise is kept depends upon the firm's ability to manage its value-delivery system. The **value-delivery system** includes all the experiences the customer will have on the way to obtaining and using the offering.

Knox and Maklan emphasize a similar theme in *Competing on Value*.[7] Too many companies create a value gap by failing to align brand value with customer value. Brand marketers try to distinguish their brand by a slogan, by a unique selling proposition, or by augmenting the basic offering with added services. But they are less successful in delivering distinctive customer value, primarily because their marketers are focused on brand development. Knox and Maklan want marketers to spend as much time influencing the company's core processes as the time spent designing the brand profile.

For customer-centered companies, customer satisfaction is both a goal and a marketing tool. Companies that achieve high customer satisfaction ratings make sure that their target market knows it. Dell Computer's meteoric growth in personal computers can be partly attributed to achieving and advertising its number-one rank in customer satisfaction. Dell's direct-to-customer business model enables it to be extremely responsive to customers while keeping costs and prices low. "There's no confusion about what the value proposition is, what the company offers, and why it's great for customers," says founder Michael Dell.[8]

Note that the main goal of the customer-centered firm is not to maximize customer satisfaction. If the company increases satisfaction by lowering its price or increasing its services, the result may be lower profits. The company might be able to increase its profitability by means other than increased satisfaction (for example, by improving manufacturing processes or investing more in R&D). Also, the company has many stakeholders, including employees, dealers, suppliers, and stockholders. Spending more to increase customer satisfaction might divert funds from increasing the satisfaction of other "partners." Ultimately, the company wants to deliver high customer satisfaction subject to delivering acceptable levels of satisfaction to other stakeholders, given its total resources. Customer satisfaction levels are particularly important because consumers can quickly spread good or bad evaluations via the Internet.

THE NATURE OF HIGH-PERFORMANCE BUSINESSES

Companies that navigate all these pitfalls to reach their customer value and satisfaction goals are **high-performance companies**. The consulting firm of Arthur D. Little proposed a four-factor model of the characteristics of a high-performance business (see Figure 3.2). According to this model, the four keys to success are stakeholders, processes, resources, and organization.[9]

Stakeholders

As its first step on the road to high performance, the business must define its stakeholders and their needs. Although businesses have traditionally paid the most attention to their stockholders, today they recognize that unless they nourish other stakeholders—customers, employees, suppliers, distributors—the business may never earn sufficient profits for the stockholders.

A business must strive to satisfy the minimum expectations of each stakeholder group while delivering above-minimum satisfaction levels for different stakeholders. For example, the company might aim to delight its customers, perform well for its employees, and deliver a threshold level of satisfaction to its suppliers. In setting these levels, the company must be careful not to violate the various stakeholder groups' sense of fairness about the relative treatment they are getting.[10]

Processes

A company can accomplish its stakeholder goals only by managing and linking work processes. High-performance companies are increasingly focusing on the need to manage core business processes such as new-product development, customer attraction and retention, and order fulfillment. They are reengineering the work flows and building cross-functional teams that are responsible for each process.[11]

At Xerox, for example, a Customer Operations Group links sales, shipping, installation, service, and billing so these activities flow smoothly into one another. Cross-functional teams are also becoming more common in government agencies and in nonprofits. As the mission of the San Diego Zoo changed from exhibition to con-

FIGURE 3.2   The High-Performance Business

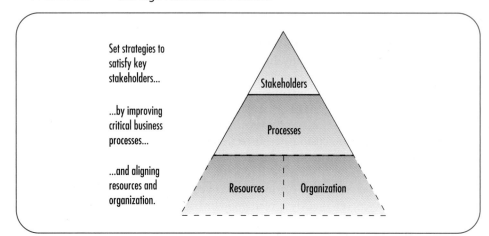

Source: P. Ranganath Nayak, Erica Drazen, and George Kastner, "The High-Performance Business: Accelerating Performance Improvement," *Prism* (First Quarter 1992), p. 6. Reprinted with permission of Arthur D. Little.

servation to education, it eliminated traditional departmental boundaries and set up cross-functional teams of gardeners, groundskeepers, and animal care experts to care for the flora and fauna in new bioclimatic zones.[12]

Resources

To carry out its business processes, a company needs resources—labor power, materials, machines, information, and energy. Traditionally, companies owned and controlled most of the resources that entered their business. Many companies today outsource less critical resources if they can be obtained at better quality or lower cost. Frequently outsourced resources include cleaning services, lawn care, and auto fleet management.

For high-performance companies, the key is to own and nurture the resources and competencies that make up the essence of the business. Nike, for example, does not manufacture its own shoes, because its Asian manufacturers are more competent in this task. But Nike nurtures its superiority in shoe design and shoe merchandising, its two core competencies. A **core competency** has three characteristics: (1) It is a source of competitive advantage in that it makes a significant contribution to perceived customer benefits; (2) it has a breadth of applications to a wide variety of markets; and (3) it is difficult for competitors to imitate.[13]

Competitive advantage also accrues to companies that possess distinctive capabilities. Whereas core competencies tend to refer to areas of special technical and production expertise, **distinctive capabilities** tend to describe excellence in broader business processes. For example, Wal-Mart has a distinctive capability in product replenishment based on its core competencies of information system design and logistics.

Organization and Organizational Culture

A company's **organization** consists of its structures, policies, and corporate culture, all of which can become dysfunctional in a rapidly changing business environment. Whereas structures and policies can be changed (with difficulty), the firm's culture is very hard to change. Yet changing the culture is often the key to implementing a new strategy successfully.

Corporate culture has been defined as "the shared experiences, stories, beliefs, and norms that characterize an organization." Sometimes corporate culture develops organically and is transmitted directly from the CEO's personality and habits to the company employees. Such is the case with computer giant Microsoft. Even as a multi-billion dollar company, Microsoft hasn't lost the hard-driving culture perpetuated by founder Bill Gates. This culture may be the biggest key to Microsoft's success and to its much-criticized dominance in the computing industry.[14]

In high-performance businesses, the organization and the corporate culture are set up to deliver superior customer value and satisfaction. Let us see how this is done.

DELIVERING CUSTOMER VALUE AND SATISFACTION

A company can only win by creating and delivering superior value. This involves the following five capabilities: understanding customer value; creating customer value; delivering customer value; capturing customer value; and sustaining customer value. To succeed, a company needs to use the concepts of a value chain and a value-delivery network.

Value Chain

Michael Porter of Harvard proposed the **value chain** as a tool for identifying ways to create more customer value.[15] Every firm is a synthesis of activities that are performed to design, produce, market, deliver, and support its product. The value chain identifies nine strategically relevant activities that create value and cost in a specific business. These consist of five primary activities and four support activities, as shown in Figure 3.3.

FIGURE 3.3   The Generic Value Chain

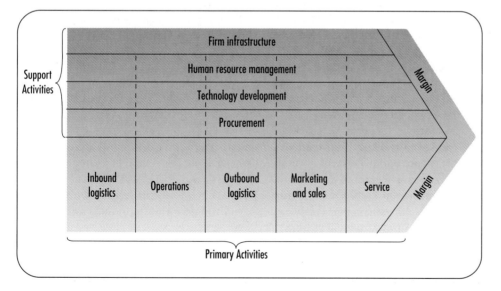

Source: Reprinted with permission of The Free Press, an imprint of Simon & Schuster, from Michael E. Porter, *Competitive Advantage. Creating and Sustaining Performance.* Copyright © 1985 by Michael E. Porter.

The firm's task is to examine its costs and performance in each value-creating activity and look for ways to improve. The firm should estimate its competitors' costs and performances as **benchmarks** against which to compare its own costs and performances. It should go further and study the "best of class" practices of the world's best companies.[16]

The firm's success depends on how well each department performs its work as well as how well the various departmental activities are coordinated. To more smoothly manage delivery of quality customer service, companies need to manage these five core business processes:[17]

- *The market sensing process.* All the activities involved in gathering market intelligence, disseminating it within the firm, and acting on it.
- *The new offering realization process.* All the activities involved in researching, developing, and launching new, high-quality offerings quickly and within budget.
- *The customer acquisition process.* All the activities involved in defining target markets and prospecting for new customers.
- *The customer relationship management process.* All the activities involved in building deeper understanding, relationships, and offerings to individual customers.
- *The fulfillment management process.* All the activities involved in receiving and approving orders, shipping the goods on time, and collecting payment.

Strong companies develop superior capabilities in managing their core processes. For example, Wal-Mart has superior strength in its stock replenishment process.

The Value Delivery Network

To be successful, a firm also needs to look for competitive advantages beyond its own operations, into the value chains of its suppliers, distributors, and customers. Many companies have partnered with specific suppliers and distributors to create a superior **value-delivery network** (also called a **supply chain**).[18] For example, Bailey Controls, which makes control systems for big factories, plugs some suppliers directly into its electronic inventory-management system as if they were internal departments. These suppliers can check Bailey's inventory levels and forecasts and then gear up to provide the materials the firm will need for the coming six months. As a result, the goods are pulled by customer demand rather than pushed by supply.

ATTRACTING AND RETAINING CUSTOMERS

In addition to working with partners through **partner relationship management (PRM)**, many companies are developing stronger customer bonds through *customer relationship management (CRM)*. Today customers are smarter, more price conscious, more demanding, less forgiving, and approached by more competitors with equal or better offers. The challenge now, says Jeffrey Gitomer, is not to produce satisfied customers, but to produce loyal customers.[19]

Attracting Customers

Companies seeking to expand sales and profits must spend considerable time and resources searching for new customers. Customer acquisition requires substantial skills in lead generation, lead qualification, and conversion of prospects into customers. After they are acquired, however, some of these customers will not be retained.

Lost Customers and Customer Lifetime Value

Too many companies suffer from high **customer churn**—namely, high customer defection. Today's companies must pay closer attention to their customer defection rate (the rate at which they lose customers). Many cellular carriers, for example, lose 25 percent of their subscribers each year at a cost estimated at $2 billion to $4 billion.

Companies can take four steps to reduce defection. First, the firm must define and measure its retention rate. For a magazine, the renewal rate is a good retention measure. For a college, it could be the first- to second-year retention rate, or the class graduation rate. Second, the company must distinguish the causes of customer attrition and identify those that can be managed better. The Forum Corporation analyzed the customers lost by 14 major companies for reasons other than leaving the area or going out of business: 15 percent switched to a better product; 15 percent found a cheaper product; and 70 percent left because of poor or little attention from the supplier. Clearly, firms can take steps to retain customers who leave because of poor service, shoddy products, or high prices.[20]

Third, the company needs to estimate how much profit it loses when it loses customers. For one customer, the lost profit is equal to the **customer lifetime value**—the present value of the profit stream that the company would have realized if the customer had not defected prematurely. Suppose a company annually loses 5 percent of its 64,000 customers due to poor service (3,200 customers). If each lost account averages $40,000 in revenue, the company loses $128 million in revenue (3,200 x $40,000). On a 10 percent profit margin, this is $12.8 million in lost profits every year.

Fourth, the company needs to figure out how much it would cost to reduce the defection rate. As long as the cost is less than the lost profit, the company should spend the money. Finally, nothing beats plain old listening to customers. Deere & Company, which makes John Deere tractors, has retired employees interviewing defectors and customers. Listening helped Deere build extraordinarily high customer loyalty. It retains nearly 98 percent of its customers in some product areas.[21]

The Need for Customer Retention

Unfortunately, most marketing theory and practice center on the art of attracting new customers rather than on retaining and cultivating existing ones. The emphasis traditionally has been on making sales rather than building relationships; on preselling and selling rather than caring for the customer afterward. Yet the key to customer retention is customer satisfaction.

A highly satisfied customer stays loyal longer, buys more, talks favorably about the company and its products, pays less attention to competitors, is less price-sensitive, offers product or service ideas, and costs less to serve than new customers because transactions are routine. Thus, a company would be wise to measure customer satisfaction regularly and try to exceed customer expectations, not merely meet them.

Although some companies try to get a sense of customer satisfaction by tallying customer complaints, 96 percent of dissatisfied customers do not complain; many just stop buying.[22] The best thing a company can do is to make it easy for customers to complain via toll-free phone numbers, suggestion forms, and e-mail—and then listen.

3M, for example, says that over two-thirds of its product-improvement ideas come from listening to customer complaints.

Listening is not enough, however. The company must respond quickly and constructively to the complaints. As Albrecht and Zemke observe: "Of the customers who register a complaint, between 54 and 70 percent will buy again if their complaint is resolved. The figure goes up to a staggering 95 percent if the customer feels the complaint was resolved quickly. Customers whose complaints were satisfactorily resolved tell an average of five people about the good treatment they received."[23]

One company long recognized for its emphasis on customer satisfaction is L.L. Bean, which runs a mail-order and Internet catalog business in clothing and equipment for rugged living. L.L. Bean has carefully blended its external and internal marketing programs. To its customers, it offers the following:[24]

100% Guarantee

All of our products are guaranteed to give 100% satisfaction in every way. Return anything purchased from us at any time if it proves otherwise. We will replace it, refund your purchase price or credit your credit card, as you wish. We do not want you to have anything from L.L. Bean that is not completely satisfactory.

To motivate its employees to serve customers well, L.L. Bean displays the following poster around its offices:[25]

What Is a Customer?

A Customer is the most important person ever in this office . . . in person or by mail.

A Customer is not dependent on us . . . we are dependent on him.

A Customer is not an interruption of our work . . . he is the purpose of it. We are not doing a favor by serving him . . . he is doing us a favor by giving us the opportunity to do so.

A Customer is not someone to argue or match wits with. Nobody ever won an argument with a Customer.

A Customer is a person who brings us his wants. It is our job to handle them profitably to him and to ourselves.

More companies are recognizing the benefits of satisfying and retaining current customers. Remember, acquiring new customers can cost five times more than the cost of satisfying and retaining current customers. On average, companies lose 10 percent of their customers each year. Yet by reducing the customer defection rate by 5 percent, companies can increase profits by 25 percent to 85 percent, depending on the industry. Also, the customer profit rate tends to increase over the life of the retained customer.[26]

Companies can strengthen customer retention in two ways. One way is to erect high switching barriers. Customers are less inclined to switch to another supplier when this would involve high capital costs, high search costs, or the loss of loyal-customer discounts. The better approach is to deliver high customer satisfaction. This makes it harder for competitors to overcome switching barriers by simply offering lower prices or switching inducements. The task of creating strong customer loyalty is called customer relationship marketing.

Customer Relationship Marketing: The Key

The goal of customer relationship marketing is to produce high customer equity. **Customer equity** is the total of the discounted lifetime values of all of the firm's customers. Rust, Zeithaml, and Lemon distinguish three drivers of customer equity: value equity, brand equity, and relationship equity.[27] This formulation integrates *value management*, *brand management*, and *relationship management* within a customer-centered focus.

- *Value equity* is the customer's objective assessment of the utility of an offering based on perceptions of its benefits relative to its costs. The subdrivers of value equity are quality, price, and convenience. Value equity makes the biggest contribution to customer equity when products are differentiated and when they are more complex and need to be evaluated.

- *Brand equity* is the customer's subjective and intangible assessment of the brand, above and beyond its objectively perceived value. The subdrivers of brand equity are customer brand awareness, customer attitude toward the brand, and customer perception of brand ethics. Brand equity is more important than the other drivers of customer equity where products are less differentiated and have more emotional impact.

- *Relationship equity* is the customer's tendency to stick with the brand, above and beyond objective and subjective assessments of its worth. Subdrivers include loyalty programs, special recognition and treatment programs, community building programs, and knowledge building programs. Relationship equity is especially important where personal relationships count for a lot and where customers tend to continue with suppliers out of habit or inertia.

Figure 3.4 shows the main steps in attracting and retaining customers. The starting point is everyone who might conceivably buy the product or service (suspects). From these the company determines the most likely prospects, who it hopes to convert into first-time customers, then into repeat customers, and then into clients, people whom the company treats as special. The next challenge is to turn clients into members by starting a membership program that offers benefits to customers who join, and then into advocates who recommend the company and its offerings to others. The ultimate challenge is to turn advocates into partners.

FIGURE 3.4   The Customer-Development Process

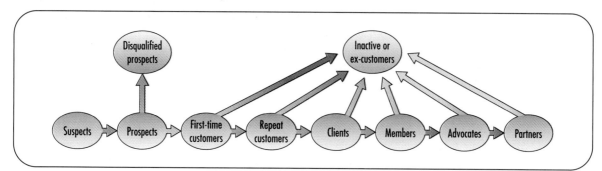

Source: See Jill Griffin, *Customer Loyalty: How to Earn It, How to Keep It* (New York: Lexington Books, 1995), p. 36. Also see Murray Raphel and Neil Raphel, *Up the Loyalty Ladder: Turning Sometime Customers into Full-Time Advocates of Your Business* (New York: HarperBusiness, 1995).

MARKETING SKILLS: WINNING BACK LOST CUSTOMERS

Customer defections are inevitable: people and companies move, have new needs, or simply lose interest in certain offerings. However, marketers can hone their skills to win back lost customers. Because former customers know the company and its offerings—and the company knows something about these customers—marketers need not spend as much to bring them back as they do to attract an entirely new customer. And if marketers carefully analyze each lost customer's profitability (as discussed later in this chapter), they can invest in winning back customers with good profit potential, which will enhance the company's bottom line.

Win-back starts with recognizing when, why, and how good customers make the decision to leave. Companies that bill monthly learn quickly when a customer leaves, as do companies that receive complaints or cancellation notices. Businesses with unscheduled or less frequent customer contacts—such as stores and Web sites—may not notice for some time. Marketers can also use informal contacts (such as a phone call from the sales rep) or formal marketing research (such as an exit interview) to uncover the reasons for good customer defections. Analyzing all this information with an open mind will reveal any patterns of dissatisfaction or internal problems. Finally, marketers can win back good customers by starting with an apology where warranted and an offer to promptly address concerns. Although price adjustments are sometimes appropriate, marketers should look for other hooks to reestablish the relationship. For instance, customers appreciate personal contact and being able to choose from alternative solutions. If the first approach fails, the company may want to communicate a different offer at a later date.

Marketers for Cellular One know that contacting customers right after they switch to another cell phone service may annoy them. Therefore, Cellular One waits one or two months before calling—enough time for customers to have a clearer assessment of why they left and of how their new service relationship is going. When Cellular One calls, some former customers come back because their new provider is not living up to their expectations. At the very least, the company gets more honest and objective feedback about why customers left and what it would take to bring them back.[28]

Some customers inevitably become inactive or drop out. Here the challenge is to reactivate dissatisfied customers through win-back strategies (see "Marketing Skills: Winning Back Lost Customers"). This is often easier than finding new customers because former customers' names and histories are known. The goal is to win back only those with strong profit potential.

How much should a company invest in building loyalty so that the costs do not exceed the gains? We need to distinguish five levels of investment in customer-relationship building:

1. *Basic marketing:* Simply selling the product.
2. *Reactive marketing:* Selling the product and encouraging customers to offer questions, comments, or complaints.
3. *Accountable marketing:* Following up after the sale to see whether the product meets expectations and to ask for improvement suggestions and any specific disappointments.

4. *Proactive marketing:* Contacting customers periodically with suggestions about improved product uses or new products.
5. *Partnership marketing:* Working continuously with customers to find ways to perform better.

Most companies practice only basic marketing when their markets contain many customers and their unit profit margins are small. Whirlpool is not going to phone each washing machine buyer to express appreciation. At best, it may set up a customer hot line or e-mail process. At the other extreme, in markets with few customers and high profit margins, most sellers will move toward partnership marketing. Boeing, for example, works closely with American Airlines in designing airplanes that fully satisfy Americans' requirements. As Figure 3.5 shows, the likely level of relationship marketing depends on the number of customers and the profit margin level.

The best relationship marketing going on today is driven by technology. Dell Computer could not customize online computer ordering for its global corporate customers without advances in Web technology. E-mail, Web sites, call centers, databases, and database software are helping to foster continuous contact between company and customer.

Forming Strong Customer Bonds

Companies that want to develop strong customer bonds can follow three value-building approaches, say Berry and Parasuraman: adding financial benefits, adding social benefits, and adding structural ties.[29]

Adding Financial Benefits   Two financial benefits that help companies bond customers more closely are frequency marketing programs and club marketing programs. **Frequency programs (FPs)** reward customers who buy frequently and/or in substantial amounts. Frequency marketing acknowledges that 20 percent of a company's customers might account for 80 percent of its business.

American Airlines was once a frequency program pioneer when it began offering free mileage credit to its customers in the early 1980s. Hotels next adopted FPs, with frequent guests receiving room upgrades or free rooms after earning so many points. Car rental firms soon started FPs, then credit-card companies began to offer points

FIGURE 3.5   Levels of Relationship Marketing

	HIGH MARGIN	MEDIUM MARGIN	LOW MARGIN
Many customers/ distributors	Accountable	Reactive	Basic or reactive
Medium number of customers/ distributors	Proactive	Accountable	Reactive
Few customers/ distributors	Partnership	Proactive	Accountable

and rebates for card usage. Today most supermarket chains offer price club cards, which provide member customers with discounts on particular items. Typically, the first company to introduce an FP gains the most benefit. After competitors respond, FPs can become a financial burden to all of the offering companies.

Many companies have created club membership programs to strengthen bonds with customers. Club membership can be open to everyone who purchases a product or service, such as a frequent flier or frequent diners club, or it can be limited to an affinity group or to those willing to pay a small fee. Although open clubs are good for building a database or snagging customers from competitors, limited membership clubs are more powerful long-term loyalty builders. Fees and membership conditions prevent those with only a fleeting interest in a company's products from joining. Limited membership clubs attract and keep those customers who are responsible for the largest portion of business.

Adding Social Benefits   Company personnel work on increasing social bonds with customers by individualizing and personalizing customer relationships. In essence, thoughtful companies turn their customers into clients. Donnelly, Berry, and Thompson draw this distinction: "Customers may be nameless to the institution; clients cannot be nameless. Customers are served as part of the mass or as part of larger segments; clients are served on an individual basis. Customers are served by anyone who happens to be available; clients are served by the professional assigned to them."[30]

Adding Structural Ties   The company may supply special equipment or computer linkages to help customers manage their orders, payroll, inventory, and so on. A good example is McKesson Corporation, a leading pharmaceutical wholesaler, which invested millions of dollars in electronic capabilities to help independent pharmacies manage inventory, order entry processes, and shelf space. The marketer's goal should be to increase the consumer's *proclivity to repurchase* the company's brand. Wunderman suggests creating structural ties with the customer by:[31]

1. *Creating long-term contracts.* A newspaper subscription replaces the need to buy a newspaper each day; a twenty-year mortgage replaces the need to re-borrow money each year.
2. *Charging less for ongoing purchases.* Offer lower prices to people who agree to be supplied regularly with a certain brand of toothpaste, detergent, or beer.
3. *Turning the product into a long-term service.* TiVo sells a personal television recorder that allows customers to personalize and automate their recording activities by subscribing to the company's extensive monthly program listings.[32]

CUSTOMER PROFITABILITY: THE ULTIMATE TEST

Ultimately, marketing is the art of attracting and keeping profitable customers. According to James Vander Putten of American Express, the best customers outspend others by ratios of 16 to 1 in retailing, 13 to 1 in the restaurant business, 12 to 1 in the airline business, and 5 to 1 in the hotel and motel industry.[33] Yet every company loses money on some of its customers. The well-known 20–80 rule says that the top 20 percent of the customers may generate as much as 80 percent of the company's profits. Sherden suggested amending the rule to read 20–80–30, to reflect the idea that the top 20 percent of customers generate 80 percent of the company's profits, half of which is lost serving the bottom 30 percent of unprofitable customers. The implication is that a company could improve its profits by "firing" its worst customers.[34]

Furthermore, it is not necessarily the company's largest customers who yield the most profit. The largest customers demand considerable service and receive the deepest discounts. The smallest customers pay full price and receive minimal service, but transaction costs reduce small customers' profitability. The midsize customers receive good service, pay nearly full price, and are often the most profitable. This is why many large firms are now invading the middle market. Major air express carriers, for instance, are finding that it does not pay to ignore the small and midsize international shippers. Programs geared toward smaller customers provide a network of drop boxes, which allow for substantial discounts over letters and packages picked up at the shipper's place of business. In addition to putting more drop boxes in place, United Parcel Service (UPS) conducts seminars to instruct exporters in the finer points of shipping overseas.[35]

What makes a customer profitable? A **profitable customer** is a person, household, or company that over time yields a revenue stream that exceeds by an acceptable amount the company's cost stream of attracting, selling, and servicing that customer. Note that the emphasis is on the lifetime stream of revenue and cost, not on one transaction's profitability. For example, Taco Bell has determined that a repeat customer is worth as much as $11,000. By sharing such estimates of lifetime value, Taco Bell's managers help employees understand the value of keeping customers satisfied.[36]

Although many firms measure customer satisfaction, most fail to measure individual customer profitability. Banks say this is because a customer uses different banking services and the transactions are logged in different departments. However, banks that have succeeded in linking customer transactions have been appalled by the number of unprofitable customers in their customer base. Some banks report losing money on over 45 percent of their customers. There are only two solutions to unprofitable customers: raise fees or reduce service support.[37]

Figure 3.6 shows a useful type of profitability analysis.[38] Customers are arrayed along the columns and products are arrayed along the rows. Each cell contains a symbol standing for the profitability of selling that product to that customer. Customer 1 is very profitable, buying three profitable products. Customer 2 represents mixed profitability, buying one profitable and one unprofitable product. Customer 3 is a losing customer, buying one profitable and two unprofitable products. What can the company do about customers 2 and 3? It can either (1) raise the price of its less profitable products or eliminate them, or (2) try to sell profitable products to the unprofitable customers. In fact, this company would benefit by encouraging unprofitable customers to switch to competitors.

Customer profitability analysis (CPA) is best conducted with the tools of an accounting technique called Activity-Based Costing (ABC). The company estimates all revenue coming from the customer, less all costs (including production and distribution costs, customer-contact costs, and the costs of all company resources that went into serving that customer). This helps the company classify customers into different profit tiers: platinum customers (most profitable), gold customers (profitable), iron customers (low profitability but desirable), and lead customers (unprofitable and undesirable). The company's job is to manage marketing investments to move iron and gold customers into higher tiers while dropping the lead customers or making them profitable by raising their prices or lowering the cost of serving them.

FIGURE 3.6   Customer-Product Profitability Analysis

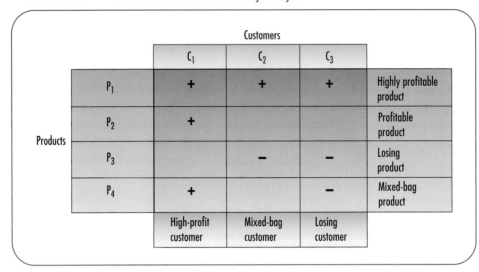

IMPLEMENTING TOTAL QUALITY MANAGEMENT

One of the major values customers expect from suppliers is high product and service quality. If companies want to stay in the race, let alone be profitable, they must adopt total quality management. **Total quality management (TQM)** is an organization-wide approach to continuously improving the quality of all of the organization's processes, products, and services. Market-leading firms see TQM as a key component of customer satisfaction and, ultimately, of profitability. According to General Electric's former chairman, John F. Welch Jr., "Quality is our best assurance of customer allegiance, our strongest defense against foreign competition, and the only path to sustained growth and earnings."[39]

The drive to produce goods of superior quality for world markets has led some countries—and groups of countries—to recognize or award prizes to companies that exemplify the best quality practices. In 1951, Japan became the first country to award a national quality prize, the Deming prize (named after W. Edwards Deming, the American statistician who taught quality improvement to postwar Japan). In the mid-1980s, the United States established the Malcolm Baldrige National Quality Award, which measures quality according to seven measures: customer focus and satisfaction, quality and operational results, management of process quality, human resource development and management, strategic quality planning, information and analysis, and senior executive leadership. FedEx, Ritz-Carlton hotels, and Custom Research are some past winners.

The European Quality Award, established in 1993, is awarded to companies that have achieved high grades on quality leadership, people management, policy and strategy, resources, processes, people satisfaction, customer satisfaction, impact on society, and business results. Europe also established the ISO 9000 standard, which has become a set of generally accepted principles for documenting quality. Earning the ISO 9000 certification involves a quality audit every six months from a registered ISO (International Standards Organization) assessor.[40]

Product and service quality, customer satisfaction, and company profitability are intimately connected. Higher quality levels result in higher levels of customer satisfaction while supporting higher prices and, often, lower costs. The well-known PIMS (Profit Impact of Market Strategy) studies show a high correlation between relative product quality and company profitability.[41]

What exactly is quality? According to the American Society for Quality Control's definition, which has been adopted worldwide, **quality** is the totality of features and characteristics of a product or service that bear on its ability to satisfy stated or implied needs.[42] This is clearly a customer-centered definition. We can say that the seller has delivered quality whenever the seller's product or service meets or exceeds the customers' expectations. A company that satisfies most of its customers' needs most of the time is called a quality company.

It is important to distinguish between *conformance* quality and *performance* quality (or grade). A Mercedes provides higher performance quality than a Hyundai: The Mercedes rides smoother, goes faster, and lasts longer. Yet both a Mercedes and a Hyundai can be said to deliver the same conformance quality if all of the units deliver their respective promised quality.

Because total quality is key to value creation and customer satisfaction, it is everyone's job, just as marketing is everyone's job. Marketing managers, in particular, have two responsibilities in a quality-centered company. First, they must participate in formulating strategies and policies to help the company win through total quality excellence. Second, they must deliver marketing quality alongside production quality. This means that every marketing activity—research, sales training, advertising, customer service, and so on—must be performed to high standards.

Marketers actually play six roles in helping their company define and deliver high-quality goods and services to target customers. First, they bear the major responsibility for correctly identifying the customers' needs and requirements. Second, they must communicate customer expectations properly to product designers. Third, they must make sure that customers' orders are filled correctly and on time. Fourth, they must check that customers have received proper instructions, training, and technical assistance in the product's use. Fifth, they must stay in touch with customers after the sale to ensure that they are—and remain—satisfied. Sixth, they must gather customer ideas for product and service improvements and convey them to the appropriate company departments. When marketers do all of this, they are making substantial contributions to total quality management and customer satisfaction, as well as to customer and company profitability.

EXECUTIVE SUMMARY

Customers are value-maximizers. They will buy from the firm they perceive offers the highest customer delivered value, defined as the difference between total customer benefits and total customer cost. Sellers who are at a delivered-value disadvantage can try to increase total customer value or decrease total customer cost.

Satisfaction is a function of the product's perceived performance and the buyer's expectations. The key to high customer loyalty is to deliver higher customer satisfaction, so many companies are aiming for total customer satisfaction. Companies that reach their customer value and satisfaction goals are high-performance businesses.

These firms recognize the dynamic relationship connecting their stakeholder groups and the need for managing core business processes. They also nurture their core competencies, which lead to distinctive capabilities that build competitive advantage. Finally, their structures, policies, and corporate culture are focused on delivering customer value and satisfaction.

The value chain identifies nine strategically relevant activities that create value and cost in a business. The five core business processes are the market sensing process, the new offering realization process, the customer acquisition process, customer relationship management, and fulfillment management. Managing these core processes means creating a value-delivery network or marketing network in which the company works with the value chains of its suppliers and distributors. Companies no longer compete—marketing networks do.

Losing profitable customers can hurt profits, so companies need to examine the percentage of customers who defect. Winning back lost customers is an important marketing activity, and often costs less than attracting first-time customers. The cost of attracting a new customer is estimated to be five times the cost of keeping a current customer. The key to retaining profitable customers is relationship marketing. Five levels of investment in customer-relationship building are basic, reactive, accountable, proactive, and partnership marketing. Companies can build stronger customer bonds by adding financial benefits, social benefits, or structural benefits.

Quality is the totality of features and characteristics of a product that bear on its ability to satisfy stated or implied needs. Today's companies must implement total quality management to remain profitable, because total quality is vital to value creation and customer satisfaction. Marketing managers must participate in formulating strategies and policies for quality excellence; they must also deliver marketing quality alongside production quality.

NOTES

1. Hubble Smith, "Caterpillar's Diversity Helps Company During Economic Slumps, Executive Says," *Las Vegas Review-Journal* (March 21, 2002), (*www.lvrj.com*); Jill Jusko, "Caterpillar Program Aims To Drive Down Costs, Improve Collaboration," *Industry Week*, September 24, 2001, (*www.industryweek.com*); Dave Mowitz, "Niche Marketing To Large Farms Helps Small Operations As Well," *Successful Farming*, December 15, 2001, p. 29; Barb Baylor Anderson, "Caterpillar Relies on Customer Input For Tractor Launch," *Agri Marketing*, November–December 2001, pp. 40+.
2. See Irwin P. Levin and Richard D. Johnson, "Estimating Price-Quality Tradeoffs Using Comparative Judgments," *Journal of Consumer Research* (June 11, 1984): 593–600. Customer perceived value can be measured as a difference or as a ratio. If total customer value is $20,000 and total customer cost is $16,000, then the customer perceived value is $4,000 (measured as a difference) or 1.25 (measured as a ratio). Ratios that are used to compare offers are often called *value-price ratios*.
3. For more on customer perceived value, see David C. Swaddling and Charles Miller, *Customer Power* (Dublin, Ohio: The Wellington Press, 2001).
4. For some provocative analysis, see Susan Fournier and David Glenmick, "Rediscovering Satisfaction," *Journal of Marketing* (October 1999): 5–23.
5. Thomas O. Jones and W. Earl Sasser, Jr., "Why Satisfied Customers Defect," *Harvard Business Review* (November–December 1995): 88–99.
6. Michael J. Lanning, *Delivering Profitable Value* (Oxford, UK: Capstone, 1998).

7. Simon Knox and Stan Maklan, *Competing on Value: Bridging the Gap Between Brand and Customer Value* (London, UK: Financial Times, 1998). See also Richard A. Spreng, Scott B. MacKenzie, and Richard W. Olshawskiy, "A Reexamination of the Determinants of Consumer Satisfaction," *Journal of Marketing*, no. 3 (July 1996): 15–32.

8. Dell Increases Its Market Share as PC Sales Slow," *New York Times*, January 22, 2001; Evan Ramstad, "Dell Fights PC Wars by Emphasizing Customer Service," *Wall Street Journal*, August 15, 1997, p. B4; "The InternetWeek Interview—Michael Dell, Chairman and CEO, Dell Computer," *InternetWeek*, April 13, 1998, p. 8.

9. See Tamara J. Erickson and C. Everett Shorey, "Business Strategy: New Thinking for the 90s," *Prism* (Fourth Quarter 1992): 19–35.

10. See Robert S. Kaplan and David P. Norton, *The Balanced Scorecard: Translating Strategy Into Action* (Boston: Harvard Business School Press, 1996), as a tool for monitoring stakeholder satisfaction.

11. See Jon R. Katzenbach and Douglas K. Smith, *The Wisdom of Teams: Creating the High-Performance Organization* (Boston: Harvard Business School Press, 1993) and Michael Hammer and James Champy, *Reengineering the Corporation* (New York: HarperBusiness, 1993).

12. Leonard L. Berry, *Discovering the Soul of Service* (New York: Free Press, 1999), pp. 188–89; David Glines, "Do You Work in a Zoo?" *Executive Excellence* 11, no. 10 (October 1994): 12–13.

13. C. K. Prahalad and Gary Hamel, "The Core Competence of the Corporation," *Harvard Business Review* (May–June 1990): 79–91.

14. "Business: Microsoft's Contradiction," *The Economist*, January 31, l998, pp. 65–67; Andrew J. Glass, "Microsoft Pushes Forward, Playing to Win the Market," *Atlanta Constitution*, June 24, l998, p. D12; Ron Chernow, "The Burden of Being a Misunderstood Monopolist," *BusinessWeek*, November 22, 1999, p. 42.

15. Michael E. Porter, *Competitive Advantage: Creating and Sustaining Superior Performance* (New York: Free Press, 1985).

16. See Robert Hiebeler, Thomas B. Kelly, and Charles Ketteman, *Best Practices: Building Your Business with Customer-Focused Solutions* (New York: Simon and Schuster, 1998).

17. Hammer and Champy, *Reengineering the Corporation*.

18. Myron Magnet, "The New Golden Rule of Business," *Fortune*, November 28, 1994, pp. 60-64.

19. See Jeffrey Gitomer, *Customer Satisfaction Is Worthless: Customer Loyalty Is Priceless: How to Make Customers Love You, Keep Them Coming Back and Tell Everyone They Know* (Austin, TX: Bard Press, l998).

20. See Frederick F. Reichheld, "Learning from Customer Defections," *Harvard Business Review* (March–April 1996): 56–69.

21. Reichheld, "Learning from Customer Defections."

22. See Technical Assistance Research Programs (TARP), *U.S. Office of Consumer Affairs Study on Complaint Handling in America*, 1986.

23. Karl Albrecht and Ron Zemke, *Service America!* (Homewood IL: Dow Jones-Irwin, l985), pp. 6–7.

24. Courtesy L.L. Bean, Freeport, Maine.

25. Ibid.

26. See Frederick F. Reichheld, *The Loyalty Effect* (Boston: Harvard Business School Press, 1996).

27. See Roland T. Rust, Valerie A. Zeithaml, and Katherine A. Lemon, *Driving Customer Equity* (New York: Free Press, 2000).

28. Jay Kassing, "Increasing Customer Retention: Profitability Isn't a Spectator Sport," *Financial Services Marketing*, March–April 2002, pp. 32+; Jill Griffin and Michael W. Lowenstein, "Winning Back a Lost Customer," *Direct Marketing*, July 2001, pp. 49 +;

John D. Cimperman, "Win-Back Starts Before Customer Is Lost," *Multichannel News*, February 19, 2001, pp. 53+.

29. Leonard L. Berry and A. Parasuraman, *Marketing Services: Competing Through Quality* (New York: Free Press, 1991), pp. 136–42. See also Richard Cross and Janet Smith, *Customer Bonding: Pathways to Lasting Customer Loyalty* (Lincolnwood, IL: NTC Business Books, 1995).

30. James H. Donnelly Jr., Leonard L. Berry, and Thomas W. Thompson, *Marketing Financial Services—A Strategic Vision* (Homewood, IL: Dow Jones-Irwin, 1985), p. 113.

31. From a privately circulated paper, Lester Wunderman, "The Most Elusive Word in Marketing," June 2000. Also see Lester Wunderman, *Being Direct* (New York: Random House, 1996).

32. J. B. Houck. "TiVo Tunes In ClientLogic for CRM." *CRMDaily.com*, May 7, 2001 (*www.crmdaily.com/perl/story/9538.html*).

33. Quoted in Don Peppers and Martha Rogers, *The One to One Future: Building Relationships One Customer at a Time* (New York: Currency Doubleday, 1993), p. 108.

34. William A. Sherden, *Market Ownership: The Art & Science of Becoming #1* (New York: Amacom, 1994), p. 77.

35. Robert J. Bowman, "Good Things, Smaller Packages," *World Trade* 6, no. 9 (October 1993): pp. 106–10.

36. Lynn O'Rourke Hayes, "Quality Is Worth 11,000 in the Bank," *Restaurant Hospitality*, March 1993, p. 68.

37. Rakesh Niraj, Mahendra Gupta, and Chakravarthi Narasimhan, "Customer Profitability in a Supply Chain," *Journal of Marketing* (July 2001): 1–16.

38. See Thomas M. Petro, "Profitability: The Fifth P of Marketing," *Bank Marketing*, September 1990, pp. 48–52; and Petro, "Who Are Your Best Customers?" *Bank Marketing*, October 1990, pp. 48–52.

39. "Quality: The U.S. Drives to Catch Up," *BusinessWeek*, November 1982, pp. 66–80; "Quality Programs Show Shoddy Results," *Wall Street Journal*, May 14, 1992, p. B1. See also Roland R. Rust, Anthony J. Zahorik, and Timothy L. Keiningham, "Return on Quality (ROQ): Making Service Quality Financially Accountable," *Journal of Marketing* 59, no. 2 (April 1995): 58–70.

40. See "Quality in Europe," *Work Study*, January–February 1993, p. 30; Ronald Henkoff, "The Hot New Seal of Quality," *Fortune*, June 28, 1993, pp. 116–20; Amy Zukerman, "One Size Doesn't Fit All," *Industry Week*, January 9, 1995, pp. 37–40; and "The Sleeper Issue of the 90s," *Industry Week*, August 15, 1994, pp. 99–100, 108.

41. Robert D. Buzzell and Bradley T. Gale, *The PIMS Principles: Linking Strategy to Performance* (New York: Free Press, 1987), ch. 6.

42. See Cyndee Miller, "U.S. Firms Lag in Meeting Global Quality Standards," *Marketing News*, February 15, 1993.

C H A P T E R   4

Winning Markets Through Strategic Planning, Implementation, and Control

In this chapter, we will address the following questions:

1. How is strategic planning carried out at the corporate, division, and business unit levels?
2. What are the major steps in the marketing process?
3. What does a marketing plan include?
4. How can a company effectively manage the marketing process?

MARKETING MANAGEMENT AT STARBUCKS

Starbucks got its start in Seattle in the 1970s selling fresh-ground coffee beans to local coffee lovers. In 1982, then-CEO Howard Schultz recognized an unfilled niche for cafés serving gourmet coffee. Seizing this opportunity as the basis for a market penetration strategy, the company built a loyal customer base in Seattle. The market development strategy marked the next phase in Starbucks' growth as it opened cafés across the Pacific Northwest, throughout North America, and finally around the world, sometimes in partnership with local companies. Then Starbucks sought to increase revenues from existing customers with a product development strategy of offering related merchandise such as CDs and Joe lifestyle magazine. Finally, Starbucks pursued diversification into grocery store aisles with Frappuccino bottled drinks, Starbucks branded ice cream, and the purchase of tea retailer Tazo Tea.

As a customer-driven company, Starbucks is always looking to add value by providing more customer benefits. For example, marketers are testing an express ordering system in which customers who have preregistered on the Web can use the phone to place a touch-tone order and have their favorite coffee or tea drink waiting at a nearby Starbucks. Social responsibility issues such as helping small coffee growers in developing countries are a high priority as well. Starbucks' senior vice president of social responsibility stresses that "corporate social responsibility adds value to a company"—a message that customers, suppliers, and other stakeholders want to hear.[1]

In earlier chapters, we addressed the question: How do companies compete successfully in today's marketplace? One part of the answer is a commitment to creating and delivering superior value to target customers. We can now add a second part: Successful companies know how to adapt to a continuously changing marketplace through **market-oriented strategic planning**, the managerial process of developing and maintaining a viable fit between the organization's objectives, skills, and resources and its changing market opportunities. The aim of strategic planning is to shape the company's businesses, products, services, and messages so they achieve targeted profits and growth. Successful firms also sharpen their expertise in organizing, implementing, and controlling marketing activities. In today's fast-paced environment, the ability to manage the entire marketing process has become an important competitive advantage.

STRATEGIC PLANNING: THREE KEY AREAS AND FOUR ORGANIZATIONAL LEVELS

Strategic planning calls for action in three key areas. The first area is managing a company's businesses as an investment portfolio. The second area involves assessing each business's strength by considering the market's growth rate and the company's position and fit in that market. The third is establishing a strategy for each business as a game plan for achieving long-term objectives.

To understand marketing management, we must understand strategic planning. Most large companies consist of four organizational levels: the corporate level, division level, business unit level, and product level. Corporate headquarters is responsible for designing a corporate strategic plan to guide the whole enterprise; it makes decisions on the amount of resources to allocate to each division, as well as on which businesses to start or eliminate. Each division establishes a plan covering the allocation of funds to each business unit within the division. Each business unit develops a strategic plan to carry that business unit into a profitable future. Finally, each product level (product line, brand) develops a marketing plan for achieving its objectives in its market.

The marketing plan operates at two levels: strategic and tactical. The **strategic marketing plan** lays out the target markets and the value proposition that will be offered, based on an analysis of the best market opportunities. The **tactical market-**

FIGURE 4.1   The Strategic Planning, Implementation, and Control Process

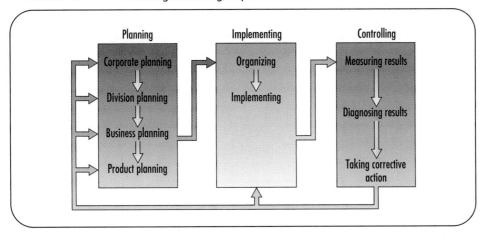

ing plan specifies the marketing tactics, including product features, promotion, merchandising, pricing, channels, and service.

The **marketing plan** is the central instrument for directing and coordinating the marketing effort. Today, teams develop marketing plans, with inputs and sign-offs from every important organizational function. These plans are then implemented at the appropriate levels of the organization, with management monitoring results and taking corrective action when necessary. The complete strategic planning, implementation, and control cycle is shown in Figure 4.1.

CORPORATE AND DIVISION STRATEGIC PLANNING

By preparing statements of mission, policy, strategy, and goals, headquarters establishes the framework within which the divisions and business units will prepare their plans. Some corporations allow their business units considerable freedom to set sales and profit goals and strategies. Others set goals for their business units but let them develop their own strategies. Still others set the goals and participate in developing in the individual business unit strategies.[2]

All corporate headquarters undertake four planning activities: defining the corporate mission; establishing strategic business units; assigning resources to each unit; and planning new businesses, downsizing, or terminating older businesses.

Defining the Corporate Mission

An organization exists to accomplish something: to make cars, lend money, provide a night's lodging, and so on. Its specific mission or purpose is usually clear when the business starts. Over time, the mission may change, to take advantage of new opportunities or respond to new market conditions. Amazon.com changed its mission from being the world's largest online bookstore to becoming the world's largest online store.

To define its mission, the company should address Peter Drucker's classic questions:[3] What is our business? Who is the customer? What is of value to the customer?

What will our business be? What should our business be? Successful companies continuously raise these questions and answer them thoughtfully and thoroughly.

Organizations develop **mission statements** to share with managers, employees, and—in many cases—customers. A clear, thoughtful mission statement provides employees with a shared sense of purpose, direction, and opportunity and guides geographically dispersed employees to work independently and collectively toward realizing the organization's goals. Motorola's mission statement, for example, is "to honorably serve the needs of the community by providing products and services of superior quality at a fair price to our customers; to do this so as to earn an adequate profit which is required for the total enterprise to grow; and by so doing provide the opportunity for our employees and shareholders to achieve their reasonable personal objectives."

Good mission statements focus on a limited number of goals, stress the company's major policies and values, and define the company's major competitive scopes. These include:

- *Industry scope.* The industry or range of industries in which a company will operate. For example, DuPont operates in the industrial market; Dow operates in the industrial and consumer markets; and 3M will go into almost any industry where it can make money.

- *Products and applications scope.* The range of products and applications that a company will supply. St. Jude Medical aims to "serve physicians worldwide with high-quality products for cardiovascular care."

- *Competence scope.* The range of technological and other core competencies that a company will master and leverage. Japan's NEC has built its core competencies in computing, communications, and components to support production of laptop computers, mobile phones, and other electronics items.

- *Market-segment scope.* The type of market or customers a company will serve. For example, Porsche makes only expensive cars; Gerber serves primarily the baby market.

- *Vertical scope.* The number of channel levels from raw material to final product and distribution in which a company will participate. At one extreme are companies with a large vertical scope; at the other extreme are firms with low or no vertical integration that may outsource design, manufacture, marketing, and physical distribution.[4]

- *Geographical scope.* The range of regions or countries in which a company operates. Some companies operate in one city or state. At the other extreme are multinationals such as Unilever and Caterpillar, which operate in almost every country in the world.

Mission statements should not be revised in response to every new economic development. However, a company must redefine its mission if that mission has lost credibility or no longer defines an optimal course for the company.[5]

Establishing Strategic Business Units (SBUs)

A business can be defined in terms of three dimensions: customer groups, customer needs, and technology.[6] For example, a company that defines its business as designing incandescent lighting systems for television studios would have television studios as its customer group; lighting as its customer need; and incandescent lighting as its technology. In line with Levitt's argument that market definitions of a business are superior to product definitions,[7] these three dimensions describe the business in terms of a customer-satisfying process, not a goods-producing process. Products are transient, but basic needs and customer groups endure forever. Transportation is a need; the horse and carriage, the automobile, the railroad, the airline, and the truck are products that satisfy that need for customers.

Large companies normally manage quite different businesses, each requiring its own strategy. An SBU has three characteristics: (1) It is a single business or collection of related businesses that can be planned separately from the rest of the company; (2) it has its own set of competitors; and (3) it has a manager responsible for strategic planning and profit performance who controls most of the factors affecting profit.

The purpose of identifying the company's strategic business units is to develop separate strategies and assign appropriate funding to the entire business portfolio. Senior managers use analytical tools to classify SBUs by profit potential. Two of the best-known business portfolio evaluation models are the Boston Consulting Group model and the General Electric model.[8]

The Boston Consulting Group Approach

The Boston Consulting Group (BCG), a leading management consulting firm, developed and popularized the growth-share matrix shown in Figure 4.2. The eight circles represent the current sizes and positions of eight business units in a hypothetical company. The size of the circle depends on the dollar volume of each business. Thus, the

FIGURE 4.2   The Boston Consulting Group's Growth-Share Matrix

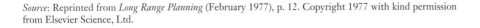

Source: Reprinted from *Long Range Planning* (February 1977), p. 12. Copyright 1977 with kind permission from Elsevier Science, Ltd.

two largest businesses are 5 and 6. The location of each business unit indicates its market growth rate and relative market share.

The market growth rate on the vertical axis indicates the annual growth rate of the market in which the business operates. *Relative market share*, which is measured on the horizontal axis, refers to the SBU's market share relative to that of its largest competitor in the segment. It serves as a measure of the company's strength in the relevant market segment.

The growth-share matrix is divided into four cells, each indicating a different type of business. *Question marks* are businesses that operate in high-growth markets but have low relative market shares. A question mark requires a lot of cash because the company is spending money on plant, equipment, and personnel. The company has to think hard about whether to keep pouring money into this business.

Stars are market leaders in a high-growth market. A star was once a question mark, but it does not necessarily produce positive cash flow; the company must still spend to keep up with the high market growth and fight off competition. *Cash cows* are former stars with large relative market share in a slow-growth market. A cash cow produces a lot of cash for the company (due to economies of scale and higher margins), paying the company's bills and supporting its other businesses. *Dogs* are businesses with weak market shares in low-growth markets.

After plotting its businesses in the growth-share matrix, a company must determine whether the portfolio has too many dogs or question marks or too few stars and cash cows. The next task is to determine what objective, strategy, and budget to assign to each SBU. Four strategies can be pursued. Building is appropriate for question marks whose market shares must grow if they are to become stars. The hold strategy is appropriate for strong cash cows if they are to continue yielding large positive cash flows. The harvest strategy is used to increase short-term cash flow regardless of long-term effect. Harvesting generally involves eliminating R&D expenditures, not replacing the physical plant and salespeople, reducing advertising expenditures, and so on. This strategy is appropriate for weak cash cows whose future is dim and from which more cash flow is needed, although it can also be used with question marks and dogs. The objective of the divest strategy is to sell or liquidate the business so resources can be better used elsewhere, an appropriate strategy for dogs and question marks that drag down company profits.

Successful SBUs move through a life cycle, starting as question marks and becoming stars, then cash cows, and finally dogs. Given this life-cycle movement, companies should be aware not only of their SBUs' current positions in the growth-share matrix (as in a snapshot), but also of their moving positions (as in a motion picture). If an SBU's expected future trajectory is not satisfactory, management should propose a new strategy to improve the likely trajectory.

The General Electric Model

An SBU's appropriate objective cannot be determined solely by its position in the growth-share matrix. If additional factors are considered, the growth-share matrix can be seen as a special case of a multifactor portfolio matrix that General Electric (GE) pioneered. In this model, shown in Figure 4.3, each business is rated in terms of two major dimensions—market attractiveness and business strength. These two factors make excellent marketing sense for rating a business. Companies are suc-

FIGURE 4.3 Market-Attractiveness Portfolio Strategies

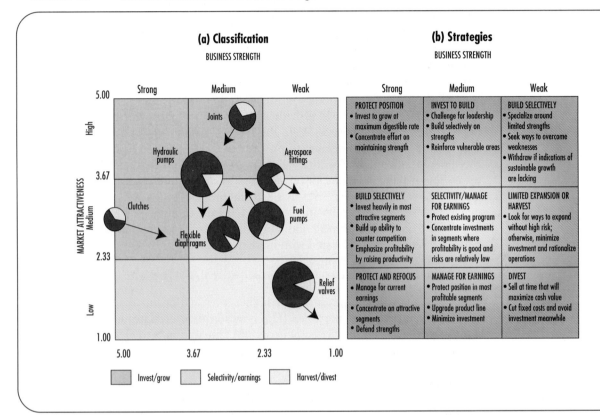

cessful to the extent that they enter attractive markets and possess the required business strengths to succeed in those markets. If one of these factors is missing, the business will not produce outstanding results. Neither a strong company operating in an unattractive market nor a weak company operating in an attractive market will do well.

Using these two dimensions, the GE matrix is divided into nine cells. The three cells in the upper-left corner indicate strong SBUs suitable for investment or growth. The diagonal cells stretching from the lower left to the upper right indicate SBUs of medium attractiveness; these should be pursued selectively and managed for earnings. The three cells in the lower-right corner indicate SBUs low in overall attractiveness, which the company may want to harvest or divest.[9]

Management should also forecast each SBU's expected position over the next 3 to 5 years given current strategy. Making this determination involves analyzing product life cycle, expected competitor strategies, new technologies, economic events, and so on. Again, the purpose is to see where SBUs are as well as where they appear to be headed.

Critique of Portfolio Models

Both the BCG and GE portfolio models have a number of benefits. They can help managers think more strategically, better understand the economics of their SBUs, improve the quality of their plans, improve communication between SBU and corporate management, identify important issues, eliminate weaker SBUs, and strengthen investment in more promising SBUs.

However, portfolio models must be used cautiously. They may lead a firm to overemphasize market-share growth and entry into high-growth businesses or to neglect its current businesses. Also, the models' results are sensitive to ratings and weights and can be manipulated to produce a desired location in the matrix. Finally, the models fail to delineate the synergies between two or more businesses, which means that making decisions for one business at a time might be risky. There is a danger of terminating a losing SBU that actually provides an essential core competence needed by several other business units. Overall, though, portfolio models have improved managers' analytical and strategic capabilities and allowed them to make better decisions than they could with mere impressions.[10]

Planning New Businesses, Downsizing Older Businesses

Corporate management often desires higher sales and profits than indicated by the projections for the SBU portfolio. The question then becomes how to grow much faster than the current businesses will permit. One option is to identify opportunities to achieve further growth within the company's current businesses (intensive growth opportunities). A second option is to identify opportunities to build or acquire businesses that are related to the company's current businesses (integrative growth opportunities). A third option is to identify opportunities to add attractive businesses unrelated to the company's current businesses (diversification growth opportunities).

- *Intensive growth.* Ansoff has proposed the product–market expansion grid as a framework for detecting new intensive growth opportunities.[11] In this grid, the company first considers whether it could gain more market share with its current products in current markets (market-penetration strategy) by encouraging current customers to buy more, attracting competitors' customers, or convincing nonusers to start buying its products. Next it considers whether it can find or develop new markets for its current products (market-development strategy). Then it considers whether it can develop new products for its current markets (product-development strategy). Later it will also review opportunities to develop new products for new markets (diversification strategy).

- *Integrative growth.* Often a business's sales and profits can be increased through backward integration (acquiring a supplier), forward integration (acquiring a distributor), or horizontal integration (acquiring a competitor). If these sources do not deliver the desired sales volume, the company should consider diversification.

- *Diversification growth.* This makes sense when good opportunities exist outside the present businesses. Three types of diversification are possible. The company could seek new products that have technological or marketing synergies with existing product lines, even though the new products themselves may appeal to a different group of customers (concentric diversification strategy). Second, the company might search for new products that appeal to its current customers but are technologically unrelated to the current product line (horizontal diversification strategy). Finally, the company might seek new businesses that have no relationship to the company's current technology, products, or markets (conglomerate diversification strategy).

Of course, companies must not only develop new businesses, but also carefully prune, harvest, or divest tired, old businesses in order to release needed resources and reduce costs. Weak businesses require a disproportionate amount of managerial attention; managers should therefore focus on growth opportunities rather than wasting energy and resources trying to save hemorrhaging businesses.

BUSINESS STRATEGIC PLANNING

The business unit strategic-planning process consists of the eight steps shown in Figure 4.4. We examine each step in the sections that follow.

Business Mission

Each business unit needs to define its specific mission within the broader company mission. Thus, a television studio-lighting-equipment company might define its mission as "The company aims to target major television studios and become their vendor of choice for lighting technologies that represent the most advanced and reliable studio lighting arrangements."

SWOT Analysis

The overall evaluation of a business's strengths, weaknesses, opportunities, and threats is called *SWOT analysis*. SWOT analysis consists of an analysis of the external and internal environments.

External Environment Analysis (Opportunity and Threat Analysis)   In general, a business unit has to monitor key *macroenvironment forces* (demographic-economic, technological, political-legal, and social-cultural) and *microenvironment actors* (customers, competitors, distributors, and suppliers) that affect its ability to earn prof-

FIGURE 4.4   The Business Strategic-Planning Process

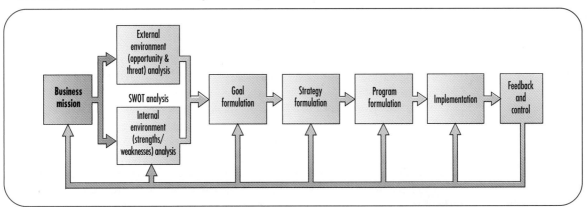

its (see Chapter 5 for more detail). Then, for each trend or development, management needs to identify the associated marketing opportunities and threats.

A **marketing opportunity** is an area of buyer need in which a company can perform profitably, such as making a buying process more efficient or providing more information and advice. Next, the company applies **market opportunity analysis (MOA)** to determine the attractiveness and success probability of each opportunity by asking five questions:

1. Can the benefits involved in the opportunity be articulated to a defined target market?
2. Can the target market(s) be located and reached with cost-effective media and trade channels?
3. Does the company have access to the capabilities and resources needed to deliver the customer benefits?
4. Can the company deliver the benefits better than any actual or potential competitors?
5. Will the financial rate of return meet or exceed the company's threshold for investment?

An **environmental threat** is a challenge posed by an unfavorable external trend or development that would lead, in the absence of defensive marketing action, to deterioration in sales or profit. Threats should be classified according to seriousness and probability of occurrence. Minor threats can be ignored; somewhat more serious threats must be carefully monitored; and major threats require the development of contingency plans that spell out changes the company can make if necessary.

Internal Environment Analysis   It is one thing to discern attractive opportunities and another to be able to take advantage of these opportunities. Each business needs to evaluate its internal strengths and weaknesses in marketing, finance, manufacturing, and organizational capabilities. Clearly, the business does not have to correct all its weaknesses, nor should it gloat about all its strengths. The big question is whether the business should limit itself to those opportunities in which it possesses the required strengths or consider better opportunities to acquire or develop certain strengths.

Sometimes a business does poorly because its departments do not work together well as a team. It is therefore critically important to assess interdepartmental working relationships as part of the internal environmental audit. Honeywell, for example, asks each department to annually rate its own strengths and weaknesses and those of the other departments with which it interacts. The notion is that each department is a "supplier" to some departments and a "customer" of other departments. If one department has weaknesses that hurt its "internal customers," Honeywell wants to correct them.

Goal Formulation

Once the company has performed a SWOT analysis, it can develop specific goals for the planning period in a process called *goal formulation*. Managers use the term *goals* to describe objectives that are specific with respect to magnitude and time.

To be effective, goals must (1) be arranged hierarchically to guide the businesses in moving from broad to specific objectives for departments and individuals; (2) be stated quantitatively whenever possible; (3) be realistic; and (4) be consistent. Other important trade-offs include: balancing short-term profit versus long-term growth; balancing deep penetration of existing markets with development of new markets; balancing profit goals versus nonprofit goals; and balancing high growth versus low risk. Each choice in this set of goal trade-offs calls for a different marketing strategy.

Strategy Formulation

Goals indicate what a business unit wants to achieve; **strategy** describes the game plan for achieving those goals. Every business strategy consists of a marketing strategy plus a compatible technology strategy and sourcing strategy. Porter has proposed three generic strategies that form a good starting point for strategic thinking: overall cost leadership, differentiation, and focus.[12]

- *Overall cost leadership.* The business works to achieve the lowest production and distribution costs so that it can price lower than competitors and win more market share. Firms pursuing this strategy must be good at engineering, purchasing, manufacturing, and physical distribution; they need less skill in marketing. Texas Instruments uses this strategy. The problem is that rivals may emerge with still lower costs, hurting a firm that has rested its whole future on cost leadership.
- *Differentiation.* The business concentrates on achieving superior performance in an important customer benefit area, such as being the leader in service, quality, style, or technology—but not leading in all of these things. Intel has established itself as a technology leader by introducing new microprocessors at breakneck speed.
- *Focus.* The business focuses on one or more narrow market segments, getting to know these segments intimately and pursuing either cost leadership or differentiation within the target segment. Airwalk shoes came to fame by focusing on the very narrow extreme-sports segment.

Firms pursuing the same strategy directed to the same target market constitute a **strategic group**. The firm that carries off that strategy best will make the most profits. Firms that do not pursue a clear strategy and try to be good on all strategic dimensions do the worst. Porter draws a distinction between operational effectiveness and strategy.[13] He defines strategy "as the creation of a unique and valuable position involving a different set of activities." A company has a strategy when it "performs different activities from rivals or performs similar activities in different ways."

Companies are also discovering that they need strategic partners if they hope to be effective. Even giant companies such as AT&T, IBM, Philips, and Siemens often cannot achieve leadership, either nationally or globally, without forming alliances with domestic or multinational companies that complement or leverage their capabilities and resources. Marketing alliances may involve products or services (licensing or jointly marketing a product); promotions (promoting a complementary offering); logistics (delivering or distributing a complementary product); or pricing (bundling offers for price discounts). The companies can designate a core group, even if it is not a formal structure, to manage and monitor such alliances.[14]

Program Formulation and Implementation

Once the business unit has developed its principal strategies, it must work out detailed supporting programs. If the business wants to attain technological leadership, it must strengthen its R&D department, gather technological intelligence, develop leading-edge products, train the technical sales force, and use ads to communicate its technological leadership.

Next, the marketing people must estimate their costs for each program. Questions arise: Is participating in a particular trade show worth it? Will a specific sales contest pay for itself? Will hiring another salesperson contribute to the bottom line? Activity-based cost (ABC) accounting should be applied to each marketing program to determine whether it is likely to produce sufficient results to justify the cost.[15]

A great marketing strategy can be sabotaged by poor implementation. Indeed, strategy is only one of seven elements, according to McKinsey & Company, that the best-managed companies exhibit.[16] In the McKinsey 7-S framework for business success, strategy, structure, and systems are considered the "hardware" of success, and style (how employees think and behave), skills (to carry out the strategy), staff (able people who are properly trained and assigned), and shared values (values that guide employees' actions) are the "software." When these software elements are present, companies are usually more successful at strategy implementation.[17] (See "Marketing Skills: Managing Implementation" for more about how marketing managers can prepare to handle this vital process.)

MARKETING SKILLS: MANAGING IMPLEMENTATION

Creative implementation can translate a good marketing strategy into great profits. Implementation management involves careful attention to detail, excellent people skills, flexibility, and a sense of urgency. First, marketers have to learn to break every program down into its component activities, identify the needed resources and their associated costs, estimate how long each activity should last and who should be responsible for it, and set up measures to monitor progress toward program objectives. Second, during the planning process, marketers must find ways of enlisting the support and enthusiasm of managers and employees in other departments that are involved (even peripherally) in implementation. This not only gets more people looking for potential implementation problems and opportunities, it injects more creativity and spreads the word about important programs.

Third, marketing managers have to become flexible enough to find workable options when dealing with unexpected twists such as late delivery of materials. Finally, marketers need to instill a sense of urgency about every phase of every program, day in and day out. Using words and action, they should communicate that implementation is critical and deserves immediate attention if the company is to achieve its objectives. One study found that grocery retailers can significantly increase sales and profits by speeding up the movement of new products to store shelves—meaning faster implementation of buying decisions.

Twinings Tea, a division of Associated British Foods, found that skillful implementation was vital to the success of its Internet program. The company wanted to use the Web to provide information and enable transactions with internal staff, suppliers, distributors, and customers while restricting access to sensitive data. Twinings managers carefully analyzed the steps and timing needed for implementation, paying particular attention to building in authorization and authentication techniques to ensure data security. They also brought in experts to handle many technical aspects of the program and carefully coordinated the program with existing supply-chain initiatives. Thanks to proficient implementation, the Twinings Web program is meeting its goals of enhancing employee, supply-chain, and customer relationships.[18]

Feedback and Control

As it implements its strategy, the firm needs to track the results and monitor new developments in the internal and external environments. Some environments are fairly stable from year to year. Other environments evolve slowly in a fairly predictable way. Still other environments change rapidly in significant and unpredictable ways. Nonetheless, the company can count on one thing: The marketplace will change. And when it does, the company will need to review and revise its implementation, programs, strategies, or even objectives.

A company's strategic fit with the environment will inevitably erode because the market environment changes faster than the company's 7-Ss. Thus a company might remain efficient while it loses effectiveness. Peter Drucker pointed out that it is more important to "do the right thing" (effectiveness) than "to do things right" (efficiency). The most successful companies excel at both.

Once an organization fails to respond to a changed environment, it has difficulty recapturing its lost position. This happened to the once-unassailable Motorola when it was slow to respond to the new digital technology used by Nokia and others, and kept rolling out analog phones.[19] Clearly, the key to organizational health is the firm's willingness to examine the changing environment and to adopt new goals and behaviors. High-performance organizations continuously monitor the environment and use flexible strategic planning to maintain a viable fit with the evolving environment.

THE MARKETING PROCESS

Planning at the corporate, division, and business levels is an integral part of the marketing process. To understand that process fully, we must first look at how a company defines its business.

The task of any business is to deliver value to the market at a profit. There are at least two views of the *value-delivery process*.[20] The traditional view is that the firm makes something and then sells it (Figure 4.5a). In this view, marketing takes place in the second half of the value-delivery process. The traditional view assumes that the company knows what to make and that the market will buy enough units to produce profits for the company.

The Value-Delivery Sequence

Companies that subscribe to this traditional view have the best chance of succeeding in economies marked by goods shortages in which consumers are not fussy about quality, features, or style. But the traditional view of the business process will not work in more competitive economies where people face abundant choices. The "mass market" is actually splintering into numerous micromarkets, each with its own wants, perceptions, preferences, and buying criteria. The smart competitor therefore must design the offer for well-defined target markets. This belief is at the core of the new view of business processes, which places marketing at the beginning of the planning process. Instead of emphasizing making and selling, companies see themselves involved in a three-phase value creation and delivery sequence (Figure 4.5b).

The first phase, choosing the value, represents the strategic "homework" that marketing must do before any product exists. The marketing staff must segment the

FIGURE 4.5   Two Views of the Value-Delivery Process

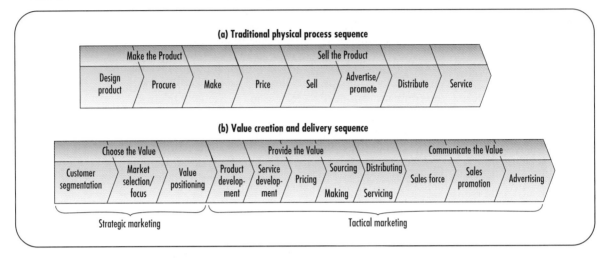

Source: Michael J. Lanning and Edward G. Michaels, "A Business Is a Value Delivery System," McKinsey Staff paper no. 41, June 1988. Copyright © McKinsey & Co., Inc.

market, select the appropriate market target, and develop the offer's value positioning. In the second phase, providing the value, marketers determine specific product features, prices, and distribution as part of tactical marketing. The task in the third phase is communicating the value. Here, further tactical marketing occurs in utilizing the sales force, sales promotion, advertising, and other promotional tools to inform the market about the product. Thus, as Figure 4.5b shows, the marketing process actually begins before there is a product and continues while it is being developed and after it becomes available.

Steps in the Marketing Process

The **marketing process** consists of analyzing marketing opportunities, researching and selecting target markets, designing marketing strategies, planning marketing programs, and organizing, implementing, and controlling the marketing effort. The four steps in the marketing process are:

1. *Analyzing market opportunities.* The marketer's initial task is to identify potential long-run opportunities given the company's market experience and core competencies. To evaluate its various opportunities, assess buyer wants and needs, and gauge market size, the firm needs a marketing research and information system (see Chapter 5). Next, the firm studies consumer markets (Chapter 6) or business markets (Chapter 7) to find out about buying behavior, perceptions, wants, and needs. Smart firms also pay close attention to competitors (Chapter 8) and look for major segments within each market that they can profitably serve (Chapter 9).

2. *Developing marketing strategies.* In this step, the marketer prepares a positioning strategy for each new and existing product's progress through the life cycle (Chapter 10), makes decisions about competitive strategy (Chapter 8), product lines and branding (Chapter 11), and designs and markets its services (Chapter 12).

3. *Planning marketing programs.* To transform marketing strategy into marketing programs, marketing managers must make basic decisions on marketing expenditures, marketing mix, and marketing allocation. The first decision is about the level of marketing expenditures needed to achieve the firm's marketing objectives. The second decision is how to divide the total marketing budget among the various tools in the marketing mix: product, price, place, and promotion (Chapters 11–17).[21] And the third decision is how to allocate the marketing budget to the various products, channels, promotion media, and sales areas.

4. *Managing the marketing effort.* In this final step (discussed later in this chapter), marketers organize the firm's marketing resources to implement and control the marketing plan. Because of surprises and disappointments as marketing plans are implemented, the company needs feedback and control.[22]

Figure 4.6 presents a grand summary of the marketing process and the factors that shape the company's marketing strategy.

Product Planning: The Nature and Contents of a Marketing Plan

Each product level (line or brand) must develop a marketing plan for achieving its goals. A typical marketing plan has eight sections:

- *Executive summary and table of contents.* This brief summary outlines the plan's main goals and recommendations; it is followed by a table of contents.
- *Current marketing situation.* This section presents relevant background data on sales, costs, profits, the market, competitors, distribution, and the macroenvironment. In turn, this information is used to carry out a SWOT analysis.

FIGURE 4.6   Factors Influencing Company Marketing Strategy

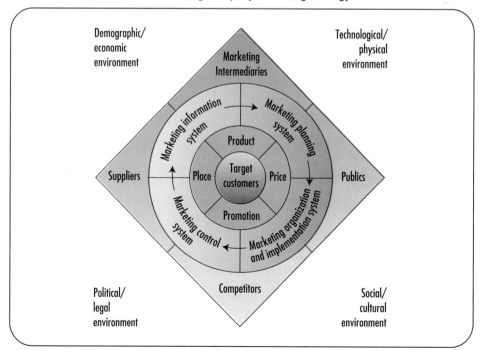

- *Opportunity and issue analysis.* Here, management reviews the main opportunities found in the SWOT analysis and identifies the key issues likely to affect the organization's attainment of its objectives.
- *Objectives.* This section outlines the plan's major financial and marketing objectives.
- *Marketing strategy.* Here the product manager defines the target segments, namely, those groups and needs the market offerings are intended to satisfy, and establishes the product line's competitive positioning. This is all done with inputs from other organizational areas to ensure proper support for effective implementation.
- *Action programs.* This section specifies the actual marketing programs, derived from the marketing strategy, to be used in achieving the objectives. Each strategy should answer these questions: What will be done? When will it be done? Who will do it? How much will it cost? How will progress be measured?
- *Financial projections.* Action plans allow the product manager to build a supporting budget with forecasted sales volume (units and average price), costs (production, physical distribution, and marketing), and projected profit. Once approved, the budget is the basis for developing plans and schedules for material procurement, production scheduling, employee recruitment, and marketing operations.
- *Controls.* This last section outlines the controls for monitoring the plan. Typically, the goals and budget are spelled out for each month or quarter so senior management can review the results each period. Sometimes contingency plans for handling specific environmental developments are included.

No two companies handle marketing planning and marketing plan content exactly the same way. Most marketing plans cover one year and vary in length; some firms take their plans very seriously, while others use them as only a rough guide to action. The most frequently cited shortcomings of marketing plans, according to marketing executives, are lack of realism, insufficient competitive analysis, and a short-run focus.

MANAGING THE MARKETING PROCESS

In addition to updating their marketing plans, companies often need to restructure business and marketing practices in response to major environmental changes such as globalization, deregulation, technology and telecommunications advances, and market fragmentation. Against this dynamic backdrop, the role of marketing in the organization must change as well. In a fully networked enterprise, every functional area can interact directly with customers. This means that marketing no longer has sole ownership of customer interactions; rather, marketing needs to integrate all customer-facing processes so customers see a single face and hear a single voice when they interact with the firm. This requires careful structuring of the marketing organization.

Organization of the Marketing Department

Modern marketing departments take numerous forms. The marketing department may be organized according to function, geographic area, products, or customer markets. Global organization is another consideration for firms that market goods or services in other countries.

Functional Organization The most common form of marketing organization consists of functional specialists (such as the sales manager and marketing research manager) who report to a marketing vice president, who coordinates their activities. The main advantage of a functional marketing organization is its administrative simplicity. However, this form loses effectiveness as products and markets increase. First, a functional organization often leads to inadequate planning for specific products and markets because products that are not favored by anyone are neglected. Second, each functional group competes with the other functions for budget and status. Therefore, the marketing vice president constantly has to weigh the claims of competing functional specialists and faces a difficult coordination problem.

Geographic Organization A company selling in a national market often organizes its sales force (and sometimes other functions, including marketing) along geographic lines. The national sales manager may supervise four regional sales managers, who each supervise six zone managers, who in turn supervise eight district sales managers, who supervise 10 sales people. Several companies are now adding *area market specialists* (regional or local marketing managers) to support the sales efforts in high-volume, distinctive markets. For example, McDonald's spends about 50 percent of its advertising budget regionally, and Krispy Kreme emphasizes local marketing to enhance customer loyalty.[23]

Product- or Brand-Management Organization Companies that produce a variety of products and brands often establish a product- (or brand-) management organization as another layer of management within the marketing function. A product manager supervises product category managers, who in turn supervise specific product and brand managers. A product-management organization makes sense if the firm's products are quite different, or if the sheer number of products is beyond the ability of a functional marketing organization to handle.

In both consumer and industrial markets, product and brand managers are responsible for product planning and competitive strategy; preparing annual marketing plans and sales forecasts; working with advertising and merchandising agencies to create programs and campaigns; stimulating support among sales reps and distributors; ongoing research into product performance, customer and dealer attitudes, opportunities and threats; and initiating product improvements to meet changing market needs.

The product-management organization allows the product manager to concentrate on developing a cost-effective marketing mix for each product, to react more quickly to marketplace changes, and to watch over smaller brands. On the other hand, it can lead to conflict and frustration when product managers are not given enough authority to carry out their responsibilities effectively. In addition, product managers become experts in their product but rarely achieve functional expertise. And appointing product managers and associate product managers for even minor products can bloat payroll costs. Also, brand managers normally move up in a few years to another brand or transfer to another company, leading to short-term thinking that plays havoc with long-term brand building. Fragmentation of markets means brand managers must increasingly please regional and local sales groups. Finally, product and brand managers tend to focus on building market share rather than on building *customer relationships*—the primary lever for value creation.

To counter these disadvantages, companies such as General Motors have eliminated brand managers; other firms have switched from product managers to product teams.[24] For example, Hallmark uses a triangular marketing team consisting of a market manager (the leader), a marketing manager, and a distribution manager; 3M uses a horizontal product team consisting of a team leader and representatives from sales, marketing, laboratory, engineering, accounting, and marketing research.

Another approach is to have each major brand run by a **brand asset management team (BAMT)** consisting of key representatives from major functions affecting the brand's performance. These BAMTs report to a BAMT Directors Committee, which reports to a Chief Branding Officer. A third alternative is to assign two or more products to each remaining manager. This is feasible where two or more products appeal to a similar set of needs.

A fourth alternative is to introduce category management, in which a company focuses on product categories to manage its brands. Kraft has changed from a classic brand-management structure, in which each brand competed for resources and market share, to a category-based structure in which category business directors (or "product integrators") lead cross-functional teams of representatives from marketing, R&D, consumer promotion, and finance. These category teams work with process teams dedicated to each product category and with customer teams dedicated to each major customer.[25] Category management is product-driven, which is why Colgate recently moved from brand management (Colgate toothpaste) to category management (toothpaste category) to a new stage called "customer-need management" (mouth care). This last step finally focuses the organization on a basic customer need.[26]

Market-Management/Customer-Management Organization   Many companies sell their products to a diverse set of markets; Canon, for instance, sells fax machines to consumer, business, and government markets. When customers fall into different user groups with distinct buying preferences and practices, a **market management organization** is desirable. A *markets manager* supervises several market managers (also called market-development managers, market specialists, or industry specialists). The market managers draw upon functional services as needed or may even have functional specialists reporting to them.

Market managers are staff (not line) people, with duties similar to those of product managers. This system has many of the same advantages and disadvantages of product management systems. Its strongest advantage is that the marketing activity is organized to meet the needs of distinct customer groups. This is why Xerox converted from geographic selling to selling by markets, as have IBM and Hewlett-Packard.

In a **customer management organization**, companies organize to understand and deal with individual customers rather than with the mass market or even market segments. Providian, for instance, has two main marketing groups: the marketing management group (which identifies new customers and new products) and the customer relations group (which maximizes the potential business from each new customer.[27]

Product-Management/Market-Management Organization   Companies that produce many products that flow into many markets may adopt a matrix organization. Consider DuPont, a pioneer in developing the matrix structure. Its textile fibers department has separate product managers for rayon and other fibers plus separate market managers for menswear and other markets. The product managers plan the sales and profits for their respective fibers, each seeking to expand the use of his or her fiber; the market managers seek to meet their market's needs rather than push a certain fiber. Ultimately, the sales forecasts from the market managers and the product managers should add to the same grand total.

A matrix organization would seem desirable in a multiproduct, multimarket company. However, this system is costly and often creates conflicts as well as questions about authority and responsibility. Still, matrix management is resurfacing because companies provide the context in which a matrix can thrive—an emphasis on flat, lean team organizations focused around business processes that cut horizontally across functions.[28]

Corporate-Divisional Organization   As multiproduct-multimarket companies grow, they often convert their larger product or market groups into separate divisions with their own departments and services. This raises the question of what marketing services and activities should be retained at corporate headquarters. Some corporations leave marketing to each division; some have a small corporate marketing staff; and some prefer to maintain a strong corporate marketing staff.

The potential contribution of a corporate marketing staff varies in different stages of the company's evolution. Most companies begin with weak marketing in their divisions and often establish a corporate staff to bring stronger marketing into the divisions through training and other services. Some members of corporate marketing might be transferred to head divisional marketing departments. As divisions become strong in their marketing, corporate marketing has less to offer them. Some companies then decide corporate marketing has done its job and proceed to eliminate the department.[29]

Global Organization   Companies that market internationally can organize in three ways. Those just going global may start by establishing an export department with a sales manager and a few assistants (and limited marketing services). As they go after global business more aggressively, they can create an international division with functional specialists (including marketing) and operating units structured geographically, according to product, or as international subsidiaries. Finally, companies that become truly global have top corporate management and staff plan worldwide operations, marketing policies, financial flows, and logistical systems. In these organizations, the global operating units report to top management, not to the head of an international division.

Building a Companywide Marketing Orientation

Many companies are beginning to realize that their organizations are not really market- and customer-driven—they are product or sales driven. Companies such as Baxter, General Motors, and Shell are working hard to reorganize themselves into true market-driven companies. The task is not easy: It requires a companywide passion for customers and changes in job and department definitions, responsibilities, incentives, and relationships. But research shows that companies "with a customer focus were almost 7 percent more productive than their competitors."[30]

To create a market- and customer-focused company, the CEO must: convince senior managers of the need to be more customer-focused; appoint a senior marketing officer and marketing task force; get outside help and guidance; change reward measurement and systems to encourage actions that build loyal, satisfied customers; hire strong marketing talent; develop strong in-house marketing training programs; install a modern marketing planning system; establish an annual marketing excellence recognition program; shift from a department focus to a process-outcome focus; and empower employees.

DuPont successfully made the transition from an inward-looking to an outward-looking orientation when it began building a "marketing community" by reorganizing divisions along market lines and holding marketing management training seminars for thousands of managers and employees. The company also established a marketing excellence recognition program and honored employees from around the world who had developed innovative marketing strategies and service improvements.[31] It takes planning and patience to get managers to accept customers as the foundation and future of the business—but it can be done, as the DuPont example shows.

Injecting More Creativity into the Organization

Although a company must be customer-oriented in today's hypercompetitive economy, it must also be creative. Instead of copying competitors' advantages and strategies, each organization has to build a capability in strategic innovation and imagination. This capability comes from assembling tools, processes, skills and measures that will enable the firm to generate more and better new ideas than its competitors.[32]

To do this, companies must watch trends and be ready to capitalize on them, which sometimes means putting innovation above risk-taking and efficiency. Companies can hire unusually creative marketers and resources, train employees to use creative techniques, address the unmet needs of customers, reward new ideas, encourage ideas from around the organization, and encourage employees to critique and challenge internal and competitive offerings.

Marketing Implementation

Organization is one factor contributing to effective **marketing implementation**, the process that turns marketing plans into action assignments and ensures that such assignments are executed in a manner that accomplishes the plan's stated objectives.[33] This part of the marketing process is critical, because a brilliant strategic marketing plan counts for little if it is not implemented properly. Whereas strategy addresses the *what* and *why* of marketing activities, implementation addresses the *who*, *where*, *when*, and *how*. Strategy and implementation are closely related in that one layer of strategy implies certain tactical implementation assignments at a lower level. For example, top management's strategic decision to "harvest" a product must be translated into specific actions and assignments.

Bonoma has identified four sets of skills for implementing marketing programs: (1) diagnostic skills (the ability to determine what went wrong); (2) identification of company level (the ability to discern whether problems occurred in the marketing function, the marketing program, or the marketing policy); (3) implementation skills (the ability to budget resources, organize effectively, motivate others); and (4) evaluation skills (the ability to evaluate results).[34] For efficient implementation and better return on marketing investments, organizations can use specialized software specifically designed to manage marketing processes, assets, and resources.

Evaluation and Control

To deal with the many surprises that occur during the implementation of marketing plans, the marketing department has to monitor and control marketing activities continuously.

TABLE 4.1   Types of Marketing Control

Type of Control	Prime Responsibility	Purpose of Control	Approaches
I. Annual-plan control	Top management Middle management	To examine whether the planned results are being achieved	• Sales analysis • Market-share analysis • Sales-to-expense ratios • Financial analysis • Market-based scorecard analysis
II. Profitability control	Marketing controller	To examine where the company is making and losing money	Profitability by: • product • territory • customer • segment • trade channel • order size
III. Efficiency control	Line and staff management Marketing controller	To evaluate and improve the spending efficiency and impact of marketing expenditures	Efficiency of: • sales force • advertising • sales promotion • distribution
IV. Strategic control	Top management Marketing auditor	To examine whether the company is pursuing its best opportunities with respect to markets, products, and channels	• Marketing-effectiveness rating instrument • Marketing audit • Marketing excellence review • Company ethical and social responsibility review

Table 4.1 lists four types of marketing control needed by companies: annual-plan control, profitability control, efficiency control, and strategic control.

Annual-Plan Control

Annual-plan control aims to ensure that the company achieves the sales, profits, and other goals established in its annual plan. The heart of annual-plan control is the four-step management by objectives process in which management sets monthly or quarterly goals; monitors the company's marketplace performance; determines the causes of serious performance deviations; and takes corrective action to close the gaps between goals and performance.

This control model applies to all levels of the organization. Top management sets sales and profit goals for the year that are elaborated into specific goals for each lower level. In turn, each product manager commits to attaining specified levels of sales and costs; each regional district and sales manager and each sales representative also commits to specific goals. Marketers today are showing a growing interest in developing better *marketing metrics* for measuring marketing performance.[35] Managers use five tools to check on plan performance: sales analysis, market-share analysis, marketing expense-to-sales analysis, financial analysis, and market-based scorecard analysis:

- *Sales analysis.* **Sales analysis** consists of measuring and evaluating actual sales in relation to goals, using two specific tools. **Sales-variance analysis** measures the relative contribution of different factors to a gap in sales performance. **Microsales analysis** looks at specific products, territories, and other elements that failed to produce expected sales. The point of these analyses is to determine what factors (pricing, lower volume, specific territories, etc.) contributed to a failure to meet sales goals.

- *Market-share analysis.* Company sales do not reveal how well the company is performing relative to competitors. To do this, management needs to track its market share. **Overall market share** is the company's sales expressed as a percentage of total market sales. **Served market share** is its sales expressed as a percentage of the total sales to its served market—all of the buyers who are able and willing to buy the product. **Relative market share** can be expressed as market share in relation to the largest competitor; a rise in relative market share means a company is gaining on its leading competitor. A useful way to analyze market-share movements is in terms of customer penetration, customer loyalty, customer selectivity, and price selectivity.

- *Marketing expense-to-sales analysis.* This is a key ratio because it allows management to be sure that the company is not overspending to achieve sales goals. Minor fluctuations in the expense-to-sales ratio can be ignored, but major fluctuations are cause for concern.

- *Financial analysis.* Management uses financial analysis to identify the factors that affect the company's rate of return on net worth.[36] The main factors are shown in Figure 4.7, along with illustrative numbers for a large chain-store retailer. To

FIGURE 4.7　Financial Model of Return on Net Worth

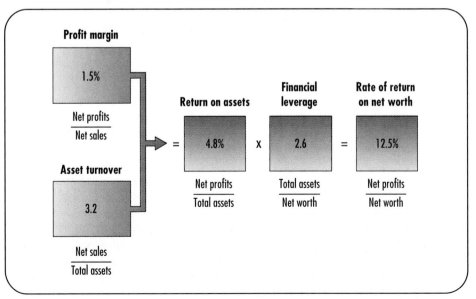

improve its return on net worth, the company must increase its ratio of net profits to its assets or increase the ratio of its assets to its net worth. The company should analyze the composition of its assets (i.e., cash, accounts receivable, inventory, and plant and equipment) and see if it can improve its asset management.[37] Tim Matanovich suggests analyzing the rate of return on marketing investment by dividing the net marketing contribution (calculated by subtracting total variable costs from total revenue) by marketing expenditures.[38]

■ *Market-based scorecard analysis.* Companies should also prepare two market-based scorecards that reflect performance and provide possible early warning signals of problems. A **customer-performance scorecard** records how well the company is doing on such customer-based measures as new customers, dissatisfied customers, lost customers, target market awareness, target market preference, relative product quality, and relative service quality. A **stakeholder-performance scorecard** tracks the satisfaction of constituencies who have a critical interest in and impact on the company's performance: employees, suppliers, banks, distributors, retailers, and stockholders.[39]

Profitability Control

Companies need to measure the profitability of their products, territories, customer groups, segments, trade channels, and order sizes. This information helps management determine whether any products or marketing activities should be expanded, reduced, or eliminated. The first step in marketing-profitability analysis is to identify the functional expenses (such as advertising and delivery) incurred for each activity. Next, the firm measures how much functional expense was associated with selling through each type of channel. Third, the company prepares a profit-and-loss statement for each type of channel.

In general, marketing-profitability analysis indicates the relative profitability of different channels, products, territories, or other marketing entities. However, it does not prove that the best course of action is to drop the unprofitable marketing entities, nor does it capture the likely profit improvement if these marginal marketing entities are dropped. Therefore, the company must examine its alternatives closely before taking corrective action.

Efficiency Control

Suppose a profitability analysis reveals poor profits for certain products, territories, or markets. This is when management must ask whether there are more efficient ways to manage the sales force, advertising, sales promotion, and distribution in connection with these marketing entities.

Some companies have established a *marketing controller* position to work on such issues and improve marketing efficiency. Marketing controllers work out of the controller's office but specialize in the marketing side of the business. At companies such as General Foods, DuPont, and Johnson & Johnson, they perform a sophisticated financial analysis of marketing expenditures and results, analyzing adherence to profit plans, helping prepare brand managers' budgets, measuring the efficiency of promotions, analyzing media production costs, evaluating customer and geographic profitability, and educating marketing personnel on the financial implications of marketing decisions.[40]

Strategic Control

From time to time, companies need to undertake a critical review of overall marketing goals and effectiveness. Each company should periodically reassess its strategic approach to the marketplace with marketing-effectiveness reviews and marketing audits.

- *The marketing-effectiveness review.* Marketing effectiveness is reflected in the degree to which a company or division exhibits the five major attributes of a marketing orientation: customer philosophy (serving customers' needs and wants), integrated marketing organization (integrating marketing with other key departments), adequate marketing information (conducting timely, appropriate marketing research), strategic orientation (developing formal marketing plans and strategies), and operational efficiency (using marketing resources effectively and flexibly). Most companies and divisions score in the fair-to-good range on measures of marketing effectiveness.[41]

- *The marketing audit.* Companies that discover marketing weaknesses should undertake a **marketing audit**, a comprehensive, systematic, independent, and periodic examination of a company's (or business unit's) marketing environment, objectives, strategies, and activities to identify problem areas and opportunities and recommend a plan of action for improving marketing performance.[42] The marketing audit examines six major marketing components: (1) the macroenvironment and task environment, (2) marketing strategy, (3) marketing organization, (4) marketing systems, (5) marketing productivity, and (6) marketing function (the 4 Ps).

Successful companies also perform marketing excellence reviews and ethical-social responsibility reviews to gain an outside-in perspective on their marketing activities.

- *The marketing excellence review.* This best-practices excellence review rates a firm's performance in relation to the best marketing and business practices of high-performing businesses. The resulting profile exposes weaknesses and strengths and highlights where the company might change to become a truly outstanding player in the marketplace.

- *The ethical and social responsibility review.* Companies need to evaluate whether they are truly practicing ethical and socially responsible marketing. Business success and continually satisfying customers and other stakeholders are closely tied to adoption and implementation of high standards of business and marketing conduct. The most admired companies abide by a code of serving people's interests, not only their own. This type of review allows management to determine how the firm is grappling with ethical issues and exhibiting a "social conscience" in its business dealings.

EXECUTIVE SUMMARY

Market-oriented strategic planning is the managerial process of developing and maintaining a viable fit among the organization's objectives, skills, and resources and its changing market opportunities. The purpose is to shape the company's businesses and products to yield the anticipated profits and growth. Strategic planning calls for action in three areas (managing the portfolio of businesses, assessing each business unit's strength, and establishing a strategy for each business), and takes place at four levels (corporate, division, business unit, and product).

Setting a corporate strategy entails defining the corporate mission; establishing strategic business units (SBUs); assigning resources to each SBU based on its market attractiveness and business strength; and planning new businesses and downsizing or terminating older businesses. Business strategic planning entails defining the business mission; analyzing external opportunities and threats; analyzing internal strengths and weaknesses; formulating goals, strategy, and programs; implementing the programs; and gathering feedback and exercising control.

The marketing process consists of four steps: analyzing market opportunities, researching and selecting target markets, developing marketing strategies, planning marketing programs, and organizing, implementing, and managing marketing effort. Each product level within a business unit must develop a marketing plan for achieving its goals. The marketing plan is one of the most important outputs of the marketing process. It should contain an executive summary and table of contents, an overview of the marketing situation, an analysis of opportunities and threats, a summary of financial and marketing objectives, an overview of marketing strategy, a description of action programs, a projected profit-and-loss statement, and a summary of the controls for monitoring the plan's progress.

In managing the marketing process, companies can organize the marketing department according to function, geographic area, products, or customer markets. Companies that market in other countries can create an export department, an international division, or a global organization. Rather than being product- or sales-driven, companies should be market- and customer-driven, exhibiting a companywide passion for customers and developing a capability in strategic creativity. Marketing implementation is the process that turns marketing plans into action assignments and ensures that execution accomplishes the plan's stated objectives. To manage the marketing process, companies can apply four types of control: annual-plan control, profitability control, efficiency control, and strategic control.

CASE PILOT

READ, INTERACT, AND TEST YOUR CASE ANALYSIS SKILLS

Case Pilot is an interactive business game. Your role is that of a marketing consultant. Your challenge is to find and solve the issues in any of seven business case studies. Each case study has five steps. Case Pilot will score, time, and provide answers after you complete each step. You should complete the steps in the order they are presented, and there are instructions for each step.

All organizations can benefit from having a market planning system that is monitored to ensure goals are achieved or that corrective action is implemented before trouble arises. Chapter 4 highlights the typical steps required in formal planning systems and how planning helps improve and control marketing activities.

Try your marketing consulting skills with the City Harborfront Preservation Society case study. Click on the Case Pilot tool at ***www.prenhall.com/kotler*** and assist the manager by answering the following questions:

1. What clues are there that the organization needs better control systems?
2. Should this business be downsized or improved?
3. What marketing decisions should be made immediately by the manager? By the Board?

NOTES

1. Bruce Finley, "Starbucks Executive Reflects on Corporate Social Responsibility," *Denver Post*, April 12, 2002, (***www.denverpost.com); "***Starbucks Pilots Telephone Express Service," *Cardline*, April 4, 2002, p.1; Brendan M. Case, "Starbucks Targets Latin America With First Mexico Shop," *Dallas Morning News*, March 26, 2002, (***www.dallasnews.com***; ***www.starbucks.com***); Howard Schultz, *Pour Your Heart Into It* (New York: Hyperion, 1997).

2. See "The New Breed of Strategic Planning," *BusinessWeek*, September 7, 1984, pp. 62–68.

3. See Peter Drucker, *Management: Tasks, Responsibilities and Practices* (New York: Harper & Row, 1973) ch. 7.

4. See "The Hollow Corporation," *BusinessWeek*, March 3, 1986, pp. 57–59. Also see William H. Davidow and Michael S. Malone, *The Virtual Corporation* (New York: HarperBusiness, 1992).

5. For more discussion, see Laura Nash, "Mission Statements—Mirrors and Windows," *Harvard Business Review* (March–April 1988): 155–56.

6. Derek Abell, *Defining the Business: The Starting Point of Strategic Planning* (Upper Saddle River, NJ: Prentice-Hall, 1980), ch. 3.

7. Theodore Levitt, "Marketing Myopia," *Harvard Business Review* (July–August 1960): 45–56.

8. See Roger A. Kerin, Vijay Mahajan, and P. Rajan Varadarajan, *Contemporary Perspectives on Strategic Planning* (Boston: Allyn & Bacon, 1990).

9. A hard decision must be made between harvesting and divesting a business. Harvesting a business will strip it of its long-run value, in which case it will be difficult to find a buyer. Divesting, on the other hand, is facilitated by maintaining a business in a fit condition in order to attract a buyer.

10. For a contrary view, however, see J. Scott Armstrong and Roderick J. Brodie, "Effects of Portfolio Planning Methods on Decision Making: Experimental Results," *International Journal of Research in Marketing* (1994): 73–84.

11. The same matrix can be expanded into nine cells by adding modified products and modified markets. See S. J. Johnson and Conrad Jones, "How to Organize for New Products," *Harvard Business Review* (May–June 1957): 49–62.

12. See Michael E. Porter, *Competitive Strategy: Techniques for Analyzing Industries and Competitors* (New York: Free Press, 1980) ch. 2.

13. Michael E. Porter, "What Is Strategy?" *Harvard Business Review* (November–December 1996): 61-78.

14. For readings on strategic alliances, see Peter Lorange and Johan Roos, *Strategic Alliances: Formation, Implementation and Evolution* (Cambridge, MA: Blackwell, 1992); and Jordan D. Lewis, *Partnerships for Profit: Structuring and Managing Strategic Alliances* (New York: Free Press, 1990).

15. See Robin Cooper and Robert S. Kaplan, "Profit Priorities from Activity-Based Costing," *Harvard Business Review* (May–June 1991): 130–35.

16. See Thomas J. Peters and Robert H. Waterman, Jr., *In Search of Excellence: Lessons from America's Best-Run Companies* (New York: Harper & Row, 1982) pp. 9–12. The same framework is used in Richard Tanner Pascale and Anthony G. Athos, *The Art of Japanese Management: Applications for American Executives* (New York: Simon & Schuster, 1981).

17. See Terrence E. Deal and Allan A. Kennedy, *Corporate Cultures: The Rites and Rituals of Corporate Life* (Reading, MA: Addison-Wesley, 1982); "Corporate Culture," *BusinessWeek*, October 27, 1980, pp. 148–60; Stanley M. Davis, *Managing Corporate Culture* (Cambridge, MA: Ballinger, 1984); and John P. Kotter and James L. Heskett, *Corporate Culture and Performance* (New York: Free Press, 1992).

18. Miles Hanson, "Fresh Ideas Are Nothing Without Implementation," *Marketing*, March 21, 2002, p. 1; "In-Store Implementation Key," *Frozen Food Age*, October 2000, p. 22;

David Prater, "The Third Time's the Charm," *Sales & Marketing Management*, September 2000, pp. 100+.

19. Stephen Baker, "The Future Goes Cellular," *BusinessWeek*, November 8, 1999, p. 74.

20. Michael J. Lanning and Edward G. Michaels, "Business Is a Value Delivery System," McKinsey Staff Paper, no. 41, June 1988 (McKinsey & Co., Inc.).

21. Perrault and McCarthy, *Basic Marketing: A Global Managerial Approach*, 13th ed. (Burr Ridge, IL: 1996).

22. Matrik G. Dekimpe and Dominique M. Hanssens, "Sustained Spending and Persistent Response: A New Look at Long-Term Profitability," *Journal of Marketing Research* (November 1999): 397-412.

23. Emily Fromm, "Steve Bumgarner: Field Marketing Coordinator, Krispy Kreme Doughnut Corp.," *Brandweek*, March 26, 2001, p. 21.

24. David Welch, "GM Brand Managers Get the Boot," *BusinessWeek*, April 22, 2002, p. 14.

25. Michael George, Anthony Freeling, and David Court, "Reinventing the Marketing Organization," *The McKinsey Quarterly*, no. 4 (1994): 43–62.

26. For further reading, see Robert Dewar and Don Shultz, "The Product Manager, an Idea Whose Time Has Gone," *Marketing Communications*, May 1998, pp. 28–35; "The Marketing Revolution at Procter and Gamble," *BusinessWeek*, July 25, 1988, pp. 72–76; Kevin T. Higgins, "Category Management: New Tools Changing Life for Manufacturers, Retailers," *Marketing News*, September 25, 1989, pp. 2, 19; George S. Low and Ronald A. Fullerton, "Brands, Brand Management, and the Brand Manager System: A Critical Historical Evaluation," *Journal of Marketing Research* (May 1994): 173–90; and Michael J. Zanor, "The Profit Benefits of Category Management," *Journal of Marketing Research*, (May 1994): pp. 202–13.

27. See Sam I. Hill, David L. Newkirk and Wayne Henderson, "Dismantling the Brandocracy," *Strategy & Business*, Issue 1, Fall 1995, pp. 4–17.

28. Richard E. Anderson, "Matrix Redux," *Business Horizons*, November–December 1994, pp. 6–10.

29. For further reading on marketing organization, see Nigel Piercy, *Marketing Organization: An Analysis of Information Processing, Power and Politics* (London: George Allen & Unwin, 1985); Robert W. Ruekert, Orville C. Walker, and Kenneth J. Roering, "The Organization of Marketing Activities: A Contingency Theory of Structure and Performance," *Journal of Marketing*, (Winter 1995): 13–25; Tyzoon T, Tyebjee, Albert V. Bruno, and Shelly H. McIntyre, "Growing Ventures Can Anticipate Marketing Stages," *Harvard Business Review* (January–February 1983): 2–4; and Andrew Pollak, "Revamping Said to be Set at Microsoft," *New York Times*, February 9, 1999, p. C1.

30. Erik Brynjolfsson and Lorin Hitt, "The Customer Counts," *Information Week*, September 9, 1996.

31. Edward E. Messikomer, "DuPont's 'Marketing Community,' " *Business Marketing*, October 1987, pp. 90–94. For an excellent account of how to convert a company into a market-driven organization, see George Day, *The Market-Driven Organization: Aligning Culture, Capabilities, and Configuration to the Market* (New York: Free Press, 1989).

32. See Gary Hamel, *Leading the Revolution* (Boston, MA.: Harvard Business School Press, 2000).

33. For more on developing and implementing marketing plans, see Marian Burk Wood, *The Marketing Plan: A Handbook* (Upper Saddle River, NJ: Prentice Hall, 2003); and H. W. Goetsch, *Developing, Implementing, and Managing an Effective Marketing Plan* (Chicago: American Marketing Association; Lincolnwood, IL: NTC Business Books, 1993).

34. Thomas V. Bonoma, *The Marketing Edge: Making Strategies Work* (New York: Free Press, 1985). Much of this section is based on Bonoma's work.

35. See Marion Debruyne and Katrina Hubbard, "Marketing Metrics," working paper series, Conference Summary, *Marketing Science Institute*, Report No. 00-119, 2000.

36. Alternatively, companies need to focus on factors affecting shareholder value. The goal of marketing planning is to increase shareholder value, which is the present value of the

future income stream created by the company's present actions. Rate-of-return analysis usually focuses on only one year's results. See Alfred Rapport, *Creating Shareholder Value*, rev. ed. (New York: Free Press, 1997).

37. For additional reading on financial analysis, see Peter L. Mullins, *Measuring Customer and Product Line Profitability* (Washington, DC: Distribution Research and Education Foundation, 1984).

38. Timothy Matanovich, "Value Measures in the Executive Suite," *Marketing Management*, Spring 2000, pp. 35-40.

39. See Robert S. Kaplan and David P. Norton, *The Balanced Scorecard* (Boston: Harvard Business School Press, 1996).

40. Sam R. Goodman, *Increasing Corporate Profitability* (New York: Ronald Press, 1982) ch. 1. Also see Bernard J. Jaworski, Vlasis Stathakopoulos, and H. Shanker Krishnan, "Control Combinations in Marketing: Conceptual Framework and Empirical Evidence," *Journal of Marketing* (January 1993): pp. 57–69.

41. For further discussion of this instrument, see Philip Kotler, "From Sales Obsession to Marketing Effectiveness," *Harvard Business Review* (November–December 1977): 67–75.

42. See Philip Kotler, William Gregor, and William Rodgers, "The Marketing Audit Comes of Age," *Sloan Management Review* (Winter 1989): 49–62.

CHAPTER 5

Understanding Markets, Market Demand, and the Marketing Environment

In this chapter, we will address the following questions:

1. What are the components of a marketing information system?

2. How can marketers improve marketing decisions through intelligence systems, marketing research, and marketing decision support systems?

3. How can demand be more accurately measured and forecasted?

4. What are the key demographic, economic, natural, technological, political-legal, and social-cultural developments in the macroenvironment?

MARKETING MANAGEMENT AT TESCO

Paying close attention to customers, competitors, and the marketing environment has helped Tesco grow into the largest grocery chain in the United Kingdom. Feeling pressure from Asda, Sainsbury's, and other competitors, Tesco's marketing managers are always searching for opportunities based on changing consumer preferences and environmental factors such as new technology. The chain recently held focus groups at dozens of supermarkets to find out which amenities (such as parking) shoppers would most like to see improved. With this feedback, the chain can proceed with remodeling plans to meet customers' needs on the local level.

The company is also market-testing an online grocery shopping service in Seoul, South Korea, similar to the service it offers in the United Kingdom and the United States. Research shows that Seoul has the dense population and Internet access penetration to support this kind of service. In addition, demand estimates play a role in Tesco's marketing decisions. Not long ago, the chain decided to reduce the price of organic milk after learning, through research, that demand would likely increase at lower price levels. In fact, demand for "natural" foods is generally on the rise, in part because some consumers see these as healthier and as less destructive to the environment. A sharp eye for these kinds of environmental developments is helping Tesco maintain its market leadership position.[1]

The marketing environment is changing at an accelerating rate, so the need for real-time market information is greater than at any time in the past. The shifts are dramatic: from local to global marketing; from buyer needs to buyer wants; from price to nonprice competition. At the same time, impressive information technologies are emerging: powerful computers, DVD players, the Internet, and more.[2]

As companies expand their geographic coverage, they need more information more quickly. As incomes improve, buyers become more selective in their choice of goods. To predict buyers' responses to different features and other attributes, sellers must turn to marketing research. As sellers increase their use of branding, product differentiation, and targeted promotions, they require information on the effectiveness of these marketing tools. This chapter first examines how marketers gather marketing information and use it for marketing decisions.

Many companies fail to see change as opportunity and ignore or resist changes until it is too late. Their strategies, structures, systems, and culture grow increasingly obsolete and dysfunctional as the environment changes. Corporations as mighty as General Motors and Sears had difficulty because they ignored macroenvironmental changes for too long. The major responsibility for identifying marketplace changes falls to marketers. More than any other group in the company, they must be trend trackers and opportunity seekers. This and later chapters examine the macroenvironmental forces that affect the company, its markets, and its competitors.

SUPPORTING MARKETING DECISIONS WITH INFORMATION, INTELLIGENCE, AND RESEARCH

Some firms have developed marketing information systems that provide managers with incredible detail about buyer wants, preferences, and behavior. Companies with superior information enjoy a competitive advantage: They can do a better job of choosing their markets, developing their offerings, and executing their marketing plans.

Every firm must organize a rich flow of information to its marketing managers for analysis, planning, implementation, and control. Companies study their managers' information needs and design marketing information systems to meet these needs. A **marketing information system (MIS)** consists of people, equipment, and procedures that gather, sort, analyze, evaluate, and distribute needed, timely, and accurate information to marketing decision makers. This information is developed from internal company records, marketing intelligence, marketing research, and marketing decision support analysis.

Internal Records System

Marketing managers rely on data from internal reports about orders, sales, prices, costs, inventory levels, receivables, payables, and so on. By analyzing this information, they can spot important opportunities and problems.

The heart of the internal records system is the order-to-payment cycle. Sales representatives, dealers, and customers dispatch orders to the firm. The sales department prepares invoices and transmits copies to various departments. Out-of-stock items are back ordered. Shipped items are accompanied by shipping and billing documents that are sent to various departments. Companies need to perform these steps quickly and accurately, because customers favor firms that can promise timely delivery. Electronic systems and intranets improve the speed, accuracy, and efficiency of the order-to-payment cycle for Wal-Mart and many other firms.[3]

Marketing managers also need timely and accurate reports on current sales. Wal-Mart, for example, knows each evening the sales of each product by store and total, so it can transmit nightly orders to suppliers for quick shipments of replacement stock. Wal-Mart shares its sales data with larger suppliers such as Procter & Gamble, expecting them to re-supply Wal-Mart stores in a timely manner.

Today many companies organize information in databases—customer databases, product databases, salesperson databases, and so forth—and then combine data from the different databases. The customer database will contain every customer's name, address, past transactions, and even demographics and psychographics (activities, interests, and opinions) in some instances. Companies warehouse these data and make them easily accessible to decision makers to better plan, target, and track marketing programs. Furthermore, analysts skilled in statistical methods can "mine" the data and garner fresh insights into neglected customer segments, recent customer trends, and other useful information. MCI, for instance, mines 1 trillion bytes of customer phoning data to craft new long-distance calling plans for different customer segments.[4]

Marketing Intelligence System

Whereas the internal records system supplies results data, the marketing intelligence system supplies happenings data. A **marketing intelligence system** is a set of procedures and sources used by managers to obtain everyday information about developments in the marketing environment. Marketing managers collect marketing intelligence by reading books, newspapers, and trade publications; talking to customers, suppliers, and distributors; checking Internet sources; and meeting with other company managers. A company can take six steps to improve the quality of its marketing intelligence.

First, it can train and motivate the sales force to spot and report new developments. Second, the company can motivate distributors, retailers, and other intermediaries to pass along important intelligence.[5] For example, Parker Hannifin, a fluid-power-products manufacturer, asks distributors to submit a copy of all invoices covering sales of its products. Parker analyzes these invoices to learn more about end users, then shares the findings with the distributors.

Third, the company can collect competitive intelligence by purchasing rivals' products; attending trade shows; scanning Web sites; attending stockholders' meetings; talking to employees, dealers, suppliers, and shippers; collecting rivals' ads; and reading business and trade publications. Fourth, the firm can set up a customer advisory panel. For example, Hitachi Data Systems regularly meets with its 20-member customer panel to discuss service, new technologies, and customers' requirements. While the firm learns about customer needs, its customers feel closer to a company that listens to their comments.[6]

Fifth, the company can purchase information from outside suppliers such as those identified in the commercial data portion of Table 5.1. These suppliers gather and store consumer-panel data at a much lower cost than the company could manage internally. Sixth, some companies have established a marketing information center to collect and circulate marketing intelligence throughout the organization.

TABLE 5.1   Selected Secondary Data Sources

Internal Sources

Company profit-loss statements, balance sheets, sales figures, sales-call reports, invoices, inventory records, and prior research reports.

Government Publications

Printed sources such as *Statistical Abstract of the United States, County and City Data Book, Industrial Outlook, Marketing Information Guide*; specialized publications such as *Annual Survey of Manufacturers, Federal Reserve Bulletin*; and Internet sources such as Census Bureau (*www.census.gov*), Fed World clearinghouse site (*www.fedworld.gov*), and Thomas legislative site (*www.thomas.loc.gov*).

Periodicals and Books

Business Periodicals Index, Standard & Poor's Industry, Moody's Manuals, Encyclopedia of Associations; marketing journals such as *Journal of Marketing, Journal of Marketing Research, Journal of Consumer Research*; trade magazines such as *Advertising Age, Sales & Marketing Management*; and business magazines such as *BusinessWeek, Fortune, Forbes, The Economist, Business 2.0*.

Business Information

On the Internet: Bloomberg financial news (*www.bloomberg.com*); C/Net coverage of technology (*www.cnet.com*); Hoover's capsules of company data (*www.hoovers.com*); SEC public company financial data (*www.sec.gov*); and National Trade Data Bank of industry trends and competition (*www.stat-usa.gov*).

Commercial Data

Nielsen (data on sales of products/brands, media audiences); MRCA Information Services (data on purchases and consumption of consumer products); Information Resources, Inc. (data on supermarket purchases and promotions); Simmons Market Research Bureau (data on media and product/brand consumption). Other sources include: Arbitron, Audit Bureau of Circulation, and Starch.

Associations

On the Internet: American Marketing Association (*www.ama.org*); CommerceNet association for Internet commerce (*www.commerce.net*); and Gale's Encyclopedia of Associations (*www.gale.com*).

International Information

On the Internet: CIA World Factbook (*www.cia.gov/cia/publications/factbook/*); the Electronic Embassy links to embassy sites (*www.embassy.org*); and the United Nations (*www.un.org*).

Marketing Research

Marketing managers often commission formal marketing studies of specific problems and opportunities, such as a market survey, a product-preference test, a sales forecast by region, or an advertising evaluation. We define **marketing research** as the systematic design, collection, analysis, and reporting of data and findings that are relevant to a specific marketing situation facing the company.

A company can obtain marketing research in a number of ways. Most large companies have their own marketing research departments.[7] At Procter & Gamble, one marketing research group is in charge of overall company advertising research, while another is in charge of market testing. Each group's staff consists of marketing research managers, supporting specialists (survey designers, statisticians, behavioral scientists), and in-house field representatives who conduct and supervise interviewing. Each year, P&G contacts over 1 million people in connection with about 1,000 research projects, often using the Internet.[8]

Small companies can hire the services of a marketing research firm or conduct research in creative and affordable ways. They can engage students or professors to design and carry out projects, they can use the Internet, and they can visit their competitors. Tom Coohill, who owns two Atlanta restaurants, gives managers a food allowance to dine out and bring back ideas. Atlanta jeweler Frank Maier Jr., who often visits out-of-town rivals, spotted and copied a dramatic way of lighting displays.[9]

Companies normally budget marketing research at 1 to 2 percent of company sales. Much of this budget is spent with outside research firms, which fall into three categories. Syndicated-service research firms such as Information Resources, Inc. gather consumer and trade information, which they sell for a fee. Custom marketing research firms design studies, carry them out, and report the findings. Specialty-line marketing research firms provide specialized services such as field interviewing.

Effective marketing research involves the five steps shown in Figure 5.1. We illustrate these steps with the following situation: Assume that American Airlines is reviewing new ideas for serving its customers. In particular, it wants to develop services for its first-class passengers, many of whom are businesspeople whose high-priced tickets pay most of the freight. Among these ideas are: (1) to supply a power plug so passengers can use their laptops longer than the 2 hours normally provided by a battery; (2) to supply an Internet connection with limited access to Web pages and e-mail messaging; (3) to offer 24 channels of satellite cable TV; and (4) to offer a system that lets each passenger create a customized play list of in-flight music and movies.

The marketing research manager is assigned to find out how first-class passengers would rate these services—particularly the Internet connection—and how much extra they would be willing to pay, if the airline decides to charge for the services.

FIGURE 5.1   Marketing Research Process

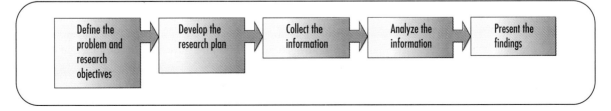

Arranging the Web connection, for example, would cost $90,000 per plane. Would enough first-class passengers be willing to pay $25 for Web access so that AA could recover its costs in a reasonable time?[10]

Step 1: Define the Problem, Decision Alternatives, and Research Objectives Marketing management must carefully define the problem to be studied. American's marketing manager and marketing researcher defined the problem this way: "Will offering an in-flight Internet service create enough incremental preference and profit for American Airlines to justify its cost against other possible investments American might make?" They agreed on these specific research objectives: (1) What types of first-class passengers would respond best to an in-flight Internet service? (2) How many first-class passengers are likely to use the Internet service at different price levels? (3) How many extra first-class passengers might choose American because of this new service? (4) How much long-term goodwill will this service add to American Airlines' image? (5) How important is Internet service to first-class passengers relative to providing other services such as a power plug or enhanced entertainment?

Not all research projects are this specific. Some research is exploratory, to shed light on the real nature of the problem and to suggest possible solutions or new ideas. Some research is descriptive, to ascertain certain magnitudes, such as how many first-class passengers would buy Internet access at $25. Some research is causal—to test a cause-and-effect relationship.

Step 2: Develop the Research Plan The second step calls for designing an efficient, affordable research plan for gathering the needed information. This entails decisions about data sources, research approaches, research instruments, sampling plan, and contact methods.

DATA SOURCES The researcher can gather secondary data, primary data, or both. Secondary data are data that were collected for another purpose and already exist somewhere. Primary data are data freshly gathered for a specific purpose or a specific research project.

Researchers usually start an investigation by examining secondary data to see whether the problem can be partly or wholly solved without collecting costlier primary data. Table 5.1 shows some of the secondary-data sources available in the United States.[11] Secondary data provide a starting point for research and offer the advantages of low cost and ready availability. When the needed data do not exist or are dated, inaccurate, incomplete, or unreliable, the researcher will have to collect primary data.

RESEARCH APPROACHES Researchers can collect primary data for marketing research in five ways: observation, focus groups, surveys, behavioral data, and experiments.

■ *Observational research.* Fresh data can be gathered by observing the relevant actors and settings. The American Airlines researchers might meander around first-class lounges in airports to hear travelers talk about different carriers, or they can fly on American and competitors' planes to observe in-flight service. This exploratory research might yield some hypotheses about how travelers perceive different carriers and their services.

■ *Focus-group research.* A **focus group** is a gathering of six to ten people who spend a few hours with a skilled moderator to discuss a product, service, organization, or other marketing entity. Many companies now conduct online focus groups to take advantage of lower cost and faster, more detailed feedback. General Motors is using the Web as a low-cost way to quickly gauge consumer reaction to vehicle features and designs.[12]

- *Survey research*. Surveys are best suited for descriptive research such as learning about people's knowledge, beliefs, preferences, and satisfaction, and measuring these magnitudes in the general population. American Airlines researchers might want to survey how many people know about American, have flown it, prefer it, and would like Internet access; as an alternative, it might ask questions of an ongoing consumer panel.

- *Behavioral data*. Customers leave traces of their purchasing behavior in store scanning data, catalog and Internet purchase records, and customer databases. Much can be learned by analyzing this data. Customers' purchases reflect their preferences and often are more reliable than their statements to researchers. People often report preferences for popular brands, yet they actually buy other brands.

- *Experimental research*. The most scientifically valid research is experimental research. Its purpose is to capture cause-and-effect relationships by eliminating competing explanations of the observed findings. American Airlines might experiment by introducing Web access on one of its regular international flights at a price of $25 one week and only $15 the next week. If the plane carried the same number of first-class passengers each week, and particular weeks made no difference, any significant difference in the number of people using the service could be related to price.

RESEARCH INSTRUMENTS   Marketing researchers can choose among a variety of research instruments in collecting primary data: questionnaires, psychological tools, mechanical devices, and qualitative measures. A questionnaire consists of a set of questions presented to respondents. Because of its flexibility, the questionnaire is by far the most common instrument used to collect primary data. Questionnaires need to be carefully developed, tested, and debugged before they are administered on a large scale. Questionnaires can contain closed-end and open-end questions. Closed-end questions specify all of the possible answers, so they are easy to interpret and tabulate. Open-end questions allow respondents to answer in their own words. They are especially useful in exploratory research, where the researcher is looking for insight into how people think rather than measuring how many people think a certain way.

Psychological tools such as laddering techniques, depth interviews, and Rorshach tests can probe a buyer's deeper beliefs and feelings. As an example of laddering, a researcher might ask a male consumer, "Why do you want to buy an SUV vehicle? " After he answers, "It is a good looking car," he is asked a follow-up question: "Why do you want a good-looking car?" Upon receiving his answer, the researcher asks: "Why is this important to you?" This continues until the researcher arrives at a deeper reason, such as "People will be more impressed with me." Another psychological tool is the Zaltman Metaphoric Elicitation Technique (ZMET), which uses metaphors to help consumers access nonverbal images.[13]

Mechanical devices are occasionally used in marketing research. Galvanometers measure the interest or emotions aroused by exposure to a specific ad or picture. An infrared eye-tracking system can study how consumers view Web sites: where their eyes land first, how long they linger, and so on. An audiometer attached to a participant's television registers when the set is on and to which channel it is tuned.[14]

Some marketers prefer more qualitative methods for gauging consumer opinion because consumer actions do not always match their answers to survey questions. Tools such as videos, pagers, and informal interviewing are helping marketers overcome the limitations of traditional research methods. For example, the ad agency Ogilvy & Mather created the Discovery Group, a research unit that creates documentary-style video by sending researchers with hand-held videocameras into consumers' homes to shoot hours of footage, which is edited to a 30-minute "highlight reel." The company uses the results to analyze consumer behavior for the benefit of its clients. Other researchers give consumers pagers and instruct them to write down what they are doing whenever paged, or hold informal interview sessions at a café or bar.

Customer prototyping, another qualitative tool, attempts to paint a realistic portrait of an individual by describing a specific customer type (e.g., "ideal customer" or "non-user") in qualitative terms. Marketers arrive at a prototype by answering questions about that person, such as "What is important to this person?" Finally, researchers use articulative interviewing to determine what social values interviewees hold dear by having them talk about broad topics such as their various roles in life and their daily activities. This format enables the marketer to draw out relevant information; the interviewee is also likely to reveal valuable information regarding his or her core beliefs and other social factors that may influence product decisions.[15]

SAMPLING PLAN   After deciding on the research approach and instruments, the marketing researcher must design a sampling plan, based on three decisions:

1. *Sampling unit: Who is to be surveyed?* The researcher must define the target population to be sampled. In the American Airlines survey, should the sampling unit be only first-class business travelers, first-class vacation travelers, or both? Once the sampling unit is determined, a sampling frame must be developed so that everyone in the target population has an equal or known chance of being sampled.

2. *Sample size: How many people should be surveyed?* Large samples give more reliable results than small samples. However, samples of less than 1 percent of a population can be reliable with a credible sampling procedure.

3. *Sampling procedure: How should the respondents be chosen?* To obtain a representative sample, a probability sample of the population should be drawn. Probability sampling allows the calculation of confidence limits for sampling error. When the cost or time involved in probability sampling is too high, marketing researchers use nonprobability sampling, even though these do not allow sampling error to be measured.

CONTACT METHODS   Once the sampling plan has been determined, the marketing researcher must decide how to contact subjects. Choices include mail, telephone, personal, or online interviews. The advantages and disadvantages of these methods are summarized in Table 5.2.

Step 3: Collect the Information   The data collection phase of marketing research is generally the most expensive and the most prone to error. In the case of surveys, four major problems arise. Respondents who are not at home must be recontacted or replaced. Other respondents will not cooperate. Still others will give biased or dishonest answers. Finally, some interviewers will be biased or dishonest.

Yet data collection methods are rapidly improving, thanks to technology. For example, Information Resources, Inc. (IRI) recruits supermarkets equipped with scan-

TABLE 5.2   Marketing Research Contact Methods

Contact Method	Advantages	Disadvantages
Mail questionnaire	Ability to reach people who would not give personal interviews or whose responses might be biased or distorted by the interviewers.	Response rate is usually low or slow.
Telephone interview	Ability to gather information quickly and clarify questions respondents do not understand; higher response rate than mail questionnaires.	Interviews must be short and not too personal; contact getting more difficult because of answering machines and suspicions about telemarketing.
Personal interview	Ability to ask more questions and record additional observations.	Most expensive contact method; requires more planning and supervision and is subject to interviewer
On-line interview	Ability to post a questionnaire on the Web or place a banner to quickly, easily recruit and survey participants.	Data may not be representative of a target population because respondents are self-selected.

ners to read the universal product code on products purchased. The firm also recruits a panel of store customers who agree to use a special card containing personal data and allow their television-viewing habits to be monitored. Because panelists receive their programs through cable television, IRI controls the ads sent to their sets and can determine, through store purchases, which ads led to more purchasing and by which customers.[16]

Step 4: Analyze the Information   The fourth step in the marketing research process is to extract findings from the collected data. The researcher first tabulates the data and then applies various statistical techniques and decision models to analyze the results. More detailed analysis is possible through marketing decision support systems, which are discussed later in this chapter.

Step 5: Present the Findings   In this step of the marketing research process, the researcher presents the major findings that are relevant to the key marketing decisions facing management. The main survey findings for the American Airlines case, for example, show that the chief reasons for using in-flight Internet service are to pass the time Web surfing and to exchange e-mail messages. Passengers would have the charge paid by their employers. About 5 first-class passengers out of every 10 would use the service at $25; about 6 would use it at $15. Thus a charge of $15 would produce less revenue ($90 = 6 × $15) than $25 ($125 = 5 × $25). By charging $25, AA would collect $125 a flight. Assuming that the same flight takes place 365 days a year, AA would annually collect $45,625 ($125 × 365). Since the investment is $90,000, AA would break even in about two years. Also, in-flight Web service would boost AA's image as an innovative airline, bring in new passengers, and build goodwill among customers.

Step 6: Make the Decision The managers who commission the research need to weigh the evidence. They know that the findings could suffer from a variety of errors. At American Airlines, if managers have little confidence in the findings, they may decide against introducing the in-flight Internet service. If they are predisposed to launching the service, the findings support their inclination. They may even decide to do more research. The decision is theirs, but the research will have provided some insight into the problem.[17]

Marketing Decision Support System

A growing number of organizations use a marketing decision support system to help marketing managers make better decisions. John Little defines a **marketing decision support system (MDSS)** as a coordinated collection of data, systems, tools, and techniques with supporting software and hardware by which an organization gathers and interprets information from business and the environment and turns it into a basis for marketing action.[18] An MDSS may include statistical tools such as multiple regression and conjoint analysis, models such as queuing models and new-product pretest models, and optimization routines such as game theory and heuristics.

Many marketing and sales software programs can help marketers design marketing research studies, segment markets, set prices and advertising budgets, analyze media, and plan sales force activity. Some models even attempt to duplicate the way expert marketers make their decisions. Lilien and Rangaswamy's *Marketing Engineering: Computer-Assisted Marketing Analysis and Planning* discusses a number of widely used modeling software tools.[19]

FORECASTING AND DEMAND MEASUREMENT

One major reason for using marketing research is to identify market opportunities. Once the research is complete, marketers must measure and forecast the size, growth, and profit potential of each market opportunity. Sales forecasts based on estimates of demand are used by finance to plan for the needed cash for investment and operations; by manufacturing to establish capacity and output levels; by purchasing to acquire the right amount of supplies; and by human resources to hire the needed number of workers. The first step is to determine which market to measure.

Which Market to Measure?

A **market** is the set of all actual and potential buyers of a market offer. The size of a market hinges on the number of buyers who might exist for a particular market offer. Although the **potential market** is the set of consumers who have a sufficient level of interest in a market offer, interest is not enough to define a market. Potential consumers must have enough income and have access to the product offer. The **available market** is thus the set of consumers who have interest, income, and access to a particular offer.

A company can go after the whole available market or concentrate on certain segments. The **target market** (also called the **served market**) is the part of the *qualified available market* (those with the interest, income, access, and qualifications to respond to a product offer) the company decides to pursue. Ultimately, the **penetrated market** is the set of consumers who buy the company's product.

These market definitions are useful tools for market planning. If the company is not satisfied with its current sales, it can try to attract more buyers from its target market; lower the qualifications of potential buyers; expand its available market by adding distribution or lowering price; or try to expand the potential market by advertising to prospects not previously targeted. Some retailers have successfully retargeted their market with new ad campaigns. When discounter Target Stores faced stiff competition from Wal-Mart and Kmart, it began running an unusual advertising campaign in the Sunday magazines of top metropolitan newspapers. With the look of department store ads, these hip spots gained Target a reputation as the "up-stairs" mass retailer and fueled the chain's expansion by targeting more affluent consumers.[20]

Demand Measurement

Once the marketer has defined its market, the next step is to estimate market demand. **Market demand** for a product is the total volume that would be bought by a defined customer group in a defined geographical area in a defined time period in a defined marketing environment under a defined marketing program. Market demand is not a fixed number but rather a function of the stated conditions. For this reason, it can be called the *market demand function*.

The dependence of total market demand on underlying conditions is illustrated in Figure 5.2a. The horizontal axis shows different possible levels of industry marketing expenditure in a given time period. The vertical axis shows the resulting demand level. The curve represents the estimated market demand associated with varying levels of industry marketing expenditure. Some base sales (called the *market minimum*, labeled Q_1 in the figure) would take place without any such expenditures. Higher levels of industry marketing expenditures would yield higher levels of demand, first at an increasing rate, then at a decreasing rate. Marketing expenditures beyond a certain

FIGURE 5.2   Market Demand Functions

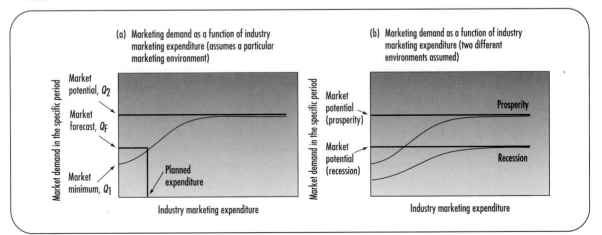

(a) Marketing demand as a function of industry marketing expenditure (assumes a particular marketing environment)

(b) Marketing demand as a function of industry marketing expenditure (two different environments assumed)

level would not stimulate much further demand, suggesting an upper limit called the *market potential* (labeled Q_2).

The total size of an *expansible market* is much affected by the level of industry marketing spending. In Figure 5.2a, the distance between Q_1 and Q_2 is relatively large. However, in a *nonexpansible market*—one not much affected by the level of marketing expenditures—the distance between Q_1 and Q_2 would be relatively small. Organizations that sell in a nonexpansible market must accept the market's size (the level of *primary demand* for the product class) and try to win a larger market share (the level of *selective demand* for the company's product).

The market demand curve shows alternative current forecasts of market demand associated with alternative possible levels of industry marketing effort in the current period. Only one level of industry marketing expenditure will actually occur; the market demand at this level is the **market forecast**. This forecast shows expected market demand, not maximum market demand.

Market potential is the limit approached by market demand as industry marketing expenditures approach infinity for a given marketing environment. The phrase "for a given marketing environment" is crucial. The market potential for many products is higher during prosperity than during recession, as illustrated in Figure 5.2b. Companies cannot do anything about the position of the market demand function, but their marketing spending can influence their location on the function.

Company Demand and Sales Forecast

Company demand is the company's estimated share of market demand at alternative levels of company marketing effort in a given time period. The company's share of market demand depends on how its marketing mix is perceived relative to that of its competitors. If other things are equal, the company's market share would depend on the size and effectiveness of its market expenditures relative to competitors. Marketing model builders have developed sales-response functions to measure how a company's sales are affected by marketing expenditures, marketing mix, and marketing effectiveness.[21]

Once marketers have estimated company demand, they next choose a level of marketing effort to produce an expected level of sales. The **company sales forecast** is the expected level of company sales based on a chosen marketing plan and an assumed marketing environment. The company sales forecast is graphed with company sales on the vertical axis and company marketing effort on the horizontal axis, as in Figure 5.2. Note that the sales forecast is the result of an assumed marketing expenditure plan.

A **sales quota** is the sales goal set for a product line, company division, or sales representative. It is primarily a managerial device for defining and stimulating sales effort. Generally, sales quotas are set slightly higher than estimated sales to stretch the sales force's effort. A **sales budget** is a conservative estimate of the expected sales volume, and is used primarily for making current purchasing, production, and cash-flow decisions. The sales budget considers the sales forecast and avoids excessive risk, so it is generally set slightly lower than the sales forecast.

Company sales potential is the sales limit approached by company demand as company marketing effort increases relative to competitors. The absolute limit of company demand is, of course, the market potential. In most cases, company sales potential is less than market potential, even when company marketing expenditures increase considerably, because each competitor has a core of loyal buyers who are not very responsive to other companies' efforts to woo them.

Estimating Current Demand

We are now ready to examine practical methods for estimating current market demand. Marketing executives want to estimate total market potential, area market potential, total industry sales, and market shares.

Total Market Potential   **Total market potential** is the maximum amount of sales that might be available to all of the firms in an industry during a given period under a given level of industry marketing effort and given environmental conditions. A common way to estimate total market potential is to estimate the potential number of buyers multiplied by the average quantity purchased by a buyer multiplied by the price.

   The most difficult component to estimate is the number of buyers for the specific product or market. Companies can start with a total population, eliminate groups that obviously would not buy the product, and do research to eliminate groups without interest or money to buy. This leaves a prospect pool of potential buyers that companies can include in the calculation of total market potential.

Area Market Potential   Companies face the problem of selecting the best territories and allocating their marketing budget optimally among these territories. Therefore, they need to estimate the market potential of different cities, states, and nations. Business marketers primarily use the market-buildup method, while consumer marketers primarily use the multiple-factor index method.

   The **market-buildup method** calls for identifying all of the potential buyers in an area and estimating their potential purchases. This works well if firms have a list of all potential buyers and a good estimate of what each will buy—data that can be difficult to gather. An efficient method makes use of the North American Industry Classification System (NAICS), a six-digit code that provides statistics that are comparable across the United States, Canada, and Mexico.[22] To compute the potential for a market, the company must estimate how many products might be used in an industry. In addition to estimating the amount of products each company might buy—multiplied by the number of companies in the market—the company must also examine the extent of market saturation, the number of competitors, the market growth rate, and other variables. Then the company adds up the market potential for all its markets.

   Consumer companies also estimate area market potentials, but because their customers are too numerous to be listed, they often use the index method. A drug marketer, for example, might assume that the market potential for drugs is directly related to population size. If Virginia has 2.28 percent of the U.S. population, the company might assume that state will account for 2.28 percent of all drugs sold. In reality, drug sales are also influenced by other factors. Thus, it makes sense to develop a multiple-factor index with each factor assigned a specific weight. For example, if Virginia has 2.00 percent of the U.S. disposable personal income, 1.96 percent of U.S. retail sales, and 2.28 percent of U.S. population, with respective weights of 0.5, 0.3, and 0.2, the buying-power index for drugs in Virginia would be:

$$0.5 \,(2.00) + 0.3 \,(1.96) + 0.2 \,(2.28) = 2.04$$

In addition to estimating total market potential and area potential, a company needs to know the actual industry sales in its market. This means identifying its competitors and estimating their sales. Some information may be available from trade associations and marketing research firms, although not for individual competitors. Business marketers typically have a harder time estimating industry sales and market shares than consumer-goods manufacturers do.

Estimating Future Demand

Forecasting is the art of anticipating what buyers are likely to do under a given set of conditions. Very few products or services lend themselves to easy forecasting of future demand. Those that do generally involve a product whose absolute level or trend is fairly constant and for which competition is nonexistent (public utilities) or stable (pure oligopolies). In most markets, total demand and company demand are not stable. Good forecasting becomes a key factor in company success. The more unstable the demand, the more critical is forecast accuracy, and the more elaborate is forecasting procedure.

Companies commonly use a three-stage procedure to prepare a sales forecast: They prepare a macroeconomic forecast first, then an industry forecast, then a company sales forecast. The macroeconomic forecast projects inflation, unemployment, interest rates, consumer spending, business investment, and other variables. The result is a forecast of gross domestic product, which is used, along with other indicators, to forecast industry sales. Finally, the company derives its sales forecast by assuming that it will win a certain market share. Methods for sales forecasting are shown in Table 5.3.

TABLE 5.3   Sales Forecast Methods

Forecast Method	Description	Use
Survey of buyers' intentions	Survey consumers or businesses about purchase probability, future finances, and expectations about the economy.	To estimate demand for industrial products, consumer durables, purchases requiring advance planning, and new products.
Composite of sales force opinions	Have sales representatives estimate how many current and prospective customers will buy the company's products.	To gather detailed forecast estimates broken down by product, territory, customer, and sales rep.
Expert Opinion	Obtain forecasts from experts such as dealers, distributors, suppliers, consultants, and trade associations; can be purchased from economic-forecasting firms.	To gather estimates from knowledgeable specialists who may offer good insights.
Past-sales analysis	Use time-series analysis, exponential smoothing, statistical demand analysis, or econometric analysis to analyze past sales.	To project future demand on the basis of an analysis of past demand.
Market-test method	Conduct a direct market test to understand customer response and estimate future sales.	To better forecast sales of new products or sales in a new area.

MACROENVIRONMENTAL TRENDS AND FORCES

Marketers find many opportunities by identifying trends in the macroenvironment. A **trend** is a direction or sequence of events that have some momentum and durability. According to futurist Faith Popcorn, a trend has longevity, is observable across several market areas and consumer activities, and is consistent with other significant indicators that occur or emerge at the same time.[23] In contrast, a **fad** is "unpredictable, short-lived, and without social, economic, and political significance."[24] A new product or marketing program is likely to be more successful if it is in line with strong trends rather than opposed to them. This is why marketers have to develop their trend-spotting skills (see "Marketing Skills: Spotting Trends"). Still, detecting a new market opportunity does not guarantee its success, even if it is technically feasible.

Companies and their suppliers, marketing intermediaries, customers, and competitors all operate in a macroenvironment of forces and trends that shape opportunities and pose threats. These forces represent "noncontrollables" which the company

MARKETING SKILLS: SPOTTING TRENDS

Futurists stress that much of our world remains the same for long periods; when this continuity is interrupted, the emerging change may endure for some time. Marketers therefore need to develop the skill of spotting trends so they can take action in time to turn a change into a profitable opportunity rather than a dangerous threat. First they must develop their "splatter vision," the ability to look at the entire environment without becoming too focused on one particular factor. Marketers who routinely concentrate on certain competitors or customers will probably miss signs of competition from an entirely new industry or signs of new customer needs. Marketers should also use their mental models of future expectations—based on sales or industry forecasts—to scan for and explain deviations. This means not only identifying anomalies but also analyzing their cause and effect to fuel timely marketing decisions.

In the ever-changing technology industry, experts develop a more accurate picture of the future using a combination of five approaches: seeing the future as an extension of the past; searching for cycles and patterns; analyzing the actions of customers and other stakeholders; monitoring technical and social events as they unfold; and watching the interaction of these four approaches to discover potential trends. The final challenge for any marketer is to understand the true nature of the trend and determine how it is likely to influence the macroenvironment and microenvironment—in particular, customers, industry players, the company, and its offerings.

For example, Herman Miller, which manufactures office furniture, has one employee surfing the Web full-time to collect breaking information about the business world, design, retailing, and other issues, then summarize the results in a daily e-mail to management. In addition, the president—who travels between headquarters in Michigan and a New York City office—carries a digital camera to photograph images that may prove helpful in identifying new design trends. Thanks to the firm's trend-spotting ability, it was an early mover in the market for small business and home-office furniture.[25]

must monitor and respond to. In the economic arena, companies and consumers are increasingly affected by global forces such as speedier transportation, communication, and financial transactions; the severe debt problems of some countries; the move toward market economies; and the growth of global brands in some product categories. Colgate-Palmolive test-marketed Total, its antibacterial plaque-fighting toothpaste, in six countries, managed by a cross-functional, international team. The test proved successful, and Total helped Colgate-Palmolive become the market leader in toothpaste.[26]

Within the rapidly changing global picture, the firm must monitor six major forces: demographic, economic, natural, technological, political-legal, and social-cultural. Although these forces will be described separately, marketers must pay attention to their interactions, because these set the stage for new opportunities as well as threats. For example, population growth (demographic) leads to resource depletion and pollution (natural environment), which leads consumers to call for more laws (political-legal). The restrictions stimulate new technological solutions and products (technology). If the solutions and products are affordable (economic forces), they may actually change attitudes and behavior (social-cultural).

Demographic Environment

Marketers monitor population trends because people make up markets. Marketers are keenly interested in the size and growth rate of the population in different cities, regions, and nations; age distribution and ethnic mix; educational levels; household patterns; and regional characteristics and movements.

Worldwide Population Growth　The world population stands at over 6.1 billion and will exceed 7.9 billion by 2025.[27] This population explosion has been a source of major concern for two reasons. First, certain resources that are needed to support this much human life (fuel, foods, and minerals) are limited and may run out at some point. Second, population growth is highest in areas that can least afford it. The less developed regions of the world currently account for 76 percent of the world population and are growing at 2 percent per year, whereas the population in the more developed countries is growing at only 0.6 percent per year. Feeding, clothing, and educating children while also providing a rising standard of living is nearly impossible in the less developed areas.

The explosive world population growth has major implications for business. A growing population does not mean growing markets unless these markets have sufficient purchasing power. Nonetheless, companies that carefully analyze their markets can find major opportunities. For example, the Chinese government limits families to one child per family. Toy marketers, in particular, see that these "little emperors" are showered with everything from candy to computers by parents, grandparents, great-grandparents, aunts, and uncles. This trend has encouraged Japan's Bandai Company, Denmark's Lego Group, and Mattel to enter the Chinese market.[28]

Population Age Mix　National populations vary in their age mix. A population can be subdivided into six age groups: preschool, school-age children, teens, young adults age 25 to 40, middle-aged adults age 40 to 65, and older adults age 65 and up. The most populous age groups shape the marketing environment. In the United States, the 78 million "baby boomers" born between 1946 and 1964 are a powerful force shaping the marketplace. Baby boomers grew up with television ads, so they are an easier market to reach than the 45 million people who were born between 1965 and 1976, dubbed Generation X. Gen-Xers are typically cynical about hard-sell marketing pitches that promise more than they can deliver.[29] The next generation is the baby boomlet, the 72 million people who were born between 1977 and 1994, a group that is highly fluent and comfortable with computer and Internet technology. Mountain Dew's use of extreme sports in advertising targeted to Gen-Xers and baby-boomlet members has helped boost the brand's share to fourth place in the soft drink category.[30]

Ethnic Markets Countries also vary in ethnic and racial makeup. The United States was originally called a "melting pot," but people now call it a "salad bowl" society, with ethnic groups maintaining their ethnic differences, neighborhoods, and cultures. Major groups within the U.S. population include whites, African Americans, Latinos (with subgroups of Mexican, Puerto Rican, and Cuban descent), and Asian Americans (with subgroups of Chinese, Filipino, Japanese, Asian Indian, and Korean descent).

Each group has certain specific wants and buying habits. Sears, for example, is targeting Latino consumers in 130 stores in southern California, Texas, Florida, and New York. "We make a special effort to staff those stores with bilingual sales personnel, to use bilingual signage, and to support community programs," says a Sears spokesperson. Yet marketers must be careful not to overgeneralize about ethnic groups. Within each ethnic group are consumers who are quite different from each other.

Educational Groups The population in any society falls into five educational groups: illiterates, high school dropouts, high school degrees, college degrees, and professional degrees. In Japan, 99 percent of the population is literate, whereas in the United States up to 15 percent of the population may be functionally illiterate. However, around 36 percent of the U.S. population is college-educated, one of the world's highest percentages; this education level fuels demand for quality books, magazines, and travel.

Household Patterns One out of eight U.S. households is "diverse" or "nontraditional," and includes single live-alones, adult live-togethers of one or both sexes, single-parent families, childless married couples, and empty nesters. More people are divorcing or separating, choosing not to marry, marrying later, or marrying without the intention to have children. Each group has a distinctive set of needs and buying habits. For example, single, separated, widowed, or divorced people need smaller apartments, smaller appliances and furniture, and food packaged in smaller sizes. Marketers must increasingly consider the special needs of nontraditional households, because they are now growing more rapidly than traditional households. Absolut Vodka targets members of the gay and lesbian market segment with advertising in *The Advocate* and other targeted publications as well as sponsorship of events such as gay and lesbian film festivals.[31]

Geographical Shifts in Population This is a period of great migratory movements between and within countries. In Eastern Europe, nationalities are reasserting themselves and forming independent countries, causing many people to seek political asylum in other nations. In the United States, many urban refugees are moving back to rural areas, bringing new marketing opportunities. Location makes a difference in goods and services preferences. Over 12 million U.S. households (more than one out of every 10) move each year, and the shift has been toward the Sunbelt states, fueling demand for air conditioning and other climate-appropriate products.[32]

Shift from a Mass Market to Micromarkets   The effect of all these changes is fragmentation of the mass market into numerous *micromarkets* differentiated by age, sex, ethnic background, education, geography, lifestyle, and other characteristics. Each group has strong preferences and is reached through increasingly targeted communication and distribution channels. More companies are shifting away from targeting a mythical "average" consumer and are instead targeting their products and marketing programs for specific micromarkets. One example is Kinko's, which targets the home office micromarket offering fax machines, fast color printers, computers loaded with popular software, and high-speed Internet connections. The company also allows time-pressured customers to order printing and binding services at Kinkos.com.[33]

Economic Environment

Markets require purchasing power as well as people. The available purchasing power in an economy depends on current income, prices, savings, debt, and credit availability. For this reason, marketers must track the trends in income and consumer-spending patterns.

Income Distribution   Nations vary greatly in level and distribution of income and industrial structure. The four types of industrial structures are: subsistence economies, which offer few marketing opportunities because most people barter excess output for simple goods and services; raw-material-exporting economies, which are rich in natural resources and represent markets for trucks and other equipment; industrializing economies, where growing industrialization is creating a growing middle class that demands new goods; and industrial economies, which are major exporters that have a sizable middle class for all sorts of goods.

Marketers often distinguish countries with five different income-distribution patterns: (1) very low incomes; (2) mostly low incomes; (3) very low, very high incomes; (4) low, medium, high incomes; and (5) mostly medium incomes. From 1973 to 1999, the income of the wealthiest 5 percent of the U.S. population grew by 65 percent, while the income for the middle fifth households grew only 11 percent. This is leading to a two-tier U.S. market, with affluent people buying expensive goods and working-class people spending more carefully on less expensive store brands. Conventional retailers who offer medium-price goods are the most vulnerable to these changes. Companies can prosper if they respond to this trend by tailoring their products and pitches to these two very different Americas.[34] Gap, for example, positions Banana Republic for higher-income shoppers, Gap for the mid-market, and Old Navy for the budget-conscious.[35]

Savings, Debt, and Credit Availability   Consumer expenditures are affected by consumer savings, debt, and credit availability. The Japanese, for example, save about 13.1 percent of their income, whereas U.S. consumers save about 4.7 percent. U.S. consumers also have a high debt-to-income ratio, which slows down further expenditures on housing and large-ticket items. Credit is very available in the United States, but lower-income borrowers pay fairly high interest rates. Marketers must pay careful attention to major changes in incomes, cost of living, interest rates, savings, and borrowing patterns because these can have a high impact on business, especially for companies whose products are geared to high-income and price-sensitive consumers.

Natural Environment

The deterioration of the natural environment is a major global concern. In many cities, air and water pollution have reached dangerous levels. In Western Europe, "green" parties have pressed for public action to reduce industrial pollution. However, legislation protecting the natural environment has hit certain industries very hard. Steel companies have had to invest in expensive pollution-control equipment and earth-friendly fuels, while automakers have had to install expensive emission controls in their vehicles. In general, marketers need to be aware of threats and opportunities related to four trends: the shortage of raw materials, the increased cost of energy, increased pollution levels, and the changing role of governments.

Shortage of Raw Materials The earth's raw materials consist of the infinite, the finite renewable, and the finite nonrenewable. Infinite resources, such as air and water, pose no immediate problem, although some groups see a long-run danger. Finite *renewable* resources, such as forests and food, must be used wisely. Forestry companies are required to reforest timberlands, for example. Finite *nonrenewable* resources such as oil will pose a serious problem as the point of depletion approaches. Firms making products that require these resources face substantial cost increases that they may be unable to pass along to customers.

Increased Energy Costs One finite nonrenewable resource, oil, has created serious problems for the world economy as oil prices have gyrated, setting off a search for alternative energy forms such as coal, solar, nuclear, and wind. Firms are also developing more energy-efficient products, such as the Toyota Prius, a car with an electric motor boosting the gasoline engine for better fuel efficiency.

Anti-Pollution Pressures Some industrial activity will inevitably damage the natural environment. However, because about 42 percent of U.S. consumers are willing to pay higher prices for "green" products, there is a large market for pollution-control solutions such as scrubbers, recycling centers, and landfill systems. Companies are showing their concern through environment-friendly programs. For example, 3M's Pollution Prevention Pays program has reduced pollution and costs; Dow's ethylene plant in Alberta uses 40 percent less energy and releases 97 percent less wastewater.[36]

Changing Role of Governments Governments vary in their concern and efforts to promote a clean environment. The German government is vigorous in its pursuit of environmental quality, partly because of the strong green movement in Germany and partly because of the ecological devastation in the former East Germany. Many nations are doing little about pollution because they lack the funds or the political will. The major hope is that companies will increasingly adopt practices that protect the natural environment.

Technological Environment

One of the most dramatic forces shaping people's lives is technology. However, every new technology is a force for "creative destruction." Autos hurt the railroads, and television hurts the newspapers. Instead of moving into the new technologies, many old industries fought or ignored them, and their businesses declined. Also, technological progress can be sporadic; for example, railroads sparked investment, and then investment petered out until the auto industry emerged. In between major innovations, the economy can stagnate, although minor innovations fill the gap. Marketers must monitor these trends in technology: the pace of change, the opportunities for innovation, varying R&D budgets, and increased regulation.

Accelerating Pace of Technological Change   Many common products, such as personal computers and fax machines, were not available decades ago. The lag between new ideas and their successful implementation is decreasing rapidly, and the time between introduction and peak production is much shorter. These technological changes are changing markets and needs. For example, technology enabling people to *telecommute*—work at home instead of traveling to offices—may reduce auto pollution, bring families closer, and create home-centered shopping and entertainment opportunities.

Unlimited Opportunities for Innovation   Scientists today are working on a startling range of new technologies (such as biotechnology and robotics) that will revolutionize products and production processes. The challenge in innovation is not only technical but also commercial—to develop affordable new products. Companies are already harnessing the power of *virtual reality*, the combination of technologies that allows users to experience three-dimensional, computer-generated environments through sound, sight, and touch. Virtual reality has helped firms to gather consumer reactions to new car designs, kitchen layouts, and other potential offerings. Technology is behind the use of smart cards for functions beyond simple payment transactions, including health-care identification, customer loyalty programs, and pay-television subscription authorization.[37]

Varying R&D Budgets   Although the United States leads the world in R&D expenditures, most is earmarked for defense. There is a need to transfer more of this money into other types of research. Many companies are still content to put their money into copying competitors' products and making minor feature and style improvements. Even basic-research companies such as DuPont and Pfizer are proceeding cautiously. Increasingly, research directed toward major breakthroughs is conducted by consortiums of companies rather than by single companies.

Increased Regulation of Technological Change   As products become more complex, the public needs to be assured of their safety. Consequently, government agencies' powers to investigate and ban potentially unsafe products have been expanded. In the United States, the Federal Food and Drug Administration must approve all drugs before they can be sold. Safety and health regulations have also increased in the areas of food, automobiles, clothing, electrical appliances, and construction. Marketers must be aware of these regulations when proposing, developing, and launching new products.

Political-Legal Environment

Marketing decisions are strongly affected by developments in the political and legal environment, which is composed of laws, government agencies, and pressure groups that influence and limit organizations and individuals. Sometimes these laws also create new opportunities for business. Mandatory recycling laws, for example, have spurred companies to make new products from recycled materials. One example is

Wellman, which makes EscoSpun Squared fiber for performance apparel from recycled soda bottles.

Legislation Regulating Business   Business legislation has three main purposes: to protect firms from unfair competition, to protect consumers from unfair business practices, and to protect society from unbridled business behavior. Over the years, legislation affecting business has steadily increased. For example, the European Community has enacted laws that cover competitive behavior, product standards, product liability, and commercial transactions; ex-Soviet nations are passing laws to promote and regulate an open market economy. The United States has laws covering issues such as competition, product safety and liability, fair trade, and packaging and labeling.[38]

At what point do the costs of regulation exceed the benefits? Although each new law may have a legitimate rationale, it may have the unintended effect of sapping initiative and retarding economic growth. Companies need a good working knowledge of business legislation, with legal review procedures and ethical standards to guide marketing managers. Internet marketers also need new parameters for conducting electronic business ethically.

Growth of Special-Interest Groups   The number and power of special-interest groups have increased over the past decades. Political-action committees (PACs) lobby government officials and pressure businesses to pay more attention to consumer rights, women's rights, senior citizen rights, minority rights, and gay rights. Many companies have public-affairs and consumer-affairs departments to deal with these groups and issues. Consumerists have won many rights, including the right to know the true interest cost of a loan and the true benefits of a product. Yet new laws and growing pressure from special-interest groups continue to add more restraints, moving many private marketing transactions into the public domain.

Social-Cultural Environment

Society shapes our beliefs, values, and norms. People absorb, almost unconsciously, a worldview that defines their relationship to themselves, others, organizations, society, nature, and the universe. Other cultural characteristics of interest to marketers include the persistence of core cultural values, the existence of subcultures, and shifts of values through time.

- *Views of themselves.* People vary in their relative emphasis on self-gratification. Today, people are more conservative: They cannot rely on continuous employment and rising income, so they are more cautious in spending and more value-driven in purchasing.

- *Views of others.* People are concerned about the homeless, crime, and other social problems. At the same time, people hunger for more lasting relationships with others. These trends portend a growing market for offerings that promote direct relations among human beings (such as health clubs) and for offerings that allow people who are alone to feel that they are not (such as video games).

- *Views of organizations.* People vary in their attitudes toward corporations, government agencies, trade unions, and other organizations. There has been an overall decline in organizational loyalty due to downsizings. As a result, companies need to find new ways to win back consumer and employee confidence through honesty and good corporate citizenship.

■ *Views of society.* People have varying attitudes toward society. Some defend it, some run it, some take what they can from it, some want to change it, some look for something deeper, and some want to leave it.[39] Consumption patterns often reflect social attitude; those who want to change it, for example, may drive more fuel-efficient cars.

■ *Views of nature.* People vary in their attitude toward nature. A long-term trend has been humankind's growing mastery of nature through technology. Recently, however, people have awakened to nature's fragility and finite resources. Businesses are responding with goods and services to increased consumer interest in hiking, camping, boating, and other outdoor activities, as well as to increased demand for "natural" food products.

■ *Views of the universe.* People vary in their beliefs about the origin of the universe and their place in it. Most Americans are monotheistic, although religious conviction and practice have varied through the years.

High Persistence of Core Values   The people living in a particular society hold many *core beliefs* and values that tend to persist. Core beliefs and values are passed on from parents to children and are reinforced by major social institutions—schools, churches, business, and government. Secondary beliefs and values are more open to change. Marketers may change secondary values but have little chance of changing core values. For instance, the nonprofit organization Mothers Against Drunk Drivers (MADD) does not try to stop the sale of alcohol, but it does promote the idea of appointing a designated driver who will not drink and lobbies to raise the legal drinking age.

Existence of Subcultures   Each society contains subcultures, groups with shared values emerging from their special life experiences or circumstances. *Star Trek* fans, Black Muslims, and Hell's Angels are all subcultures whose members share common beliefs, preferences, and behaviors. To the extent that subcultural groups exhibit different wants and consumption behavior, marketers can target particular subcultures. For instance, marketers love teenagers because they are trendsetters in fashion, music, entertainment, and attitudes. Marketers know that if they attract someone as a teen, they will probably keep that customer for years. Frito-Lay, which draws 15 percent of its sales from teens, has seen more chip-snacking by grown-ups. "We think it's because we brought them in as teenagers," says a Frito-Lay marketing director.[40]

Shifts of Secondary Cultural Values Through Time

Although core values are fairly persistent, cultural swings do take place, bringing new marketing opportunities or threats. Just as rock music and musicians had a major impact on young people's hairstyles and clothing in the 1960s, contemporary heroes and activities such as U2's Bono, Tiger Woods, and extreme sports are influencing the attitudes and behavior of young people today.

EXECUTIVE SUMMARY

Three developments make the need for marketing information greater than in the past: the rise of global marketing, the emphasis on buyers' wants, and the trend toward nonprice competition. Marketing managers therefore need a marketing information system (MIS) to assess information needs, develop the needed information, and distribute that information in a timely manner. An MIS consists of (a) an internal records system with information on the order-to-payment cycle and sales reporting systems; (b) a marketing intelligence system to obtain everyday information about developments in the marketing environment; (c) marketing research for the systematic design, collection, analysis, and reporting of data and findings that are relevant to a specific marketing situation; and (d) a computerized marketing decision support system to help marketers make and implement better decisions.

Companies can conduct their own marketing research or hire other companies to do it for them. The marketing research process consists of: defining the problem, alternatives, and objectives; developing the research plan; collecting the information; analyzing the information; presenting the findings to management; and making the decision. In conducting research, firms must decide whether to collect primary data or use secondary data. They must also decide which research approach (observation, focus groups, surveys, behavioral data, or experiments) and which research instrument (questionnaire, psychological tools, mechanical devices, or qualitative measures) to use. In addition, they have to decide on a sampling plan and contact methods.

One purpose of marketing research is to discover market opportunities. Then the company must evaluate its opportunities carefully and decide which markets to enter, based on sales forecasts of market and company demand. To estimate current demand, companies look at total market potential, area market potential, industry sales, and market share. To estimate future demand, companies survey buyers' intentions, solicit sales input, gather expert opinions, analyze past demand, or engage in market testing.

Marketers are responsible for identifying significant macroenvironmental changes, especially opportunities and threats posed by trends in six environmental forces. In the demographic environment, they must look at population growth; changes in age, ethnic composition, and educational levels; the rise of nontraditional households; geographic population shifts; and the move to micromarketing.

Within the economic environment, marketers should focus on income distribution and savings, debt, and credit availability. Within the natural environment, they need to watch raw-materials shortages, higher energy costs, anti-pollution pressures, and the changing role of governments in environmental protection. In the technological environment, they should note the faster pace of technological change, opportunities for innovation, varying R&D budgets, and increased governmental regulation. Within the political-legal environment, marketers must be aware of laws regulating business practices and of the influence of special-interest groups. Within the social-cultural environment, they must understand how people view themselves, others, organizations, society, nature, and the universe; how products fit with core and secondary cultural values; and how to address the needs of different subcultures.

CASE PILOT

READ, INTERACT AND TEST YOUR CASE ANALYSIS SKILLS

A very challenging question for all marketers is how can demand be more accurately measured and forecasted, especially for new products or services? Chapter 5 details various ways to conduct valid and reliable research so that the right products reach the right consumer targets.

Practice being a marketing consultant for the Big Wind case study and click on the Case Pilot tool at *www.prenhall.com/kotler*. This new business has developed a special windmill but needs help in deciding what to do next. See if you can answer the following questions:

1. What type of research should URS do?
2. Will different research methods be required to assess the demand for farmers versus small businesses?
3. What market opportunities are there for this product?

NOTES

1. "Tesco.com Turns a Profit," *EuropeMedia*, April 11, 2002, (*www.vandusseldorp.com*); Mark Kleinman, "Shoppers to Give Tesco Store Input," *Marketing*, March 28, 2002, p. 2; "Tesco Defends Price Reduction," *Grocer*, March 16, 2002, p. 4; "Safeway Blues as Shoppers Switch," *Grocer*, March 16, 2002, p. 22; "Tesco Trials Online Shopping in Seoul," *Grocer*, March 16, 2002, p. 14.
2. See James C. Anderson and James A. Narus, *Business Market Management: Understanding, Creating and Delivering Value* (Upper Saddle River, NJ: Prentice Hall, 1998), ch. 2.
3. "The Dot-Com Within Ford," *U.S. News & World Report*, February 7, 2000, p. 34; Amy Feldman, "How Big Can It Get," *Money*, December 1999, pp. 158–64.
4. John Verity, "A Trillion-Byte Weapon," *BusinessWeek*, July 31, 1995, pp. 80–81.
5. James A. Narus and James C. Anderson, "Turn Your Industrial Distributors into Partners," *Harvard Business Review* (March–April 1986): 66–71.
6. Don Peppers, "How You Can Help Them," *Fast Company*, October–November 1997, pp. 128–36.
7. See *1994 Survey of Market Research, eds.* Thomas Kinnear and Ann Root (Chicago: American Marketing Association, 1994).
8. John Gaffney, "How Do You Feel About a $44 Tooth-Bleaching Kit?" *Business 2.0*, September 2001, 126–127.
9. Kevin J. Clancy and Robert S. Shulman, *Marketing Myths That Are Killing Business* (New York: McGraw-Hill, 1994) p. 58; Phaedra Hise, "Comprehensive CompuServe," *Inc*, June 1994, p. 109; "Business Bulletin: Studying the Competition," *Wall Street Journal*, pp. A1–5.
10. For background information on in-flight Internet service, see "In-Flight Dogfight," *Business 2.0*, January 9, 2001, pp. 84–91.
11. For an excellent annotated reference to major secondary sources of business and marketing data, see Gilbert A. Churchill Jr., *Marketing Research: Methodological Foundations*, 6th ed. (Fort Worth, TX: Dryden, 1995).
12. Rick Whiting, "Virtual Focus Group," *Information Week*, July 30, 2001, pp. 53+.
13. Kevin Lane Keller, *Strategic Brand Management* (Upper Saddle River, NJ: Prentice Hall, 1998) pp. 317–18; and Daniel H. Pink, "Metaphor Marketing," *Fast Company*, April 1998, p. 214.
14. Elizabeth Millard, "Spool of Thought," *Business 2.0*, October 1999, pp. 219, 221; Roger D. Blackwell, James S. Hensel, Michael B. Phillips, and Brian Sternthal, *Laboratory Equipment for Marketing Research* (Dubuque, IA: Kendall/Hunt, 1970); and Wally Wood, "The Race to Replace Memory," *Marketing and Media Decisions*, July 1986, pp. 166–67. See also Gerald Zaltman, "Rethinking Market Research: Putting People Back In," *Journal of Marketing Research* 34, no. 4 (November 1997): 424–37.
15. David Goetzl, "O&M Turns Reality TV Into Research Tool," *Advertising Age*, July 10, 2000; Brian Wansink, "New Techniques to Generate Key Marketing Insights," *American Marketing Association: Marketing Research*, Summer, 2000.

16. For further reading, see Joanne Lipman, "Single-Source Ad Research Heralds Detailed Look at Household Habits," *Wall Street Journal*, February 16, 1988, p. 39; Joe Schwartz, "Back to the Source," *American Demographics*, January 1989, pp. 22–26; and Magid H. Abraham and Leonard M. Lodish, "Getting the Most Out of Advertising and Promotions," *Harvard Business Review* (May–June 1990): 50–60.

17. See Kevin J. Clancy and Peter C. Krieg, *Counterintuitive Marketing: How Great Results Come from Uncommon Sense* (New York: The Free Press, 2000).

18. John D. C. Little, "Decision Support Systems for Marketing Managers," *Journal of Marketing* (Summer 1979): 11.

19. Gary L. Lilien and Arvind Rangaswamy, *Marketing Engineering*, 2nd ed. (Upper Saddle River, NJ: Prentice Hall, 2002).

20. Janet Moore and Ann Merrill, "Target Market," *Minneapolis-St. Paul Star Tribune*, July 27, 2001; "Hitting the Bulls-Eye: Target Sets Its Sights on East Coast Expansion," *Newsweek*, October 11, 1999.

21. For further discussion, see Gary L. Lilien, Philip Kotler, and K. Sridhar Moorthy, *Marketing Models* (Upper Saddle River, NJ: Prentice Hall, 1992).

22. For more information on NAICS, check the *U.S. Bureau of the Census* Web site, (*www.census.gov/epcd/www/naics.html*).

23. See Faith Popcorn, *The Popcorn Report* (New York: HarperBusiness, 1992).

24. Gerald Celente, *Trend Tracking* (New York: Warner Books, 1991).

25. Riza Cruz, "This Design Exec Manages 31 People Spread Over Two States," *Business 2.0*, April 2002, p. 115; Cynthia G. Wagner, "Top 10 Reasons to Watch Trends," *The Futurist*, March–April 2002, pp. 68+; Wayne Burkan, "Developing Your Wide-Angle Vision," *The Futurist*, March 1998, pp. 35+; Edward Cornish, "How We Can Anticipate Future Events," *The Futurist*, July 2001, pp. 26+; "Techniques for Forecasting," *The Futurist*, March 2001, p. 56.

26. Christine Bittar, "Total Whitening Joins Sparkling White, Whitening Sensitive SKUs. Got That?" *Brandweek*, October 2, 2000, p. 7; Pam Weisz, "Border Crossings: Brands Unify Image to Counter Cult of Culture," *Brandweek*, October 31, 1994, pp. 24–28.

27. See "World Population Profile: 1998—Highlights," *U.S. Census Bureau*, March 18, 1999 (*www.census.gov/ipc/www/wp98001.html*).

28. Sally D. Goll, "Marketing: China's (Only) Children Get the Royal Treatment," *Wall Street Journal*, February 8, 1995, p. B1.

29. Bill Stoneman, "Beyond Rocking the Ages: An Interview with J. Walker Smith," *American Demographics*, May 1998, pp. 45–49; Margot Hornblower, "Great X," Time, June 9, 1997, pp. 58–59; Bruce Horowitz, "Gen X in a Class by Itself," *USA Today*, September 23, 1996, p. B1.

30. "Top-10 U.S. Soft Drink Companies and Brands for 2000," *Beverage Digest*, February 15, 2001.

31. Susan Kastner, "A Tiny Agency's Ingenious Campaign Has Turned the Vodka into a Cult for Both Drinkers and Advertisers," *Toronto Star*, January 26, 1997; Stuart Elliot, "Absolute Customizes a Campaign to Salute GLAAD, *New York Times*, February 22, 2001.

32. Dan Fost, "Americans on the Move," *American Demographics*, Tools Supplement, January–February 1997, pp. 10–13.

33. Lauri J. Flynn, "Not Just a Copy Shop Any Longer, Kinko's Pushes Its Computer Services," *New York Times*, July 6, 1998, p. D1 (*www.kinkos.com*).

34. David Leonhardt, "Two-Tier Marketing," *BusinessWeek*, March 17, 1997, pp. 82–90.

35. Barbara Lippert, "Tailor-Made," *Adweek*, May 10, 1999 (*www.gap.com*, *www.oldnavy.com*).

36. Francoise L. Simon, "Marketing Green Products in the Triad," *The Columbia Journal of World Business* (Fall and Winter 1992): 268–85; and Jacquelyn A. Ottman, *Green*

Marketing: Responding to Environmental Consumer Demands (Lincolnwood, IL: NTC Business Books, 1993).

37. Patricia Sabatini, "Getting Smarter for Years, All-in-One Smart Cards Have Been on the Horizon," *Pittsburgh Post-Gazette*, July 1, 2001; "Europeans Prove Themselves Adept with Smart Cards," *Associated Press*, February 2, 2001.

38. See Dorothy Cohen, Legal Issues on Marketing Decision Making (Cincinnati: South-Western, 1995).

39. Arnold Mitchell of the Stanford Research Institute, private publication.

40. Laura Zinn, "Teens: Here Comes the Biggest Wave Yet," *BusinessWeek*, April 11, 1994, pp. 76–86.

CHAPTER 6

Analyzing Consumer Markets and Buyer Behavior

In this chapter, we will address the following questions:

1. How do cultural, social, personal, and psychological factors influence consumer buying behavior?
2. How does the consumer make a purchasing decision?

MARKETING MANAGEMENT AT WHIRLPOOL

Whirlpool, which makes and markets home appliances around the world, constantly looks at what consumers do and what drives their behavior. Its staff anthropologists go into people's homes, observe how consumers use appliances, and talk with household members. As a result, the company learned that in busy families, women are not the only ones doing the laundry. Knowing this, the company's engineers developed color-coded washer and dryer controls to make it easier for kids and men to pitch in.

In addition, Whirlpool's managers observed the trend toward "extreme nesting," consumers investing time and money in decorating their homes, preparing home-cooked meals, and entertaining friends and family at home. In response, Whirlpool developed the Inspired Chef business unit to sell KitchenAid equipment through cooking classes held in consumer's homes. Further, the company responded to increased Internet usage by establishing a Web site where consumers can quickly and easily file warranty claims. To give consumers new ideas, Whirlpool teamed up with Lowe's Home Improvement Warehouse for an Innovation Tour in which a huge van parks at local Lowe's stores to showcase cutting-edge appliances in professionally-designed kitchens.[1]

The aim of marketing is to meet and satisfy target customers' needs and wants. The field of **consumer behavior** studies how individuals, groups, and organizations select, buy, use, and dispose of goods, services, ideas, or experiences to satisfy their needs and desires. Understanding consumer behavior is never simple, because customers may say one thing but do another. They may not be in touch with their deeper motivations, and they may respond to influences or change their minds at the last minute.

Like Whirlpool, all marketers can profit from understanding how and why consumers buy. On the other hand, not understanding your customer's motivations and preferences can hurt. When Wal-Mart entered Latin American markets, it replicated its U.S. store design: narrow aisles crowded with merchandise and many products with red, white, and blue banners. However, Latin American shoppers need wider aisles because they come with larger families, and they perceived the red, white, and blue banners as Yankee imperialism—two reasons why initial sales were disappointing.[2]

Studying customers provides clues for developing new products, product features, prices, channels, messages, and other marketing-mix elements. This chapter explores consumers' buying dynamics; the next chapter explores the dynamics of business buyers.

HOW AND WHY CONSUMERS BUY

The starting point for understanding consumer buying behavior is the stimulus-response model shown in Figure 6.1. Both marketing and environmental stimuli enter the buyer's consciousness. In turn, the buyer's characteristics and decision process lead to certain purchase decisions. The marketer's task is to understand what happens in the buyer's consciousness between the arrival of outside stimuli and the purchase decision.

A consumer's buying behavior is influenced by cultural, social, personal, and psychological factors. Cultural factors exert the broadest and deepest influence.

FIGURE 6.1   Model of Consumer Buyer Behavior

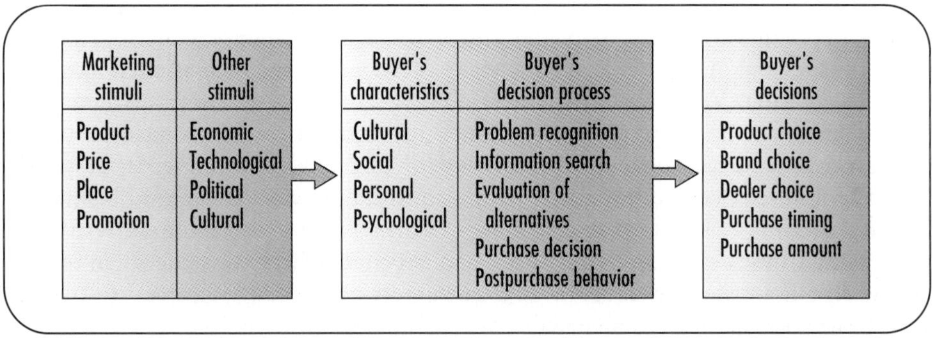

Marketing stimuli	Other stimuli	Buyer's characteristics	Buyer's decision process	Buyer's decisions
Product	Economic	Cultural	Problem recognition	Product choice
Price	Technological	Social	Information search	Brand choice
Place	Political	Personal	Evaluation of	Dealer choice
Promotion	Cultural	Psychological	alternatives	Purchase timing
			Purchase decision	Purchase amount
			Postpurchase behavior	

Cultural Factors

Culture, subculture, and social class are particularly important influences on consumer buying behavior. **Culture** is the most fundamental determinant of a person's wants and behavior. A child growing up in the United States is exposed to these broad cultural values: achievement and success, activity, efficiency and practicality, progress, material comfort, individualism, freedom, external comfort, humanitarianism, and youthfulness.[3]

Each culture consists of smaller **subcultures** that provide more specific identification and socialization for their members. Subcultures include nationalities, religions, racial groups, and geographic regions. Many subcultures make up important market segments, leading marketers to tailor products and marketing programs to their needs. Such programs are known as **diversity marketing**, a practice pioneered by large companies like AT&T, Sears Roebuck, and Coca-Cola. Diversity marketing grew out of marketing research showing that ethnic and demographic niches did not always respond favorably to mass-market advertising. Latinos, for example, the fastest-growing U.S. subculture, are targeted by Dallas-based Carnival Food Stores, among other marketers. When the chain uses Spanish language promotions, customers are more responsive.[4]

Social classes are relatively homogeneous and enduring divisions in a society. They are hierarchically ordered and their members share similar values, interests, and behavior (see Table 6.1). Social classes reflect income as well as occupation, education, and other indicators. Those within each social class tend to behave more alike than do persons from different social classes. Also, within the culture, persons are perceived as occupying inferior or superior positions according to social class. Social class is indicated by a cluster of variables rather than by any single variable.

Still, individuals can move from one social class to another—up or down—during their lifetime. Because social classes often show distinct product, brand, and media preferences, some marketers focus their efforts on one social class. Neiman Marcus, for example, focuses on the upper classes, offering top-quality merchandise in upscale stores with personal services geared to these customers' needs.

Social Factors

In addition to cultural factors, a consumer's behavior is influenced by such social factors as reference groups, family, and social roles and statuses.

Reference Groups **Reference groups** consist of all of the groups that have a direct (face-to-face) or indirect influence on a person's attitudes or behavior. Groups having a direct influence on a person are called **membership groups**. Some **primary groups** are family, friends, neighbors, and co-workers, with whom individuals interact fairly continuously and informally. **Secondary groups**, such as professional and trade-union groups, tend to be more formal and require less continuous interaction. Reference groups expose people to new behaviors and lifestyles, influence attitudes and self-concept, and create pressures for conformity that may affect product and brand choices.

People are also influenced by groups to which they do not belong. **Aspirational groups** are those the person hopes to join; **dissociative groups** are those whose values or behavior an individual rejects.

TABLE 6.1   Selected Characteristics of Major U.S. Social Classes

1. *Upper Uppers (less than 1%)*	The social elite who live on inherited wealth. They give large sums to charity, run the debutante balls, maintain more than one home, and send their children to the finest schools. They are a market for jewelry, antiques, homes, and vacations. They often buy and dress conservatively. Although small as a group, they serve as a reference group to the extent that their consumption decisions are imitated by the other social classes.
2. *Lower Uppers (about 2%)*	Persons, usually from the middle class, who have earned high income or wealth through exceptional ability in their professions or business. They tend to be active in social and civic affairs and to buy the symbols of status for themselves and their children. They include the nouveau riche, whose pattern of conspicuous consumption is designed to impress those below them.
3. *Upper Middles (12%)*	These persons possess neither family status nor unusual wealth and are primarily concerned with "career." They are professionals, independent businesspersons, and corporate managers who believe in education and want their children to develop professional or administrative skills. Members of this class are civic-minded and home-oriented. They are the quality market for good homes, clothes, furniture, and appliances.
4. *Middle Class (32%)*	Average-pay white- and blue-collar workers who live on "the right side of town." Often, they buy popular products to keep up with trends. Twenty-five percent own imported cars, and most are concerned with fashion. The middle class believes in spending more money on "worthwhile experiences" for their children and steering them toward a college education.
5. *Working Class (38%)*	Average-pay blue-collar workers and those who lead a working-class lifestyle, whatever their income, school background, or job. The working class depends heavily on relatives for economic and emotional support, for tips on job opportunities, for advice, and for assistance. A working-class vacation means staying in town, and "going away" means to a lake or resort no more than two hours away. The working class tends to maintain sharp sex-role divisions and stereotyping.
6. *Upper Lowers (9%)*	Upper lowers are working, although their living standard is just above poverty. They perform unskilled work and are very poorly paid. Often, upper lowers are educationally deficient.
7. *Lower Lowers (7%)*	Lower lowers are on welfare, visibly poverty stricken, and usually out of work. Some are not interested in finding a permanent job, and most are dependent on public aid or charity for income.

Sources: Richard P. Coleman, "The Continuing Significance of Social Class to Marketing," *Journal of Consumer Research* (December 1983): 265–80; Richard P. Coleman and Lee P. Rainwater, *Social Standing in America: New Dimension of Class* (New York: Basic Books, 1978).

Although marketers try to identify target customers' reference groups, the level of reference-group influence varies among products and brands. Manufacturers of products and brands with strong group influence must reach and influence the opinion leaders in these reference groups. An **opinion leader** is the person in informal product-related communications who offers advice or information about a product or product category.[5] Marketers try to reach opinion leaders by identifying demographic and psychographic characteristics associated with opinion leadership, identifying the preferred media of opinion leaders, and directing messages at the opinion leaders. For example, the clothing retailer Abercrombie and Fitch, which targets college students, hires college students as in-store brand representatives—"leaders who have charisma, who portray the image of the brand."[6]

Family   The family is the most important consumer-buying organization in society, and it has been researched extensively.[7] The **family of orientation** consists of one's parents and siblings. From parents, a person acquires an orientation toward religion, politics, and economics as well as a sense of personal ambition, self-worth, and love.[8] A more direct influence on the everyday buying behavior of adults is the **family of procreation**—namely, one's spouse and children.

Marketers are interested in the roles and relative influence of the husband, wife, and children in the purchase of a large variety of products and services. These roles vary widely in different cultures and social classes. Vietnamese Americans, for example, are more likely to adhere to the model in which the man makes large-purchase decisions. In the United States, husband-wife involvement has traditionally varied widely by product category, so marketers need to determine which member has the greater influence in choosing particular products.

Traditional household purchasing patterns are changing, with baby-boomer husbands and wives shopping jointly for products once thought to be under the separate control of one spouse or the other.[9] For this reason, marketers of products traditionally purchased by one spouse may need to start thinking of the other as a possible purchaser, as Cadillac is doing with accessories designed to appeal to female car buyers.[10]

Another shift in buying patterns is an increase in the amount of money spent and influence wielded by children and teens.[11] Children age 2 to 14 indirectly influence an estimated $300 billion in annual household purchases. Indirect influence means that parents know the brands, product choices, and preferences of their children without hints or outright requests; direct influence refers to children's hints, requests, and demands.

Because the fastest route to Mom and Dad's wallets may be through Junior, many successful companies are showing off their products to children in promotions—and soliciting marketing information from them through the Internet. Controversy over this practice led to the enactment of the Children's Online Privacy Protection Act, which prevents Web sites from asking children for personal data (or using or disclosing the data) without parental permission.[12]

Roles and Statuses   A person participates in many groups, such as family, clubs, or organizations. The person's position in each group can be defined in terms of role and status. A **role** consists of the activities that a person is expected to perform. Each role carries a **status**. A Supreme Court justice has more status than a sales manager, and a sales manager has more status than an office clerk. People choose products that communicate their role and status in society. Company presidents often drive Mercedes, wear expensive suits, and drink Chivas Regal scotch. Savvy marketers are aware of the status symbol potential of their products and brands.

Personal Factors

The third factor affecting consumer buying decisions is personal characteristics, including the buyer's age, stage in the life cycle, occupation, economic circumstances, lifestyle, personality and self-concept.

Age and Stage in the Life Cycle   People buy different goods and services over a lifetime. They eat baby food in the early years, most foods in the growing and mature years, and special diets in the later years. Taste in clothes, furniture, and recreation is also age-related, which is why smart marketers are attentive to the influence of age.

Similarly, consumption is shaped by the **family life cycle**. The traditional family life cycle covers a series of stages in adult lives, starting with independence from parents and continuing into marriage, child rearing, empty-nest years, retirement, and later life. Marketers often choose a specific family life-cycle group as their target market. Yet target households are not always family based: There are also single households, gay households, and cohabitor households. In addition, research has identified psychological life-cycle stages, indicating that adults experience certain "passages" or "transformations" in life.[13] Marketers should pay close attention to how changing life circumstances—divorce, widowhood, remarriage—influence consumption behavior.

Occupation and Economic Circumstances   Occupation also influences a person's consumption pattern. A blue-collar worker will buy work clothes, while a company president will buy expensive suits and a country club membership. Marketers try to identify the occupational groups that are more interested in their products and services, and sometimes tailor their products for certain occupations. Software manufacturers, for example, design special programs for lawyers, physicians, and other occupational groups.

Product choice is greatly affected by a consumer's economic circumstances: spendable income (level, stability, and time pattern), savings and assets (including the percentage that is liquid), debts, borrowing power, and attitude toward spending versus saving. Marketers of income-sensitive goods must track trends in personal income, savings, and interest rates. If a recession is likely, marketers can redesign, reposition, and reprice their products to offer more value to target customers.

Lifestyle   People from the same subculture, social class, and occupation may actually lead quite different lifestyles. A **lifestyle** is a person's pattern of living in the world as expressed in activities, interests, and opinions. Lifestyle portrays the "whole person" interacting with his or her environment. Marketers search for relationships between their products and lifestyle groups. For example, a computer manufacturer might find that most computer buyers are achievement-oriented. The marketer may then aim its brand more clearly at the achiever lifestyle.

Psychographics is the science of measuring and categorizing consumer lifestyles. One of the most popular classifications based on psychographic measurements is SRI International's Values and Lifestyles (VALS) framework. The VALS 2 system classifies all U.S. adults into eight groups based on psychological attributes drawn from survey responses to demographic, attitudinal, and behavioral questions, including questions about Internet usage.[14] The major tendencies of these groups are:

- *Actualizers*. Successful, sophisticated, active, "take-charge" people whose purchases often reflect cultivated tastes for relatively upscale, niche-oriented products.
- *Fulfilleds*. Mature, satisfied, comfortable, and reflective people who favor durability, functionality, and value in products.
- *Achievers*. Successful, career- and work-oriented consumers who favor established, prestige products that demonstrate success.
- *Experiencers*. Young, vital, enthusiastic, impulsive, and rebellious people who spend much of their income on clothing, fast food, and entertainment.
- *Believers*. Conservative, conventional, and traditional people who favor familiar products and established brands.

- *Strivers*. Uncertain, insecure, approval-seeking, resource constrained consumers who favor stylish products that emulate the purchases of wealthier people.

- *Makers*. Practical, self-sufficient, traditional, and family-oriented people who favor products with a practical or functional purpose, such as tools and fishing equipment.

- *Strugglers*. Elderly, resigned, passive, concerned, and resource-constrained consumers who are cautious and loyal to favorite brands.

Lifestyle segmentation schemes vary by culture. McCann-Erickson London, for example, has identified these British lifestyles: Avant-Gardians (interested in change); Pontificators (traditionalists); Chameleons (follow the crowd); and Sleepwalkers (contented underachievers). The advertising agency D'Arcy, Masius, Benton & Bowles has identified five segments of Russian consumers: Merchants, Cossacks, Students, Business Executives, and Russian Souls.[15]

Personality and Self-Concept Each person has a distinct personality that influences buying behavior. **Personality** refers to the distinguishing psychological characteristics that lead to relatively consistent and enduring responses to environment. Personality is often described in terms of such traits as self-confidence, dominance, autonomy, deference, sociability, defensiveness, and adaptability.[16]

Personality can be useful in analyzing consumer behavior. The idea is that brands also have personalities, and that consumers are likely to choose brands whose personalities match their own. **Brand personality** is the specific mix of human traits that may be attributed to a particular brand. Jennifer Aaker's research has identified five brand personality traits: sincerity, excitement, competence, sophistication, and ruggedness.[17]

Marketers often try to develop brand personalities that will attract consumers with the same **self-concept**. Yet it is possible that a person's *actual self-concept* (how she views herself) differs from her *ideal self-concept* (how she would like to view herself) and from her *others-self-concept* (how she thinks others see her). Which self will she try to satisfy in making a purchase? Self-concept theory has had a mixed record of success in predicting consumer responses to brand images.[18]

Psychological Factors

A person's buying choices are influenced by the psychological factors of motivation, perception, learning, beliefs, and attitudes.

Motivation A person has many needs at any given time. Some needs are *biogenic*; they arise from physiological states of tension such as hunger, thirst, and discomfort. Other needs are *psychogenic*; they arise from psychological states of tension such as the need for recognition, esteem, or belonging. A need becomes a motive when it is aroused to a sufficient level of intensity. A **motive** is a need that is sufficiently pressing to drive the person to act.

Psychologists have developed theories of human motivation. Three of the best known—the theories of Sigmund Freud, Abraham Maslow, and Frederick Herzberg—carry quite different implications for consumer analysis and marketing strategy.

Sigmund Freud assumed that the psychological forces shaping people's behavior are largely unconscious, and that people cannot fully understand their own motivations. A technique called *laddering* can be used to trace a person's motivations from the stated instrumental ones to the more terminal ones. Then the marketer can decide at what level to develop the message and appeal.[19] In line with Freud's theory, consumers react not only to the stated capabilities of specific brands, but also to other, less conscious cues. Shape, size, weight, material, color, and brand name can all trigger certain associations and emotions.

Abraham Maslow sought to explain why people are driven by particular needs at particular times.[20] His theory is that human needs are arranged in a hierarchy, from the most to the least pressing. In order of importance, these five categories are physiological, safety, social, esteem, and self-actualization needs. A consumer will try to satisfy the most important need first; when that need is satisfied, the person will try to satisfy the next most pressing need. Maslow's theory helps marketers understand how various products fit into the plans, goals, and lives of consumers.

Frederick Herzberg developed a two-factor theory that distinguishes *dissatisfiers* (factors that cause dissatisfaction) from *satisfiers* (factors that cause satisfaction).[21] The absence of dissatisfiers is not enough; satisfiers must be actively present to motivate a purchase. For example, a computer that comes without a warranty would be a dissatisfier. Yet the presence of a product warranty would not act as a satisfier or motivator of a purchase, because it is not a source of intrinsic satisfaction with the computer. Ease of use would, however, be a satisfier for a computer buyer. In line with this theory, marketers should avoid dissatisfiers that might unsell their products. They should also identify and supply the major satisfiers or motivators of purchase, because these satisfiers determine which brand consumers will buy.

Perception   A motivated person is ready to act, yet how that person actually acts is influenced by his or her perception of the situation. **Perception** is the process by which an individual selects, organizes, and interprets information inputs to create a meaningful picture of the world.[22] Perception depends not only on physical stimuli, but also on the stimuli's relation to the surrounding field and on conditions within the individual. The key word is individual. Individuals can have different perceptions of the same object because of three perceptual processes: selective attention, selective distortion, and selective retention.

People are exposed to many daily stimuli such as ads; most of these stimuli are screened out—a process called **selective attention**. The result is that marketers must work hard to attract consumers' attention. Through research, marketers have learned that people are more likely to notice stimuli that relate to a current need; this is why car shoppers notice car ads but not appliance ads. Furthermore, people are more likely to notice stimuli that they anticipate—such as foods promoted on a food Web site. And people are more likely to notice stimuli whose deviations are large in relation to the normal size of the stimuli, such as a banner ad offering a $100 discount (not just $5).

Even noticed stimuli do not always come across the way that marketers intend. **Selective distortion** is the tendency to twist information into personal meanings and interpret information in a way that fits our preconceptions. Unfortunately, marketers can do little about selective distortion.

People forget much that they learn but tend to retain information that supports their attitudes and beliefs. Because of **selective retention**, we are likely to remember good points mentioned about a product we like and forget good points mentioned about competing products. Selective retention explains why marketers use drama and repetition in messages to target audiences.

Learning   When people act, they learn. **Learning** involves changes in an individual's behavior that arise from experience. Most human behavior is learned. Theorists believe that learning is produced through the interplay of drives, stimuli, cues, responses, and reinforcement. A **drive** is a strong internal stimulus that impels action. **Cues** are minor stimuli that determine when, where, and how a person responds.

Suppose you buy an IBM computer. If your experience is rewarding, your response to computers and IBM will be positively reinforced. Later, when you want to buy a printer, you may assume that because IBM makes good computers, it also makes good printers. You have now generalized your response to similar stimuli. A counter-tendency to generalization is **discrimination**, in which the person learns to recognize differences in sets of similar stimuli and adjust responses accordingly. Applying learning theory, marketers can build up demand for a product by associating it with strong drives, using motivating cues, and providing positive reinforcement.

Beliefs and Attitudes   Through doing and learning, people acquire beliefs and attitudes that, in turn, influence buying behavior. A **belief** is a descriptive thought that a person holds about something. Beliefs may be based on knowledge, opinion, or faith, and they may or may not carry an emotional charge. Of course, manufacturers are very interested in the beliefs that people have about their products and services. These beliefs make up product and brand images, and people act on their images. If some beliefs are wrong and inhibit purchase, the manufacturer will want to launch a campaign to correct these beliefs.[23]

Global marketers need to remember that buyers often hold distinct beliefs about brands or products based on their country of origin. Studies have found, for example, that the impact of country of origin varies with product type. Consumers want to know where a car was made but not the origin of the lubricating oil. In addition, attitudes toward country of origin can change over time. When a product's place of origin turns off consumers, the company can consider co-production with a foreign company that has a better name. Another alternative is to hire a well-known celebrity to endorse the product. Or the company can adopt a strategy to achieve world-class quality in the local industry, as is the case with Belgian chocolates and Colombian coffee.

This is what South African wineries are attempting to do as their wine exports increase. South African wines have been hurt by the perception that the country's vineyards are primitive in comparison to those in other countries and that wine farmers are continuing crude labor practices. In reality, South Africa's wine farmers have improved the lives of their workers. "Wine is such a product of origin that we cannot succeed if South Africa doesn't look good," says the chief executive of the Ko-operatieve Wijnbouwers Vereniging, the farmers' co-op that dominates the industry.[24]

Attitudes are just as important as beliefs for influencing buying behavior. An **attitude** is a person's enduring favorable or unfavorable evaluations, emotional feelings, and action tendencies toward some object or idea.[25] People have attitudes toward almost everything: religion, politics, clothes, music, food. Attitudes put them into a frame of mind of liking or disliking an object, moving toward or away from it. Attitudes lead people to behave in a fairly consistent way toward similar objects. Because attitudes economize on energy and thought, they are very difficult to change; to change a single attitude may require major adjustments in other attitudes.

Thus, a company would be well advised to fit its product into existing attitudes rather than to try to change people's attitudes. Of course, trying to change attitudes can pay off occasionally. Consider milk. Consumption had been in decline for 20 years when the California Milk Processor Board kicked off the "Got Milk?" ad campaign to highlight the inconvenience and annoyance of running out of milk. Within the first year of the campaign, the number of Californians who reported consuming milk several times a week rose from 72 to 78 percent. Then the National Fluid Milk Processor Education Program bought the rights to the "Got Milk?" tagline and began using it in multimillion dollar national advertising campaigns.[26]

THE CONSUMER BUYING DECISION PROCESS

Marketers have to go beyond the various influences on buyers and develop an understanding of how consumers actually make their buying decisions. Specifically, marketers must identify who makes the buying decision, the types of buying decisions, and the stages in the buying process.

Buying Roles

Marketers can identify the buyer for many products easily. In the United States, men normally choose their shaving equipment, and women choose their pantyhose. Still, marketers must be careful, because buying roles can change. After the giant British chemical firm ICI discovered that women made 60 percent of the decisions on the brand of household paint, it began advertising its DeLux brand to women.

We can distinguish five roles that people might play in a buying decision. An *initiator* first suggests the idea of buying the product or service. An *influencer* is the person whose view or advice influences the decision. A *decider* actually decides whether to buy, what to buy, how to buy, or where to buy. A *buyer* makes the actual purchase, while a *user* consumes or uses the product or service.

Buying Behavior

Consumer decision making varies with the type of buying decision. The decisions to buy toothpaste, a tennis racket, a personal computer, and a new car are all very different. In general, complex and expensive purchases are likely to involve more buyer deliberation and more participants. As shown in Table 6.2, Assael distinguished four types of consumer buying behavior, based on the degree of buyer involvement and the degree of differences among brands:[27]

Complex buying behavior applies to high-involvement products such as personal computers. Buyers may not know what attributes to consider in these products, so they do research. Knowing this, marketers can help educate buyers about product attributes, differentiate and describe the brand's features, and motivate store personnel and others to influence the final brand choice.

Dissonance-reducing buyer behavior applies to high-involvement products such as carpeting. Carpeting is expensive and self-expressive, yet the buyer may consider most brands in a given price range to be the same. After buying, the consumer might experience dissonance that stems from noticing certain disquieting features or hearing favorable things about other brands. Marketers should therefore supply beliefs and evaluations that help consumers feel good about their brand choices.

Habitual buying behavior applies to low-involvement products such as salt. Consumers keep buying the same brand out of habit, not due to strong brand loyalty,

TABLE 6.2   Four Types of Consumer Buying Behavior

	High Involvement	Low Involvement
Significant Differences between Brands	*Complex buying behavior*— applies when product is expensive, bought infrequently, risky, and self-expressive; buyer first develops beliefs about the product, then develops attitudes about it, and finally makes a thoughtful choice.	*Variety-seeking buying behavior*— applies when buyer switches brands for the sake of variety rather than dissatisfaction; buyer has some beliefs about the product, chooses a brand with little evaluation, and evaluates the product during consumption.
Few Differences between Brands	*Dissonance-reducing behavior*— applies when the product is expensive, bought infrequently, and risky; buyer shops around and buys fairly quickly, then later experiences dissonance but stays alert to information supporting the purchase decision.	*Habitual buying behavior*— applies when the product is low-cost and frequently purchased; buyers do not pass through normal sequence of belief, attitude, and behavior but instead make decisions based on brand familiarity.

Source: Modified from Henry Assael, *Consumer Behavior and Marketing Action* (Boston: Kent Publishing Co., 1987), p. 87. Copyright © 1987 by Wadsworth, Inc. Printed by permission of Kent Publishing Co., a division of Wadsworth, Inc.

because they are passive recipients of information conveyed by advertising. Ad repetition creates brand familiarity rather than brand conviction. Marketers of such products can use price and sales promotions to entice new customers to try their products.

Variety-seeking buying behavior applies to low-involvement products such as cookies. In this category, consumers switch brands often because they want more variety. The market leader will therefore try to encourage habitual buying behavior by dominating the shelf space, keeping shelves stocked, and running frequent reminder ads. Challenger firms will encourage variety seeking by offering lower prices, coupons, free samples, and ads that present reasons for trying something new.

The Stages of the Buying Decision Process

Smart companies will immerse themselves in trying to understand the customer's overall experience in learning about a product, making a brand choice, using the product, and even disposing of it. Trying to understand the customer's behavior in connection with a product has been called mapping the customer's *consumption system*,[28] *customer activity cycle*,[29] or *customer scenario*.[30] This can be done for such activity clusters as doing laundry, preparing for a wedding, or buying a car. Buying a car, for example, involves a cluster of activities, including choosing the car, financing the purchase, buying insurance, buying accessories, and so on. Professor Sawhney views these activities as constituting a **metamarket** and calls firms that help customers navigate through these activities **metamediaries**.[31] Edmunds.com, for instance, is a metamediary that provides unbiased information and resources for buying autos and related services.

Figure 6.2 shows a five-stage model of the consumer buying process. Starting with problem recognition, the consumer passes through the stages of information

FIGURE 6.2   Five-Stage Model of the Consumer Buying Process

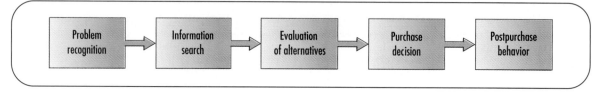

search, evaluation of alternatives, purchase decision, and postpurchase behavior. Clearly, the consumer buying process starts long before the actual purchase and has consequences long afterward.[32] Although the model implies that consumers pass sequentially through all five stages in buying a product, consumers sometimes skip or reverse some stages. However, we use this model because it captures the full range of considerations that arise when a consumer faces a highly involving new purchase.[33]

Problem Recognition   The buying process starts when the buyer recognizes a problem or need. This need can be triggered by internal stimuli (such as feeling hunger or thirst) or external stimuli (such as seeing an ad) that then becomes a drive. By gathering information from a number of consumers, marketers can identify the most frequent stimuli that spark interest in a product category. They can then develop marketing strategies that trigger consumer interest and lead to the second stage in the buying process.

Information Search   An aroused consumer will be inclined to search for more information, the second stage of the process. We can distinguish between two levels of arousal. At the milder search state of *heightened attention*, a person simply becomes more receptive to information about a product. At the *active information search* level, a person surfs the Internet, talks with friends, and visits stores to learn more about the product. Consumer information sources include personal sources (family, friends, neighbors, acquaintances), commercial sources (advertising, Web sites, salespersons, dealers, packaging, displays), public sources (mass media, consumer-rating organizations), and experiential sources (handling, examining, using the product). The consumer usually receives the most information from commercial sources, although the most influential information comes from personal sources.

Through gathering information, the consumer learns about competing brands and their features. The first box in Figure 6.3 shows the *total set* of brands available to the consumer. The individual consumer will come to know only a subset of these brands (*awareness set*). Some of these brands will meet initial buying criteria (*consideration set*). As the person gathers more information, only a few brands will remain as strong contenders (*choice set*). The person makes a final choice from this set.[34]

Figure 6.3 makes it clear that a company must strategize to get its brand into the prospect's awareness set, consideration set, and choice set. The company must also identify the other brands in the consumer's choice set so it can plan competitive appeals. In addition, the company should identify the consumer's information sources and evaluate their relative importance so it can prepare effective communications.

Evaluation of Alternatives   How does the consumer process competitive brand information and make a final judgment? There are several evaluation processes; the

FIGURE 6.3   Successive Sets Involved in Consumer Decision Making

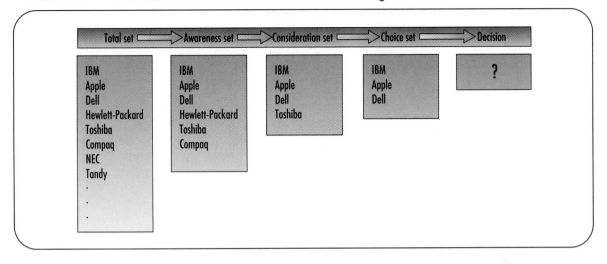

most current models view the process as being cognitively oriented, meaning that consumers form judgments largely on a conscious and rational basis.

Some basic concepts underlie consumer evaluation processes. As noted earlier, the consumer is trying to satisfy a need. In seeking certain benefits from the product solution, the consumer sees each product as a bundle of attributes with varying abilities of delivering the benefits to satisfy this need. However, the attributes of interest to buyers vary by product. For example, the attributes sought in a camera might be picture sharpness, camera size, and price. In addition, consumers vary as to which product attributes they see as most relevant and the importance they attach to each attribute. Knowing that consumers pay the most attention to attributes that deliver the benefits they seek, marketers can segment their markets according to the attributes that are salient to different consumer groups.

The consumer develops a set of *brand* beliefs about where each brand stands on each attribute. The set of beliefs about a particular brand, which make up the **brand image,** will vary with the consumer's experiences as filtered by the effects of selective perception, selective distortion, and selective retention.

Ultimately, consumers develop attitudes toward various brand alternatives through an attribute evaluation procedure.[35] Suppose, for example, that Linda Brown has narrowed her choice set to four computers (A, B, C, D) on the basis of four attributes: memory capacity, graphics capability, size and weight, and price. If one computer dominated the others on all of the criteria, we could predict that Linda would choose it. But her choice set consists of brands that vary in their appeal. She sees A as having the best memory capacity, B as having the best graphics capability, C as having the best size and weight, and D as having the best price.

Like most buyers, Linda is considering several attributes in her purchase decision, each with a particular weight. She has assigned 40 percent of the importance to the computer's memory capacity, 30 percent to graphics capability, 20 percent to size and weight, and 10 percent to price. To find Linda's perceived value for each computer, multiply her weights by the scores indicating her beliefs about each computer's attributes. So for computer A, if she assigns a score of 10 for memory capacity, 8 for graphics capability, 6 for size and weight, and 4 for price, the overall score would be:

$$0.4\,(10) + 0.3\,(8) + 0.2\,(6) + 0.1\,(4) = 8.0$$

Calculating the scores for all of the other computers that Linda is evaluating would show which one has the highest perceived value.[36] This is critical, because a manufacturer who knows how buyers evaluate alternatives and form preferences can take steps to influence buyer decisions. In the case of computers, a manufacturer might redesign the computer (a technique called real repositioning), alter consumer beliefs about the brand (psychological repositioning), alter consumer beliefs about competitors' brands (competitive depositioning), alter the importance weights (to persuade buyers to attach more importance to attributes in which the brand excels), call attention to neglected attributes (such as styling), or shift the buyer's ideals (to persuade buyers to change ideal levels on one or more attributes).[37]

Purchase Decision   In the fourth stage, the consumer forms preferences among the brands in the choice set and may also form an intention to buy the most preferred brand. However, two factors can intervene between the purchase intention and the purchase decision.[38]

The first factor is the *attitudes of others*. The extent to which another person's attitude reduces one's preferred alternative depends on two things: (1) the intensity of the other person's negative attitude toward the consumer's preferred alternative, and (2) the consumer's motivation to comply with the other person's wishes.[39] The influence of others becomes even more complex when several people close to the buyer hold contradictory opinions and the buyer wants to please them all. **Infomediaries** that publish consumer or professional evaluations also influence decisions.

The second factor is *unanticipated situational factors* that may erupt to change the purchase intention. A consumer could lose his job, some other purchase might become more urgent, or a store salesperson may turn him or her off, which is why preferences and even purchase intentions are not completely reliable predictors of purchase behavior. A consumer's decision to modify, postpone, or avoid a purchase decision is heavily influenced by *perceived risk*.[40] The amount of perceived risk varies with the amount of money at stake, the amount of attribute uncertainty, and the amount of consumer self-confidence. Consumers develop routines for reducing risk, such as decision avoidance, information gathering from friends, and preference for national brand names and warranties. Smart marketers study the factors that provoke a feeling of risk in consumers and then provide information and support to reduce the perceived risk.

Postpurchase Behavior   In the fifth stage of the process, after purchasing the product, the consumer will experience some level of satisfaction or dissatisfaction. Thus, the marketer's job does not end when the product is bought. Marketers must monitor postpurchase satisfaction, postpurchase actions, and postpurchase product uses.

The buyer's satisfaction with a purchase is a function of the closeness between the buyer's expectations and the product's perceived performance.[41] If performance falls short of expectations, the customer is *disappointed*; if it meets expectations, the customer is *satisfied*; if it exceeds expectations, the customer is *delighted*. These feelings influence whether the customer buys the product again and talks favorably or unfavorably about it to others. The importance of postpurchase satisfaction suggests that product claims must truthfully represent the product's likely performance. Some sellers might even understate performance levels so that consumers experience higher-than-expected satisfaction.

The buyer's satisfaction or dissatisfaction after a product purchase will influence subsequent behavior. Satisfied consumers will be more likely to purchase the product again. This has been confirmed by the data on automobile brand choice, which show a high correlation between satisfaction with the last brand bought and intention to rebuy the brand. One survey showed that 75 percent of Toyota buyers were highly satisfied and about 75 percent intended to buy a Toyota again; 35 percent of Chevrolet buyers were highly satisfied and about 35 percent intended to buy a Chevrolet again. Satisfied customers also tend to say good things about the brand to others, which is why many marketers say: "Our best advertisement is a satisfied customer."[42] (Measuring satisfaction is the focus of "Marketing Skills: Gauging Customer Satisfaction," below).

Dissatisfied consumers may abandon or return the product; seek information that confirms its high value; take public action by complaining to the company, going to a lawyer, or complaining to government agencies and other groups; or take private

MARKETING SKILLS: GAUGING CUSTOMER SATISFACTION

Over and over, research has shown that satisfying customers pays off in repeat purchasing, forming a solid foundation for profitability. This is why marketers need the vital skill of gauging customer satisfaction. This skill requires a working knowledge of marketing research coupled with a sensitivity for customer concerns. Start by defining the goal as it relates specifically to customer satisfaction: Is the purpose to pinpoint problems? To identify elements of the offering that are particularly strong contributors to satisfaction? To tease out concerns of loyal customers? This helps focus the research design on the critical data to be gathered.

Now marketers build on their knowledge of customer behavior and attitudes to encourage participation in the study. The key is understanding not only what will entice customers to participate but also what discourages participation. Volvo of North America, for example, heard from its dealers that car buyers felt "surveyed to death." So the company slimmed down its customer satisfaction survey from 33 questions to 20 and invited customers to respond on the Internet, by phone, or by mail. Knowing its busy customers are tech-savvy, the Mandarin Oriental Hotel in Hong Kong set up its satisfaction survey so customers can answer using a Palm Pilot or any other PDA. Marketers should communicate research findings internally to highlight good news, act on bad news, and plan new ways of satisfying customers. Finally, continuously surveying customers or repeating research at regular intervals allows marketers to follow satisfaction trends and determine the effect of changes.

McAlister's Deli, an 81-unit restaurant chain based in Mississippi, gets valuable customer satisfaction data from research that costs only $100 per unit per year. "For our little chain, meeting guest-service needs matters as much as menu appeal," observes the company chairman. McAlister's Deli proved that paying close attention to customer satisfaction can boost unit sales—even though the chain does no media advertising.[43]

actions such as not buying the product or warning friends.[44] In these cases, the seller has done a poor job of satisfying the customer.[45]

Marketers can use postpurchase communications to reduce product returns and order cancellations.[46] Computer companies, for example, might send e-mail messages to new buyers congratulating them on having selected a fine computer, place ads showing satisfied brand owners, solicit customer suggestions for improvements, and provide channels for speedy resolution of customer complaints.

Also, marketers should monitor how buyers use and dispose of the product after purchase. The various options that are open to consumers are shown in Figure 6.4. If consumers store the product and never use it, the product is probably not very satisfying, and word-of-mouth will not be strong. If they sell or trade the product, new-product sales will be depressed.

Consumers sometimes find new uses for a product, as Avon discovered when its customers talked about Skin-So-Soft bath oil and moisturizer as an insect repellant. This prompted Avon to seek and receive Environmental Protection Agency approval so it could officially tout Skin-So-Soft as a triple-action product serving as an insect repellent, waterproof sunscreen, and moisturizer. Another unusual use for this product is to remove lime deposits from shower doors.[47]

If consumers throw the product away, the marketer needs to know how they dispose of it, especially if it can hurt the environment. Increased public awareness of recycling and ecological concerns as well as consumer complaints about having to throw away beautiful bottles led French perfume maker Rochas to think about introducing a new, refillable fragrance line.

FIGURE 6.4   How Consumers Use or Dispose of Products

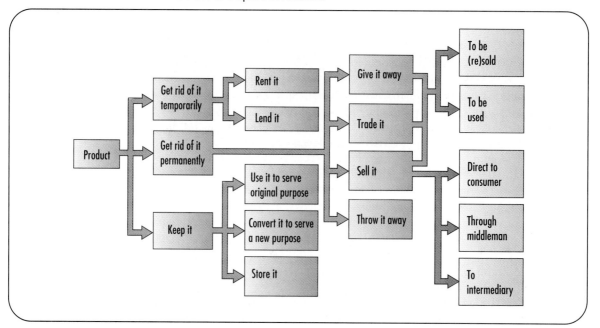

Source: From Jacob Jacoby, Carol K. Benning, and Thomas F. Dietvorst, "What About Disposition?" *Journal of Marketing* (July 1977): 23. Reprinted with permission of the American Marketing Association.

EXECUTIVE SUMMARY

Consumer behavior is influenced by four factors: cultural (culture, subculture, and social class), social (reference groups, family, and social roles and statuses), personal (age, stage in the life cycle, occupation, economic circumstances, lifestyle, personality, and self-concept), and psychological (motivation, perception, learning, beliefs, and attitudes). Research into all of these factors can provide clues as to how marketers can reach and serve consumers more effectively.

To understand how consumers actually make their buying decisions, marketers must identify who makes and influences the buying decision. People can be initiators, influencers, deciders, buyers, or users, and different marketing campaigns might be targeted to each participant. Marketers must also examine buyers' levels of involvement and the number of brands available to determine whether consumers are engaging in complex buying behavior, dissonance-reducing buying behavior, habitual buying behavior, or variety-seeking buying behavior.

The typical five-stage consumer buying process consists of problem recognition, information search, evaluation of alternatives, purchase decision, and postpurchase behavior. The marketer's job is to understand the buyer's behavior at each stage and what influences are operating. The attitudes of others, unanticipated situational factors, and perceived risk may all affect the decision to buy, as will consumers' levels of postpurchase satisfaction, the company's postpurchase actions, and consumers' postpurchase use and disposal of the product. Satisfied customers will continue to purchase; dissatisfied customers will stop purchasing the product and are likely to spread the word among their friends.

NOTES

1. Tim Wilson, "Whirlpool Puts Warranties Online," *InternetWeek*, November 19, 2001, p. 16; "Whirlpool and Lowe's Home Improvement Warehouse, Wilkesboro, N.C., Have Begun an Innovation Tour," *Appliance Manufacturer*, October 2001, p. 16; Fara Warner, "Recipe for Growth," *Fast Company*, October 2001, pp. 40+; Tobi Elkin, "Product Pampering," *Brandweek*, June 16, 1997, pp. 38–40; Tim Stevens, "Lights, Camera, Innovation!" *IndustryWeek*, July 19, 1999, (***www.industryweek.com***); Rekha Balu, "Whirlpool Gets Real with Customers," *Fast Company*, December 1999, pp. 74, 76.
2. Adrienne Sanders, "Yankee Imperialism," *Forbes*, December 13, 1999, p. 56.
3. See Leon G. Schiffman and Leslie Lazar Kanuk, *Consumer Behavior*, 7th ed. (Upper Saddle River, NJ: Prentice Hall, 2000).
4. Carole Radice, "Hispanic Consumers: Understanding a Changing Market," *Progressive Grocer*, February 1997, pp. 109–14.
5. Ibid.
6. Abigail Goodman, "Store Most Likely to Succeed," *Los Angeles Times*, April 3, 1999.
7. See Rosann L. Spiro, "Persuasion in Family Decision Making," *Journal of Consumer Research*, March 1983, pp. 393–402; Lawrence H. Wortzel, "Marital Roles and Typologies as Predictors of Purchase Decision Making for Everyday Household Products: Suggestions for Research," in *Advances in Consumer Research*, Vol. 7, ed. Jerry C. Olson (Chicago: American Marketing Association, 1989) pp. 212–15; David J. Burns, "Husband-Wife Innovative Consumer Decision Making: Exploring the Effect of Family Power," *Psychology & Marketing*, May–June 1992, pp. 175–89; Robert Boutilier, "Pulling the Family's Strings," *American Demographics*, August 1993, pp. 44–48. For cross-cultural

comparisons of husband–wife buying roles, see John B. Ford, Michael S. LaTour, and Tony L. Henthorne, "Perception of Marital Roles in Purchase-Decision Processes: A Cross-Cultural Study," *Journal of the Academy of Marketing Science*, (Spring 1995): 120–31.

8. George Moschis, "The Role of Family Communication in Consumer Socialization of Children and Adolescents," *Journal of Consumer Research* (March 1985): 898–913.

9. Marilyn Lavin, "Husband-Dominant, Wife-Dominant, Joint: A Shopping Typology for Baby Boom Couples?" *Journal of Consumer Marketing* 10, no. 3 (1993): 33–42.

10. Matt Nauman, "Cadillac Attracts New Buyer Groups with Escalade Sport-Utility," *San Jose Mercury News*, January 19, 2001.

11. James U. McNeal, "Tapping the Three Kids' Markets," *American Demographics*, April 1998, pp. 37–41.

12. Robert Strohmeyer, "COPPA Out," *Smart Business*, August 1, 2001, p. 42.

13. See Lawrence Lepisto, "A Life Span Perspective of Consumer Behavior," in *Advances in Consumer Research*, vol. 12, ed. Elizabeth Hirshman and Morris Holbrook (Provo, UT: Association for Consumer Research, 1985), p. 47. Also see Gail Sheehy, *New Passages: Mapping Your Life Across Time* (New York: Random House, 1995).

14. Arnold Mitchell, *The Nine American Lifestyles* (New York: Warner Books), pp. viii–x, 25–31; Personal communication from the VALS™ Program, Business Intelligence Center, SRI Consulting, Menlo Park, CA, February 1, 1996. See also Wagner A. Kamakura and Michel Wedel, "Lifestyle Segmentation with Tailored Interviewing," *Journal of Marketing Research* 32, no. 3 (August 1995): 308–17.

15. Stuart Elliott, "Sampling Tastes of a Changing Russia," *New York Times*, April 1, 1992, pp. D1, D19.

16. See Harold H. Kassarjian and Mary Jane Sheffet, "Personality and Consumer Behavior: An Update," in *Perspectives in Consumer Behavior*, ed. Harold H. Kassarjian and Thomas S. Robertson (Glenview, IL: Scott Foresman, 1981), pp. 160–80.

17. Jennifer Aaker, "Dimensions of Measuring Brand Personality," *Journal of Marketing Research*, 34 (August 1997): 347–56.

18. See M. Joseph Sirgy, "Self-Concept in Consumer Behavior: A Critical Review," *Journal of Consumer Research* (December 1982): 287–300.

19. See Thomas J. Reynolds and Jonathan Gutman, "Laddering Theory, Method, Analysis, and Interpretation," *Journal of Advertising Research* (February–March 1988): 11–34.

20. Abraham Maslow, *Motivation and Personality* (New York: Harper & Row, 1954) pp. 80–106.

21. See Frederick Herzberg, *Work and the Nature of Man* (Cleveland, OH: William Collins, 1966); and Henk Thierry and Agnes M. Koopman-Iwerna, "Motivation and Satisfaction," in *Handbook of Work and Organizational Psychology*, ed. P. J. Drenth (New York: John Wiley, 1984), pp. 141–42.

22. Bernard Berelson and Gary A. Steiner, *Human Behavior: An Inventory of Scientific Findings* (New York: Harcourt Brace Jovanovich, 1964) p. 88.

23. See Alice M. Tybout, Bobby J. Calder, and Brian Sternthal, "Using Information Processing Theory to Design Marketing Strategies," *Journal of Marketing Research*, (February 1981): 73–79.

24. "International: Old Wine in New Bottles," *The Economist*, February 21, 1998, p. 45.

25. See David Krech, Richard S. Crutchfield, and Egerton L. Ballachey, *Individual in Society* (New York: McGraw-Hill, 1962), ch. 2.

26. Melanie Wells, "Got a Milk Mustache? Campaign's Popularity Staying Fresh," *USA Today Ad Track*, July 13, 1999 (*www.usatoday.com*); Jill Venter, "Milk Mustache Campaign Is a Hit with Teens," *St. Louis Post-Dispatch*, April 1, 1998, p. E1; Dave Fusaro, "The Milk Mustache," *Dairy Foods*, April 1997, p. 75; Judann Pollack, "Milk: Kurt Graetzer," *Advertising Age*, June 30, 1997, p. S1; "Milk: Branding a Commodity," in Kevin Lane Keller, *Strategic Brand Management* (Upper Saddle River, NJ: Prentice Hall, 1998).

27. See Henry Assael, *Consumer Behavior and Marketing Action* (Boston: Kent, 1987), ch. 4.

28. Harper W. Boyd Jr. and Sidney Levy, "New Dimensions in Consumer Analysis," *Harvard Business Review* (November–December 1963): 129–40.

29. Sandra Vandermerwe, *Customer Capitalism: Increasing Returns in New Market Spaces* (London: Nicholas Brealey Publishing), ch. 11.

30. See Patricia B. Seybold, "Get Inside the Lives of Your Customers," *Harvard Business Review* (May 2001): 81–89.

31. Mohanbir Sawhney, "Making New Markets," *Business 2.0*, May 1999, pp. 116–21.

32. Marketing scholars have developed several models of the consumer buying process. See John A. Howard and Jagdish N. Sheth, *The Theory of Buyer Behavior* (New York: Wiley, 1969); and James F. Engel, Roger D. Blackwell, and Paul W. Miniard, *Consumer Behavior*, 8th ed. (Fort Worth, TX: Dryden, 1994).

33. See William P. Putsis, Jr. and Narasimhan Srinivasan, "Buying or Just Browsing? The Duration of Purchase Deliberation," *Journal of Marketing Research* (August 1994): 393–402.

34. See Chem L. Narayana and Rom J. Markin, "Consumer Behavior and Product Performance: An Alternative Conceptualization," *Journal of Marketing*, (October 1975): 1–6. See also Wayne S. DeSarbo and Kamel Jedidi, "The Spatial Representation of Heterogeneous Consideration Sets," *Marketing Science* 14, no. 3, pt. 2 (1995), 326–42; and Lee G. Cooper and Akihiro Inoue, "Building Market Structures from Consumer Preferences," *Journal of Marketing Research* 33, no. 3 (August 1996): 293–306.

35. See Paul E. Green and Yoram Wind, *Multiattribute Decisions in Marketing: A Measurement Approach* (Hinsdale, IL: Dryden, 1973), ch. 2; Leigh McAlister, "Choosing Multiple Items from a Product Class," *Journal of Consumer Research* (December 1979): 213–24.

36. This expectancy-value model was developed by Martin Fishbein, "Attitudes and Prediction of Behavior," in *Readings in Attitude Theory and Measurement*, ed. Martin Fishbein (New York: John Wiley, 1967), pp. 477–92. For a critical review, see Paul W. Miniard and Joel B. Cohen, "An Examination of the Fishbein-Ajzen Behavioral-Intentions Model's Concepts and Measures," *Journal of Experimental Social Psychology* (May 1981): 309–39.

37. See Harper W. Boyd Jr., Michael L. Ray, and Edward C. Strong, "An Attitudinal Framework for Advertising Strategy," *Journal of Marketing*, (April 1972): 27–33.

38. See Jagdish N. Sheth, "An Investigation of Relationships Among Evaluative Beliefs, Affect, Behavioral Intention, and Behavior," in *Consumer Behavior: Theory and Application*, ed. John U. Farley, John A. Howard, and L. Winston Ring (Boston: Allyn & Bacon, 1974), pp. 89–114.

39. See Fishbein, "Attitudes and Prediction of Behavior."

40. See Raymond A. Bauer, "Consumer Behavior as Risk Taking," in *Risk Taking and Information Handling in Consumer Behavior*, ed. Donald F. Cox (Boston: Division of Research, Harvard Business School, 1967); and James W. Taylor, "The Role of Risk in Consumer Behavior," *Journal of Marketing* (April 1974): 54–60.

41. See Priscilla A. La Barbera and David Mazursky, "A Longitudinal Assessment of Consumer Satisfaction/Dissatisfaction: The Dynamic Aspect of the Cognitive Process," *Journal of Marketing Research* (November 1983): 393–404.

42. See Barry L. Bayus, "Word of Mouth: The Indirect Effects of Marketing Efforts," *Journal of Advertising Research* (June–July 1985): 31–39.

43. Jack Hayes, "Industry Execs: Best Customer Feedback Info Is 'Real' Thing," *Nation's Restaurant News*, March 18, 2002, pp. 4+; Leslie Wood and Michael Kirsch, "Performing Your Own Satisfaction Survey," *Agency Sales Magazine*, February 2002, pp. 26; Arlena Sawyers, "Volvo Trims Fat from Buyer Survey," *Automotive News*, February 4, 2002, p. 50; "Palm Pilot = Painless Poll," *Cornell Hotel & Restaurant Administration Quarterly*, April 2001, p. 9.

44. See Albert O. Hirschman, *Exit, Voice, and Loyalty* (Cambridge, MA: Harvard University Press, 1970).

45. See Mary C. Gilly and Richard W. Hansen, "Consumer Complaint Handling as a Strategic Marketing Tool," *Journal of Consumer Marketing* (Fall 1985): 5–16.

46. See James H. Donnelly Jr. and John M. Ivancevich, "Post-Purchase Reinforcement and Back-Out Behavior," *Journal of Marketing Research* (August 1970): 399–400.

47. Beverly Beyette, "Strange But True: Cheez Whiz Works in Laundry," *Los Angeles Times*, October 22, 2000; Pam Weisz, "Avon's Skin-So-Soft Bugs Out," *Brandweek*, June 6, 1994, p. 4.

CHAPTER 7

Analyzing Business Markets and Buyer Behavior

In this chapter, we will address the following questions:

1. What is the business market, and how does it differ from the consumer market?
2. How do institutions and government agencies buy?
3. What buying situations do organizational buyers face?
4. Who participates in business buying, and what are the influences on business buying decisions?
5. How do business buyers make their decisions?

MARKETING MANAGEMENT AT COVISINT

Buying in volume pays off in lower prices and improved efficiency. That's the philosophy behind Covisint, a huge online auto-parts exchange originally set up by Ford, DaimlerChrysler, and General Motors, later joined by Renault-Nissan, Peugeot Citroen, and Mitsubishi. Covisint has attracted 4,600 participating suppliers and facilitates more than $50 billion annually in auction purchases. DaimlerChrysler, for example, recently solicited suppliers' bids to provide 1,200 automotive body parts in 80 combinations. Offline, the process would have taken weeks; through Covisint, the online auction lasted just four days. Two auto manufacturers are already taking advantage of this buying efficiency to order everything they need for two new models through Covisint.

Covisint's marketing managers know the site must continually add innovative services to satisfy its business customers. Although auctions are its mainstay, the site also helps buyers obtain suppliers' quotes for particular goods and services; hosts company-specific trading networks for Ford and other manufacturers; hosts catalog sites for suppliers such as Delphi Automotive; and provides systems to support closer collaboration between manufacturers and their suppliers. Suppliers like Covisint because they can adapt their operations to one site rather than adapting to six different automakers. Now Covisint is requesting that participating suppliers bring their suppliers onto the exchange. This will drive transaction costs down while enlarging the pool of suppliers available to collaborate on meeting the needs of participating buyers.[1]

Business organizations like Ford and Mitsubishi do not only sell. They also buy vast quantities of raw materials, manufactured components, plants and equipment, supplies, and business services. Over 13 million business, institutional, and government organizations in the United States alone—plus millions more in other countries—represent a huge, lucrative buying market for goods and services purchased from both domestic and international suppliers. Sellers need to understand these organizations' needs, resources, policies, and buying procedures.

WHAT IS ORGANIZATIONAL BUYING?

Webster and Wind define **organizational buying** as the decision-making process by which formal organizations establish the need for purchased products and services and identify, evaluate, and choose among alternative brands and suppliers.[2] Just as no two consumers buy in exactly the same way, no two organizations buy in exactly the same way. Therefore, business sellers work hard to distinguish clusters of customers that buy in similar ways and then create suitable marketing strategies for reaching those targeted business segments. However, the business market differs from the consumer market in a number of significant ways.

The Business Market Versus the Consumer Market

The **business market** consists of all the organizations that acquire goods and services used in the production of other products or services that are sold, rented, or supplied to other customers. The major industries making up the business market are agriculture, forestry, and fisheries; mining; manufacturing; construction; transportation; communication; public utilities; banking, finance, and insurance; distribution; and services.

More dollars and items are involved in sales to business buyers than to consumers. Consider the process of producing and selling a simple pair of shoes. Hide dealers must sell hides to tanners, who sell leather to shoe manufacturers, who sell shoes to wholesalers, who sell shoes to retailers, who finally sell them to consumers. Each party in the supply chain has to buy many other goods and services, which means every business seller is a business buyer, as well. To add value, many business sellers use the Internet to help business buyers do their jobs. Cisco Systems, for example, invites customers to go online to put together different network router components and see prices before they buy. One customer, Sprint, found that Cisco's system slashed the time needed to complete networking projects from 60 days to as little as 35 days.[3]

From the number and size of buyers to geographical location, demand, and buying behaviors, business markets have a number of characteristics that contrast sharply with those of consumer markets. These characteristics are described in Table 7.1

Understanding the impact of these characteristics can help a supplier target business buyers more effectively. Pittsburgh-based Cutler-Hammer, for example, sells circuit breakers and other electrical equipment to industrial manufacturers such as Ford Motor. As its product line grew larger and more complex, C-H developed "pods" of salespeople that focus on a particular geographical region, industry, or market concentration. Each individual brings expertise about a product that the other members of the team can take to the customer. Now salespeople can leverage their co-workers' knowledge to sell to increasingly sophisticated buying teams, instead of working in isolation.[4]

Specialized Organizational Markets

The overall business market includes institutional and government organizations in addition to profit-seeking companies. However, the buying goals, needs, and methods of these two organizational markets are generally different from those of businesses, something firms must keep in mind when planning their business marketing strategies.

The Institutional Market   The **institutional market** consists of schools, hospitals, nursing homes, prisons, and other institutions that provide goods and services to people in their care. Many of these organizations have low budgets and captive clienteles. For example, hospitals have to decide what quality of food to buy for their patients. The buying objective here is not profit, because the food is provided to the patients as part of the total service package. Nor is cost minimization the sole objective, because poor food will cause patients to complain and hurt the hospital's reputation. The hospital purchasing agent has to search for institutional food vendors whose quality meets or exceeds a certain minimum standard and whose prices are low. Knowing this, many food vendors set up a separate division to respond to the special needs of institutional buyers. Thus, Heinz will produce, package, and price its ketchup differently to meet the different requirements of hospitals, colleges, and prisons.

Being a supplier of choice for the nation's schools or hospitals means big business for marketers such as Allegiance Healthcare. This firm has become the largest U.S. supplier of medical, surgical, and laboratory products. Through its ValueLink stockless inventory program, Allegiance delivers ordered products to more than 150 hospitals when and where staff members need them. Under the old system, the most needed items were inevitably in short supply, while the rarely used items were available in great number. By using Allegiance's ValueLink system, hospitals save an average of $500,000 or more yearly and gain faster, easier access to the items they need.[5]

The Government Market   In most countries, government organizations are a major buyer of goods and services. The U.S. government, for example, buys goods and services valued at $200 billion, making it the largest customer in the world. The number of individual purchases is equally staggering: Over 20 million individual contract actions are processed every year. Although the cost of most items purchased is

TABLE 7.1 Characteristics of Business Markets

Characteristic	Description	Example
Fewer buyers	Business marketers normally deal with far fewer buyers than do consumer marketers.	Goodyear Tire Company aims to get orders from buyers for the Big Three U.S. automakers (General Motors, Ford, and DaimlerChrysler).
Larger buyers	Buyers for a few large firms do most of the purchasing in many industries.	Major companies are big customers in industries such as aircraft engines and defense weapons.
Close supplier-customer relationship	With the smaller customer base and the importance and power of the larger customers, suppliers are frequently required to customize offerings, practices, and performance to meet the needs of individual customers.	Tooling supplier Stillwater Technologies shares office and manufacturing space with key customer Motoman, a supplier of industrial robots, to minimize delivery distances and enhance their symbiotic working relationship.[1]
Geographically concentrated buyers	More than half of the U.S. business buyers are concentrated in seven states: New York, California, Pennsylvania, Illinois, Ohio, New Jersey, and Michigan, which helps to reduce selling costs.	Because the Big Three U.S. automakers have their U.S. headquarters in the Detroit area, industry suppliers head there on sales calls.
Derived demand	Demand for business goods is ultimately derived from demand for consumer goods, so business marketers must monitor the buying patterns of ultimate consumers.	The Big Three U.S. automakers are seeing higher demand for steel-bar products, mostly derived from consumers' demand for minivans and other light trucks, which consume far more steel than cars.
Inelastic demand	Total demand for many business goods and services is inelastic and not much affected by price changes, especially in the short run, because producers cannot make quick production changes.	Shoe manufacturers will not buy much more leather if the price of leather falls. Nor will they buy much less leather if the price rises unless they can find satisfactory substitutes.
Fluctuating demand	Demand for business products tends to be more volatile than demand for consumer products. An increase in consumer demand can lead to a much larger increase in demand for plant and equipment needed to produce the additional output.	An increase of only 10% in consumer demand for computers might result in a 200% increase in business demand for related parts, supplies, and services; a 10% drop in consumer demand for computers might cause a complete collapse in business demand.
Professional purchasing	Trained purchasing agents follow organizational purchasing policies, constraints, and requirements to buy business products. Many of the buying instruments—such as proposals and purchase contracts—are not typical of consumer buying.	Programs on the Cisco Systems Web site allow purchasing agents to research, select, and price new networking systems at any hour and obtain speedy online answers about products, orders, and service.[2]
Multiple buying influences	More people typically influence business buying decisions. Buying committees are common in the purchase of major goods; marketers have to send well-trained sales reps and often sales teams to deal with these well-trained buyers.	Metal supplier Phelps Dodge uses an "account management approach" to reach all the key people who influence business buying decisions in customer organizations.[3]
Multiple sales calls	With more people involved in the process, it takes multiple sales calls to win most business orders, and the sales cycle can take years.	In the case of major capital equipment sales, customers may take multiple attempts to fund a project, and the sales cycle—between quoting a job and delivering the product—is often measured in years.[4]

TABLE 7.1   Characteristics of Business Markets (continued)

Characteristic	Description	Example
Direct purchasing	Business buyers often buy directly from manufacturers rather than through intermediaries, especially items that are technically complex or expensive.	Southwest Airlines, Air Madagascar, and other airlines around the world buy airplanes directly from Boeing.
Reciprocity	Business buyers often select suppliers who also buy from them.	A paper manufacturer buys chemicals from a chemical company that buys a considerable amount of its paper.
Leasing	Many industrial buyers lease rather than buy heavy equipment to conserve capital, get the latest products, receive better service, and gain tax advantages. The lessor often makes more profit and sells to customers who could not afford outright purchase.	General Electric leases truck and car fleets, aircraft, commercial trailers, railcars, and other major equipment products to business buyers.

Sources: [1]John H. Sheridan, "An Alliance Built on Trust," *IndustryWeek*, March 17, 1997, pp. 66–70; [2]Andy Reinhardt, "Meet Mr. Internet," *BusinessWeek*, September 13, 1999, pp. 128–40; [3]Minda Zetlin, "It's All the Same to Me," *Sales & Marketing Management*, February 1994, pp. 71–75; [4]Michael Collins, "Breaking into the Big Leagues," *American Demographics*, January 1996, p. 24.

between $2,500 and $25,000, the government also makes purchases in the billions of dollars (often for technology).

Government organizations typically require suppliers to submit bids, and they normally award the contract to the lowest bidder. In some cases, they take into account a supplier's superior quality or reputation for on-time performance. Because their spending decisions are subject to public review, government organizations require considerable documentation from suppliers, who often complain about excessive paperwork, bureaucracy, regulations, decision-making delays, and shifts in procurement personnel.

Consider the experience of ADI Technology Corporation. The U.S. government accounts for about 90 percent of its nearly $6 million in annual revenues. Yet managers at this professional services company often shake their heads at all the work that goes into winning coveted government contracts. A comprehensive bid proposal will run from 500 to 700 pages, and ADI's president estimates that the firm has spent as much as $20,000, mostly in worker hours, to prepare a single bid proposal.

Fortunately, the federal government has been putting reforms in place to streamline buying procedures. Now the government is moving all purchasing online, with the use of Web-based technologies such as digital signatures.[6] Several federal agencies that act as purchasing agents for the U.S. government have set up Web-based catalogs, allowing defense and civilian agencies to buy everything from medical and office supplies to clothing through online purchasing. The General Services Administration, for example, sells through its Web site and creates links connecting buyers with contract suppliers.

Some companies, such as Gateway, Rockwell, Kodak, and Goodyear, make a special effort to anticipate the needs and projects of the government market. Firms that participate in the product specification phase, gather competitive intelligence, prepare bids carefully, and produce strong communications to enhance their companies' reputations are more likely to succeed in this market.

Business Buying Situations

Business buyers in companies, institutions, and government organizations face many decisions in the course of making a purchase. The number of decisions depends on the type of buying situation. Robinson and others distinguish three types of buying situations: the straight rebuy, the modified rebuy, and the new task.[7]

- *Straight rebuy.* The straight rebuy is a buying situation in which the purchasing department reorders on a routine basis (e.g., office supplies, bulk chemicals). The buyer chooses from suppliers on an "approved list." These suppliers make an effort to maintain product and service quality. They often propose automatic reordering systems to help purchasing agents save time. The "out-suppliers" attempt to offer something new or to exploit dissatisfaction with a current supplier. Out-suppliers try to get a small order and then enlarge their purchase share over time.

- *Modified rebuy.* The modified rebuy is a situation in which the buyer wants to modify product specifications, prices, delivery requirements, or other terms. The modified rebuy usually involves additional decision participants on both sides. The in-suppliers become nervous and have to protect the account; the out-suppliers see an opportunity to gain some business.

- *New task.* The new task is a buying situation in which a purchaser buys a product or service for the first time (e.g., office building, new security system). The greater the cost or risk, the larger the number of decision participants and the greater their information gathering—and therefore the longer the time to decision completion.[8]

New-task buying passes through several stages: awareness, interest, evaluation, trial, and adoption.[9] Communication tools' effectiveness varies at each stage. Mass media are most important during the initial awareness stage, salespeople have their greatest impact at the interest stage, and technical sources are most important during the evaluation stage.

The business buyer makes the fewest decisions in the straight-rebuy situation and the most in the new-task situation. In the new-task situation, the buyer has to determine product specifications, price limits, delivery terms and times, service terms, payment terms, order quantities, acceptable suppliers, and the selected supplier. Different participants influence each decision, and the order in which these decisions are made can vary. The new-task situation is, therefore, the business marketer's greatest opportunity and challenge. For this reason, marketers should try to reach as many key buying influencers as possible and provide helpful information and assistance. Because of the complicated selling involved in new-task situations, many companies use a *missionary sales force* consisting of their best salespeople.

Systems Buying and Selling   Many business buyers prefer to buy a total solution to their problem from one seller. This practice, called **systems buying**, originated with government purchases of major weapons and communication systems. The government solicited bids from *prime contractors*, who would assemble the package or system. The winning contractor then bid out and assembled the system from subcomponents purchased from other contractors. Thus, the prime contractor was providing a **turnkey solution**, so-called because the buyer simply turns one key to get the job done.

Sellers have increasingly recognized that buyers like to purchase in this way, and many have adopted systems selling as a marketing tool. **Systems selling** can take different forms. For example, many auto parts manufacturers now sell whole systems, such as the seating system, the braking system, or the door system. A variant on systems selling is *systems contracting*, in which a single supply source provides the buyer with all required MRO supplies (maintenance, repair, and operating supplies). This lowers the buyer's costs because the seller maintains the inventory, less time is spent on supplier selection, and the buyer enjoys price protection during the life of the contract. The seller benefits from lower operating costs because of steady demand and reduced paperwork.

Systems selling is a key industrial marketing strategy in bidding to build large-scale industrial projects such as dams, steel factories, and pipelines. Project engineering firms must compete on price, quality, reliability, and other attributes to win these contracts. For example, when the Indonesian government requested bids to build a cement factory near Jakarta, a U.S. firm made a proposal that included choosing the site, designing the cement factory, hiring the construction crews, assembling the materials and equipment, and turning over the finished factory to the Indonesian government. The Japanese bidder's proposal included all of these services, plus hiring and training the factory workers, exporting the cement, and using the cement to build roads and office buildings around Jakarta. Although the Japanese proposal was more costly, it won. This is true system selling: The firm took the broadest view of its customer's needs.

PARTICIPANTS IN THE BUSINESS BUYING PROCESS

Who buys the trillions of dollars' worth of goods and services needed by business organizations? Purchasing agents are influential in straight-rebuy and modified-rebuy situations, whereas other department personnel are more influential in new-buy situations. Engineering personnel carry the most influence in selecting product components, and purchasing agents dominate in selecting suppliers.[10]

Webster and Wind call the decision-making unit of a buying organization the **buying center**. The buying center is composed of "all those individuals and groups who participate in the purchasing decision-making process, who share some common goals and the risks arising from the decisions."[11] The buying center includes organizational members who play any of seven roles in the purchase decision process:[12]

1. *Initiators.* People who request that something be purchased, including users or others.

2. *Users.* Those who will use the product or service; often, users initiate the buying proposal and help define product requirements.

3. *Influencers.* People who influence the buying decision, including technical personnel. They often help define specifications and provide information for evaluating alternatives.

4. *Deciders.* Those who decide on product requirements or on suppliers.

5. *Approvers.* People who authorize the proposed actions of deciders or buyers.

6. *Buyers.* People who have formal authority to select the supplier and arrange the purchase terms, including high-level managers. Buyers may help shape product specifications, but their major role is selecting vendors and negotiating.

7. *Gatekeepers.* People who have the power to prevent sellers or information from reaching members of the buying center; examples are purchasing agents, receptionists, and telephone operators.

To target their efforts properly, business marketers have to determine: Who are the major decision participants? What decisions do they influence? What is their level of influence? What evaluation criteria do they use? When a buying center includes many participants, the business marketer will not have the time or resources to reach all of them. Small sellers concentrate on reaching the key buying influencers. Larger sellers go for multilevel in-depth selling to reach as many buying-center participants as possible. Their salespeople virtually "live" with their high-volume customers. In general, companies will have to rely more heavily on communications to reach hidden buying influences and keep their current customers informed.[13]

The buying center can be highly dynamic, so business marketers need to periodically review their assumptions about who is participating. For years, Kodak sold X-ray film to hospital lab technicians, not noticing that buying decisions were increasingly being made by professional administrators. As sales declined, Kodak hurriedly revised its targeting strategy.

Major Influences on Business Buying

Business buyers respond to many influences when they make their decisions. When supplier offerings are similar, buyers can satisfy the purchasing requirements with any supplier, and they place more weight on the personal treatment they receive. When supplier offerings differ substantially, buyers are more accountable for their choices and pay more attention to economic factors. In addition to culture, business buyers respond to four main influences: environmental, organizational, interpersonal, and individual (see Figure 7.1).[14]

Environmental Factors   Within the macroenvironment, business buyers pay close attention to numerous economic factors, including interest rates and levels of production, investment, and consumer spending. In a recession, business buyers reduce their

FIGURE 7.1   Major Influences on Business Buying Behavior

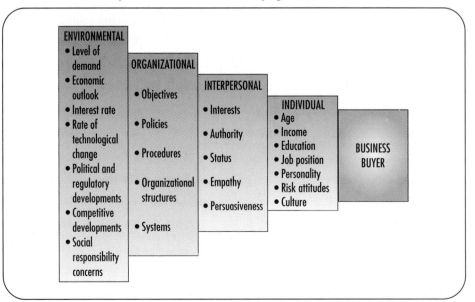

investment in plant, equipment, and inventories. Business marketers can do little to stimulate total demand in recessionary periods; they can only fight harder to increase or maintain their share of demand.

Companies that fear materials shortages often buy and hold large inventories and sign long-term contracts with suppliers to ensure steady availability. In fact, DuPont, Ford, and other major companies regard long-term *supply planning* as a major responsibility of their purchasing managers.

Business buyers also actively monitor technological, political-regulatory, and competitive developments. For example, environmental concerns can cause changes in business buyer behavior. A printing firm might favor suppliers that carry recycled papers or use environmentally safe ink. One buyer claimed, "We push suppliers with technical expertise to be more socially conscious."

Organizational Factors   Business marketers need to be aware of current trends in organizational purchasing. First, spurred by competitive pressures, companies are staffing their purchasing departments with MBAs who aspire to top management— like Thomas Stallkamp, DaimlerChrysler's former executive vice president of procurement and supply, known for cutting costs and streamlining manufacturing.[15] These new, more strategically positioned "procurement departments" seek out the best value from fewer and better suppliers. At Caterpillar and other multinationals, purchasing departments have become "strategic supply departments" with responsibility for global sourcing and partnering. In response to this trend, business marketers must correspondingly upgrade their sales personnel to match the higher caliber of the business buyers.

In addition, business buying is moving toward cross-functional teams. Most purchasing professionals describe their job as more strategic, technical, team-oriented, and involving more responsibility than ever before. Sixty-one percent of buyers surveyed said the buying group was more involved in new-product design and development than it was five years ago. More than half of the buyers now participate in cross-functional teams, with suppliers well represented.[16]

Many companies with multiple divisions have recentralized their purchasing, identifying materials purchased by several divisions and buying them centrally to gain more purchasing clout. Individual divisions can buy from other sources if they can get a better deal, but centralized purchasing usually produces substantial savings. For the business marketer, this means dealing with fewer and higher-level buyers, and using a national account sales group to deal with large corporate buyers.

More companies are decentralizing some purchasing by empowering employees to purchase small-ticket items such as binders or coffee makers, often using corporate purchasing cards issued by credit-card firms. Companies distribute the cards to supervisors, clerks, and secretaries; the cards incorporate codes that set credit limits and restrict usage. National Semiconductor's purchasing chief says these cards have cut processing costs from $30 an order to a few cents, allowing buyers and suppliers to spend less time on paperwork and more time on building relationships.[17]

Further, online procurement is growing rapidly, with dramatic and far-reaching implications. So far, businesses mostly buy MRO supplies online. However, a growing number, such as General Electric, buy nearly all supplies online to shave transaction and personnel costs, reduce time between order and delivery, cut paperwork, and consolidate purchasing. Internet purchasing can help forge closer relations between partners and buyers, and it levels the playing field between large and small suppliers. However, it may potentially erode supplier-buyer loyalty and open the door to possible security disasters.[18]

Business buyers are increasingly initiating or accepting long-term contracts with reliable suppliers. For example, General Motors wants to buy from fewer suppliers who are willing to locate close to its plants and produce high-quality components. In addition, business marketers are setting up Extranets so major customers can enter and transmit purchase orders electronically. Also, many companies have set up incentive systems to reward purchasing managers for good buying performance, in much the same way that sales personnel receive bonuses for good selling performance. These systems are leading purchasing managers to pressure sellers for the best terms. Many purchasing executives are also working on building a seamless supply chain management system, from the purchase of raw materials to the on-time arrival of finished goods to end users.

Another trend is toward lean production, which enables manufacturers to produce a more high-quality product at lower cost, in less time, using less labor. Lean production incorporates just-in-time (JIT) production, stricter quality control, frequent and reliable supply delivery, suppliers close to customers, computerized purchasing, stable production schedules made available to suppliers, and single sourcing with early supplier involvement. JIT II, the next level of customer-supplier partnerships, focuses on reducing the costs and time in day-to-day purchasing transactions by locating supplier employees at the customer's site in place of buyers and materials planners. Bose Corporation pioneered this arrangement with G&F Industries as its first in-plant supplier. Says G&F's Christ Labonte, "It's a fresh, nontraditional agreement based on trust. After people get comfortable in their partnering, they start turning up rocks they wouldn't have turned up and revealing causes that were sacred cows."[19]

Interpersonal and Individual Factors   Buying centers usually include several participants with differing interests, authority, status, empathy, and persuasiveness. The business marketer is not likely to know what kind of group dynamics take place during the buying decision process. Therefore, marketers need to find out as much as possible about individual buying center participants and their interaction and then train their employees to be attuned to the influence of interpersonal factors.

Each buyer carries personal motivations, perceptions, and preferences, as influenced by the buyer's age, income, education, job position, personality, attitudes toward risk, and culture. Buyers definitely exhibit different buying styles. For example, some younger, highly educated buyers are experts at conducting rigorous, computerized analyses of competitive proposals before choosing a supplier. Other buyers are "toughies" from the old school and pit competitors against one another.

Cultural Factors   Marketers should study the culture and customs of each country or region where they sell their products to better understand how cultural factors can affect business buyers. For example, in Germany, businesspeople prefer to be introduced by their full, correct titles, and they shake hands at both the beginning and the end of business meetings. As another example, both Korean and Japanese businesspeople observe Confucian ethics based on respect for authority and the primacy of the group over the individual.[20] Such attitudes and practices permeate marketing transac-

MARKETING SKILLS: MARKETING ACROSS CULTURES

All people are *not* basically alike. This is just one premise to keep in mind when developing the skill of marketing across cultural boundaries—a vital skill in today's global marketplace. Language differences aside, marketers assume that people from other cultures have different customs, beliefs, preferences, and values, at least until they can confirm similarities with their own cultures. Marketers should research the other culture to learn what to say and do in both business and social settings, because many cultures value a good buyer-seller relationship more than they value price or other aspects of the offering itself. Just as important, marketers should find out (and emulate) how people in the other culture communicate respect and avoid making judgements based on cultural differences.

In addition, marketers need to understand how businesspeople in other cultures prefer to communicate (are phone calls more acceptable than e-mails?), how they perceive time (are schedules only approximate?) how they make decisions (is consensus a requirement?), and other differences that can affect the buying center. Above all, marketers must be flexible—willing and able to adapt their behavior and attitudes to accommodate cultural differences.

Consider the skill needed by marketers for Intercomp, a software firm based in Israel with offices in Michigan. Intercomp's marketers are constantly dealing with businesspeople from other nations—sometimes with people from more than one nation on a single project. Not long ago, two of its marketing managers flew to Munich to meet with two managers from a high-tech German company that was weighing the purchase of Intercomp's software. Over a three-hour lunch, the four discussed their favorite foods and travel destinations, but not business. "The lunch was such a cultivation of our partnership," remembers Intercomp's marketing director, who says the software firm would not have clinched the sale without taking the time to build the relationship.[21]

tions with organizations based in other nations (see "Marketing Skills: Marketing Across Cultures").

THE PURCHASING/PROCUREMENT PROCESS

Business buying passes through eight stages called *buyphases*, as identified by Robinson and associates in the *buygrid* framework shown in Table 7.2.[22] In modified-rebuy or straight-rebuy situations, some of these stages are compressed or bypassed. For example, in a straight-rebuy situation, the buyer normally has a favorite supplier or a ranked list of suppliers, so the supplier search and proposal solicitation stages are skipped. The sections that follow examine each of the eight stages for a typical new-task buying situation.

Problem Recognition

The buying process begins when someone in the company recognizes a problem or need that can be met by acquiring a good or service. The recognition can be triggered by internal or external stimuli. Internally, problem recognition commonly occurs

TABLE 7.2   Buygrid Framework: Major Stages (Buyphases) of the Industrial Buying Process in Relation to Major Buying Situations (Buyclasses)

		New Task	Buyphases Modified Rebuy	Straight Rebuy
Buyphases	1. Problem recognition	Yes	Maybe	No
	2. General need description	Yes	Maybe	No
	3. Product specification	Yes	Yes	Yes
	4. Supplier search	Yes	Maybe	No
	5. Proposal solicitation	Yes	Maybe	No
	6. Supplier selection	Yes	Maybe	No
	7. Order-routine specification	Yes	Maybe	No
	8. Performance review	Yes	Yes	Yes

Source: Adapted from Patrick J. Johnson, Charles W. Faris, and Yoram Wind, *Industrial Buying and Creative Marketing* (Boston: Allyn & Bacon, 1967), p. 14.

when a firm decides to develop a new product and needs new equipment and materials, when a machine breaks down and requires new parts, when purchased material turns out to be unsatisfactory, and when a purchasing manager senses an opportunity to obtain lower prices or better quality. Externally, problem recognition can occur when a buyer gets new ideas at a trade show, sees an ad, or is contacted by a sales representative offering a better product or a lower price. Business marketers can stimulate problem recognition by direct mail, telemarketing, effective Internet communications, and calling on prospects.

General Need Description and Product Specification

Once a problem has been recognized, the buyer has to determine the needed item's general characteristics and the required quantity. For standard items, this is not a very involved process. For complex items, the buyer will work with others—engineers, users, and so on—to define the needed characteristics. These may include reliability, durability, price, or other attributes. In this stage, business marketers can assist buyers by describing how their products would meet such needs.

The buying organization now develops the item's technical specifications. Often, the company will assign a **product value analysis** engineering team to the project. Product value analysis is a cost-reduction approach in which components are studied to determine if they can be redesigned or standardized or made by cheaper production methods. The PVA team will examine the high-cost components in a given product, because 20 percent of the parts usually account for 80 percent of the costs of manufacturing it. The team will also identify overdesigned product components that last longer than the product itself, then decide on the optimal product characteristics. Tightly written specifications will allow the buyer to refuse components that are too expensive or that fail to meet the specified standards. Suppliers can also use product value analysis as a tool for positioning themselves to win an account.

Supplier Search

The buyer now tries to identify the most appropriate suppliers, by examining trade directories, doing a computer search, phoning other firms for recommendations, scanning trade advertisements, and attending trade shows. However, these days the most likely place to look is on the Internet. *Vertical hubs* focus on industries (plastics, steel, chemicals, paper) and *functional hubs* focus on specific functions (logistics, media buying, advertising, energy management). Companies also manage e-procurement through direct extranet links to major suppliers, buying alliances with other industry members, and company buying sites.

The supplier's task is to get listed in major online catalogs or services, communicate with buyers, and build a good reputation in the marketplace. Suppliers who lack capacity or have a poor reputation will be rejected, while those who qualify may be visited by buyer's agents, who will examine their facilities and meet their personnel. After evaluating each company, the buyer will end up with a short list of qualified suppliers.

Proposal Solicitation

In this stage, the buyer invites qualified suppliers to submit proposals. When the item is complex or expensive, the buyer will require a detailed written proposal from each qualified supplier. After evaluating the proposals, the buyer will invite a few suppliers to make formal presentations.

Business marketers must be skilled in researching, writing, and presenting proposals. Their written proposals should be marketing documents that describe value and benefits in customer terms, not just technical documents. Oral presentations should inspire confidence, positioning their company's capabilities and resources so that they stand out from the competition.

A supplier must become qualified or, in some cases, become certified, so it will be invited to submit proposals. Consider the hurdles that Xerox has set up for suppliers. Only suppliers that meet ISO 9000 international quality standards qualify for certification. Suppliers must also complete the Xerox Multinational Supplier Quality Survey, participate in Xerox's Continuous Supplier Involvement process, and undergo rigorous quality training and evaluation based on the Malcolm Baldrige National Quality Award criteria. Not surprisingly, only 176 companies worldwide have qualified.[23]

Supplier Selection

Before selecting a supplier, the buying center will specify desired supplier attributes (such as product reliability and service reliability) and indicate their relative importance. It will then rate each supplier on these attributes to identify the most attractive one.

The buyer may attempt to negotiate with preferred suppliers for better prices and terms before making the final selection. Despite moves toward strategic sourcing, partnering, and participation in cross-functional teams, buyers still spend a lot of time haggling over price, which remains a key criterion for supplier selection.[24] Marketers can counter a buyer's request for a lower price in several ways. They may be able to show that the "life-cycle cost" of using their product is lower than that of competitors' products. They can also cite the value of the services the buyer now receives, especially where those services are superior to those offered by competitors.

Hewlett-Packard, for example, has worked hard to become a "trusted advisor" to its customers, selling specific solutions to their unique problems. HP has discovered that some companies want a partner and others simply want a product that works. The company estimates that the trusted-advisor approach has contributed to 60 percent growth of its high-end computer business.[25]

As part of the supplier selection process, buying centers must decide how many suppliers to use. In the past, many companies preferred a large supplier base to ensure adequate supplies and to obtain price concessions. Out-suppliers would try to get in the door by offering an especially low price. Increasingly, however, companies are reducing the number of suppliers. Companies such as Ford, Motorola, and AlliedSignal have cut the number of suppliers anywhere from 20 percent to 80 percent. The suppliers who remain are responsible for larger component systems, for achieving continuous quality and performance improvements, and for lowering prices annually by a given percentage.

There is even a trend toward single sourcing arrangements with only one supplier. The *Knoxville News-Sentinel* and the *New York Daily News* newspapers both rely on one source for newsprint. This makes it easier to control newsprint inventories and maintain paper consistency to avoid the time and cost of changing presses for different papers.[26]

Order-Routine Specification

After selecting suppliers, the buyer negotiates the final order, listing the technical specifications, the quantity needed, the delivery schedule, and so on. In the case of MRO items, buyers are moving toward blanket contracts rather than periodic purchase orders. A **blanket contract** establishes a long-term relationship in which the supplier promises to resupply the buyer as needed at agreed-upon prices over a specified period. Because the seller holds the stock, blanket contracts are sometimes called **stockless purchase plans**. The buyer's computer automatically sends an order to the seller when stock is needed.

Blanket contracting leads to more single-source buying and ordering of more items from that single source. This system locks suppliers in tighter with the buyer and makes it difficult for out-suppliers to break in unless the buyer becomes dissatisfied with the in-supplier's prices, quality, or service.

Performance Review

In the final stage of the buying process, the buyer periodically reviews the performance of the chosen supplier(s) using one of three methods. The buyer may contact the end users and ask for their evaluations; the buyer may rate the supplier on several criteria using a weighted score method; or the buyer might aggregate the cost of poor supplier performance to come up with adjusted costs of purchase, including price. The performance review may lead the buyer to continue, modify, or end the relationship with the supplier. To stay in the running for future purchases, suppliers should monitor the same variables that are monitored by the product's buyers and end users.

EXECUTIVE SUMMARY

Organizational buying is the decision-making process by which formal organizations establish the need for purchased products and services, and then identify, evaluate, and choose among alternative brands and suppliers. The business market consists of all of the organizations that acquire goods and services used in the production of other products or services that are sold, rented, or supplied to others: profit-seeking companies, institutions, and government agencies.

Compared to consumer markets, business markets generally have fewer and larger buyers, a closer customer-supplier relationship, and more geographically concentrated buyers. Demand in the business market is derived from demand in the consumer market and fluctuates with the business cycle. Nonetheless, the total demand for many business goods and services is quite price-inelastic. Marketers need to be aware of the nature and influence of these and other characteristics of business markets, which affect the way organizations buy.

Three types of buying situations are the straight rebuy, the modified rebuy, and the new task. Systems buying is a practice in which the buyer wants to purchase a total solution to its problem from one seller. Some marketers use systems selling when bidding on large-scale industrial projects. The buying center—which is the decision-making unit of a buying organization—consists of initiators, users, influencers, deciders, approvers, buyers, and gatekeepers.

To influence the buying center, marketers must be aware of environmental, organizational, interpersonal, individual, and cultural factors. The buying process consists of eight stages called buyphases: (1) problem recognition, (2) general need description, (3) product specification, (4) supplier search, (5) proposal solicitation, (6) supplier selection, (7) order-routine specification, and (8) performance review. Although all these stages are involved in a new-task buying situation, some may be skipped or compressed in modified-rebuy or straight-rebuy situations.

CASE PILOT

READ, INTERACT, AND TEST YOUR CASE ANALYIS SKILLS

In the world of marketing, business markets are much larger than consumer markets. For example, all businesses, governments, and institutions need a wide variety of products and services. Chapter 7 details how business markets differ from consumer markets and outlines variables to consider when marketing to these business segments.

The manager in the Advantage Transportation Systems case study has to make crucial marketing decisions concerning his company's business markets. Click on the Case Pilot tool at *www.prenhall.com/kotler* and help the manager by answering the following questions:

1. What should the company do about the new business contract?
2. How could the competition impact the marketing efforts?
3. What steps should the manager take to resolve the marketing issues?

NOTES

1. Ralph Kisiel, "English: Covisint Getting Stronger; Profitability in 2002 Is Exchange's Top Priority," *Automotive News*, April 8, 2002, p. 6; "Southfield, Mich., Automotive Online Business Reshapes Itself," *Detroit Free Press*, April 4, 2002, (*www.freep.com*); David

Hannon, "Online Buy Gains Speed: Web-Based Buying Cuts Costs and Streamlines Sourcing for the Hard-Hit Auto Industry," *Purchasing*, February 7, 2002, pp. 22 +.

2. Frederick E. Webster Jr. and Yoram Wind, *Organizational Buying Behavior* (Upper Saddle River, NJ: Prentice Hall, 1972), p. 2.

3. Shawn Tully, "How Cisco Mastered the Net," *Fortune*, August 17, 1998, pp. 107-110.

4. Robert Hiebeler, Thomas B. Kelly, and Charles Ketteman, *Best Practices: Building Your Business with Customer-Focused Solutions* (New York: Arthur Andersen/Simon & Schuster, 1998), pp. 122–24.

5. Hiebeler, Kelly, and Ketteman, *Best Practices*, pp. 124–26.

6. Laura M. Litvan, "Selling to Uncle Sam: New, Easier Rules," *Nation's Business*, March 1995, pp. 46–48; Ellen Messmer, "Feds Do E-Commerce the Hard Way," *Network World*, April 13, 1998, pp. 31–32; Anna Muoio, "Fast Agency, Slow Government," *Fast Company*, December 1999, pp. 344, 346, 348.

7. Patrick J. Robinson, Charles W. Faris, and Yoram Wind, *Industrial Buying and Creative Marketing* (Boston: Allyn & Bacon, 1967).

8. See Daniel H. McQuiston, "Novelty, Complexity, and Importance as Causal Determinants of Industrial Buyer Behavior," *Journal of Marketing* (April 1989): 66–79; and Peter Doyle, Arch G. Woodside, and Paul Mitchell, "Organizational Buying in New Task and Rebuy Situations," *Industrial Marketing Management*, February 1979, pp. 7–11.

9. Urban B. Ozanne and Gilbert A. Churchill, Jr., "Five Dimensions of the Industrial Adoption Process," *Journal of Marketing Research* (August 1971): 322–28.

10. See Donald W. Jackson Jr., Janet E. Keith, and Richard K. Burdick, "Purchasing Agents' Perceptions of Industrial Buying Center Influence: A Situational Approach," *Journal of Marketing* (Fall 1984): 75–83.

11. Webster and Wind, *Organizational Buying Behavior*, p. 6.

12. Ibid., pp. 78–80.

13. Ibid.

14. Webster and Wind, *Organizational Buying Behavior*, pp. 33–37.

15. Sara Lorge, "Purchasing Power," *Sales & Marketing Management*, June 1998, pp. 43–46; Joann Muller, "The One-Year Itch at Daimler-Chrysler," *BusinessWeek*, November 15, 1999, p. 42.

16. Tim Minahan, "OEM Buying Survey—Part 2: Buyers Get New Roles but Keep Old Tasks," *Purchasing*, July 16, 1998, pp. 208–209.

17. Shawn Tully, "Purchasing's New Muscle," *Fortune*, February 20, 1995; Mark Fitzgerald, "Decentralizing Control of Purchasing," *Editor and Publisher*, June 18, 1994, pp. 8, 10.

18. Robert Yoegel, "The Evolution of B-to-B Selling on the 'Net,' " *Target Marketing*, August 1998, p. 34; Andy Reinhardt, "Extranets: Log On, Link Up, Save Big," *BusinessWeek*, June 22, 1998, p. 134; John Evan Frook, "Buying Behemoth—By Shifting $5B in Spending to Extranets, GE Could Ignite a Development Frenzy," *InternetWeek*, August 17, 1998, p. 1; John Jesitus, "Procuring an Edge," *IndustryWeek*, June 23, 1997, pp. 56–62.

19. Lance Dixon, "JLG Industries Offers JIT II Advice," *Purchasing*, January 15, 1998, p. 39.

20. (Germany, Japan) Teresa C. Morrison, Wayne A. Conaway, and Joseph J. Douress, *Dun & Bradstreet's Guide to Doing Business Around the World* (New York: Prentice Hall, 1997); (Korean) "Tips, Tricks and Pitfalls to Avoid when Doing Business in the Tough but Lucrative Korean Market," *Business America*, June 1997, p. 7.

21. Betsy Cummings, "Selling Around the World," *Sales & Marketing Management*, May 2001, p. 70; Mary Schroeder, "Pru Picks Intercomp for OTC Trading System Interface," *Securities Industry News*, January 29, 2001; Rhonda Coast, "Understanding Cultural Differences Is a Priority," *Pittsburgh Business Times*, February 11, 2000, p. 13; John V. Thill and Courtland L. Bovée, *Excellence in Business Communication*, 5th ed. (Upper Saddle River, NJ: Prentice Hall, 2002) ch. 3.

22. Robinson, Faris, and Wind, *Industrial Buying and Creative Marketing*.

23. See "Xerox Multinational Supplier Quality Survey," *Purchasing*, January 12, 1995, p. 112.

24. Minahan, "OEM Buying Survey—Part 2." To see how the Internet is affecting supplier selection, see Kevin Ferguson, "Purchasing in Packs," *BusinessWeek*, November 1, 1999, pp. EB32–38.

25. Rick Mullin, "Taking Customer Relations to the Next Level," *The Journal of Business Strategy*, January–February 1997, pp. 22–26.

26. Donna Del Moro, "Single-Source Newsprint Supply," *Editor & Publisher*, October 25, 1997, pp. 42–45.

CHAPTER 8

Dealing with the Competition

In this chapter, we will address the following questions:

1. How can a company identify its primary competitors and ascertain their strategies, objectives, strengths and weaknesses, and reaction patterns?
2. How can a company design a competitive intelligence system?
3. Should a company position itself as market leader, challenger, follower, or nicher?
4. How can a company balance a customer versus competitor orientation?

MARKETING MANAGEMENT AT PROCTER & GAMBLE

Procter & Gamble (P&G) is one of the world's most skillful marketers of consumer packaged goods. Its brands lead 19 of the 39 categories in which the company competes; its average market share is almost 25 percent. P&G achieved its success by expanding the total market, defending against rivals, and building market-share profitably. The company is always studying its customers and its competitors, so it has in-depth knowledge of its markets and its customers' needs. It is an active product innovator, devoting $1.2 billion (3.4 percent of sales) annually to research and development. Management takes a long-term approach to capitalizing on opportunities and will invest considerable time and money to succeed in its target markets. Just as important, P&G constantly improves the quality of its products and reevaluates core brands like Tide to find new ways of boosting share and profitability.

In defending its market share, P&G has been known to invest heavily in outpromoting new competitive brands and preventing them from gaining a foothold. Its hefty ad budget is among the largest in the industry, and it has developed creative online programs to promote new products and boost existing brands. One involves a nationwide network of teenage "advocates" to communicate new product information; another uses e-mail newsletters to build awareness and sales of five P&G household cleaning brands. Through its sales force, the company also maintains close ties with Wal-Mart and other intermediaries. Thus, P&G's success is based on the effective orchestration of myriad factors that contribute to market leadership.[1]

This chapter examines the role of competition within markets and industries and explores how companies can position themselves relative to competitors. Because markets have become so competitive, understanding customers is no longer enough. Companies must pay keen attention to competition and design and operate systems for gathering continuous intelligence about competitors.[2]

COMPETITIVE MARKETS AND COMPETITORS

Today, competition is not only rife, but growing more intense every year. Many U.S., European, and Japanese companies are setting up production in lower-cost countries and bringing cheaper goods to market. Thus, it is more important than ever for companies to study competition from the viewpoint of the market and the industry.

Market Attractiveness

In analyzing competition, Michael Porter has identified five forces that determine the intrinsic, long-run profit attractiveness of a market or market segment: industry competitors, potential entrants, substitutes, buyers, and suppliers. His model is shown in Figure 8.1

FIGURE 8.1   Five Forces That Determine Market Attractiveness

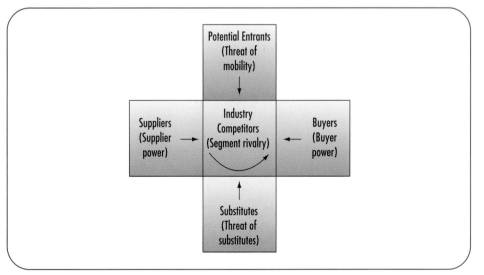

Source: Reprinted with the permission of the Free Press, an imprint of Simon & Schuster, from Michael E. Porter, *Competitve Advantage: Creating and Sustaining Superior Performance.* Copyright © 1985 by Michael E. Porter.

The threats these forces pose are:

1. *Threat of intense segment rivalry.* A segment is unattractive if it already contains numerous, strong, or aggressive competitors. It is even more unattractive if the segment is stable or declining, if a great deal of plant capacity is being added, if fixed costs are high, if exit barriers are high, or if competitors have high stakes in staying in the segment. These conditions will lead to frequent price wars, advertising battles, and new-product introductions—making competition more expensive.

2. *Threat of new entrants.* A segment's attractiveness varies with the height of its entry and exit barriers.[3] The most attractive segment has high entry barriers and low exit barriers (see Figure 8.2), so few new firms can enter, while poor-performing firms can exit easily. Profit potential is high when both entry and exit barriers are high, but firms face more risk because poorer-performing firms stay in and fight it out. When entry and exit barriers are both low, firms enter and leave the industry easily, and the returns are stable and low. The worst case is when entry barriers are low and exit barriers are high: Firms can enter during good times but find it hard to leave during bad times. The result is chronic overcapacity and depressed earnings for all.

3. *Threat of substitute products.* A segment is unattractive when there are actual or potential substitutes for the product. Substitutes place a limit on prices and on the profits that a segment can earn. The company has to monitor the price trends in substitutes closely. If technology advances or competition increases in these substitute industries, prices and profits in the segment are likely to fall.

4. *Threat of buyers' growing bargaining power.* A segment is unattractive if the buyers possess strong or growing bargaining power. Buyers' bargaining power grows when they become more concentrated or organized, when the product represents a significant fraction of the buyers' costs, when the product is undifferentiated, when the buyers' switching costs are low, when buyers are price sensitive, or when buyers can integrate upstream. To compete, sellers might select buyers with less power to negotiate, switch suppliers, or develop superior offers that strong buyers cannot refuse.

5. *Threat of suppliers' growing bargaining power.* A segment is unattractive if the company's suppliers are able to raise prices or reduce quantity supplied. Suppliers tend to be powerful when they are concentrated or organized, when there are few substitutes, when the supplied product is an important input, when the costs of switching suppliers are high, and when suppliers can integrate downstream. The best defenses are to build win-win relations with suppliers or use multiple supply sources.

FIGURE 8.2 Barriers and Profitability

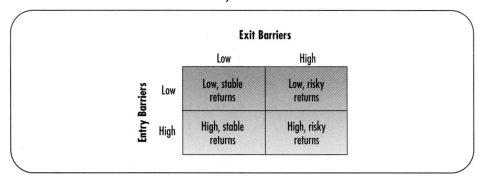

Identifying Competitors

It would seem a simple task for a company to identify its competitors. Coca-Cola knows that Pepsi-Cola is its major competitor; Sony knows that Matsushita is a major competitor. However, the range of a company's actual and potential competitors is actually much broader. A company is more likely to be hurt by emerging competitors or new technologies than by current competitors.

In recent years, many businesses failed to look to the Internet for their most formidable competitors. The Barnes & Noble and Borders bookstore chains used to compete to see who could build the most megastores. While these chains battled for retail dominance, Jeffrey Bezos built Amazon.com with an almost unlimited selection of books. Now Barnes & Noble and Borders are playing catch-up online, even as Amazon.com grows beyond $3 billion in annual sales.[4]

Such "competitor myopia"—a focus on current competitors rather than latent ones—can render a business extinct. Encyclopaedia Britannica, for example, was invited but refused to provide content for Microsoft's Encarta CD-ROM-based encyclopedia. When introduced, the Encarta sold for only $50, making Encyclopaedia Britannica's $1,250 set of 32 volumes look less appealing to parents. This situation forced Encyclopaedia Britannica to change its business model by dismissing its home sales force and offering free online access to the encyclopedia; it sought to generate revenues via Web advertising sales.[5]

The businesses with the most to fear from Internet technology are the world's middlemen, such as travel agencies, car dealers, insurance brokers, real estate brokers, stockbrokers, and employee placement firms. By facilitating direct contact between buyers and sellers, the Internet is causing *disintermediation*—the displacement of traditional intermediaries—and opening up great opportunities for businesses such as Expedia.com and Monster.com to form customer relationships. Although the Internet has given rise to a new breed of competitors for traditional middlemen, it has also opened up opportunities for companies in every industry to provide human intermediaries who will lead consumers through the maze.

Industry Concept of Competition

An **industry** is a group of firms that offer a product or class of products that are close substitutes for each other. Industries are classified according to number of sellers; degree of product differentiation; presence or absence of entry, mobility, and exit barriers; cost structure; degree of vertical integration; and degree of globalization.

Number of Sellers and Degree of Differentiation   The starting point for describing an industry is to specify the number of sellers and determine whether the product is homogeneous or highly differentiated. These characteristics give rise to four industry structure types. In a *pure monopoly*, only one firm provides a certain product or service in a certain country or area (such as a local gas company). An unregulated monopolist might charge a high price, do little or no advertising, and offer minimal service. If partial substitutes are available and there is some danger of competition, the monopolist might invest in more service and technology. A regulated monopolist is required to charge a lower price and provide more service as a matter of public interest.

In an *oligopoly*, a small number of (usually) large firms produce products that range from highly differentiated to standardized. In *pure oligopoly*, a few companies produce essentially the same commodity (such as oil), so all have difficulty charging more than the going price. If competitors match services, the only way to gain a competitive advantage is through lower costs. In *differentiated oligopoly*, a few companies offer products (such as autos) partially differentiated by quality, features, styling, or services. Each competitor may seek leadership in one attribute, attract customers seeking that attribute, and charge a premium for that attribute.

Monopolistic competition means that many competitors are able to differentiate their offers in whole or part (restaurants are a good example). Competitors focus on market segments where they can better meet customer needs and charge more. In *pure competition*, many competitors offer the same product and service, so, without differentiation, all prices will be the same. No competitor will advertise unless advertising can create psychological differentiation (such as cigarettes), in which case the industry is actually monopolistically competitive.

An industry's competitive structure can change over time. For example, the maker of the Palm Pilot handheld computerized organizer initially enjoyed a pure monopoly, because no similar products existed at that time. Soon, however, a few other companies entered the industry, turning it into an oligopoly. As Handspring and additional competitors introduced products, the industry took on a monopolistically competitive structure. When demand growth slows, however, some competitors will probably exit, returning the industry to an oligopoly.[6]

Entry, Mobility, and Exit Barriers   Industries differ greatly in ease of entry. It is easy to open a new restaurant but difficult to enter the aircraft industry. Major *entry barriers* include high capital requirements; economies of scale; patents and licensing requirements; scarce locations, raw materials, or distributors; and reputation requirements. Even after a firm enters an industry, it may face *mobility barriers* in trying to enter more attractive market segments.

Firms often face *exit barriers*,[7] such as legal or moral obligations to customers, creditors, and employees; government restrictions; low asset salvage value; lack of alternative opportunities; high vertical integration; and emotional barriers. Many firms stay in an industry as long as they cover their variable costs and some or all of their fixed costs; their continued presence, however, dampens profits for everyone.

Cost Structure   Each industry has a certain cost burden that shapes much of its strategic conduct. For example, steelmaking involves heavy manufacturing and raw-material costs; toy manufacturing involves heavy distribution and marketing costs. Firms strive to reduce their main costs. The steel firm with the most cost-efficient plant will have a great advantage over other steel companies.

Degree of Vertical Integration   Many companies benefit from integrating backward or forward (**vertical integration**). For example, major oil producers carry on oil exploration, oil drilling, oil refining, chemical manufacture, and service-station operation. Vertical integration often lowers costs, and the company gains a larger share of the value-added stream. In addition, a vertically integrated firm can manage prices and costs in different parts of the value chain to earn profits where taxes are lowest. On the other hand, vertical integration may cause high costs in certain parts of the value chain and restrict a firm's strategic flexibility. This is why firms are increasingly outsourcing activities that can be done better and more cheaply by specialists.

Degree of Globalization   Some industries are highly local (such as lawn care); others are global (such as oil, aircraft engines, and cameras). Companies in global industries need to compete on a global basis if they are to achieve economies of scale and keep up with the latest advances in technology.[8]

Market Concept of Competition

In addition to the industry approach, companies need to identify competitors using the market approach: Competitors are those that satisfy the same customer need. For example, a customer who buys word processing software really wants "writing ability"—a need that can be satisfied by pencils, pens, or typewriters. The market concept of competition opens up a broader set of actual and potential competitors that companies must identify and analyze.

Rayport and Jaworski suggest profiling a company's direct and indirect competitors by mapping the buyer's steps in obtaining and using the product. Figure 8.3 illustrates their *competitor map* of Eastman Kodak in the film business. The center shows consumer activities such as buying a camera and buying film. The first outer ring lists Kodak's main competitors with respect to each consumer activity: Olympus for buying a camera, Fuji for purchasing film, and so on. The second outer ring lists indirect competitors—HP, cameraworks.com—who may become direct competitors. This analysis highlights a company's opportunities and challenges.[9]

FIGURE 8.3   Competitor Map—Eastman Kodak

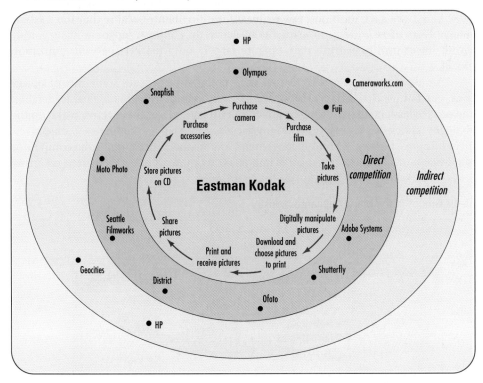

Source: Jeffrey F. Rayport and Bernard J. Jaworski, *e-Commerce* (New York: McGraw-Hill, 2001), p. 53.

COMPETITOR ANALYSIS

Once a company identifies its primary competitors, it must ascertain their characteristics, specifically their strategies, objectives, strengths and weaknesses, and reaction patterns.

Strategies

A group of firms that follow the same strategy in a given target market is called a **strategic group**.[10] Suppose a company wants to enter the major appliance industry. What is its strategic group? It develops the chart shown in Figure 8.4 and discovers four strategic groups based on product quality and level of vertical integration. Group A has one competitor (Maytag), group B has three (General Electric, Whirlpool, and Sears), group C has four, and group D has two. This analysis shows that the height of the entry barriers differs for each group. If the company successfully enters a group, this analysis identifies who will be its key competitors. Changes can occur, so a company must continuously monitor its competitors' strategies over time.

Objectives

Once a company has identified its main competitors and their strategies, it must ask: What is each competitor seeking in the marketplace? What drives each competitor's behavior? Although one initial assumption is that competitors strive to maximize profits, companies differ in the weights they put on short-term versus long-term profits. Most U.S. firms seek short-term profit maximization mainly because they must satisfy stockholders or risk losing investors' confidence. In contrast, Japanese firms readily accept lower profits because they operate largely on a market-share-maximization model.

An alternative assumption is that each competitor pursues some mix of objectives: current profitability, market-share growth, cash flow, technological leadership, and service leadership. Knowing how a competitor weighs each objective will help the company anticipate its reactions. Many factors can shape a competitor's objectives, including size, history, current management, and financial situation. If the competitor is a division of a larger company, it is important to know whether the parent company

FIGURE 8.4   Strategic Groups in the Major Appliance Industry

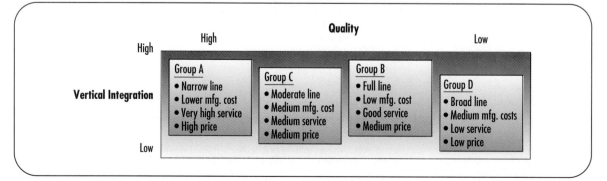

is running it for growth or milking it.[11] Finally, a company must monitor its competitors' expansion plans and, as appropriate, try to establish mobility barriers to block or slow rivals' growth.

Strengths and Weaknesses

Whether competitors can carry out their strategies and reach their goals depends on their resources and capabilities. This is why marketers need to gather information on each competitor's strengths and weaknesses. According to the Arthur D. Little consulting firm, a firm will occupy one of six competitive positions in the target market:[12]

- *Dominant.* This firm controls the other competitors' behavior and has many strategic options.
- *Strong.* This firm can take independent action without endangering its long-term position and can maintain its long-term position regardless of competitors' actions.
- *Favorable.* This firm has an exploitable strength and a better opportunity to improve its position.
- *Tenable.* This firm's performance is sufficient for it to remain in business, but it exists at the sufferance of the dominant company and has less opportunity to improve its position.
- *Weak.* This firm has unsatisfactory performance and an opportunity for improvement; it must change or exit.
- *Nonviable.* This firm has unsatisfactory performance and no opportunity for improvement.

To gauge strengths and weaknesses, a company should monitor share of market, share of mind, and share of heart for each competitor (see Table 8.1). In general, companies that make steady gains in share of mind and heart will inevitably gain market share and profitability.

Reaction Patterns

Companies react differently to competitive attacks: some are slow; some respond only to certain attacks, such as price cuts; others react quickly and strongly to any assault. Bruce Henderson observes that much depends on the industry's competitive equilibrium.[13] *If competitors are nearly identical and make their living in the same way, then their competitive equilibrium is unstable.* Perpetual conflict characterizes industries such as

TABLE 8.1 Gauging a Competitor's Strengths and Weaknesses

Basis of Analysis	Description
1. Share of market	The competitor's share of the target market
2. Share of mind	The percentage of customers who name the competitor when asked to "name the first company that comes to mind in this industry"
3. Share of heart	The percentage of customers who name the competitor when asked to "name the company from whom you would prefer to buy the product"

steel or newsprint, where differentiation is hard to maintain. Equilibrium will be upset if a firm lowers its price to relieve overcapacity; price wars are frequent.

If a single major factor is the critical factor, then the competitive equilibrium is unstable. This occurs in industries where cost-differentiation opportunities exist through economies of scale, advanced technology, or experience. Any company that achieves a cost breakthrough can cut its price and win market share at the expense of others, which can defend their market shares only at great cost; price wars are frequent.

If multiple competitive factors can be critical, each competitor may have some advantage and be differentially attractive to some customers. The more factors that may provide an advantage (in service, quality, and so on), the more competitors who can coexist in a segment defined by the preference for the factor trade-offs they offer. *The fewer the number of critical competitive variables, the fewer the number of competitors.* If only one factor is critical, no more than two or three competitors are likely to coexist. *A ratio of 2 to 1 in market share between any two competitors seems to be the equilibrium point at which it is neither practical nor advantageous for either competitor to increase or decrease share.* At this level, the costs of extra promotion or distribution would outweigh the gains in market share.

THE COMPETITIVE INTELLIGENCE SYSTEM

Every company needs a competitive intelligence system to track its competitors and the competitive trends in the industry and the market. Such a system need not be computerized, although the Internet and computer databases can be very useful. Once the system is up and running, it will provide a stream of intelligence to support competitive strategy decisions.

Designing the Competitive Intelligence System

The four main steps in designing a competitive intelligence system are: setting up the system, collecting the data, evaluating and analyzing the data, then disseminating information and responding to queries.

The first step calls for identifying vital types of competitive information, identifying the best information sources, and assigning someone to manage the system and its services. In smaller companies that cannot afford a formal competitive intelligence office, specific executives should be assigned to watch specific competitors. Then any manager who needs to know about a specific competitor would contact the corresponding in-house expert.[14]

In the second step, the data are collected on a continuous basis from the field (sales force, channels, suppliers, market research firms, trade associations), from people who do business with competitors, from observing competitors, and from published data. A vast store of data on both domestic and international firms is available via CD-ROM and online services. Companies can learn a great deal from Web sites maintained by competitors and by trade associations. For example, when the controller of Stone Container's specialty-packaging division checked a trade association Web site, he found that a rival had won an award for a new process using ultraviolet-resistant lacquers. The site revealed the machines' configuration and run rate, which Stone's engineers used to replicate the process.[15]

The third step is evaluating and analyzing the data. Here, company managers check the data they have collected for validity and reliability. Then they interpret the findings and organize the results so users can conveniently find what they need. The fourth step is to disseminate the information to relevant decision makers and answer managers' inquiries. With a well-designed system, company managers receive timely data about competitors via phone calls, e-mails, bulletins, newsletters, and reports. Managers can also request information when they need help interpreting a competitor's move, when they need to know a rival's weaknesses and strengths, or when they want to discuss a competitor's likely response to a contemplated company move.

Selecting Competitors to Attack and to Avoid

With good competitive intelligence, managers will find it easier to evaluate their competitive situations and then formulate appropriate competitive strategies. They can assess how customers view their firm and their competitors using a technique called customer value analysis.

Customer Value Analysis   Very often, managers conduct a **customer value analysis** to reveal the company's strengths and weaknesses relative to various competitors. The company first asks customers what attributes and performance levels they look for in choosing a product and vendors. Next, the company asks customers to rate the importance of these different attributes and describe where they see the company's and competitors' performances on each attribute.

Then the company must examine how customers in each targeted segment rate its performance against a particular competitor on an attribute-by-attribute basis. If the company's offer exceeds the competitor's offer on all important attributes, the company can charge a higher price (thereby earning higher profits), or it can charge the same price and gain more market share. Of course, the company must periodically redo its studies of customer value and competitors' standings as the economy, technology, products, and features change.

Classes of Competitors   After the company has conducted its customer value analysis, it can focus its attack on one of the following classes of competitors: strong versus weak competitors, close versus distant competitors, or "good" versus "bad" competitors.

Most companies aim at weak competitors, because this requires fewer resources per share point gained. Yet, in attacking weak competitors, the firm will barely improve its own capabilities. Thus, the firm should also compete with strong competitors to keep up with the best. Even strong competitors have some weaknesses, and the firm may prove to be a worthy opponent. In addition, most companies compete with competitors who most resemble them. For instance, Chevrolet competes with Ford, not with Jaguar. At the same time, a company should avoid trying to destroy the closest competitor. One risk is that a much larger competitor will buy out the weakened rival; another risk is that additional, stronger competitors will enter the market.

Finally, every industry contains "good" and "bad" competitors.[16] A company should support its good competitors and attack its bad competitors. Good competitors play by the industry's rules, make realistic assumptions about the industry's growth potential, set prices in reasonable relation to costs, favor a healthy industry, limit themselves to a portion or segment of the industry, motivate others to lower costs or improve differentiation, and accept the general level of their share and profits. Bad competitors try to buy share rather than earn it, take large risks, invest in overcapacity, and upset industrial equilibrium.

DESIGNING COMPETITIVE STRATEGIES

A company can gain further insight into its competitive position by classifying its competitors and itself according to the role each plays as market leader, market challenger, market follower, or market nicher. On the basis of this classification, the company can take specific actions in line with its current and desired roles.

Market-Leader Strategies

Many industries contain one firm that is the acknowledged market leader, with the largest share of the relevant product market. This market leader usually leads the other firms in price changes, new-product introductions, distribution coverage, and promotional intensity. Some of the best-known market leaders are Microsoft (computer software), Procter & Gamble (consumer packaged goods), Caterpillar (earthmoving equipment), Coca-Cola (soft drinks), McDonald's (fast food), and Gillette (razor blades).

Unless a dominant firm enjoys a legal monopoly, it must maintain constant vigilance to avoid missing key developments. One development might be competitive product innovations; Motorola's analog cell phones, for example, suffered when Nokia's and Ericsson's digital models took over. Or the leader might continue to spend conservatively while a challenger spends liberally, it might experience higher costs cutting into profits, or it might misjudge its competition and get left behind. Another risk is that the dominant firm might look old-fashioned against newer, peppier rivals. For example, Levi Strauss lost ground in jeans against more stylish brands and newer competitors such as Diesel.[17]

Remaining number one calls for action on three fronts. First, the leader must expand total market demand. Second, it must protect its current market share through good defensive and offensive actions. Third, the firm can try to further increase its market share, even if market size remains constant.

Expanding the Total Market   The dominant firm normally gains the most when the total market expands. If Americans take more photographs, Kodak stands to gain the most because it sells most of the country's film. If Kodak can convince more Americans to buy cameras and take photos, take photos on more occasions, or take more photos on each occasion, Kodak will benefit considerably. In general, the market leader should aim for new users, new uses, and more usage of its products.

In identifying new users, marketers can try to attract buyers who are unaware of the company's product or who are resisting it because of price or lack of certain features. A company can search for new users among buyers who might use the product but do not (*market-penetration strategy*), those who have never used it (*new-market segment strategy*), or those who live elsewhere (*geographical-expansion strategy*).

Also, companies can expand markets by discovering and promoting new uses for the product. For example, cereal manufacturers would gain if they could promote cereal eating on occasions other than breakfast—perhaps as a snack. Sometimes customers discover new uses. After sales of Arm & Hammer's baking soda had drifted downward for 125 years, the company learned that consumers use the product as a refrigerator deodorant. It heavily promoted this use and succeeded in getting half of all U.S. homes to place an open box of baking soda in the refrigerator. When Arm & Hammer discovered that consumers use the product to quell kitchen grease fires, it promoted that use with great results.

A third strategy is to convince people to use more product per use occasion. France-based Michelin Tire, for example, wanted French car owners to drive their cars more miles per year—thus leading to more tire replacement. The company conceived the idea of rating restaurants around France. Once it began promoting many of the best restaurants in southern France, Parisians began taking weekend drives to Provence and the Riviera. Michelin also published guidebooks with maps and lists of sights along the way to encourage additional driving.

Defending Market Share While trying to expand total market size, the dominant firm must continuously defend its current business. The leader is like a large elephant being attacked by a swarm of bees, some domestic and some foreign. Coca-Cola must guard against Pepsi-Cola; Gillette against Bic; Hertz against Avis; McDonald's against Burger King; General Motors against Ford; and Kodak against Fuji.

What can the market leader do to defend its terrain? The most constructive response is *continuous innovation*. The leader leads the industry in developing new product and customer services, distribution effectiveness, and cost cutting. It keeps increasing its competitive strength and value to customers. Here, the best defense is a good offense. For example, International Gaming Technology, a manufacturer of slot machines and video poker machines, has maintained a 64 percent domestic market share. How? By forming partnerships with casino operators and competitive gaming manufacturers to develop innovative new equipment. The firm spends aggressively on R&D, is dedicated to customer service, and involves customers throughout the sales process, from initial product development to final placement on the casino floor.[18]

Even when it does not launch offensives, the market leader must leave no major flanks exposed. It must keep its costs down, and its prices must reflect the value that customers see in the brand. In addition, the leader must consider what segments to defend (even at a loss) and what segments to surrender. The aim of defensive strategy is to reduce the probability of attack, divert attacks to less threatening areas, and lessen their intensity. A dominant firm can use six defense strategies, which are shown in Figure 8.5:[19]

1. *Position defense.* This approach involves building superior brand power, making the brand almost impregnable. For instance, Heinz let Hunt's mount a costly attack in the ketchup market without striking back. Hunt's expensive strategy failed, and Heinz continues to enjoy over 50 percent U.S. market share, compared with Hunt's 17 percent share.[20]

2. *Flank defense.* The market leader should also erect outposts to protect a weak front or possibly serve as an invasion base for counterattack. Heublein's brand Smirnoff, which had a 23 percent share of the U.S. vodka market, was attacked by the Wolfschmidt brand, priced at $1 less per bottle. Heublein raised Smirnoff's price by $1 and increased advertising; in addition, it launched another brand to compete with Wolfschmidt and a brand to sell for less than Wolfschmidt, thus protecting Smirnoff's flanks.

FIGURE 8.5   Defense Strategies

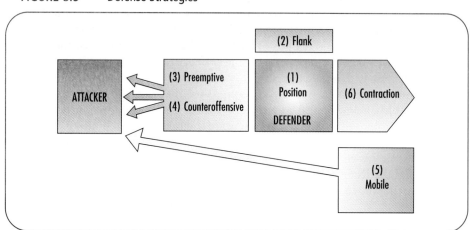

3. *Preemptive defense.* A more aggressive maneuver is to attack before a rival starts its offense, which can be done in several ways. A company can hit one competitor here, another there, and keep everyone off balance. Or it can try to envelop the market, as Seiko has done with 3,000 watch models distributed worldwide.[21] Other strategies focus on sustained price attacks or sending out market signals to dissuade competitors from attacking.[22]

4. *Counteroffensive defense.* When attacked, most leaders will counterattack. One effective counterattack is to invade the attacker's main market so it will have to defend the territory. Another approach is to use economic or political clout to deter the attacker. For example, the leader may subsidize lower prices for a vulnerable product with revenue from more profitable products, prematurely announce a forthcoming product upgrade to prevent customers from buying the competitor's product, or lobby legislators to take political action that would hurt the competition.

5. *Mobile defense.* Here, the leader stretches its domain over new territories that can serve as future centers for defense and offense, using market broadening and market diversification. With *market broadening*, the company shifts its focus from the current product to the underlying generic need. The company gets involved in R&D across the whole range of technology associated with that need, which is how "petroleum" companies recast themselves as "energy" companies to enter oil, nuclear, hydroelectric, and other industries. *Market diversification* into unrelated industries is the other alternative. When U.S. tobacco companies like Philip Morris acknowledged the growing curbs on cigarette smoking, they moved into unrelated industries such as beer and foods.

6. *Contraction defense.* Large companies sometimes recognize that they can no longer defend all of their territory. The best course of action then appears to be *planned contraction* (also called *strategic withdrawal*), giving up weaker territories and reassigning resources to stronger territories. This move consolidates competitive strength in the market and concentrates mass at pivotal positions. Heinz, General Mills, and Georgia-Pacific are among the companies that have used the contraction defense to prune product lines in recent years.

Expanding Market Share   Market leaders can improve their profitability by increasing their market share. Depending on the market, one share point can be worth tens of millions of dollars. A one-share-point gain in coffee is worth $48 million, and in soft drinks, $120 million! No wonder normal competition has turned into marketing warfare. Because the cost of buying higher market share may far exceed its revenue value, a company should consider three factors before pursuing increased market share. The first factor is the possibility of provoking antitrust action: Jealous competitors may cry "monopoly" if a dominant firm makes further inroads. This happened to Verizon when it came under attack from competitors and consumers for "anti-competitive" practices in Pennsylvania. Controlling 90 percent of the state's local phone lines, Verizon announced it would enter the long-distance market. In response, the state's Public Utilities Commission ordered Verizon to establish "functional structural separation" of its retail and wholesale units.[23]

The second factor is economic cost. Profitability may fall, not rise, with further market-share gains after a certain level, driving the cost of gaining share higher than the value. Here, a leader must recognize that "holdout" customers may dislike the company, be loyal to competitive suppliers, have unique needs, or prefer dealing with smaller suppliers. Also, the cost of legal work, public relations, and lobbying rises with market share. Pushing for higher market share is less justified when there are few scale or experience economies, unattractive market segments exist, buyers want multiple sources of supply, and exit barriers are high. Some market leaders have even increased profitability by selectively decreasing market share in weaker areas.[24]

The third factor is that companies might pursue the wrong marketing-mix strategy in their bid for higher market share and therefore fail to increase profits. Companies that win more market share by cutting price are buying, not earning, a larger share, and their profits may be lower. Each of these factors is associated with potential risks and rewards that must be weighed before a company makes its choice.

Market-Challenger Strategies

Firms that occupy second, third, and lower ranks in an industry are often called runner-up, or trailing, firms. Some, such as Colgate, Ford, Avis, and Pepsi-Cola, are quite large in their own right. These firms can adopt one of two postures. They can attack the leader and other competitors in an aggressive bid for further market share (market challengers), or they can not "rock the boat" (acting like market followers). Market challengers can use the following competitive attack strategies.

Defining the Strategic Objective and Opponent(s) A market challenger must first define its strategic objective; most aim to increase market share. Then the challenger must decide whom to attack. Attacking the market leader is a high-risk, but potentially high-payoff strategy if the leader is not serving the market well. Another way to attack the leader is to out-innovate it across the whole segment. Xerox wrested the copy market from 3M by developing a better copying process; later, Canon grabbed a large chunk of Xerox's market by introducing desk copiers. If the attacking company goes after the market leader, its objective might be to grab a certain share. Bic is under no illusion that it can topple Gillette in the razor market—it is simply seeking a larger share.

A second choice for the market challenger is to attack firms of its own size that are underperforming and underfinanced. These firms have aging products, charge excessive prices, or are not satisfying customers in other ways. A third choice is to attack small local and regional firms, perhaps gobbling up these smaller competitors as some beer companies have done.

Choosing a General Attack Strategy   Given clear opponents and objectives, what attack options are available? We can distinguish among five attack strategies, as shown in Figure 8.6: frontal, flank, encirclement, bypass, and guerilla attacks.

In a pure *frontal attack*, the attacker matches its opponent's product, advertising, price, and distribution. The principle of force says that the side with the greater resources will win, unless the defender enjoys a terrain advantage. A modified frontal attack, such as undercutting an opponent's price, can work if the market leader does not retaliate and if the competitor convinces the market that its product is equal to the leader's.

A *flank attack* can be directed along two strategic dimensions. In a geographical attack, the challenger spots areas where the opponent is underperforming. For example, some of IBM's rivals, such as Honeywell, chose to set up strong sales branches in medium- and smaller-size cities that were relatively neglected by IBM. Another flanking strategy is to serve uncovered market needs, as Miller Brewing Company did when it introduced light beer.

A flanking strategy is another name for identifying shifts in market segments that are causing gaps to develop, then rushing in to fill the gaps and develop them into strong segments. Flank attacks are particularly attractive to a challenger with fewer resources and are much more likely to be successful than frontal attacks.

The encirclement maneuver is an attempt to capture a wide slice of the enemy's territory through a "blitz"—launching a grand offensive on several fronts. Encirclement makes sense when the challenger commands superior resources and believes a swift

FIGURE 8.6   Attack Strategies

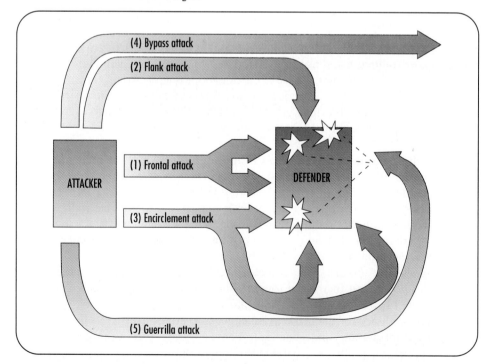

encirclement will break the opponent's will. For example, in taking a stand against archrival Microsoft, Sun Microsystems licensed its Java software for all types of consumer devices. Now Java has been licensed by more than 200 companies and used by more than 2.5 million software developers.[25]

The most indirect assault strategy is the *bypass*. It involves bypassing the enemy and attacking easier markets to broaden one's resource base. This strategy offers three lines of approach: diversifying into unrelated products, diversifying into new geographical markets, and leapfrogging into new technologies to supplant existing products. For example, PepsiCo used a bypass when it bought Tropicana as a weapon in its war against Coca-Cola. Tropicana's 42 percent share of the orange juice market outshines Coke-owned Minute-Maid's 24 percent share. Next, Pepsi obtained the Gatorade brand by buying its owner, Quaker Oats. Gatorade boasts over an 80 percent share of the sports drink market—overshadowing Coke's Powerade brand.[26]

Guerrilla warfare consists of waging small, intermittent attacks to harass and demoralize the opponent and eventually secure permanent footholds. The guerrilla challenger uses both conventional and unconventional means of attack, such as selective price cuts, intense promotional blitzes, and attention-getting activities. Consider the way upstart The Princeton Review used guerrilla marketing against its established rival in test preparation services, Kaplan Educational Centers. Princeton Review's ads brashly advised, "Friends don't let friends take Kaplan" while touting Princeton Review's smaller, livelier classes. Princeton's founder also posted horror stories about Kaplan on the Internet. Ultimately, this guerrilla warfare paid off: Princeton is now one of the market leaders in test preparation.

Normally, guerrilla warfare is practiced by a smaller firm against a larger one. A guerrilla campaign can be costly, although less expensive than a frontal, encirclement, or flank attack (see "Marketing Skills: Guerrilla Marketing"). Still, guerrilla warfare must be backed by a stronger attack if the challenger hopes to beat the opponent.

Choosing a Specific Attack Strategy   Having chosen a broad attack strategy, the company must now develop more specific attack strategies, such as:

- *Price-discount.* The challenger can offer a comparable product at a lower price. This works if (1) the challenger can convince buyers that its product and service are comparable to the leader's; (2) buyers are price-sensitive; and (3) the leader refuses to cut price despite the competitor's attack.

- *Lower-price goods.* The challenger can offer an average- or low-quality product at a much lower price. Little Debbie Snack Cakes are priced lower than Drake's and outsell Drake's by 20 to 1. Firms that use this strategy, however, can be attacked by firms with even lower prices.

- *Prestige goods.* A challenger can launch a higher-quality product and charge more than the leader. Mercedes gained on Cadillac in the U.S. market by offering a higher-quality car at a higher price.

- *Product proliferation.* The challenger can attack the leader by offering more product variety, giving buyers more choice. Samsung, for instance, is challenging market leader Sony with a wide variety of consumer electronics products, including flat-screen televisions and lightweight laptop computers.[28]

- *Product innovation.* The challenger can pursue product innovation, such as the way 3M enters new markets by introducing a product improvement or breakthrough.

- *Improved services.* The challenger can offer new or better services, as JetBlue Airways does by providing roomier leather seats and personal viewing screens with a choice of 24 satellite television channels.[29]

- *Distribution innovation.* A challenger might develop a new distribution channel. For example, 1800Contacts has built its business selling contact lenses by mail and online.

- *Manufacturing cost reduction.* The challenger might achieve lower manufacturing costs through more efficient purchasing, lower labor costs, and/or more modern production equipment.

- *Intensive advertising promotion.* Some challengers attack by boosting advertising and promotion spending, a strategy that can work if the challenger's product or advertising message is superior.

A challenger's success depends on combining several strategies to improve its position over time.

Market-Follower Strategies

Theodore Levitt has argued that a strategy of *product imitation* might be as profitable as a strategy of *product innovation*.[30] The innovator bears the expense of developing the new product, getting it into distribution, and educating the market. The reward for all

MARKETING SKILLS: GUERRILLA MARKETING

Who needs guerrilla marketing skills? Any marketer who wants to attack and grab share from the market leader without risking the higher cost and provocation of a frontal attack. Guerrilla marketing became popular in the 1980s after Jay Conrad Levinson published his first of many books on the subject. To start, guerrilla marketers must think creatively about how to attract maximum customer attention and achieve marketing objectives with minimal investment; then test the idea internally and/or locally to spot potential problems and opportunities for improvement before bringing it to national markets.

During planning, guerilla marketers must anticipate stakeholders' reactions to controversial techniques or messages and be sensitive to legal and ethical concerns. "Guerrilla marketing does not mean being socially irresponsible or taking liberties with the law and ethics of doing business," stresses Levinson. They must plan for how results will be measured and then closely monitor progress during the program. Finally, they must be prepared to move quickly by either modifying or dropping a non-performing guerrilla campaign in favor of a new idea.

To illustrate, when Van's Harley-Davidson in Gloversville, New York, wanted to build store traffic, it decided on a provocative but imaginative promotion. Rather than use a conventional approach such as a price promotion, the store advertised a special "cat shoot" event at the store. Local newspapers quickly published front-page stories investigating the event while the store's manager fielded calls from animal welfare advocates, the police, and municipal officials. When people arrived for the "cat shoot," they were invited to pay $1 for three paintball shots at a giant cardboard cartoon cat—with proceeds going to the local Humane Society. Traffic got a big boost, and the store polished its reputation for being a good corporate citizen.[27]

this work and risk is normally market leadership—even though another firm can then copy or improve on the new product. Although it probably will not overtake the leader, the follower can achieve high profits because it did not bear any of the innovation expense.

Many companies prefer to follow rather than challenge the leader. This pattern is common in industries such as steel and chemicals, where few opportunities exist for product differentiation and image differentiation, service quality is often comparable, and price sensitivity is high. Short-run grabs for market share provoke retaliation, so most firms present similar offers to buyers, usually by copying the leader; this keeps market shares highly stable.

Four broad strategies for market followers are:

- *Counterfeiter.* The counterfeiter duplicates the leader's product and package and sells it on the black market or through disreputable dealers. Both Apple Computer and Rolex have been plagued by counterfeiters, especially in the Far East.
- *Cloner.* The cloner emulates the leader's products, name, and packaging, with slight variations. For example, Ralcorp Holding sells imitations of name-brand cereals in lookalike boxes at lower prices.[31]
- *Imitator.* The imitator copies some things from the leader but maintains differentiation in terms of packaging, advertising, pricing, and so on. The leader does not respond as long as the imitator does not attack the leader aggressively.
- *Adapter.* The adapter adapts or improves the leader's products, perhaps for different markets. S&S Cycle, for example, supplies engines to firms that build Harley-like cruiser bikes. It buys a new Harley-Davidson bike every year and takes the engine apart to see what it can improve upon.[32]

Normally, a follower earns less than the leader. For example, a study of food processing companies found that only the top two firms were profitable. Thus, followership is not always a rewarding path.

Market-Nicher Strategies

An alternative to being a follower in a large market is to be a leader in a small market, or niche. Smaller firms normally avoid competing with larger firms by targeting small markets of little or no interest to the larger firms. For example, Logitech International expanded worldwide by making every variation of computer mouse imaginable. This niche success enabled the company to expand into other growing niches, such as joysticks and Internet video cameras.[33]

Even large companies are now setting up business units or brands for specific niches, the way Anheuser-Busch has established Red Wolf beer. The key idea in nichemanship is specialization. Table 8.2 shows the specialist roles open to nichers. However, because niches can weaken, the firm must continually create new niches, expand niches, and protect its niches. By developing strength in two or more niches, the company increases its chances for survival. It gets to know the target customers so well that it can meet their needs better than competitors—and can charge a substantial price over costs. Thus the nicher achieves *high margin*, whereas the mass marketer achieves *high volume*.

TABLE 8.2   Specialized Niche Roles

Niche Specialty	Description
End-user specialist	The firm specializes in serving one type of end-use customer.
Vertical-level specialist	The firm specializes at some vertical level of the production-distribution value chain.
Customer-size specialist	The firm concentrates on selling to small, medium-size, or large customers.
Specific-customer specialist	The firm limits its selling to one or a few customers.
Geographic specialist	The firm sells only in a certain locality, region, or area of the world.
Product or product-line specialist	The firm carries or produces only one product line or product.
Product-feature specialist	The firm specializes in producing a certain type of product or product feature.
Job-shop specialist	The firm customizes its products for individual customers.
Quality-price specialist	The firm operates at the low- or high-quality ends of the market.
Service specialist	The firm offers one or more services not available from competitors.
Channel specialist	The firm specializes in serving only one channel of distribution.

Balancing Customer and Competitor Orientations

We have stressed the importance of a company's positioning itself competitively as a market leader, challenger, follower, or nicher. Yet a company must not spend all of its time focusing on competitors. We can distinguish between two types of companies: competitor-centered and customer-centered.

A *competitor-centered company* looks at each situation in terms of what competitors are doing (increasing distribution, cutting prices, introducing new services) and then formulates competitive reactions (increasing advertising expenditures, meeting price cuts, increasing the sales-promotion budget). This kind of planning has both pluses and minuses. On the positive side, the company develops a fighter orientation, training its marketers to be alert for weaknesses in its competitors' and its own position. On the negative side, the company is too reactive. Rather than formulating and executing a consistent customer-oriented strategy, it determines its moves based on its competitors' moves rather than its own goals.

A *customer-centered company* focuses more on customer developments in formulating its strategies. Its marketers might learn through research, for example, that the total market is growing at 4 percent annually, while the quality-sensitive segment is growing at 8 percent annually. They might also find that the deal-prone customer segment is growing fast, but these customers do not stay with any supplier for very long. And they might find that more customers are asking for a 24-hour hot line, which no one else offers. In response, this company could put more effort into reaching and satisfying the quality segment, avoid cutting prices, and research the possibility of installing a hot line.

Clearly, the customer-centered company is in a better position to identify new opportunities and set a strategy toward long-run profits. By monitoring customer

needs, it can decide which customer groups and emerging needs are the most important to serve, given its resources and objectives. Successful companies monitor both
customers and competitors carefully.

EXECUTIVE SUMMARY

To prepare an effective marketing strategy, a company must study its competitors as
well as its actual and potential customers. The closest competitors are those seeking to
satisfy the same customers and needs and making similar offers; latent competitors are
those who may offer new or other ways to satisfy the same needs. The company can
identify competitors by using both industry and market-based analyses, then analyze
competitors' strategies, objectives, strengths, weaknesses, and reaction patterns.

Through a competitive intelligence system, companies can continuously collect,
analyze, and disseminate competitive information to provide managers with timely
information about competitors so they can more easily formulate appropriate strategies. In selecting which competitors to attack and which to avoid, managers conduct a
customer value analysis, which reveals the company's strengths and weaknesses relative to competitors. The aim is to determine the benefits that customers want and how
they perceive the relative value of competitors' offers.

A firm can gain further insight by classifying competitors and itself according to
their roles as market leader, challenger, follower, or nicher. To remain dominant, the
market leader looks for ways to expand total market demand, attempts to protect its
current market share, and perhaps tries to increase its market share.

A market challenger attacks the market leader and other competitors in an
aggressive bid for more market share. After defining their strategic objectives and
opponents, challengers can choose from five types of general attack (frontal, flank,
encirclement, bypass, guerrilla) and a number of more specific attack strategies. A
market follower is a runner-up firm that is willing to maintain its market share and not
rock the boat. A follower can play the role of counterfeiter, cloner, imitator, or
adapter. A market nicher serves small market segments that are not being served by
larger firms. The key to nichemanship is specialization; multiple niching is generally
preferable to single niching. As important as a competitive orientation is in today's
global markets, companies should not overdo the competitive emphasis. Instead, companies should balance their monitoring of both customers and competitors.

NOTES

1. Jack Neff, "Management: P&G vs. Martha," *Advertising Age*, April 8, 2002, p. 24; "The
   Tide Is Turning at P&G," *BusinessWeek*, April 8, 2002, pp. 44+; Karen Benezra, "Get Me
   Results!" *Brandweek*, March 25, 2002, p. 16; Ronald Henkoff, "P&G: New & Improved,"
   Fortune, October 14, 1995, pp. 151–60.
2. See Leonard M. Fuld, *The New Competitor Intelligence: The Complete Resource for Finding,
   Analyzing, and Using Information About Your Competitors* (New York: John Wiley, 1995);
   John A. Czepiel, *Competitive Marketing Strategy* (Upper Saddle River, NJ: Prentice Hall,
   1992).
3. Michael E. Porter, *Competitive Strategy* (New York: Free Press, 1980) pp. 22–23.
4. Keith Regan, "Analysts Look for Amazon Sales Growth to Balance Q1 Red Ink,"
   E-Commerce Times, April 22, 2002 *(www.ecommercetimes.com/perl/story/17378.html)*;

Keith Regan, "Amazon Posts First-Ever Profit," *E-Commerce Times*, January 22, 2002 *(www.ecommercetimes.com/perl/story/15926.html)*; Leslie Kaufman with Saul Hansell, "Holiday Lessons in Online Retailing," *New York Times*, January 2, 2000, sec. 3, pp. 1, 14.

5. Jonathan Gaw, "Britannica Gives In and Gets Online," *Los Angeles Times*, October 19, 2000, p. A1; Jerry Useem, "Withering Britannica Bets It All on the Web," *Fortune*, November 22, 1999, pp. 344, 348.

6. Ian Fried and Richard Shim, "Handheld Industry Sees Hope in Wireless," *CNET News.com*, January 16, 2002 *(news.com.com/2100-1040-814416.html)*; Cliff Edwards, "Palm's Market Starts To Melt in Its Hands," *BusinessWeek*, June 4, 2001, p. 42.

7. See Kathryn Rudie Harrigan, "The Effect of Exit Barriers Upon Strategic Flexibility," *Strategic Management Journal* 1 (1980): 165–76.

8. Porter, *Competitive Strategy*, ch. 13.

9. Jeffrey F. Rayport and Bernard J. Jaworski, *E-Commerce* (New York: McGraw Hill, 2001), p. 53.

10. Ibid., ch. 7.

11. William E. Rothschild, *How to Gain (and Maintain) the Competitive Advantage* (New York: McGraw-Hill, 1989), ch. 5.

12. See Robert V. L. Wright, *A System for Managing Diversity* (Cambridge, MA: Arthur D. Little, December 1974).

13. The following section has been drawn from Bruce Henderson's various writings, including "The Unanswered Questions, The Unsolved Problems" (paper delivered in a speech at Northwestern University in 1986); *Henderson on Corporate Strategy* (New York: Mentor, 1982); and "Understanding the Forces of Strategic and Natural Competition," *Journal of Business Strategy* (Winter 1981): 11–15.

14. For more discussion, see Leonard M. Fuld, *Monitoring the Competition* (New York: John Wiley, 1988).

15. "Spy/Counterspy," *Context* (Summer 1998): 20–21.

16. Michael E. Porter, *Competitive Advantage* (New York: Free Press, 1985) ch. 6.

17. Brad Stone, "Jean Therapy for Levi's," *Newsweek*, April 15, 2002, pp. 42+; Bernhard Warner, "Levi's Internet Blues Keep Keepin' On," *The Industry Standard*, November 8, 1999 *(www.thestandard.com/subject/ecommerce)*.

18. Erika Rasmusson, "The Jackpot," *Sales & Marketing Management*, June 1998, pp. 35–41.

19. These six defense strategies, as well as the five attack strategies, are taken from Philip Kotler and Ravi Singh, "Marketing Warfare in the 1980s," *Journal of Business Strategy* (Winter 1981): 30–41. For additional reading, see Gerald A. Michaelson, *Winning the Marketing War: A Field Manual for Business Leaders* (Lanham, MD: Abt Books, 1987); Al Ries and Jack Trout, *Marketing Warfare* (New York: McGraw-Hill, 1990); Jay Conrad Levinson, *Guerrilla Marketing* (Boston, MA: Houghton-Mifflin Co., 1984); and Barrie G. James, *Business Wargames* (Harmondsworth, England: Penguin Books, 1984).

20. "Leader of the Pack," *Pittsburgh Post-Gazette*, April 1, 2000.

21. "Seiko," *Hoover's Capsules*, January 2000 *(www.hoovers.com)*.

22. See Porter, *Competitive Strategy*, ch. 4.

23. Yochi J. Dreazen and Shawn Young, "Regulators Stop Short of a Verizon Split," *Wall Street Journal*, March 23, 2001, p. A3.

24. Philip Kotler and Paul N. Bloom, "Strategies for High Market-Share Companies," *Harvard Business Review* (November–December 1975): 63–72. Also see Porter, *Competitive Advantage*, pp. 221–26.

25. Daniel Lyons, "Solar Power," *Forbes*, January 22, 2001, p. 82; Robert D. Hof, "A Java in Every Pot? Sun Aims to Make It the Language of All Smart Appliances," *BusinessWeek*, July 27, 1998, p. 71.

26. Robert J. O'Harrow Jr., "PepsiCo to Acquire Quaker for $14 Billion," *Washington Post*, December 5, 2000, p. E1; Holman W. Jenkins Jr., "Business World: On a Happier Note, Orange Juice," *Wall Street Journal*, September 23, 1998, p. A23.

27. Shari Caudron, "Guerrilla Tactics," *IndustryWeek*, July 16, 2001, pp. 53+; "If You Can't Stand the Heat, Stay Out of the Streets," *Brandweek*, November 12, 2001, p. 36.
28. William J. Holstein, "Samsung's Golden Touch," *Fortune*, April 1, 2002, pp. 89–94.
29. Amy Goldwasser, "Something Stylish, Something Blue," *Business 2.0*, February 2002, pp. 94–96.
30. Theodore Levitt, "Innovative Imitation," *Harvard Business Review*, September–October 1966, pp. 63ff. Also see Steven P. Schnaars, *Managing Imitation Strategies: How Later Entrants Seize Markets from Pioneers* (New York: Free Press, 1994).
31. Greg Burns, "A Fruit Loop by Any Other Name," *BusinessWeek*, June 26, 1995, pp. 72, 76.
32. Stuart F. Brown, "The Company that Out-Harleys Harley," *Fortune*, September 28, 1998, pp. 56–57.
33. Antonio Ligi, "The Bottom Line: Logitech Plots Its Escape from Mouse Trap," *Dow Jones Newswire*, February 20, 2001; Allen J. McGrath, "Growth Strategies with a '90s Twist," *Across the Board*, March 1995, pp. 43–46.

CHAPTER 9

Identifying Market Segments and Selecting Target Markets

In this chapter, we will address the following questions:

1. How can a company identify the segments that make up a market?
2. What criteria can a company use to choose the most attractive target markets?

MARKETING MANAGEMENT AT HALLMARK CARDS

Hallmark has a card for every person and every occasion. The market leader in the greeting-card market rigorously segments the consumer market to identify segments and niches for new products and product lines. Its marketers segment by race, religion, occasion, age, national origin, price-sensitivity, and other variables. For example, the Hallmark En Español brand covers more than 1,000 cards designed for Hispanic Americans; the Mahogany brand targets African American card buyers; the Tree of Life brand targets Jewish Americans; the Fresh Ink brand targets 18-to-39-year-old women; and the Warm Wishes brand—priced at 99 cents—targets price-sensitive card buyers.

Once the company has established an overall brand for cards targeting a specific segment, it creates one or more product lines geared to attractive subsegments. The Mahogany brand covers not only a line of Kwanza holiday cards but also a Legacy of

Greatness line recognizing African Americans for their contributions to society. The Tree of Life brand serves as an umbrella for 300 cards, including various holiday cards and occasion-oriented cards, such as Bar and Bat Mitzvah celebrations. Building on this segmentation strategy, Hallmark expects to boost revenues beyond $10 billion by 2010.[1]

A company cannot serve everyone in broad markets such as greeting cards (for consumers) and computers (for businesses), because the customers are too numerous and diverse in their buying requirements. This is why marketers look for specific market segments that they can serve more effectively. Instead of scattering their marketing efforts (a "shotgun" approach), they focus on the buyers whom they have the greatest chance of satisfying (a "rifle" approach).

    Target marketing requires marketers to take three major steps: (1) Identify and profile distinct groups of buyers who might require separate products or marketing mixes (market segmentation); (2) select one or more market segments to enter (market targeting); and (3) establish and communicate the product's key distinctive benefits to the target market (market positioning). This chapter focuses on the first two steps; the following chapter will discuss positioning strategy.

USING MARKET SEGMENTATION

Sellers that use **mass marketing** engage in the mass production, distribution, and promotion of one product for all buyers. Henry Ford epitomized this strategy when he offered the Model T Ford "in any color, as long as it is black." Coca-Cola also used mass marketing when it sold only one kind of Coke in a 6.5-ounce bottle.

    The argument for mass marketing is that it creates the largest potential market, which leads to the lowest costs, which in turn can lead to lower prices or higher margins. However, critics point to increased splintering of the market, which makes mass marketing more difficult. According to Regis McKenna, "[Consumers] have more ways to shop: at giant malls, specialty shops, and superstores; through mail-order catalogs, home shopping networks, and virtual stores on the Internet. And they are bombarded with messages pitched through a growing number of channels: broadcast and narrow-cast television, radio, on-line computer networks, the Internet, telephone services such as fax and telemarketing, and niche magazines and other print media."[2]

    This proliferation of media and distribution channels is making it increasingly difficult to reach a mass audience. Some claim that mass marketing is dying. Not surprisingly, many companies are turning to **micromarketing** at one of four levels: segments, niches, local areas, and individuals.

Segment Marketing

A **market segment** consists of a group of customers who share a similar set of wants, such as car buyers who are primarily seeking low-cost transportation and those seeking a luxurious driving experience. However, a *segment* is not a *sector*. "Young, middle-income car buyers" is a **sector**, not a segment, because these buyers will differ in what they want in a car.

    Because the wants of segment members are similar but not identical, Anderson and Narus urge marketers to present flexible market offerings instead of one standard offering to all of a segment's members.[3] A **flexible market offering** consists of the product and service elements that all segment members value, plus *discretionary options* (for an additional charge) that some members value. For example, Delta Airlines offers economy passengers a seat, food, and soft drinks, but it charges extra for alcoholic beverages.

Niche Marketing

A **niche** is a more narrowly defined group seeking a distinctive mix of benefits. Marketers usually identify niches by dividing a segment into subsegments. For example, the segment of heavy smokers includes two niches: those who are trying to stop smoking and those who don't care.

In an attractive niche, customers have a distinct set of needs; they will pay a premium to the firm that best satisfies their needs; the niche is not likely to attract other competitors; the nicher gains certain economies through specialization; and the niche has size, profit, and growth potential. Whereas segments are fairly large and attract several competitors, niches are fairly small and may attract one or two rivals. Still, giants such as IBM can and do lose pieces of their market to nichers: Dalgic and Leeuw labeled this confrontation "guerrillas against gorillas."[4]

Hallmark and many other giants have, therefore, turned to niche marketing. In Germany, for example, Tetra Food supplies 80 percent of the food for tropical fish; Hohner holds 85 percent of the world's harmonica market; and Becher has 50 percent of the world's oversized umbrella market. These firms succeed in their niches because they are dedicated to their customers, offer superior service, and innovate continuously.[5]

The low cost of Internet marketing has led small start-ups to serve niches. In fact, 15 percent of all commercial Web sites with fewer than 10 employees take in more than $100,000, and 2 percent ring up more than $1 million. The recipe for Internet niching success: Choose a hard-to-find product that customers don't need to see and touch. Consider Steve Warrington's successful online venture selling ostriches and related products (*www.ostrichesonline.com*). Launched for next to nothing on the Web, the business has 10,000 customers in 100 countries buying ostrich meat, feathers, leather jackets, videos, and eggshells.[6]

Local Marketing

Target marketing is leading to marketing programs tailored to the needs and wants of local customer groups (trading areas, neighborhoods, even individual stores). Citibank, for instance, adjusts its banking services in each branch depending on neighborhood demographics; Kraft helps supermarket chains identify the cheese assortment and shelf positioning that will optimize cheese sales in low-, middle-, and high-income stores and in different ethnic neighborhoods.

Proponents of local marketing see national advertising as wasteful because it fails to address local needs. Opponents argue that local marketing drives up manufacturing and marketing costs by reducing economies of scale. Logistical problems become magnified when companies try to meet varying local requirements, and a brand's overall image might be diluted if the product and message vary in different localities.

Individual Marketing

The ultimate level of segmentation leads to "segments of one," "customized marketing," or "one-to-one marketing."[7] In past centuries, consumers were served as individuals: The tailor fitted suits and the cobbler designed shoes for each individual. Now technology is enabling companies to mass-customize their offerings. **Mass customization** is a company's ability to prepare individually designed products, programs, and communications on a mass basis to meet each customer's requirements.[8]

For example, Andersen Windows, a $1 billion Minnesota-based manufacturer of residential windows, turned to mass customization after additions to its product line led to fat, unwieldy catalogs and a bewildering array of choices for homeowners and contractors. Then the firm equipped 650 showrooms with an interactive computer catalog linked directly to the factory. Using this catalog, salespeople help customers customize each window, check the design for structural soundness, and generate a price quote. Andersen has also developed a "batch of one" manufacturing process in which everything is made to order, reducing its finished parts inventory (a major cost to the company).[9]

Patterns of Market Segmentation

Market segments can be built up in many ways. One common method is to identify *preference segments.* Suppose ice cream buyers are asked how much they value sweetness and creaminess as two product attributes. Three different patterns can emerge:

- *Homogeneous preferences.* Figure 9.1a shows a market where all the consumers have roughly the same preferences, so there are no natural segments. We predict that existing brands would be similar and cluster around the middle of the scale in both sweetness and creaminess.
- *Diffused preferences.* At the other extreme, consumer preferences may be scattered throughout the space (Figure 9.1b), indicating great variance in consumer preferences. One brand might position in the center to appeal to most people; if several brands are in the market, they are likely to position throughout the space and show real differences to reflect consumer-preference differences.

FIGURE 9.1   Basic Market-Preference Patterns

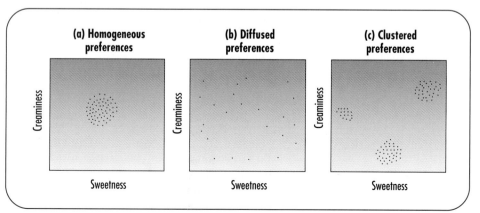

■ *Clustered preferences.* The market might reveal distinct preference clusters, called *natural market segments* (Figure 9.1c). The first firm in this market might position in the center to appeal to all groups, choose the largest market segment (*concentrated marketing*), or develop several brands for different segments. If the first firm has only one brand, competitors would enter and introduce brands in the other segments.

Market-Segmentation Process

Market researchers advocate a *needs-based market segmentation approach.* Roger Best proposed the seven-step process in Table 9.1. Because segments can change over time, market segmentation must be done periodically.

Companies can uncover new segments by researching the hierarchy of attributes that customers consider when choosing a brand, a process called **market partitioning**. For instance, some car buyers might first decide on the national origin of the manufacturer (*nation-dominant hierarchy*); others might first decide on brand (*brand-dominant hierarchy*), type of vehicle (*type-dominant*), or price (*price-dominant*). One segment might therefore be made up of buyers who are type/price/brand dominant; another might be made up of buyers who are quality/service/type dominant. Each segment may have distinct demographics, psychographics, and mediagraphics.[10]

Effective Segmentation

Not all segmentation is useful. For example, table salt buyers could be divided into blond and brunette customers, but hair color is not relevant to the purchase of salt. Furthermore, if all salt buyers buy the same amount of salt each month, believe all salt

TABLE 9.1   Steps in Segmentation Process

	Description
1. Needs-Based Segmentation	Group customers into segments based on similar needs and benefits sought by customer in solving a particular consumption problem.
2. Segment Identification	For each needs-based segment, determine which demographics, lifestyles, and usage behaviors make the segment distinct and identifiable (actionable).
3. Segment Attractiveness	Using predetermined segment attractiveness criteria (such as market growth, competitive intensity, and market access), determine the overall attractiveness of each segment.
4. Segment Profitability	Determine segment profitability.
5. Segment Positioning	For each segment, create a "value proposition" and product-price positioning strategy based on that segment's unique customer needs and characteristics.
6. Segment "Acid Test"	Create "segment storyboards" to test the attractiveness of each segment's positioning strategy.
7. Marketing-Mix Strategy	Expand segment positioning strategy to include all aspects of the marketing mix: product, price, promotion, and place.

Source: Adapted from Robert J. Best, *Market-Based Management* (Upper Saddle River, NJ: Prentice Hall, 2000).

is the same, and pay only one price for salt, this market would
mentable from a marketing perspective. To be useful, market segm

- *Measurable*. The size, purchasing power, and characteristics of
  measured.
- *Substantial*. The segments are large and profitable enough to
  the largest possible homogeneous group worth pursuing with
- *Accessible*. The segments can be effectively reached and serve
- *Differentiable*. The segments are conceptually distinguishabl
  ently to different marketing mixes. If two segments respond i
  offer, they are not separate segments.
- *Actionable*. Effective programs can be formulated for attract
  segments.

SEGMENTING CONSUMER AND BUSINESS MARKETS

Because of the inherent differences between consumer and business markets, marketers cannot use exactly the same variables to segment both. Instead, they use one
broad group of variables as the basis for consumer segmentation and another broad
group for business segmentation.

Bases for Segmenting Consumer Markets

In segmenting consumer markets, marketers can apply geographic, demographic, psychographic, and behavioral variables (see Table 9.2). Once the segments are formed,
the marketer sees whether different characteristics are associated with each consumer-
response segment. For example, the researcher might examine whether car buyers
who want "quality" rather than "low price" differ in their geographic, demographic,
and psychographic makeup. This will determine whether the segments are useful for
marketing purposes.

Geographic Segmentation   **Geographic segmentation** calls for dividing the market into different geographical units such as nations, states, regions, counties, cities, or
neighborhoods. The company can operate in one or a few geographic areas or operate
in all but pay attention to local variations. Pillsbury can even segment down to the zip
code level, using sophisticated software to analyze customer data according to preferences, suggestions, and purchasing patterns. This segmentation allows the company
to target specific marketing campaigns and establish the products to be stocked in
local grocery stores.[11]

Demographic Segmentation   In **demographic segmentation**, the market is
divided into groups on the basis of age and the other variables (Table 9.2.) One reason
this is the most popular segmentation method is that consumer wants, preferences,
and usage rates are often associated with demographic variables. Another reason is
that demographic variables are easier to measure. Even when the target market is
described in nondemographic terms (say, a personality type), the link back to demographic characteristics is needed to estimate the size of the target market and the
media that can be used to reach it.

BLE 9.2   Major Segmentation Variables for Consumer Markets

Geographic	
Region	Pacific, Mountain, West North Central, West South Central, East North Central, East South Central, South Atlantic, Middle Atlantic, New England
City or metro size	Under 5,000; 5,000–20,000; 20,000–50,000; 50,000–100,000; 100,000–250,000; 250,000–500,000; 500,000–1,000,000; 1,000,000–4,000,000; 4,000,000 or over
Density	Urban, suburban, rural
Climate	Northern, southern
Demographic	
Age	Under 6, 6–11, 12–19, 20–34, 35–49, 50–64, 65+
Family size	1–2, 3–4, 5+
Family life cycle	Young, single; young, married, no children; young, married, youngest child under 6; young, married, youngest child 6 or over; older, married, with children; older, married, no children under 18; older, single; other
Gender	Male, female
Income	Under $10,000; $10,000–$15,000; $15,000–$20,000; $20,000–$30,000; $30,000–$50,000; $50,000–$100,000; $100,000 and over
Occupation	Professional and technical; managers, officials, and proprietors; clerical sales; craftspeople; forepersons; operatives; farmers; retired; students; homemakers; unemployed
Education	Grade school or less; some high school; high school graduate; some college; college graduate
Religion	Catholic, Protestant, Jewish, Muslim, Hindu, other
Race	White, Black, Asian, Hispanic
Generation	Baby boomers, Generation Xers
Nationality	North American, South American, British, French, German, Italian, Japanese
Social class	Lower lowers, upper lowers, working class, middle class, upper middles, lower uppers, upper uppers
Psychographic	
Lifestyle	Culture-oriented, sports-oriented, outdoor-oriented
Personality	Compulsive, gregarious, authoritarian, ambitious
Behavioral	
Occasions	Regular occasion, special occasion
Benefits	Quality, service, economy, speed
User status	Nonuser, ex-user, potential user, first-time user, regular user
Usage rate	Light user, medium user, heavy user
Loyalty status	None, medium, strong, absolute
Readiness stage	Unaware, aware, informed, interested, desirous, intending to buy
Attitude toward product	Enthusiastic, positive, indifferent, negative, hostile

Here is how demographic variables can be used to segment consumer markets:

- *Age and life-cycle stage.* Consumer wants and abilities change with age, as Gerber realized when it decided to expand beyond baby foods because the market was growing more slowly due to lower birthrates, babies staying on formula longer, and children moving to solid foods sooner. The company hopes that parents who buy its baby food will go on to buy its Graduates foods for 1- to 3-year olds.[12] People also differ in their **life stage,** a major concern such as going through a divorce or buying a new home—concerns that marketers address with stage-specific offerings. However, age and life cycle can be tricky variables. For example, Ford originally designed its Mustang automobile to appeal to young people who wanted an inexpensive sports car. But when Ford found that all age groups were buying the car, it realized that the market was not the chronologically young, but the psychologically young.

- *Gender.* Gender segmentation has long been applied in clothing, cosmetics, and magazines. Occasionally other marketers notice an opportunity for gender segmentation. The Internet site iVillage.com reaped the benefits of gender segmentation after initially trying to appeal to a broader market. Noticing that Parent Soup and other offerings for women were the most popular, iVillage soon evolved into the leading women's online site, buying up women.com and other firms.[13]

- *Income.* Income segmentation is a long-standing practice in such categories as automobiles, boats, clothing, cosmetics, and travel. However, income does not always predict the best customers for a given product. The most economical cars are not bought by the really poor, but rather by those who think of themselves as poor relative to their status aspirations; medium-price and expensive cars tend to be purchased by the overprivileged segments of each social class.

- *Generation.* Each generation is profoundly influenced by the times in which it grows up—the music, movies, politics, and events of that period. Demographers call these groups *cohorts.* Because members of a cohort share the same experiences and have similar outlooks and values, effective marketing appeals use the icons and images that are prominent in the targeted cohort's experience. Schewe, Meredith, and Karlovich distinguish seven cohort groups, from the Depression cohort (in their 80s) to the Generation Y cohort (in their teens and 20s).[14]

- *Social class.* Social class strongly influences preference in cars, clothing, home furnishings, leisure activities, reading habits, and retailers, which is why many firms design products for specific social classes. However, the tastes of social classes can change over time. The 1990s were about ostentation for the upper classes; affluent tastes now run toward more utilitarian products.[15]

Psychographic Segmentation   In *psychographic segmentation,* buyers are divided into different groups on the basis of lifestyle, personality, or values. People within the same demographic group can exhibit very different psychographic profiles.

- *Lifestyle.* People exhibit many more lifestyles than are suggested by the seven social classes, and the offerings they buy express their lifestyles. Meat seems an unlikely product for lifestyle segmentation, but one Kroger supermarket in Nashville found that segmenting self-service meat products by lifestyle, not by type of meat, had a big payoff. This store created sections in the meat case such as "Meals in Minutes" and "Kids Love This Stuff" (hot dogs, hamburger patties, and the like). Focusing on lifestyle needs helped Kroger's boost both sales and profits.[16] Lifestyle segmentation does not always work: Nestlé introduced a brand of decaffeinated coffee for "late nighters," and it failed.

■ *Personality.* Marketers can endow their products with *brand personalities* that correspond to targeted consumer personalities. For instance, a brand may appear sincere (Gateway Computer), exciting (Nike), or rugged (Timberland).[17]

■ *Values.* **Core values** are the belief systems that underlie consumer attitudes and behaviors. Core values go much deeper than behavior or attitude, and determine, at a basic level, people's choices and desires over the long term. Marketers who use this segmentation variable believe that by appealing to people's inner selves, it is possible to influence purchase behavior. Although values often differ from culture to culture, Roper Reports has identified six values segments stretching across 35 countries: strivers (who focus on material and professional goals), devouts (who consider tradition and duty very important), altruists (who are interested in social issues), intimates (who value close personal relationships and family), fun seekers (who tend to be younger and usually male), and creatives (who are interested in education, knowledge, and technology).[18]

Behavioral Segmentation   In **behavioral segmentation,** buyers are divided into groups on the basis of their knowledge of, attitude toward, use of, or response to a product. Many marketers believe that behavioral variables—occasions, benefits, user status, usage rate, loyalty status, buyer-readiness stage, and attitude—are the best starting points for segmentation.

■ *Occasions.* Buyers can be distinguished according to the occasions when they develop a need, and purchase or use a product. For example, air travel is triggered by business, vacation, or family occasions, so an airline can specialize in one of these occasions. Thus, charter airlines serve groups of people who fly to a vacation destination. Occasion segmentation can help firms expand product usage, as the Curtis Candy Company did by urging consumers to buy candy for trick-or-treaters at Halloween. A company can also consider needs that arise from critical life events or transitions. This can alert service providers such as banks, lawyers, and employment counselors to ways in which they can help.[19]

■ *Benefits.* Buyers can be classified according to the benefits they seek. One study of travelers uncovered three benefit segments: those who travel to be with family, those who travel for adventure or education, and those who enjoy the "gambling" and "fun" aspects of travel.[20]

■ *User status.* Markets can be segmented into nonusers, ex-users, potential users, first-time users, and regular users of a product. The company's market position also influences its focus. Market leaders focus on attracting potential users, whereas smaller firms try to lure users away from the leader.

■ *Usage rate.* Markets can be segmented into light, medium, and heavy product users. Heavy users are often a small percentage of the market but account for a high percentage of total consumption. Marketers usually prefer to attract one heavy user rather than several light users, and they vary their promotional efforts accordingly. However, heavy users either are extremely loyal to one brand or are always looking for the lowest price and, therefore, never stay loyal to a brand.

- *Loyalty status.* Buyers can be divided into four groups according to brand loyalty status: hard-core loyals (who always buy one brand), split loyals (who are loyal to two or three brands), shifting loyals (who shift from one brand to another), and switchers (who show no loyalty to any brand).[21] Each market consists of different numbers of these four types of buyers; thus, a *brand-loyal market* has a high percentage of hard-core loyals. Companies have difficulty gaining more market share in such markets, and new competitors have difficulty breaking in. One caution: What appears to be brand loyalty may actually reflect habit, indifference, a low price, a high switching cost, or the nonavailability of other brands. Thus, marketers must carefully interpret what is behind observed purchasing patterns.

- *Buyer-readiness stage.* A market consists of people in different stages of readiness to buy a product: Some are unaware of the product, some are aware, some are informed, some are interested, some desire the product, and some intend to buy. The relative numbers make a big difference in designing the marketing program.

- *Attitude.* Five attitude groups can be found in a market: enthusiastic, positive, indifferent, negative, and hostile. So, for example, workers in a political campaign use the voter's attitude to determine how much time to spend with that voter. They may thank enthusiastic voters and remind them to vote, reinforce those who are positively disposed, try to win the votes of indifferent voters, and spend no time trying to change the attitudes of negative and hostile voters.

Multiattribute Segmentation (Geoclustering)   Marketers are increasingly combining several variables in an effort to identify smaller, better-defined target groups. Thus, a bank may not only identify a group of wealthy retired adults, but within that group may distinguish several segments depending on current income, assets, savings, and risk preferences.

One of the most promising developments in multiattribute segmentation is *geoclustering*, which yields richer descriptions of consumers and neighborhoods than does traditional demographics. Geoclustering can help a firm answer such questions as: Which clusters (neighborhoods or zip codes) contain our most valuable customers? How deeply have we already penetrated these segments? Which markets provide the best opportunities for growth?

Claritas Inc. has developed a geoclustering approach called PRIZM (Potential Rating Index by Zip Markets), classifying U.S. residential neighborhoods into 62 lifestyle groupings called PRIZM Clusters.[22] The groupings consider 39 factors in the broad categories of education and affluence, family life cycle, urbanization, race and ethnicity, and mobility. They cover specific geographic areas defined by zip code, zip + 4, census tract, and block group.

Each cluster has a descriptive title, such as *American Dreams* and *Rural Industria*. Within each cluster, members tend to lead similar lives, drive similar cars, have similar jobs, and read similar magazines. The *American Dreams* cluster, for example, is upscale and ethnic—a big-city mosaic of people likely to buy imported cars, read *Essence* magazine, and bank with a home computer. In contrast, *Rural Industria* contains young families in heartland offices and factories whose lifestyle is typified by trucks, fishing trips, and auto racing enthusiasm.[23]

Geoclustering captures the increasing diversity of the American population. Moreover, it can make microsegments more accessible even to smaller firms because of lower database costs, more sophisticated software, increased data integration, and wider use of the Internet.[24]

Bases for Segmenting Business Markets

Business markets can be segmented with some variables that are employed in consumer market segmentation, such as geography, benefits sought, and usage rate. Yet business marketers can also use several other variables. Bonoma and Shapiro proposed segmenting the business market with the variables shown in Table 9.3. The demographic variables are the most important, followed by the operating variables—down to the personal characteristics of the buyer.

A company should first decide which industries it wants to serve. Then, within a chosen target industry, the company can further segment by company size, possibly setting up separate operations for selling to large and small customers. Small businesses, in particular, have become a Holy Grail for business marketers, both on and off

TABLE 9.3   Major Segmentation Variables for Business Markets

Demographic

1. *Industry*: Which industries should we serve?

2. *Company size*: What size companies should we serve?

3. *Location*: What geographical areas should we serve?

Operating Variables

4. *Technology*: What customer technologies should we focus on?

5. *User or nonuser status*: Should we serve heavy users, medium users, light users, or nonusers?

6. *Customer capabilities*: Should we serve customers needing many or few services?

Purchasing Approaches

7. *Purchasing-function organization*: Should we serve companies with highly centralized or decentralized purchasing organizations?

8. *Power structure*: Should we serve companies that are engineering dominated, financially dominated, and so on?

9. *Nature of existing relationships*: Should we serve companies with which we have strong relationships or simply go after the most desirable companies?

10. *General purchase policies*: Should we serve companies that prefer leasing? Service contracts? Systems purchases? Sealed bidding?

11. *Purchasing criteria*: Should we serve companies that are seeking quality? Service? Price?

Situational Factors

12. *Urgency*: Should we serve companies that need quick and sudden delivery or service?

13. *Specific application*: Should we focus on certain applications of our product rather than all applications?

14. *Size of order*: Should we focus on large or small orders?

Personal Characteristics

15. *Buyer-seller similarity*: Should we serve companies whose people and values are similar to ours?

16. *Attitudes toward risk*: Should we serve risk-taking or risk-avoiding customers?

17. *Loyalty*: Should we serve companies that show high loyalty to their suppliers?

Source: Adapted from Thomas V. Bonoma and Benson P. Shapiro, *Segmenting the Industrial Market* (Lexington, MA: Lexington Books, 1983).

the Internet.[25] Small businesses are responsible for 50 percent of the U.S. gross domestic product, according to the Small Business Administration—and this segment is growing faster than the large company segment.

IBM, already successful in marketing to corporate giants, is targeting small businesses (with 1,000 or fewer employees) and further targeting the subsegment of minority-owned small businesses. IBM's strategy is to devote some field salespeople exclusively to small and medium-size businesses, hire executives responsible for targeting subsegments, and become more involved in professional groups frequented by minority small-business owners.[26]

Marketers can be more effective even within mature commodity industries if they use segmentation for better targeting. For example, Rangan, Moriarty, and Swartz found four business segments within the steel strapping industry:[27]

1. *Programmed buyers.* Buyers who see the product as not very important to their operation. This is a very profitable segment: The buyers view the product as a routine purchase item, usually paying full price and receiving below-average service.

2. *Relationship buyers.* Buyers who regard the product as moderately important and are knowledgeable about competitive offerings. They get a small discount and a modest amount of service and prefer the vendor as long as the price is not far out of line. This is the second most profitable segment.

3. *Transaction buyers.* Buyers who see the product as very important to their operations. They are price- and service-sensitive and receive some discounts, but they know the competition and will switch for a better price, even sacrificing some service.

4. *Bargain hunters.* Buyers who see the product as very important and demand low prices and top service. They know the alternative suppliers, bargain hard, and are ready to switch if dissatisfied. The company needs these buyers for volume purposes, but they are not very profitable.

Rackham and DeVincentis proposed a segmentation scheme classifying business buyers into three groups, each warranting a different sales approach: price-oriented customers (transactional selling); solution-oriented customers (consultative selling); and strategic-value customers (enterprise selling).[28] Clearly, segmentation can help a business marketer develop an appropriate marketing mix for each targeted segment.[29]

MARKET TARGETING STRATEGIES

Once the firm has identified its market-segment opportunities, it has to evaluate each segment and decide how many and which ones to target.

Evaluating and Selecting Market Segments

In evaluating different market segments, the firm must look at two factors: the segment's overall attractiveness, and the company's objectives and resources. First, the firm must ask whether a potential segment has the characteristics that make it generally attractive, such as size, growth, profitability, scale economies, and low risk. Second, the firm must consider whether investing in the segment makes sense given the firm's objectives and resources. Some attractive segments could be dismissed because they do not mesh with the company's long-term objectives; some should be dismissed if the company lacks one or more of the competencies needed to offer superior value (see "Marketing Skills: Evaluating Segments").

Having evaluated different segments, the company can consider five patterns of target market selection, as shown in Figure 9.2.

Single-Segment Concentration Volkswagen concentrates on the small-car market, while Porsche concentrates on the sports car market. Through concentrated marketing, these firms gain a thorough understanding of the chosen segment's needs and achieve a strong market presence. Furthermore, each firm enjoys operating economies by specializing in its production, distribution, and promotion; if it gains leadership, it can earn a high return on investment.

However, concentrated marketing involves risks: the segment may turn sour because of changes in buying patterns or new competition. For these reasons, many companies prefer to operate in more than one segment.

Selective Specialization Here the firm selects a number of segments, each objectively attractive and appropriate. There may be little or no synergy among the segments, but each segment promises to be a moneymaker. This strategy has the advan-

---

MARKETING SKILLS: EVALUATING SEGMENTS

Determining which of the identified segments a company should enter is a high-stakes activity, because choosing the wrong segment(s) can waste money and divert attention from more profitable segments. Therefore, marketers need to develop the vital skill of evaluating segments. To start, they must establish criteria to use in weighing a segment's attractiveness. These may be market growth measures such as size and growth potential; competitive intensity measures such as number of competitors and ease of market entry; and market access measures such as channel access and fit with company resources. This analysis shows which segments are more attractive on each measure.

Now the marketer has to establish the criteria for screening out unsuitable segments, such as segments that would be illegal or controversial for the company to target. Some companies use the potential for significant risks—such as imminent political unrest—to eliminate particular segments. The next step is to estimate the likely sales and profits from the remaining segments and use these figures, along with the attractiveness criteria, to rank the segments. Some marketers determine the order of entry by calculating a composite score for each segment, giving priority to segments with the highest scores (unless the company's strategy or mission requires another ranking method).

Delta Education, based in New Hampshire, has used segmentation to fuel sales growth past $50 million in annual revenues. The company sells science and math products on the Web, through stores, and through catalogs. Among the criteria it uses to evaluate segments are: average sales and profits; frequency of purchasing; and recency of purchase. Applying these criteria, Delta ranked multiple-purchase segments ahead of single-purchase segments and more-recent-purchase segments ahead of less-recent-purchase segments. "The faster [customers] get from that first order to that second order," says Delta's head of sales and marketing, "the better their lifetime value and retention."[30]

FIGURE 9.2 Five Patterns of Target Market Selection

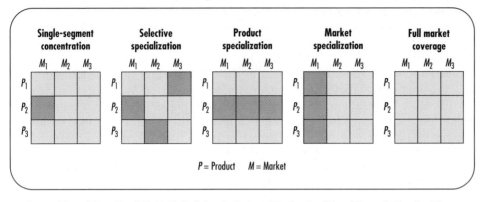

Source: Adapted from Derek F. Abell, *Defining the Business: The Starting Point of Strategic Planning* (Upper Saddle River, NJ: Prentice Hall, 1980), ch. 8, pp. 192–96.

tage of diversifying the firm's risk. Consider a radio broadcaster that wants to appeal to both younger and older listeners. Emmis Communications owns New York's WRKS-RM, which describes itself as "smooth R&B [rhythm and blues] and classic soul" and appeals to older listeners, as well as WQHT-FM, which plays hip-hop (urban street music) for under-25 listeners.[31]

Product Specialization Another approach is to specialize in making a certain product for several segments. An example would be a microscope manufacturer that sells microscopes to university laboratories, government laboratories, and commercial laboratories. The firm makes different microscopes for different customer groups and builds a strong reputation in the specific product area. The downside risk is that the product may be supplanted by an entirely new technology.

Market Specialization Here, the firm concentrates on serving many needs of a particular customer group. An example would be a firm that sells an assortment of products only to university laboratories. The firm gains a strong reputation in serving this customer group and becomes a channel for further products that the customer group can use. The downside risk is that the customer group may suffer budget cuts.

Full Market Coverage The firm attempts to serve all customer groups with all the products they might need. Only very large firms such as IBM (computer market), General Motors (vehicle market), and Coca-Cola (drink market) can undertake a full market coverage strategy. Large firms can cover a whole market through undifferentiated marketing or differentiated marketing.

In *undifferentiated marketing*, the firm ignores segment differences and goes after the whole market with one market offer. It designs a product and a marketing program that will appeal to the broadest number of buyers, then uses mass distribution backed by mass advertising to create a superior product image. The narrow product line keeps down costs of research and development, production, inventory, transportation, marketing research, advertising, and product management; the undifferentiated advertising program keeps down advertising costs. Presumably, the company can turn its lower costs into lower prices to win over price-sensitive customers.

In *differentiated marketing*, the firm operates in several market segments and designs different programs for each segment. General Motors does this with its various vehicle brands and models; Intel does this with chips and programs for consumer, business, small business, networking, digital imaging, and video markets.[32] Differentiated marketing typically creates more total sales than undifferentiated marketing. However, it also increases the firm's costs for product modification, manufacturing, administration, inventory, and promotion.

Because differentiated marketing leads to both higher sales and higher costs, we cannot generalize regarding this strategy's profitability. Still, companies should be cautious about oversegmenting their market. If this happens, they may want to use *countersegmentation* to broaden their customer base. As an example, Smith Kline Beecham introduced Aquafresh toothpaste to attract three benefit segments simultaneously: those seeking fresh breath, whiter teeth, and cavity protection.

Targeting Multiple Segments and Supersegments

Very often, companies start marketing to one segment, then expand to others. For example, Motorola used the results of a 25-nation segmentation study to create four sub-brands for its mobile phones, each appealing to a different segment. Accompli is for customers seeking leading-edge wireless technology; Timeport is for business users who view phones as a tool; V. is for status-seeking users who want the latest styles and technology; and Talkabout is for users who want everyday calling capabilities.[33]

In targeting more than one segment, a company should examine segment interrelationships on the cost, performance, and technology side. A company carrying fixed costs, such as a sales force or store outlets, can add products to absorb and share some costs. Economies of scope can be just as important as economies of scale. Moreover, companies should look beyond isolated segments to target a **supersegment,** a set of segments that share some exploitable similarity. For example, many symphony orchestras target people with broad cultural interests, rather than only those who attend concerts.

Still, a company's invasion plans can be thwarted when it confronts blocked markets. This problem calls for **megamarketing,** the strategic coordination of economic, psychological, political, and public-relations skills to gain the cooperation of a number of parties in order to enter or operate in a given market. Pepsi used megamarketing to enter India after Coca-Cola left the market. First, it worked with a local business group to gain government approval for its entry over the objections of domestic soft-drink companies and anti-multinational legislators. Pepsi also offered to help India export enough agricultural products to more than cover the cost of importing soft-drink concentrate and promised economic development for some rural areas. By winning the support of these and other interest groups, Pepsi was finally able to crack the Indian market.

Ethical Choice of Market Targets

Market targeting sometimes generates public controversy.[34] The public is concerned when marketers take unfair advantage of vulnerable groups (such as children) or disadvantaged groups (such as inner-city poor people), or promote potentially harmful products. For example, the cereal industry has been criticized for marketing to children. Critics worry that high-powered appeals presented through the mouths of animated characters will lead children to eat too much sugared cereal or poorly balanced breakfasts.

As another example, G. Heileman Brewing drew fire when it extended its Colt 45 malt liquor line with Powermaster, which has 5.9 percent alcohol. Federal officials, industry leaders, black activists, and the media charged that Heileman was targeting African Americans extensively with this product.[35]

Not all attempts to target children, minorities, or other segments draw criticism. Colgate-Palmolive's Colgate Junior toothpaste has special features designed to get children to brush longer and more often. Also, black-owned ICE theaters noticed that although moviegoing by blacks has surged, there is a dearth of inner-city theaters, so it began opening theaters in Chicago and other cities. ICE partners with the black communities in which it operates, using local radio stations to promote films and featuring favorite foods at concession stands.[36]

Thus the issue is not who is targeted, but rather how and for what purpose.[37] Socially responsible marketing calls for targeting and positioning that serve not only the company's interests but also the interests of the targeted segments.

EXECUTIVE SUMMARY

Target marketing involves three activities: market segmentation, market targeting, and market positioning. Markets can be targeted at four levels: segments, niches, local areas, and individuals. Market segments are large, identifiable groups within a market. A niche is a more narrowly defined group. Many marketers localize their marketing programs for certain trading areas, neighborhoods, and even individual stores. More marketers now practice individual marketing and mass customization.

The major segmentation variables for consumer markets are geographic, demographic, psychographic, and behavioral, used singly or in combination. Business marketers can use all of these variables along with operating variables, purchasing approaches, and situational factors. To be useful, market segments must be measurable, substantial, accessible, differentiable, and actionable.

Once a firm has identified its market-segment opportunities, it has to evaluate the various segments and decide how many and which ones to target. In evaluating segments, managers look at the segment's attractiveness indicators and the company's objectives and resources. In choosing which segments to target, the company can focus on a single segment, selected segments, a specific product, a specific market, or the full market. In targeting the full market, it can use either differentiated or undifferentiated marketing. Marketers should choose target markets in a socially responsible manner by ensuring that the targeting serves the interests of the market being targeted as well as the company.

NOTES

1. "AG, Hallmark Build on Ethnic Diversity," *MMR*, October 15, 2001, pp. 37+; "New Arrangements at Hallmark," *Promo*, May 1, 2001, pp. 77+; Beth Whitehouse, "Season's Greetings," *Newsday*, December 11, 2000, p. B6.
2. Regis McKenna, "Real-Time Marketing," *Harvard Business Review*, July–August 1995, p. 87.

3. See James C. Anderson and James A. Narus, "Capturing the Value of Supplementary Services," *Harvard Business Review* (January–February 1995): 75–83.

4. See Tevfik Dalgic and Maarten Leeuw, "Niche Marketing Revisited: Concept, Applications, and Some European Cases," *European Journal of Marketing* 28, no. 4 (1994): 39–55.

5. Hermann Simon, *Hidden Champions* (Boston: Harvard Business School Press, 1996); "Hohner Expands with New U.S. Headquarters," *Music Trades*, February 2000, p. 48.

6. Paul Davidson, "Entrepreneurs Reap Riches from Net Niches," *USA Today*, April 20, 1998, p. B3, (***www.ostrichesonline.com***).

7. See Don Peppers and Martha Rogers, *The One to One Future: Building Relationships One Customer at a Time* (New York: Currency/Doubleday, 1993).

8. B. Joseph Pine II, *Mass Customization* (Boston: Harvard Business School Press, 1993); B. Joseph Pine II, Don Peppers, and Martha Rogers, "Do You Want to Keep Your Customers Forever?" *Harvard Business Review* (March–April 1995): 103–14.

9. "Creating Greater Customer Value May Require a Lot of Changes," *Organizational Dynamics*, Summer 1998, p. 26.

10. For a market-structure study of the hierarchy of attributes in the coffee market, see Dipak Jain, Frank M. Bass, and Yu-Min Chen, "Estimation of Latent Class Models with Heterogeneous Choice Probabilities: An Application to Market Structuring," *Journal of Marketing Research* (February 1990): 94–101.

11. Roger Crockett, "Pillsbury's New Software Will Let the Food Giant Slice and Dice Reams of Data, Changing Everything About How It Caters to Consumers," *BusinessWeek*, April 3, 2000, p. EB78.

12. Leah Rickard, "Gerber Trots Out New Ads Backing Toddler Food Line," *Advertising Age*, April 11, 1994, pp. 1, 48.

13. Valerie Seckler, "TVillage Posts Pro Forma Profit, Buys Direct Marketing Firm," *WWD*, February 13, 2002, p. 16; Lisa Napoli, "A Focus on Women at iVillage.com," *New York Times*, August 3, 1998, p. D6; Linda Himelstein, "I Am Cyber-Woman. Hear Me Roar," *BusinessWeek*, November 15, 1999, p. 40.

14. Geoffrey E. Meredith and Charles D. Schewe with Janice Karlovich, *Defining Markets, Defining Moments* (New York: Hungrey Minds, 2002).

15. Andrew E. Serwer, "42,496 Secrets Bared," *Fortune*, January 24, 1994, pp. 13–14; Kenneth Labich, "Class in America," *Fortune*, February 7, 1994, pp. 114–26.

16. "Lifestyle Marketing," *Progressive Grocer*, August 1997, pp. 107–10.

17. See Jennifer Aaker, "Dimensions of Brand Personality," *Journal of Marketing Research* (August 1997): 347–56.

18. Tom Miller, "Global Segments from 'Strivers' to 'Creatives,' " *Marketing News*, July 20, 1998, p. 11.

19. Cathy Goodwin and James W. Gentry, "Life Transition as a Basis for Segmentation," *Journal of Segmentation in Marketing* 4, no. 1 (2000).

20. Junu Bryan Kim, "Taking Comfort in Country: After Decade of '80s Excess, Marketers Tap Easy Lifestyle as Part of Ad Messages," *Advertising Age*, January 11, 1993, pp. S1–S4.

21. This classification was adapted from George H. Brown, "Brand Loyalty—Fact or Fiction?" *Advertising Age*, June 1952–January 1953, a series. See also Peter E. Rossi, R. McCulloch, and G. Allenby, "The Value of Purchase History Data in Target Marketing," *Marketing Science* 15, no. 4 (1996): 321–40.

22. Other leading suppliers of geodemographic data are ClusterPlus (by Donnelly Marketing Information Services) and C.A.C.I. International, which offers ACORN.

23. Christina Del Valle, "They Know Where You Live—and How You Buy," *BusinessWeek*, February 7, 1994, p. 89.

24. See Michael J. Weiss, *The Clustering of America* (New York: Harper & Row, 1988).

25. Jesse Berst, "Why Small Business Is Suddenly Big Business," *ZDNet AnchorDesk*, November 29, 1999, *(www.anchordesk.com)*; Michele Marchetti, "Dell Computer," *Sales & Marketing Management*, October 1997, pp. 50–53.

26. Geoffrey Brewer, "Lou Gerstner Has His Hands Full," *Sales & Marketing Management*, May 1998, pp. 36–41.

27. V. Kasturi Rangan, Rowland T. Moriarty, and Gordon S. Swartz, "Segmenting Customers in Mature Industrial Markets," *Journal of Marketing* (October 1992): 72–82.

28. Neil Rackham and John DeVincentis, Rethinking the Sales Force: Redefining Selling to Create and Capture Customer Value (New York: McGraw-Hill, 1999) ch. 1.

29. For another interesting approach to segmenting the business market, see John Berrigan and Carl Finkbeiner, *Segmentation Marketing: New Methods for Capturing Business* (New York: HarperBusiness, 1992).

30. Roger J. Best, *Market-Based Management*, 2nd ed (Upper Saddle River, NJ: Prentice Hall, 2000), pp. 111–14; Marian Burk Wood, *The Marketing Plan: A Handbook* (Upper Saddle River, NJ: Prentice Hall, 2003), pp. 63–65; Patricia Odell, "A-Plus," *Direct*, September 15, 2000, p. E7.

31. Wendy Brandes, "Advertising: Black-Oriented Radio Tunes into Narrower Segments," *Wall Street Journal*, February 13, 1995, p. B5; "Emmis Reports Record Third Quarter" Emmis, *PR Newswire*, December 21, 1999 (*www.prnewswire.com*).

32. Tom Davey, "Intel Reorganization Reflects Changing Market," *Information Week Online*, November 25, 1999 (*www.informationweek.com*).

33. Bhanu Pande, "Upwardly Mobiles," *Business Standard*, May 30, 2000, p. 1 (*www.motorola.com*).

34. See Bart Macchiette and Roy Abhijit, "Sensitive Groups and Social Issues," *Journal of Consumer Marketing* 11, no. 4 (1994): 55–64.

35. N. Craig Smith and Elizabeth Cooper-Martin, "Ethics and Target Marketing: The Role of Product Harm and Consumer Vulnerability," *Journal of Marketing* (July 1997): 11–20.

36. Roger O. Crockett, "They're Lining Up for Flicks in the 'Hood,'" *BusinessWeek*, June 8, 1998, pp. 75–76.

37. See "Selling Sin to Blacks," *Fortune*, October 21, 1991, p. 100; Martha T. Moore, "Putting on a Fresh Face," *USA Today*, January 3, 1992, pp. B1, B2; Dorothy J. Gaiter, "Black-Owned Firms Are Catching an Afrocentric Wave," *Wall Street Journal*, January 8, 1992, p. B2; and Maria Mallory, "Waking Up to a Major Market," *BusinessWeek*, March 23, 1992, pp. 70–73.

CHAPTER 10

Developing, Positioning, and Differentiating Products Through the Life Cycle

In this chapter, we will address the following questions:

1. What challenges does a company face in developing and introducing new products?
2. What are the main stages in developing new products, and how can they be managed better?
3. What factors affect the rate at which consumers adopt new products?
4. What marketing strategies are appropriate at each stage of the product life cycle?
5. How can a company choose and communicate an effective positioning in the market?

MARKETING MANAGEMENT AT RED BULL

Red Bull, a caffeine-enhanced soft drink, has gotten a huge global boost from smart marketing throughout the product life cycle. Made by the Austrian subsidiary of a company based in Thailand, the product is popular in 83 countries because its marketers are "keeping the shared Red Bull brand positioning alive in all markets," says marketing manager Sanit Wangvicha. What sets Red Bull apart is its blend of caffeine, vitamins, amino acids, and other ingredients; in addition, the brand has an edgy, extreme image that is quite different from Coca-Cola and other established brands.

Red Bull has built its mystique by sending "Mobile Energy Teams" of young marketers to launch the drink through sampling in local night clubs, bars, sporting events, student haunts, and other venues. In the United States, Red Bull started sampling in San Francisco, Venice Beach, and Santa Monica. Over time, it expanded into convenience stores, restaurants, and supermarkets in these test markets. Only then did Red Bull target larger markets like Miami, Chicago, and Atlanta. By building a buzz to boost sales, Red Bull broke into the ranks of the top 10 U.S. carbonated soft drinks after only four years. Looking ahead, Red Bull is seeking more sales growth with the introduction of LunAqua, a caffeine-enhanced bottled water, and other new products.[1]

New product development can shape a company's future. Customers constantly want new products (such as Red Bull), and competitors are always vying to provide them: Coca-Cola introduced KMX, and Anheuser-Busch introduced 180 to enter the energy-drink market. Consumer-product firms churn out over 31,000 new products (including line extensions and new brands) every year. However, not every new product catches on, and those that do are adopted by customers at different rates.

Companies normally reformulate their marketing strategy several times during a product's life as economic conditions change, competitors launch new assaults, and the product passes through new stages of buyer interest and requirements. Consequently, companies must plan strategies that are appropriate to each stage in the product's life cycle and try to extend each product's life and profitability, knowing that no product lasts forever. The key to setting one offering apart from its competitors is to create a distinctive position in the market throughout the product's life cycle.

CHALLENGES IN NEW PRODUCT DEVELOPMENT

Companies that fail to develop new products are putting themselves at great risk. Over time, existing products are vulnerable to changing customer needs and tastes, new technologies, shortened product life cycles, and increased competition. Yet new-product development also entails considerable risk: Texas Instruments lost $660 million before leaving the home computer business; RCA lost $500 million on its videodisc players; the British-French Concorde aircraft will never recover its investment; and the bankrupt Iridium satellite phone system cost Motorola and its partners billions of dollars.[2]

A company can add new products in two ways: through acquisition (buying another company, buying another firm's patent, or buying a license or franchise) or through development (using its own laboratories, hiring independent researchers, or hiring a new-product-development firm). Moreover, there is more than one category of new products.

Types of New Products

Even though thousands of products are offered for the first time each year, less than 10 percent are entirely new and innovative. Booz, Allen & Hamilton has identified six categories of new products:[3]

1. *New-to-the-world products.* New, innovative products that create an entirely new market, such as Palm personal digital assistants.

2. *New product lines.* New products that allow a company to enter an established market for the first time, such as Fuji's brand of disks for Zip drives.

3. *Additions to existing product lines.* New products that supplement a company's established product lines (package sizes, flavors, and so on), such as Hallmark's e-mail greeting cards.

4. *Improvements and revisions of existing products.* New products that provide improved performance or greater perceived value and replace existing products, such as Windows XP.

5. *Re-positionings.* Existing products that are targeted to new markets or market segments, such as repositioning Johnson & Johnson's Baby Shampoo for adults as well as youngsters.

6. *Cost reductions.* New products that provide similar performance at lower cost, such as Intel's Celeron chip.

The new-to-the-world category involves the greatest cost and risk because these products are new to both the company and the marketplace, so positive customer response is far from certain. That's why most new-product activities are improvements on existing products. At Sony, for example, over 80 percent of new-product activity is undertaken to modify and improve existing Sony products. Even new-product improvements are not guaranteed to succeed, however.

Why New Products Fail—and Succeed

New products are failing at a disturbing rate. Recent studies put the failure rate of new U.S. consumer products at 95 percent and new European consumer products at 90 percent.[4] Some of the reasons for new-product failure are: a high-level executive pushes a favorite idea in spite of negative market research findings; the idea is good, but the market size is overestimated; the product is not well designed; the product is incorrectly positioned, ineffectively advertised, or overpriced; development costs are higher than expected; or competitors fight back harder than expected.

What can a company do to develop successful new products? Cooper and Kleinschmidt found that unique, superior products succeed 98 percent of the time, compared to products with a moderate advantage (58 percent success) or minimal advantage (18 percent success).[5] Madique and Zirger studied successful product launches in the electronics industry and found greater success when the firm has a better understanding of customer needs; a higher performance-to-cost ratio; a head-start in introducing the product before competitors; a higher expected contribution margin; a higher budget for promoting and launching the product; more use of cross-functional teamwork; and stronger top-management support.[6]

MANAGING NEW PRODUCTS: IDEAS TO STRATEGY

The process of developing new products spans eight stages, each with a particular set of marketing challenges and questions to answer (see Figure 10.1). If the company cannot answer "yes" to the key question at each of the first six stages, the new product will be dropped; in the final two stages, the company has the option of further devel-

FIGURE 10.1   The New-Product Development Decision Process

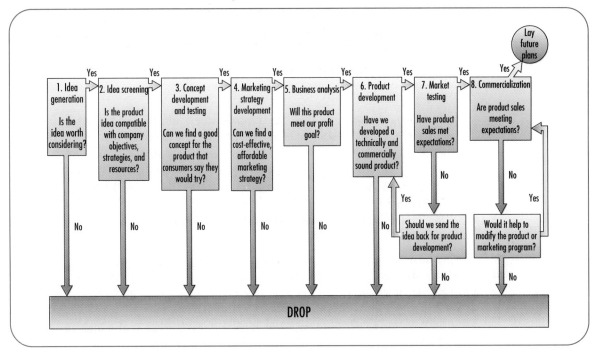

opment or modification rather than dropping the new product. This section covers the stages from idea to strategy and analysis; the following section covers the stages from product development through commercialization.

Idea Generation

The marketing concept holds that customer needs and wants are the logical place to start the search for new product ideas. Hippel has shown that the highest percentage of ideas for new industrial products originates with customers.[7] Many of the best ideas come from asking customers to describe their problems with current products. For instance, in an attempt to grab a foothold in steel wool soap pads, 3M asked consumer focus groups about problems with these products. The most frequent complaint was that the pads scratched expensive cookware. This sparked the idea for the successful Scotch-Brite Never Scratch pad.[8] In addition to customers, new-product ideas can come from many sources: scientists, competitors, employees, channel members, sales reps, top management, inventors, patent attorneys, university and commercial laboratories, industrial consultants, advertising agencies, research firms, and industry publications.

Idea Screening

The second step is to screen out weaker ideas, because product-development costs rise substantially with each successive development stage. Most companies require new-product ideas to be described on a standard form for review by a new-product committee. The description states the product idea, target market, and competition, along with estimates of market size, product price, development time and costs, manufacturing costs, and rate of return. The committee reviews each idea against criteria such as: Does the product meet a need and offer superior value? Will the new product deliver the expected sales volume, sales growth, and profit? Ideas that survive this screening move on to the concept development stage.

Concept Development

A *product idea* is a possible product the company might offer to the market. In contrast, a *product concept* is an elaborated version of the idea expressed in meaningful consumer terms. A product idea can be turned into several concepts by asking: Who will use this product? What primary benefit will it provide? When will people consume or use it? By answering such questions, a company can often form several product concepts, select the single most promising concept, and create a *product-positioning map* for it. Figure 10.2a shows the positioning of a product concept, a low-cost instant breakfast drink, compared to other breakfast foods already on the market.

Next, the product concept has to be turned into a brand concept. To transform the concept of a low-cost instant breakfast drink into a brand concept, the company must decide how much to charge and how calorific to make its drink. Figure 10.2b shows a brand-positioning map reflecting the positions of three instant breakfast drink brands. The gaps on this map indicate that the new brand concept would have to be distinctive in the medium-price, medium-calorie market or the high-price, high-calorie market.

Concept Testing

Concept testing involves presenting the product concept to appropriate target consumers and getting their reactions. The concepts can be presented symbolically or physically. However, the more the tested concepts resemble the final product or experience, the more dependable concept testing is. In the past, creating physical prototypes was costly and time-consuming, but computer-aided design and manufacturing programs have changed that. Today firms use *rapid prototyping* to design products on a

FIGURE 10.2   Product and Brand Positioning

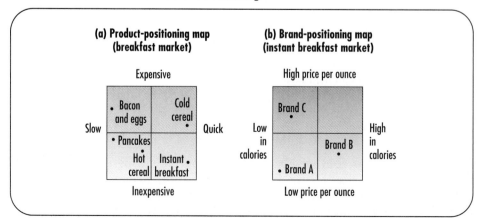

computer and then create plastic models to obtain feedback from potential consumers.[9] Companies are also using *virtual reality* to test product concepts.

Many companies use *customer-driven engineering* to design new products. Customer-driven engineering attaches high importance to incorporating customer preferences in the design. National Semiconductor uses the Internet to enhance its customer-driven engineering by offering design tools online and tracking what customers search for on its Web site. Sometimes, says the Web services manager, it is more important to know when a customer did not find a product than when he did. That helps the firm shrink the time needed to identify market niches and create new products.[10]

Marketing Strategy Development

After a successful concept test, the new-product manager will draft a three-part preliminary marketing-strategy plan for introducing the new product into the market. The first part describes the target market's size, structure, and behavior; the planned product positioning; and the sales, market share, and profit goals sought in the first few years. The second part outlines the planned price, distribution strategy, and marketing budget for the first year. The third part describes the long-run sales and profit goals and marketing-mix strategy over time. This plan forms the basis for the business analysis that is conducted before management makes a final decision on the new product.

Business Analysis

In this stage, the company evaluates the proposed new product's business attractiveness by preparing sales, cost, and profit projections to determine whether these satisfy company objectives. If they do, the concept can move to the product-development stage. This cannot be a static process: As new information emerges, the business analysis must be revised and expanded accordingly.

Estimating Total Sales   Management needs to estimate whether sales will be high enough to yield a satisfactory profit. Total estimated sales are the sum of estimated first-time sales, replacement sales, and repeat sales. For one-time purchased products, such as an engagement ring, sales rise at the beginning, peak, and later approach zero as the number of potential buyers is exhausted; if new buyers keep entering the market, the curve will not drop to zero. Infrequently purchased products—such as automobiles and industrial equipment—exhibit replacement cycles that are dictated by physical wearing out or by obsolescence due to changing styles, features, and performance; sales forecasting calls for estimating first-time sales and replacement sales separately.

For frequently purchased products, such as nondurables like soap, the number of first-time buyers initially increases and then decreases as fewer buyers are left (assuming a fixed population). Repeat purchases occur soon, providing that the product satisfies some buyers. The sales curve eventually falls to a plateau representing a level of steady repeat-purchase volume; by this time, the product is no longer a new product.

Estimating Costs and Profits   Management should also analyze expected costs and profits based on estimates prepared by the R&D, manufacturing, marketing, and finance departments. Companies use other financial measures to evaluate new-product proposals. The simplest is **break-even analysis**, in which management estimates how many units of the product the company will have to sell to break even with the given price and cost structure.

The most complex method of estimating profit is **risk analysis**. Here, three estimates (optimistic, pessimistic, and most likely) are obtained for each uncertain variable affecting profitability under an assumed marketing environment and marketing strategy for the planning period. The computer simulates possible outcomes and computes a rate-of-return probability distribution showing the range of possible rates of returns and their probabilities.[11]

MANAGING NEW PRODUCTS: DEVELOPMENT TO COMMERCIALIZATION

If the product concept passes the business analysis test, it is developed into a physical product. Up to now, it has existed only as a description, drawing, or prototype. This step involves a large jump in investment. If the company determines that the idea cannot be translated into a technically and commercially feasible product, the accumulated project cost will be lost—except for any useful information gained in the process.

Product Development

The job of translating target customer requirements into a working prototype is helped by a set of methods known as *quality function deployment* (QFD). This methodology takes the list of desired *customer attributes* (CAs) generated by market research and turns them into a list of *engineering attributes* (EAs) that the engineers can use. For example, customers of a proposed truck may want a certain acceleration rate (CA). Engineers turn this into the required horsepower and other engineering equivalents (EAs). QFD allows firms to measure the trade-offs and costs of satisfying customer requirements; it also improves communication among marketing, engineering, and manufacturing.[12]

Next, the firm uses QFD to develop one or more physical versions of the product concept. The goal is to find a prototype that customers believe embodies the key attributes described in the product-concept statement, that performs safely under normal use, and that can be produced within the budget. The rise of the World Wide Web has driven more rapid prototyping and more flexible development; prototype-driven firms such as Yahoo! and Microsoft cherish quick-and-dirty tests and experiments.[13]

When the prototypes are ready, they are put through rigorous functional tests and customer tests. *Alpha testing* means testing the product within the firm to see how it performs in different applications. After refining the prototype further, the company moves to *beta testing*, enlisting customers to use the prototype and give feedback. Beta testing is most useful when the potential customers are heterogeneous, the potential applications are not fully known, several decision makers are involved in purchasing the product, and opinion leadership from early adopters is sought.[14]

Consumer testing can take a variety of forms, from bringing consumers into a laboratory to giving them samples to use in their homes. In-home placement tests are common with many consumer products. For example, when DuPont developed new synthetic carpeting, it installed free carpeting in several homes in exchange for the homeowners' willingness to report their likes and dislikes about the carpeting.

Market Testing

After management is satisfied with functional and psychological performance, the product is ready to be dressed up with a brand name and packaging, and put to a market test. The new product is introduced into an authentic setting to learn how large the market is and how consumers and dealers react to handling, using, and repurchasing the product.

Consumer-Goods Market Testing   In testing consumer products, the company seeks to estimate four variables: trial, first repeat purchase, adoption, and purchase frequency. The company hopes to find all of these variables at high levels. In some cases, however, it will find many consumers trying the product but few rebuying it. Or it might find high permanent adoption but low purchase frequency (as with gourmet frozen foods).

Four major methods of consumer-goods market testing are sales-wave research, simulated test marketing, controlled test marketing, and test markets. In *sales-wave research*, consumers who initially try the product at no cost are reoffered the product, or a competitor's product, at slightly reduced prices, as many as three to five times (sales waves). The company notes how many customers select its product again and their reported level of satisfaction.

Simulated test marketing requires asking 30–40 qualified buyers to answer questions about brand familiarity and product preferences. These buyers are invited to look at commercials or print ads, including one for the new product; then they receive money and go into a store where they can make purchases. The company notes how many people buy the new brand and competing brands as a test of the ad's relative effectiveness in simulating trial. Consumers are also asked why they bought or did not buy; nonbuyers receive a free sample of the new product and are reinterviewed later to determine product attitudes, usage, satisfaction, and repurchase intention.[15]

In *controlled test marketing*, a research firm manages a panel of stores that will carry new products for a fee. The company with the new product specifies the number of stores and geographic locations it wants to test. The research firm delivers the product to the stores and controls shelf position; number of facings, displays, and point-of-purchase promotions; and pricing. Sales results can be measured through electronic scanners at the checkout. The company can also evaluate the impact of local advertising and promotions.

In full-blown *test markets*, the company chooses a few representative cities, the sales force sells the trade on carrying the product and giving it good exposure, and the company unleashes a complete advertising and promotion campaign in these markets. Marketers must decide on the number and location of test cities, length of the test, what to track, and what action to take. Today, many firms are skipping extended test marketing and relying instead on faster and more economical market-testing methods, such as smaller test areas and shorter test periods.

Business-Goods Market Testing   Business goods also benefit from market testing. Expensive industrial goods and new technologies will normally undergo both alpha and beta testing. In addition, new business products are sometimes market-tested at trade shows. Trade shows such as the annual American Booksellers Association convention draw a large number of buyers who view many new products in a few days. The vendor can observe how much interest buyers show in the new product, how they react to various features and terms, and how many express purchase intentions or place orders. The disadvantage of trade shows is that they reveal the product to competitors; therefore, the vendor should be ready to make any changes and launch the product soon after the trade show.

Commercialization

If the company goes ahead with commercialization, it will face its largest costs to date. The company will have to contract for manufacture or build or rent a full-scale manufacturing facility. Plant size will be a critical decision. When Quaker Oats launched its 100 Percent Natural breakfast cereal, it built a smaller plant than called for by the sales forecast. Demand so exceeded the forecast that for about a year the company could not supply enough of the product to stores. Although Quaker Oats was gratified with the response, the low forecast cost it a considerable amount of profit.

In addition to promotion, major decisions during this stage include timing, geographic strategy, target-market prospects, and introductory market strategy. Marketing timing is critical. If a firm learns that a competitor is nearing the end of its development work, it can choose: *first entry* (being first to market, locking up key distributors and customers, and gaining reputational leadership; however, if the product is not thoroughly debugged, it can acquire a flawed image); *parallel entry* (launching at the same time as a rival may gain both products more attention); or *late entry* (waiting until a competitor has born the cost of educating the market and revealed problems to avoid).

The company must also decide whether to launch the new product in one locality, one region, several regions, the national market, or the international market. Smaller companies often select one city for a blitz campaign, entering other cities one at a time; in contrast, large companies usually launch within a whole region and then move to the next region, although companies with national distribution generally launch new models nationally. More firms are rolling out new products simultaneously around the globe, a challenge in coordinating activities and obtaining agreement on strategy and tactics.

Within the rollout markets, the company must target its initial distribution and promotion to the best prospect groups. Presumably, the company has already profiled the prime prospects—who would ideally be early adopters, heavy users, and opinion leaders who are able to be reached at a low cost.[16] The company should rate the various prospect groups on these characteristics and target the best group to generate strong sales as soon as possible, motivate the sales force, and attract further prospects.

Finally, the company must develop an action plan for introducing the new product into the rollout markets. To coordinate the many activities involved in launching a new product, management can use network-planning techniques such as **critical path scheduling (CPS)**, which uses a master chart to show the simultaneous and sequential activities that must take place to launch the product. By estimating how much time each activity takes, the planners can estimate the project's completion time. A delay in any activity on the critical path will delay the entire project.[17]

THE CONSUMER ADOPTION PROCESS

Adoption is an individual's decision to become a regular user of a product. How do potential customers learn about new products, try them, and adopt or reject them? In the past, companies used a mass-market approach to introduce new products, on the assumption that most people are potential adopters. Yet consumers have different levels of interest in new products and brands. The theory of innovation diffusion and consumer adoption helps firms identify and target people who adopt products before the majority of consumers in a market.

Stages in the Adoption Process

An **innovation** refers to any good, service, or idea that is *perceived* by someone as new. The idea may have a long history, but it is an innovation to the person who sees it as new. Innovations take time to spread through the social system. Rogers defines the **innovation diffusion process** as "the spread of a new idea from its source of invention or creation to its ultimate users or adopters."[18] The adoption process focuses on the mental process through which a consumer passes from first hearing about an innovation to adoption.

Adopters of new products move through five stages: (1) *awareness* (consumer becomes aware of the innovation but has no information about it); (2) *interest* (consumer is stimulated to seek information); (3) *evaluation* (consumer considers whether to try the innovation); (4) *trial* (consumer tries the innovation to estimate its value); and (5) *adoption* (consumer decides to make full and regular use of the innovation).

Factors Influencing the Adoption Process

As Figure 10.3 shows, people adopt new products at different rates: Innovators are the first to adopt something new, while laggards are the last. Rogers defines a person's innovativeness as "the degree to which an individual is relatively earlier in adopting

FIGURE 10.3 Adopter Categorization on the Basis of Relative Time of Adoption of Innovation

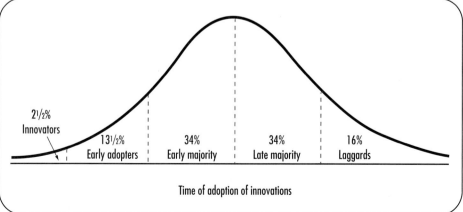

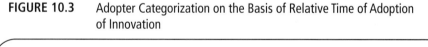

Source: Redrawn from Everett M. Rogers, *Diffusion of Innovations* (New York: The Free Press, 1983).

new ideas than the other members of his social system." Because people differ in their readiness to try new products, there are pioneers and early adopters for each product. After a slow start, an increasing number of people adopt the innovation, the number reaches a peak, and then it diminishes as fewer nonadopters remain.

Another factor affecting adoption is **personal influence**, the effect one person has on another's attitude or purchase probability. Although personal influence is greater in some situations and for some individuals, it is more important in the evaluation stage of the adoption process than in the other stages. It generally has more influence on late adopters and is more important in risky situations, as well.

Five characteristics influence the rate of adoption of an innovation. The first is *relative advantage*—the degree to which the innovation appears superior to existing products. The second is *compatibility*, the degree to which the innovation matches consumers' values and experiences. Third is *complexity*—the degree to which the innovation is relatively difficult to understand or use. Fourth is *divisibility*—the degree to which consumers can try the innovation on a limited basis. Fifth is *communicability*, the degree to which the benefits are observable or describable to others. Marketers must research and consider these factors in designing a new product and its marketing program.[19]

Finally, organizations vary in their readiness to adopt innovations. Adoption is associated with variables in the organization's environment, the organization itself (size, profits, pressure to change), and its managers. Other forces come into play when trying to get a product adopted into organizations that receive the bulk of their funding from the government. And a controversial or innovative product can be squelched by negative public opinion.

MARKETING THROUGH THE PRODUCT LIFE CYCLE

In today's dynamic marketing environment, a company's marketing strategy must change as the product, market, and competitors change over time. Here, we describe the concept of the product life cycle (PLC) and the changes that companies make as the product passes through each stage of the life cycle.

Product Life Cycles

To say that a product has a life cycle is to assert four things: (1) Products have a limited life; (2) product sales pass through distinct stages with different challenges, opportunities, and problems for the seller; (3) profits rise and fall at different stages of the product life cycle; and (4) products require different marketing, financial, manufacturing, purchasing, and human resource strategies in each stage. Most product life-cycle curves are portrayed as a bell-shape (Figure 10.4).

This PLC curve is typically divided into four stages.[20] In *introduction*, sales grow slowly as the product is introduced in the market, and profits are nonexistent due to heavy expenses incurred to launch the product. *Growth* is a period of rapid market acceptance and substantial profit improvement. In *maturity*, sales growth slows because the product has achieved acceptance by most potential buyers, and profits stabilize or decline because of increased competition. In *decline*, sales drift downward and profits erode. Table 10.1 summarizes the characteristics, objectives, and strategies associated with each stage.

FIGURE 10.4   Sales and Profit Life Cycles

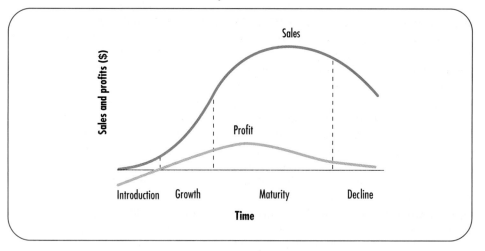

TABLE 10.1   Summary of Product Life-Cycle Characteristics, Objectives, and Strategies

		Introduction	Growth	Maturity Decline
Characteristics				
Sales		Low sales	Rapidly rising sales	Peak sales	Declining sales
Costs		High cost per customer	Average cost per customer	Low cost per customer	Low cost per customer
Profits		Negative	Rising profits	High profits	Declining profits
Customers		Innovators	Early adopters	Middle majority	Laggards
Competitors		Few	Growing Number	Stable number beginning to decline	Declining number
Marketing Objectives				
		Create product awareness and trial	Maximize market share	Maximize profit while defending market share	Reduce expenditure and milk the brand
Strategies				
Product		Offer a basic product	Offer product extensions, service, warranty	Diversify brands and items	Phase out weak models
Price		Charge cost-plus	Price to penetrate	Price to match or best market competitors'	Cut price
Distribution		Build selective distribution	Build intensive distribution	Build more intensive distribution	Go selective: phase out unprofitable outlets
Advertising		Build product awareness among early adopters and dealers	Build awareness and interest in the mass-market	Stress brand differences and benefits	Reduce to level needed to retain hard-core loyals
Sales Promotion		Use heavy sales promotion to entice trial	Reduce to take advantage of heavy consumer demand	Increase to encourage brand switching	Reduce to minimal level

Sources: Chester R. Wasson, *Dynamic Competitive Strategy and Product Life Cycles* (Austin, TX: Austin Press, 1978); John A. Weber, "Planning Corporate Growth with Inverted Product Life Cycles," *Long Range Planning* (October 1976): 12–29; Peter Doyle, "The Realities of the Product Life Cycle," *Quarterly Review of Marketing* (Summer 1976).

Marketing Strategies: Introduction Stage

Because it takes time to roll out a new product and fill dealer pipelines, sales growth tends to be slow at this stage. Buzzell identified several causes for the slow growth: delays in the expansion of production capacity, technical problems ("working out the bugs"), delays in obtaining adequate distribution through retail outlets, and customer reluctance to change established behaviors.[21] Sales of expensive new products are retarded by additional factors such as product complexity and fewer buyers.

Profits are negative or low in the introduction stage because of low sales and heavy distribution and promotion expenses. Much money is needed to attract distributors. Promotional expenditures are high because of the need to inform potential consumers, induce trial, and secure distribution. Firms focus on those buyers who are the most ready to buy, usually higher-income groups. Prices tend to be high because costs are high.

Companies must decide when to enter the market with a new product. Most studies indicate that the market pioneer gains the most advantage. Such pioneers as Amazon.com, Cisco, Coca-Cola, eBay, Eastman Kodak, Hallmark, and Microsoft developed sustained market dominance.

However, the pioneer advantage is not inevitable. Schnaars studied 28 industries in which the imitators surpassed the innovators and found several weaknesses among the failing pioneers, including new products that were too crude, were improperly positioned, or appeared before there was strong demand; product-development costs that exhausted the innovator's resources; a lack of resources to compete against entering larger firms; and managerial incompetence or unhealthy complacency. Successful imitators thrived by offering lower prices, improving the product more continuously, or using brute market power to overtake the pioneer.[22] Tellis and Golder identify the following factors as underpinning long-term market leadership: vision of a mass market; persistence; relentless innovation; financial commitment; and asset leverage.[23]

Still, the pioneer knows that competition will eventually enter the market and cause prices and its market share to fall. As competition and market share stabilize, buyers will no longer pay a price premium; some competitors will withdraw at this point, and the pioneer can build further share if it chooses.[24]

Marketing Strategies: Growth Stage

The growth stage is marked by a rapid climb in sales. Early adopters like the product, and additional consumers start buying it. Attracted by the opportunities, new competitors enter with new product features and expanded distribution. Prices remain where they are or fall slightly, depending on how fast demand increases. Companies maintain or increase their promotional expenditures to meet competition and to continue to educate the market, but sales rise much faster than promotional expenditures.

Profits increase during this stage as promotion costs are spread over a larger volume and unit manufacturing costs fall faster than price declines owing to the producer learning effect. During this stage, the firm uses several strategies to sustain rapid market growth as long as possible: improving product quality and adding new product features and improved styling; adding new models and flanker products; entering new market segments; increasing distribution coverage and entering new distribution channels; shifting from product-awareness advertising to product-preference advertising; and lowering prices to attract the next layer of price-sensitive buyers.

Marketing Strategies: Maturity Stage

At some point, the rate of sales growth will slow, and the product will enter a stage of relative maturity. This stage normally lasts longer than the previous stages, and poses formidable challenges to marketing management. *Most products are in the maturity stage of the life cycle, and most marketing managers cope with the problem of marketing the mature product.*

Three strategies for the maturity stage are market modification, product modification, and marketing-mix modification. Using market modification, the company might try to expand the market for its mature brand by working to expand the number of brand users. This is accomplished by *converting nonusers*; *entering new market segments* (as Johnson & Johnson did when promoting baby shampoo for adult use); or *winning competitors' customers* (the way Pepsi-Cola tries to woo Coca-Cola users). Volume can also be increased by convincing current brand users to increase their usage of the brand.

With product modification, managers try to stimulate sales by modifying the product's characteristics through quality improvement, feature improvement, or style improvement. *Quality improvement* aims at increasing the product's functional performance—its durability, reliability, and speed. *Feature improvement* adds new features that build the company's image as an innovator and win the loyalty of market segments that value these features. However, feature improvements are easily imitated; unless there is a permanent gain from being first, the improvement might not pay off in the long run.[25]

Product managers can try to stimulate sales by modifying other marketing-mix elements such as prices, distribution, advertising, sales promotion, personal selling, and services. For example, Goodyear boosted its market share from 14 to 16 percent in a year when it began selling tires through Wal-Mart, Sears, and Discount Tire.[26] Sales promotion has more impact at this stage because consumers have reached an equilibrium in their buying patterns, and psychological persuasion (advertising) is not as effective as financial persuasion (sales-promotion deals). Although brand managers use sales promotion because its effects are quicker and more visible, excessive sales-promotion activity can hurt the brand's image and long-run profit performance.

Marketing Strategies: Decline Stage

Sales decline for a number of reasons, including technological advances, shifts in consumer tastes, and increased competition. All of these factors lead to overcapacity, increased price cutting, and profit erosion. As sales and profits decline, some firms withdraw from the market. Those remaining may reduce the number of products they offer. They may withdraw from smaller market segments and weaker trade channels, and they may cut their promotion budget and reduce their prices further.

In a study of company strategies in declining industries, Harrigan identified five possible decline strategies:

1. Increasing the firm's investment (to dominate the market or strengthen competitive position)

2. Maintaining the firm's investment level until industry uncertainties are resolved

3. Decreasing the firm's investment level selectively, by dropping unprofitable customer groups, while simultaneously strengthening the firm's investment in lucrative niches

4. Harvesting ("milking") the firm's investment to recover cash quickly

5. Divesting the business quickly by disposing of assets as advantageously as possible.[27]

The appropriate decline strategy depends on the industry's relative attractiveness and the company's competitive strength in that industry. Pitney Bowes, which dominates the postage-meter market, faced critics who said that faxes and e-mail would hurt its profits. In response, Pitney recast itself as a messaging company and developed software to help business customers document and track product movement and payments.[28]

If the company were choosing between harvesting and divesting, its strategies would be quite different. *Harvesting* calls for gradually reducing a product's or business's costs while trying to maintain its sales. The first costs to cut are R&D costs and plant and equipment investment. The company might also reduce product quality, sales force size, marginal services, and advertising expenditures. It would try to cut these costs without letting customers, competitors, and employees know what is happening. Harvesting is an ethically ambivalent strategy, and it is difficult to execute, but it can substantially increase the company's current cash flow.[29]

Critique of the Product Life Cycle Concept

The PLC concept helps interpret product and market dynamics. It can be used for planning and control, although it is less useful as a forecasting tool because sales histories exhibit diverse patterns, and the stages vary in duration. Critics claim that life-cycle patterns are too variable in their shape and duration. They also say that marketers can seldom tell what stage the product is in: A product may appear to be mature when it is actually in a plateau prior to another upsurge. One final criticism is that the PLC pattern is the result of marketing strategies rather than an inevitable course that sales must follow. Marketers must therefore be careful when using the PLC.

POSITIONING AND DIFFERENTIATION STRATEGY

Companies need to develop and communicate a distinctive positioning for each offering throughout the product life cycle. **Positioning** is the act of designing the company's offering and image to occupy a distinctive place in the target market's mind. The end result of positioning is the successful creation of a market-focused *value proposition*, a cogent reason why the target market should buy the product.

Two Views of Positioning

The word *positioning* was popularized by two advertising executives, Al Ries and Jack Trout. They see positioning as a creative exercise done with an existing product:

> Positioning starts with a product. A piece of merchandise, a service, a company, an institution, or even a person. . . . But positioning is not what you do to a product. Positioning is what you do to the mind of the prospect. That is, you position the product in the mind of the prospect.

Ries and Trout argue that well-known products generally hold a distinctive position in customers' minds; Coca-Cola, for example, holds the position of world's largest soft-drink firm. To compete against this kind of position, a rival can strengthen its own current position in the consumer's mind (the way 7-Up advertised itself as the Uncola);

grab an unoccupied position (as Snapple did with its tea-based beverages), *de-position* or *re-position* the competition; or imply that it is in the club with the "best."[30]

Treacy and Wiersema propose a different positioning framework called *value disciplines*.[31] Within its industry, a firm could aspire to be the *product leader*, the *operationally excellent firm*, or the *customer intimate firm*. This is based on the notion that every market contains a mix of three types of customers. Some customers favor the firm that is advancing the technological frontier (product leadership); other customers want highly reliable performance (operational excellence), and still others want responsiveness in meeting their individual needs (customer intimacy). To succeed, a business should become the best at one of these value disciplines, perform adequately in the other disciplines, and continue improving in all the disciplines to fend off rivals.

How Many Ideas to Promote in Positioning?

Each company must decide how many ideas (e.g., benefits, features) to stress in its positioning. Ries and Trout favor one consistent positioning message.[32] With this approach, each brand is touted as "number one" on a particular attribute, such as "best

MARKETING SKILLS: MANAGING POSITIONING

Effective positioning extends well beyond advertising and promotion. Marketers need to manage positioning through every customer contact point, from online and telephone communication to personal sales and service. If the company does not back up its positioning strategy with consistent and appropriate actions, customers will—at the very least—be confused about what the company or brand stands for. To sharpen their skills in managing positioning, marketers can start by analyzing the positioning statement. What exact position does the company want to achieve in the minds of the target market? What need does this positioning address, and why would customers value this position?

Learning to take the customer's viewpoint is an integral part of this skill. Marketers should consider how the customer perceives the interaction and what the customer expects at each contact point. The next step is to formulate a strategy for managing the positioning at every contact point, including complaint handling. Marketers need to implement this strategy with training and guidelines to keep managers and employees focused on the communication and service requirements that support the desired position—as perceived by customers. Finally, firms must carefully monitor customer reaction and competitive activity for signs that the positioning or the way it is translated into day-to-day activities should be changed.

A good example of a company that carefully manages its positioning is Ritz-Carlton Hotels. Based on its "best-in-quality" positioning, the company provides employees with 120 hours of training every year. Employees learn the 20 rules that govern customer contacts, such as answering calls within three rings. Employees constantly note customer preferences and enter the details into a database used to tailor each customer's room and service offerings during subsequent visits. When a problem arises, Ritz employees apologize and correct the mistake. By managing its positioning at every contact point, Ritz has built a global reputation for legendary service.[35]

quality," "best service," "lowest price," or "most advanced technology." If a company hammers away at one positioning and delivers on it, it will probably be best known and recalled for this strength.

Not everyone sticks to single-benefit positioning. Smith Kline Beecham promotes its Aquafresh toothpaste as offering three benefits: anticavity protection, better breath, and whiter teeth. The firm therefore formulated the toothpaste so it squeezes out of the tube in three colors, visually confirming the three benefits.

Communicating the Positioning

To communicate a company or brand positioning, a marketing plan should include a *positioning statement* following the form: To (*target group and need*) our (*Brand*) is (*concept*) that (*point-of-difference*).[33] The *Mountain Dew* positioning is: "To young, active soft-drink consumers who have little time for sleep, Mountain Dew is the soft drink that gives you more energy than any other brand because it has the highest level of caffeine. With Mountain Dew, you can stay alert and keep going even when you haven't been able to get a good night's sleep."[34]

Once the company has developed a clear positioning strategy, it must communicate that positioning through all facets of the marketing mix and manage it through every point of contact (see "Marketing Skills: Managing Positioning").

Adding Further Differentiation

The task of positioning is to deliver a central idea about a company or an offering to the target market. Positioning simplifies what we think of the entity. Differentiation goes beyond to spin a complex web of differences characterizing that entity. **Differentiation** is the process of adding a set of meaningful and valued differences to distinguish the company's offering from competitors' offerings.

All products can be differentiated to some extent.[36] But not all brand differences are meaningful or worthwhile. A difference is stronger if it satisfies the following criteria:

- *Important*. The difference delivers a highly valued benefit to enough buyers.
- *Distinctive*. The difference is delivered in a distinctive way.
- *Superior*. The difference is superior to other ways of obtaining the benefit.
- *Preemptive*. The difference cannot be copied easily by competitors.
- *Affordable*. The buyer can afford to pay for the difference.
- *Profitable*. The company will find it profitable to introduce the difference.

Differentiation Tools

Even in commodity-type industries, some real or image differentiation is possible. Here we examine how a company can differentiate its market offering along five dimensions: product, services, personnel, channel, and image (Table 10.2).

Product Differentiation   Physical products vary in their potential for differentiation. At one extreme are products that allow little variation: chicken, steel, aspirin. Yet even here, some differentiation is possible: Procter & Gamble offers several laundry detergent brands, each with its own identity. At the other extreme are products that

TABLE 10.2   Differentiation Variables

Product	Services	Personnel	Channel	Image
Form	Ordering ease	Competence	Coverage	Symbols
Features	Delivery	Courtesy	Expertise	Media
Performance	Installation	Credibility	Performance	Atmosphere
Conformance	Customer training	Reliability		Events
Durability	Customer consulting	Responsiveness		
Reliability	Maintenance and repair	Communication		
Repairability	Miscellaneous			
Style				
Design				

can be highly differentiated, such as cars and furniture. Here the seller faces an abundance of design parameters, including:[37]

- *Form.* Many products can be differentiated in *form*—the product's size, shape, or physical structure. Consider the many possible forms taken by products such as aspirin, which can be differentiated by dosage size, shape, coating, and action time.
- *Features.* Features are the characteristics that supplement the product's basic function. Marketers start by asking recent buyers about additional features that would improve satisfaction, then determining which would be profitable to add, given the potential market, cost, and price.
- *Performance quality.* **Performance quality** is the level at which the product's primary characteristics operate. The Strategic Planning Institute found a significantly positive correlation between relative product quality and return on investment. Yet there are diminishing returns to higher performance quality, so marketers must choose a level suited to the target market and rivals' performance levels.
- *Conformance quality.* Buyers expect products to have a high **conformance quality**, which is the degree to which all of the produced units are identical and meet the promised specifications. The problem with low conformance quality is that the product will disappoint some buyers.
- *Durability.* **Durability**, a measure of the product's expected operating life under natural or stressful conditions, is important for products such as vehicles and appliances. However, the extra price must not be excessive, and the product must not be subject to rapid technological obsolescence.
- *Reliability.* Buyers normally will pay a premium for high **reliability**, a measure of the probability that a product will not malfunction or fail within a specified period. Maytag, for instance, has an outstanding reputation for reliable home appliances.
- *Repairability.* Buyers prefer products that are easy to repair. **Repairability** measures the ease of fixing a product when it malfunctions or fails. An automobile made with standard parts that are easily replaced has high repairability. Ideal repairability would exist if users could fix the product themselves with little cost or time.
- *Style.* Style describes the product's look and feel to the buyer. Buyers are normally willing to pay a premium for products that are attractively styled. Aesthetics have played a key role in such brands as Absolut vodka, Apple computers, Godiva choco-

late, and Harley-Davidson motorcycles.[38] Style can create distinctiveness that is difficult to copy; however, strong style does not always mean high performance.

- *Design*. As competition intensifies, design offers a potent way to differentiate and position a company's products and services.[39] Design is the integrating force that incorporates all of the qualities just discussed; this means the designer has to figure out how much to invest in form, feature development, performance, conformance, durability, reliability, repairability, and style. To the company, a well-designed product is one that is easy to manufacture and distribute. To the customer, a well-designed product is one that is pleasant to look at and easy to open, install, use, repair, and dispose of. The designer has to take all of these factors into account.

Services Differentiation   When the physical product cannot be differentiated easily, the key to competitive success may lie in adding valued services and improving their quality. The main service differentiators are:

- *Ordering ease* refers to how easy it is for the customer to place an order with the company. Baxter Healthcare eased the ordering process by supplying hospitals with computers through which they send orders to Baxter for delivery directly to individual departments and wards.[40] Similarly, consumers can easily order groceries for home delivery through Web-based services such as Peapod.[41]

- *Delivery* refers to how well the product or service is delivered to the customer, covering speed, accuracy, and customer care. Deluxe Corp. has built a reputation for shipping out custom-printed checks one day after receiving an order—without being late once in 18 years—to fuel continued profitable growth.[42]

- *Installation* refers to the work done to make a product operational in its planned location. Buyers of heavy equipment expect good installation service. Differentiation by installation is particularly important for companies that offer complex products.

- *Customer training* refers to training the customer's employees to use the vendor's equipment properly and efficiently. General Electric not only sells and installs expensive X-ray equipment in hospitals, but also trains users.

- *Customer consulting* refers to data, information systems, and advising services that the seller offers to buyers. For example, the Rite Aid drugstore chain's communications program, called the Vitamin Institute, provides customers with research so they can make more educated judgments and feel comfortable asking for help. On the Web, Rite Aid offers more health-related consultation information.[43]

- *Maintenance and repair* describes the service program for helping customers keep products in good working order, an important consideration for many products.

Personnel Differentiation   Companies can gain a strong competitive advantage through having better-trained people. Singapore Airlines enjoys an excellent reputation in large part because of its flight attendants. The McDonald's people are courteous, the IBM people are professional, and the Disney people are upbeat. The sales forces of such companies as General Electric, Cisco, Frito-Lay, Northwestern Mutual Life, and Pfizer enjoy an excellent reputation.[44] Well-trained personnel exhibit competence, courtesy, credibility, reliability, responsiveness, and communication.[45]

Channel Differentiation   Companies can achieve competitive advantage through the way they design their distribution channels' coverage, expertise, and performance. Caterpillar's success in the construction-equipment industry is based partly on superior channel development. Its dealers are found in more locations, are better trained, and perform more reliably than competitors' dealers. Dell Computers has also distinguished itself by developing and managing superior direct-marketing channels using telephone and Internet sales.[46]

Image Differentiation   Buyers respond differently to company and brand images. *Identity* comprises the ways that a company aims to identify or position itself or its product, whereas *image* is the way the public perceives the company or its products. Image is affected by many factors beyond the company's control. The shoe and apparel maker Vans, for example, has a countercultural, aggressive image that contrasts with mainstream competitors such as Nike and Reebok.[47] An effective image establishes the product's character and value proposition; conveys the character in a distinctive way; and delivers emotional power beyond a mental image. For the image to work, it must be conveyed through every communication vehicle and brand contact, including logos, media, and special events.

EXECUTIVE SUMMARY

New products are essential to a company's long-term success. Although the rate of new product failure is disturbingly high, companies can improve their chances of success by creating products with a high product advantage. The new-product development process covers idea generation, screening, concept development and testing, marketing strategy development, business analysis, product development, market testing, and commercialization. The company must decide in each stage whether the idea should be dropped or moved to the next stage.

The consumer-adoption process is the process by which customers learn about new products, try them, and adopt or reject them. In this process, consumers progress from awareness through interest, evaluation, trial, and adoption. The process is influenced by many factors beyond the marketer's control, including consumers' and organizations' willingness to try new products, personal influences, and the characteristics of the new product or innovation.

Companies normally reformulate marketing strategy several times during a product's life cycle. The introduction stage is marked by slow growth and minimal profits as the new product gains distribution. Then the product enters a growth stage marked by rapid sales and increasing profits. The company attempts to improve the product, enter new market segments and distribution channels, and reduce prices slightly. In the maturity stage, sales growth slows and profits stabilize, causing the firm to try to modify the market, the product, or the marketing mix to renew sales growth. When the product starts to decline, the firm must determine whether to increase, maintain, or decrease its investment; harvest the product; or divest as advantageously as possible.

Throughout the life cycle, marketers need to develop and communicate a distinctive positioning for each product. Positioning is the act of designing the offering and image to occupy a distinctive place in the target market's mind. Many marketers advocate positioning according to a single product benefit, although double- and triple-benefit positioning can be successful if used carefully. Differentiation is the process of adding a set of meaningful and valued differences to distinguish the company's offering from competitors' offerings. A difference is worth establishing to the extent it is important, distinctive, superior, preemptive, affordable, and profitable. Companies can differentiate their offerings along five dimensions: product, services, personnel, channel, and image.

NOTES

1. "Sales of Red Bull Beverage in United States Grow to 10.5 Million Cases," *Bangkok Post*, March 14, 2002 (***www.bangkokpost.com***); "Global Trends," *Prepared Foods*, January 2002, p. 13; Hank Behar, "Running of the Bull," *Beverage World*, December 15, 2001, p. 18; Libby Estell, "Raging Bull," *Incentive*, January 2002, p. 25; Claire Phoenix, "Red Bull— Fact and Function," *Soft Drinks World*, February 2001.
2. Christopher Power, "Flops," *BusinessWeek*, August 16, 1993, pp. 76–82. (American Marketing Association, 1990); Eric M. Olson, Stanley F. Slater, and Andrew J. Czaplewski, "The Iridium Story: A Marketing Disconnect?" *Marketing Management*, Summer 2000, pp. 54–57.
3. *New Products Management for the 1980s* (New York: Booz, Allen & Hamilton, 1982).
4. See Deloitte and Touche, "Vision in Manufacturing Study," Deloitte Consulting and Kenan-Flagler Business School, March 6, 1998; A.C. Nielsen, "New Product Introduction—Successful Innovation/Failure: Fragile Boundary," A.C. Nielsen BASES and Ernst & Young Global Client Consulting, June 24, 1999.
5. Robert G. Cooper and Elko J. Kleinschmidt, *New Products: The Key Factors in Success* (Chicago: American Marketing Association, 1990).
6. Modesto A. Madique and Billie Jo Zirger, "A Study of Success and Failure in Product Innovation: The Case of the U.S. Electronics Industry," *IEEE Transactions on Engineering Management*, November 1984, pp. 192–203.
7. Eric von Hippel, "Lead Users: A Source of Novel Product Concepts," *Management Science*, July 1986, pp. 791–805. Also see his *The Sources of Innovation* (New York: Oxford University Press, 1988); and "Learning from Lead Users," in *Marketing in an Electronic Age*, ed. Robert D. Buzzell (Cambridge, MA: Harvard Business School Press, 1985), pp. 308–17.
8. Constance Gustke, "Built to Last," *Sales & Marketing Management*, August 1997, pp. 78–83.
9. "The Ultimate Widget: 3-D 'Printing' May Revolutionize Product Design and Manufacturing," *U.S. News & World Report*, July 20, 1992, p. 55.
10. Rick DeMeis, "Prototypes Delivered Overnight," *Design News*, January 21, 2002, p. 67; Dan Deitz, "Customer-Driven Engineering," *Mechanical Engineering*, May 1996, p. 68; "In Search of e-Success," *Chief Executive*, January 2000, pp. 54–61.
11. See David B. Hertz, "Risk Analysis in Capital Investment," *Harvard Business Review* (January–February 1964): 96–106.
12. See John Hauser, "House of Quality," *Harvard Business Review* (May–June 1988): 63–73. Customer-driven engineering is also called "quality function deployment." See Lawrence R. Guinta and Nancy C. Praizler, *The QFD Book: The Team Approach to Solving Problems and Satisfying Customers Through Quality Function Deployment* (New York: AMACOM, 1993); V. Srinivasan, William S. Lovejoy, and David Beach, "Integrated Product Design for Marketability and Manufacturing," *Journal of Marketing Research* (February 1997): 154–63.
13. Tom Peters, *The Circle of Innovation* (New York: Alfred A. Knopf, 1997) p. 96; Mark Borden, "Keeping Yahoo Simple—and Fast," *Fortune*, January 10, 2000, pp. 167–68. See also Rajesh Sethi, "New Product Quality and Product Development Teams," *Journal of Marketing* (April 2000): 1–14.
14. Peters, *The Circle of Innovation*, p. 99.
15. Christopher Power, "Will it Sell in Podunk? Hard to Say," *BusinessWeek*, August 10, 1992, pp. 46–47.

16. Philip Kotler and Gerald Zaltman, "Targeting Prospects for a New Product," *Journal of Advertising Research* (February 1976):7–20.

17. For details, see Keith G. Lockyer, *Critical Path Analysis and Other Project Network Techniques* (London: Pitman, 1984). Also see Arvind Rangaswamy and Gary L. Lilien, "Software Tools for New Product Development," *Journal of Marketing Research* (February 1997): 177–84.

18. The following discussion leans heavily on Everett M. Rogers, *Diffusion of Innovations* (New York: Free Press, 1962). Also see his third edition, published in 1983.

19. See Hubert Gatignon and Thomas S. Robertson, "A Propositional Inventory for New Diffusion Research," *Journal of Consumer Research* (March 1985): 849–67; Vijay Mahajan, Eitan Muller, and Frank M. Bass, "Diffusion of New Products: Empirical Generalizations and Managerial Uses," *Marketing Science*, 14, no. 3, part 2 (1995): G79–G89; Fareena Sultan, John U. Farley, and Donald R. Lehmann, "Reflection on 'A Meta-Analysis of Applications of Diffusion Models,'" *Journal of Marketing Research* (May 1996): 247–49; Minhi Hahn, Sehoon Park, and Andris A. Zoltners, "Analysis of New Product Diffusion Using a Four-Segment Trial-Repeat Model," *Marketing Science*, 13, no. 3 (1994): 224–47.

20. Some authors distinguished additional stages. Wasson suggested a stage of competitive turbulence between growth and maturity. See Chester R. Wasson, *Dynamic Competitive Strategy and Product Life Cycles* (Austin, TX: Austin Press, 1978). Maturity describes a stage of sales growth slowdown and saturation, a stage of flat sales after sales have peaked.

21. Robert D. Buzzell, "Competitive Behavior and Product Life Cycles," in *New Ideas for Successful Marketing*, eds. John S. Wright and Jack Goldstucker (Chicago: American Marketing Association, 1956), p. 51.

22. Steven P. Schnaars, *Managing Imitation Strategies* (New York: Free Press, 1994).

23. Gerald Tellis and Peter Golder, *Will & Vision: How Latecomers Can Grow to Dominate Markets* (New York: McGraw-Hill, 2001).

24. John B. Frey, "Pricing Over the Competitive Cycle," speech presented at the 1982 Marketing Conference, Conference Board, New York.

25. Stephen M. Nowlis and Itamar Simmonson, "The Effect of New Product Features on Brand Choice," *Journal of Marketing Research* (February 1996): 36–46.

26. Allen J. McGrath, "Growth Strategies with a '90s Twist," *Across the Board*, March 1995, pp. 43–46.

27. Kathryn Rudie Harrigan, "Strategies for Declining Industries," *Journal of Business Strategy* (Fall 1980): 27.

28. "Pitney Bowes Launches New Transportation Management Software," *Managing Logistics*, January 2002, p. 9; Claudia H. Deutsch, "Pitney Bowes Survives Faxes, E-Mail and the Internet, *New York Times*, August 18, 1998, p. D1; Matthew Lubanko, "Pitney Bowes Faces E-Foes Despite Lion's Share of the Market," *Hartford Courant*, March 18, 2000, p. E1.

29. See Philip Kotler, "Harvesting Strategies for Weak Products," *Business Horizons*, August 1978, pp. 15–22; and Laurence P. Feldman and Albert L. Page, "Harvesting: The Misunderstood Market Exit Strategy," *Journal of Business Strategy* (Spring 1985): 79–85.

30. Al Ries and Jack Trout, *Positioning: The Battle for Your Mind* (New York: Warner Books, 1982).

31. Michael Treacy and Fred Wiersema, *The Disciplines of Market Leaders* (Reading, MA.: Addison-Wesley, 1994).

32. Ries and Trout, *Positioning*.

33. See Bobby J. Calder and Steven J. Reagan, "Brand Design," in Dawn Iacobucci, ed. *Kellogg on Marketing* (New York: John Wiley & Sons, Inc., 2001), p. 61.

34. The Mountain Dew example is taken from Alice M. Tybout and Brian Sternthal, "Brand Positioning," in Dawn Iacobucci, ed. *Kellogg on Marketing* (New York: John Wiley & Sons, Inc., 2001), p. 54.

35. "Positioning Your Product," *Association Management*, August 2001, p. 34; Susan Burns, "See How They Glow," *Sarasota Magazine*, March 2002, pp. 67+; Camilla Palmer, "Time for Tea to Establish a New Brand Positioning," *Campaign*, June 1, 2001, p. 19.

36. Theodore Levitt, "Marketing Success Through Differentiation—of Anything," *Harvard Business Review* (January–February 1980).

37. Some of these bases are discussed in David A. Garvin, "Competing on the Eight Dimensions of Quality," *Harvard Business Review* (November–December 1987): 101–9.

38. See Bernd Schmitt and Alex Simonson, *Marketing Aesthetics: The Strategic Management of Brand, Identity, and Image* (New York: Free Press, 1997).

39. See Philip Kotler, "Design: A Powerful but Neglected Strategic Tool," *Journal of Business Strategy*, Fall 1984, pp. 16–21. Also see Christopher Lorenz, *The Design Dimension* (New York: Basil Blackwell, 1986).

40. William C. Copacino and Jonathan L.S. Byrnes, "How to Become a Supply Chain Master," *Supply Chain Management Review*, March–April 2002, pp. S37+.

41. "Online Grocers Try to Extend Their Shelf Life," *Christian Science Monitor*, February 12, 2001, p. 16.

42. Amanda Fung, "Small-Biz, Home Offices Fuel Deluxe's Profits," *American Banker*, April 22, 2002, p. 18.

43. Susan Hirsh, "At Rite Aid, the Medicine 'Is Working,'" *Baltimore Sun*, January 10, 2001, p. 1C; Christine Bittar, "The Rite Stuff," *Brandweek*, September 14, 1998, pp. 28–29.

44. See "The 25 Best Sales Forces," *Sales & Marketing Management*, July 1998, pp. 32–50.

45. For a similar list, see Leonard L. Berry and A. Parasuraman, *Marketing Services: Competing Through Quality* (New York: Free Press, 1991), p. 16.

46. Erin Davies, "Selling Sex and Cat Food," *Fortune*, June 9, 1997, p. 36.

47. Katherine Bowers, "Skating Its Way to the Top," *WWD*, February 7, 2002, p. 14, (*www.vans.com*).

CHAPTER 11

Setting Product and Brand Strategy

In this chapter, we will address the following questions:

1. What are the characteristics of products?
2. How can a company build and manage its product mix and product lines?
3. How can a company make better brand decisions?
4. How can packaging and labeling be used as marketing tools?

MARKETING MANAGEMENT AT ARTS & ENTERTAINMENT (A&E) NETWORK

A&E is building Biography, its nightly look at famous figures, into its trademark masterbrand, crossing a spectrum of media to reach a broad audience. Since its inception in 1987, the cable series has profiled over 1,000 people. Using line extension, A&E executives are moving this brand into new formats. Biography videos are sold through direct response, through catalogs, online, and in dedicated sections of some Barnes & Noble bookstores. The Biography Web site profiles 22,000 personalities and attracts more than 400,000 monthly visitors. And A&E now offers a separate Biography cable channel, a Biography magazine (with 700,000 subscribers), Biography books, Biography board games and calendars, and Biography music CDs.

Features that prove popular in one medium are added to Biography offerings in other media to support brand building. For example, "Born on This Day," which first appeared on the Web site, also airs on the Biography channel. The quiz "Who Am I?" debuted in the magazine and also airs on the cable channel. When people enjoy these and other features, they develop a closer bond with the Biography brand, turning it into a major asset for A&E.[1]

Product is a key element in the market offering. This holds true whether the product is a television show (offered by Arts & Entertainment Network), an Internet access service (offered by Earthlink), a hamburger (offered by Wendy's), a DVD player (offered by Sony), a sweater (offered by Benetton), or a chocolate bar (offered by Nestlé). Marketing-mix planning begins with formulating an offering to meet customers' needs or wants.

In this chapter, we examine the concept of product, basic brand decisions and packaging, and labeling issues. In Chapter 12, we look at how companies design and manage services; in Chapter 13, we explore pricing decisions. All three elements—product, services, and price—must be meshed into a competitively attractive offering.

THE PRODUCT AND THE PRODUCT MIX

A **product** is anything that can be offered to a market to satisfy a want or need. Products include *physical goods, services, experiences, events, persons, places, properties, organizations, information,* and *ideas.* The customer will judge the offering by three basic elements: product features and quality, services mix and quality, and price appropriateness (Figure 11.1). As a result, marketers must think about the level of each product's features, benefits, and quality.

Product Levels

Marketers plan their market offering at five levels, as shown in Figure 11.2.[2] Each level adds more customer value, and together the levels constitute a **customer value hierarchy**. The most fundamental level is the **core benefit**: the fundamental service or benefit that the customer is really buying. A hotel guest is buying "rest and sleep." The purchaser of a drill is buying "holes." Marketers must see themselves as providing product benefits, not merely product features.

At the second level, the marketer has to turn the core benefit into a **basic product**. Thus, a hotel room includes a bed, bathroom, and towels. At the third level, the marketer prepares an **expected product**, a set of attributes and conditions that buyers normally expect when they buy this product. Hotel guests expect a clean bed, fresh towels, and so on. Because most hotels can meet this minimum expectation, the traveler normally will settle for whichever hotel is most convenient or least expensive.

FIGURE 11.1   Components of the Market Offering

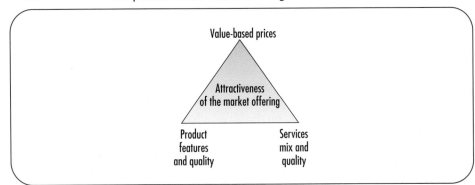

FIGURE 11.2   Five Product Levels

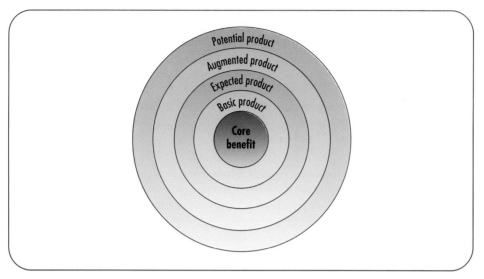

At the fourth level, the marketer prepares an **augmented product** that exceeds customer expectations. A hotel might include high-speed Internet access, fresh flowers, and express check-in and checkout. Today's competition essentially takes place at the product-augmentation level. (In less developed countries, competition takes place mostly at the expected product level.) Product augmentation leads the marketer to look at the user's total **consumption system**: the way the user performs the tasks of getting, using, fixing, and disposing of the product.[3] As Levitt notes: "The new competition is not between what companies produce in their factories, but between what they add to their factory output in the form of packaging, services, advertising, customer advice, financing, delivery, and other things that people value."[4]

However, product augmentation adds cost, so the marketer must determine whether customers will pay enough to cover the extra cost (of high-speed Internet access in a hotel room, for example). Moreover, augmented benefits soon become expected benefits, which means that competitors have to search for still other features and benefits. And as companies raise the price of their augmented product, some competitors can offer a "stripped-down" version at a much lower price. Thus, the hotel industry has seen the growth of fine hotels offering augmented products (Ritz-Carlton) as well as lower-cost lodgings offering basic products (Motel 6).

At the fifth level stands the **potential product**, which encompasses all of the possible augmentations and transformations the product might undergo in the future. Here, a company searches for entirely new ways to satisfy its customers and distinguish its offer. For example, Procter & Gamble invites coffee lovers to customize a coffee blend at personalblends.com.

Product Classifications

Marketers also must understand how to classify the product on the basis of three characteristics: durability, tangibility, and consumer or industrial use. Each product classification is associated with a different marketing-mix strategy.[5]

- *Durability and tangibility. Nondurable goods* are tangible goods that are normally consumed in one or a few uses (such as beer and soap). Because these goods are consumed quickly and purchased frequently, the appropriate strategy is to make them available in many locations, charge only a small markup, and advertise heavily to induce trial and build preference. *Durable goods* are tangible goods that normally survive many uses (such as refrigerators). These products normally require more personal selling and service, command a higher margin, and require more seller guarantees. *Services* are intangible, inseparable, variable, and perishable products (such as haircuts or cell phone service), so they normally require more quality control, supplier credibility, and adaptability.

- *Consumer-goods classification.* Classified according to consumer shopping habits, these products include: **convenience goods** that are usually purchased frequently, immediately, and with a minimum of effort, such as newspapers; **shopping goods** that the customer, in the process of selection and purchase, characteristically compares on the basis of suitability, quality, price, and style, such as furniture; **specialty goods** with unique characteristics or brand identification, such as cars, for which a sufficient number of buyers are willing to make a special purchasing effort; and **unsought goods** that consumers do not know about or do not normally think of buying, such as smoke detectors. Dealers that sell specialty goods need not be conveniently located but must communicate their locations to buyers; unsought goods require more advertising and personal sales support.

- *Industrial-goods classification.* **Materials and parts** are goods that enter the manufacturer's product completely. Raw materials can be either *farm products* (e.g., wheat) or *natural products* (e.g., lumber). Farm products are sold through intermediaries; natural products are generally sold through long-term supply contracts, for which price and delivery reliability are key purchase factors. *Manufactured materials and parts* fall into two categories: *component materials* (iron) and *component parts* (small motors); again, price and supplier reliability are important considerations. **Capital items** are long-lasting goods that facilitate developing or managing the finished product. They include *installations* (such as factories) and *equipment* (such as trucks and computers), both sold through personal selling. **Supplies and business services** are short-lasting goods and services that facilitate developing or managing the finished product, including *maintenance and repair services* and *business advisory services.*

Product Mix

A **product mix** (also called **product assortment**) is the set of all products and items that a particular marketer offers for sale. Kodak's product mix consists of two strong product lines: information products and image products. NEC's product mix consists of communication products and computer products.

A company's product mix can be described in terms of width, length, depth, and consistency. The *width* refers to how many different product lines the company carries. The *length* refers to the total number of items in the mix. The *depth* of a product mix refers to how many variants of each product are offered. The *consistency* refers to how closely related the product lines are in end use, production requirements, distribution channels, or some other way.

These four product-mix dimensions permit the company to expand its business by adding new product lines, thus widening its product mix; lengthening each product line; deepening the product mix by adding more variants; and pursuing more product-line consistency.

PRODUCT-LINE DECISIONS

Especially in large companies such as Kodak and NEC, the product mix consists of a variety of product lines. In offering a product line, the company normally develops a basic platform and modules that can be expanded to meet different customer requirements. As one example, many home builders show a model home to which additional features can be added, enabling the builders to offer variety while lowering production costs.

Product-Line Analysis

To support decisions about which items to build, maintain, harvest, or divest, product-line managers need to analyze the sales and profits as well as the market profile of each item. The manager must calculate each item's percentage contribution to total sales and profits. A high concentration of sales in a few items means line vulnerability. On the other hand, the firm may consider eliminating items that deliver a low percentage of sales and profits—unless these exhibit strong growth potential.

   The manager must also review how the line is positioned against competitors' lines. A useful tool is a product map showing which competitive products compete against the company's products on specific features or benefits. This helps management identify different market segments and determine how well the firm is positioned to serve the needs of each. After performing these analyses, the product-line manager has to make decisions about product-line length, line modernization, line featuring, and line pruning.

Product-Line Length

Companies seeking high market share and market growth will carry longer lines; companies emphasizing high profitability will carry shorter lines of carefully chosen items. **Line stretching** occurs when a firm lengthens its product line.

   With a downmarket stretch, a firm introduces a lower price line. However, moving downmarket can be risky. When Kodak introduced Funtime film to counter lower-priced brands, the price was not low enough to match the lower-priced competitive products. After regular customers started buying Funtime—cannibalizing the core brand—Kodak withdrew Funtime.

   With an upmarket stretch, a company enters the high end of the market for more growth, higher margins, or to position itself as a full-line manufacturer. All of the leading Japanese automakers have launched an upscale automobile: Toyota launched Lexus; Nissan launched Infinity; and Honda launched Acura. Note that these marketers invented new names rather than using their own names.

   Companies serving the middle market can stretch their product lines in both directions, as the Marriott Hotel group did by adding the Renaissance to serve the upper end of the upscale market, the Courtyard to serve the upper mid-scale segment, and Fairfield Inns for the lower mid-scale segment.[6] By basing the development of these brands on distinct consumer targets with unique needs, Marriott ensures against overlap between brands.

A product line can also be lengthened by adding more items within the present range. There are several motives for *line filling*: reaching for incremental profits, trying to satisfy dealers who complain about lost sales because of missing items in the line, trying to utilize excess capacity, trying to be the leading full-line company, and trying to plug holes to keep out competitors.

Line Modernization, Featuring, and Pruning

Product lines need to be modernized. This happens continuously in rapidly changing markets, where timing is critical to avoid hurting sales of current products or losing sales to competitors. In *line featuring*, the manager showcases one or a few items in the line to attract customers, lend prestige, or achieve other goals. If one end of the line is selling well and the other end is not, the company may use featuring to boost demand for the slower sellers, especially if those items are produced in a factory that is idled by lack of demand. In addition, managers must periodically review the entire line for pruning, identifying weak items through sales and cost analysis. They may also prune when the company is short of production capacity or demand is slow.

BRAND DECISIONS

Branding is a major issue in product strategy. Well-known brands command a price premium and enable companies to build a brand-loyal market. Developing a branded product requires considerable long-term investment, especially for advertising, promotion, and packaging.

What Is a Brand?

Perhaps the most distinctive skill of professional marketers is their ability to create, maintain, protect, and enhance brands. The American Marketing Association defines a **brand** as a name, term, sign, symbol, or design, or a combination of these, intended to identify the goods or services of one seller or group of sellers and to differentiate them from those of competitors.

In essence, a brand identifies the seller or maker. Whether it is a name, trademark, logo, or another symbol, a brand is a seller's promise to deliver a specific set of features, benefits, and services consistently to the buyers. The best brands convey a warranty of quality. But a brand is an even more complex symbol.[7] It can convey up to six levels of meaning (see Table 11.1).

A brand can be better positioned by associating its name with a desirable benefit, the way FedEx is associated with guaranteed overnight delivery. However, promoting a brand on only one benefit can be risky, because a new competitive brand may more effectively deliver that benefit or buyers may start to place less importance on the benefit. Successful brands therefore work to engage customers on a deeper level by touching a universal emotion.[8]

Building Brand Identity

Building the brand identity requires additional decisions about the brand's *name, logo, colors, tagline,* and *symbol*. Going beyond these elements, marketers must believe that they are offering a contract to the customer regarding how the brand will perform—

TABLE 11.1   Levels of Brand Meaning

Meaning	Description	Example
Attributes	A brand brings to mind certain attributes.	Mercedes suggests expensive, well-built, durable, high-prestige vehicles.
Benefits	Attributes must be translated into functional and emotional benefits.	The attribute "durable" could translate into the functional benefit "I won't have to buy another car for several years."
Values	The brand says something about the producer's values.	Mercedes stands for high performance, safety, and prestige.
Culture	The brand may represent a certain culture.	Mercedes represents German culture: organized, efficient, high quality.
Personality	The brand can project a certain personality.	Mercedes may suggest a no-nonsense boss (person) or a reigning lion (animal).
User	The brand suggests the kind of customer who buys or uses the product.	Mercedes vehicles are more likely to be bought by 55-year-old top managers than by 20-year-old store clerks.

and the contract must be honest. Motel 6, for instance, promotes clean rooms and low prices but does not imply that its room furniture is expensive.

At best, a brand campaign will create name recognition, brand knowledge, and possibly some brand preference, but it does not create brand bonding. **Brand bonding** occurs when customers experience the company as delivering on its benefit promise, through all of their contacts with employees and communications.

The Schultzes urge marketing managers to use a new approach to brand-building in the new economy. First, managers should clarify and use their corporate values to support the brand. Second, they need to engage all employees and managers in living the value proposition. Third, companies need to create positive customer experiences at every contact point. Fourth, companies should define the brand's basic essence to be delivered in every market. Fifth, firms must use the brand-value proposition to drive their strategy, operations, and product development. Finally, companies need to measure brand-building results according to measures such as customer retention and customer advocacy.[9]

Brand Equity

Brands vary in the amount of power and value they have in the marketplace. At one extreme are brands that are not known by most buyers. Then there are brands for which buyers have a fairly high degree of *brand awareness*. Beyond this are brands with a high degree of *brand acceptability*. Next are brands that enjoy a high degree of *brand preference*. Finally there are brands that command a high degree of *brand loyalty*. Aaker distinguished five levels of customer attitude toward a brand:

1. Customer will change brands, especially for price reasons. No brand loyalty.
2. Customer is satisfied. No reason to change the brand.
3. Customer is satisfied and would incur costs by changing brand.
4. Customer values the brand and sees it as a friend.
5. Customer is devoted to the brand.

Brand equity is highly related to how many customers are in classes 3, 4, or 5. Aaker says it is also related to the degree of brand recognition, perceived brand quality, strong mental and emotional associations, and other assets such as patents, trademarks, and channel relationships.[10]

Brand equity is the positive differential effect that knowing the brand name has on customer response to the product or service. High brand equity allows a company to enjoy reduced marketing costs because of high brand awareness and loyalty, gives a company more leverage in bargaining with distributors and retailers, permits the firm to charge more because the brand has higher perceived quality, allows the firm to more easily launch extensions because the brand has high credibility, and offers some defense against price competition. In contrast, **brand valuation** refers to estimating the total financial value of the brand. Among the world's most valuable brands are Coca-Cola, Microsoft, General Electric, Nokia, and McDonald's.[11]

Some analysts see brands as outlasting a company's specific products and facilities, so brands become the company's major enduring asset. Yet every powerful brand really represents a set of loyal customers. Brand equity is thus a major contributor to *customer equity*. This suggests that the proper focus of marketing planning is to extend *customer lifetime value*, with brand management serving as a major marketing tool.

Unfortunately, some companies mismanage their brands. This happened to Snapple almost as soon as Quaker Oats bought the beverage marketer for $1.7 billion in 1994. Snapple became a hit thanks to grassroots marketing and distribution through small outlets and convenience stores. Analysts said that because Quaker did not understand the brand's appeal, it made the mistake of changing the ads and the distribution. Snapple lost so much money and share that Quaker sold it for $300 million to Triarc in 1997; Triarc revived the brand and sold it to Cadbury Schweppes for $1.5 billion in 2000.[12] Marketers for brands such as Snapple need particular skills, as discussed in "Marketing Skills: Building a Cult Brand".

Branding Challenges

Branding poses several challenges: whether or not to brand; how to handle brand sponsorship; choosing a brand name; deciding on brand strategy; and whether to reposition a brand later (Figure 11.3).

To Brand or Not to Brand? The first decision is whether to develop a brand name for a product. Branding is such a strong force today that hardly anything goes unbranded, including salt, oranges, nuts and bolts, and a growing number of fresh food products such as chicken and turkey.

In some cases, there has been a return to "no branding" of certain staple consumer goods and pharmaceuticals. Generics are unbranded, plainly packaged, less expensive versions of common products such as spaghetti or paper towels. They offer standard or lower quality at a price that is as much as 20 percent to 40 percent lower than nationally advertised brands and 10 percent to 20 percent lower than retailer private-label brands. The lower price is made possible by lower-quality ingredients, lower-cost labeling and packaging, and minimal advertising.

Sellers brand their products, despite the costs, because they gain a number of advantages: The brand makes it easier for the seller to process orders; the seller's brand name and trademark legally protect unique product features; branding allows sellers to attract loyal, profitable customers and offers some protection from competi-

MARKETING SKILLS: BUILDING A CULT BRAND

Some brands provoke such strong customer loyalty that they attain cult status—Harley-Davidson motorcycles, for instance. Building a cult brand can significantly increase sales and profits without expensive promotions and without appealing to a mass market, making this skill particularly important for marketers launching unconventional or niche products. Several competencies contribute to this skill. First is the ability to create a "buzz" by stirring excitement among opinion leaders in the targeted segment and creating a sense of close community. Imagination is the key—widespread, ordinary advertising would dilute the effect. SoBe, for example, sends its SoBe Love Bus to alternative music concerts and sports events to sample its beverages and bring new customers into the fold.

Next, marketers need to enhance the product's appeal through supply and distribution. A new product that is readily available everywhere will seem less special. This is why Acid cigars are sold through only 500 U.S. retailers and the company's Web site and why Screaming Eagle vineyards produces just 500 cases of wine per year. Marketers can also provide a framework for brand-based communities like the Harley Owners Group; bringing enthusiasts together for special events will reinforce and expand the brand experience.

Entrepreneur Peter van Stolk has honed his skills in making Jones Soda a cult hit. After struggling to obtain shelf space in food stores, van Stolk decided to place his products in untraditional outlets such as record stores, hair salons, and tattoo parlors. Customers who tried the colorful soft drinks began asking for it in other stores, paving the way for distribution in convenience stores. The entrepreneur adds a community flavor by putting photos of loyal customers on bottle labels and encouraging interaction on his Web site. Thanks to van Stolk's skill in building a cult brand, Jones Soda's annual revenues are $19 million and climbing.[13]

tion; branding helps the seller segment markets by offering different brands with different features for different benefit-seeking segments; and strong brands help build the corporate image, easing the way for new brands and wider acceptance by distributors and customers.

Distributors and retailers want brands because they make the product easier to handle, indicate certain quality standards, strengthen buyer preferences, and make it

FIGURE 11.3 An Overview of Branding Decisions

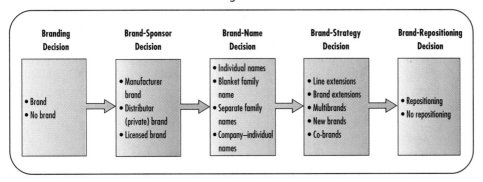

easier to identify suppliers. For their part, customers find that brand names help them distinguish quality differences and shop more efficiently.

Brand-Sponsor Decision   A manufacturer has several options regarding brand sponsorship. The product may be launched as a *manufacturer brand* (sometimes called a national brand), a *distributor brand* (also called reseller, store, house, or private brand), or a *licensed brand name*. Another alternative is for the manufacturer to produce some output under its own name and some under reseller labels. John Deere and IBM sell virtually all of their output under their own brand names, whereas Whirlpool produces both under its own name and under distributors' names (Sears Kenmore appliances).

Although manufacturers' brands dominate, large retailers and wholesalers have been developing their own brands by contracting production from willing manufacturers. Sears has created names such as Diehard batteries and Craftsman tools that command brand preference and even brand loyalty. Retailers such as Gap sell mostly own-brand merchandise. Sainsbury, Britain's largest food chain, sells 50 percent store-label goods, and its operating margins are six times those of U.S. retailers (U.S. supermarkets average 19.7 percent private-brand sales).

Intermediaries sponsor their own brands because these brands are more profitable: They are produced at a low cost by manufacturers with excess capacity. Other costs, such as research and development, advertising, sales promotion, and physical distribution, are also much lower. As a result, the private brander can charge less and make a higher margin. Second, retailers develop exclusive store brands to differentiate themselves from competitors.

In years past, consumers viewed the brands in a category arranged in a *brand ladder*, with their favorite brand at the top and remaining brands in descending order of preference. There are now signs that this ladder is being replaced with a consumer perception of *brand parity*—that many brands are equivalent.[14] Instead of a strongly preferred brand, consumers buy from a set of acceptable brands, choosing whichever is on sale that day.

Today's consumers are also more price sensitive, because a steady barrage of coupons and price specials has trained them to buy on price. In fact, over time, companies have reduced advertising to 30 percent of their total promotion budget, weakening brand equity. Moreover, the endless stream of brand extensions and line extensions has blurred brand identity and led to a confusing amount of product proliferation.

Of course, one of the factors that is changing the entire branding landscape is the Internet. While some "born digital" companies like America Online (AOL) and Amazon.com have used the Internet to gain brand recognition seemingly overnight, other companies have poured millions of dollars into online advertising with little effect on brand awareness or preference. Now packaged-goods powerhouses are trying different approaches to Web marketing. Procter & Gamble, for example, is focusing much of its online marketing on brands with narrow target audiences. The company has turned Pampers.com into the Pampers Parenting Institute, reaching out to customers by addressing issues of concern to new or expectant parents.[15]

Companies are also becoming adept at achieving solid brand recognition through less conventional marketing approaches. For example, over half of all U.S.

households are familiar with the America Online (AOL) brand. That's because AOL has blanketed the country for years with free software and free trial offers. The company has also put product samples in unlikely places such as inside cereal boxes and airline meals. AOL's marketers believe that consumers need to try the service to appreciate its benefits. Once consumers try AOL, the company reasons that the user-friendly program will lure them to subscribe—a philosophy that has helped build a subscriber base more than four times as large as the nearest competitor.[16]

Brand-Name Decision   Manufacturers and service companies who brand their products must choose which brand names to use. Four strategies are available, as shown in Table 11.2.

Once a company decides on its brand-name strategy, it must choose a specific brand name. The company could choose the name of a person (Estée Lauder), location (American Airlines), quality (Duracell), lifestyle (Weight Watchers), or an artificial name (eBay). Among the desirable qualities for a brand name are the following:[17]

- *It should suggest something about the product's benefits.* Examples: Beauty-rest, Priceline.com.
- *It should suggest product qualities.* Examples: Spic and Span, Jiffy Lube
- *It should be easy to pronounce, recognize, and remember.* Examples: Tide, Amazon.com
- *It should be distinctive.* Examples: Kodak, Yahoo!
- *It should not carry poor meanings in other countries and languages.* Example: Nova is a poor name for a car sold in Spanish-speaking countries because it means "doesn't go."

TABLE 11.2   Brand-Name Strategies

Strategy	Examples	Rationale
Individual names	General Mills (Bisquick, Gold Medal, Betty Crocker)	The firm does not tie its reputation to the product's; if the product fails or seems low quality, the company's name or image is not hurt.
Blanket family names	Campbell's, Heinz, General Electric	The firm spends less on development because there is no need for "name" research or heavy ad spending to create brand-name recognition; also, product sales are likely to be strong if the manufacturer's name is good.
Separate family names	Sears (Kenmore for Appliances, Craftsman for tools); Kuwait's Burgan Bank (Burgan Bank for the physical branches, BeeeBank.com for the Web-based bank)	Where a firm offers quite different products, separate family names are more appropriate than one blanket family name.
Company trade name with individual product names	Kellogg (Kellogg's Rice Krispies, Kellogg's Raisin Bran)	The company name legitimizes while the individual name individualizes each product.

Many firms strive to build a unique brand name that eventually will become intimately identified with the product category. Examples are Kleenex, Kitty Litter, Levi's, Jell-O, Popsicle, Scotch Tape, and Xerox. Federal Express officially shortened its marketing identity to FedEx because the term has become a synonym for "to ship overnight." Yet identifying a brand name with a product category may threaten the company's exclusive rights to that name. Cellophane and shredded wheat are now in the public domain and available for any manufacturer to use.

Given the rapid growth of the global marketplace, companies must be careful to choose brand names that are meaningful worldwide and pronounceable in other languages. Companies should also take care to avoid names owned by someone in another country. Anheuser-Busch, for example, cannot use the name "Budweiser" in Germany.

Brand Strategy Decision Brand strategy varies according to whether the brand is a functional brand, an image brand, or an experiential brand.[18] Consumers purchase a *functional brand* to satisfy a functional need such as to shave or to clean clothes. Functional brands rely heavily on "product" and or "price" features. *Image brands* arise with products or services that are difficult to differentiate or assess quality or that convey a statement about the user—typically something positive. *Experiential brands* involve the consumer beyond simply acquiring the product. The consumer encounters "people" and "place" with these brands, as happens in a visit to a Starbuck's coffee shop or DisneyWorld.

Over time, each type of brand can be developed further. A company can introduce **line extensions** (existing brand name extended to new sizes or flavors in the existing product category), **brand extensions** (brand names extended to new-product categories), **multibrands** (new brand names introduced in the same product category), **new brands** (new brand name for a new category product), and **co-branding** (combining two or more well-known brand names).

LINE EXTENSIONS Line extensions introduce additional items in the same product category under the same brand name, such as new flavors, forms, colors, added ingredients, and package sizes. The vast majority of new products (such as "lite" versions of existing foods) are actually line extensions.

Line extension involves risks and has provoked heated debate among marketing professionals.[19] On the downside, extensions may lead to the brand name losing its specific meaning; Ries and Trout call this the "line-extension trap."[20] A consumer asking for a Coke in the past would receive a 6.5-ounce bottle. Today the seller must ask: New, Classic, or Cherry Coke? Regular or diet? With or without caffeine? Bottle or can? Line extensions of strong brands, symbolic brands, brands with strong advertising and promotion support, and early market entrants are more successful; a company's size and marketing competence also play a role.[21]

Line extensions have a much higher chance of survival than do brand-new products. Some marketing executives defend line extensions as the best way to build a business. Kimberly-Clark's Kleenex unit has had great success with line extensions. "We try to get facial tissue in every room of the home," says one Kimberly-Clark executive. "If it is there, it will get used." This philosophy led to 20 varieties of Kleenex facial tissues, including a line for children.

BRAND EXTENSIONS A company may use its existing brand name to launch new products in other categories, the way Honda has put its name on snowblowers, lawnmowers, and other products. A recent trend in corporate brand-building is licensing the company name to manufacturers of a wide range of products—from bedding to shoes. Harley-Davidson, for example, uses licensing to reach audiences outside its core market, with branded armchairs for women and a Barbie doll for future generations of Harley purchasers.[22]

Brand-extension strategy offers many of the same advantages as line extensions, but it involves risks. One is that the new product might disappoint buyers and damage their respect for the company's other products. Another is **brand dilution,** which occurs when consumers stop associating a brand with a specific product or highly similar products and think less of the brand.

MULTIBRANDS, NEW BRANDS, AND CO-BRANDS   A company will often introduce additional brands in the same product category. Sometimes the firm is trying to establish different features or appeal to different buying motives. A **multibrand** strategy enables the company to lock up more distributor shelf space and to protect its major brand by setting up *flanker brands*. Seiko uses one brand for higher-priced watches (Seiko Lasalle) and another for lower-priced watches (Pulsar) to protect its flanks. Ideally, a company's brands within a category should cannibalize the competitors' brands and not each other. At the very least, net profits from multibrands should be larger despite some cannibalism.[23]

When a company launches products in a new category, it may find that none of its current brand names are appropriate. If Timex decides to make toothbrushes, it is not likely to call them Timex toothbrushes. Yet establishing a new U.S. brand for a mass-consumer-packaged good can cost $100 million, making this an extremely critical decision.

A rising phenomenon is the emergence of **co-branding** (also called **dual branding**), in which two or more well-known brands are combined in an offer. Each brand sponsor expects that the other brand will strengthen preference or purchase intention. With co-packaged products, each brand hopes to reach a new audience by associating with the other brand.

Co-branding takes a variety of forms. One is *ingredient co-branding*, as when Volvo advertises that it uses Michelin tires or Betty Crocker's brownie mix includes Hershey's chocolate syrup. Another form is *same-company co-branding*, as when General Mills advertises Trix and Yoplait yogurt. Still another form is *joint venture co-branding*, as in the case of General Electric and Hitachi lightbulbs in Japan. Finally, there is *multiple-sponsor co-branding*, in which three or more firms become involved in one offer, as Toyota and six other Japanese firms have done in creating the WiLL brand.[24]

Many manufacturers make components—motors, computer chips, carpet fibers—that enter into final branded products, and whose individual identity normally gets lost. These manufacturers hope their brand will be featured as part of the final product. Intel's consumer-directed brand campaign convinced many people to buy only PCs with "Intel Inside." As a result, many PC manufacturers buy chips from Intel at a premium price rather than buying equivalent chips from other suppliers.

Brand Auditing and Repositioning   Companies need to periodically audit their brands' strengths and weaknesses. One tool, Kevin Keller's *brand report card*, is designed to assess 10 characteristics of a brand.[25] A company will occasionally discover that it may have to reposition a brand because of new competitors or changing customer preferences. Consider Schwinn, the leading U.S. bicycle manufacturer, which has repositioned itself several times since the late 1800s. First it was geared toward boys and their fathers, then toward family bikes, then toward fitness bikes. However, as dirt bikes and mountain bikes became more popular, young bikers saw the Schwinn brand as irrelevant until the company began making these products and cultivated a fun, daring, quality brand image.

PACKAGING AND LABELING

Most physical products have to be packaged and labeled. Some packages—such as the Coke bottle—are world famous. Many marketers have called packaging a fifth P, along with price, product, place, and promotion; however, packaging and labeling are usually treated as an element of product strategy.

Packaging

Packaging includes all the activities of designing and producing the container for a product. The container is called the **package**, and it might include up to three levels of material. Old Spice aftershave lotion is in a bottle (*primary package*) that is in a cardboard box (*secondary package*) that is in a corrugated box (*shipping package*) containing six dozen boxes of Old Spice.

Several factors have contributed to packaging's growing use as a potent marketing tool:

- *Self-service.* The typical supermarket shopper passes by some 300 items per minute. Given that 53 percent of all purchases are made on impulse, an effective package attracts attention, describes features, creates confidence, and makes a favorable impression.
- *Consumer affluence.* Rising consumer affluence means consumers are willing to pay a little more for the convenience, appearance, dependability, and prestige of better packages.
- *Company and brand image.* Packages contribute to instant recognition of the company or brand. Campbell Soup estimates that the average shopper sees its red and white can 76 times a year, the equivalent of $26 million worth of advertising.
- *Innovation opportunity.* Innovative packaging can bring benefits to consumers and profits to producers. Toothpaste pump dispensers, for example, have captured 12 percent of the toothpaste market because they are more convenient and less messy.

Developing an effective package for a new product requires several decisions. The first task is to establish the packaging concept, defining what the package should *be* or *do* for the particular product. Then decisions must be made on other elements—size, shape, materials, color, text, and brand mark, plus the use of any "tamperproof" devices. All packaging elements must be in harmony and must fit with the product's pricing, advertising, and other marketing elements. Next come *engineering tests* to ensure that the package stands up under normal conditions; visual *tests*, to ensure that the script is legible and the colors harmonious; *dealer tests*, to ensure that dealers find the packages attractive and easy to handle; and *consumer tests*, to ensure favorable response.

Tetra Pak, a major Swedish multinational, provides an example of the power of innovative packaging. The firm invented an "aseptic" package that enables milk and other perishable liquid foods to be distributed without refrigeration. This allows dairies to distribute milk over a wider area without investing in refrigerated trucks and facilities. Supermarkets can carry Tetra Pak packaged products on ordinary shelves, saving on expensive refrigerator space. The firm's motto is "the package should save more than it costs."

Labeling

Every physical product must carry a label, which may be a simple tag attached to the product or an elaborately designed graphic that is part of the package. Labels perform several functions. First, the label *identifies* the product or brand—for instance, the name Sunkist stamped on oranges. The label might also *grade* the product, the way canned peaches are grade labeled A, B, and C. The label may *describe* the product: who made it, where it was made, when it was made, what it contains, how it is to be used, and how to use it safely. Finally, the label might *promote* the product through attractive graphics.

Labels eventually become outmoded and need freshening up. The label on Ivory soap has been redone 18 times since the 1890s, with gradual changes in the size and design of the letters. The label on Orange Crush soft drink was substantially changed when competitors' labels began to picture fresh fruits, thereby pulling in more sales. In response, Orange Crush developed a label with new symbols to suggest freshness and with much stronger and deeper colors.

Legal concerns about labels and packaging stretch back to the early 1900s and continue today. The Food and Drug Administration (FDA) recently took action against the potentially misleading use of such descriptions as "light" and "low fat." Meanwhile, consumerists are lobbying for additional labeling laws to require *open dating* (to describe product freshness), *unit pricing* (to state the product cost in standard measurement units), *grade labeling* (to rate the quality level), and *percentage labeling* (to show the percentage of each important ingredient).

EXECUTIVE SUMMARY

Product strategy calls for coordinated decisions on the product mix, product lines, brands, and packaging and labeling. The marketer needs to think through the five levels of the product: core benefit (the fundamental benefit or service the customer is really buying), basic product, expected product (a set of attributes that buyers expect), augmented product (additional services and benefits that distinguish the company's offer from the competition), and potential product (all of the augmentations and transformations the product might ultimately undergo).

Products can be classified in several ways. In terms of durability and reliability, products can be nondurable goods, durable goods, or services. In the consumer-goods category are convenience goods, shopping goods, specialty goods, and unsought goods. In the industrial-goods category are materials and parts, capital items, and supplies and business services.

A product mix is the set of all products and items offered for sale by the marketer. This mix can be classified according to width, length, depth, and consistency, providing four dimensions for developing the company's marketing strategy. To support product decisions, product-line managers first analyze each product's sales, profits, and market profile. Managers can then change their product-line strategy by line stretching or line filling, modernizing products, featuring certain products, and by pruning to eliminate less profitable products.

Branding is a major product-strategy issue. In formulating brand strategy, firms must decide whether or not to brand; whether to produce manufacturer brands, or distributor or private brands; which brand name to use, and whether to use line extensions, brand extensions, multibrands, new brands, or co-brands. The best brand names suggest the product's benefits or qualities; are easy to pronounce, recognize, and remember; are distinctive; and do not carry negative meanings or connotations in other countries or languages.

Many physical products have to be packaged and labeled. Well-designed packages create convenience value for customers and promotional value for producers. Marketers first develop a packaging concept and then test it functionally and psychologically to make sure it achieves its desired objectives and is compatible with public policy and environmental concerns. Physical products also require labeling for identification and possible grading, description, and product promotion. Sellers may be required by law to present certain information on the label.

NOTES

1. "Biography—the Industry," *Multichannel News*, April 22, 2002, pp. 8A+; "In the Beginning," *Multichannel News*, April 22, 2002, pp. 12A+; (***www.biography.com***).
2. This discussion is adapted from Theodore Levitt, "Marketing Success through Differentiation—of Anything," *Harvard Business Review* (January–February 1980): 83–91. The first level, core benefit, has been added to Levitt's discussion.
3. See Harper W. Boyd Jr. and Sidney Levy, "New Dimensions in Consumer Analysis," *Harvard Business Review* (November–December 1963): 129–40.
4. Theodore Levitt, *The Marketing Mode* (New York: McGraw-Hill, 1969) p. 2.
5. For some definitions, see *Dictionary of Marketing Terms*, ed. Peter D. Bennett (Chicago: American Marketing Association, 1995). Also see Patrick E. Murphy and Ben M. Enis, "Classifying Products Strategically," *Journal of Marketing* (July 1986): 24–42.
6. John P. Walsh, "Marriott Refines Renaissance Brand," *Hotel & Motel Management*, October 1, 2001, p. 3.
7. See Jean-Noel Kapferer, *Strategic Brand Management: New Approaches to Creating and Evaluating Brand Equity* (London: Kogan Page, 1992) pp. 38ff; Jennifer L. Aaker, "Dimensions of Brand Personality," *Journal of Marketing Research* (August 1997): 347–56. For an overview of academic research on branding, see Kevin Lane Keller, "Branding and Brand Equity," in *Handbook of Marketing* eds., Bart Weitz and Robin Wensley (Sage Publications: in press).
8. Marc Gobe, *Emotional Branding* (New York: Allworth Press, 2001); B.H. Schmitt and A. Simonson, *Marketing Aesthetics: The Strategic Management of Brands, Identity and Image* (New York: Free Press, 1997); B.H. Schmitt, *Experiential Marketing: How to Get Customers to Sense, Feel, Think, Act, and Relate to Your Company and Brands* (New York: Free Press, 1999).
9. Heidi F. Schultz and Don E. Schultz, "Why the Sock Puppet Got Sacked," *Marketing Management*, July–August 2001, pp. 34–39.
10. David A. Aaker, *Building Strong Brands* (New York: Free Press, 1995). See also Kevin Lane Keller, *Strategic Brand Management: Building, Measuring, and Managing Brand Equity*

(Upper Saddle River, NJ: Prentice-Hall, 1998) and D. A. Aaker and E. Joachimsthaler, *Brand Leadership* (New York: Free Press, 2000).

11. "The Best Global Brands," *BusinessWeek*, August 6, 2001, pp. 50-64. For a discussion of how to calculate brand value, see Kevin L. Keller, *Strategic Brand Management: Building, Measuring, and Managing Brand Equity* (Upper Saddle River, NJ: Prentice Hall, 1998) pp. 361–63.

12. Margaret Webb Pressler, "The Power of Branding," *Washington Post*, July 27, 1997, p. H1; "Cadbury Is Paying Triarc $1.45 Billion for Snapple Unit," *Baltimore Sun*, September 19, 2000.

13. Jeanie Casison, "Innovation Sensation," *Incentive*, April 2002, pp. 44+; Melanie Wells, "Cult Brands," *Forbes*, April 16, 2001, pp. 150+.

14. See Paul S. Richardson, Alan S. Dick, and Arun K. Jain, "Extrinsic and Intrinsic Cue Effects on Perceptions of Store Brand Quality," *Journal of Marketing* (October 1994): 28–36.

15. Saul Hensell, "Selling Soap Without the Soap Operas, Mass Marketers Seek Ways to Build Brands on the Web," *New York Times*, August 24, 1998, p. D1.

16. Marc Gunther, "Understanding AOL's Grand Unified Theory of the Media Cosmos," *Fortune*, January 8, 2001, p. 72; Patricia Nakache, "Secrets of the New Brand Builders," *Fortune*, June 22, 1998, pp. 167–70; John Ellis, "Digital Matters: 'People Need a Haven from the Web That's on the Web,'" *Fast Company*, January–February 2000, pp. 242–46.

17. See Kim Robertson, "Strategically Desirable Brand Name Characteristics," *Journal of Consumer Marketing*, Fall 1989, pp. 61–70.

18. Adapted from Alice M. Tybout and Gregory S. Carpenter, "Creating and Managing Brands," *Kellogg on Marketing*, ed. Dawn Iacobucci (New York: John Wiley & Son, 2001), pp. 74–98; See also C. W. Park, S. Milberg, and R. Lawson, "Evaluation of Brand Extensions: The Role of Product Feature Similarity and Brand Concept Consistency," *Journal of Consumer Research* 18 (1991): 185–93.

19. Robert McMath, "Product Proliferation," *Adweek Superbrands 1995 Supplement*, 1995, pp. 34–40; John A. Quelch and David Kenny, "Extend Profits, Not Product Lines," *Harvard Business Review* (September–October 1994): 153–60; and Bruce G. S. Hardle, Leonard M. Lodish, James V. Kilmer, David R. Beatty, et al., "The Logic of Product-Line Extensions," *Harvard Business Review* (November–December 1994): 53–62.

20. Al Ries and Jack Trout, *Positioning: The Battle for Your Mind* (New York: McGraw-Hill, 1981).

21. From Srinivas K. Reddy, Susan L. Holak, and Subodh Bhat, "To Extend or Not to Extend: Success Determinants of Line Extensions," *Journal of Marketing Research* (May 1994): 243–62. See also Morris A. Cohen, Jehoshua Eliashberg, and Teck H. Ho, "An Anatomy of a Decision-Support System for Developing and Launching Line Extensions," *Journal of Marketing Research* (February 1997): 117–29; V. Padmanabhan, Surendra Rajiv, and Kannan Srinivasan, "New Products, Upgrades, and New Releases: A Rationale for Sequential Product Introduction," *Journal of Marketing Research* (November 1997): 456–72.

22. Constance L. Hays, "No More Brand X: Licensing of Names Adds to Image and Profit," *New York Times*, June 12, 1998.

23. See Mark B. Taylor, "Cannibalism in Multibrand Firms," *Journal of Business Strategy* (Spring 1986): 69–75.

24. Campbell Gray, "Marketing, Japan: Will WiLL Fade Away?" *Advertising Age*, April 8, 2002, p. 17; Bernard L. Simonin and Julie A. Ruth, "Is a Company Known by the Company It Keeps? Assessing the Spillover Effects of Brand Alliances on Consumer Brand Attitudes," *Journal of Marketing Research* (February 1998): 30–42. See also C. W. Park, S. Y. Jun, and A. D. Shocker, "Composite Branding Alliances: An Investigation of Extension and Feedback Effects," *Journal of Marketing Research* 33 (1996): 453–66.

25. Kevin Lane Keller, "The Brand Report Card," *Harvard Business Review* (January–February 2000): 147–57.

CHAPTER 12

Designing and Managing Services

In this chapter, we will address the following questions:

1. How are services defined and classified?
2. How can service firms improve their differentiation, quality, and productivity?
3. How can goods-producing companies improve their customer support services?

MARKETING MANAGEMENT AT E*TRADE

E*TRADE burst onto the Internet in 1996 as an alternative to traditional full-price, full-service brokerage firms. Using a low-price, self-service strategy to target tech-savvy Generation Xers, the company quickly became the third-largest U.S. online broker, with $53 billion in customer assets. CEO Christos Cotsakos and his marketing team know that customers expect prompt and accurate execution of securities trades. Customers also want timely information about financial markets, tax and investment questions, and financial planning—available with just a few clicks on the company's Web site.

Now E*TRADE is expanding into a virtual supermarket of financial services. Customers can open checking and savings accounts online through E*TRADE Bank and use the company's network of 11,000 ATMs; take out a mortgage online through E*Mortgage; use high-speed day-trade and professional trading facilities in 19 U.S. locations; and visit one of five E*TRADE financial centers in major U.S. cities. Another point of differentiation is service delivery through E*TRADE Zones located inside Target SuperStores. To reinforce its brash brand image and showcase its expanded offerings, the company spends heavily on Super Bowl promotions and year-round ad campaigns. More promotions and new services are planned as financial services competition heats up.[1]

One of the megatrends of recent years has been the phenomenal growth of services. In the United States, service jobs now account for 79 percent of all jobs and 74 percent of gross domestic product. On the other hand, since 1994, satisfaction has dropped among customers of U.S. banks, airlines, stores, and hotels. These trends have led to a growing interest in the special challenges and opportunities of services marketing.[2]

THE NATURE OF SERVICES

Service industries are quite varied. The *government sector*, with its courts, employment services, hospitals, loan agencies, military services, police and fire departments, post office, regulatory agencies, and schools, is in the service business. The *private nonprofit sector*, with its museums, charities, churches, colleges, foundations, and hospitals, is in the service business. A good part of the *business sector*, with its airlines, banks, hotels, insurance firms, Internet service providers, law firms, consulting firms, medical practices, and Web-based services, is in the service business. Many workers in the *manufacturing sector*, such as computer operators, accountants, and legal staff, are really service providers, making up a "service factory" providing services to the "goods factory." And manufacturers and distributors often use a service strategy to differentiate themselves.

A **service** is any act or performance that one party can offer to another that is essentially intangible and does not result in the ownership of anything. Its production may or may not be tied to a physical product.

Categories of Service Mix

As the previous examples show, services are often part of a company's total offering. Five categories of an offering's service mix can be distinguished:

1. *Pure tangible good.* The offering is a tangible good such as soap, with no services.
2. *Tangible good with accompanying services.* The offering consists of a tangible good accompanied by one or more services. General Motors, for example, offers repairs, warranty fulfillment, and other services along with its cars and trucks.
3. *Hybrid.* The offering consists of equal parts of goods and services. For example, people patronize restaurants for both food and service.
4. *Major service with accompanying minor goods and services.* The offering consists of a major service along with additional services or supporting goods. For example, airline passengers are buying transportation service, but they get snacks or meals, as well.
5. *Pure service.* The offering consists primarily of a service; examples include baby-sitting and psychotherapy.

Characteristics of Services and their Marketing Implications

Services have four major characteristics that greatly affect the design of marketing programs: intangibility, inseparability, variability, and perishability.

Intangibility Unlike physical products, services cannot be seen, tasted, felt, heard, or smelled before they are bought. The person getting a face lift cannot see the exact results before the purchase, just as the patient in the psychiatrist's office cannot know the exact outcome.

To reduce uncertainty, buyers will look for signs or evidence of the service quality. They will draw inferences about quality from the place, people, equipment, communication material, symbols, and price that they see. Therefore, the service provider's task is to "manage the evidence," to "tangibilize the intangible."[3] Whereas product marketers are challenged to add abstract ideas, service marketers are challenged to add physical evidence and imagery to abstract offers. This is why Allstate uses the slogan "You're in good hands with Allstate," as one example.

Inseparability   Services are typically produced and consumed simultaneously, unlike physical goods, which are manufactured, put into inventory, distributed through resellers, and consumed later. If a person renders the service, then the provider is part of the service. Because the client is also present as the service is produced, provider-client interaction is a special feature of services marketing—both provider and client affect the outcome.

Often, buyers of services have strong provider preferences. Several strategies exist for getting around this limitation. One is higher pricing in line with the provider's limited time. Another is having the provider work with larger groups or work faster. A third alternative is to train more service providers and build up client confidence, as H&R Block has done with its national network of trained tax consultants.

Variability   Because services depend on who provides them and when and where they are provided, they are highly variable. Knowing this, service firms can take three steps toward quality control. The first is recruiting the right service employees and providing them with excellent training. This is crucial regardless of whether employees are highly skilled professionals or low-skilled workers.

For example, the California-based Horn Group handles public relations for Silicon Valley software firms and technology consultants. Founder Sabrina Horn invests heavily in training her employees and building morale and enthusiasm. She has developed education programs on everything from how to write a press release to how to manage an account. Employees also receive tuition reimbursement for continuing education and earn awards for special dedication.[4]

The second step is standardizing the service-performance process throughout the organization. Companies can do this by preparing a *service blueprint* that depicts every service event and process in a flowchart. This allows management to identify potential fail points and then plan improvements. The third step—taken by E*TRADE and many other service firms—is monitoring customer satisfaction through suggestion and complaint systems, customer surveys, and comparison shopping.

Perishability   Services cannot be stored; once an airplane takes off or a movie starts, any unsold seats cannot be held for future sale. Perishability is not a problem when demand is steady, but fluctuating demand can cause problems. For example, public-transportation companies have to own much more equipment because of higher rush-hour demand. Service providers can deal with perishability in a number of ways. Table 12.1 shows some strategies proposed by Sasser for matching demand and supply in a service business.[5]

For example, Club Med cultivates nonpeak demand at its worldwide resorts using e-mail to pitch unsold, discounted room and air packages to consumers who

TABLE 12.1   Strategies for Improving the Match Between Demand and Supply

Demand-Side Strategies	Supply-Side Strategies
Use differential pricing to shift demand from peak to off-peak periods; movie theaters and car rental firms do this by lowering prices during off-peak periods.	*Hire part-time employees* to meet peak demand; restaurants, stores, and Web-based businesses often bring in temporary staffers to help out during holidays and other peak periods.
Cultivate nonpeak demand to build sales during off-peak periods; hotels do this with their weekend minivacation packages.	*Introduce peak-time efficiency* routines to keep productivity high during periods of high demand; paramedics often assist physicians during busy periods.
Develop complementary services to provide alternatives for customers during peak periods; many banks do this by providing drop-off boxes for deposits and payments.	*Increase consumer participation* to speed transactions; this is one reason why many supermarkets are installing self-service checkouts where shoppers scan and bag their own groceries.
Install reservation systems to better manage demand levels; airlines, hotels, and physicians employ such systems extensively.	*Plan facilities for future expansion* to increase supply; an amusement park can buy surrounding land for later development as demand increases.
	Share services with other providers to help manage demand; hospitals can do this by sharing medical-equipment purchases and scheduling.

Source: Adapted from W. Earl Sasser, "Match Supply and Demand in Service Industries," *Harvard Business Review* (November–December 1976): 133–40.

have signed up for notification. Customers learn by mid-week what packages are available that weekend, at discounts of 30 to 40 percent off the standard price.[6]

MARKETING STRATEGIES FOR SERVICE FIRMS

In addition to the traditional four Ps of marketing, service providers must pay attention to three more Ps suggested by Booms and Bitner for services marketing: *people, physical evidence*, and *process*.[7] Because most services are provided by people, the selection, training, and motivation of employees can make a huge difference in customer satisfaction. Ideally, service employees should exhibit competence, a caring attitude, responsiveness, initiative, problem-solving ability, and goodwill.

Companies should also try to demonstrate their service quality through *physical evidence* and *presentation*. Thus, a hotel such as the Four Seasons will develop a look and observable style of handling customers that embodies its intended customer value proposition (in this case, luxury accommodations). Also, service companies can choose among different *processes* to deliver their service. For instance, McDonald's outlets offer self-service, while Olive Garden restaurants offer table service.

A service encounter is affected by both visible and invisible elements (see Figure 12.1). Consider a customer visiting a bank to get a loan (service X). The customer sees other customers waiting for this and other services. The customer also sees a physical environment (the building, interior, equipment, and furniture) as well as bank personnel. Not visible is a whole "backroom" production process and organization system that supports the visible business. Thus, the service outcome, and whether or not people will be satisfied and remain loyal to a service provider, are influenced by a host of variables.[8]

FIGURE 12.1 Elements in a Service Encounter

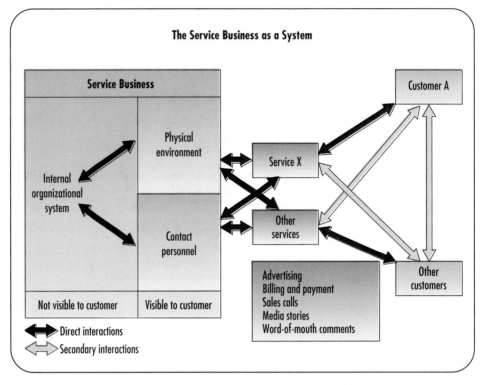

Source: Slightly modified from P. Eigler and E. Langeard, "A Conceptual Approach to the Service Offering," in *Proceedings of the EAARM X Annual Convention Conference*, ed. H. Hartvig Larson and S. Heede (Copenhagen School of Economics and Business Administration, 1981).

In view of this complexity, Gronroos has argued that service marketing requires not only external marketing, but also internal and interactive marketing (Figure 12.2).[9] *External marketing* describes the normal work to prepare, price, distribute, and promote the service to customers. *Internal marketing* describes the work to train and motivate employees to serve customers well. Berry has argued that the most important contribution the marketing department can make is to be "exceptionally clever in getting everyone else in the organization to practice marketing."[10]

Interactive marketing describes the employees' skill in serving the client. Because the client judges service not only by its *technical quality* (e.g., Was the surgery successful?) but also by its *functional quality* (e.g., Did the surgeon show concern and inspire confidence?),[11] service providers must deliver services that are "high touch" as well as "high tech."[12]

Consider how Charles Schwab, the nation's largest discount brokerage house, uses the Internet to deliver both high-tech and high-touch services. One of the first major brokerage firms to provide Web-based trading, Schwab today has 7.7 million customers in its online trading network. Its Web site offers financial and company information, real-time stock quotes, account data, after-hours trading, and detailed securities research. Schwab continues to lead its competitors by providing superior service (online, via phone, and in local branches) as well as innovative products and discount prices.[13]

FIGURE 12.2 Three Types of Marketing in Service Industries

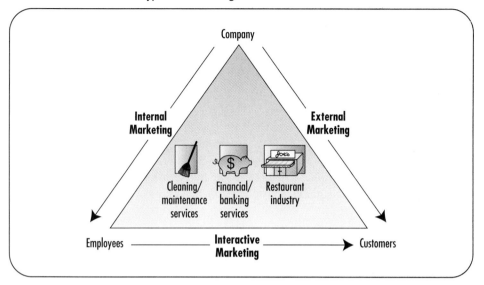

In some cases, customers cannot judge the technical quality of a service even after they have received it, as shown in Figure 12.3.[14] At the left are goods that are high in *search qualities*—characteristics the buyer can evaluate before purchase. In the middle are goods and services that are high in *experience qualities*—characteristics the buyer can evaluate after purchase. At the right are services that are high in *credence qualities*—characteristics the buyer normally finds hard to evaluate even after consumption.[15]

FIGURE 12.3 Continuum of Evaluation for Different Types of Products

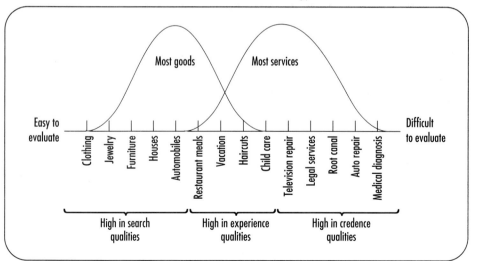

Source: Valerie A. Zeithaml. "How Consumer Evaluation Processes Differ Between Goods and Services," in *Marketing of Services*, ed. James H. Donnelley and William R. George. Reprinted with permission of the American Marketing Association, 1981.

Because services are generally high in experience and credence qualities, there is more risk in their purchase. As a result, service buyers rely more on word of mouth than on advertising when selecting a provider. They also rely heavily on price, personnel, and physical cues to judge quality, and are highly loyal to service providers who satisfy them.

Given these issues, service firms face three key marketing tasks: increasing *competitive differentiation*, *service quality*, and *productivity*. Although these interact, we will examine each separately.

Managing Differentiation

Service marketers frequently complain about the difficulty of differentiating their services on more than price alone. Price is a major marketing focus in service industries such as communications, banking, transportation, and energy, which have experienced intense price competition since deregulation. In a deregulated environment, the success of E*TRADE and other discount Web-based brokerages shows that many customers have little loyalty to established firms when they can save money by trading online. To the extent that customers view a service as fairly homogeneous, they care less about the provider than the price. The alternative to price competition in services marketing is to develop a differentiated offer, delivery, or image.

In developing a differentiated offer, companies can include innovative features. The customer expects the *primary service package*, but *secondary service features* can be added. Marriott, for example, offers hotel rooms (primary service package) with connections for computers, fax machines, and e-mail (secondary service features). Although most service innovations are easily copied, the company that regularly introduces new features will gain a succession of temporary competitive advantages and earn a reputation for innovation.

A service company can also differentiate itself by designing a better and faster delivery system. There are three levels of differentiation.[16] The first is *reliability*: some suppliers are more reliable in their on-time delivery, order completeness, and order-cycle time. The second is *resilience*: some suppliers are better at handling emergencies, product recalls, and answering inquiries. The third is *innovativeness*: some suppliers create better information systems and find other ways to help the customer.

Some service companies differentiate their image through symbols and branding. Prudential uses the Rock of Gibraltar as its corporate symbol to signify strength and stability. Differentiation through branding is a specialty of the charge-card division of American Express. Worldwide, millions of people "can't leave home without it." Yet credit cards like Visa and MasterCard have invaded Amex's turf, and customers are flocking to no-fee credit cards with frequent-flier miles and other benefits. Fighting back, Amex launched benefit-enhanced products such as the "Blue Card," aimed at upscale 25- to 35-year-olds—and attracted 6 million Blue cardholders in less than three years.[17]

Managing Service Quality

The service quality of a firm is tested at each service encounter. Customers form expectations from past experiences, word of mouth, and advertising. After receiving the service, they compare the perceived service with the expected service. If the perceived service falls below the expected service, customers are disappointed. If the per-

FIGURE 12.4   Service-Quality Model

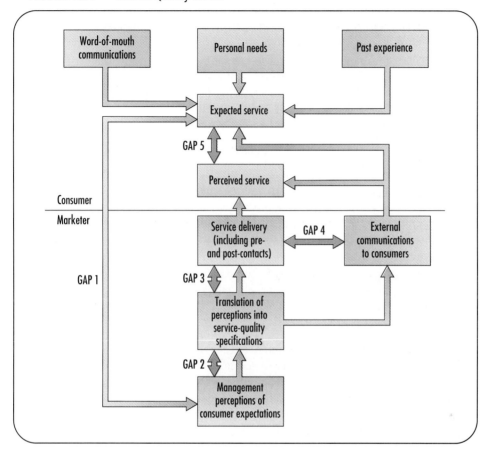

Source: A Parasuraman, Valerie A. Zeithaml, and Leonard L. Berry, "A Conceptual Model of Service Quality and Its Implications for Future Research," *Journal of Marketing* (Fall 1985): 44. Reprinted with permission of the American Marketing Association. The model is more fully discussed or elaborated in Valerie A. Zeithmal and Mary Jo Bitner, *Services Marketing* (New York: McGraw-Hill, 1996), ch. 2.

ceived service meets or exceeds their expectations, they are apt to use the provider again.

Parasuraman, Zeithaml, and Berry formulated a service-quality model that highlights the main requirements for delivering high service quality.[18] The model, shown in Figure 12.4, identifies five gaps that cause unsuccessful service delivery:

1. *Gap between consumer expectation and management perception.* Management does not always correctly perceive what customers want. Hospital administrators may think that patients want better food, but patients may be more concerned with nurse responsiveness.

2. *Gap between management perception and service-quality specification.* Management might correctly perceive the customers' wants but not set a specified performance standard. Hospital administrators may tell the nurses to give "fast" service without specifying it quantitatively.

3. *Gap between service-quality specifications and service delivery.* Personnel might be poorly trained, or incapable or unwilling to meet the standard; or they may be held to conflicting standards, such as taking time to listen to customers and serving them fast.

4. *Gap between service delivery and external communications.* Customer expectations are affected by statements made by company representatives and ads. If a hospital brochure shows an attractive room, but the patient finds an unappealing room, communications have distorted the customer's expectations.

5. *Gap between perceived service and expected service.* This gap occurs when the consumer misperceives the service quality. The physician may keep visiting the patient to show care, but the patient may interpret this as an indication that something really is wrong.

In addressing these gaps and pursuing service quality, well-managed service companies share the following common practices: a strategic concept, top-management commitment to quality, high standards, systems for monitoring service performance and customer complaints, and an emphasis on employee as well as customer satisfaction.

Strategic Concept   Top service companies are "customer obsessed." These firms have a clear sense of their target customers and their needs, and use a distinctive strategy to satisfy these needs.

Top-Management Commitment   Companies such as Marriott, Disney, and McDonald's are thoroughly committed to service quality. Every month, their management looks not only at financial performance but also at service performance. Top-management commitment can be demonstrated in various ways. Founder Sam Walton of Wal-Mart required the following employee pledge: "I solemnly swear and declare that every customer that comes within 10 feet of me, I will smile, look them in the eye, and greet them, so help me Sam."

High Standards   The best service providers set high service-quality standards. Citibank aims to answer phone calls within 10 seconds and customer letters within two days. Service standards must be set *appropriately* high. A 98 percent accuracy standard may sound good, but it would result in FedEx losing 64,000 packages a day, 10 misspelled words on each page, 400,000 misfilled prescriptions daily, and unsafe drinking water eight days a year. Companies can be distinguished between those offering "merely good" service and those offering "breakthrough" service aiming at 100 percent defect-free service.[19]

Monitoring Systems   Top firms regularly audit service performance, both their own and their competitors'. They use a number of measurement devices: comparison shopping, ghost shopping, customer surveys, suggestion and complaint forms, service-audit teams, and letters to the president. General Electric sends out 700,000 response cards a year asking households to rate its service people's performance; Citibank checks continuously on measures of accuracy, responsiveness, and timeliness.

When designing customer feedback mechanisms, service marketers need to ask the right questions, as United Parcel Service (UPS) discovered. UPS always assumed that on-time delivery was its customers' paramount concern, and based its definition of quality on the results of time-and-motion studies. UPS's surveys included questions about whether customers were pleased with delivery time and whether they thought the company could be any speedier. Yet when the company asked about service improvements, it found that customers wanted more face-to-face contact with drivers. If drivers could stop to answer questions, customers might get practical advice on shipping. Taking its service a step further, UPS allows customers to track shipments, order supplies, and send documents securely from its Web site.[20]

Satisfying Customer Complaints   Studies show that although customers are dissatisfied with their purchases about 25 percent of the time, only about 5 percent complain. The other 95 percent either feel that complaining is not worth the effort, or that they don't know how or to whom to complain. Of the 5 percent who complain, only about half report a satisfactory resolution. Yet the need to resolve a customer problem in a satisfactory manner is critical. On average, a satisfied customer tells three people about a good product experience, but the average dissatisfied customer gripes to 11 people. If each of them tells still other people, the number of people exposed to bad word of mouth may grow exponentially.

Customers whose complaints are satisfactorily resolved often become more company-loyal than customers who were never dissatisfied. About 34 percent of customers who register major complaints will buy again from the company if their complaint is resolved, and this number rises to 52 percent for minor complaints. If the complaint is resolved quickly, between 52 percent (major complaints) and 95 percent (minor complaints) will buy again from the company.[21]

According to Tax and Brown, companies that encourage disappointed customers to complain—and also empower employees to remedy the situation on the spot—achieve higher revenues and greater profits than companies that lack a systematic approach for addressing service failures.[22] They also found that companies that are effective at resolving complaints:

- Develop hiring criteria and training programs that take into account employees' service-recovery role.
- Develop guidelines for service recovery that focus on achieving fairness and customer satisfaction (see "Marketing Skills: Service Recovery").
- Remove barriers that make it difficult for customers to complain, while developing effective response systems. Pizza Hut prints its toll-free number on all pizza boxes. When a customer complains, Pizza Hut sends voice mail to the store manager, who must call the customer within 48 hours and resolve the complaint.
- Maintain customer and product databases that let the company analyze types and sources of complaints and adjust its policies accordingly.

Satisfying Both Employees and Customers   Excellent service companies know that positive employee attitudes will promote stronger customer loyalty. These firms recruit the best employees they can find, offer a career rather than just a job, provide solid training and support, and offer rewards for good performance. They also reinforce customer-centered attitudes at every opportunity.

Yet training employees to be friendly can cause problems. The Safeway supermarket chain found this out when it instituted an aggressive program to build employee friendliness toward customers, with rules such as: Make eye contact with all customers, smile, and greet each customer. The store employed "mystery shoppers" to secretly grade workers. Those who were graded "poor" are sent for more training.

MARKETING SKILLS: SERVICE RECOVERY

Service missteps can hurt customer relationships and, in severe cases, send formerly loyal customers in search of competitors. By developing good service recovery skills, however, marketers can turn a tense situation into an opportunity for strengthening customer ties. Good service recovery starts with an intense focus on understanding and meeting customers' needs. With this background, marketers can map potential problem areas and identify potential solutions to be implemented if problems arise. In planning for service recovery, consider cross-training and empowerment so employees can solve problems without bouncing customers from one department to another.

The ability to listen carefully and tactfully ask questions (of the customer and the employees involved) will help clarify the problem. Apologize when appropriate and offer a solution that is acceptable to the customer and fits with the company's objectives. Finally, tell the customer what will happen and when, then follow through to see that the problem was resolved as promised and that the customer is satisfied with the outcome.

At Xerox, management recognizes that "resolving the problem quickly is the best way to respond to the customer's needs," says one executive. Through ongoing training and top-down support for empowerment, the company has found numerous ways to streamline processes and speed up service recovery for customer satisfaction. Xerox employees are expected to quickly solve customer problems and check up on the results. Just as important, they are experienced in investigating underlying causes and finding ways to turn problems into opportunities for improvement.[23]

Although surveys showed that customers liked the program, many employees admitted being stressed out and several quit over the plan.[24]

Managing Productivity

Service firms are under great pressure to keep costs down and increase productivity. There are seven approaches to improving service productivity:

1. Have service providers work more skillfully. Top service companies such as Starbucks seek to hire and foster more skillful workers through better selection and training.

2. Increase the quantity of service by surrendering some quality. Doctors working for some HMOs have moved toward handling more patients and giving less time to each patient.

3. Industrialize the service by adding equipment and standardizing production. Levitt recommended that companies adopt a "manufacturing attitude" toward producing services as represented by McDonald's assembly-line approach to fast-food retailing, culminating in the "technological hamburger."[25]

4. Reduce or make obsolete the need for a service by inventing a product solution, the way wash-and-wear clothing reduced the need for commercial laundries.

5. Design a more effective service. For example, hiring paralegal workers reduces the need for more expensive legal professionals.

6. Present customers with incentives to substitute their own labor for company labor. FedEx has turned customers into shippers; E*TRADE allows customers to enter their own securities trades.

7. Use technology to give better customer service and make service workers more productive. Companies such as Cisco Systems that use their Web sites to empower customers can lessen workloads, capture valuable customer data, and increase the value of their businesses.

MANAGING PRODUCT SUPPORT SERVICES

A growing number of product-based industries now offer a service bundle. Manufacturers of equipment such as small appliances, computers, and tractors generally have to provide *product support services*. In fact, product support service is a major battleground for competitive advantage. Some equipment companies, such as John Deere, make over 50 percent of their profits from these services. In the global marketplace, companies that make a good product but provide poor local service support are seriously disadvantaged. This is why Subaru contracted to use the Australian Volkswagen dealer network to provide parts and service when it began selling its autos in that market.

To design the best service support program, a manufacturer must identify the services its customers most value. In general, customers worry about three things.[26] First, they are concerned about reliability and *failure frequency*. A farmer may tolerate a combine that breaks down once a year, but not more often. The second issue is *downtime duration*. The longer the downtime, the higher the cost, which is why customers count on *service dependability*—the seller's ability to fix the product quickly or at least provide a loaner.[27] The third issue is *out-of-pocket costs* of maintenance and repair. Customers worry about the amount they will have to spend on regular maintenance and repair costs.

A buyer considers all of these factors when choosing a vendor. As part of the decision process, the buyer tries to estimate the **life-cycle cost**, which is the product's purchase cost plus the discounted cost of maintenance and repair less the discounted salvage value. Sellers must therefore consider customer costs and the options for diffusing customer worries when designing presale and postsale support services.

Presale Service Strategy

Before any sale can be made, the marketer has to design an appealing and competitive service offer that will attract customers. In the case of expensive equipment, such as medical equipment, manufacturers offer *facilitating services* such as installation, repairs, and financing. They may also add *value-augmenting services*. Herman Miller, a leading office-furniture company, offers quality products coupled with: (1) Five-year product warranties; (2) quality audits after installation; (3) guaranteed move-in dates; (4) trade-in allowances on furniture systems products; and (5) easy online ordering.

A manufacturer can offer and charge for enhanced product support services in different ways. One specialty organic chemical company provides a standard offering plus a basic level of services. If the customer wants additional services, it can pay extra or increase its annual purchases to a higher level, in which case additional services would be included. Many companies sell add-on *service contracts* with variable lengths and different deductibles so customers can choose the service level they want beyond the basic service package.

Postsale Service Strategy

In providing postsale service, most companies progress through a series of stages. Manufacturers usually start out by running their own parts and service department, because they want to stay close to their products and learn about any problems right away. They also find it expensive and time-consuming to train others. Often, they discover that they can make good money running the parts-and-service business—and, if they are the only supplier of certain parts, they can charge a premium price. In fact, many equipment manufacturers price their equipment low and compensate by charging high prices for parts and service. This explains why competitors sometimes manufacture the same or similar parts and sell them to customers or intermediaries for less.

Over time, manufacturers—especially those who expand into global markets—switch more maintenance and repair services to authorized distributors and dealers. These intermediaries are closer to customers, operate in more locations, and can offer quicker service. Manufacturers still make a profit on the parts but leave the servicing profit to their intermediaries. Still later, independent service firms emerge. Over 40 percent of auto-service work is now done outside franchised automobile dealerships, by independent garages and chains such as Midas Muffler. Independent service organizations handle computers, telecommunications products, and other items, typically offering lower price or faster service than offered by the manufacturer or authorized intermediaries.

Ultimately, some large business customers may prefer to handle their own maintenance and repair services. A company with several hundred personal computers, printers, and related equipment might find it cheaper to have its own service personnel on site. These companies typically press the manufacturer for a lower product price because they are providing their own services.

Major Trends in Customer Service

Lele has noted a number of recent customer service trends.[28] Equipment manufacturers are building more reliable and more easily fixable equipment. One reason is the shift from electromechanical to electronic equipment, which has fewer breakdowns and is more easily repaired. Modular and disposable products also facilitate self-servicing by customers. In addition, customers are becoming more sophisticated about buying product support services and are pressing for "services unbundling." They want separate prices for each service element and the right to select just the elements they want.

Increasingly, customers dislike having to deal with a multitude of service providers that handle different types of equipment. In response, some third-party service organizations have begun servicing a greater range of equipment.[29] Service contracts (also called *extended warranties*), in which sellers agree to provide free maintenance and repair services for a specified period of time at a specified contract price, may diminish in importance. Some new car warranties now cover 100,000 miles before servicing. The increase in disposable or never-fail equipment makes customers less inclined to pay from 2 percent to 10 percent of the purchase price every year for a service.

Another trend is the rapid increase in customer service choices, which is holding down service prices and profits. Equipment manufacturers increasingly have to figure out how to make money on their equipment independent of service contracts. Add to these trends the use of call centers and the Internet to deliver service, advice, and maintenance or repair information around the clock, which is improving customer service, reducing customer complaints, and reinforcing long-term customer relationships.

EXECUTIVE SUMMARY

A service is any act or performance that one party offers to another that is essentially intangible and does not result in the ownership of anything. Its production may or may not be tied to a tangible product. Services are intangible, inseparable, variable, and perishable. Each characteristic poses challenges and requires certain strategies. Marketers must find ways to give tangibility to intangibles, to increase the productivity of service providers, to increase and standardize the quality of the service provided, and to match the supply of services during peak and nonpeak periods with market demand.

Service marketing strategy covers three additional Ps: people, physical evidence, and process. Successful services marketing calls not only for external marketing, but also for internal marketing to motivate employees and interactive marketing to emphasize both "high-tech" and "high-touch" elements.

Because services are generally high in experience and credence qualities, there is more risk in their purchase. The service organization therefore faces three tasks in marketing: It must differentiate its offer, delivery, or image; it must manage service quality in order to meet or exceed customers' expectations; and it must manage productivity by getting employees to work more skillfully, increasing the quantity of service by surrendering some quality, industrializing the service, inventing new product solutions, designing more effective services, offering customers incentives to substitute their own labor for company labor, or using technology to save time and money.

Even product-based companies must provide support services for their customers. To provide the best support, a manufacturer must identify and prioritize the services that customers value most. The service mix includes both presale services (such as facilitating services and value-augmenting services) and postsale services (customer service departments, repair and maintenance services).

NOTES

1. Deborah Bach, "E-Trade Group Bulking Up for Onsite Trade War," *American Banker*, April 12, 2002, p. 2; John Helyar, "At E*TRADE, Growing Up Is Hard to Do," *Fortune*, March 18, 2002, pp. 88+; Doug Desjardins, "Beyond-the-Box Deals Open Frontiers," *DSN Retailing Today*, April 8, 2002, p. 62; Sam Zuckerman, "E*TRADE Loses $5.2 Million Despite Late Business Surge," *San Francisco Chronicle*, January 20, 2000 (*www.sfgate.com*).
2. Diane Brady, "Why Service Stinks," *BusinessWeek*, October 23, 2000, pp. 119–128; Ronald Henkoff, "Service Is Everybody's Business," *Fortune*, June 27, 1994, pp. 48–60. Also see G. Lynn Shostack, "Breaking Free from Product Marketing," *Journal of Marketing* (April 1977): 73–80; Leonard L. Berry, "Services Marketing Is Different," *Business*, May–June 1980, pp. 24–30; Eric Langeard, John E. G. Bateson, Christopher H. Lovelock, and

Pierre Eiglier, *Services Marketing: New Insights from Consumers and Managers* (Cambridge, MA: Marketing Science Institute, 1981); Karl Albrecht and Ron Zemke, *Service America! Doing Business in the New Economy* (Homewood, IL: Dow Jones-Irwin, 1986); Karl Albrecht, *At America's Service* (Homewood, IL: Dow Jones-Irwin, 1988); Benjamin Scheider and David E. Bowen, *Winning the Service Game* (Boston: Harvard Business School Press, 1995); and Leonard L. Berry, *Discovering the Soul of Service* (New York: Free Press, 1999).

3. See Theodore Levitt, "Marketing Intangible Products and Product Intangibles," *Harvard Business Review* (May–June 1981): 94–102; and Berry, "Services Marketing Is Different."

4. Lewis P. Carbone and Stephan H. Haeckel, "Engineering Customer Experiences," *Marketing Management*, Winter 1994; "Creating a Corporate Culture," *PR Newswire*, May 17, 1999.

5. See W. Earl Sasser, "Match Supply and Demand in Service Industries," *Harvard Business Review* (November–December 1976): 133–40.

6. Carol Krol, "Case Study: Club Med Uses E-Mail to Pitch Unsold, Discounted Packages," *Advertising Age*, December 14, 1998, p. 40; "It's Raining Hard on Club Med," *BusinessWeek*, February 4, 2002, p. 28.

7. See B. H. Booms and M. J. Bitner, "Marketing Strategies and Organizational Structures for Service Firms," in *Marketing of Services*, eds. J. Donnelly and W. R. George (Chicago: American Marketing Association, 1981) pp. 47–51.

8. Keaveney has identified more than 800 critical behaviors of service firms that cause customers to switch services. These behaviors fit into eight categories ranging from price, inconvenience, and core service failure to service encounter failure, failed employee response to service failures, and ethical problems. See Susan M. Keaveney, "Customer Switching Behavior in Service Industries: An Exploratory Study," *Journal of Marketing* (April 1995): 71–82. See also Michael D. Hartline and O. C. Ferrell, "The Management of Customer-Contact Service Employees: An Empirical Investigation," *Journal of Marketing* (October 1996): 52–70; Lois A. Mohr, Mary Jo Bitner, and Bernard H. Booms, "Critical Service Encounters: The Employee's Viewpoint," *Journal of Marketing* (October 1994): 95–106; Linda L. Price, Eric J. Arnould, and Patrick Tierney, "Going to Extremes: Managing Service Encounters and Assessing Provider Performance," *Journal of Marketing* (April 1995): 83–97.

9. Christian Gronroos, "A Service Quality Model and Its Marketing Implications," *European Journal of Marketing* 18, no. 4 (1984): 36–44.

10. Leonard Berry, "Big Ideas in Services Marketing," *Journal of Consumer Marketing*, (Spring 1986): 47–51. See also Walter E. Greene, Gary D. Walls, and Larry J. Schrest, "Internal Marketing: The Key to External Marketing Success," *Journal of Services Marketing* 8, no. 4 (1994): 5–13; John R. Hauser, Duncan I. Simester, and Birger Wernerfelt, "Internal Customers and Internal Suppliers," *Journal of Marketing Research* (August 1996): 268–80.

11. Gronroos, "A Service Quality Model," pp. 38–39.

12. See Philip Kotler and Paul N. Bloom, *Marketing Professional Services* (Upper Saddle River, NJ: Prentice-Hall, 1984).

13. "Can Schwab Hang On to Its Heavy Hitters?" *BusinessWeek*, January 31, 2000, p. 46; "USA: Charles Schwab Web Site Ready for Questioning," *Reuters English News Service*, May 22, 2001.

14. See Valarie A. Zeithaml, "How Consumer Evaluation Processes Differ Between Goods and Services," in Donnelly and George, eds., *Marketing of Services*, pp. 186–90.

15. Amy Ostrom and Dawn Iacobucci, "Consumer Trade-offs and the Evaluation of Services," *Journal of Marketing*, January 1995, pp. 17–28.

16. William C. Copacino, *Supply Chain Management* (Boca Raton, Fl.: St. Lucie Press, 1997).

17. Suzanne Bidlake, "John Crewe, American Express Blue Card," *Advertising Age International*, December 14, 1998, p. 10; Sue Beenstock, "Blue Blooded," *Marketing*, June

4, 1998, p. 14; Pamela Sherrid, "A New Class Act at AMEX," *U.S. News & World Report*, June 23, 1997, pp. 39–40.

18. A. Parasuraman, Valarie A. Zeithaml, and Leonard L. Berry, "A Conceptual Model of Service Quality and Its Implications for Future Research," *Journal of Marketing* (Fall 1985): 41–50. See also Susan J. Devlin and H. K. Dong, "Service Quality from the Customers' Perspective," *Marketing Research: A Magazine of Management & Applications*, Winter 1994, pp. 4–13; William Boulding, Ajay Kalra, and Richard Staelin, "A Dynamic Process Model of Service Quality: From Expectations to Behavioral Intentions," *Journal of Marketing Research* (February 1993): 7–27.

19. See James L. Heskett, W. Earl Sasser, Jr., and Christopher W. L. Hart, *Service Breakthroughs* (New York: Free Press, 1990).

20. "Web Watch: UPS Online Courier," *Sales & Marketing Management*, April 2002, p. 23; David Greising, "Quality: How to Make It Pay," *BusinessWeek*, August 8, 1994, pp. 54–59.

21. See John Goodman, *Technical Assistance Research Program (TARP)*, U.S. Office of Consumer Affairs Study on Complaint Handling in America, 1986; Albrecht and Zemke, *Service America!*; Berry and Parasuraman, *Marketing Services*; Roland T. Rust, Bala Subramanian, and Mark Wells, "Making Complaints a Management Tool," *Marketing Management* 1, no. 3 (1992): 41–45; Stephen S. Tax, Stephen W. Brown, and Murali Chandrashekaran, "Customer Evaluations of Service Complaint Experiences: Implications for Relationship Marketing," *Journal of Marketing* (April 1998): 60–76.

22. Stephen S. Tax and Stephen W. Brown, "Recovering and Learning from Service Failure," *Sloan Management Review*, Fall 1998, pp. 75–88.

23. Julie Demers, "Service Drives a New Program," *CMA Management*, May 2002, pp. 36+; Robert Geier, "How to Create Disaster Recovery Plans for Customer Contact Operations," *Customer Contact Management Report*, January 2002, pp. 1+; Don Merit, "Dealing with Irate Customers," *American Printer*, October 2001, p. 66.

24. Kirstin Downey Grimsley, "Service with a Forced Smile; Safeway's Courtesy Campaign Also Elicits Some Frowns," *Washington Post*, October 18, 1998, p. A1. See also Suzy Fox, "Emotional Value: Creating Strong Bonds with Your Customers," *Personnel Psychology*, April 1, 2001, pp. 230–34.

25. Theodore Levitt, "Production-Line Approach to Service," *Harvard Business Review*, September–October 1972, pp. 41–52; see also his "Industrialization of Service," *Harvard Business Review*, September–October 1976, pp. 63–74.

26. See Milind M. Lele and Uday S. Karmarkar, "Good Product Support Is Smart Marketing," *Harvard Business Review* (November–December 1999): 124–32.

27. Research on the effects of service delays on service evaluations: Shirley Taylor, "Waiting for Service: The Relationship between Delays and Evaluations of Service," *Journal of Marketing*, April 1994, pp. 56–69; Michael K. Hui and David K. Tse, "What to Tell Customers in Waits of Different Lengths," *Journal of Marketing* (April 1996): 81–90.

28. Milind M. Lele, "How Service Needs Influence Product Strategy," *Sloan Management Review*, Fall 1986, pp. 63–70.

29. However, see Ellen Day and Richard J. Fox, "Extended Warranties, Service Contracts, and Maintenance Agreement: A Marketing Opportunity?" *Journal of Consumer Marketing* (Fall 1985): 77–86.

CHAPTER 13

Designing Pricing Strategies and Programs

In this chapter, we will address the following questions:

1. How should a company price a new good or service?
2. How should the price be adapted to meet varying circumstances and opportunities?
3. When should the company initiate a price change, and how should it respond to competitive price changes?

MARKETING MANAGEMENT AT INTEL

Pricing has long been a vital marketing tool for Intel, the world's leading maker of computer chips. Intel's share of the global microprocessor market is more than three times that of competitor Advanced Micro Devices (AMD). However, now that market growth has slowed, one company's share gain means another company's share loss. Both Intel and AMD are therefore using price cuts to retain share and build volume to lower costs—even at the expense of profits. After lowering prices almost monthly during one recent year (even slashing one chip's price by more than half), Intel's profit margins dropped to 48 percent, compared with 60 percent only one year earlier.

Intel sets different prices for different products in its mix. The latest high-end Pentium chips carry a premium price, whereas Celeron chips, which have less functionality, are priced lower to compete with lower-priced chips from rival AMD. Intel also sets different prices for different customer types, based on volume. Giant manufacturers like Dell who buy 10,000 chips or more at a time pay much less than smaller assemblers who buy in batches of 1,000 chips or less. Close attention to pricing helped Intel dominate the chip market and boosted annual sales past $26 billion.[1]

All for-profit organizations and many nonprofit organizations set prices on their offerings. Whether the price is called rent (for an apartment), tuition (for education), fare (for travel), or interest (for borrowed money), the concept is the same. Throughout most of history, prices were set by negotiation between buyers and sellers. Setting one price for all buyers arose with the development of large-scale retailing at the end of the nineteenth century, when Woolworth's and other stores followed a "strictly one-price policy" because they carried so many items and had so many employees.

Today, the Internet is partially reversing the fixed pricing trend. Online auction sites like eBay.com make it easy for buyers and sellers to negotiate prices on thousands of items. Priceline.com invites customers to state the price they want to pay for airline tickets, hotel rooms, and other services, then checks whether any seller is willing to meet that price. Other technologies are allowing sellers to collect data about customers' buying habits, preferences—even spending limits—so they can tailor their products and prices.[2]

In the entire marketing mix, price is the one element that produces revenue; the others produce costs. Price is also one of the most flexible elements: It can be changed quickly, unlike product features and channel commitments. Although price competition is a major problem facing companies, many do not handle pricing well. The most common mistakes are: Pricing is too cost-oriented; price is not revised often enough to capitalize on market changes; price is set independent of the rest of the marketing mix rather than as an intrinsic element of market-positioning strategy; and price is not varied enough for different product items, market segments, and purchase occasions.

SETTING THE PRICE

A firm must set a price for the first time when it develops a new product, introduces its regular product into a new distribution channel or geographical area, and enters bids on new contract work. Price is also a key element used to support a product's quality positioning. Because a firm, in developing its strategy, must decide where to position its product on price and quality, there can be competition between price-quality segments (see Figure 13.1).

In setting a product's price, marketers follow a six-step procedure: (1) selecting the pricing objective; (2) determining demand; (3) estimating costs; (4) analyzing competitors' costs, prices, and offers; (5) selecting a pricing method; and (6) selecting the final price (see Figure 13.2).

Step 1: Selecting the Pricing Objective

A company can pursue any of five major objectives through pricing: survival, maximum current profit, maximum market share, maximum market skimming, or product-quality leadership. *Survival* is a short-term objective that is appropriate for companies plagued with overcapacity, intense competition, or changing consumer wants. As long as prices cover variable costs and some fixed costs, the company can stay in business.

FIGURE 13.1   Nine Price-Quality Strategies

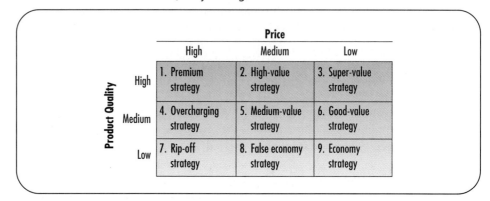

To *maximize current profits*, companies estimate the demand and costs associated with alternative prices and then choose the price that produces maximum current profit, cash flow, or return on investment. However, by emphasizing current profits, the company may sacrifice long-run performance by ignoring the effects of other marketing-mix variables, competitors' reactions, and legal restraints on price.

Firms choosing the objective of *maximum market share* believe that higher sales volume will lead to lower unit costs and higher long-run profit. With this **market-penetration pricing**, the firms set the lowest price, assuming the market is price sensitive. This is appropriate when the market is highly price sensitive, so a low price stimulates market growth; production and distribution costs fall with accumulated production experience; and a low price discourages competition.

Many companies favor setting high prices to "skim" the market. This *market-skimming pricing* objective makes sense when enough buyers have high current demand; the unit costs of producing a small volume are not so high that they cancel the advantage of charging what the traffic will bear; the high initial price does not attract more competitors; and the high price communicates the image of a superior product.

Companies such as Maytag that aim to be *product-quality leaders* will offer premium products at premium prices. Because they offer top quality plus innovative features that deliver wanted benefits, these firms can charge more. Maytag can charge much more for its Neptune washers—double what most other washers cost—because the appliances use less water and electricity and prolong the life of clothing by being less abrasive. Maytag's strategy is to encourage buyers to trade up to new models before their existing appliances wear out.[3]

FIGURE 13.2   Setting Pricing Policy

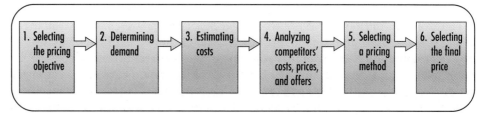

Nonprofit and public organizations may adopt other pricing objectives. A university aims for *partial cost recovery*, knowing that it must rely on private gifts and public grants to cover the remaining costs, while a nonprofit theater company prices its productions to fill the maximum number of seats. As another example, a social services agency may set prices geared to the varying incomes of clients.

Step 2: Determining Demand

Each price will lead to a different level of demand and therefore will have a different impact on a company's marketing objectives. A demand curve shows the relationship between alternative prices and the resulting current demand. Normally, demand and price are inversely related: The higher the price, the lower the demand. For prestige goods, the demand curve sometimes slopes upward because some consumers take the higher price to signify a better product. Still, if the price is too high, the level of demand may fall.

Price Sensitivity   The demand curve shows the market's probable purchase quantity at alternative prices, summing the reactions of many individuals who have different price sensitivities. The first step in estimating demand is to understand what affects price sensitivity. Nagle and Holden say customers are less price sensitive when:

- The product is more distinctive,
- Buyers are less aware of substitutes,
- Buyers cannot easily compare the quality of substitutes,
- The expenditure is a lower part of buyer's total income,
- The expenditure is small compared to the total cost of the end product,
- Part of the cost is borne by another party,
- The product is used in conjunction with assets previously bought,
- The product is assumed to have more quality, prestige, or exclusiveness, and
- Buyers cannot store the product.[4]

Now that instant price comparisons are available online, some (but not all) customers have become more price sensitive. More than ever, companies need to understand the price sensitivity of targeted customers and the trade-offs that people are willing to make between price and product characteristics. Some utility companies are even branding energy, marketing it, and differentiating their offerings. Vermont-based Green Mountain, an electric power company, learned through research that a large market of prospects were concerned with the environment and willing to pay more to protect it. Because Green Mountain is a "green" power provider—using energy from natural gas, water, wind, and solar sources—customers are willing to pay higher prices to help the environment by purchasing its power.[5]

Estimating Demand Curves   Companies can use one of three basic methods to estimate their demand curves. The first involves statistically analyzing past prices, quantities sold, and other factors to estimate their relationships. However, building a model and fitting the data with the proper techniques calls for considerable skill.

The second approach is to conduct price experiments, as when Bennett and Wilkinson systematically varied the prices of several products sold in a discount store and observed the results.[6] An alternative here is to charge different prices in similar territories to see how sales are affected. Still another approach is to test prices using the Internet, being careful not to alienate customers.

The third approach is to ask buyers how many units they would buy at different proposed prices.[7] However, buyers might understate their purchase intentions at higher prices to discourage the company from setting higher prices. In measuring the price-demand relationship, the marketer must control for various factors that will influence demand, such as competitive response. Also, if the company changes other marketing-mix factors besides price, the effect of the price change itself will be hard to isolate.[8]

Price Elasticity of Demand   Marketers need to know how responsive, or elastic, demand would be to a change in price. If demand hardly changes with a small change in price, we say the demand is *inelastic*. If demand changes considerably, it is *elastic*.

Demand is likely to be less elastic when (1) there are few or no substitutes or competitors; (2) buyers do not readily notice the higher price; (3) buyers are slow to change their buying habits and search for lower prices; and (4) buyers think the higher prices are justified. If demand is elastic, sellers will consider lowering the price to produce more total revenue. This makes sense as long as the costs of producing and selling more units do not increase disproportionately.[9]

Price elasticity depends on the magnitude and direction of the contemplated price change. It may be negligible with a small price change and substantial with a large price change; it may differ for a price cut versus a price increase. Finally, long-run price elasticity may differ from short-run elasticity. Buyers may continue to buy from their current supplier after a price increase but they may eventually switch suppliers. The distinction between short-run and long-run elasticity means that sellers will not know the total effect of a price change until time passes.

Step 3: Estimating Costs

Whereas demand sets a ceiling on the price the company can charge for its product, costs set the floor. The company wants to charge a price that covers its cost of producing, distributing, and selling the product and provides a fair return for its effort and risk.

Types of Costs and Levels of Production   A company's costs take two forms—fixed and variable. **Fixed costs** (also known as **overhead**) are costs that do not vary with production or sales revenue, such as payments for rent, heat, interest, salaries, and other bills that must be paid regardless of output.

Variable costs vary directly with the level of production. For example, each calculator produced by Texas Instruments (TI) involves a cost of plastic, microprocessing chips, packaging, and the like. These costs tend to be constant per unit produced, but they are called variable because their total varies with the number of units produced.

Total costs consist of the sum of the fixed and variable costs for any given level of production. **Average cost** is the cost per unit at that level of production; it is equal to total costs divided by production. Management wants to charge a price that will at least cover the total production costs at a given level of production.

To price intelligently, management needs to know how its costs vary with different levels of production. A firm's cost per unit is high if only a few units are produced every day, but as production increases, fixed costs are spread over a higher level of production results in each unit, bringing the average cost down. At some point, however, higher production will lead to higher average cost because the plant becomes inefficient (due to problems such as machines breaking down more often). By calculating costs for different-sized plants, a company can identify the optimal plant size and production level to achieve economies of scale and bring down the average cost.

Accumulated Production Suppose TI runs a plant that produces 3,000 hand calculators per day. As TI gains experience producing calculators, its methods improve. Workers learn shortcuts, materials flow more smoothly, and procurement costs fall. The result, as Figure 13.3 shows, is that average cost falls with accumulated production experience. Thus, the average cost of producing the first 100,000 hand calculators is $10 per calculator. When the company has produced the first 200,000 calculators, the average cost has fallen to $9. After its accumulated production experience doubles again to 400,000, the average cost is $8. This decline in the average cost with accumulated production experience is called the **experience curve or learning curve**.

Now suppose TI competes against firms A and B in this industry. TI is the lowest-cost producer at $8, having produced 400,000 units in the past. If all three firms sell the calculator for $10, TI makes $2 profit per unit, A makes $1 per unit, and B breaks even. The smart move for TI would be to lower its price to $9 to drive B out of the market; even A will consider leaving. Then TI will pick up the business that would have gone to B (and possibly A). Furthermore, price-sensitive customers will enter the market at the lower price. As production increases beyond 400,000 units, TI's costs will drop even more, restoring its profits even at a price of $9. TI has used this aggressive pricing strategy repeatedly to gain market share and drive others out of the industry.

Experience-curve pricing is risky because aggressive pricing may give the product a cheap image. This strategy also assumes that the competitors are weak and not willing to fight. Finally, the strategy may lead the firm into building more plants to meet demand while a competitor innovates a lower-cost technology and enjoys lower costs, leaving the leader stuck with old technology.

Differentiated Marketing Offers Today's companies try to adapt their offers and terms to different buyers. Thus, a manufacturer will negotiate different terms with dif-

FIGURE 13.3 The Experience Curve

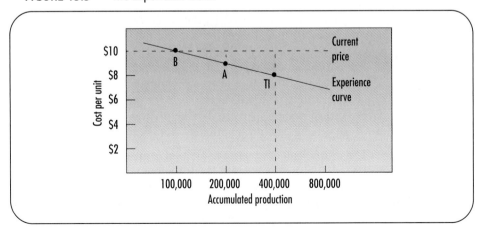

ferent retail chains, meaning the costs and profits will differ with each chain. To estimate the real profitability of dealing with different retailers, the manufacturer needs to use **activity-based cost (ABC) accounting** instead of standard cost accounting.[10]

ABC accounting tries to identify the real costs associated with serving different customers. Both the variable costs and the overhead costs must be tagged back to each customer. Companies that fail to measure their costs correctly are not measuring their profit correctly, and they are likely to misallocate their marketing effort. Identifying the true costs arising in a customer relationship also enables a company to explain its charges better to the customer.

Target Costing   Costs change with production scale and experience. They can also change as a result of a concentrated effort by the company's designers, engineers, and purchasing agents to reduce them. Many Japanese firms use a method called **target costing**.[11] First, they use market research to establish a new product's desired functions, then they determine the price at which the product will sell given its appeal and competitors' prices. They deduct the desired profit margin from this price, leaving the target cost they must achieve.

Next, the firms examine each cost element—design, engineering, manufacturing, sales—and look for ways to reengineer components, eliminate functions, and bring down supplier costs. The objective is to bring the final cost projections into the target cost range. If they cannot succeed, they may decide against developing the product because it could not sell for the target price and make the target profit. When they can succeed, profits are likely to follow.

Step 4: Analyzing Competitors' Costs, Prices, and Offers

Within the range of possible prices determined by market demand and company costs, the firm must take into account its competitors' costs, prices, and possible price reactions. If the firm's offer is similar to a major competitor's offer, then the firm will have to price close to the competitor or lose sales. If the firm's offer is inferior, it will not be able to charge more than the competitor charges. If the firm's offer is superior, it can charge more—remembering, however, that competitors might change their prices at any time.

Step 5: Selecting a Pricing Method

The three Cs—the customers' demand schedule, the cost function, and competitors' prices—are major considerations in setting price (see Figure 13.4). First, costs set a floor to the price. Second, competitors' prices and the price of substitutes provide an orienting point. Third, customers' assessment of unique product features establishes the ceiling price. Companies must therefore select a pricing method that includes one or more of these considerations. We will examine seven price-setting methods: markup pricing, target-return pricing, perceived-value pricing, value pricing, going-rate pricing, auction-type pricing, and group pricing.

Markup Pricing   The most elementary pricing method is to add a standard **markup** to the product's cost. Construction companies do this when they submit job bids by estimating the total project cost and adding a standard markup for profit. Similarly, lawyers and accountants typically price by adding a standard markup on their time and costs.

FIGURE 13.4 The Three Cs Model for Price Setting

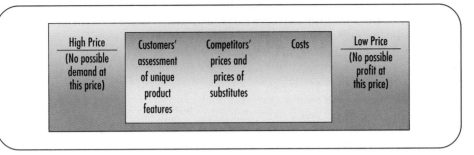

Suppose a toaster manufacturer has the following costs and sales expectations:

Variable cost per unit	$ 10
Fixed cost	300,000
Expected unit sales	50,000

The manufacturer's unit cost is given by:

$$\text{Unit cost} = \text{variable cost} + \frac{\text{fixed costs}}{\text{unit sales}} = \$10 + \frac{\$300,000}{50,000} = \$16$$

If the manufacturer wants to earn a 20 percent markup on sales, its markup price is:

$$\text{Markup price} = \frac{\text{unit cost}}{(1 - \text{desired return on sales})} = \frac{\$16}{1 - 0.2} = \$20$$

The manufacturer charges dealers $20 per toaster and makes a profit of $4 per unit. If the dealers want to earn 50 percent on their selling price, they will mark up the toaster to $40. This is equivalent to a cost markup of 100 percent.

Do standard markups make logical sense? Generally, no. Any pricing method that ignores current demand, perceived value, and competition is not likely to lead to the optimal price. Markup pricing works only if the marked-up price actually brings in the expected level of sales.

Companies introducing a new product often price it high, hoping to recover their costs as rapidly as possible. But a high-markup strategy could be fatal if a competitor is pricing low. This happened to Philips, the Dutch electronics manufacturer, in pricing its videodisc players. Philips wanted to make a profit on each videodisc player. Meanwhile, Japanese competitors priced low and succeeded in building their market share rapidly, which in turn pushed down their costs substantially.

Markup pricing remains popular for a number of reasons. First, sellers can determine costs much more easily than they can estimate demand. By tying the price to cost, sellers simplify the pricing task. Second, when all firms in the industry use this pricing method, prices tend to be similar, which minimizes price competition. Third, many people feel that cost-plus pricing is fairer to both buyers and sellers: Sellers do not take advantage of buyers when demand becomes acute, and sellers earn a fair return on investment.

Target-Return Pricing In **target-return pricing**, the firm determines the price that would yield its target rate of return on investment (ROI). Target pricing is used by many firms, including General Motors, which prices its automobiles to achieve a 15–20 percent ROI.

Suppose the toaster manufacturer in the previous example has invested $1 million and wants to earn a 20 percent return on its invested capital. The target-return price is given by the following formula:

$$\text{Target -return price} = \frac{\text{unit cost} + \text{desired return} \times \text{invested capital}}{\text{unit sales}}$$

$$= \$16 + \frac{.20 \times \$1,000,000}{50,000} = \$20$$

The manufacturer will realize this 20 percent ROI provided its costs and estimated sales turn out to be accurate, but what if sales do not reach 50,000 units? The manufacturer can prepare a break-even chart to learn what would happen at other sales levels (Figure 13.5). Note that fixed costs remain the same regardless of sales volume, while variable costs, which are not shown in the figure, rise with volume. Total costs equal the sum of fixed costs and variable costs; the total revenue curve rises with each unit sold.

According to this break-even chart, the total revenue and total cost curves cross at 30,000 units. This is the break-even volume. It can be verified by the following formula:

$$\text{Break-even volume} = \frac{\text{fixed cost}}{\text{price} - \text{variable cost}} = \frac{\$300,000}{\$20 - \$10} = 30,000$$

If the manufacturer sells 50,000 units at $20, it carns a $200,000 profit on its $1 million investment. But much depends on price elasticity and competitors' prices, two elements ignored by target-return pricing. In practice, the manufacturer needs to consider different prices and estimate their probable impacts on sales volume and

FIGURE 13.5   Break-Even Chart

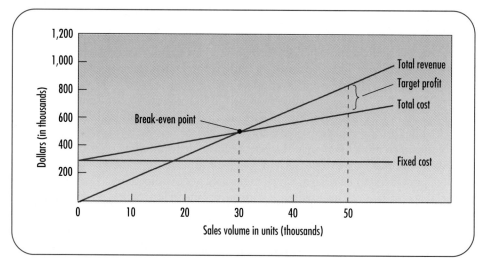

profits. The manufacturer should also search for ways to lower fixed or variable costs, because lower costs will decrease its required break-even volume.

Perceived-Value Pricing   An increasing number of companies base price on customers' *perceived value*. They must deliver the value promised by their value proposition, and the customer must perceive this value. They use the other marketing-mix elements, such as advertising, to communicate and enhance perceived value in buyers' minds.[12]

For example, when DuPont developed a new synthetic carpet fiber, it demonstrated that carpet manufacturers could afford to pay as much as $1.40 per pound for the new fiber and still make their target profit. DuPont calls the $1.40 the *value-in-use price*. But pricing the new material at $1.40 per pound would leave the carpet manufacturers indifferent. So DuPont set the price lower than $1.40 to induce carpet manufacturers to adopt the new fiber. In this situation, DuPont used its cost only to judge whether there was enough profit to go ahead with the new product.

The key to perceived-value pricing is to deliver more value than the competitor and demonstrate this to prospective buyers. Basically, a company needs to research the customer's value drivers and understand the customer's decision-making process. The company can try to determine its offering's value through managerial judgments, focus groups, the value of analogous products, conjoint analysis, and other methods.[13]

Value Pricing   **Value pricing** is a method in which the company charges a fairly low price for a high-quality offering. IKEA, Southwest Airlines, and Wal-Mart practice value pricing. Value pricing is not a matter of simply setting lower prices on one's products compared to those of competitors. It is a matter of reengineering the company's operations to become a low-cost producer without sacrificing quality, and lowering prices significantly to attract a large number of value-conscious customers.

An important type of value pricing is **everyday low pricing (EDLP)**, which takes place at the retail level. Retailers using EDLP pricing charge a constant, everyday low price with few or no price promotions and special sales. These constant prices eliminate week-to-week price uncertainty and can be contrasted to the "high-low" pricing of promotion-oriented competitors. In **high-low pricing**, the retailer charges higher prices on an everyday basis but then runs frequent promotions in which prices are temporarily lowered below the EDLP level.[14] Wal-Mart is the king of EDLP, offering only a few sale items every month; Saturn dealerships also offer EDLP.

The most important reason retailers adopt EDLP is that constant sales and promotions are costly and erode consumer confidence in the credibility of everyday prices. Consumers also have less time and patience for such time-honored traditions as watching for specials and clipping coupons. Yet promotions are an excellent way to create excitement and draw shoppers. For this reason, EDLP is not a guarantee of success. As supermarkets face heightened competition from store rivals and alternative channels, many are drawing shoppers using a combination of high-low and EDLP strategies, with increased advertising and promotions.[15]

Going-Rate Pricing   In **going-rate pricing**, the firm bases its price largely on competitors' prices. The firm might charge the same, more, or less than its major competitor(s) charges. In oligopolistic industries that sell a commodity such as steel, paper, or fertilizer, firms normally charge the same price. The smaller firms "follow the leader," changing their prices when the leader's prices change rather than when their own demand or costs change. Some firms may charge a slight premium or discount, but they typically preserve the amount of difference. When costs are difficult to measure or competitive response is uncertain, firms adopt the going price because it seems to reflect the industry's collective wisdom as to the price that will yield a fair return and not jeopardize industrial harmony.

Auction-Type Pricing   Auction-type pricing is growing more popular, especially with the growth of the Internet. One major use of auctions is to dispose of excess inventories or used goods; another is to procure goods and services at lower prices (see "Marketing Skills: Planning Online Auctions"). Companies need to be aware of the three major types of auctions and their pricing procedures.

In *English auctions* (*ascending bids*), one seller puts up an item and bidders raise the offer price until the top price is reached. English auctions are often used to sell antiques, cattle, real estate, used equipment, and vehicles. In *Dutch auctions* (*descending bids*), one seller may propose pricing to many buyers or one buyer may solicit bids from many sellers. In the first kind, an auctioneer announces a high price for a product and then slowly decreases the price until a bidder accepts the price. In the other, the buyer announces something that he wants to buy and then potential sellers com-

---

MARKETING SKILLS: ONLINE AUCTIONS

Businesses around the world are embracing online auctions to keep costs down and expand their roster of suppliers and customers. Thus, marketers need to know how to plan and manage an online auction, especially one in which the company solicits bids from suppliers to supply certain components, materials, equipment, or services. Companies sometimes start by experimenting with a few auctions to buy low-risk products that are available from more than a handful of suppliers. The first step is to define what the company wants to buy, including detailed specifications of quality and other attributes.

Next, the marketer alerts suppliers that are known as qualified to provide such products, allowing several weeks' lead time so the suppliers can prepare documentation or bids in advance. New suppliers may be required to show that they can meet the quality level, delivery dates, and other specifications in order to bid. When soliciting bids for multiple items, a firm must decide whether suppliers will be allowed to bid only on selected items. Once the auction begins, marketers will be busy reviewing bids and proposals and posting bids to keep the auction running smoothly. At the close, marketers should notify all participants of the buying decision and thank everyone for participating.

Sainsbury's Supermarkets, a large U.K. chain, uses online auctions to obtain bids for making private label products such as frozen foods, meat, cosmetics, and beverages. In planning these auctions, quality is as important as price. "In most cases, product samples are evaluated before the auction to ensure all are competing on a 'level playing field,'" says a Sainsbury's executive. "Any products which fall short on quality attributes are simply not included in the auction. At the same time, we want to source at the best price for that quality." Not every auction saves money, but the company has enjoyed an overall financial benefit and plans to step up its use of online auctions in the future.[16]

pete to get the sale by offering the lowest price. Each seller sees the last bid and decides whether to go lower.

In *sealed-bid auctions*, each would-be supplier submits only one bid and does not know the other bids. The U.S. government often uses this method to procure supplies. A supplier will not bid below its cost but cannot bid too high for fear of losing the job. To solve this dilemma, the company estimates the profit and the probability of winning with each price bid. By multiplying the profit by the probability of winning the bid on the basis of that price, the company can calculate the expected profit for each bid. For a firm that makes many bids, this method is a way of playing the odds to achieve maximum profits in the long run. However, firms that bid only occasionally or that badly want to win certain contracts will not find it advantageous to use the expected-profit criterion.

Group Pricing   The Internet is facilitating a method whereby consumers and business buyers join groups to buy at a lower price. For instance, industrial buyers can go to the Weatherchem site to see the price of raw materials at different sales volume levels. If enough buyers order sufficient quantities for the same shipping date, the price will drop for all participants. In one instance, buyers from 11 North American firms signed up to buy a certain product for the same shipment date; group buying enabled them to save more than 25 percent.[17] A major drawback is that some buyers will not wait for the volume order to be executed.

Step 6: Selecting the Final Price

The previous pricing methods narrow the range from which the company selects its final price. In selecting that price, the company must consider additional factors: psychological pricing, gain-and-risk-sharing pricing, the influence of other marketing-mix elements on price, company pricing policies, and the impact of price on other parties.

Psychological Pricing   Many consumers use price as an indicator of quality. Image pricing is especially effective with ego-sensitive products such as perfumes and expensive cars. A $100 bottle of perfume might contain $10 worth of scent, but gift givers pay $100 to communicate their high regard for the receiver. Similarly, price and quality perceptions of cars interact:[18] Higher-priced cars are perceived to possess high quality; higher-quality cars are likewise perceived to be higher priced than they actually are. In general, when information about true quality is unavailable, price acts as a signal of quality.

When looking at a particular product, buyers carry in their minds a **reference price** formed by noticing current prices, past prices, or the buying context. Sellers often manipulate these reference prices. A seller may situate its product among expensive products to imply that it belongs in the same class. Reference-price thinking is also created by stating a high manufacturer's suggested price, by indicating that the product was priced much higher originally, or by pointing to a rival's high price.[19]

Often sellers set prices that end in an odd number, believing that customers who see a television priced at $299 instead of $300 will perceive the price as being in the $200 range rather than the $300 range. Another explanation is that odd endings convey the notion of a discount or bargain, which is why both toysrus.com and etoys.com set prices ending in 99. But if a company wants a high-price image instead of a low-price image, it should avoid the odd-ending tactic.[20]

Gain-and-Risk-Sharing Pricing   Buyers may resist a seller's proposal because of a high perceived level of risk. The seller has the option of offering to absorb part or all of the risk if it fails to deliver the promised value. This happened when Baxter, a medical products firm, proposed an information management system that would save Columbia/HCA, a health-care provider, millions of dollars over eight years. After Columbia balked, Baxter offered to write a check for the difference if the full savings were not realized—and Baxter got the order.

Baxter could have further proposed that if its system saved Columbia more than the targeted amount, Baxter would share in some of the additional savings—essentially sharing in the gain as well as the risk. An increasing number of firms, especially business marketers who promise great savings, may have to stand ready to guarantee promised savings, and possibly participate if the gains are much greater than expected.

The Influence of Other Marketing-Mix Elements   The final price must take into account the brand's quality and advertising relative to competition. When Farris and Reibstein examined the relationships among relative price, relative quality, and relative advertising for 227 consumer businesses, they found that brands with average relative quality but high relative advertising budgets were able to charge premium prices. Consumers seemed willing to pay higher prices for known products than for unknown products. Also, brands with high relative quality and high relative advertising obtained the highest prices, while brands with low quality and advertising had the lowest prices. Finally, the positive relationship between high prices and high advertising held most strongly late in the product life cycle for market leaders.[21]

Company Pricing Policies   The price must be consistent with company pricing policies. To accomplish this, many firms set up a pricing department to develop policies and establish or approve decisions. The aim is to ensure that the salespeople quote prices that are reasonable to customers and profitable to the company.

Impact of Price on Other Parties   Management must also consider the reactions of other parties to the contemplated price, including distributors, dealers, and the sales force. How will competitors react? Will suppliers raise their prices when they see the company's price? Will the government intervene and prevent this price from being charged?

Marketers need to know the laws regulating pricing. U.S. legislation outlaws price-fixing, so sellers must set prices without talking to competitors. Many federal, state, and local laws protect consumers against deceptive pricing practices. For example, it is illegal for a company to set artificially high "regular" prices, then announce a "sale" at prices close to previous everyday prices.

ADAPTING THE PRICE

Companies usually do not set a single price, but rather a pricing structure that reflects variations in geographical demand and costs, market-segment requirements, purchase timing, order levels, delivery frequency, guarantees, service contracts, and other factors. As a result of discounts, allowances, and promotional support, a company rarely realizes the same profit from each unit of a product that it sells. Here we will examine several price-adaptation strategies: geographical pricing, price discounts and allowances, promotional pricing, discriminatory pricing, and product-mix pricing.

Geographical Pricing

In geographical pricing, the company decides how to price its products to different customers in different locations and countries. For example, should the company charge distant customers more to cover higher shipping costs, or set a lower price to win additional business? Another issue is how to get paid. This is particularly critical when foreign buyers lack sufficient hard currency to pay for their purchases. Many buyers want to offer other items in payment in a practice known as **countertrade**, which accounts for 15–25 percent of world trade and takes several forms:[22]

- *Barter.* The direct exchange of goods, with no money and no third party involved. Eminence S.A., a clothing maker in France, bartered $25 million worth of U.S.-produced underwear and sportswear to customers in eastern Europe in exchange for transportation, magazine advertising space, and other goods and services.
- *Compensation deal.* The seller is paid partly in cash and partly in products. A British aircraft manufacturer used this approach to sell planes to Brazil for 70 percent cash and the rest in coffee.
- *Buyback arrangement.* The seller sells a plant or equipment and accepts products manufactured with the supplied equipment as partial payment. A U.S. chemical firm built a plant for an Indian company and accepted partial payment in cash and the remainder in chemicals manufactured at the plant.
- *Offset.* The seller receives full cash payment but agrees to spend much of the cash in that country within a stated period. For example, PepsiCo sells its cola syrup to Russia for rubles and buys Russian vodka at a certain rate for sale in the United States.

Price Discounts and Allowances

Most companies will adjust their list price and give discounts and allowances for early payment, volume purchases, and off-season buying, as shown in Table 13.1. However, companies must do this carefully or their profits will be much less than planned.[23]

Promotional Pricing

Companies can use any of seven promotional pricing techniques to stimulate early purchase (see Table 13.2). However, promotional pricing strategies are often a zero-sum game. If they work, competitors copy them, reducing their effectiveness. If they do not work, they waste money that could have been put into marketing tools such as building up product quality and service or strengthening product image through advertising.

Discriminatory Pricing

Companies often adjust their basic price to accommodate differences in customers, products, locations, and so on. **Price discrimination** occurs when a company sells a product or service at two or more prices that do not reflect a proportional difference in costs. Sellers may set different prices for different classes of buyers, as in these cases:

- *Customer-segment pricing.* Different customer groups pay different prices for the same offering. For example, museums often charge a lower admission fee to students and senior citizens.

- *Product-form pricing.* Different versions of the product are priced differently but not proportionately to their respective costs. Evian may price a 48-ounce bottle of mineral water at $2, while its 1.7 ounce moisturizer spray sells for $6.

- *Image pricing.* Some companies price the same product at two different levels based on image differences. A perfume manufacturer can put its perfume in one bottle with a certain brand and image, priced at $10 an ounce; the same perfume in another bottle with a different name and image could be priced at $30 an ounce.

- *Channel pricing.* Coca-Cola carries a different price depending on whether it is purchased in a fine restaurant, a fast-food restaurant, or a vending machine.

- *Location pricing.* The same product is priced differently at different locations even though the costs are the same; for example, theaters often vary seat prices according to audience preferences for different locations.

- *Time pricing.* Prices are varied by season, day, or hour. Public utilities use time pricing, varying energy rates to commercial users by time of day and weekend versus weekday. Airlines use **yield pricing** to offer lower prices on unsold inventory before it expires.[24]

Price discrimination works when (1) the market is segmentable and the segments show different intensities of demand; (2) members in the lower-price segment

TABLE 13.1   Price Discounts and Allowances

Cash Discounts:	A *cash discount* is a price reduction to buyers who pay their bills promptly. A typical example is "2/10, net 20," which means that payment is due within 30 days and that the buyer can deduct 2 percent by paying the bill within 10 days. Such discounts are customary in many industries.
Quantity Discounts:	A *quantity discount* is a price reduction to those buyers who buy large volumes. A typical example is "$10 per unit for less than 100 units; $9 per unit for 100 or more units." Quantity discounts must be offered equally to all customers and must not exceed the cost savings to the seller associated with selling large quantities. They can be offered on a noncumulative basis (on each order placed) or a cumulative basis (on the number of units ordered over a given period).
Functional Discounts:	*Functional discounts* (also called *trade discounts*) are offered by a manufacturer to trade-channel members if they will perform certain functions, such as selling, storing, and record keeping. Manufacturers may offer different functional discounts to different trade channels but must offer the same functional discounts within each channel.
Seasonal Discounts:	A *seasonal discount* is a price reduction to buyers who buy merchandise or services out of season. Ski manufacturers will offer seasonal discounts to retailers in the spring and summer to encourage early ordering. Hotels, motels, and airlines will offer seasonal discounts in slow selling periods.
Allowances:	*Allowances* are extra payments designed to gain reseller participation in special programs. *Trade-in allowances* are price reductions granted for turning in an old item when buying a new one. Trade-in allowances are most common in durable-goods categories. *Promotional allowances* are payments or price reductions to reward dealers for participating in advertising and sales support programs.

TABLE 13.2   Promotional Pricing Techniques

Technique	Description	Example
Loss-leader pricing	Stores drop the price on well-known brands to stimulate additional store traffic.	Wal-Mart cuts the price of selected toys to attract shoppers before Christmas.
Special-event pricing	Sellers establish special prices in certain seasons to draw in more customers.	Staples offers special prices on stationery items during a back-to-school sale.
Cash rebates	Manufacturers offer cash rebates to encourage purchase of their products within a specified period; this helps clear inventories without cutting the stated price.	Mazda advertises cash rebates on the purchase of selected previous-year models to clear these vehicles out of dealer inventory.
Low-interest financing	Instead of cutting its price, the company can offer customers low-interest financing.	Ford offers low- or no-interest financing to encourage the purchase of selected vehicles.
Longer payment terms	Sellers stretch loans over longer periods and thus lower the monthly payments that customers pay.	Auto companies and mortgage banks use this approach because consumers are more concerned with affordable payments than with the interest rate.
Warranties and service contracts	Companies can promote sales by adding a free or low-cost warranty or service contract.	Real estate brokers offer special warranties on selected homes to expedite sales.
Psychological discounting	Used legitimately, this involves offering the item at substantial savings from the normal price.	A jewelry store lowers the price of a diamond ring and advertises "Was $359, now $299."

cannot resell the product to the higher-price segment; (3) competitors cannot undersell the firm in the higher-price segment; (4) the cost of segmenting and policing the market does not exceed the extra revenue derived from price discrimination; (5) the practice does not breed customer resentment and ill will; and (6) the particular form of price discrimination is not illegal (practices such as predatory pricing—selling below cost with the intention of destroying competition—are against the law).[25]

Technology helps sellers practice price discrimination. For example, a company can use software to monitor customers' movements online and then customize offers and prices. At the same time, sellers can use the Internet to easily compare prices and offers from thousands of suppliers and to name their own price for certain goods and services.

Product-Mix Pricing

Price-setting logic must be modified when the product is part of a product mix. In this case, the firm searches for a set of prices that maximizes profits on the total mix. Pricing a product line is difficult because the various products have demand and cost interrelationships and are subject to different degrees of competition. We can distinguish six situations involving product-mix pricing:

- *Product-line pricing.* Many sellers use well-established price points (such as $200, $400, and $600 for suits) to distinguish the products in their line. The seller's task is to establish perceived-quality differences that justify the price differences.

- *Optional-feature pricing.* Automakers and other firms offer optional products, features, and services along with their main product. Pricing these options is a sticky problem because companies must decide which items to include in the standard price and which to offer as options.

- *Captive-product pricing.* Some products require the use of ancillary, or **captive**, products. In the razor industry, manufacturers often price their razors low and set high markups on blades. However, there is a danger in pricing the captive product too high in the aftermarket (the market for ancillary supplies to the main product). Caterpillar, for example, makes high aftermarket profits by pricing parts and service high. This practice has given rise to "pirates," who counterfeit the parts and sell them to "shady tree" mechanics who install them, sometimes without passing on the cost savings to customers. Meanwhile, Caterpillar loses sales.[26]

- *Two-part pricing.* Many service firms use **two-part pricing**, which consists of a fixed fee plus a variable usage fee. Telephone customers pay a minimum monthly fee plus charges for calls beyond a certain area. The challenge is how much to charge for the basic service and how much for the variable usage. The fixed fee should be low enough to induce purchase; the profit can then be made on the usage fees.

- *By-product pricing.* The production of certain goods—meats, chemicals, and so on—often results in by-products, which can be priced according to their value to customers. Any income earned on the by-products will make it easier for the company to charge less for the main product if competition forces it to do so. Sometimes companies do not realize how valuable their by-products are. Until Zoo-Doo Compost Company came along, many zoos did not realize that one of their by-products—manure—could be an excellent source of additional revenue.[27]

- *Product-bundling pricing.* Sellers often bundle their products and features at a set price. An auto manufacturer, for instance, might offer an option package at less than the cost of buying all of the options separately. Because customers may not have planned to buy all of the components, the savings on the price bundle must be substantial enough to induce them to buy the bundle.[28]

INITIATING AND RESPONDING TO PRICE CHANGES

Firms often face the need to cut or raise prices in certain situations. Here we will examine the challenges of initiating price cuts, initiating price increases, reacting to price changes, and responding to competitors' price changes. For an overview of strategic pricing options involving marketing-mix variables, see Table 13.3.

Initiating Price Cuts

Several circumstances might lead a firm to cut prices. One is excess plant capacity: If the firm needs additional business but cannot generate it through increased sales effort or other measures, it may initiate a price cut. In doing so, however, the company risks triggering a price war. Another circumstance is a declining market share, which

TABLE 13.3   Marketing-Mix Alternatives

Strategic Options	Reasoning	Consequences
1. Maintain price and perceived quality. Engage in selective customer pruning.	Firm has higher customer loyalty. It is willing to lose poorer customers to competitors.	Smaller market share. Lowered profitability.
2. Raise price and perceived quality.	Raise price to cover rising costs. Improve quality to justify higher prices.	Smaller market share. Maintained profitability.
3. Maintain price and raise perceived quality.	It is cheaper to maintain price and raise perceived quality.	Smaller market share. Short-term decline in profitability. Long-term increase in profitability.
4. Cut price partly and raise perceived quality.	Must give customers some price reduction but stress higher value of offer.	Maintained market share. Short-term decline in profitability. Long-term maintained profitability.
5. Cut price fully and maintain perceived quality.	Discipline and discourage price competition.	Maintained market share. Short-term decline in profitability.
6. Cut price fully and reduce perceived quality.	Discipline and discourage price competition and maintain profit margin.	Maintained market share. Maintained margin. Reduced long-term profitability.
7. Maintain price and reduce perceived quality.	Cut marketing expense to combat rising costs.	Smaller market share. Maintained margin. Reduced long-term profitability.
8. Introduce an economy model.	Give the market what it wants.	Some cannibalization but higher total volume.

may prompt the firm to cut prices as a way of regaining share. In addition, companies sometimes initiate price cuts in a drive to *dominate the market through lower costs*. Either the company starts with lower costs than those of its competitors or it initiates price cuts in the hope of gaining market share and lower costs.

When considering price cutting, marketers need to be aware of three possible traps: Customers may assume that lower-priced products have lower quality; a low price buys market share but not market loyalty because the same customers will shift to any lower-price firm; and higher-priced competitors may cut their prices and still have longer staying power because of deeper cash reserves.

Initiating Price Increases

A successful price increase can raise profits considerably. For example, if the company's profit margin is 3 percent of sales, a 1 percent price increase will increase profits by 33 percent if sales volume does not drop. In many cases, firms increase prices just to maintain profits in the face of *cost inflation*. This occurs when rising costs—unmatched by productivity gains—squeeze profit margins, leading firms to regularly increase prices. In fact, companies often raise their prices by more than the cost increase in anticipation of further inflation or government price controls in a practice called *anticipatory pricing*.

Another factor leading to price increases is *overdemand*. When a company cannot supply all of its customers, it can use one of the following pricing techniques:

- *Delayed quotation pricing.* The company does not set a final price until the product is finished or delivered. This is prevalent in industries with long production lead times.
- *Escalator clauses.* The company requires the customer to pay today's price and all or part of any inflation increase that occurs before delivery, based on some specified price index. Such clauses are found in contracts involving major industrial projects.
- *Unbundling.* The company maintains its price but removes or prices separately one or more elements that were part of the former offer, such as free delivery or installation.
- *Reduction of discounts.* The company no longer offers its usual cash and quantity discounts.

Instead of raising prices, companies can respond to higher costs or overdemand in other ways, as shown in Table 13.3. When raising prices, avoid being perceived as a price gouger. Companies should maintain a sense of fairness about any price increase and, where possible, give customers advance notice so they can do forward buying or shop around. It is also a good idea to fully explain sharp increases in understandable terms.

Reactions to Price Changes

Any price change can provoke a response from the firm's stakeholders. Savvy marketers pay close attention to customers' reactions, because customers often question the motivation behind price changes.[29] A price cut can be interpreted in different ways: The item is about to be replaced by a new model; the item is faulty and not selling well; the firm is in trouble; the price will drop even further; the quality has been cut. A price increase, which would normally deter sales, may suggest that an item is "hot" and is a good value.

Competitors are most likely to react to a price change when there are few firms offering the product, the product is homogeneous, and buyers are highly informed. Anticipating reaction is complicated because each rival may have different interpretations of a company's price cut: One may think the company is trying to steal the market; another may believe that the company wants all suppliers to reduce prices to stimulate total demand. To understand possible competitive reactions, companies must continuously monitor and analyze its rivals' activities.

Responding to Competitors' Price Changes

How should a firm respond to a price cut that is initiated by a competitor? In markets characterized by high product homogeneity, the firm should search for ways to enhance its augmented product; if it cannot find any, it will have to meet the price reduction. If the competitor raises its price in a homogeneous product market, the other firms might not match it, unless the price increase will benefit the industry as a whole. Then the leader will have to rescind the increase.

In nonhomogeneous product markets, a firm has more latitude to consider the following issues: Why did the competitor change the price? Is it to steal the market, to utilize excess capacity, to meet changing cost conditions, or to lead an industrywide price change? Does the competitor plan to make the price change temporary or permanent? What will happen to the company's market share and profits if it does not respond? Are other companies going to respond? What are the competitor's and other firms' responses likely to be to each possible reaction?

Market leaders often face aggressive price cutting by smaller competitors trying to build market share, the way Amazon.com has attacked Barnes and Noble. The brand leader can respond by:

- *Maintaining price and profit margin*, believing that (1) it would lose too much profit if it reduced its price, (2) it would not lose much market share, and (3) it could regain market share when necessary. However, the risk is that the attacker may get more confident, the leader's sales force may get demoralized, and the leader can lose more share than expected. Then the leader may panic, lower price to regain share, and find that regaining market share is more difficult and costly than expected.
- *Maintaining price while adding value* to its product, services, and communications. This may be less expensive than cutting price and operating at a lower margin.
- *Reducing price* to match the competitor's price, because its costs fall with volume, it would lose market share in a price-sensitive market, and it would be hard to rebuild market share once it is lost, even though this will cut short-term profits.
- *Increasing price and improving quality* by introducing a new brand to bracket the attacking brand.
- *Launching a low-price fighter line* or creating a separate lower-price brand to combat competition.

The best response varies with the situation. Management should consider the product's stage in the life cycle, its importance in the company's portfolio, the competitor's intentions and resources, the market's price and quality sensitivity, the behavior of costs with volume, and the company's alternative opportunities.

EXECUTIVE SUMMARY

Price is the only one of the four Ps that produces revenue. In setting prices, a company follows a six-step procedure: (1) Select the pricing objective, (2) determine demand, (3) estimate costs, (4) analyze competitors' costs, prices, and offers, (5) select a pricing method, and (6) select the final price.

Companies usually establish a pricing structure that reflects variations in geographical demand and costs, market-segment requirements, purchase timing, order levels, and other factors. Several price-adaptation strategies are available: (1) geographical pricing; (2) price discounts and allowances; (3) promotional pricing; (4) discriminatory pricing, and (5) product-mix pricing, which includes setting prices for product lines, optional features, captive products, two-part items, by-products, and product bundles.

After developing pricing strategies, firms often have to change prices by initiating price cuts or price increases. In these situations, companies need to consider how stakeholders will react to price changes. In addition, marketers must develop strategies for responding to competitors' price changes. The firm's strategy often depends on whether it is producing homogeneous or nonhomogeneous products. Market leaders who are attacked by lower-priced competitors can choose to maintain price, raise the perceived quality of their product, reduce price, increase price and improve quality, or launch a low-price fighter line.

NOTES

1. Craig Zarley, "Intel Less Aggressive in Latest Price Cut," *Computer Reseller News*, March 18, 2002, p. 115; Edward F. Moltzen, "Casualties of Price War," *Computer Reseller News*, July 30, 2001, pp. 14+; Ken Popovich, "Earnings Be Damned, Chip Makers Say," *eWeek*, July 16, 2001, p. 14.
2. Amy E. Cortese, "Good-Bye to Fixed Pricing?" *BusinessWeek*, May 4, 1998, pp. 71–84.
3. Juan Koncius, "A New Spin on Doing Your Laundry," *Washington Post*, April 12, 2001, p. A1; Steve Gelsi, "Spin-Cycle Doctor," *Brandweek*, March 10, 1997, pp. 38–40; Tim Stevens, "From Reliable to 'Wow,'" *IndustryWeek*, June 22, 1998, pp. 22–26.
4. Thomas T. Nagle and Reed K. Holden, *The Strategy and Tactics of Pricing*, 2d ed. (Upper Saddle River, NJ: Prentice Hall, 1995) ch. 4. Consumers are also concerned about whether a price seems "fair" or "reasonable," as noted in Thomas T. Nagle and Reed K. Holden, *The Strategy and Tactics of Pricing*, 3rd ed. (Upper Saddle River, NJ: Prentice Hall, 2002) ch. 4.
5. Kevin J. Clancy, "At What Profit Price?" *Brandweek*, June 23, 1997, pp. 24–28; "GreenMountain.com Begins Supplying Cleaner Electricity to Pennsylvania State Government," *PR Newswire*, January 4, 2000.
6. See Sidney Bennett and J. B. Wilkinson, "Price-Quantity Relationships and Price Elasticity Under In-Store Experimentation," *Journal of Business Research* (January 1974): 30–34.
7. John R. Nevin, "Laboratory Experiments for Estimating Consumer Demand—A Validation Study," *Journal of Marketing Research* (August 1974): 261–68; and Jonathan Weiner, "Forecasting Demand: Consumer Electronics Marketer Uses a Conjoint Approach to Configure Its New Product and Set the Right Price," *Marketing Research: A Magazine of Management & Applications*, Summer 1994, pp. 6–11.
8. For an excellent summary of the various methods for estimating price sensitivity and demand, see Nagle and Holden, *The Strategy and Tactics of Pricing*, ch. 13.
9. For summary of elasticity studies, see Dominique M. Hanssens, Leonard J. Parsons, and Randall L. Schultz, *Market Response Models: Econometric and Time Series Analysis* (Boston: Kluwer Academic Publishers, 1990) pp. 187–91.
10. See Robin Cooper and Robert S. Kaplan, "Profit Priorities from Activity-Based Costing," *Harvard Business Review* (May–June 1991): 130–35.
11. See "Japan's Smart Secret Weapon," *Fortune*, August 12, 1991, p. 75.
12. Tung-Zong Chang and Albert R. Wildt, "Price, Product Information, and Purchase Intention: An Empirical Study," *Journal of the Academy of Marketing Science* (Winter 1994): 16–27. See also G. Dean Kortge and Patrick A. Okonkwo, "Perceived Value Approach to Pricing," *Industrial Marketing Management*, May 1993, pp. 133–40.
13. See James C. Anderson, Dipak C. Jain, and Pradeep K. Chintagunta, "Customer Value Assessment in Business Markets: A State-of-Practice Study," *Journal of Business-to-Business Marketing* 1, no. 1 (1993): 3–29.
14. Stephen J. Hoch, Xavier Dreze, and Mary J. Purk, "EDLP, Hi-Lo, and Margin Arithmetic," *Journal of Marketing* (October 1994): 16–27; Rajiv Lal and R. Rao, "Supermarket Competition: The Case of Everyday Low Pricing," *Marketing Science* 16, no. 1 (1997): 60–80.
15. Becky Bull, "No Consensus on Pricing," *Progressive Grocer*, November 1998, pp. 87–90.
16. Joel Oberman, "Auction Advice from Europe's eFoodmanager," *Private Label Buyer*, March 2002, p. 17; "Sainsbury's Will Increase Auction Use," *Private Label Buyer*, March

2002, p. 16; Richard Karpinski, "Manufacturer Takes Auctions In-House," *InternetWeek*, November 12, 2001, p. 27; Chris Clark, "Five Auction Steps," *Purchasing*, June 21, 2001, p. S24.

17. David Needle, "Group Buying Forges Ahead Despite Mercata Shut Down," *Internet.com*, January 4, 2001 (***http://siliconvalley.internet.com/news***); Erika Morphy, "New E-Commerce App Promises to Goose B2B Spending," *CRM Daily.com*, August 13, 2001 (***www.crmdaily.com/perl/story/12733.html***).

18. Gary M. Erickson and Johny K. Johansson, "The Role of Price in Multi-Attribute Product-Evaluations," *Journal of Consumer Research* (September 1985): 195–99.

19. K. N. Rajendran and Gerard J. Tellis, "Contextual and Temporal Components of Reference Price," *Journal of Marketing* (January 1994): 22–34.

20. Eric Anderson and Duncan Simeter, "The Role of Price Endings: Why Stores May Sell More at $49 than at $44," unpublished conference paper, April 2001.

21. Paul W. Farris and David J. Reibstein, "How Prices, Expenditures, and Profits Are Linked," *Harvard Business Review* (November–December 1979): 173–84. See also Makoto Abe, "Price and Advertising Strategy of a National Brand Against Its Private-Label Clone: A Signaling Game Approach," *Journal of Business Research* (July 1995): 241–50.

22. See Michael Rowe, *Countertrade* (London: Euromoney Books, 1989); P. N. Agarwala, *Countertrade: A Global Perspective* (New Delhi: Vikas Publishing House, 1991); and Christopher M. Korth, ed., *International Countertrade* (New York: Quorum Books, 1987).

23. See Michael V. Marn and Robert L. Rosiello, "Managing Price, Gaining Profit," *Harvard Business Review* (September–October 1992): 84–94. See also Gerard J. Tellis, "Tackling the Retailer Decision Maze: Which Brands to Discount, How Much, When, and Why?" *Marketing Science* 14, no. 3, pt. 2 (1995): 271–99.

24. Robert E. Weigand, "Yield Management: Filling Buckets, Papering the House," *Business Horizons*, September–October 1999, pp. 55–64.

25. For more information on specific types of price discrimination that are illegal, see Henry R. Cheeseman, *Business Law* (Upper Saddle River, NJ: Prentice Hall, 2001).

26. See Robert E. Weigand, "Buy In–Follow On Strategies for Profit," *Sloan Management Review*, Spring 1991, pp. 29–37.

27. Susan Krafft, "Love, Love Me Doo," *American Demographics*, June 1994, pp. 15–16.

28. See Gerald J. Tellis, "Beyond the Many Faces of Price: An Integration of Pricing Strategies," *Journal of Marketing* (October 1986): 155. This article also analyzes and illustrates other pricing strategies.

29. For an excellent review, see Kent B. Monroe, "Buyers' Subjective Perceptions of Price," *Journal of Marketing Research* (February 1973): 70–80.

CHAPTER 14

Designing and Managing Value Networks and Marketing Channels

In this chapter, we will address the following questions:

1. What is a value network and marketing-channel system?
2. What work is performed by marketing channels?
3. What decisions do companies face in designing, managing, evaluating, and modifying their channels?
4. What trends are taking place in channel dynamics?
5. How can channel conflict be managed?

MARKETING MANAGEMENT AT CARMAX

CarMax, founded in 1993, has reduced the risk that usually surrounds used-car purchases. Instead of calling classified ads to buy someone else's vehicle or negotiating with a slick used-car salesperson, customers who visit one of 35 CarMax used-car superstores start by discussing their needs with a sales associate. Then they preview different vehicles on a computer kiosk, check the fixed price—no haggling allowed—and arrange financing if needed. Each vehicle has undergone a 110-point mechanical inspection and comes with a 5-day money-back guarantee plus a 30-day comprehensive warranty. Salespeople are paid a commission on the number of cars sold rather than their value, so they have no incentive to push higher-priced cars. Start to finish, a typical purchase takes less than one hour.

The streamlined purchasing process is not the only reason for CarMax's success. Over the years, the company has developed a system for buying good, low-mileage vehicles from consumers and wholesale auctions to create the best mix of makes, models, and colors to match customer demand at each superstore location. One Texas CarMax might feature luxury sedans and upscale sport-utility vehicles; just one town over, the CarMax store might stock pickup trucks and mid-level sport-utility vehicles. The combination of customized superstore inventories and superior customer service has helped CarMax push annual sales beyond $3.2 million.[1]

Companies are increasingly taking a *value network* view of their businesses by examining the supply chain that links raw materials, components, and manufactured goods to manage the way products are made available to final consumers. The term *supply chain* suggests a *make-and-sell* view of the business; a better term might be *demand chain* because it suggests a *sense-and-respond* view of the market, the way CarMax operates. The starting point is a customer segment with certain needs, to which the company responds by organizing resources to prepare an offering. Intermediaries such as CarMax play important roles in helping a company make products available to buyers, which is why a company must actively manage its ever-evolving value network.

WHAT IS A VALUE NETWORK AND MARKETING CHANNEL SYSTEM?

A **value network** is a system of partnerships and alliances that a firm creates to source, augment, and deliver its offerings. For example, Palm, the leading manufacturer of handheld computing devices, works with a large community of suppliers and assemblers of semiconductor components, plastic cases, LCD displays, and accessories. The community also includes off-line and online resellers and 45,000 software developers who have created over 5,000 applications for the Palm operating system.

The value-network perspective yields several insights. First, a company can estimate whether more money is made upstream or downstream, in case it might want to integrate backward or forward. Second, it is more aware of disturbances anywhere in the supply chain that might cause costs, prices, or supplies to change suddenly. Third, value-network partners can link through technology for faster, less costly, and more accurate communications, transactions, and payments.

Palm, like most producers, does not sell directly to the final users. Between producer and consumer stands a set of intermediaries that perform a variety of functions; these intermediaries constitute **marketing channels** (also called trade or distribution channels), sets of interdependent organizations involved in the process of making a product or service available for use or consumption.[2] Marketing channel decisions are among the most critical facing management, because the chosen channels intimately affect all the other marketing decisions. As one example, the firm's sales force and advertising decisions depend on how much training and motivation its dealers need.

Another reason these decisions are so critical is that they involve relatively long-term commitments to other firms. When an automaker signs up independent dealers to sell its vehicles, the automaker cannot simply buy them out one day and replace them with company-owned outlets. Corey observed: "A distribution system . . . is a key external resource. Normally it takes years to build, and it is not easily changed. It ranks in importance with key internal resources such as manufacturing, research, engineering, and field sales personnel and facilities. It represents a significant corporate commitment to large numbers of independent companies whose business is distribution—and to the particular markets they serve. It represents, as well, a commitment to a set of policies and practices that constitute the basic fabric on which is woven an extensive set of long-term relationships."[3]

Many companies manage **hybrid** channels by selling in different ways to different markets or inviting customers to choose the channel they prefer. The key is to make sure these channels work well together and to accommodate each target segment's preferred ways of doing business.

WHAT WORK IS PERFORMED BY MARKETING CHANNELS?

Why would a producer delegate some of the selling job to intermediaries? Although delegation means relinquishing some control over how and to whom the products are sold, producers gain several advantages by using channel intermediaries. First, many producers lack the financial resources to carry out direct marketing. For example, General Motors sells its cars through more than 8,100 dealer outlets in North America alone. Even this corporate giant would be hard-pressed to raise the cash to buy out its dealers.

Second, direct marketing is not feasible for some products. The William Wrigley Jr. Company would not find it practical to open gum stores or sell gum online. Wrigley finds it easier to work through a network of privately owned distribution organizations. Finally, producers who do establish their own channels can often earn a greater return by increasing their investment in their main business. If a company earns a 20 percent rate of return on manufacturing and only a 10 percent return on retailing, it does not make sense to undertake its own retailing.

Intermediaries normally achieve superior efficiency in making goods widely available and accessible to target markets. Through their contacts, experience, specialization, and scale of operation, these specialists usually offer the firm more than it can achieve on its own. According to Stern and El-Ansary, "Intermediaries smooth the flow of goods and services . . . This procedure is necessary in order to bridge the discrepancy between the assortment of goods and services generated by the producer and the assortment demanded by the consumer. The discrepancy results from the fact that manufacturers typically produce a large quantity of a limited variety of goods, whereas consumers usually desire only a limited quantity of a wide variety of goods."[4]

Figure 14.1 shows how working through intermediaries can cut costs. Part (a) shows three producers, each using direct marketing to reach three customers, for a total of nine contacts. Part (b) shows the three producers working through one distributor, who contacts the three customers, for a total of only six contacts. Clearly, working through a distributor is more efficient in such situations.

FIGURE 14.1   How a Distributor Effects Economy of Effort

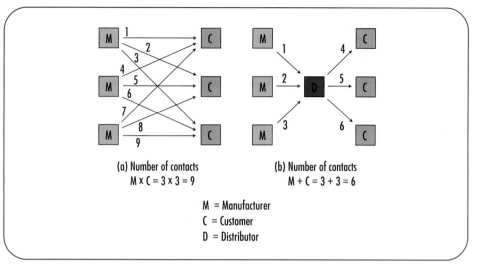

(a) Number of contacts
M x C = 3 x 3 = 9

(b) Number of contacts
M + C = 3 + 3 = 6

M = Manufacturer
C = Customer
D = Distributor

Channel Functions and Flows

A marketing channel performs the work of moving goods from producers to consumers, overcoming the time, place, and possession gaps that separate goods and services from those who need or want them. Members of the marketing channel perform a number of key functions:

- They gather information about potential and current customers, competitors, and other parts of the marketing environment.
- They develop and disseminate persuasive communications to stimulate purchasing.
- They reach agreement on price and other terms so that transfer of ownership or possession can be effected.
- They place orders with manufacturers.
- They acquire the funds to finance inventories at different levels in the marketing channel.
- They assume risks connected with carrying out channel work.
- They provide for the successive storage and movement of physical products.
- They provide for buyers' payment of bills through banks and other financial institutions.
- They oversee actual transfer of ownership from one organization or person to another.

Some functions (physical, title, and promotion) constitute a *forward flow* of activity from the company to the customer; other functions (ordering and payment) constitute a *backward flow* from customers to the company. Still others (information, negotiation, finance, and risk taking) occur in both directions. Five flows are illustrated in Figure 14.2 for the marketing of forklift trucks. If these flows were superimposed in one diagram, the tremendous complexity of even simple marketing channels would be apparent.

FIGURE 14.2 Five Marketing Flows in the Marketing Channel for Forklift Trucks

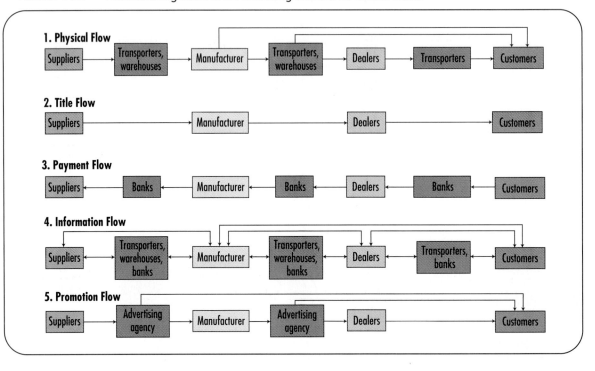

The question is not *whether* these channel functions need to be performed—they must be—but rather *who* is to perform them. All channel functions have three things in common: They use up scarce resources; they can often be performed better through specialization; and they can be shifted among channel members. If a manufacturer shifts some functions to intermediaries, its costs and prices go down, but the intermediaries will charge more to cover their increased responsibilities. Still, if the intermediaries are more efficient than the manufacturer, the prices to consumers should be lower. If consumers perform some functions themselves, they should enjoy still lower prices. In general, changes in channel institutions reflect the discovery of more efficient ways to combine or separate the economic functions that provide assortments of products to target customers.

Channel Levels

The producer and the final customer are part of every channel. We will use the number of intermediary levels to designate the length of a channel. Figure 14.3a illustrates several consumer-goods marketing channels of different lengths, while Figure 14.3b illustrates industrial marketing channels.

A **zero-level channel** (also called a *direct-marketing channel*) consists of a manufacturer selling directly to the final customer through Internet selling, door-to-door sales, home parties, mail order, telemarketing, TV selling, and other methods. A **one-level channel** contains one selling intermediary, such as a retailer. A **two-level channel** contains two intermediaries; a three-level channel contains three intermediaries.

FIGURE 14.3 Consumer and Industrial Marketing Channels

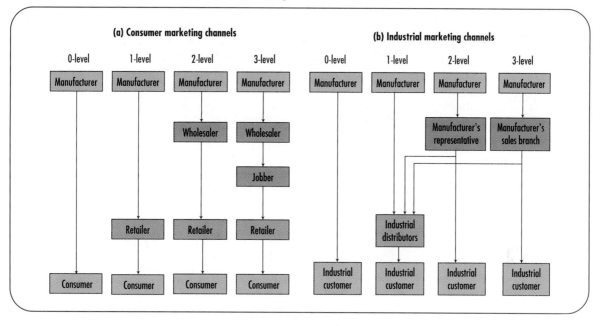

From the producer's point of view, obtaining information about end users and exercising control becomes more difficult as the number of channel levels increases.

Channels normally describe a forward movement of products. One can also talk about *reverse-flow channels*, which bring products back for reuse (such as refillable bottles), refurbishing for resale, recycling, or disposal. Several intermediaries play a role in these channels, including manufacturers' redemption centers, community groups, traditional intermediaries such as soft-drink intermediaries, trash-collection specialists, recycling centers, trash-recycling brokers, and central-processing warehousing.[5]

Service Sector Channels

Producers of services and ideas also face the problem of making their output available and accessible to target populations. For instance, schools develop "educational-dissemination systems" and hospitals develop "health-delivery systems." These institutions must determine agencies and locations for reaching a population that is spread out over an area. As Internet technology advances, service industries such as retailing, banking, travel, and securities trading are harnessing this channel for customer interaction. CarMax, for example, encourages consumers to search for used cars among the 14,000 vehicles listed on its Web site (*www.carmax.com*).

CHANNEL-DESIGN DECISIONS

A new firm typically starts as a local operation selling in a limited market through existing intermediaries. The problem at this point is not deciding on the best channels, but convincing the available intermediaries to handle the firm's line. If the firm is successful, it might enter new markets and select different channels in response to the opportunities and conditions in the different markets.

In managing its intermediaries, the firm must determine how much effort to devote to push versus pull strategy. In a **push strategy**, the manufacturer uses its sales force and trade promotion to induce intermediaries to carry, promote, and sell the product. In a **pull strategy**, the manufacturer uses advertising and promotion to induce consumers to ask intermediaries for the product. When designing a channel system, management must analyze customer needs, establish channel objectives, and identify and evaluate major channel alternatives.

Analyzing Customers' Desired Service Output Levels

Because the point of a marketing channel is to make a product available to customers, the marketer must understand what its target customers actually want. Channels produce five service outputs:

1. *Lot size*. The number of units the channel permits a typical customer to purchase on one occasion. In buying cars for its fleet, Hertz prefers a channel from which it can buy a large lot size; a household wants a channel that permits buying a lot size of one.

2. *Waiting time*. The average time customers of that channel wait for receipt of the goods. Customers normally prefer fast delivery channels.

3. *Spatial convenience*. The degree to which the marketing channel makes it easy for customers to purchase the product. As CarMax opens more superstores, it will offer even greater spatial convenience.

4. *Product variety*. The assortment breadth provided by the channel. Normally, customers prefer a greater assortment, which increases the chance of finding what they need.

5. *Service backup*. The add-on services (credit, delivery, installation, repairs) provided by the channel. The greater the service backup, the greater the work provided by the channel.[6]

Providing greater service outputs means increased channel costs and higher prices for customers, just as a lower level means lower costs and prices. The success of discount resellers (online and off-line) indicates that many consumers will accept lower outputs if they can save money.

Establishing Objectives and Constraints

The company needs to develop channel objectives related to the targeted service output levels. According to Bucklin, under competitive conditions, channel institutions should arrange their functional tasks to minimize total channel costs with respect to desired levels of service outputs.[7] Producers can usually identify several market segments that desire differing service output levels. Thus, effective planning means determining which market segments to serve and the best channels to use in each case.

Channel objectives vary with product characteristics. For instance, perishable products require more direct channels, whereas bulkier products require channels that minimize the shipping distance and the amount of handling in the movement from producer to consumer. In contrast, nonstandardized products, such as custom-built machinery, typically are sold directly by company sales representatives.

Channel design must also take into account the strengths and constraints of working with different types of intermediaries. As one example, manufacturers' reps can contact customers at a low cost per customer because the total cost is shared by several clients, but the selling effort per customer will be less intense than if each company's reps did the selling. In addition, channel design can be constrained by such factors as competitors' channels, the marketing environment, and country-by-country legal regulations and restrictions. U.S. law looks unfavorably upon channel arrangements that tend to substantially lessen competition or create a monopoly.

Identifying Major Channel Alternatives

The next step is to identify channel alternatives. Most companies now use a mix of channels to reach different segments at the least cost. These are described by (1) the types of available intermediaries, (2) the number of intermediaries needed, and (3) the terms and responsibilities of each channel member.

Types of Intermediaries   Intermediaries known as *merchants*—such as wholesalers and retailers—buy, take title to, and resell the merchandise. *Agents*—brokers, manufacturers' representatives, and sales agents—search for customers and may negotiate on the producer's behalf but do not take title to the goods. *Facilitators*—transportation companies, independent warehouses, banks, and advertising agencies—assist in the distribution process but neither take title to goods nor negotiate purchases or sales. Increasingly, companies are searching for innovative marketing channels to reach new or existing customers. Consider the numerous variations on the Book-of-the-Month Club idea, including monthly club purchases of CDs, flowers, fruit, even quilt patterns.

Number of Intermediaries   In deciding how many intermediaries to use, companies can use one of three strategies: exclusive, selective, or intensive distribution. **Exclusive distribution** means severely limiting the number of intermediaries. Firms such as automakers use this approach when they want to maintain control over the service level and service outputs offered by the resellers. Often it involves *exclusive dealing* arrangements, in which the resellers agree not to carry competing brands.

Selective distribution involves the use of more than a few but less than all of the intermediaries who are willing to carry a particular product. In this way, the producer avoids dissipating its efforts over too many outlets, and it gains adequate market coverage with more control and less cost than intensive distribution. Disney uses selective distribution for its videos and DVDs, selling through movie rental chains, company stores, other retailers, online retailers, and Disney's catalog and online site.[8]

Intensive distribution consists of the manufacturer placing the goods or services in as many outlets as possible. This strategy is generally used for items such as tobacco products, soap, snack foods, and gum, products for which the consumer requires a great deal of location convenience.

Terms and Responsibilities of Channel Members   The producer must determine the rights and responsibilities of participating members when considering channel alternatives. From an ethical perspective, each channel member must be treated respectfully and given the opportunity to be profitable.[9] The main elements in channel relations are: price policies; conditions of sale; territorial rights; and the services to be performed by each party.

Price policy calls for the producer to establish a price list and a schedule of discounts and allowances that intermediaries see as equitable and sufficient. **Conditions of sale** refer to the producer's payment terms and guarantees for each sale. Most producers grant cash discounts to distributors for early payment; they may also offer guarantees against defective merchandise or price declines.

Territorial rights define the distributors' territories and the terms under which the producer will enfranchise other distributors. Distributors normally expect to receive full credit for all sales in their territory, whether or not they did the selling. Mutual services and responsibilities must be carefully spelled out, especially in franchised and exclusive-agency channels. McDonald's provides franchisees with a building, promotional support, a record-keeping system, training, and technical assistance. In turn, franchisees must satisfy company standards regarding physical facilities, cooperate with promotional programs, and buy beef and other supplies from specified vendors.[10]

Evaluating the Major Alternatives

Once the company has identified its major channel alternatives, it must evaluate each alternative against appropriate economic, control, and adaptive criteria.

- *Economic criteria.* Each channel alternative will produce a different level of sales and costs, so producers must estimate the costs of selling different volumes through each channel versus the added value (see Figure 14.4). For example, in comparing a company sales force to a manufacturer's sales agency, the producer would estimate the variable cost of commissions paid to representatives and the fixed cost of rent payments for a sales office. By comparing its costs at different sales levels, the company can determine which alternative appears to be the most profitable. Companies that

FIGURE 14.4   The Value-Adds Versus Costs of Different Channels

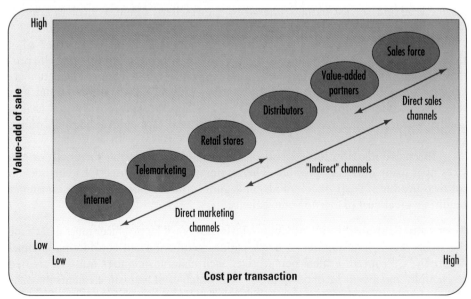

Source: Oxford Associates, adapted from Dr. Rowland T. Moriarty, Cubex Corp.

can switch their customers to lower-cost channels without losing sales or service quality will gain a *channel advantage*.[11]

- *Control and adaptive criteria.* Producers must consider how much channel control they require, since they will have less control over members they do not own. Outside agents may concentrate on customers who buy the most, but not necessarily of the producer's goods. Furthermore, agents might not master the details of every product they carry. To develop a channel, the members must make some mutual commitments for a specified period of time. Yet these commitments invariably reduce the producer's ability to respond to a changing marketplace. In volatile or uncertain environments, producers need channels and policies that provide high adaptability.

CHANNEL-MANAGEMENT DECISIONS

After a company has chosen a channel alternative, it must select, train, motivate, and evaluate the individual intermediaries. Because neither the marketing environment nor the product life cycle remains static, the company must be ready to modify these channel arrangements over time.

Selecting Channel Members

During the selection process, producers should determine what characteristics distinguish the better intermediaries. They will want to evaluate number of years in business, other lines carried, growth and profit record, solvency, cooperativeness, and reputation. If the intermediaries are sales agents, producers will want to evaluate the number and character of other lines carried and the size and quality of the sales force. If the intermediaries are retailers that want exclusive distribution, the producer will want to evaluate locations, future growth potential, and type of clientele.

Selection can be a lengthy process. Consider the experience of Japan's Epson Corporation. A leading manufacturer of computer printers, Epson decided to add computers to its product line but chose to recruit new distributors rather than sell through existing distributors. The firm hired a recruiting firm to find candidates who (1) had distribution experience with major appliances, (2) were willing and able to set up their own distributorships, (3) would accept Epson's financial arrangements, and (4) would handle only Epson equipment, although they could stock other companies' software. After the recruiting firm found qualified candidates, Epson terminated its existing distributors and began selling through the new channel members. Despite this time-consuming, detailed selection process, Epson never succeeded as a computer maker.[12]

Training Channel Members

Companies need to plan and implement careful training programs for their intermediaries because end users view these partners as the company. Microsoft, for example, requires third-party service engineers who work with its software applications to complete a number of courses and take certification exams. Those who pass are formally recognized as Microsoft Certified Professionals and can use this designation to promote business.

Motivating Channel Members

Companies should look at their channel members in the same way they look at their end users. This means determining intermediaries' needs and then tailoring the channel positioning to provide superior value to these intermediaries. To improve intermediaries' performance, the company should provide training, market research, and other capability-building programs. The company must also constantly reinforce that its intermediaries are partners in the joint effort to satisfy customers. More sophisticated companies go beyond merely gaining cooperation and instead try to forge a long-term partnership with channel members. The manufacturer communicates clearly what it expects from its distributors in the way of market coverage and other channel issues and may establish a compensation plan for adhering to these policies.

Too many manufacturers think of their distributors and dealers as customers rather than as working partners. Up to now, we have treated manufacturers and distributors as separate organizations. But many manufacturers are distributors of related products made by other manufacturers, and some distributors also own or contract for the manufacture of in-house brands. JCPenney sells branded jeans by manufacturers such as Levi Strauss in addition to Original Arizona Jeans, the retailer's own private label.[13] This situation, which is common in the jeans industry and in many others, complicates the process of selecting and motivating channel members.

Evaluating Channel Members

Producers must periodically evaluate intermediaries' performance against such standards as sales-quota attainment, average inventory levels, customer delivery time, treatment of damaged and lost goods, and cooperation in promotional and training programs (see "Marketing Skills: Evaluating Intermediaries.") A producer will occasionally discover that it is paying too much to particular intermediaries for what they are actually doing. For example, a manufacturer that was compensating a distributor for holding inventories found that the stock was actually held in a public warehouse at the manufacturer's expense. Producers should therefore set up functional discounts in which they pay specified amounts for the intermediary's performance of each agreed-upon service. Underperformers need to be counseled, retrained, remotivated, or terminated.

Modifying Channel Arrangements

Channel arrangements must be reviewed periodically and modified when distribution is not working as planned, consumer buying patterns change, the market expands, new competition arises, innovative distribution channels emerge, or the product moves into later stages in the product life cycle.

No marketing channel remains effective over the entire product life cycle. Early buyers might be willing to pay for high value-added channels, but later buyers will switch to lower-cost channels. Lele developed the grid in Figure 14.5 to show how marketing channels have changed for PCs and designer apparel at different product life-cycle stages. As the grid indicates, products in the introductory stage enter the market through specialist channels that attract early adopters. As interest grows, higher-volume channels appear (dedicated chains, department stores), offering some services, but not as many as the previous channels. In the maturity stage, growth is slowing, so some competitors move into lower-cost channels (mass merchandisers). In

MARKETING SKILLS: EVALUATING INTERMEDIARIES

How important is it for marketers to evaluate and manage suppliers, wholesalers, retailers, and other intermediaries? One company found, through rigorous analysis, that unpredictable supplier deliveries was causing it to hold $200 million in excess inventory to guard against out-of-stock conditions. By evaluating its suppliers on the basis of standards such as on-time delivery, this company slashed its costs—and began to manage intermediaries through charge-backs based on performance problems.

Start by determining how suppliers (and their suppliers) as well as distributors (and their reseller-customers) can influence the company's performance. Sometimes a tiny widget supplied by one minor supplier can be a pivotal ingredient in the production process, which makes that supplier's on-time delivery and product quality particularly critical. Another important step is to translate companywide strategic goals and measurements into specific targets and measures for value-network members. At Cisco, corporate targets for customer satisfaction are translated into detailed intermediary measures of on-time deliveries, defect rates, and similar elements (targets and measures will vary by company and industry—and should not conflict). Good communication will help intermediaries understand the company's expectations and encourage information sharing for mutual benefit. Finally, measure and reward performance on an ongoing basis to keep the network efficient, reactive, and reliable.

Delphi Automotive Systems has an unusual perspective on evaluation. After being spun off from General Motors, Delphi had to establish itself as a leader in vehicle systems manufacturing, a desirable supplier for automakers, and a desirable customer for suppliers. Although GM still comprises 70 percent of its sales, Delphi uses the Internet to provide up-to-date stock and order information so customers can better manage their inventory and production plans. Despite its $2.5 billion in annual purchases, the company buys a lower volume of electronics parts than networking and telecommunications giants; as a result, when parts are scarce, the company has not always been able to get what it needs. Therefore, Delphi added long-term vision and industry commitment to the standards it uses to evaluate suppliers.[14]

decline, even lower-cost channels emerge (mail-order, discount Web sites, off-price discounters).[15]

Adding or dropping an individual channel member requires an incremental analysis to determine what the firm's profits would look like with and without this intermediary. Sometimes a producer considers dropping all intermediaries whose sales are below a certain amount. For example, Navistar once noticed that 5 percent of its dealers sold fewer than three or four trucks a year. It cost the company more to service these dealers than their sales were worth, but dropping the dealers could have system-wide repercussions. The unit costs of producing trucks would be higher because the overhead would be spread over fewer trucks, some employees and equipment would be idled, some customers would go to competitors, and other dealers might become insecure. All of these factors have to be taken into account before modifying channel arrangements.

FIGURE 14.5   Channel Value Added and Market Growth Rate

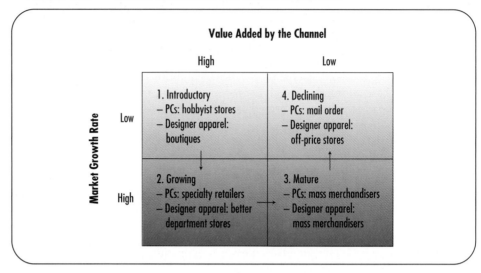

The most difficult decision involves revising the overall channel strategy.[16] Distribution channels can become outmoded over time, as a gap arises between the existing distribution system and the ideal system that would satisfy target customers' (and producers') requirements. For example, Avon had to modify its traditional door-to-door system for selling cosmetics as more women entered the workforce. The company arranged for select branches of JCPenney to sell a separate product line, dubbed beComing, which differs in price, packaging, and content from the products sold by Avon representatives. It also began selling directly to customers on the Internet.[17]

CHANNEL DYNAMICS

In the ever-changing marketing environment, distribution channels do not stand still. New wholesaling and retailing institutions emerge, and new channel systems evolve. We look next at the recent growth of vertical, horizontal, and multichannel marketing systems and see how these systems cooperate, conflict, and compete.

Vertical Marketing Systems

One of the most significant channel developments is the rise of vertical marketing systems. A **conventional marketing channel** comprises an independent producer, wholesaler(s), and retailer(s). Each is a separate business seeking to maximize its own profits, even if this goal reduces profit for the system as a whole. No channel member has complete or substantial control over other members.

A **vertical marketing system (VMS)**, by contrast, comprises the producer, wholesaler(s), and retailer(s) acting as a unified system. One channel member, the *channel captain*, owns the others, franchises them, or has so much power that they all cooperate. The channel captain can be the producer, the wholesaler, or the retailer. VMSs arose as a result of strong channel members' attempts to control channel behavior and eliminate conflict from independent channel members pursuing their own objectives. They achieve economies through size, bargaining power, and elimination of duplicated services. VMSs have become the dominant mode of distribution in the U.S. consumer marketplace, serving between 70 percent and 80 percent of the total market. There are three types of VMS: corporate, administered, and contractual.

A *corporate VMS* combines successive stages of production and distribution under single ownership. Vertical integration is favored by companies that desire a high level of control over their channels. For example, Sears obtains over 50 percent of the goods it sells from companies that it partly or wholly owns.

An *administered VMS* coordinates successive stages of production and distribution through one member's size and power. Manufacturers of a dominant brand are able to secure strong trade cooperation and support from resellers. Thus Kodak, Gillette, Procter & Gamble, and Campbell Soup can command cooperation from their resellers in connection with displays, shelf space, promotions, and price policies.

A *contractual VMS* consists of independent firms at different levels of production and distribution integrating their programs on a contractual basis to obtain more economies or sales impact than they could achieve alone. Johnston and Lawrence call them "value-adding partnerships" (VAPs).[18] Contractual VMSs are of three types:

1. *Wholesaler-sponsored voluntary chains* organize groups of independent retailers to better compete with large chains. Wholesalers such as Drug Guild work with participating retailers (in this case, independent pharmacies) to standardize selling practices and achieve buying economies so the group can compete with chains.

2. *Retailer cooperatives* arise when the stores take the initiative and organize a new business entity to carry on wholesaling and possibly some production. Members of retail cooperatives such as ServiStar concentrate their purchases through the co-op and jointly plan their advertising; members share in profits in proportion to their purchases.

3. *Franchise organizations* are created when a channel member called a *franchisor* links several successive stages in the production-distribution process. Franchises include manufacturer-sponsored retailer franchises (Ford and its dealers); manufacturer-sponsored wholesaler franchises (Coca-Cola and its bottlers); and service-firm-sponsored retailer franchises (Ramada Inn and its motel franchisees).

Horizontal Marketing Systems

Another channel development is the **horizontal marketing system**, in which two or more unrelated companies pool resources or programs to exploit a particular opportunity. Each company lacks the capital, know-how, production, or marketing resources to venture alone, or fears the risk. The companies might work together on a temporary or permanent basis or create a joint venture company. H&R Block, for instance, arranged to provide car insurance information to its customers on behalf of GEICO insurance.

Multichannel Marketing Systems

Once, many companies sold to a single market through a single channel. Today, with the proliferation of customer segments and channel possibilities, more companies have adopted multichannel marketing. **Multichannel marketing** occurs when a single firm uses two or more marketing channels to reach one or more customer segments.

As one example, the Parker-Hannifin Corporation (PHC) sells pneumatic drills to the lumber, fishing, and aircraft industries. Instead of selling through one industrial distributor, PHC established three separate channels—forestry equipment distributors, marine distributors, and industrial distributors. There appears to be little conflict because each type of distributor sells to a separate target segment.

By adding more channels, companies can gain three important benefits. The first is increased market coverage—companies often add a channel to reach a customer segment that its current channels cannot reach. The second is lower channel cost—companies may add a new channel to lower the cost of selling to an existing customer group (selling by phone rather than personally visiting small customers). The third is more customized selling—companies may add a channel whose selling features fit customer requirements better (adding a technical sales force to sell more complex equipment).

However, new channels typically introduce conflict and control problems. First, different channels may end up competing for the same customers. Second, as the new channels become more independent, the company may have difficulty maintaining cooperation among all of the members.

Conflict, Cooperation, and Competition

No matter how well channels are designed and managed, there will be some conflict, if for no other reason than the interests of independent business entities do not always coincide. Here we examine three questions: What types of conflict arise in channels? What causes channel conflict? What can be done to resolve conflict situations?

Types of Conflict and Competition   *Vertical channel conflict* means conflict between different levels within the same channel. As one example, General Motors came into conflict with its dealers in trying to enforce policies on service, pricing, and advertising.

Horizontal channel conflict involves conflict between members at the same level within the channel. Horizontal channel conflict erupted, for instance, when some Pizza Inn franchisees complained that other Pizza Inn franchisees were cheating on ingredients, maintaining poor service, and hurting the brand image.

Multichannel conflict exists when the manufacturer has established two or more channels that sell to the same market. For instance, when Mattel began selling toys and children's apparel on its Barbie.com Web site—and mailed a catalog to 4 million U.S. households, retailers perceived this as channel conflict. Mattel noted that online and catalog sales would initially contribute very little to Barbie's sales; it also did not advertise the site's e-commerce capabilities, viewing it as a relationship-building tool.[19]

Causes of Channel Conflict   Why does channel conflict erupt? One major cause is *goal incompatibility*. For example, the manufacturer may want to achieve rapid market penetration through a low-price policy. The dealers, in contrast, may prefer to work with high margins for short-run profitability. Sometimes conflict arises from *unclear roles and rights*. This is what happened when IBM started selling PCs to large accounts through its own sales force while its licensed dealers were also trying to sell to large accounts. Territory boundaries and credit for sales often produce conflict in such situations.

By adding new channels, a company faces the possibility of channel conflict, as the Mattel example indicated. Conflict can also stem from differences in perception, as when the producer is optimistic about the short-term economic outlook and wants dealers to carry more inventory, while its dealers are more pessimistic about future prospects. At times, conflict can arise because of the intermediaries' great dependence on the manufacturer. The fortunes of exclusive dealers, such as auto dealers, are greatly affected by the manufacturer's product and pricing decisions, creating high potential for conflict.

Managing Channel Conflict   Some channel conflict can be constructive and lead to more dynamic adaptation in a changing environment. Too much conflict can be dysfunctional, however, so the challenge is not to eliminate conflict but to manage it better. There are several mechanisms for effective conflict management.[20]

One method is to adopt superordinate goals. Here, channel members come to an agreement on the fundamental goal they are jointly seeking (survival, market share, high quality, or customer satisfaction). They usually do this when the channel faces an outside threat, such as a more efficient competing channel, an adverse piece of legislation, or a shift in consumer desires.

Another approach is to exchange persons between channel levels. General Motors executives might work briefly in some dealerships, and some dealers might work in GM's dealer policy department, to help participants appreciate the other's viewpoint.

Cooptation is an effort by one organization to win the support of the leaders of another organization by including them in advisory councils, boards of directors, trade associations, and the like. As long as the initiating organization treats the leaders seriously and listens to their opinions, cooptation can reduce conflict.

With chronic or acute conflict, diplomacy, mediation, or arbitration may be needed. *Diplomacy* takes place when each side sends a person or group to meet with its counterpart to resolve the conflict. *Mediation* means having a skilled, neutral third party reconcile the two parties' interests. *Arbitration* occurs when the two parties agree to present their arguments to an arbitrator and accept the arbitration decision.

Legal and Ethical Issues in Channel Relations

For the most part, companies are legally free to develop whatever channel arrangements suit them. In fact, the law seeks to prevent companies from using exclusionary tactics that might keep competitors from using a channel. Here we briefly consider the legality of exclusive dealing, exclusive territories, tying agreements, and dealers' rights.

With **exclusive dealing**, the seller allows only certain outlets to carry its products and requires that these dealers not handle competitors' products. Both parties benefit from exclusive arrangements: The seller obtains more loyal and dependable outlets, and the dealers obtain a steady source of supply of special products and stronger seller support. Exclusive arrangements are legal as long as they do not substantially lessen competition or tend to create a monopoly, and both parties have voluntarily entered into the agreement.

Exclusive dealing often includes exclusive territorial agreements. The producer may agree not to sell to other dealers in a given area, or the dealer may agree to sell only in its own territory. The first practice increases dealer enthusiasm and commitment and is perfectly legal—a seller has no legal obligation to sell through more outlets than it wishes. The second practice, whereby the producer tries to keep a dealer from selling outside its territory, is a major legal issue.

The producer of a strong brand sometimes sells it to dealers only if they will take some or all of the rest of the line. This practice is called full-line forcing. Such **tying agreements** are not necessarily illegal, but they do violate U.S. law if they tend to lessen competition substantially.

A producer's right to terminate dealers is somewhat restricted. In general, sellers can drop dealers "for cause," but not if, for instance, the dealers refuse to cooperate in a doubtful legal arrangement, such as exclusive dealing or tying agreements.

EXECUTIVE SUMMARY

Most producers do not sell their goods directly to final users. Between producers and final users stands one or more marketing channels, a set of marketing intermediaries performing a variety of functions. Companies use intermediaries when they lack the financial resources to carry out direct marketing, when direct marketing is not feasible, and when they can earn more by doing so. The use of intermediaries largely boils down to their superior efficiency in making goods widely available and accessible to target markets. The most important functions performed by intermediaries are gathering information, handling promotion, handling negotiation, placing orders, arranging financing, taking risks, and facilitating physical possession, payment, and title.

Manufacturers have many alternatives for reaching a market. They can sell direct through a zero-level channel or use one-, two-, or three-level channels. Deciding which type(s) of channel to use calls for analyzing customer needs, establishing channel objectives, and identifying and evaluating the major alternatives. The company must also determine whether to distribute its product exclusively, selectively, or intensively, and it must clearly spell out each channel member's rights and responsibilities.

Effective channel management calls for selecting intermediaries, then training and motivating them. The goal is to build a long-term, mutually profitable partnership. Individual members must be periodically evaluated and overall channel arrangements may need to be modified as market conditions change. Three of the most important trends in channel dynamics are the growth of vertical marketing systems, horizontal marketing systems, and multichannel marketing systems.

All marketing channels have the potential for conflict and competition resulting from goal incompatibility, poorly defined roles and rights, perceptual differences, or interdependent relationships. Companies can manage conflict by striving for superordinate goals, exchanging people among two or more channel levels, coopting the support of leaders in different parts of the channel, and through diplomacy, mediation, or arbitration to resolve chronic or acute conflict. Management must consider certain legal and ethical issues with regard to channel practices such as exclusive dealing or territories, tying agreements, and dealers' rights.

NOTES

1. Arlena Sawyers, "CarMax Doubles Profit, Plans More Stores," *Automotive News*, April 8, 2002, p. 16; Arlena Sawyers, "CarMax Shows There's Life in Big-Box Concept," *Automotive News*, March 4, 2002, p. 4; Terry Box, "CarMax Success Comes From

Matching Outlets, Automobiles," *Dallas Morning News*, November 2, 2001 (*www.dallasnews.com*); Mike Brennan, "Mavericks Are Changing Way Cars Are Sold," *Detroit Free Press*, January 6, 1998, p. 28.

2. Louis W. Stern and Adel I. El-Ansary, *Marketing Channels*, 5th ed. (Upper Saddle River, NJ: Prentice Hall, 1996).

3. E. Raymond Corey, *Industrial Marketing: Cases and Concepts*, 4th ed. (Upper Saddle River, NJ: Prentice Hall, 1991), ch. 5.

4. Stern and El-Ansary, *Marketing Channels*, pp. 5–6.

5. For additional information on reverse-flow channels, see Marianne Jahre, "Household Waste Collection as a Reverse Channel—A Theoretical Perspective," *International Journal of Physical Distribution and Logistics* 25, no. 2 (1995): 39–55; and Terrance L. Pohlen and M. Theodore Farris II, "Reverse Logistics in Plastics Recycling," *International Journal of Physical Distribution and Logistics* 22, no. 7 (1992): 35–37.

6. Louis O. Bucklin, Competition and Evolution in the Distributive Trades (Upper Saddle River, NJ: Prentice Hall, 1972). Also see Stern and El-Ansary, Marketing Channels.

7. Louis P. Bucklin, A Theory of Distribution Channel Structure (Berkeley: Institute of Business and Economic Research, University of California, 1966).

8. Edward Helmore, "Media: Why House of Mouse Is Haunted by Failures," *The Observer*, February 11, 2001, p. 10; (*www.disney.com*).

9. For more on relationship marketing and the governance of marketing channels, see Jan B. Heide, "Interorganizational Governance in Marketing Channels," *Journal of Marketing* (January 1994): 71–85.

10. See Alby Gallun, "Greenberg's Mantra: Keep the Franchising Beefs to a Minimum," *Crain's Chicago Business*, April 30, 2001, p. 20.

11. See Lawrence G. Friedman and Timothy R. Furey, *The Channel Advantage: Going to Marketing with Multiple Sales Channels* (Butterworth-Heinemann, 1999). They suggest measuring a channel's profitability by the expense-to-revenue ratio (E/R), the average transaction cost divided by the average order size. The average transaction cost is found by dividing the total expense in operating the channel by the total number of transactions. The lower the E/R, the more profitable the channel.

12. Arthur Bragg, "Undercover Recruiting: Epson America's Sly Distributor Switch," *Sales and Marketing Management*, March 11, 1985, pp. 45–49.

13. "Turnaround Twins: Levi and J.C. Penney," *BusinessWeek Online*, April 24, 2002 (*www.businessweek.com/bwdaily/dnflash/apr2002/nf20020424_4206.htm*).

14. Miles Cook and Rob Tyndall, "Lessons from the Leaders," *Supply Chain Management Review*, November–December 2001, pp. 22+; Jennifer Baljko Shah, "Staying Efficient Despite Tough Marketing Dynamics," *EBN*, August 27, 2001, p. 33.

15. Miland M. Lele, *Creating Strategic Leverage* (New York: John Wiley, 1992) pp. 249–51.

16. For an excellent report on this issue, see Howard Sutton, *Rethinking the Company's Selling and Distribution Channels*, research report no. 885, Conference Board, 1986, p. 26.

17. "A Makeover Has Avon Looking Good," *BusinessWeek Online*, January 22, 2002 (*www.businessweek.com/bwdaily/dnflash/jan2002/nf20020122_8624.htm*); Emily Nelson, "Avon Goes Store to Store," *Wall Street Journal*, September 18, 2000, p. B1.

18. Russell Johnston and Paul R. Lawrence, "Beyond Vertical Integration—The Rise of the Value-Adding Partnership," *Harvard Business Review* (July–August 1988): 94–101. See also Judy A. Siguaw, Penny M. Simpson, and Thomas L. Baker, "Effects of Supplier Market Orientation on Distributor Market Orientation and the Channel Relationship: The Distribution Perspective," *Journal of Marketing* (July 1998): 99–111; Narakesari Narayandas and Manohar U. Kalwani, "Long-Term Manufacturer–Supplier Relationships: Do They Pay Off for Supplier Firms?" *Journal of Marketing* (January 1995): 1–16.

19. Lisa Bannon, "Selling Barbie Online May Pit Mattel vs. Stores," *Wall Street Journal*, November 17, 2000, p. B1.

20. This section draws on Stern and El-Ansary, *Marketing Channels*, ch. 6.

CHAPTER 15

Managing Retailing, Wholesaling, and Market Logistics

In this chapter, we will address the following questions:

1. What are the major types of organizations in this sector?
2. What marketing decisions do organizations in this sector make?
3. What are the major trends in this sector?

MARKETING MANAGEMENT AT MALL OF AMERICA

The gigantic Mall of America in Bloomington, Minnesota, is the largest in the United States. When this 520-store super-regional mall opened in 1992, its marketers set the ambitious goal of attracting 40 million visitors a year. Within 5 years it was drawing 43 million visitors, thanks to a campaign marketing the mall as a "must see" destination for power shoppers and tourists alike. In addition to advertising throughout the Midwest, marketers work with airlines and bus companies to arrange travel tours from across the United States and other countries.

Sears, Bloomingdale's, Macy's, and Nordstrom are the four department store anchors. In between are hundreds of specialty stores (including five Gap stores and three Victoria's Secrets), 34 eateries, and entertainment areas such as Camp Snoopy, Underwater Adventures, General Mills' Cereal Adventure, Lego Imagination Center, a golf course, Chapel of Love wedding center, plus nightclubs and cinemas. To build a sense of community, Mall of America promotes its Mall Walker fitness program, cause-related activities, special events such as a Weather Channel eco-celebration, and a secure parking lot reserved for women and staffed by women. Each store has its own promotion strategy of advertising, sales, contests, samples, and displays. As a result of savvy marketing, the mall's specialty stores ring up $450 per square foot in average annual sales, compared with $325 for typical mall stores.[1]

In the previous chapter, we examined intermediaries from the viewpoint of manufacturers and service providers who want to build and manage value networks and marketing channels. In this chapter, we view these intermediaries—retailers, wholesalers, and logistical organizations—as forging their own marketing strategies.

Many use strategic planning, advanced information systems, and sophisticated marketing tools, measuring performance more on a return-on-investment basis than on a profit-margin basis. They segment their markets carefully, hone their targeting and positioning, and aggressively pursue market expansion and diversification strategies.

RETAILING

Retailing includes all of the activities involved in selling goods or services directly to final consumers for personal, nonbusiness use. A **retailer** or **retail store** is any business enterprise whose sales volume comes primarily from retailing. Any organization that sells to final consumers—whether a manufacturer, wholesaler, or retailer—is engaged in retailing. It does not matter *how* the goods or services are sold (by person, mail, telephone, vending machine, or Internet) or *where* they are sold (in a store, on the street, or in the consumer's home).

Types of Retailers

Retailers exhibit great variety, and new forms keep emerging. The most important types of retail stores are described in Table 15.1

Like products, retail-store types pass through stages of growth and decline that can be described as the *retail life cycle*.[2] A type emerges, enjoys a period of accelerated growth, reaches maturity, and then declines. Older retail forms took many years to reach maturity; newer retail forms reach maturity much more quickly. Department stores took 80 years to reach maturity, whereas warehouse retail outlets reached maturity in 10 years; Internet retailers are approaching maturity in even less time.[3]

New store types emerge, according to the wheel-of-retailing hypothesis, after conventional retail-store types increase their services and raise their prices to cover the cost. In turn, these higher costs provide an opportunity for new retail forms to emerge with lower prices and less service.[4] Retailers can offer one of four levels of service:

1. *Self-service:* The cornerstone of all discount stores, self-service allows customers to save money by carrying out their own locate-compare-select process.
2. *Self-selection:* Customers find their own goods, although they can ask for help.
3. *Limited service:* These retailers carry more shopping goods, and customers need more information and assistance. The stores also offer services (such as credit and merchandise-return privileges).

TABLE 15.1   Major Store Retailer Types

Specialty Store: Narrow product line with a deep assortment, such as apparel stores, sporting-goods stores, furniture stores, florists, and bookstores. A clothing store would be a *single-line store*, a men's clothing store would be a *limited-line store*, and a men's custom-shirt store would be a *superspecialty store*. Example: The Body Shop.

Department Store: Several product lines—typically clothing, home furnishings, and household goods—with each line operated as a separate department managed by specialist buyers or merchandisers. Example: Sears.

Supermarket: Relatively large, low-cost, low-margin, high-volume, self-service operation designed to serve total needs for foods and household products. Example: Kroger.

Convenience Store: Relatively small store located near residential area, open long hours 7 days a week, and carrying a limited line of high-turnover convenience products at slightly higher prices. Example: 7-Eleven.

Discount Store: Standard merchandise sold at lower prices with lower margins and higher volumes. Example: All-purpose: Wal-Mart; Specialty: Circuit City.

Off-Price Retailer: Merchandise bought at less than regular wholesale prices and sold at less than retail; often leftover goods, overruns, and irregulars. These include *factory outlets* owned and operated by manufacturers (example: Mikasa); *independent off-price retailers* owned and run by entrepreneurs or by divisions of larger retail corporations (example: T.J. Maxx); *warehouse* (or *wholesale*) *clubs* selling a limited selection of brand-name groceries, appliances, clothing, other goods at deep discounts to consumers who pay membership fees (example: Costco).

Superstore: Averages 35,000 square feet of selling space, traditionally aimed at meeting consumers' total needs for routinely purchased food and nonfood items; usually includes services such as laundry, dry cleaning, shoe repair, check cashing, and bill paying. *Category killers* carry a deep assortment in a particular category and have a knowledgeable staff (example: Staples). Superstores include *combination stores* that carry food and drugs in an average 55,000 square feet of selling space (example: Jewel stores) and *hypermarkets* with up to 220,000 square feet of space combining supermarket, discount, and warehouse retailing (example: France's Carrefour).

Sources: For further reading, see Leah Rickard, "Supercenters Entice Shoppers," *Advertising Age*, March 29, 1995, pp. 1–10; Debra Chanil, "Wholesale Clubs: A New Era?" *Discount Merchandiser*, November, 1994, pp. 33–51; Julie Nelson Forsyth, "Department Store Industry Restructures for the 90s," *Chain Store Executive* (August 1993): pp. 29A–30A; John Milton Fogg, "The Giant Awakens," *Success*, March 1995, p. 51; J. Douglas Eldridge, "Nonstore Retailing: Planning for a Big Future," *Chain Store Age Executive* (August 1993): 34A–35A.

4. *Full service:* Salespeople are ready to assist in the locate-compare-select process. The high staffing cost, the higher proportion of specialty goods, slower-moving items, and more services add up to high-cost retailing.

By combining these different service levels with different assortment breadths, we can distinguish four broad retail positioning strategies:

1. *Bloomingdale's:* Stores with a broad product assortment and high value added; they pay close attention to store design, product quality, service, and image, and they enjoy a high profit margin.

2. *Tiffany:* Stores with a narrow product assortment and high value added; they cultivate an exclusive image and tend to operate on high margin and low volume.

3. *Sunglass Hut:* With a narrow line and low value added, these stores keep costs and prices low by centralizing buying, merchandising, advertising, and distribution.

4. *Wal-Mart:* With a broad line and low value added, these stores keep prices low to create an image of being a place for bargains, and they make up for low margins with high volume.

Although the overwhelming majority of goods and services is sold through stores, *nonstore retailing*—especially online retailing—has been growing much faster than store retailing. Nonstore retailing falls into four major categories: (1) *direct selling*, a $9 billion industry with over 600 companies (such as Avon) selling door-to-door or at home; (2) *direct marketing*, with roots in direct-mail and catalog marketing (L.L. Bean) and encompassing telemarketing (1-800-FLOWERS), television direct-response marketing (QVC), and online shopping (Amazon.com); (3) *automatic vending*, used for items such as cigarettes, candy, and newspapers; and (4) *buying service*, a storeless retailer serving a specific clientele—usually employees of large organizations—who are entitled to buy from retailers that have agreed to provide discounts in return for membership.

Many stores remain independently owned, but an increasing number are part of some form of **corporate retailing** (see Table 15.2). Such organizations achieve economies of scale and have greater purchasing power, wider brand recognition, and better trained employees.

Retailer Marketing Decisions

In the past retailers held customers by offering convenient location, special or unique assortments of goods, greater or better services, and store credit cards. All of this has changed. Today, national brands such as Calvin Klein and Levi Strauss are found in most department stores, in their own shops, in merchandise outlets, and in off-price discount stores; the result is that store assortments have grown more alike.

Service differentiation also has eroded. Many department stores have trimmed services while many discounters have increased services. Customers have become smarter shoppers. They do not want to pay more for identical brands, especially when service differences have diminished. Nor do they need credit from a particular store, because bank credit cards are almost universally accepted. Effective differentiation

TABLE 15.2   Major Types of Retail Organizations

Corporate Chain Store: Two or more outlets commonly owned and controlled, employing central buying and merchandising, and selling similar lines of merchandise. Such stores buy in large quantities at lower prices, and hire corporate specialists to deal with pricing, promotion, merchandising, inventory control, and sales forecasting. Example: Tower Records.

Voluntary Chain: A wholesaler-sponsored group of independent retailers engaged in bulk buying and common merchandising. Example: Independent Grocers Alliance (IGA).

Retailer Cooperative: Independent retailers who set up a central buying organization and conduct joint promotion efforts. Example: Ace Hardware.

Consumer Cooperative: A retail firm owned by its customers. In consumer co-ops, residents contribute money to open their own store, vote on policies, elect managers, and receive patronage dividends.

Franchise Organization: Contractual association between a franchiser (manufacturer, wholesaler, service organization) and franchisees (independent businesspeople who buy the right to own and operate one or more units). Example: Jiffy Lube.

Merchandising Conglomerate: A free-form corporation that combines several diversified retailing lines and forms under central ownership, along with some integration of distribution and management. Example: Allied Domeq PLC operates Dunkin' Donuts and Baskin-Robbins.

therefore requires savvy marketing decisions about target market, product assortment and procurement, services and store atmosphere, price, promotion, and place, as suggested by the Mall of America example.

Target Market   A retailer's most important decision concerns the target market. Until the target market is defined and profiled, the retailer cannot make consistent decisions on product assortment, store decor, advertising messages and media, price, and service levels.

Some retailers have defined their target markets quite well. Consider The Limited, founded by Leslie Wexner as a single store targeting young fashion-conscious women. All aspects of the store—clothing assortment, fixtures, music, colors, and personnel—were orchestrated for this target consumer. A decade later Wexner's original customers were no longer in the "young" group, so he started Express to catch the new "youngs." He also started or acquired targeted chains such as Victoria's Secret, Lerner's, and Bath and Body Works. Today, The Limited operates 5,400 stores in the United States plus global catalog and e-commerce sites, ringing up over $10 billion in annual sales.[5]

Product Assortment and Procurement   The retailer's product assortment—*breadth* and *depth*—must match the target market's shopping expectations. Thus, a restaurant can offer a narrow and shallow assortment (small lunch counters), a narrow and deep assortment (delicatessen), a broad and shallow assortment (cafeteria), or a broad and deep assortment (large restaurant). Next, the retailer must develop a product-differentiation strategy. Some possibilities are to feature national brands not available at competing retailers (Saks uses this strategy); to feature mostly private branded merchandise (Gap uses this strategy); to feature the latest or newest merchandise first (The Sharper Image uses this strategy); or to offer customizing services (Harrod's of London uses this strategy).[6]

A growing number of stores are using **direct product profitability (DPP)** to measure a product's handling costs (receiving, moving to storage, paperwork, selecting, checking, loading, and space cost) from the time it reaches the warehouse until a customer buys it in the store. Resellers who have adopted DPP learn to their surprise that the gross margin on a product often has little relation to the direct product profit. Some high-volume products may have such high handling costs that they are less profitable and deserve less shelf space than some low-volume products.

Services and Store Atmosphere   The *services mix* is a key tool for differentiating a particular store. For example, a store may offer prepurchase services such as telephone and mail orders, advertising, window and interior display, fitting rooms, shopping hours, fashion shows, and trade-ins. Another option is to offer postpurchase services such as shipping and delivery, gift wrapping, adjustments and returns, alterations and tailoring, installations, and engraving. Finally, some stores emphasize ancillary services such as check cashing, parking, restaurants, repairs, interior decorating, credit, rest rooms, and baby-attendant service.

Atmosphere is another differentiation tool in the store's arsenal. Every store has a physical layout that makes it hard or easy to move around, as well as a "look." The store must embody a planned atmosphere that suits the target market and draws consumers toward purchase. The Kohl's department store chain uses a racetrack model to convey customers past all the merchandise in the store, along with a middle aisle for shoppers in a hurry. This loop yields much higher per-square-foot revenues than other retailers.[7]

Price Decision   Pricing is a key positioning factor and must be decided in relation to the target market, the mix of products and services, and the competition. All retailers would like to achieve both high volumes and high gross margins, but the two usually do not go together. Most retailers fall into the *high-markup, lower-volume group* (fine specialty stores) or the *low-markup, higher-volume group* (mass merchandisers and discount retailers).

Many retailers periodically put low prices on some items to serve as traffic builders or loss leaders, run occasional storewide sales, and plan markdowns on slower-moving merchandise. For example, shoe retailers expect to sell 50 percent of their shoes at the normal markup, 25 percent at a 40 percent markup, and the remaining 25 percent at cost.

Still, some retailers have abandoned high-low "sales pricing" in favor of everyday low pricing (see Chapter 13). Feather cites a study showing that supermarket chains practicing everyday low pricing are often more profitable than those practicing sales pricing.[8] Clearly, pricing is a key marketing decision that affects the bottom line.

Promotion Decision   Retailers can use a wide range of promotion tools to generate traffic and purchases: advertising, special sales, money-saving coupons, frequent shopper rewards, in-store sampling, and in-store couponing. Online retailers can use the same promotional tools; Amazon.com, for example, periodically offers free shipping on orders over $99, which encourages customers to buy more.[9] Each retailer must use promotion tools that support and reinforce its image positioning. Fine stores place tasteful ads in high-fashion magazines and carefully train salespeople to greet customers, interpret their needs, and handle complaints. Off-price retailers promote the idea of bargains and large savings, while conserving on service and sales assistance.

Place Decision   Retailers say that the three keys to success are "location, location, and location," because customers usually choose the most convenient place to shop. Stores have five major location choices, as shown in Table 15.3. Given the relationship between

TABLE 15.3   Location Options for Retailers

Location	Description
General business district	"Downtown," the oldest and most heavily trafficked city area; rents are normally high but a renaissance is bringing shoppers back to many cities.
Regional shopping center	Large suburban mall containing 40–200 stores and, generally, one or more anchor stores such as JCPenney; draws customers from 5–20 mile radius; offers generous parking, one-stop shopping and other facilities; the most successful malls charge high rents and may get a share of stores' sales.
Community shopping center	Smaller mall with one anchor store and 20–40 smaller stores.
Strip mall (shopping strip)	A cluster of stores, usually housed in one long building.
Location within a larger store or operation	Concession space rented by McDonald's and other retailers inside the unit of a larger retailer or an operation such as an airport.

high traffic and high rents, retailers need to support location decisions with assessment methods such as traffic counts, surveys of shoppers' habits, and analysis of competitive locations.[10] Several software models for site location have also been formulated.[11]

Trends in Retailing

Some of the main developments that retailers and manufacturers need to take into account in planning competitive strategies are:

1. *New retail forms and combinations continually emerge.* Bank branches have opened in supermarkets; gas stations include food stores that make more profit than the gas operation; bookstores feature coffee shops. Even old retail forms are reappearing: Peddler's carts are now in major U.S. malls, airports, and train stations.

2. *Competition is increasingly intertype.* Different types of retailers—discount stores, department stores, Web sites—all compete for the same consumers by carrying the same type of merchandise.

3. *Growth of giant retailers.* Huge retail organizations have the information technology, logistical systems, and buying power to provide immense volumes of products at appealing prices to masses of consumers.

4. *Technology is a critical competitive tool.* Computers help retailers generate better forecasts, control inventory costs, order from suppliers electronically, communicate with outlets, and sell to customers. Technology is also raising productivity through checkout scanning systems, electronic funds transfer, and sophisticated merchandise-handling systems.

5. *Global expansion of major retailers.* Retailers with unique formats and strong brand positioning are increasingly expanding into other countries.[12] Many U.S. retailers, such as McDonald's and Wal-Mart, have gone global to boost profits, as have Italy's Benetton chain, France's Carrefour hypermarkets, and Sweden's IKEA chain.[13]

6. *Selling an experience.* More retailers are adding fun and community, often inviting people to congregate—resulting in more coffeehouses, tea shops, juice bars, bookshops, and brew pubs. Riding this wave, Starbucks doubled in size to more than 5,300 units in less than four years by marketing the café experience.[14] See "Marketing Skills: Experience Marketing" for more on this vital skill.

7. *Competition between store-based and non-store-based retailing.* Non-store-based retailers are successfully competing with store-based retailers for customers and purchases. Retailers that once sold only through catalogs are now reaching customers via the Internet, stores, and other channels.[15] In turn, store retailers such as Wal-Mart are adding Web sites and other non-store retail channels.

WHOLESALING

Wholesaling includes all of the activities involved in selling goods or services to those who buy for resale or business use. Wholesaling excludes manufacturers and farmers (because they are engaged primarily in production) and retailers. Wholesalers (also called *distributors*) differ from retailers in a number of ways. First, wholesalers pay less attention to promotion, atmosphere, and location because they are dealing with business customers rather than final consumers. Second, wholesale transactions are usually larger than retail transactions, and wholesalers usually cover a larger trade area than retailers. Third, wholesalers and retailers comply with different legal regulations and taxes.

MARKETING SKILLS: EXPERIENCE MARKETING

Now that most national brands are available through multiple channels and shoppers perceive few real differences between retailers, experience marketing has emerged as a way for a store to set itself apart. Experts advise starting with a thorough understanding of what customers in the targeted segment value and expect. Then think about how to build relationships with these customers by enhancing the store's atmosphere through a sensory experience (feel, look, sound, smell, or taste). Not only must the experience be unique, it must also be brand appropriate and memorable.

A very basic experience might be built around a particular sense; for example, the scent of fresh coffee or baked goods in a food store. The starbucks store experience includes a rich coffee aroma (smell), soft jazz playing in the background (sound), comfortable seating (feel), and hip appointments (look). Ideally, the goal is to create a positive in-store experience that will be "entertaining, educational, aesthetic, and escapist all at once," says one marketer.

When Toys "R" Us built a 110,000-square-foot flagship in New York City, it installed a 60-foot-tall Ferris wheel with decorated gondolas based on familiar children's toys and characters. Every day, 3,000 customers pay $2.50 each (donated to charity) to board this ride. The store's Jurassic Park exhibit includes a lifelike, towering T-Rex; also in the store are several New York skyscrapers replicated 25 feet tall in Lego blocks and an 18-foot-long roller coaster made from K'Nex parts. With all these special exhibits plus music, toy sounds, and flashing neon lights, Toys 'R' Us has made its shopping experience more fun and unforgettable for customers of all ages.[16]

Why don't manufacturers sell directly to retailers or final consumers rather than through wholesalers? The main reason is efficiency: wholesalers are often better at handling one or more of these functions:

- *Selling and promoting.* Wholesalers provide a sales force that helps manufacturers reach many small business customers at a relatively low cost.
- *Buying and assortment building.* Wholesalers can select items and build the assortments their customers need, saving customers considerable work.
- *Bulk breaking.* Wholesalers achieve savings for their customers through buying in large lots and breaking the bulk into smaller units.
- *Warehousing.* Wholesalers generally hold inventories, reducing the inventory costs and risks to suppliers and customers.
- *Transportation.* Wholesalers can often provide quicker delivery because they are closer to buyers.
- *Financing.* Many wholesalers finance customers by granting credit, and they finance suppliers by ordering early and paying bills on time.
- *Risk bearing.* Some wholesalers absorb part of the risk by taking title and bearing the cost of theft, damage, spoilage, and obsolescence.
- *Market information.* Wholesalers supply information to suppliers and customers regarding competitors' activities, new products, price developments, and so on.

■ *Management services and counseling.* Wholesalers often help retailers train staff, plan store layouts and displays, and set up accounting and inventory-control systems. They may also help industrial customers with training and technical services.

The Growth and Types of Wholesaling

Wholesalers, like retailers, vary in type and function. Some take title to the products they handle, while others do not; some perform multiple functions, while others are more specialized. The major types of wholesalers are shown in Table 15.4.

TABLE 15.4 Major Wholesaler Types

Merchant Wholesalers: Independently owned businesses that take title to the merchandise they handle. Called jobbers, distributors, or mill supply houses, these are either full service or limited service.

Full-Service Wholesalers: Carry stock, maintain a sales force, offer credit, make deliveries, and provide management assistance. *Wholesale merchants* sell primarily to retailers and provide a full range of services; *industrial distributors* sell to manufacturers only and provide several services—carrying stock, offering credit, and providing delivery.

Limited-Service Wholesalers: Offer fewer services to suppliers and customers. *Cash-and-carry wholesalers* have a limited line of fast-moving goods and sell to small retailers for cash. *Truck wholesalers* primarily sell and deliver a limited line of semiperishable merchandise to supermarkets, small groceries, hospitals and others. *Drop shippers* operate in bulk industries, such as coal; upon receiving an order, they select a manufacturer, who ships the merchandise directly to the customer, with the drop shipper retaining title and assuming the risk until delivery is complete. *Rack jobbers* serve grocery and drug retailers—mostly in nonfood items—and retain title to goods, billing retailers only for goods sold to consumers; their delivery people set up displays, price goods, keep them fresh, and keep inventory records. *Producers' cooperatives* assemble farm produce to sell in local markets, distributing profits to members at the end of the year. *Mail-order wholesalers* have no sales staff; instead, they send catalogs to retail, industrial, and institutional customers and fill orders by mail or another transportation method.

Brokers and Agents: Do not take title to goods, and perform only a few functions—mainly facilitating buying and selling—for which they earn a commission of 2–6 percent of the selling price. They generally specialize by product line or customer type.

Brokers: Chief function is bringing buyers and sellers together and assisting in negotiation. They are paid by the party who hired them and do not carry inventory, finance goods, or assume risk. The most familiar examples are food brokers, real estate brokers, and insurance brokers.

Agents: Represent either buyers or sellers on a more permanent basis. *Manufacturers' agents* represent two or more manufacturers of complementary lines, following a written agreement covering pricing policy, territories, order-handling procedure, delivery service and warranties, and commissions. *Selling agents* have contractual authority to sell a manufacturer's entire output in such product areas as textiles and industrial machinery. *Purchasing agents* have a long-term relationship with buyers and make purchases for them, often receiving, inspecting, warehousing, and shipping merchandise to buyers. *Commission merchants*, used most often in agricultural marketing, take physical possession of products and negotiate sales.

Manufacturers' and Retailers' Branches and Offices: Wholesaling operations conducted by sellers or buyers themselves rather than through independent wholesalers. Sales branches and offices are set up by manufacturers to improve inventory control, selling, and promotion. *Sales branches*, which carry inventory, are found in lumber and other industries. *Sales offices*, which do not carry inventory, are most prominent in dry-goods industries. *Purchasing offices* operate similarly to brokers but are part of the buyer's organization; many retailers set up purchasing offices in major market centers.

Miscellaneous Wholesalers: Specialized types of wholesalers, including agricultural assemblers, which buy the agricultural output of many farms; petroleum bulk plants and terminals, which consolidate the petroleum output of many wells; and auction companies, which auction cars and other items to dealers and other businesses.

Wholesaling has been growing in the United States. One reason is the establishment of larger factories located far from buyers; another is the increasing need for adapting product quantities, packages, and features to the needs of intermediate and final users. Consider how McKesson uses technology to meet the needs of its diverse customer base. McKesson stocks and manages medical supplies and drugs for hospitals, doctors, nursing homes, and pharmacies. It allows pharmacies and other customers to use the McKesson Web site to transmit and track orders. In addition, the system automatically reorders replenishment stock from drug manufacturers so McKesson can fill customers' orders.[17]

Wholesaler Marketing Decisions

Wholesaler-distributors have faced mounting pressures in recent years from new sources of competition, demanding customers, new technologies, and more direct-buying programs by large buyers. In response, the industry has been working to increase asset productivity by better managing inventories and receivables. Wholesalers have also had to revisit their strategic decisions on target markets, product assortment and services, price, promotion, and place.

Target Market In defining their target markets, wholesalers can choose a target group of customers by size (only large retailers), type of customer (convenience stores only), need for service (customers needing credit), or other criteria. Within the target group, they can identify the most profitable customers and build relationships through value-added offers such as automatic replenishment systems or training. They can also discourage less-profitable customers by requiring larger orders or adding surcharges to smaller ones.

Product Assortment and Services The wholesalers' "product" is their assortment. They are under great pressure to carry a full line and maintain sufficient stock for immediate delivery, yet the costs of carrying huge inventories can kill profits. This is why wholesalers are constantly reexamining how many lines to offer and carrying only the more profitable ones. They are also identifying services that help strengthen customer relationships and determining which should be dropped or charged for. The key is to find a distinct mix of services valued by customers.

Price Decision Wholesalers usually mark up the cost of goods by a conventional percentage, say 20 percent, to cover expenses. Expenses may run 17 percent of the gross margin, leaving a profit margin of approximately 3 percent. In grocery wholesaling, the average profit margin is often less than 2 percent. Wholesalers are now experimenting with new pricing approaches: Some are trying to cut margin on selected lines in order to win important new customers; others are asking suppliers for a special price break that can be turned into an opportunity to increase the supplier's sales.

Promotion Decision In general, wholesalers rely on their sales force to achieve promotional objectives. Yet most wholesalers see selling as a single salesperson talking to a single customer instead of a team effort to sell and service major accounts. Wholesalers would benefit from adopting some of the image-building techniques used by retailers. They need to develop an overall promotion strategy involving trade advertising, sales promotion, and publicity and make greater use of supplier promotion materials and programs.

Place Decision Progressive wholesalers have been improving materials-handling procedures and costs by developing automated warehouses and improving their supply capabilities through advanced information systems. For example, W. W. Grainger, Inc. is one of the largest U.S. distributors of equipment, components, and supplies, offering more than 500,000 products through 400 sales offices and a comprehensive Web site. It maintains national, regional, and zone distribution centers for better product availability, faster order fulfillment, and convenient customer-delivery service.[18]

Trends in Wholesaling

For a while, wholesalers seemed to be headed for a significant decline as large manufacturers, and retailers such as Wal-Mart, moved aggressively into direct buying. Yet savvy wholesalers have rallied to the challenge, adapting their services to meet their suppliers' and target customers' changing needs as a way of adding value to the channel. They have also reduced operating costs by investing in advanced materials-handling technology and information systems.

After interviewing leading industrial distributors, Narus and Anderson identified four ways that wholesalers can strengthen relationships with manufacturers: (1) seek a clear agreement with their manufacturers about their expected functions in the marketing channel; (2) gain insight into manufacturers' requirements by visiting plants and attending conventions and trade shows; (3) fulfill commitments by meeting volume targets, paying promptly, and providing feedback of customer information to manufacturers; and (4) offer value-added services to help suppliers.[19]

Wholesaling still faces considerable challenges. The industry remains vulnerable to fierce resistance to price increases and the winnowing out of suppliers based on cost and quality. And the trend toward vertical integration, in which manufacturers try to control or own their intermediaries, is still strong.

MARKET LOGISTICS

The process of getting goods to customers has traditionally been called physical distribution. Physical distribution starts at the factory, where managers choose warehouses and transportation carriers that will deliver products to final destinations in the desired time or at the lowest cost. Physical distribution has been expanded into the broader concept of **supply chain management (SCM)**. Supply chain management starts before physical distribution, covering procurement of inputs (raw materials, components, and equipment); conversion into finished products; and product movement to final destinations. An even broader perspective calls for studying the suppliers' suppliers. The supply chain perspective can help a company identify superior suppliers and distributors and help them improve productivity, which ultimately brings down the company's costs.

Unfortunately, the supply chain view sees markets only as destination points and amounts to a linear view of the flow. As noted in Chapter 14, the *value network* view includes suppliers and its suppliers' suppliers and its immediate customers and their end customers. The value network includes valued relations with other stakeholders such as government agencies. The company should first consider its target market's requirements and then design the supply chain backward from that point, a view known as **demand chain planning. Market logistics** means planning the infrastructure to meet demand, then implementing and controlling the physical flows of materials and final goods from points of origin to points of use to meet customer needs at a profit. The result is the most efficient way to deliver value to customers.

The market logistics task calls for **integrated logistics systems (ILS)**, involving materials management, material flow systems, and physical distribution, abetted by information technology. Third-party suppliers, such as FedEx Logistics Services or Ryder Integrated Logistics, often participate in designing or managing these systems. For example, Volvo, working with FedEx, set up a warehouse in Memphis with a complete stock of truck parts. A dealer who needs a part in an emergency calls a toll-free number; FedEx ships the part for same-day delivery to the airport, the dealership, or the repair site.

Market logistics links several activities, starting with sales forecasting, which helps the company schedule distribution, production, and inventory levels. In turn, production plans indicate the materials that the purchasing department must order. These materials arrive through inbound transportation, enter the receiving area, and are stored in raw-material inventory and later converted into finished goods. Finished-goods inventory is the link between customer orders and manufacturing activity. Customers' orders draw down the finished-goods inventory level, and manufacturing activity builds it up. Finished goods flow off the assembly line and pass through packaging, in-plant warehousing, shipping-room processing, outbound transportation, field warehousing, and customer delivery and servicing.

Management has become concerned about the total cost of market logistics, which can amount to 30–40 percent of the product's cost. The grocery industry alone thinks it can decrease its annual operating costs by 10 percent, or $30 billion, by revamping market logistics. A typical box of breakfast cereal spends 104 days chugging through a labyrinth of intermediaries to reach the supermarket.[20] No wonder experts call market logistics "the last frontier for cost economies." Lower logistics costs permit lower prices, higher profit margins, or both. Although market logistics can be costly, a well-planned program can be a potent marketing tool, bringing in additional customers and boosting profits through better service, faster cycle time, or lower prices.

Consider Supervalu, a Minnesota-based wholesaler-retailer of dry groceries. The firm has implemented "cross-docking," in which products are moved from the supplier's truck through the distribution center and directly onto a store-bound truck. Attracted by the promise of savings on time and labor, Supervalu is cross-docking up to 25 percent of its products. This has reduced the total number of inventory days on hand for the 1.5 billion cases of goods the wholesaler ships every year.[21]

On the other hand, companies can lose customers when they fail to supply goods on time. Kodak found this out when it launched a national ad campaign for a new instant camera before it had delivered enough stock to the stores. Customers who could not find the camera bought competing models instead.

Market-Logistics Objectives

Many companies state their market-logistics objective as "getting the right goods to the right places at the right time for the least cost." Unfortunately, no market-logistics system can simultaneously maximize customer service and minimize distribution cost.

Maximum customer service implies large inventories, premium transportation, and multiple warehouses, all of which raise market-logistics costs.

Given that market-logistics activities involve strong trade-offs, decisions must be made on a total system basis. The starting point is to study what customers require and what competitors offer. Customers are interested in on-time delivery, supplier willingness to meet emergency needs, careful handling of merchandise, and supplier willingness to take back defective goods and resupply them quickly.

The company must then research the relative importance of these service outputs. For example, service-repair time is very important to buyers of copying equipment. Knowing this, Xerox developed a service-delivery standard that "can put a disabled machine anywhere in the continental United States back into operation within 3 hours after receiving the service request." It then designed a service division of personnel, parts, and locations to deliver on this promise.

The company must also consider competitors' service standards, seeking to match or exceed those levels. Still, the objective is to maximize profits, not sales, which means looking at the costs of providing higher service levels. Some companies offer less service and charge a lower price; others offer more service and charge a premium price. In the end, the company must establish some service promise to the market. One appliance manufacturer set these service standards: to deliver at least 95 percent of the dealer's orders within 7 days of order receipt, to fill the dealer's orders with 99 percent accuracy, to answer dealer inquiries on order status within 3 hours, and to ensure that damage to merchandise in transit does not exceed 1 percent.

The company must design a system that will minimize the cost of achieving its logistical objectives. Each possible market-logistics system will lead to the following cost:

$$M = T + FW + VW + S$$

where

   M = total market-logistics cost of proposed system;
   T = total freight cost of proposed system;
   FW = total fixed warehouse cost of proposed system;
   VW = total variable warehouse costs (including inventory) of proposed system; and
   S = total cost of lost sales due to average delivery delay under proposed system.

Choosing a market-logistics system calls for examining the total cost (M) associated with different systems and selecting the system that minimizes it. If S is hard to measure, the company should aim to minimize $T + FW + VW$ for a target level of customer service.

Market-Logistics Decisions

Companies make four major decisions with regard to market logistics: How should orders be handled? Where should stocks be located? How much stock should be held? How should goods be shipped?

Order Processing   Most companies want to shorten the *order-to-payment cycle*—the elapsed time between an order's receipt, delivery, and payment. This cycle involves many steps, including order transmission by the salesperson, order entry and customer credit check, inventory and production scheduling, order shipment, and receipt of payment. The longer this cycle takes, the lower the customer's satisfaction and the lower the company's profits.

Still, companies are making great progress. General Electric, for example, operates an information system that checks the customer's credit standing and determines whether and where the ordered items are in stock. The system then issues an order to ship, bills the customer, updates the inventory records, orders new stock, and notifies the sales representative that the order is on the way—in less than 15 seconds.

Warehousing   Every manufacturer has to store finished goods until they are sold because production and consumption cycles rarely match. The storage function helps to smooth discrepancies between production and quantities desired by the market. Two warehousing options are storage warehouses, which hold goods for moderate-to-long periods, and distribution warehouses, which receive goods from company plants and suppliers and move them out as soon as possible. Having more stocking locations means that goods can be delivered to customers more quickly, but it also means higher warehousing costs, which is why many firms are reassessing their warehousing arrangements. When National Semiconductor closed six storage warehouses and set up a central distribution warehouse in Singapore, it was able to cut its standard delivery time by 47 percent, cut distribution costs by 2.5 percent, and boost sales by 34 percent.[22]

Newer *automated warehouses* are equipped with advanced materials-handling systems under the control of a central computer. The computer reads store orders and directs lift trucks and electric hoists to gather goods according to bar codes, move them to loading docks, and issue invoices. Automated warehouses save money by reducing worker injuries, labor costs, pilferage, and breakage while improving inventory control. For instance, when Helene Curtis replaced its six antiquated warehouses with a new $32 million facility, it cut its distribution costs by 40 percent.[23]

Inventory   Inventory levels represent a major market-logistics decision. Salespeople would like to have enough stock to fill all customer orders immediately, but this is not cost effective. *Inventory cost increases at an increasing rate as the customer service level approaches 100 percent.* To make an informed decision, management needs to determine how much sales and profits would increase as a result of carrying larger inventories and promising faster order fulfillment times.

Crafting an inventory strategy means knowing when to order and how much to order. As inventory draws down, management must know at what stock level to place a new order. This stock level is called the *order (reorder) point*. An order point of 20 means reordering when the stock falls to 20 units. The order point should balance the risks of stockout against the costs of overstock.

The other decision is how much to order. The larger the quantity ordered, the less frequently an order has to be placed. Here, the company is balancing order-processing costs against inventory-carrying costs. *Order-processing costs* for a manufacturer consist of *setup costs* and *running costs* (operating costs when production is running). If setup costs are low, the manufacturer can produce the item often, and the average cost per item is stable and equal to the running costs. If setup costs are high, however, the manufacturer can cut the average cost per unit by producing a long run and carrying more inventory.

Order-processing costs must be compared with *inventory-carrying costs*. The larger the average stock carried, the higher the inventory-carrying costs, including storage charges, cost of capital, taxes and insurance, and depreciation and obsolescence. This means that marketing managers who want their companies to carry larger inventories need to show that the larger inventories would produce incremental gross profit that exceeds the incremental carrying costs.

The optimal order quantity can be determined by analyzing the sum of order-processing costs and inventory-carrying costs at different order levels. As in Figure 15.1, the order-processing cost per unit decreases with the number of units ordered because the costs are spread over more units. Inventory-carrying charges per unit increase with the number of units ordered because each unit remains longer in inventory. The two cost curves are summed vertically into a total-cost curve. The lowest point on the total-cost curve is projected down on the horizontal axis to find the optimal order quantity Q^*.[24]

Just-in-time production methods have changed inventory-planning practices. With **just-in-time (JIT) production**, supplies arrive at the factory when they are needed. If the suppliers are dependable, then the manufacturer can carry much lower levels of inventory and still meet customer-order-fulfillment standards. Tesco, the large British supermarket chain, has an innovative JIT market logistics system. Management reduced costly backroom storage space by arranging twice-a-day delivery of replenishment stock. Instead of using three trucks to deliver frozen, refrigerated, and regular goods, it designed new trucks with three compartments to carry all these goods in one trip. The ultimate answer to carrying *near-zero inventory* is to build to order, as Dell Computer does.

Transportation   Transportation choices affect product pricing, on-time delivery performance, and the condition of the goods on arrival, all of which influence customer satisfaction. In shipping goods to its warehouses, dealers, and customers, the company can choose among rail, air, truck, waterway, and pipeline, using such criteria as speed, frequency, dependability, capability, availability, traceability, and cost. For speed, air and truck are the prime contenders; for low cost, waterway and pipeline are appropriate.

FIGURE 15.1   Determining Optimal Order Quantity

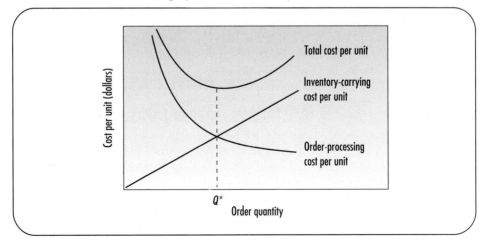

Shippers are increasingly combining two or more transportation modes, thanks to containerization. **Containerization** consists of putting the goods in boxes or trailers that are easy to transfer between two transportation modes. *Piggyback* describes the use of rail and trucks; *fishyback*, water and trucks; *trainship*, water and rail; and *airtruck*, air and trucks. Each coordinated mode offers specific advantages. For example, piggyback is cheaper than trucking alone, yet provides flexibility and convenience.

In deciding on transportation modes, shippers have three broad choices. If the shipper owns its own truck or air fleet, the shipper becomes a *private carrier*. A *contract carrier* is an independent organization that sells transportation services to others on a contract basis. A *common carrier* provides services between predetermined points on a schedule, and is available to all shippers at standard rates.

Market Logistics Lessons

Companies have learned several major lessons in handling market logistics. First, they need a senior vice president as the single point of contact for all logistical elements and for accountability for both cost and customer satisfaction. Second, this executive should meet frequently with sales and operations people to review inventory, costs, and service and satisfaction issues and achievements—as well as to discuss any needed changes. Third, software and systems are increasingly critical for competitively superior logistics performance. In the end, market-logistics strategies must be derived from business strategies, rather than solely from cost considerations.

EXECUTIVE SUMMARY

Retailing includes all of the activities involved in selling goods or services directly to final consumers for personal, nonbusiness use. Retailers include store retailing, nonstore retailing, and retail organizations. Like products, retail-store types pass through stages of growth and decline. Major types of retail stores are specialty stores, department stores, supermarkets, convenience stores, discount stores, off-price retailers, and superstores.

Although most goods and services are sold through stores, nonstore retailing has been growing much faster. The major types of nonstore retailing are direct selling, direct marketing, automatic vending, and buying services. An increasing number of retailers are part of corporate retailing and achieve many economies of scale, such as greater purchasing power, wider brand recognition, and better trained employees. Retailers must make decisions about target markets, product assortment and procurement, services and store atmosphere, price, promotion, and place, taking into account major industry trends.

Wholesaling includes all of the activities involved in selling goods or services to those who buy for resale or business use. Manufacturers use wholesalers because wholesalers can perform certain functions better and more cost effectively than the manufacturer can, such as selling and promoting, buying and assortment building, bulk breaking, warehousing, transportation, financing, risk bearing, dissemination of market information, and training and consulting.

Types of wholesalers include merchant wholesalers; full-service and limited-service wholesalers; brokers; agents; manufacturers' and retailers' sales branches, sales offices, and purchasing offices; and miscellaneous wholesalers such as agricultural assemblers. The most successful wholesalers adapt their services to meet suppliers' and target customers' needs, adding value to the channel. Wholesalers must decide on target markets, product assortment and services, price, promotion, and place.

Producers must decide on market logistics—the best way to store and move goods and services to market destinations. Logistics decisions cover order processing, warehousing, inventory, and transportation. Information technology has led to major gains in logistical efficiency. Although market logistics can be costly, a well-planned program can be a potent tool in competitive marketing. The ultimate goal of market logistics is to meet customers' requirements in an efficient and profitable way.

NOTES

1. "A Lot of Their Own," *Chain Store Age*, April 2002, p. 31; "Mall of America," *Chain Store Age*, February 2002, p. 153; Jerry Gerlach and James Janke, "The Mall of America as a Tourist Attraction," *Focus*, Summer 2001, pp. 32+; "Mall Bawl," *Promo*, August 1, 2001, p. 57.

2. William R. Davidson, Albert D. Bates, and Stephen J. Bass, "Retail Life Cycle," *Harvard Business Review* (November–December 1976): 89–96.

3. See Jeffrey Davis, "Chasing Retail's Tail," *Business 2.0*, January 2000, p. 172.

4. Stanley C. Hollander, "The Wheel of Retailing," *Journal of Marketing* (July 1960): 37–42.

5. David Moin, "Wexner, Lieutenants Push Divisions, Brands Beyond Limited Appeal," *WWD*, October 11, 2001, p. 1; Hoover's Company Capsules, 1999; Limited Annual Report, 2001.

6. Laurence H. Wortzel, "Retailing Strategies for Today's Marketplace," *Journal of Business Strategy* (Spring 1987): 45–56.

7. Cametta Coleman, "Kohl's Retail Racetrack," *Wall Street Journal*, March 1, 2000.

8. Frank Feather, *The Future Consumer* (Toronto: Warwick Publishing, 1994) p. 171. Also see Stephen J. Hoch, Xavier Dreeze, and Mary E. Purk, "EDLP, Hi-Lo, and Margin Arithmetic," *Journal of Marketing* (October 1994): 1–15.

9. Robert D. Hof, "The Shipping News," *BusinessWeek*, May 6, 2002, p. 42.

10. R. L. Davies and D. S. Rogers, eds., *Store Location and Store Assessment Research* (New York: John Wiley, 1984).

11. See Sara L. McLafferty, *Location Strategies for Retail and Service Firms* (Lexington, MA: Lexington Books, 1987).

12. For further discussion of retail trends, see Louis W. Stern and Adel I. El-Ansary, *Marketing Channels*, 5th ed. (Upper Saddle River, NJ: Prentice Hall, 1996).

13. Shelley Donald Coolidge, "Facing Saturated Home Markets, Retailers Look to Rest of World," *Christian Science Monitor*, February 14, 1994, p. 7; Carla Rapoport with Justin Martin, "Retailers Go Global," *Fortune*, February 20, 1995, pp. 102–108; Amy Feldman, "Wal-Mart: How Big Can It Get?" *Money*, December 1999, pp. 158–64; Kerry Capell and Heidi Dawley, "Wal-Mart's Not-So-Secret British Weapon," *BusinessWeek*, January 24, 2000, p. 132.

14. "Starbucks Corp.," *Nation's Restaurant News Daily NewsFax*, April 5, 2002, p. 1.

15. Kate Mason, "Nuts & Bolts," *Target Marketing*, September 2001, p. 18.

16. Tim Palmer, "Sensing a Winner," *Grocer*, January 26, 2002, pp. 40+; "Go Live with a Big Brand Experience," *Marketing*, October 26, 2000, pp. 45+; Russell Pearlman, "Where the Toys Are," *SmartMoney*, May 2002, pp. 34–36; Kelly Barbieri, "Toys 'R' Us Becomes Big Wheel in Times Square," *Amusement Business*, April 29, 2002, p. 10.

17. Hoover's Company Profiles, 1999; Michael Liedtke, "Online Goes Offline at McKesson HBOC," *Pittsburgh Post-Gazette*, February 27, 2001, p. B4.

18. Susan E. Fisher, "W. W. Grainger Procures Success on the Web," *Info World*, December 10, 1999 (***www.infoworld.com***); "Annual Meetings: Grainger Out to Build Distribution Efficiency," *Crain's Chicago Business*, May 6, 2002, p. 12.

19. James A. Narus and James C. Anderson, "Contributing as a Distributor to Partnerships with Manufacturers," *Business Horizons*, September–October 1987. Also see James D. Hlavecek and Tommy J. McCuistion, "Industrial Distributors—When, Who, and How," *Harvard Business Review* (March–April 1983): 96–101.

20. Ronald Henkoff, "Delivering the Goods," *Fortune*, November 28, 1994, pp. 64–78.

21. Susan Reda, "Crossdocking: Can Supermarkets Catch Up?" *Stores*, February, 1998; Supervalu 2001 Annual Report; Deena M. Amato-McCoy, "Cross-Docking at Supervalu," *Convenience Store News*, March 5, 2001, p. 92.

22. Henkoff, "Delivering the Goods," pp. 64–78.

23. Rita Koselka, "Distribution Revolution," *Forbes*, May 25, 1992, pp. 54–62.

24. The optimal order quantity is given by the formula $Q^* = 2DS/IC$, where D = annual demand, S = cost to place one order, and I = annual carrying cost per unit. Known as the economic-order quantity formula, it assumes a constant ordering cost, a constant cost of carrying an additional unit in inventory, a known demand, and no quantity discounts. For more, see Richard J. Tersine, *Principles of Inventory and Materials Management*, 4th ed. (Upper Saddle River, NJ: Prentice Hall, 1994).

CHAPTER 16

Designing and Managing Integrated Marketing Communications

In this chapter, we will address the following questions:

1. What are the major steps in developing an effective integrated marketing communications program?
2. What steps are involved in developing an advertising program?
3. How can companies exploit the marketing potential of sales promotion, public relations, direct marketing, and e-marketing?

MARKETING MANAGEMENT AT YAHOO!

"Do you Yahoo!?" Since 1996, that tagline has appeared on numerous television commercials, print ads, and other marketing communications geared toward consumers. Initially, Yahoo! used public relations to build awareness by emphasizing its site's user-friendliness—and garnered 600 press mentions in the first six months of operation. Early on, nearly 60 search sites competed with Yahoo! but now its major competitors are MSN and America Online. Yahoo! has therefore changed its focus from establishing its brand to differentiating its brand through humorous ads with eye-catching graphics and a clear, consistent message promoting the site as "the only place you need to go on the Internet to find things, to connect with people, or to buy," says an executive with the company's advertising agency.

Users indicate on the marketing preferences page what types of contacts they are willing to receive from Yahoo! and its partners, such as e-mail and telemarketing offers. Lately, the company has increased its use of direct marketing to promote various fee-based services to its 237 million users. Although targeted e-mail and splashy banner ads are mainstays, the company also is testing direct-mail offers. For example, consumers can sign up for online personal ads ($19.95 monthly); run a fantasy football team ($24.95 per team); or ask astrology questions ($14.95 per question). Coordinating all its communications has helped Yahoo! boost annual revenues beyond $700 million.[1]

Modern marketing calls for more than developing a good product, pricing it attractively, and making it accessible. Companies must also communicate with present and potential stakeholders as well as the general public. For Yahoo! and most companies, the question is not whether to communicate but rather what to say, to whom, and how often.

The marketing communications mix consists of advertising, sales promotion, public relations and publicity, personal selling, and direct marketing. However, the product's styling and price, the package's shape and color, the salesperson's manner and dress, the store's decor—all communicate something to buyers. In fact, every *brand contact* delivers an impression that can affect a customer's view of the company. Therefore, the entire marketing mix must be integrated to deliver a consistent message and strategic positioning. This chapter explores marketing communications, with a closer look at advertising, sales promotion, public relations, direct marketing, and e-marketing. Chapter 17 discusses the sales force and personal selling.

DEVELOPING EFFECTIVE MARKETING COMMUNICATIONS

Today communications is seen as an interactive dialogue between the company and its customers that takes place during the preselling, selling, consuming, and postconsuming stages. Companies are asking not only "How can we reach our customers?" but also "How can our customers reach us?" Sellers now use a variety of communication platforms to stay in touch with customers, as shown in Table 16.1. Increasingly, it is the newer technologies, such as the Internet, that have encouraged more firms to use targeted communication for one-to-one dialogues with customers and other stakeholders.

There are eight steps to follow in developing an effective marketing communications program: (1) identify the target audience, (2) determine the communication objectives, (3) design the message, (4) select the communication channels, (5) establish the communications budget, (6) decide on the media mix, (7) measure the results, and (8) manage the integrated marketing communication process.

Step 1: Identify the Target Audience

The first step is to identify a clear target audience: potential buyers of the company's products, current users, deciders, or influencers; individuals, groups, particular publics, or the general public. The target audience is a critical influence on the firm's

TABLE 16.1   Common Communication Platforms

Advertising	Sales Promotion	Public Relations	Personal Selling	Direct Marketing
Print and broadcast ads	Contests, games, sweepstakes, lotteries	Press kits	Sales presentations	Catalogs
Packaging–outer		Speeches	Sales meetings	Mailings
Packaging inserts	Premiums and gifts	Seminars	Incentive programs	Telemarketing
Motion pictures	Sampling	Annual reports	Samples	Electronic shopping
Brochures and booklets	Fairs and trade shows	Charitable donations	Fairs and trade shows	TV shopping
Posters and leaflets	Exhibits	Sponsorships		Fax mail
Directories	Demonstrations	Publications		E-mail
Reprints of ads	Coupons	Community relations		Voice mail
Billboards	Rebates	Lobbying		
Display signs	Low-interest financing	Identity media		
Point-of-purchase displays	Entertainment	Company magazine		
Audiovisual material	Trade-in allowances	Events		
Symbols and logos	Continuity programs			
Videotapes	Tie-ins			

decisions about what to say, how to say it, when to say it, where to say it, and to whom to say it.

A major part of audience analysis is assessing the audience's current image of the company, its products, and its competitors. **Image** is the set of beliefs, ideas, and impressions that a person holds regarding an object. People's attitudes and actions toward an object such as a product or service are highly conditioned by that object's image. In assessing image, marketers research the audience's familiarity with the product, then they ask respondents who know the product how they feel about it.

If most respondents have unfavorable feelings toward the product, the organization needs to overcome a negative image problem, which requires great patience because images persist long after the organization has changed. Once people have a certain image, they perceive what is consistent with that image. It will take highly disconfirming information to raise doubts and open their minds—but it can be done.

Step 2: Determine the Communication Objectives

The marketing communicator must now decide on the desired audience response, seeking a *cognitive*, *affective*, or *behavioral* response. That is, the marketer might want to put something into the consumer's mind, change an attitude, or get the consumer to act. The four best-known models of consumer-response stages are presented in Figure 16.1.

All of these models assume that the buyer passes through a cognitive, affective, and behavioral stage, in that order. This "learn-feel-do" sequence is appropriate when the audience has high involvement with a product category that is perceived to have high differentiation, as in purchasing an automobile. An alternative sequence, "do-feel-learn," is relevant when the audience has high involvement but perceives little or no differentiation within the product category, as in purchasing aluminum siding. A

FIGURE 16.1   Response Hierarchy Models

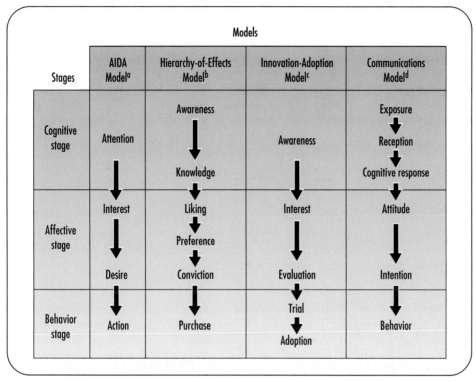

Sources: [a]E. K. Strong, *The Psychology of Selling* (New York: McGraw-Hill, 1925), p. 9; [b]Robert J. Lavidge and Gary A. Steiner, "A Model for Predictive Measurements of Advertising Effectiveness," *Journal of Marketing* (October, 1961): 61; [c]Everett M. Rogers, *Diffusion of Innovation* (New York: The Free Press, 1962), p. 79–86; [d]Various sources.

third sequence, "learn-do-feel," is relevant when the audience has low involvement and perceives little differentiation within the category, as in purchasing salt. By choosing the right sequence, the marketer can do a better job of planning communications.[2]

Step 3: Design the Message

Having defined the desired response, the communicator moves to developing an effective message. Ideally, the message should gain *attention*, hold *interest*, arouse *desire*, and elicit *action* (AIDA model—see the first column of Figure 16.1). Few messages actually take the target audience all the way from awareness through purchase, but the AIDA framework suggests the desirable qualities of any communication. Formulating the message involves decisions about message content, structure, format, and source.

Message Content   In determining message content, management searches for an appeal, theme, idea, or unique selling proposition. There are three types of appeals. *Rational appeals* engage self-interest by claiming the product will produce certain benefits such as value or performance. It is widely believed that industrial buyers are most responsive to rational appeals because they are knowledgeable about the product, trained to recognize value, and accountable to others for their choices. Consumers, when they buy certain big-ticket items, also tend to gather information and estimate benefits.

Emotional appeals attempt to stir up negative or positive emotions that will motivate purchase. Negative appeals such as fear, guilt, and shame are used to get people to do things (brush their teeth) or stop doing things (smoking). Companies can also use positive emotional appeals such as humor, love, pride, and joy. The online financial services firm E*Trade, for example, uses high-profile humorous ads to differentiate itself. The ads score well in consumer polls and encourage positive attitudes toward the firm.[3]

Moral appeals are directed to the audience's sense of what is right and proper. These are often used to exhort people to support social causes. An example is the appeal "Silence = Death," which is the slogan of Act-Up, the AIDS Coalition to Unleash Power.

Multinational companies wrestle with a number of challenges in developing message content for global campaigns. First, they must decide whether the product is appropriate for a country. Second, they must make sure the targeted market segment is both legal and customary. Third, they must decide if the style of the ad is acceptable. And fourth, they must decide whether ads should be created at headquarters or locally. Coca-Cola, for example, has a pool of ads that can be customized for local audiences.[4]

Message Structure   Message effectiveness depends on structure as well as content. For example, a one-sided presentation praising a product might seem to be more effective than two-sided arguments that also mention shortcomings. Yet two-sided messages may be more appropriate, especially when some negative association must be overcome. In this spirit, Heinz ran the message "Heinz Ketchup is slow good."[5] Two-sided messages are more effective with more educated audiences and those who are initially opposed.[6]

The order in which arguments are presented is also important.[7] In a one-sided message, presenting the strongest argument first establishes audience attention and interest. This is important in newspapers and other media where the audience often does not attend to the whole message. With a captive audience, however, a climactic presentation might be more effective. In a two-sided message, if the audience is initially opposed, the communicator might start with the other side's argument and conclude with the strongest argument.[8]

Message Format   The communicator must develop a strong message format. In a print ad, the communicator has to decide on headline, copy, illustration, and color. For radio, the communicator has to choose words, voice qualities, and vocalizations. If the message is carried on television or in person, all of these elements plus nonverbal clues have to be planned. If the message is carried by the product or its packaging, the communicator has to consider color, texture, scent, size, and shape. Web-based messages can combine aspects of print, radio, and television messages with special effects and interactivity to attract, retain, and reinforce audience interest. BMW combined entertainment and advertising when it posted minifilms featuring its cars on a special Web site and used television spots to attract 3 million visitors to the site in just six weeks.[9]

Message Source   Messages delivered by attractive or popular sources achieve higher attention and recall, which is why advertisers often use celebrities as spokespeople. In particular, messages delivered by highly credible sources are more persuasive, so pharmaceutical companies have doctors testify about product benefits because doctors have high credibility.

Three factors underlying source credibility are expertise, trustworthiness, and likability.[10] *Expertise* is the specialized knowledge the communicator possesses to back the claim. *Trustworthiness* is related to how objective and honest the source is perceived to be. Friends are trusted more than strangers or salespeople, and people who are not paid to endorse a product are seen as more trustworthy than people who are paid.[11] *Likability* describes the source's attractiveness; qualities like candor, humor, and naturalness make a source more likable. The most credible source would score high on all three factors.

Step 4: Select the Communication Channels

The communicator must select efficient communication channels to carry the message. For example, pharmaceutical salespeople can rarely wrest more than five minutes' time from a busy physician. Because personal selling is expensive, the industry has added multiple channels to build physician preference for specific branded drugs through ads in medical journals, direct mail, sampling, telemarketing, Web sites, and conferences. In general, firms can use two types of communication channels: personal and nonpersonal.

Personal Communication Channels   Personal communication channels involve two or more persons communicating directly with each other face to face, person to audience, over the telephone, or through e-mail. These channels derive their effectiveness through individualized presentation and feedback. Kiehl's, which makes skincare products, does not advertise or create exciting packaging; instead, it gives away free samples to anyone entering its stores, encouraging widespread word-of-mouth and positive publicity.[12]

Companies can stimulate personal influence channels to work on their behalf by:

- *Identifying influential individuals and companies and devoting extra effort to them.*[13] In industrial selling, the entire industry might follow the market leader in adopting innovations.
- *Creating opinion leaders by supplying certain people with the product on attractive terms.* A new tennis racket might be offered initially to high school tennis teams at a special low price.
- *Working through community influentials such as local disk jockeys and heads of civic organizations.* When Ford introduced the Thunderbird, it sent invitations to executives offering a free car to drive for the day; 10 percent of the respondents indicated that they would become buyers, and 84 percent said they would recommend the car to a friend.
- *Using influential or believable people in testimonial advertising.* This is why Nike and other companies hire top athletes such as Tiger Woods as spokespeople.
- *Developing advertising with high "conversation value."* Ads with high conversation value often have a slogan that becomes part of the national vernacular, such as Nike's "Just do it."
- *Developing word-of-mouth referral channels to build business.* Professionals such as accountants will often encourage clients to recommend their services.

- *Establishing an electronic forum.* Toyota owners who use Internet services such as America Online can share experiences online.
- *Using viral marketing.* Online marketers can use **viral marketing**, a form of word of mouth, to draw attention to their sites.[14] This involves passing along company-developed products, services, or information from user to user.

Nonpersonal Communication Channels   Nonpersonal channels include media, atmospheres, and events. *Media* consist of print media (newspapers, magazines, direct mail), broadcast media (radio, television), network media (telephone, cable, satellite, wireless), electronic media (audiotape, videotape, CD-ROM, DVD, Web page), and display media (billboards, signs, posters). Most nonpersonal messages come through paid media.

Atmospheres are "packaged environments" that create or reinforce the buyer's leanings toward product purchase. Law offices, for instance, are decorated with fine rugs and furniture to communicate "stability" and "success."[15] *Events* are occurrences such as news conferences, grand openings, and other activities designed to communicate particular messages to target audiences. Department stores often arrange special events to maintain a sophisticated, cultured image in the minds of shoppers.

Nonpersonal channels of mass communication affect personal attitudes and behavior through a two-step flow-of-communication process. Ideas often flow from media sources to opinion leaders and from these to the less media-involved population groups. This two-step flow has several implications. First, the influence of nonpersonal channels on public opinion is mediated by opinion leaders, people whose opinions are sought or who carry their opinions to others. Second, the two-step flow shows that people interact primarily within their own social group and acquire ideas from their group's opinion leaders. Third, two-step communication suggests that marketers using nonpersonal channels should direct messages specifically to opinion leaders and let them carry the message to others. This is why many software makers give opinion leaders a preview of new programs.

Step 5: Establish the Marketing Communications Budget

Industries and companies vary considerably in how much they spend on promotion. Expenditures might amount to 30–50 percent of sales in the cosmetics industry but only 5–10 percent in the industrial-equipment industry, with company-to-company variations. Four common methods for deciding on a budget include:

- *Affordable method.* Many companies set the promotion budget at what management thinks the firm can afford. However, this method ignores the role of promotion as an investment and the immediate impact of promotion on sales volume; it also leads to an uncertain annual budget, making long-range planning difficult.
- *Percentage-of-sales method.* Many firms set promotion expenditures at a specified percentage of sales (either current or anticipated) or of the sales price. Supporters say this method links promotion expenditures to the movement of corporate sales over the business cycle; focuses attention on the interrelationship of promotion cost, selling price, and unit profit; and encourages stability when competing firms spend approximately the same percentage. On the other hand, this method views sales as the determiner of promotion rather than as the result; it provides no logical basis for

choosing the specific percentage; nor does it allow for determining the promotion budget each product and territory deserves.

- *Competitive-parity method.* Some companies set their promotion budget to achieve share-of-voice parity with competitors. Although proponents say that competitors' expenditures represent the collective wisdom of the industry and that maintaining competitive parity prevents promotion wars, neither argument is valid. Company reputations, resources, opportunities, and objectives differ so much that promotion budgets are hardly a guide. Furthermore, there is no evidence that competitive parity discourages promotional wars.

- *Objective-and-task method.* Here, marketers develop promotion budgets by defining specific objectives, determining the tasks that must be performed to achieve these objectives, and estimating the costs of performing these tasks. The sum of these costs is the proposed promotion budget. This method has the advantage of requiring management to spell out assumptions about the relationship among dollars spent, exposure levels, trial rates, and regular usage.

Step 6: Decide on the Marketing Communications Mix

Companies must decide how to allocate the budget over the five promotional tools. Even in the same industry, companies differ considerably in their media and channel choices. Avon concentrates on personal selling, whereas Cover Girl advertises heavily. Because companies are always searching for more efficiency by substituting one promotional tool for another, they must be careful to coordinate all of their marketing functions.

Promotional Tools   Each promotional tool has its own unique characteristics and costs, as the following overview indicates.[16] Personal selling will be discussed in Chapter 17; the rest of these tools are discussed later in this chapter.

- *Advertising.* Advertising can be used to forge a long-term image for a product (Coca-Cola ads) or trigger quick sales (a Sears ad for a weekend sale). Advertising can reach geographically dispersed buyers efficiently. Certain forms of advertising (TV advertising) require a large budget; other forms (newspaper advertising) do not.

- *Sales promotion.* Sales-promotion tools—coupons, contests, premiums, and the like—offer three key benefits: (1) communication (gaining attention that may lead the consumer to the product); (2) incentive (incorporating some concession or inducement that gives value to the consumer); and (3) invitation (including a distinct invitation to engage in the transaction now). Sales promotion can be used for short-run effects such as dramatizing product offers and boosting sales.

- *Public relations and publicity.* The appeal of public relations and publicity is based on three qualities: (1) high credibility (news stories and features are more authentic and credible than ads); (2) ability to catch buyers off guard (reaching prospects who prefer to avoid salespeople and advertisements); and (3) dramatization (the potential for dramatizing a company or product).

- *Direct marketing.* All forms of direct marketing—direct mail, telemarketing, Internet marketing—share four characteristics: They are (1) nonpublic (normally addressed to a specific person); (2) customized (prepared to appeal to the addressed individual); (3) up-to-date (can be prepared very quickly); and (4) interactive (can be changed depending on the person's response).

- *Personal selling.* Qualities of personal selling include: (1) personal confrontation (an immediate and interactive relationship between two or more persons); (2) cultivation (all kinds of relationships can spring up, ranging from a matter-of-fact selling relationship to a deep personal friendship); and (3) response (the buyer feels under some obligation for having listened to the sales talk).

Factors in Setting the Marketing Communications Mix In developing their promotion mix, companies must consider the type of product market, customer readiness to make a purchase, stage in the product life cycle, and market rank. First, consumer and business markets tend to require different promotional allocations. Although advertising is used less than sales calls in business markets, it still plays a significant role in building awareness and comprehension, is an efficient reminder of the product, generates leads, legitimizes the company and products, and reassures customers about purchases. Personal selling can also be effective in consumer markets, by helping to persuade dealers to take more stock and display more of the product, build dealer enthusiasm, sign up more dealers, and grow sales at existing accounts.

Second, promotional tools vary in cost effectiveness at different stages of buyer readiness, as shown in Figure 16.2. Advertising and publicity are most important in the awareness-building stage. Customer comprehension is affected primarily by advertising and personal selling, while customer conviction is influenced mostly by personal selling. Closing the sale is influenced mostly by personal selling and sales promotion. Reordering is also affected mostly by personal selling and sales promotion, and somewhat by reminder advertising.

Third, promotional tools vary in cost effectiveness at different stages of the product life cycle. Advertising and publicity are most cost effective in the introduction stage; then all the tools can be toned down in the growth stage because demand is

FIGURE 16.2 Cost-Effectiveness of Different Promotional Tools at Different Buyer-Readiness Stages

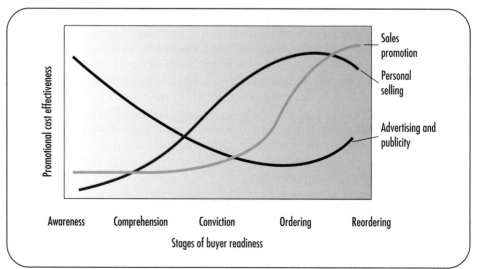

building word of mouth. Sales promotion, advertising, and personal selling grow more important in the maturity stage. In the decline stage, sales promotion continues strong, advertising and publicity are reduced, and salespeople give the product minimal attention.

Finally, market leaders derive more benefit from advertising than from sales promotion. Conversely, smaller competitors gain more by using sales promotion in their marketing communications mix.

Step 7: Measure Results

After implementing the promotional plan, the company must measure its impact. Members of the target audience are asked whether they recognize or recall the message, how many times they saw it, what points they recall, how they felt about the message, and their previous and current attitudes toward the product and company. The communicator should also collect behavioral measures of audience response, such as how many people bought the product, liked it, and talked to others about it.

Suppose 80 percent of the targeted customers are aware of the brand, 60 percent have tried it, and only 20 percent who tried it are satisfied. The communications program has effectively created awareness, but the product failed to meet consumer expectations. However, if 40 percent of the targeted customers are aware of the brand and only 30 percent have tried it—but 80 percent of those who tried it are satisfied—communications should be strengthened to take advantage of the brand's power.

Step 8: Manage the Integrated Marketing Communications Process

Given the fragmenting of mass markets, the proliferation of new media, and the growing sophistication of consumers, companies need to use a wider range of tools and messages through integrated marketing communications. As defined by the American Association of Advertising Agencies, **integrated marketing communications (IMC)** is a concept of marketing communications planning that recognizes the added value of a comprehensive plan evaluating the strategic roles of a variety of communications disciplines—such as advertising, direct response, sales promotion, and public relations—and combines these disciplines to provide clarity, consistency, and maximum communications' impact through the seamless integration of discrete messages.

For example, Beck's North America recently launched a $10 million IMC campaign to promote Beck's Beer among 21- to 34-year-old men. The company used 60 percent of its budget to buy television advertising on ESPN/ABC Sports networks. The remaining 40 percent went to Internet advertising on ESPN.com, radio advertising on ESPN radio, print advertising in *ESPN Magazine*, and sponsorships and promotions at sporting events.

Integrated marketing communications produces stronger message consistency and greater sales impact; it also gives someone responsibility to unify the company's various brand images and messages. Properly implemented, IMC improves the firm's ability to reach the right customers with the right messages at the right time and in the right place.[17]

DEVELOPING AND MANAGING THE ADVERTISING CAMPAIGN

Advertising is any paid form of nonpersonal presentation and promotion of ideas, goods, or services by an identified sponsor. Advertisers include not only business firms but also museums, charitable organizations, and government agencies that direct messages to target publics. Ads are a cost-effective way to disseminate messages, whether to build brand preference for Absolut vodka or to educate people about the dangers of drugs.

In developing an advertising program, marketing managers start by identifying the target market and buyer motives. Then they make five critical decisions, known as the five Ms: *Mission*: What are the advertising objectives? *Money*: How much can be spent? *Message*: What message should be sent? *Media*: What media should be used? *Measurement*: How should the results be evaluated? These decisions are summarized in Figure 16.3 and described in the following sections.

Setting Advertising Objectives

An **advertising goal** (or **objective**) is a specific communication task and achievement level to be accomplished with a specific audience in a specific period. Advertising objectives can be classified according to whether their aim is to inform, persuade, remind, or reinforce. *Informative advertising* aims to create awareness and knowledge of new products or new features of existing products. Thus, DVD makers initially had to inform consumers of the benefits of this technology.

Persuasive advertising aims to create liking, preference, conviction, and purchase of a good or service. Chivas Regal attempts to persuade consumers that it delivers

FIGURE 16.3   The Five Ms of Advertising

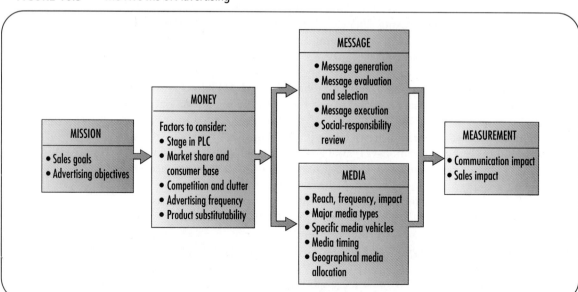

more taste and status than other Scotch whiskey brands. Some persuasive advertising is comparative advertising, which explicitly compares two or more brands.[18]

Reminder advertising aims to stimulate repeat purchase of products. Thus, Coca-Cola ads primarily remind people to purchase Coca-Cola. *Reinforcement advertising* seeks to convince current purchasers that they made the right choice. Car ads often depict satisfied customers enjoying special features of their new vehicle.

The advertising objective should emerge from a thorough analysis of the current marketing situation. If the product class is mature, the company is the market leader, and brand usage is low, the proper objective should be to stimulate more usage. If the product class is new, the company is not the market leader, but the brand is superior to the leader, the proper objective is to convince the market of the brand's superiority.

Deciding on the Advertising Budget

Management should consider these five factors when setting the advertising budget:[19]

1. *Product life cycle stage.* New products typically receive large budgets to build awareness and to gain consumer trial. Established brands usually are supported with lower budgets as a ratio to sales.

2. *Market share and consumer base.* High-market-share brands usually require less advertising expenditure as a percentage of sales to maintain their share. To build share by increasing market size requires larger advertising expenditures. On a cost-per-impression basis, it is less expensive to reach consumers of a widely used brand than to reach consumers of low-share brands.

3. *Competition and clutter.* In a market with many competitors and high advertising spending, a brand must advertise more heavily to be heard. Even clutter from non-competing advertisements creates a need for heavier advertising.

4. *Advertising frequence.* The number of repetitions needed to convey the brand's message to customers has an important impact on the advertising budget.

5. *Product substitutability.* Brands in a commodity class (cigarettes, beer, soft drinks) require heavy advertising to establish a differential image. Advertising is also important when a brand offers unique benefits or features.

Choosing the Advertising Message

Advertising campaigns vary in creativity. In 1997, Taco Bell launched television spots featuring a chihuahua saying, "Yo Quiero Taco Bell," meaning "I want some Taco Bell." The campaign resonated with the chain's 18- to 35-year-old customers; sales shot up 4.3 percent in the campaign's first year. By late 2000, with sales dropping, the company replaced the dog with a campaign featuring singing and dancing twentysomethings; boosted by new-product advertising, Taco Bell's sales were up again in 2002.[20]

In developing a creative strategy, advertisers follow four steps: message generation, message evaluation and selection, message execution, and social responsibility review.

Message Generation   Creative people can use several methods to generate possible advertising appeals. Many proceed inductively by talking to consumers, dealers, experts, and competitors, while others use a deductive framework. How many alternative ad themes should the advertiser create before choosing? The more ads that are created, the higher the probability of finding an excellent one. This is a balancing act, because creating alternative ads raises costs, even with the use of computerized tools.

Message Evaluation and Selection A good ad normally focuses on one core selling proposition. Twedt suggested that messages be rated on *desirability*, *exclusiveness*, and *believability*.[21] When the March of Dimes searched for an advertising theme to raise money for its fight against birth defects, managers brainstormed several messages. They asked a group of young parents to rate each for interest, distinctiveness, and believability, assigning up to 100 points for each. "Seven hundred children are born each day with a birth defect" scored 70, 62, and 80 on interest, distinctiveness, and believability, whereas "Your next baby could be born with a birth defect" scored 58, 51, and 70. The first message outperformed the second on all accounts.[22] Advertisers need market research to determine which appeal works best.

Message Execution The message's impact depends not only upon what is said but also on how it is said. Some ads aim for *rational positioning* and others for *emotional positioning*. U.S. ads typically present an explicit feature or benefit with a rational appeal, such as "gets clothes cleaner," while Japanese ads tend to be less direct and appeal more to the emotions.

Message execution can be decisive for highly similar products, such as detergents, cigarettes, coffee, and vodka. The Swedish brand Absolut became the largest selling imported vodka in the United States by mounting a well-integrated targeting, packaging, and advertising strategy geared toward sophisticated, upwardly mobile, affluent drinkers. The distinctively shaped bottle is used as the centerpiece of most ads. Now the brand rings up more than $1 billion in worldwide sales every year.[23]

In preparing an ad campaign, the advertiser usually prepares a *copy strategy statement* describing the objective, content, support, and tone of the desired ad. Any message can be presented in a number of execution styles: slice of life, lifestyle, fantasy, mood or image, musical, personality symbol, technical expertise, scientific evidence, and testimonial. For example, Rogaine extra-strength for men uses testimonial advertising featuring celebrities, with the promise of growing back more hair than its predecessor.[24]

The actual words in an ad must be memorable and attention-getting to make an impression on the audience. The following themes listed on the left would have had much less impact without the creative phrasing on the right:

Theme	Creative Copy
Milk is good for you.	Got milk? (Milk industry)
Use our credit card, get cash back.	It pays to Discover (Discover card)
No hard sell, just a good car.	Drivers wanted (Volkswagen)
Dependable, long-lasting vehicles.	Like a rock (Chevrolet)

Format elements such as ad size, color, and illustration will affect an ad's impact as well as its cost. A minor rearrangement of mechanical elements can improve attention-getting power. Larger-size ads gain more attention, though not necessarily by as much as their difference in cost. Four-color illustrations increase ad effectiveness as well as ad cost. Still, by carefully planning the relative dominance of different elements, companies can achieve better message delivery.

Social Responsibility Review Advertisers and their agencies must be sure their "creative" advertising does not overstep social and legal norms. Most marketers work hard to communicate openly and honestly with consumers. Still, abuses occur, and public policymakers have developed a substantial body of laws and regulations to govern advertising. Under U.S. law, for example, companies must avoid false or deceptive advertising and cannot use bait-and-switch advertising to attract buyers under false pretenses.[25] To be socially responsible, advertisers try not to offend ethnic groups, racial minorities, or special-interest groups. For instance, a commercial for Black Flag insecticide was altered after a veterans group protested the playing of Taps over dead bugs.[26] Some companies, such as the Canadian mutual fund firm Ethical Funds, build their ad campaigns around social responsibility.[27]

Developing Media Strategies

The next task is to choose media to carry the message. Here, the steps are: deciding on reach, frequency, and impact; choosing among media types; selecting specific media vehicles; deciding on media timing; and deciding on geographical media allocation.

Deciding on Reach, Frequency, and Impact   **Media selection** means finding the most cost-effective media to deliver the desired number of exposures to the target audience. What do we mean by the desired number of exposures? Presumably, the advertiser is seeking a certain response from the target audience—for example, a certain level of product trial. The rate of product trial will depend, among other things, on the level of brand awareness. The effect of exposures on audience awareness depends on the exposures' reach, frequency, and impact:

- *Reach (R)*. The number of different persons or households that are exposed to a particular media schedule at least once during a specified period.
- *Frequency (F)*. The number of times within the specified time period that an average person or household is exposed to the message.
- *Impact (I)*. The qualitative value of an exposure through a given medium (thus a food ad in *Good Housekeeping* would have a higher impact than in the *Police Gazette*).

Although audience awareness will be greater with higher reach, frequency, and impact, there are important trade-offs among these elements. The media planner must figure out the most cost-effective combination of reach, frequency, and impact. Reach is most important when launching new products, flanker brands, extensions of well-known brands, or infrequently purchased brands, or when going after an undefined target market. Frequency is most important where there are strong competitors, a complex story to tell, high consumer resistance, or a frequent-purchase cycle.[28]

Many advertisers believe that a target audience needs a large number of exposures for the advertising to work; too few repetitions will hardly be noticed. Others doubt the value of high ad frequency, believing that after people see the same ad a few times, they either act on it, get irritated, or stop noticing it. Krugman asserted that three exposures to an advertisement might be enough.[29] Another factor arguing for repetition is that of forgetting. The higher the forgetting rate associated with a brand, product category, or message, the higher the warranted level of repetition. But repetition is not enough. Ads wear out and viewers tune out, so advertisers need fresh executions of the message.

Selecting Media and Vehicles   The media planner has to know the capacity of the major media types to deliver reach, frequency, and impact. The costs, advantages, and limitations of the major media are profiled in Table 16.2

TABLE 16.2   Profiles of Major Media Types

Medium	Advantages	Limitations
Newspapers	Flexibility; timeliness; good local market coverage; broad acceptance; high believability	Short life; poor reproduction quality; small "pass-along" audience
Television	Combines sight, sound, and motion; appealing to the senses; high attention; high reach	High absolute cost; high clutter; fleeting exposure; less audience selectivity
Direct mail	Audience selectivity; flexibility; no ad competition within the same medium; personalization	Relatively high cost; "junk mail" image
Radio	Mass use; high geographic and demographic selectivity; low cost	Audio presentation only; lower attention than television; nonstandardized rate structures; fleeting exposure
Magazines	High geographic and demographic selectivity; credibility and prestige; high-quality reproduction; long life; good pass-along readership	Long ad purchase lead time; some waste circulation; no guarantee of position
Outdoor	Flexibility; high repeat exposure; low cost; low competition	Limited audience selectivity; creative limitations
Yellow Pages	Excellent local coverage; high believability; wide reach; low cost	High competition; long ad purchase lead time; creative limitations
Newsletters	Very high selectivity; full control; interactive opportunities; relatively low cost	Costs could run away
Brochures	Flexibility; full control; can dramatize messages	Overproduction could lead to runaway costs
Telephone	Many users; opportunity to give a personal touch	Relatively high cost unless volunteers are used
Internet	High selectivity; interactive possibilities; relatively low cost	Relatively new media with a low number of users in some countries

Media planners choose among these media categories by considering four main variables. First is the target audience's media habits. For example, radio, television, and the Internet are effective media for reaching teenagers. Second is the product. Media types have different potentials for demonstration, visualization, explanation, believability, and color. Third is the message. A message announcing a major sale tomorrow will require radio, TV, or newspaper; a message containing technical data might require specialized magazines or mailings. Fourth is cost. Television is more expensive than newspaper and radio advertising. What counts is the cost-per-thousand exposures.

Rust and Oliver see the proliferation of newer media such as the World Wide Web hastening the death of traditional mass-media advertising as we know it. They see a greater amount of direct producer-consumer interaction, with benefits to both parties. Producers gain more information about their customers; customers gain greater control because they can choose whether to receive an advertising message.[30] Marketers are also using creative and unexpected ad placements to grab customers' attention: logos and products electronically added to television broadcasts; ads and logos applied to store floors; and ads transmitted to wireless device users.[31]

Given all of these media choices, the media planner must first decide on how to allocate the budget to the major media types. Then the media planner searches for the most cost-effective media vehicles within each chosen media type—relying on media measurement services for estimates of audience size, composition, and media cost.

Audience size can be measured according to: *circulation*, the number of physical units carrying the advertising; *audience*, the number of people exposed to the vehicle (with pass-on readership, a print vehicle's audience will be larger than circulation figures suggest); *effective audience*, the number of people with target audience characteristics exposed to the vehicle; and *effective ad-exposed audience*, the number of people with target audience characteristics who actually saw the ad.

Knowing the audience size, media planners can calculate the cost-per-thousand persons reached by a vehicle. If a full-page ad in Newsweek costs $84,000 and the estimated readership is 3 million people, the cost of exposing the ad to 1,000 persons is approximately $28. The same ad in *BusinessWeek* may cost $30,000 but reach only 775,000 persons—at a cost per thousand of about $39. The media planner then ranks each magazine by cost per thousand and favors magazines with the lowest cost per thousand for reaching target consumers. The magazines themselves often put together a "reader profile" for their advertisers, summarizing the characteristics of the magazine's readers with respect to age, income, residence, marital status, and leisure activities.

Deciding on Media Timing In choosing media, the advertiser faces both a macroscheduling and a microscheduling problem. The macroscheduling problem is scheduling the advertising in relation to seasons and the business cycle. Suppose 70 percent of a product's sales occur between June and September. The firm can vary its advertising expenditures to follow the seasonal pattern, to oppose the seasonal pattern, or to be constant throughout the year. Most firms pursue a seasonal policy, although advertising in the off-season may boost sales and consumption without hurting seasonal consumption.

The microscheduling problem calls for allocating advertising expenditures within a short period to obtain maximum impact. Over a given period, advertising messages can be concentrated ("burst" advertising), dispersed continuously, or dispersed intermittently. The advertiser must also decide whether to leave ad messages level, increase them, decrease them, or alternate them in the schedule.

In launching a new product, the advertiser can choose among ad continuity, concentration, flighting, and pulsing. **Continuity** means scheduling exposures evenly throughout a given period. Generally, advertisers use this method when markets are expanding, with frequently purchased items, and in narrowly-defined buyer categories. **Concentration** calls for spending all of the advertising dollars in a single period, which makes sense for products with one selling season or holiday. **Flighting** calls for advertising for a period, followed by a hiatus with no advertising, followed by a second period of advertising activity. It is used when funding is limited, the purchase cycle is relatively infrequent, and with seasonal items. **Pulsing** is continuous advertising at low-weight levels reinforced periodically by waves of heavier activity.[32] Those who favor pulsing feel that the audience will learn the message more thoroughly, and money can be saved.

Deciding on Geographical Allocation In allocating media geographically, the company should consider area differences in market size, advertising response, media efficiency, competition, and profit margins. The company makes "national buys" when it places ads on national TV or radio networks or in nationally circulated publications. It makes "spot buys" when it buys TV or radio time in just a few markets or in regional editions of national publications. The company makes "local buys" when it uses local advertising media. Despite its efficiency, however, national (and international) advertising may fail to adequately address differing local situations, such as market-to-market variations in share and competitive standing.

FIGURE 16.4   Formula for Measuring Sales Impact of Advertising

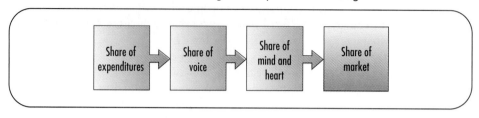

Evaluating Advertising Effectiveness

Good planning and control of advertising depend on measures of advertising effectiveness. Yet the amount of fundamental research on advertising effectiveness is appallingly small. Most advertisers try to measure the communication effect of an ad—its potential effect on awareness, knowledge, or preference—as well as the ad's sales effect.

Communication-effect research seeks to determine whether an ad is communicating effectively. Called *copy testing*, it can be done before an ad is placed (pretesting) and after it is placed (posttesting). Advertisers also need to posttest the overall impact of a completed campaign.

Sales-effect research is complex because sales are influenced by many factors beyond advertising, such as product features, price, and availability, as well as competitors' actions. The sales impact is easiest to measure in direct-marketing situations and hardest to measure in brand or corporate-image-building advertising. One approach is shown in Figure 16.4: A company's *share of advertising expenditures* produces a *share of voice* that earns a *share of consumers' minds and hearts* and ultimately a *share of market*. Peckham studied the relationship between share of voice and share of market for several consumer products over a number of years and found a 1-to-1 ratio for established products and a 1.5–2.0 to 1.0 ratio for new products.[33]

SALES PROMOTION

Sales promotion, a key ingredient in many marketing campaigns, consists of a diverse collection of incentive tools, mostly short term, designed to stimulate trial, or quicker or greater purchase, of particular products or services by consumers or the trade.[34] Whereas advertising offers a *reason* to buy, sales promotion offers an *incentive* to buy. Sales promotion includes tools for *consumer promotion* (samples, coupons, cash refund offers, prices off, premiums, prizes, patronage rewards, free trials, warranties, tie-in promotions, cross-promotions, point-of-purchase displays, and demonstrations); *trade promotion* (prices off, advertising and display allowances, and free goods), and *business- and sales-force promotion* (trade shows, contests for sales reps, and specialty advertising).

In years past, the advertising-to-sales-promotion ratio was about 60 : 40. Today, in many consumer-packaged-goods companies, sales promotion accounts for 65–75 percent of the promotion budget. Several factors have contributed to this trend, particularly in consumer markets.[35] Internal factors include the following: Promotion is now more accepted by top management as an effective sales tool, more product managers are qualified to use sales-promotion tools, and product managers are under greater pressure to increase current sales. External factors include: The number of brands has increased, competitors use promotions frequently, many brands are seen as similar, consumers are more price-oriented, the trade demands more deals from manufacturers, and advertising efficiency has declined because of rising costs, media clutter, and legal restraints.

Purpose of Sales Promotion

Sales-promotion tools can be used to achieve a variety of objectives. Sellers use incentive-type promotions to attract new triers, to reward loyal customers, and to increase the repurchase rates of occasional users. Sales promotions often attract the brand switchers, who are primarily looking for low price, good value, or premiums, so sales promotions are unlikely to turn them into loyal users. Sales promotions used in markets of high brand similarity produce a high sales response in the short run but little permanent gain in market share. In markets of high brand dissimilarity, however, sales promotions can alter market shares permanently.

One challenge is to balance short- and long-term objectives when combining advertising and sales promotion. Advertising typically acts to build long-term brand loyalty, but the question of whether or not sales promotion weakens brand loyalty over time is subject to different interpretations. Sales promotion, with its incessant prices off, coupons, deals, and premiums, may devalue the product offering in the buyers' minds. Therefore, companies need to distinguish between price promotions (which focus only on price) and added-value promotions (intended to enhance brand image).

When a brand is price promoted too often, the consumer begins to buy it mainly when it goes on sale. So there is risk in putting a well-known brand leader on promotion over 30 percent of the time.[36] Farris and Quelch counter that sales promotion enables manufacturers to adjust to short-term variations in supply and demand, test list prices, sell more than they would ordinarily sell at the list price, adapt programs to different consumer segments, induce consumers to try new products, and lead to more varied retail formats. On the consumer side, sales promotion helps consumers feel satisfied as smart shoppers when they take advantage of specials.[37]

Major Decisions in Sales Promotion

In using sales promotion, a company establishes its objectives, selects the tools, develops the program, pretests the program, implements and controls it, and evaluates the results.

- *Establishing objectives.* Sales-promotion objectives are derived from broader promotion objectives, which are derived from more basic marketing objectives for the product. For consumers, objectives include encouraging purchase of larger-size units, building trial among nonusers, and attracting switchers away from competitors' brands. For retailers, objectives include persuading retailers to carry new items and higher levels of inventory, encouraging off-season buying, offsetting competitive promotions, building brand loyalty, and gaining entry into new retail outlets. For the sales force, objectives include encouraging support of a new product or model, encouraging more prospecting, and stimulating off-season sales.[38]

- *Selecting consumer-promotion tools.* The main consumer-promotion tools are summarized in Table 16.3. We can distinguish between *manufacturer promotions* and

TABLE 16.3 Major Consumer-Promotion Tools

Samples: Offer of a free amount of a product or service.

Coupons: Certificates offering a stated saving on the purchase of a specific product.

Cash Refund Offers (rebates): Provide a price reduction after purchase: Consumer sends a specified "proof of purchase" to the manufacturer who "refunds" part of the purchase price by mail.

Price Packs (cents-off deals): Promoted on the package or label, these offer savings off the product's regular price.

Premiums (gifts): Merchandise offered at low or no cost as an incentive to buy a particular product.

Frequency Programs: Provide rewards for the consumer's frequency and intensity in buying company products or services.

Prizes (contests, sweepstakes, games): *Prizes* offer consumers the chance to win cash, trips, or merchandise as a result of purchasing something. A *contest* calls for consumers to submit an entry to be examined by judges who will select the best entries. A *sweepstakes* asks consumers to submit their names for a drawing. A *game* presents consumers with something every time they buy—bingo numbers, missing letters—that might help them win a prize.

Patronage Awards: Values in cash or points given to reward patronage of a certain seller.

Free Trials: Inviting prospects to try the product free in the hope that they will buy the product.

Product Warranties: Explicit or implicit promises by sellers that the product will perform as specified or that the seller will fix it or refund the customer's money during a specified period.

Tie-in Promotions: Two or more brands or companies team up on coupons, refunds, and contests to increase pulling power.

Cross-Promotions: Using one brand to advertise another noncompeting brand.

Point-of-Purchase (POP) Displays and Demonstrations: Displays and demonstrations that take place at the point of purchase or sale.

retailer promotions. The former are illustrated by the auto industry's frequent use of rebates and gifts to motivate test-drives and purchases; the latter include price cuts, retailer coupons, and retailer contests or premiums. We can also distinguish between sales-promotion tools that are "consumer-franchise building," reinforcing the consumer's brand understanding, and those that are not. The former imparts a selling message along with the deal, as in the case of coupons that include a selling message. Sales-promotion tools that are not consumer-franchise building include price-off packs, premiums that are unrelated to a product, contests and sweepstakes, consumer refund offers, and trade allowances. In one study, sales promotion combined with

TABLE 16.4 Major Trade-Promotion Tools

Price-Off (off-invoice or off-list): A straight discount off the list price on each case purchased during a stated time period.

Allowance: An amount offered in return for the retailer's agreeing to feature the manufacturer's products in some way. An *advertising allowance* compensates retailers for advertising the manufacturer's product. A *display allowance* compensates them for carrying a special product display.

Free Goods: Offers of extra cases of merchandise to intermediaries who buy a certain quantity or who feature a certain flavor or size.

Source: For more information, see Betsy Spethman, "Trade Promotion Redefined," *Brandweek*, March 13, 1995, pp. 25–32.

TABLE 16.5   Major Business and Sales Force Promotion Tools

Trade Shows and Conventions: Industry associations organize annual trade shows and conventions where firms selling products and services to this industry buy space and set up booths and displays to demonstrate their products. Participating vendors expect several benefits, including generating new sales leads, maintaining customer contacts, introducing new products, meeting new customers, selling more to present customers, and educating customers with publications, videos, and other audiovisual materials.

Sales Contests: A *sales contest* aims at inducing the sales force or dealers to increase sales over a stated period, with prizes going to those who succeed. Incentives work best when they are tied to measurable and achievable sales objectives (such as finding new accounts or reviving old accounts) for which employees feel they have an equal chance.

Specialty Advertising: Specialty advertising consists of useful, low-cost items (such as calendars) bearing the company's name and address, and sometimes an advertising message, that salespeople give to prospects and customers.

feature advertising boosted sales volume by 19 percent; when point-of-purchase display was added, sales volume increased by 24 percent.[39]

- *Selecting trade-promotion tools.* Manufacturers use a number of trade-promotion tools (Table 16.4) to (1) persuade an intermediary to carry the product, (2) persuade an intermediary to carry more units, (3) induce retailers to promote the brand by featuring, display, and price reduction, and (4) stimulate retailers and their salespeople to push the product. Today, giant retailers have more power to demand trade promotion at the expense of consumer promotion and advertising.[40]

- *Selecting business- and sales force promotion tools.* Companies spend billions of dollars on business- and sales-force-promotion tools (Table 16.5) to gather business leads, impress and reward customers, and motivate the sales force to greater effort. Companies typically develop budgets for each business-promotion tool that remain fairly constant from year to year.

- *Developing the program.* In deciding to use a particular incentive, marketers must consider: (1) the *size* of the incentive (a certain minimum is necessary if the promotion is to succeed; a higher level will produce more sales response but at a diminishing rate); (2) the *conditions* for participation (whether to offer the incentive to everyone or to select groups); (3) the *duration*; (4) the *distribution vehicle* (each will have a different level of reach, cost, and impact); (5) the *timing*; and (6) the *total sales-promotion budget* (including administrative costs and incentive costs).

- *Pretesting the program.* Although most sales-promotion programs are designed on the basis of experience, marketers should pretest to see if the tools are appropriate, the incentive optimal, and the presentation method efficient. Strang says that promotions usually can be tested quickly and inexpensively and that large companies should test alternative strategies in selected market areas with each national promotion.[41]

- *Implementing and evaluating the program.* Implementation planning must cover *lead time* (to prepare the program before the launch) and *sell-in time* (beginning with the launch and ending when approximately 95 percent of the deal merchandise is in the hands of consumers). Manufacturers can evaluate sales-promotion effectiveness using sales data, consumer surveys, and experiments (see Chapter 5 for more details).

PUBLIC RELATIONS

Not only must the company relate constructively to customers, suppliers, and dealers, but it must also relate to a large number of interested publics. A **public** is any group that has an actual or potential interest in or impact on a company's ability to achieve its objectives. **Public relations (PR)** involves a variety of programs that are designed to promote or protect a company's image or its individual products.

The wise company takes concrete steps to manage successful relations with its key publics. PR departments typically perform five functions: (1) *press relations* (presenting news and information about the organization in the most positive light); (2) *product publicity* (publicizing specific products); (3) *corporate communication* (promoting understanding of the organization through internal and external communications); (4) *lobbying* (dealing with legislators and government officials to promote or defeat legislation and regulation); and (5) *counseling* (advising management about public issues and company positions and image during both good times and crises).[42]

Marketing Public Relations

Many companies are turning to **marketing public relations (MPR)** to directly support corporate or product promotion and image making. MPR, like financial PR and community PR, serves a special constituency, namely the marketing department.[43] MPR plays an important role in:

- *Assisting in the launch of new products.* The success of toys such as the Pokemon line owes a great deal to clever publicity.
- *Assisting in repositioning a mature product.* New York City had bad press in the 1970s until the "I Love New York" campaign began.
- *Building interest in a product category.* Companies and industry groups use MPR to expand consumption of products such as pork and milk.
- *Influencing specific target groups.* McDonald's sponsors special neighborhood events in Latino and African American communities to build goodwill.
- *Defending products that have encountered public problems.* Johnson & Johnson's masterly use of MPR helped save Tylenol from extinction following two incidents involving poison-tainted Tylenol capsules.
- *Building the corporate image in a way that reflects favorably on its products.* Richard Branson's publicity stunts have created a bold, upstart image for his U.K.-based Virgin Group.

As the power of mass advertising weakens, marketing managers are turning to MPR to cost-effectively build awareness and brand knowledge and to reach local communities and specific audiences. The company does not pay for the space or time obtained in the media; it pays only for a staff to develop and circulate the stories and manage certain events. A story picked up by the news media could be worth millions of dollars in equivalent advertising—and would be more credible than advertising.

Major Decisions in Marketing PR

In considering when and how to use MPR, management must establish the marketing objectives, choose the messages and vehicles, implement the plan carefully, and evaluate the results. The main tools of MPR are described in Table 16.6.[44]

TABLE 16.6   Major Tools in Marketing PR

Publications: Companies rely extensively on published materials to reach and influence their target markets. These include annual reports, brochures, articles, company newsletters and magazines, and audiovisual materials.

Events: Companies can draw attention to new products or other company activities by arranging special events like news conferences, seminars, outings, trade shows, exhibits, contests and competitions, and anniversaries that will reach the target publics.

Sponsorships: Companies can promote their brands and corporate name by sponsoring sport and cultural events and highly regarded causes.

News: One of the major tasks of PR professionals is to find or create favorable news about the company, its products, and its people, and get the media to accept press releases and attend press conferences.

Speeches: Increasingly, company executives must field questions from the media or give talks at trade associations or sales meetings, and these appearances can build the company's image.

Public-Service Activities: Companies can build goodwill by contributing money and time to good causes.

Identity Media: Companies need a visual identity that the public immediately recognizes. The visual identity is carried by company logos, stationery, brochures, signs, business forms, business cards, buildings, uniforms, and dress codes.

- *Establishing the marketing objectives*. MPR can build *awareness* of a product, service, person, organization, or an idea; add *credibility* by communicating a message in an editorial context; boost sales force and dealer *enthusiasm*; and hold down *promotion costs* because it costs less than media advertising. Harris suggests PR and direct-response marketing work together to achieve objectives such as building marketplace excitement before media advertising breaks, building a core customer base, building a one-to-one relationship with consumers, turning satisfied customers into advocates, and influencing the influentials.[45]

- *Choosing messages and vehicles*. The MPR expert must identify or develop interesting stories to tell about the product. If there are few stories, the expert should propose newsworthy events to sponsor as a way of stimulating media coverage. For example, when Anheuser-Busch sponsored a Black World Championship Rodeo in Brooklyn, the event attracted more than 5,000 spectators.

- *Implementing and evaluating the plan*. PR implementation must be handled with care. A great story is easy to place, but other stories might not get past busy editors. One of the chief assets of publicists is their personal relationship with media editors. MPR's contribution to the bottom line is difficult to measure because it is used along with other promotional tools. The easiest measure is the number of *exposures* obtained in the media. A better measure would be changes in product awareness, comprehension, or attitude resulting from the MPR campaign (after allowing for the effect of other promotional tools). The most satisfactory measure is sales-and-profit impact, allowing the company to determine its return on MPR investment.

DIRECT MARKETING

Direct marketing is the use of consumer-direct channels to reach and deliver goods and services to customers without intermediaries. These channels include direct mail, catalogs, telemarketing, interactive TV, kiosks, Web sites, and mobile devices. Direct marketers seek a measurable response, typically a customer order. This is sometimes called **direct-order marketing**. Today, many direct marketers use direct marketing to build long-term customer relationships by sending birthday cards, information, or small premiums to strengthen customer bonds over time.[46]

The Growth of Direct Marketing

Sales through direct-marketing channels (catalogs, direct mail, and telemarketing) are growing every year. Whereas U.S. retail sales grow around 3 percent annually, catalog and direct-mail sales grow at about double that rate. Direct sales include sales to the consumer market (53 percent), business-to-business sales (27 percent), and fund raising by charitable institutions (20 percent).[47] Electronic marketing is growing even faster, with 6.8 million orders placed weekly, adding up to $785 million in purchases.[48]

The Benefits of Direct Marketing

Consumers find home shopping fun, convenient, and hassle-free; it saves time; introduces a larger selection of merchandise; and allows comparative shopping. Business customers also benefit by learning about products and services without meeting salespeople. Direct marketers benefit, as well. They can buy mailing lists for almost any segment (left-handed people, millionaires); customize and personalize messages; build relationships over time; reach the most interested prospects at the right moment; easily test alternative media and messages; and easily measure campaign results.

Integrated Direct Marketing

Companies are recognizing the importance of integrating their marketing communications. Some companies appoint a chief communications officer (CCO) to supervise specialists in advertising, sales promotion, public relations, and direct marketing. The aim is to set the right overall communication budget and best allocation of funds to each communication tool through integrated marketing communications.

How can direct marketing be integrated in campaign planning? Imagine a marketer using a single tool in a "one-shot" effort to reach and sell a prospect. An example of a *single-vehicle, single-stage campaign* is a one-time mailing offering a cookware item. A *single-vehicle, multiple-stage campaign* would involve successive mailings to the same prospect. Magazine publishers, for example, send about four renewal notices to a household before giving up. A more powerful approach is the *multiple-vehicle, multiple-stage campaign*. Consider the following sequence:

News campaign about a new product → Paid ad with a response mechanism → Direct mail or e-mail → Outbound telemarketing → Face-to-face sales call → Ongoing communication

Roman says that the use of response compression—deploying multiple media a tightly defined time frame—increases message reach and impact. The idea is to deploy a sequence of messages with precise timing intervals in the hope of generating incremental sales and profits that exceed the costs involved.

Major Channels for Direct Marketing

Direct marketers can use a number of channels for reaching individual prospects and customers. These include face-to-face selling, direct mail, catalog marketing, telemarketing, TV and other direct-response media, kiosk marketing, and e-marketing.

Face-To-Face Selling   The original and oldest form of direct marketing is the field sales call. Most industrial firms rely heavily on a professional sales force to locate prospects, develop them into customers, and grow the business. Or they hire manufacturers' representatives and agents to carry out the direct-selling task. Many consumer companies use a direct-selling force: insurance agents, stockbrokers, and distributors working for direct-sales organizations such as Avon, Amway, and Tupperware.

Direct Mail   Direct-mail marketing involves sending an offer, announcement, reminder, or other item to a person. Using highly selective mailing lists, direct marketers send out millions of mail pieces each year—letters, flyers, and other "salespeople with wings." Some marketers mail audiotapes, videotapes, CDs, and computer disks to prospects and customers. Tesco, the U.K.'s largest retailer, mails personalized letters and coupons to its 14 million shoppers—and enjoys an average coupon redemption rate of 90 percent.

Direct mail is popular because it permits target market selectivity, can be personalized, is flexible, and allows early testing and response measurement. Although the cost per thousand people reached is higher than with mass media, the people reached are better prospects for purchases and charitable contributions. Newer forms of mail delivery include: *fax mail*, sending sale or special event announcements to fax machines or computers set up to receive faxes; *e-mail* (short for *electronic mail*), sending a message, file, image, or Web page from one computer to another; and *voice mail*, leaving voice messages on recipients' voice mailboxes. In constructing a direct-mail campaign, direct marketers follow the five steps in Table 16.7.

Catalog Marketing   Catalog marketing occurs when companies mail full-line merchandise catalogs, specialty consumer catalogs, or business catalogs in print, on CD, or online to selected people. The Direct Marketing Association estimates there are up to 10,000 mail-order catalogs of all kinds. Catalog marketing has gotten a big boost from the Internet—about three-quarters of catalog companies also do business online. The Lands' End Web site, for example, gets 180,000 e-mail queries a year, surpassing the firm's print-mail response.[49]

Catalog companies must carefully manage their customer lists to avoid duplication of names; carefully control inventory; offer quality merchandise to minimize returns; and project a distinctive image. Some companies distinguish themselves by adding literary or information features to their catalogs, sending swatches, sending gifts to key customers, or donating to good causes. Others invite customers to view their Web-based catalogs for more information or to check product availability.

Catalogs are catching on in Asia and Europe. In just a few years foreign catalogs—mainly from the United States and Europe—have won 5 percent of the $20 billion Japanese mail-order market. A full 90 percent of L.L. Bean's international sales come from Japan. U.S. catalog firms prosper in Japan because they offer high-quality merchandise for specific segments. American catalogs often feature two other items unusual in Japan: a lifetime, no-questions-asked guarantee and pictures of top models.

TABLE 16.7   Steps in Developing a Direct-Mail Campaign

Step	Description
1. Set objectives	Establish objectives by which campaign success will be measured, such as producing orders from prospects, generating prospect leads, strengthening customer relationships, and informing and educating customers for later offers. An order-response rate of 2 percent is considered good for many products.
2. Identify target markets	The best customer targets are those who bought most recently, who buy frequently, and who spend the most. Consumer prospects can be identified on the basis of such variables as age, sex, income, education, previous mail-order purchases, purchase occasions, and lifestyle; business prospects can be identified on the basis of buying center role and other variables. Once the target market is defined, the direct marketer needs to obtain specific names by acquiring mailing lists and building databases.
3. Define the offer	According to Nash, the offer strategy consists of five elements: the product, the offer, the medium, the distribution method, and the creative strategy. Fortunately, all of these elements can be tested. In addition to these elements, the direct-mail marketer has to decide on five components of the mailing itself: the outside envelope, sales letter, circular, reply form, and reply envelope.
4. Test the elements	Direct marketing allows companies to test, under real marketplace conditions, the efficacy of different elements, such as product features, copy, prices, media, or mailing lists.
5. Measure results	By adding up the campaign costs, the firm can determine in advance the needed break-even response rate, net of returned merchandise and bad debts. Even when a specific campaign fails to break even, it can still be profitable over the customer lifetime, because of increased awareness and future intention to buy. A customer's ultimate value is not revealed by a purchase response to a particular mailing but by the expected profit made on all future purchases, net of acquisition and maintenance costs.

Sources: Based in part on information in Bob Stone, *Successful Direct Marketing Methods*, 6th ed. (Lincolnwood, IL: NTC Business Books, 1996); and Edward L. Nash, *Direct Marketing: Strategy, Planning, Execution*, 3rd ed. (New York: McGraw-Hill, 1995).

By putting their catalogs on the Internet, companies such as Eddie Bauer have better access to global consumers than ever before.

Telemarketing   **Telemarketing** is the use of the telephone operators and call centers to attract prospects, sell to existing customers, and provide service by taking orders and answering questions. Companies use call centers for *inbound telemarketing* (receiving calls from customers) and *outbound telemarketing* (initiating calls to prospects and customers.) Telemarketing is a major direct-marketing tool. Telemarketers annually sell $482 billion worth of products and services to consumers and businesses.

Telemarketing is increasingly used in business as well as consumer marketing. Raleigh Bicycles uses telemarketing to reduce the amount of personal selling needed for contacting its dealers. In the first year, sales force travel costs were reduced by 50 percent and sales in a single quarter went up 34 percent. Telemarketing, as it improves with the use of videophones, will increasingly replace, though never eliminate, more expensive field sales calls. Effective telemarketing depends on choosing the right tele-marketers, training them well, offering performance incentives, and being sensitive to privacy issues.

Direct-Response Television Marketing Two forms of direct-response television marketing have become prominent in recent years. One is *direct-response TV advertising* through 30- and 60-minute infomercials that resemble documentaries. These often include testimonials and a toll-free number for ordering or getting further information. This format is particularly good for selling complex or expensive goods and services, which is why Philips, Humana Healthcare, Bose, and many other firms have used infomercials.[50]

A second approach is *home shopping channels*, television channels dedicated to selling merchandise and services. For example, the Home Shopping Network and the QVC network promote attractive prices on such products as jewelry, lamps, and power tools. Viewers call a toll-free number to order and receive delivery within 48 hours. QVC also supplements its television network with a shopping Web site.[51]

Kiosk Marketing A kiosk is a small building or structure that houses a selling or information unit. The term describes newsstands, refreshment stands, and free-standing carts whose vendors sell watches, costume jewelry, and other items often seen along the aisles in a mall. It also covers computer-linked vending machines and "customer-order-placing machines" placed in stores, airports, and other locations to sell directly to consumers.

E-Marketing The newest channels for direct marketing are electronic. The Internet today functions as an information source, an entertainment source, a communication channel, a transaction channel, and even a distribution channel. As discussed in Chapter 2, the Internet provides marketers and customers with opportunities for much greater *interaction* and *individualization*. Instead of beaming messages in a monologue for a mass audience, marketers can now customize communications to create dialogues with specific individuals, thereby strengthening customer relationships. A key technique in e-marketing is permission marketing.

According to Seth Godin, author of *Permission Marketing*, most promotion amounts to "interruption marketing." This approach is becoming less effective because as more companies increase promotional spending to get attention, they create more clutter and wind up reaching fewer people; they then spend even more and get even less.[52]

Instead, Godin advocates **permission marketing**, using the Internet's interactivity to let customers have a say in what is sent to them. Godin compares permission-based marketing to dating; if a company conducts itself well and earns trust in its initial contacts, customers will be willing to receive subsequent offers. As a result, permission marketing is anticipated (customers expect to hear from the company), personal (tailored to recipients), and relevant (recipients are interested in the offer). Once marketers have permission to communicate, the response rate is 10 times better than response to Internet ad banners.[53] "Marketing Skills: Permission Marketing" explains this vital skill.

Properly planned and executed, an e-mail campaign can build customer relationships and boost profits. E-mail costs a fraction of what a direct-mail campaign

MARKETING SKILLS: PERMISSION MARKETING

Permission marketing has become popular because it is extremely targeted, can build relationships, and is cost-effective. How do marketers develop this skill? According to Seth Godin, the first step is to learn to calculate a customer's worth over the duration of a typical relationship. This determines what the company can afford to spend on acquiring a new customer. Then the marketer creates a series of communications (e-mail messages, letters, and so on) to engage customers in a dialogue. Each message must educate the customer about the value of the company's offers, be customizable as the company learns more about the customer, and provide an incentive (such as more information or a discount) for the customer to respond and continue the relationship. Always ask for a response so results can be measured.

As the interchange continues, the marketer may change or add incentives (customized where appropriate) to encourage the customer to keep granting permission. Over time, the marketer gains the customer's trust and can ask for permission to send additional offers. In this way, the marketer builds a valuable, profitable core of customers who respond at ever-higher levels of permission marketing.

Pop Secret Microwave Popcorn has used permission marketing to build brand and product loyalty. The company recently showcased its NASCAR sponsorship on the package, at state fairs, in banner ads, in an e-mail campaign, and on the brand's Web site. The incentive was a $25,000 sweepstakes contest inviting consumers to guess which color car Richard Petty would drive in an upcoming race. The 90,000 entrants were asked whether they wanted to receive e-mail reminders about the contest and future offers; subsequent messages asked permission to send further offers. The majority of entrants agreed to future contacts, building a customer base that is "really interested in things related to the brand and the product," says an official at Pop Secret's ad agency.[54]

costs. Microsoft used to spend approximately $70 million yearly on paper-based campaigns. Now it sends out 20 million e-mail messages every month at a significant savings. To maintain permission for such communication, marketers must remember to make it easy for customers to unsubscribe at any point.[55]

EXECUTIVE SUMMARY

The marketing communications mix consists of five major modes of communication: advertising, sales promotion, public relations and publicity, personal selling, and direct marketing. Developing effective marketing communications involves eight steps: (1) Identify the target audience, (2) determine the communication objectives, (3) design the message, (4) select the communication channels, (5) establish the total communications budget, (6) decide on the communications mix, (7) measure the communications' results, and (8) manage the integrated marketing communication process.

Integrated marketing communications (IMC) recognizes the added value of a comprehensive plan that evaluates the strategic roles of a variety of communications disciplines and combines these disciplines to provide clarity, consistency, and maximum communications' impact through the seamless integration of discrete messages.

Advertising is any paid form of nonpersonal presentation and promotion of ideas, goods, or services by an identified sponsor. Developing an advertising program involves setting objectives, setting a budget, choosing the advertising message, determining how the message will be generated, evaluating and selecting messages, executing the message, developing media strategies, and evaluating the results.

Sales promotion consists of a diverse group of incentive tools, mostly short term, designed to stimulate trial or quicker or greater purchase of particular products by consumers or the trade. Sales promotion includes tools for consumer promotion, trade promotion, and business- and sales force promotion. In using sales promotion, as in using advertising, a company must set its objectives, select the tools, develop the program, pretest the program, implement and control it, and evaluate the results.

Public relations involves a variety of programs designed to promote or protect a company's image or its individual products. Marketing public relations (MPR) is often used to support corporate or product promotion and image-building through publications, events, news, speeches, public-service activities, and identity media.

Direct marketing is an interactive marketing system that uses one or more media to effect a measurable response or transaction at any location. Major channels for direct marketing include face-to-face selling, direct mail, catalog marketing, telemarketing, direct-response marketing, kiosk marketing, and e-marketing.

NOTES

1. Tobi Elkin, "Internet Strategies: Yahoo! Increases Direct Marketing," *Advertising Age*, April 22, 2002, p. 20; Ann M. Mack, "No More Funny Stuff," *Adweek*, March 4, 2002, pp. 23+; Tia O'Brien, "Secrets of Spin," *Upside*, June 1, 1999.
2. See Michael L. Ray, *Advertising and Communications Management* (Upper Saddle River, NJ: Prentice Hall, 1982).
3. Susanne Craig, "E*Trade to Cut Marketing Even as Its Losses Narrow," *Wall Street Journal*, April 12, 2001, p. B13; "Bank on It," *Brandweek*, December 11, 2000.
4. Betsy McKay, "Coca-Cola Restructuring Effort Has Yet to Prove Effective," *Asian Wall Street Journal*, March 2, 2001, p. N4; James Kynge and Mure Dickie, "Coke forced to Dump Taiwanese Diva," *Financial Times*, May 25, 2000, p. C12.
5. See Ayn E. Crowley and Wayne D. Hoyer, "An Integrative Framework for Understanding Two-Sided Persuasion," *Journal of Consumer Research* (March 1994): 561–74.
6. See C. I. Hovland, A. A. Lumsdaine, and F. D. Sheffield, *Experiments on Mass Communication*, vol. 3 (Princeton, NJ: Princeton University Press, 1948) ch. 8; and Crowley and Hoyer, "An Integrative Framework." For an alternative viewpoint, see George E. Belch, "The Effects of Message Modality on One- and Two-Sided Advertising Messages," in *Advances in Consumer Research*, eds. Richard P. Bagozzi and Alice M. Tybout (Ann Arbor, MI: Association for Consumer Research, 1983) pp. 21–26.
7. Curtis P. Haugtvedt and Duane T. Wegener, "Message Order Effects in Persuasion: An Attitude Strength Perspective," *Journal of Consumer Research* (June 1994): 205–18; H. Rao Unnava, Robert E. Burnkrant, and Sunil Erevelles, "Effects of Presentation Order and Communication Modality on Recall and Attitude," *Journal of Consumer Research* (December 1994):481–90.
8. See Brian Sternthal and C. Samuel Craig, *Consumer Behavior: An Information Processing Perspective* (Upper Saddle River, NJ: Prentice Hall, 1982) pp. 282–84.

9. Michael McCarthy, "BMW Drives into New Ad World," *USA Today*, June 6, 2001, p. B3.

10. Herbert C. Kelman and Carl I. Hovland, "Reinstatement of the Communication in Delayed Measurement of Opinion Change," *Journal of Abnormal and Social Psychology* 48 (1953): 327–35.

11. David J. Moore, John C. Mowen, and Richard Reardon, "Multiple Sources in Advertising Appeals: When Product Endorsers Are Paid by the Advertising Sponsor," *Journal of the Academy of Marketing Science* (Summer 1994): 234–43.

12. Rob Eder, "Chain Drug Can Learn a Thing or Two from Kiehl's," *Drug Store News*, August 6, 2001, p. 12.

13. Michael Cafferky has identified four kinds of people that companies try to reach to stimulate word-of-mouth referrals: opinion leaders, marketing mavens, influentials, and product enthusiasts. For more, see *Let Your Customers Do the Talking* (Chicago: Dearborn Financial Publishing, 1995) pp. 30–33.

14. See Emanuel Rosen, *The Anatomy of Buzz* (New York: Currency, 2000) ch. 12.

15. See Philip Kotler, "Atmospherics as a Marketing Tool," *Journal of Retailing* (Winter 1973–1974): 48–64.

16. Sidney J. Levy, *Promotional Behavior* (Glenview, IL: Scott, Foresman, 1971) ch. 4.

17. See Don E. Shultz, Stanley I. Tannenbaum, and Robert F. Lauterborn, *Integrated Marketing Communications: Putting It Together and Making It Work* (Lincolnwood, IL: NTC Business Books, 1992); and Ernan Roman, *Integrated Direct Marketing: The Cutting-Edge Strategy for Synchronizing Advertising, Direct Mail, Telemarketing, and Field Sales* (Lincolnwood, IL: NTC Business Books, 1995).

18. See William L. Wilkie and Paul W. Farris, "Comparison Advertising: Problem and Potential," *Journal of Marketing* (October 1975): 7–15.

19. See Donald E. Schultz, Dennis Martin, and William P. Brown, *Strategic Advertising Campaigns* (Chicago: Crain Books, 1984) pp. 192–97.

20. Bob Garfield, "Perspicacious Pooch Scores for Taco Bell," *Advertising Age*, March 9, 1998, p. 53; Jennifer Ordonez, "Managers & Managing: Taco Bell's President Set to Improve Sales," *Wall Street Journal*, February 27, 2001, p. 27; "Taco Bell," *Nation's Restaurant News Daily NewsFax*, February 1, 2002, p. 1.

21. Dik Warren Twedt, "How to Plan New Products, Improve Old Ones, and Create Better Advertising," *Journal of Marketing* (January 1969): 53–57.

22. See William A. Mindak and H. Malcolm Bybee, "Marketing Application to Fund Raising," *Journal of Marketing* (July 1971): 13–18.

23. James B. Amdorfer, "Absolut Ads Sans Bottle Offer a Short-Story Series," *Advertising Age*, January 12, 1998, p. 8; Shelly Branch, "Absolut's Latest Ad Leaves Bottle Behind," *Wall Street Journal*, May 3, 2001, p. B9.

24. Yumiko Ono, "Bulletins from the Battle of Baldness Drug—Sports Figures Tout Rogaine for Pharmacia," *Wall Street Journal*, December 19, 1997, p. B1.

25. For further reading, see Dorothy Cohen, *Legal Issues in Marketing Decision Making* (Cincinnati, OH: South-Western, 1995).

26. Kevin Goldman, "Advertising: From Witches to Anorexics: Critical Eyes Scrutinize Ads for Political Correctness," *Wall Street Journal*, May 19, 1994, p. B1.

27. Adapted from Sandra Cordon, "Where High Road Meets Bottom Line: Ethical Mutual Funds Avoid Companies Deemed Socially Irresponsible," *The London Free Press*, October 9, 1998, p. D3; "Ethical Funds Launches 4 New Mutual Funds," *Ethical Funds*, January 17, 2000 (*www.ethicalfunds.com*).

28. Schultz et al., *Strategic Advertising Campaigns*, p. 340.

29. See Herbert E. Krugman, "What Makes Advertising Effective?" *Harvard Business Review* (March–April 1975): 98.

30. Roland T. Rust and Richard W. Oliver, "Notes and Comments: The Death of Advertising," *Journal of Advertising* (December 1994): 71–77.

31. Michael McCarthy, "Ads Are Here, There, Everywhere," *USA Today*, June 19, 2001; Michael McCarthy, "Critics Target 'Omnipresent' Ads," *USA Today*, April 16, 2001.

32. See also Hani I. Mesak, "An Aggregate Advertising Pulsing Model with Wearout Effects," *Marketing Science*, Summer 1992, pp. 310–26; and Fred M. Feinberg, "Pulsing Policies for Aggregate Advertising Models," *Marketing Science*, Summer 1992, pp. 221–34.

33. See J. O. Peckham, *The Wheel of Marketing* (Scarsdale, NY: printed privately, 1975) pp. 73–77.

34. From Robert C. Blattberg and Scott A. Neslin, *Sales Promotion: Concepts, Methods, and Strategies* (Upper Saddle River, NJ: Prentice Hall, 1990).

35. Roger A. Strang, "Sales Promotion—Fast Growth, Faulty Management," *Harvard Business Review* (July-August 1976): 116–19.

36. For a summary of the research on whether promotion erodes the consumer franchise of leading brands, see Blattberg and Neslin, *Sales Promotion*.

37. See Paul W. Farris and John A. Quelch, "In Defense of Price Promotion," *Sloan Management Review*, Fall 1987, pp. 63–69.

38. For a model for setting sales promotions objectives, see David B. Jones, "Setting Promotional Goals: A Communications Relationship Model," *Journal of Consumer Marketing* 11, no. 1 (1994): 38–49.

39. See John C. Totten and Martin P. Block, *Analyzing Sales Promotion: Text and Cases*, 2d ed. (Chicago: Dartnell, 1994) pp. 69–70.

40. See Paul W. Farris and Kusum L. Ailawadi, "Retail Power: Monster or Mouse?" *Journal of Retailing* (Winter 1992): 351–69.

41. Strang, *Sales Promotion*, p. 120.

42. Adapted from Scott M. Cutlip, Allen H. Center, and Glen M. Broom, *Effective Public Relations*, 8th ed. (Upper Saddle River, NJ: Prentice Hall, 1997).

43. For an excellent account, see Thomas L. Harris, *The Marketer's Guide to Public Relations* (New York: John Wiley, 1991). Also see *Value-Added Public Relations* (Chicago: NTC Business Books, 1998).

44. For more on cause-related marketing, see P. Rajan Varadarajan and Anil Menon, "Cause-Related Marketing: A Co-Alignment of Marketing Strategy and Corporate Philanthropy," *Journal of Marketing*, (July 1988): 58–74.

45. Adapted from Thomas L. Harris, "PR Gets Personal," *Direct Marketing*, April 1994, pp. 29–32.

46. The terms *direct-order marketing* and *direct-relationship marketing* were suggested as subsets of direct marketing by Stan Rapp and Tom Collins in *The Great Marketing Turnaround* (Upper Saddle River, NJ: Prentice Hall, 1990).

47. *Direct Marketing Magazine*, 516-716-6700.

48. *Industry Standard*, February 12, 2001, p. 86.

49. Bruce Horovitz, "Catalog Craze Delivers Holiday Deals," *USA Today*, December 1, 1998, p. 3B.

50. Jim Edwards, "The Art of the Infomercial," *Brandweek*, September 3, 2001, pp. 14+.

51. Miriam Hill, "QVC, the Shopping Network, Reaches and Makes Millions," *Philadelphia Inquirer*, April 28, 2002 (*www.philly.com*).

52. Seth Godin, "Permission Marketing," *Credit Union Executive*, January 2001, pp. 42+.

53. "Permission-Based Marketing Gets in Your In-Box," *TechWeb*, May 12, 2001.

54. Gina Bernacchi, "Permission Marketing: A New Path for Your Appeals," *Non-Profit Times*, March 15, 2002, p. 23; L. Erwin, "The Secret Behind Permission-Based Marketing," *Point of Purchase*, February 2001, p. 41; Godin, "Permission Marketing," pp. 42+.

55. Seth Godin, *Permission Marketing* (New York: Simon & Schuster, 1999).

CHAPTER 17

Managing the Sales Force

In this chapter, we will address the following questions:

1. What decisions do companies face in designing a sales force?
2. How do companies recruit, select, train, supervise, motivate, and evaluate a sales force?
3. How can salespeople improve their selling, negotiating, and relationship-building skills?

MARKETING MANAGEMENT AT TIFFANY

The name *Tiffany* brings to mind expensive jewelry, and the famous retailer cultivates its classy image in every aspect of its marketing. Tiffany's newspaper and magazine ads feature glittery jewelry ranging up to $100,000. A purchase in its Fifth Avenue flagship in New York City (or in one of its 125 worldwide store locations) can be like an investment—the average engagement-ring purchase at Tiffany runs $10,000. Therefore, management carefully trains the retail sales staff to serve as consultants.

Because buyers are not typically jewelry experts, salespeople are trained to offer advice and information about the quality and cut of stones, the suitability of various settings, and the choices available at various prices. Even when selling less expensive items such as a box of stationery, salespeople know that part of the purchase is the experience and prestige of shopping at Tiffany. They also know that a satisfied customer is a potential repeat customer. In addition to its retail sales staff, Tiffany has 155 sales reps to serve corporate customers ordering distinctive business gifts or personalized items for employee recognition. New corporate reps receive training for 6 to 8 weeks. Only when they have demonstrated their mastery of sales skills, jewelry knowledge, and Tiffany products are corporate reps allowed to deal with customers.[1]

Personal selling is a mainstay of nonprofit as well as for-profit organizations. College recruiters are the university's sales force arm; the U.S. Agricultural Extension Service uses specialists to sell farmers on new farming methods. On the business side, no one debates the importance of the sales force in the marketing mix. However, companies are sensitive to the high and rising costs (salaries, commissions, bonuses, travel expenses, and benefits) of maintaining a sales force. Because the average cost of a personal sales call ranges from $250 to $500, and closing a sale typically requires four calls, the total cost to complete a sale can range from $1,000 to $2,000. Not surprisingly, companies are seeking to substitute other selling methods—including mail, phone, fax, and e-mail—to reduce field sales expenses. They also are working to increase sales force productivity through better selection, training, supervising, motivation, and compensation.

DESIGNING THE SALES FORCE

Personal selling is a key element in promotion. Sales personnel serve as the company's personal link to the customers. But not all sales representatives do the same kind of selling. McMurry has distinguished six types of sales representatives, ranging from the least to the most creative types of selling:[2]

1. *Deliverer.* A salesperson whose major task is the delivery of a product (milk or fuel).
2. *Order taker.* A salesperson who acts predominantly as an inside order taker (behind a counter) or outside order taker (calling on supermarket managers).
3. *Missionary.* A salesperson whose major task is to build goodwill or to educate the actual or potential user, rather than to sell (the medical "detailer" representing a pharmaceutical firm).
4. *Technician.* A salesperson with a high level of technical knowledge (the engineering salesperson who is primarily a consultant to client companies).
5. *Demand creator.* A salesperson who relies on creative methods for selling tangible products (vacuum cleaners or siding) or intangibles (insurance or education).
6. *Solution vendor.* A salesperson whose expertise lies in solving a customer's problem, often with a system of the firm's goods and services (such as computer systems).

In general, salespeople perform one or more of the following tasks: prospecting (searching for prospects or leads); targeting (deciding how to allocate their time among prospects and customers); communicating (conveying information about the company's products); selling (approaching, presenting, answering objections, and closing sales); servicing (consulting on problems, rendering technical assistance, arranging financing, expediting delivery); information gathering (conducting market research and doing intelligence work); and allocating (deciding which customers will get scarce products during shortages).

Because of the expense, companies have to look carefully at the design of the sales force, including the development of sales force objectives and strategy, structure, size, and compensation (see Figure 17.1).

Sales Force Objectives and Strategy

Each company needs to define the specific objectives its sales force will achieve. Increasingly, companies are setting objectives for sales reps based not only on sales volume and profitability targets, but also on their ability to create customer satisfaction, as the Tiffany example shows.

FIGURE 17.1   Designing a Sales Force

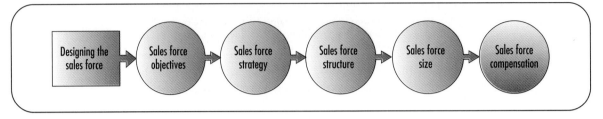

To implement the firm's sales objectives, a common strategy is for sales representatives to act as "account managers," arranging fruitful contact among people in the buying and selling organizations. Selling increasingly calls for teamwork requiring the support of other personnel, such as: top management, especially when national accounts or major sales are at stake; technical people, who supply technical information and service to the customer; customer service representatives, who provide installation, maintenance, and other services; and an office staff, consisting of sales analysts, order expediters, and administrative personnel. DuPont has used a team orientation. Finding that corn growers needed a herbicide that could be applied less often, DuPont appointed a team of chemists, sales and marketing executives, and regulatory specialists to tackle the problem. They created a product that captured $57 million in sales during its first year.[3]

Once the company decides on objectives and strategy, it can use either a direct or a contractual sales force. A **direct (company) sales force** consists of full- or part-time paid employees who work exclusively for the company. This sales force includes inside sales personnel who conduct business from the office using the telephone, fax, and e-mail, and receive visits from prospective buyers, and field sales personnel who travel and visit customers. A **contractual sales force** consists of manufacturers' reps, sales agents, and brokers, who are paid a commission based on sales.

Sales Force Structure

The sales force strategy has implications for the sales force structure. If the company sells one product line to one end-using industry with customers in many locations, it would use a territorial sales force structure. If the company sells many products to many types of customers, it might need a product or market sales force structure. Table 17.1 summarizes the most common sales force structures.

Companies typically single out major accounts (also called key accounts, national accounts, global accounts, or house accounts) for special attention. The largest accounts may have a strategic account management team, consisting of cross-functional personnel who are permanently assigned to one customer and may even maintain offices at the customer's facility. For example, Procter & Gamble has a strategic account team working with Wal-Mart in Bentonville, Arkansas. This arrangement has saved P&G and Wal-Mart $30 billion jointly through supply chain improvements.[4] See "Marketing Skills: Major Account Management" for more on this important aspect of personal selling.

TABLE 17.1   Sales Force Structures

Territorial: Each sales representative is assigned an exclusive territory. This results in a clear definition of responsibilities and increases the rep's incentive to cultivate local business and personal ties. Travel expenses remain relatively low, because each rep travels within a small area.

Product: The importance of sales reps' knowing their products, together with the development of product divisions and product management, has led many companies to structure their sales forces along product lines. This is particularly useful for product lines that are technically complex, highly unrelated, or very numerous.

Market: Companies often specialize their sales forces along industry or customer lines. Market specialization helps the sales force become knowledgeable about specific customer needs, but the major disadvantage is that customers are scattered throughout the country, requiring extensive travel.

Complex: When a company sells a diverse product line to many types of customers over a broad geographical area, it often combines several structures, with sales forces specialized by territory-product, territory-market, product-market, and so on. A sales representative might then report to one or more line and staff managers.

Established companies need to revise their sales force structure as market and economic conditions change. A study at British Airways, for example, revealed that the sales force excelled in business-to-consumer sales but needed to focus more on business-to-business sales. So the airline added "key account" managers to "focus on accounts that delivered the most value."[6]

MARKETING SKILLS: MAJOR ACCOUNT MANAGEMENT

Major accounts represent considerable sales and profit potential, which is why companies often assign major account managers to work with these important customers. On average, each major account manager works with nine specific accounts, reporting to the national sales manager (who reports to the vice president of marketing and sales). Major accounts normally receive more favorable pricing based on their purchasing volume. However, they look more for added value than a price advantage and appreciate the personal attention and advice from a major account manager.

What do major account managers do? They act as the single point of contact between buyer and seller; understand and respond to customer needs and decision processes; look for ways to add value through appropriate solutions to customer problems; negotiate contracts with their customers; and provide tailored, responsive customer service. To be effective, they need communication, marketing, management, and financial expertise. One major account manager says, "My position must not be as a salesman, but as a 'marketing consultant' to our customers and a salesman of my company's capabilities as opposed to my company's products."

California Eastern Laboratories (CEL), which sells semiconductor components to electronics manufacturers, piloted a major account management program with one key client, Motorola. Within four years, its sales to Motorola had increased 566 percent. CEL then added three more major account managers to work closely with other large customers. Rather than simply shift its top salespeople into these positions, the company carefully chose employees with both sales and marketing experience, paving the way for closer, more productive relationships with customers.[5]

Sales Force Size

Once the company clarifies its sales force strategy and structure, it is ready to consider sales force size, based on the number of customers it wants to reach. One widely-used method for determining sales force size is the five-step *workload approach*: (1) group customers into size classes by annual sales volume; (2) establish call frequencies, the number of calls to be made per year on each account in a size class; (3) multiply the number of accounts in each size class by the call frequency to arrive at the total yearly sales call workload; (4) determine the average number of calls a sales rep can make per year; and (5) divide the total annual calls (calculated in step 3) required by the average annual calls made by a rep (in step 4) to see how many reps are needed.

Suppose the company has 1,000 A accounts and 2,000 B accounts; A accounts require 36 calls a year (36,000 calls yearly), and B accounts require 12 calls a year (totaling 24,000 calls). The company therefore needs a sales force that can make 60,000 sales calls a year. If the average rep can make 1,000 calls a year, the company would need 60,000/1,000, or 60 sales representatives.

Some companies are reducing their sales forces by leveraging the Internet to maintain customer relationships. Bethlehem Steel, for instance, cut its sales force in half a few years ago and invited customers to view product inventories, place orders, and track deliveries on its Web site.[7]

Sales Force Compensation

The compensation package is a critical element in attracting top-quality sales reps. The level and components of a compensation plan must bear some relation to the "going market price" for the type of sales job and required abilities. If the market price for salespeople is well defined, the individual firm has little choice but to pay the going rate. However, published data on industry sales force compensation levels are infrequent and generally lack sufficient detail.

The company must next determine the four components of sales force compensation—a fixed amount, a variable amount, expense allowances, and benefits. The *fixed amount*, a salary, is intended to satisfy the sales reps' need for income stability. The *variable amount*, which might be commissions, a bonus, or profit sharing, is intended to stimulate and reward greater effort. *Expense allowances* enable sales reps to meet the expenses involved in travel, lodging, dining, and entertaining. *Benefits*, such as paid vacations and life insurance, provide security and job satisfaction. Fixed compensation receives more emphasis in jobs with a high ratio of nonselling to selling duties and in jobs in which the selling task is technically complex and involves teamwork. Variable compensation receives more emphasis in jobs in which sales are cyclical or depend on individual initiative.

Fixed and variable compensation give rise to three basic types of compensation plans—straight salary, straight commission, and combination salary and commission. Only one-fourth of all firms use either a straight-salary or straight-commission method, while three-quarters use a combination of the two, though the relative proportion of salary versus incentives varies widely.[8]

Straight-salary plans provide sales reps with a secure income, make them more willing to perform nonselling activities, and give them less incentive to overstock customers. These plans are easy to administer and they lower turnover. Straight-commission plans attract higher sales performers, provide more motivation, require less supervision, and control selling costs. Combination plans offer the benefits of both plans while reducing their disadvantages. Such plans allow companies to link the variable portion of a salesperson's pay to a wide variety of strategic goals. Some see a trend toward deemphasizing volume measures in favor of factors such as gross profitability, customer satisfaction, and customer retention. For example, IBM partly rewards salespeople on the basis of customer satisfaction as measured by customer surveys.[9]

MANAGING THE SALES FORCE

Effective management of the sales force is needed to implement the company's chosen sales force design and achieve its sales objectives. Sales force management covers the steps in recruiting and selecting, training, supervising, motivating, and evaluating representatives (see Figure 17.2).

Recruiting and Selecting Sales Representatives

At the heart of a successful sales force is the selection of effective representatives. One survey revealed that the top 27 percent of the sales force brought in over 52 percent of the sales. Beyond differences in productivity is the great waste in hiring the wrong people. When a rep quits, the costs of finding and training a new rep, plus the cost of lost sales, can run up to $100,000—and a sales force with many new hires is less productive.[10]

In selecting sales reps, the company can start by asking customers what traits they prefer in salespeople. Most customers want honest, reliable, knowledgeable, and helpful reps. Another approach is to look for traits that are common to successful salespeople. Garfield concluded that supersales performers exhibit risk taking, a powerful sense of mission, a problem-solving bent, care for the customer, and careful planning.[11] Mayer and Greenberg noted that the effective salesperson has *empathy*, the ability to feel as the customer does, and *ego drive*, a strong personal need to make the sale.[12]

After management develops selection criteria, the next step is to recruit applicants by various means, including soliciting names from current sales reps, using employment agencies, placing print and online job ads, and contacting graduating college students. Selection procedures can vary from an informal interview to prolonged testing and interviewing. Although test scores are only one information element in a set that includes personal characteristics, references, past employment history, and interviewer reactions, they are weighted quite heavily by such companies as IBM,

FIGURE 17.2   Managing the Sales Force

Procter & Gamble, and Gillette. Gillette claims that tests have reduced turnover by 42 percent and have correlated well with the subsequent progress of new reps.

Training Sales Representatives

Today's customers expect salespeople to have deep product knowledge, offer ideas to improve customer operations, and be efficient and reliable. These demands have required companies to make a much higher investment in training their sales reps.

Companies use training to help sales reps: know and identify with the company; learn about the company's products; know customers' and competitors' characteristics; make effective sales presentations; and understand sales procedures and responsibilities. Training time and method varies with the complexity of the selling task and the type of person recruited into the sales organization. Training often involves a variety of methods, including role playing, audio- and videotapes, CD-ROMs, and Web-based distance learning. For instance, IBM uses a computerized self-study system in which trainees practice sales calls with an on-screen actor portraying a buying executive.

Supervising Sales Representatives

Companies vary in how closely they supervise sales reps. Reps paid mostly on commission generally receive less supervision, while those who are salaried and must cover definite accounts are likely to receive substantial supervision. In the course of supervising sales reps, successful companies set norms for calls on customers and prospects, and they help reps make the most efficient use of sales time.

Norms for Customer Calls   The average salesperson makes about four calls a day, down from five in the previous decade. The downward trend is due to higher use of the phone, fax, and e-mail, plus increased reliance on automated ordering systems and fewer cold calls due to better market research information. How many calls should a company make on a particular account each year? Research shows that additional calls generally produce more sales, but companies still need to determine whether the increase in sales justifies the increase in sales costs. Research suggests that sales reps may spend too much time selling to smaller, less profitable accounts when they should focus on larger, more profitable accounts.[13]

Norms for Prospect Calls   Companies often specify how much time reps should spend prospecting for new accounts. Spector Freight, for instance, wants sales representatives to spend 25 percent of their time prospecting and to stop calling on a prospect after three unsuccessful calls. Other companies set prospect and customer norms based on product sales, specifying, for example, that reps spend 85 percent of their time selling established products and 15 percent selling new products. Companies set up prospecting standards because many reps, left to their own devices, will spend most of their time with current customers, who are known quantities, rather than with prospects, who might never buy. Some firms rely on a missionary sales force to open new accounts.

Using Sales Time Efficiently   Studies confirm that the best sales reps are those who manage their time effectively.[14] One popular efficiency tool is configurator software to automate the ordering process. DAA Solutions configurator software, for example, allows sales reps to help customers access pricing information, production schedules, and customize orders in minutes.[15]

Another tool is *time-and-duty analysis*, which helps reps understand how they spend their time and how they might increase their productivity. In general, sales reps spend time in (1) preparation (getting information and planning call strategy); (2) travel (which can be more than 50 percent of total time); (3) food and breaks (some portion of every workday); (4) waiting (to see buyers); (5) selling (time spent with the buyer); and (6) administration (writing reports, billing, and so on).

With so many duties, it is no wonder that actual face-to-face selling time can amount to as little as 29 percent of total working time![16] To improve sales force productivity, many companies train their reps in the use of "phone power;" simplify record-keeping; and use the computer and the Internet to develop call and routing plans, to supply customer and competitive information, and to generate leads for sales reps.

Seeking to reduce the time demands on their outside sales force, many firms have increased the size and responsibilities of their inside sales force. Inside salespeople are of three types. *Technical support people* provide technical information and answers to customers' questions. *Sales assistants* provide clerical backup for the outside reps by confirming appointments, carrying out credit checks, following up on deliveries, and answering customers' questions. *Telemarketers* use the phone to find new leads, qualify and sell to them, reactivate old accounts, and give more attention to neglected accounts.

Motivating Sales Representatives

Some sales representatives will put forth their best effort without any special coaching. The majority of reps, however, require more encouragement and special incentives. This is especially true of field selling, which can be frustrating because reps usually work alone, keep irregular hours, are often away from home, lack the authority to do what is necessary to win an account, and sometimes lose large orders they worked hard to obtain.

Studying sales rep motivation, Churchill, Ford, and Walker developed a model indicating that the higher the salesperson's motivation, the greater his or her effort.[17] Greater effort will lead to greater performance, greater performance will lead to greater rewards, greater rewards will lead to greater satisfaction, and greater satisfaction will reinforce motivation. The model thus implies that sales managers must be able to convince salespeople that they can sell more by working harder or by being trained to work smarter, and that the rewards for better performance are worth the extra effort.

According to this research, the most-valued reward was pay, followed by promotion, personal growth, and sense of accomplishment. The least-valued rewards were liking and respect, security, and recognition. Thus, salespeople are highly motivated by pay and the chance to get ahead and satisfy their intrinsic needs, and less motivated by compliments and security. However, the researchers also found that the importance of motivators varied with demographic characteristics. Financial rewards were mostly valued by older, longer-tenured reps and those with large families, while rewards such as recognition were more valued by young reps who were unmarried or had small families and usually more formal education. Motivators vary across countries. Whereas money is the top motivator of 37 percent of U.S. salespeople, only 20 percent of salespeople in Canada feel the same way. Salespeople in Australia and New Zealand were the least motivated by money.[18]

Sales Quotas   Many companies set annual sales quotas based on dollar sales, unit volume, margin, selling effort or activity, and product type. Management often ties salesperson compensation to degree of quota fulfillment. Sales quotas are developed from the annual marketing plan. Management first prepares a sales forecast, which becomes the basis for planning production, workforce size, and financial requirements. Then the firm can establish sales quotas for regions and territories, often setting the total higher than the sales forecast to encourage managers and salespeople to perform at their best levels. If they fail to make their quotas, the company nevertheless might make its sales forecast.

Each area sales manager divides the area's quota to arrive at an individual quota for each sales rep. A common approach to individual quotas is to set the individual rep's quota at least equal to the person's last year's sales plus some fraction of the difference between area sales potential and last year's sales. The more the rep reacts favorably to pressure, the higher the fraction should be.

Some companies are dropping or deemphasizing quotas to avoid stressing short-term results at the cost of long-term customer satisfaction.[19] Siebel Systems, for example, sets no quotas but instead uses metrics such as customer satisfaction, repeat business, and profitable revenues. This has helped Siebel capture 80 percent market share.[20]

Supplementary Motivators   Companies use additional motivators to stimulate sales force effort. One motivator is the periodic *sales meeting*, a social occasion that also serves as an important tool for education, communication, and motivation. Many companies sponsor *sales contests* to spur the sales force to a special selling effort above what is normally expected. The contest should present a reasonable opportunity for enough salespeople to win. At IBM, about 70 percent of the sales force qualifies for the 100 percent Club; the reward is a trip capped off by a recognition dinner and a special pin.

Whether a sales contest focuses on a specific product or products during a limited period or generally recognizes top revenue earners for the period, the reward should be commensurate with the achievement. Reps who are well paid and whose earnings are based in large part on commissions are more likely to be motivated by a trip, a trophy, or merchandise than by a check of equal value.

Evaluating Sales Representatives

We have been describing the *feed-forward* aspects of sales supervision—how management communicates what sales reps should be doing and motivates them to do it. But good feed-forward requires good *feedback*, which means getting regular information from reps to evaluate their performance.

Sources of Information   Management can obtain information about reps in several ways, including sales reports, personal observation, customer letters and complaints, customer surveys, and conversations with other sales representatives. Many companies require their representatives to develop an annual territory marketing plan outlining their program for developing new accounts and increasing business from existing accounts. This report casts sales reps into the role of market managers and profit centers. Sales managers study these plans, make suggestions, and use them to develop sales quotas.

Sales reps write up completed activities on *call reports* and, in addition, submit expense reports, new-business reports, lost-business reports, and reports on local business and economic conditions. These reports provide raw data from which sales managers can monitor sales performance by: (1) average number of sales calls per rep per day, (2) average sales call time per contact, (3) average revenue per sales call, (4) average cost per sales call, (5) entertainment cost per sales call, (6) percentage of orders per hundred sales calls, (7) number of new customers per period, (8) number of lost customers per period, and (9) sales force cost as a percentage of total sales.

Formal Evaluation   Sales reports, along with other observations, supply the raw materials for evaluation. There are several approaches to conducting evaluations. One type of evaluation compares the rep's current performance to that individual's past performance and to overall company averages on key performance indicators. These comparisons help management pinpoint specific areas for improvement. For example, if one rep's average gross profit per customer is lower than the company's average, that rep could be concentrating on the wrong customers or not spending enough time with each customer.

Evaluations can also assess the rep's knowledge of the firm, products, customers, competitors, territory, and responsibilities; relevant personality characteristics; and any problems in motivation or compliance.[21] The sales manager can also check that salespeople know and observe the law. For example, under U.S. law, salespeople's statements must match the product's advertising claims. In selling to businesses, salespeople may not offer bribes to purchasing agents or others influencing a sale; they may not obtain or use competitors' technical or trade secrets through bribery or industrial espionage. Finally, salespeople must not disparage competitors or competing products by suggesting things that are not true.[22]

PRINCIPLES OF PERSONAL SELLING

Personal selling is an ancient art that has spawned many principles. Among these are three major aspects we will examine here: sales professionalism, negotiation, and relationship marketing (see Figure 17.3).[23]

FIGURE 17.3   Managing the Sales Force: Improving Effectiveness

Sales Professionalism

In the course of instilling professionalism, sales-training approaches try to convert a salesperson from a passive order taker into an active order getter. Order takers operate on the assumption that customers know their own needs, resent attempts to influence them, and prefer courteous and self-effacing salespersons. There are two basic approaches in training salespersons to be order getters: a sales-oriented approach and a customer-oriented approach.

The *sales-oriented approach* trains the person in the stereotyped high-pressure techniques traditionally used in selling automobiles. This form of selling assumes that customers are not likely to buy except under pressure, that they are influenced by a slick presentation, and that they will not be sorry after signing the order—or, if they are, that it doesn't matter. The *customer-oriented approach* trains salespeople in customer problem solving. The rep learns to listen and ask questions in order to identify customer needs and come up with sound product solutions. This approach assumes that customers have latent needs that constitute opportunities, that they appreciate constructive suggestions, and that they will be loyal to sales reps who have their long-term interests at heart.

No approach works best in all circumstances. Yet most professional sales-training programs agree on the major steps involved in any effective sales process (see Figure 17.4). Here is how these steps are applied in industrial selling:[24]

- *Prospecting and qualifying.* The first step is to identify and qualify prospects. Companies can generate leads by examining data sources (newspapers, directories, CD-ROMs, Web sites); exhibiting at trade shows; asking customers, suppliers, dealers, and bankers for referrals; contacting trade associations; engaging in speaking and writing activities to draw attention; using the telephone, mail, and the Internet to find leads; and dropping in unannounced (cold canvassing). Companies then qualify the leads by mail or phone to assess their level of interest and financial capacity. The hot prospects are turned over to the field sales force, while the warm prospects are turned over to the telemarketing unit for follow-up.

- *Preapproach.* The salesperson needs to learn as much as possible about the prospect company (what it needs, who is involved in the purchase decision) and its buyers (their personal characteristics and buying styles) by consulting trade and database sources. The salesperson sets call objectives to qualify the prospect, gather information, or make an immediate sale. Another task is to decide on whether to use a personal visit, a phone call, or a letter. The best timing should also be considered because many prospects are busy at certain times. Finally, the salesperson should plan an overall sales strategy for the account.

FIGURE 17.4   Major Steps in Effective Selling

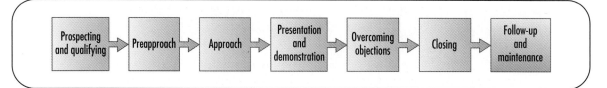

- *Approach*. The salesperson must decide how to get the relationship off to a good start. The salesperson might consider wearing clothes similar to what the buyers typically wear, show courtesy and attention to the buyer, and avoid distracting mannerisms. In a meeting, the rep should open with a positive statement and then concentrate on understanding the buyer's needs through careful questioning and active listening.

- *Presentation and demonstration*. The salesperson now tells the product "story" using a *features, advantages, benefits,* and *value* approach. Companies have developed three different styles of sales presentation. The oldest is the *canned approach*, a memorized sales talk covering the main points. It assumes that the buyer is passive and can be moved to purchase by the use of the right stimulus words, pictures, and actions. The *formulated approach* first identifies the buyer's needs and buying style and then uses an approach formulated to this type of buyer. The *need-satisfaction approach* starts with a search for the customer's real needs, after which the salesperson takes on the role of a knowledgeable consultant to help the customer save or make more money.

- *Overcoming objections*. Customers typically pose objections during the presentation or when asked for the order. To handle these objections, the salesperson maintains a positive approach, asks the buyer to clarify the objection, asks questions that lead the buyer to answer his or her own objection, denies the validity of the objection, or turns the objection into a reason for buying. Handling and overcoming objections is a part of the broader skills of negotiation, discussed in the next section of this chapter.

- *Closing*. Now the salesperson attempts to close the sale using one of several techniques. The rep can ask for the order, recapitulate the points of agreement, offer to help write up the order, ask whether the buyer wants A or B, get the buyer to make minor choices such as color or size, or indicate what the buyer will lose if the order is not placed now. The rep might offer the buyer an inducement to close, such as a special price, an extra quantity, or a token gift.

- *Follow-up and maintenance*. Follow-up and maintenance are necessary to ensure customer satisfaction and repeat business. Immediately after closing, the salesperson should cement any details on delivery time, purchase terms, and other matters that are important to the customer. The salesperson should schedule a follow-up call when the initial order is received to check on proper installation and training. The purpose is to detect any problems, assure the buyer of the salesperson's interest, and reduce any cognitive dissonance that might have arisen. The salesperson should also develop a maintenance and growth plan for the account.

Negotiation

Salespeople involved in business-to-business deals, in particular, need negotiating skills as they work with customers to reach agreement on price and other terms of sale without making concessions that will hurt profitability. To be effective in sales negotiation, reps must be well prepared and have planning skill, knowledge of subject matter being negotiated, the ability to think clearly and rapidly under pressure and uncertainty, the ability to express thoughts verbally, listening skill, judgment and general intelligence, integrity, the ability to persuade others, and patience.[25] These attributes come into play when it is appropriate to negotiate with a customer or prospect.

When to Negotiate   According to Dobler, negotiation is appropriate for concluding a sale when many factors bear not only on price, but also on quality and service;

business risks cannot be accurately predetermined; a long period of time is required to produce the product purchased; and production is interrupted often because of numerous change orders.[26]

There is an obvious advantage in knowing the other party's reservation price and in making one's own reservation price seem higher (for a seller) or lower (for a buyer) than it really is. The openness with which buyers and sellers reveal their reservation prices depends upon the bargainers' personalities, the negotiation circumstances, and expectations about future relations.

Formulating a Negotiation Strategy Successful salespeople prepare a strategic plan before meeting their buyers and making tactical decisions during negotiation sessions. A **negotiation strategy** is a commitment to an overall approach that has a good chance of achieving the negotiator's objectives. Some negotiators pursue a "hard" strategy, whereas others maintain that a "soft" strategy yields more favorable results. Fisher and Ury propose a strategy of "principled negotiation." In this strategy, the parties (1) actively listen to each other's viewpoint, (2) focus on their interests rather than on their personal differences or positions, (3) search for options that offer mutual gain, and (4) insist on objective criteria to assess the solution.[27]

Fisher and Ury suggest that if the other party is more powerful, the best tactic is to know one's BATNA—Best Alternative to a Negotiated Agreement. By identifying the alternatives if a settlement is not reached, the company sets a standard against which any offer can be measured. Knowing its BATNA protects the company from being pressured into accepting unfavorable terms from a more powerful opponent.

What should a firm's negotiators do when the other side uses a take-it-or-leave-it tactic or seats them with the sun in their eyes? The negotiators should recognize the tactic, raise the issue explicitly, and question the tactic's legitimacy and desirability—in other words, negotiate over it. If this fails, the company should resort to its BATNA and terminate the negotiation until the other side changes its tactics. Meeting such tactics with defending principles is more productive than counterattacking with tricky tactics.

Relationship Marketing

The principles of personal selling and negotiation thus far described are transaction-oriented because their purpose is to close a specific sale. However, in many cases, the company is seeking to build a long-term supplier-customer relationship by demonstrating that it can serve the account's needs in a superior way over the long run. More companies are therefore emphasizing relationship marketing rather than transaction marketing, as discussed in Chapter 1. This has come about because larger customers are often global and prefer suppliers that can sell and deliver a coordinated set of products and services to many locations; quickly solve problems that arise in different locations; and work closely with customer teams to improve products and processes.

When a relationship management program is properly implemented throughout the organization, the organization will focus as much on managing its customers as on managing its products. At the same time, companies should realize that relationship marketing is not effective in all situations. Ultimately, companies must judge which segments and customers will respond profitably to relationship management.

EXECUTIVE SUMMARY

Salespeople—the company's link to its customers—perform one or more of these tasks: prospecting, targeting, communicating, selling, servicing, information gathering, and allocating. Designing the sales force requires making decisions regarding objectives, strategy, structure, size, and compensation. First the company must define the specific objectives the sales force will achieve and select the approaches and type of sales force that will be most effective.

Choosing the structure entails dividing territories by geography, product, or market (or some combination). Estimating how large the sales force needs to be involves estimating the total workload and how many sales hours (and hence salespeople) will be needed. Compensating the sales force entails determining what types of salaries, commissions, bonuses, expense accounts, and benefits to give, and how much weight customer satisfaction should have in determining total compensation.

There are five steps involved in managing the sales force: (1) recruiting and selecting sales representatives; (2) training reps in sales techniques and in the company's products, policies, and customer-satisfaction orientation; (3) supervising the sales force by establishing norms for customer and prospect calls and helping reps to use their time efficiently; (4) motivating the sales force, balancing quotas, monetary rewards, and supplementary motivators; and (5) evaluating individual and group sales performance.

Three major aspects of personal selling are sales professionalism, negotiation, and relationship marketing. Most trainers see professional selling as a seven-step process: prospecting and qualifying customers, preapproach, approach, presentation and demonstration, overcoming objections, closing, and follow-up and maintenance. Professional selling often requires negotiation, the art of arriving at transaction terms that satisfy both parties. Many firms are deemphasizing transaction-oriented marketing in favor of relationship marketing, which focuses on developing long-term, mutually beneficial relationships between two parties.

NOTES

1. Kate Fitzgerald, "Jewelers Out to Protect Cachet," *Advertising Age*, March 11, 2002, p. S2; Sarah Lorge, "A Priceless Brand," *Sales & Marketing Management*, October 1998, pp. 102–10; Leigh Gallagher, "All-You-Can-Eat Breakfast at Tiffany's," *Forbes*, April 15, 2002, p. 40.
2. Adapted from Robert N. McMurry, "The Mystique of Super-Salesmanship," *Harvard Business Review* (March–April 1961): 114. Also see William C. Moncrief III, "Selling Activity and Sales Position Taxonomies for Industrial Salesforces," *Journal of Marketing Research* (August 1986): 261–70.
3. Christopher Power, "Smart Selling: How Companies Are Winning Over Today's Tougher Customer," *BusinessWeek*, August 3, 1992, pp. 46–48.
4. See John F. Martin and Gary S. Tubridy, "Major Account Management," in *AMA Management Handbook*, ed. John J. Hampton (New York: Amacom, 1994) pp. 3-25–3-27; Sanjit Sengupta, Robert E. Krapfel, and Michael A. Pusateri, "The Strategic Sales Force," *Marketing Management*, Summer 1997, pp. 29–34; Robert S. Duboff and Lori Underhill Sherer, "Customized Customer Loyalty," *Marketing Management*, Summer 1997, pp. 21–27; Tricia Campbell, "Getting Top Executives to Sell," *Sales & Marketing Management*, October 1998, p. 39.

5. Michele Marchetti, "A Hiring Decision You Can't Afford to Screw Up," *Sales & Marketing Management*, June 1999, pp. 13+; Martin and Tubridy, "Major Account Management," in *AMA Management Handbook*; Sengupta, Krapfel, and Pusateri, "The Strategic Sales Force;" Duboff and Sherer, "Customized Customer Loyalty."

6. "BA Shake-Up 'Not Due to New Scheme,'" *Travel Trade Gazette UK & Ireland*, May 7, 2001.

7. Philip B. Clark and Sean Callahan, "Sales Staffs: Adapt or Die," *B to B*, April 10, 2000.

8. Luis R. Gomez-Mejia, David B. Balkin, and Robert L. Cardy, *Managing Human Resources* (Upper Saddle River, NJ: Prentice Hall, 1995) pp. 416–18.

9. "What Salespeople Are Paid," *Sales & Marketing Management*, February 1995, pp. 30–31; Christopher Power, "Smart Selling: How Companies Are Winning Over Today's Tougher Customer," *BusinessWeek*, August 3, 1992, pp. 46–48; William Keenan Jr., ed., *The Sales & Marketing Management Guide to Sales Compensation Planning*: *Commissions, Bonuses & Beyond* (Chicago: Probus Publishing, 1994).

10. George H. Lucas Jr., A. Parasuraman, Robert A. Davis, and Ben M. Enis, "An Empirical Study of Sales Force Turnover," *Journal of Marketing* (July 1987): 34–59.

11. See Charles Garfield, Peak Performers: *The New Heroes of American Business* (New York: Avon Books, 1986); "What Makes a Supersalesperson?" *Sales & Marketing Management*, August 23, 1984, p. 86; "What Makes a Top Performer?" *Sales & Marketing Management*, May 1989; and Timothy J. Trow, "The Secret of a Good Hire: Profiling," *Sales & Marketing Management*, May 1990, pp. 44–55.

12. David Mayer and Herbert M. Greenberg, "What Makes a Good Salesman?" *Harvard Business Review* (July–August 1964): 119–25.

13. Michael R. W. Bommer, Brian F. O'Neil, and Beheruz N. Sethna, "A Methodology for Optimizing Selling Time of Salespersons," *Journal of Marketing Theory and Practice* (Spring 1994): 61–75.

14. See Thomas Blackshear and Richard E. Plank, "The Impact of Adaptive Selling on Sales Effectiveness Within the Pharmaceutical Industry," *Journal of Marketing Theory and Practice* (Summer 1994):106–25.

15. Paul Mann, "Success Mode," *Manufacturing Systems*, September 2000.

16. Dartnell Corporation, 30th Sales Force Compensation Survey.

17. See Gilbert A. Churchill Jr., Neil M. Ford, and Orville C. Walker Jr., *Sales Force Management: Planning, Implementation and Control*, 4th ed. (Homewood, IL: Irwin, 1993). Also see Jhinuk Chowdhury, "The Motivational Impact of Sales Quotas on Effort," *Journal of Marketing Research* (February 1993): 28–41; Murali K. Mantrala, Prabhakant Sinha, and Andris A. Zoltners, "Structuring a Multiproduct Sales Quota-Bonus Plan for a Heterogeneous Sales Force: A Practical Model-Based Approach," *Marketing Science* 13, no. 2 (1994): 121–44; Wujin Chu, Eitan Gerstner, and James D. Hess, "Costs and Benefits of Hard-Sell," *Journal of Marketing Research* (February 1995): 97–102.

18. "What Motivates U.S. Salespeople?" *American Salesman*, February 1994, pp. 25, 30.

19. Eilene Zimmerman, "Quota Busters," *Sales & Marketing Management*, January 2001, pp. 59-63.

20. Betsy Cummings, "Getting Reps to Live Your Mission," *Sales & Marketing Management*, October 2001, p. 15.

21. See Philip M. Posdakoff and Scott B. MacKenzie, "Organizational Citizenship Behaviors and Sales Unit Effectiveness," *Journal of Marketing Research* (August 1994): 351–63.

22. For further reading, see Dorothy Cohen, *Legal Issues in Marketing Decision Making* (Cincinnati, OH: South-Western, 1995) and Henry R. Cheeseman, *Contemporary Business Law*, 3rd edition (Upper Saddle River, NJ: Prentice Hall, 2000).

23. For an excellent summary of the skills needed by sales representatives and sales managers, see Rolph Anderson and Bert Rosenbloom, "The World Class Sales Manager: Adapting to Global Megatrends," *Journal of Global Marketing* 5, no. 4 (1992): 11–22.

24. Some of the following discussion is based on W. J. E. Crissy, William H. Cunningham, and Isabella C. M. Cunningham, *Selling: The Personal Force in Marketing* (New York: John Wiley, 1977) pp. 119–29.

25. For additional reading, see Howard Raiffa, *The Art and Science of Negotiation* (Cambridge, MA: Harvard University Press, 1982); Max H. Bazerman and Margaret A. Neale, *Negotiating Rationally* (New York: Free Press, 1992); James C. Freund, *Smart Negotiating* (New York: Simon & Schuster, 1992); Frank L. Acuff, *How to Negotiate Anything with Anyone Anywhere Around the World* (New York: American Management Association, 1993); and Jehoshua Eliashberg, Gary L. Lilien, and Nam Kim, "Searching for Generalizations in Business Marketing Negotiations," *Marketing Science* 14, no. 3, pt. 1 (1995): G47–G60.

26. See Donald W. Dobler, *Purchasing and Materials Management*, 5th ed. (New York: McGraw-Hill, 1990).

27. Adapted from Roger Fisher and William Ury, *Getting to Yes: Negotiating Agreement Without Giving In*, rev. ed. (Boston: Houghton Mifflin, 1992) p. 57.

Glossary

Advertising any paid form of nonpersonal presentation and promotion of ideas, goods, or services, by an identified sponsor (p. 312)

Attitude person's enduring favorable or unfavorable evaluations, emotional feelings, and action tendencies toward some object or idea (p. 119)

Belief descriptive thought that a person holds about something (p. 119)

Brand name, term, sign, symbol, or design, or a combination of these, intended to identify the goods or services of one seller or group of sellers and to differentiate them from those of the competitors (p. 8)

Business Services short-lasting goods and services that facilitate developing or managing the finished product (p. 214)

Capital Items long-lasting goods that facilitate developing or managing the finished product (p. 214)

Company Demand company's estimated share of market demand at alternative levels of company marketing effort in a given time period (p. 96)

Company Sales Forecast expected level of company sales based on a chosen marketing plan and an assumed marketing environment (p. 96)

Convenience Goods products purchased frequently, immediately, and with a minimum of effort (p. 214)

Customer Database organized collection of comprehensive data about individual customers, prospects, or suspects that is current, accessible, and actionable for marketing purposes such as lead generation, lead qualification, sales, and maintenance of customer relationships (p. 34)

Customer Perceived Value difference between total customer value and total customer cost (p. 38)

Database Marketing process of building, maintaining, and using customer databases and other databases (products, suppliers, resellers) for the purpose of contacting and transacting (p. 34)

Differentiation act of designing a set of meaningful differences to distinguish the company's offering from competitors' offerings (p. 204)

Direct Marketing interactive marketing system that uses one or more advertising media to effect a measurable response and/or transaction at any location (p. 323)

Environmental Threat challenge posed by an unfavorable external trend or development that would lead, in the absence of defensive marketing action, to deterioration in sales or profit (p. 66)

Image set of beliefs, ideas, and impressions that a person holds regarding an object (p. 304)

Learning changes in an individual's behavior that arise from experience (p. 119)

Lifestyle person's pattern of living in the world as expressed in activities, interests, and opinions (p. 116)

Market set of all actual and potential buyers of a market offer (p. 94)

Market Demand total volume that would be bought by a defined customer group in a defined geographical area in a defined time period in a defined marketing environment under a defined marketing program (p. 95)

Marketing societal process by which individuals and groups obtain what they need and want through creating, offering, and exchanging products and services of value freely with others (p. 6)

Marketing Audit comprehensive, systematic, independent, and periodic examination of a company's (or SBU's) marketing environment, objectives, strategies, and activities to identify problem areas and opportunities and recommend a plan of action for improving the company's marketing performance (p. 80)

Marketing Channels sets of interdependent organizations involved in the process of making a product or service available for use or consumption (p. 267)

Marketing Concept holds that the key to achieving organizational goals consists of the company being more effective than its competitors in creating, delivering, and communicating customer value to its chosen target markets (p. 13)

Marketing Decision Support System (MDSS) coordinated collection of data, systems, tools, and techniques with supporting software and hardware by which an organization gathers and interprets information from business and environment and turns it into a basis for marketing action (p. 94)

Marketing Information System (MIS) people, equipment, and procedures that gather, sort, analyze, evaluate, and distribute needed, timely, and accurate information to marketing decision makers (p. 86)

Marketing Implementation process that turns marketing plans into action assignments and ensures that such assignments are executed in a manner that accomplishes the plan's stated objectives (p. 76)

Marketing Intelligence System set of procedures and sources used by managers to obtain everyday information about developments in the marketing environment (p. 87)

Marketing Management process of planning and executing the conception, pricing, promotion, and distribution of ideas, goods, services to create exchanges that satisfy individual and organizational goals (p. 6)

Marketing Mix set of marketing tools that the firm uses to pursue its marketing objectives in the target market (p. 11)

Marketing Opportunity area of buyer need in which a company can perform profitably (p. 66)

Marketing Process analyzing market opportunities, researching and selecting target markets, designing market strategies, planning marketing programs, and organizing, implementing, and controlling the market effort (p. 70)

Marketing Research systematic design, collection, analysis, and reporting of data and findings that are relevant to a specific marketing situation facing the company (p. 89)

Market-Oriented Strategic Planning managerial process of developing and maintaining a viable fit among the organization's objectives, skills, and resources and its changing market opportunities (p. 58)

Market Potential limit approached by market demand as industry marketing expenditures approach infinity for a given marketing environment (p. 96)

Materials goods that enter the manufacturer's product completely (p. 214)

Media Selection finding the most cost-effective media to deliver the desired number of exposures to the target audience (p. 315)

Negotiation Strategy commitment to an overall approach that has a good chance of achieving the negotiator's objectives (p. 344)

Organizational Buying decision-making process by which formal organizations establish the need for purchased products and services and identify, evaluate, and choose among alternative brands and suppliers (p. 132)

Packaging activities of designing and producing the container for a product (p. 224)

Parts goods that enter the manufacturer's product completely (p. 214)

Perception process by which an individual selects, organizes, and interprets information inputs to create a meaningful picture of the world (p. 118)

Personality distinguishing psychological characteristics that lead to relatively consistent and enduring responses to environment (p. 117)

Positioning act of designing the company's offering and image to occupy a distinctive place in the target market's mind (p. 202)

Product Assortment set of all products and items that a particular marketer offers for sale (p. 214)

Product Concept holds that consumers favor those products that offer the most quality, performance, or innovative features (p. 13)

Production Concept holds that consumers prefer products that are widely available and inexpensive (p. 12)

Product Mix   set of all products and items that a particular marketer offers for sale (p. 214)

Product Value Analysis   approach to cost reduction in which components are carefully studied to determine if they can be redesigned or standardized or made by cheaper methods of production (p. 142)

Profitable Customer   a person, household, or company that over time yields a revenue stream that exceeds by an acceptable amount the company's cost stream of attracting, selling, and servicing that customer (p. 51)

Public   any group that has an actual or potential interest in or impact on a company's ability to achieve its objectives (p. 322)

Public Relations (PR)   variety of programs that are designed to promote or protect a company's image or its individual products (p. 322)

Reference Groups   all the groups that have a direct (face-to-face) or indirect influence on a person's attitudes or behavior (p. 113)

Retailer   any business enterprise whose sales volume comes primarily from retailing (p. 285)

Retail Store   any business enterprise whose sales volume comes primarily from retailing (p. 285)

Sales Budget   conservative estimate of the expected sales volume, and is used primarily for making current purchasing, production, and cash-flow decisions (p. 96)

Sales Promotion   key ingredient in many marketing campaigns, consists of a diverse collection of incentive tools, mostly short term, designed to stimulate trial, or quicker or greater purchase, of particular products or services by consumers or the trade (p. 318)

Sales Quota   sales goal set for a product line, company division, or sales representative (p. 96)

Satisfaction   a person's feelings of pleasure or disappointment resulting from comparing a product's perceived performance (or outcome) in relation to his or her expectations (p. 40)

Selling Concept   holds that consumers and businesses, if left alone, will ordinarily not buy enough of the organization's products (p. 13)

Service   any act or performance that one party can offer to another that is essentially intangible and does not result in the ownership of anything (p. 229)

Shopping Goods   products that the customer, in the process of selection and purchase, characteristically compares on the basis of suitability, quality, price, and style (p. 214)

Societal Marketing Concept   holds that the organization's task is to determine the needs, wants, and interests of target markets and to deliver the desired satisfactions more effectively and efficiently than competitors in a way that preserves or enhances the consumer's and the society's well-being (p. 17)

Specialty Goods   products with unique characteristics or brand identification (p. 214)

Supplies   short-lasting goods and services that facilitate developing or managing the finished product (p. 214)

Total Customer Cost   bundle of costs that customers expect to incur in evaluating, obtaining, using, and disposing of the product or service (p. 38)

Total Customer Value   bundle of benefits that customers expect from a given product or service (p. 38)

Total Quality Management (TQM)   an organization-wide approach to continuously improving the quality of all the organization's processes, products, and services (p. 52)

Trend   direction or sequence of events that have some momentum and durability (p. 99)

Unsought Goods   products that consumers do not know about or do not normally think of buying (p. 214)

Wholesaling   all of the activities involved in selling goods or services to those who buy for resale or business use (p. 290)

Index

Note: The letters *f* or *t* next to a page number indicate a figure or table.

A

Aaker, J., 117
ABC accounting, 250
Accounting, activity-based cost, 250
Accumulated production, 249, *249f*
Activity-based cost (ABC) accounting, 250
Activity-based costing (ABC), 51
ADI Technology Corporation, 135
Adoption, described, 197
Advanced Micro Devices (AMD), 244
Advertisement(s)
    banner, 32
    browser, 32
Advertising
    budget for, 313
    critical decisions in, 312, *312f*
    defined, 312
    goal of, 312–313
    informative, 312
    media strategies in, development of, 315–318, *316t*
    message in, 313–315
    objectives of, 312–313
    persuasive, 312–313
    reinforcement, 313
    reminder, 312–313
Affiliate programs, 32
Age
    as factor in buying behavior, 115–116
    of population, in demographic environment, 100–102
Albrecht, K., 46
Allegiance Healthcare, 133
Alliances programs, 32
Alpha testing, 194
Amazon.com, 220
AMD. *See* Advanced Micro Devices (AMD)
America Online (AOL), 220
American Airlines, 49

American Association of Advertising Agencies, 311
American Dreams, 179
American Express, 50, 234
American Marketing Association, 6, 216
American Society for Quality Control, 53
Anheuser-Busch, 165, 189
Annual-plan control, in marketing process, 77–79, *78f*
Anticipative marketer, 14
Anticipatory pricing, 261
Anti-pollution pressures, 103
Appeal(s)
    emotional, 306
    moral, 306
    rational, 305–306
Area market potential, 97–98
Arts & Entertainment (A&E) network, marketing management at, 211–212
Aspirational groups, 113
Atmosphere
    service's, in retailing, 288–289
    store's, in retailing, 288–289
Attention, selective, 118
Attitude(s), buying behavior and, 119–120
Auction-type pricing, 254–255
Audience, target, in marketing communications, 303–304
Audit, marketing, 80
Auditing, brand, 223–224
Augmented product, 213, *213f*
Available market, 94
Average cost, 248
Avon, 126

B

B2B. *See* Business-to-business (B2B)
B2C. *See* Business-to-consumer (B2C)
Bailey Controls, 44
BAMT. *See* Brand asset management team (BAMT)
Banner ads, 32
Basic product, 212, *213f*

BATNA (Best Alternative to a Negotiated Agreement), 344
Beck's North America, 311
Behavior(s)
    buyer, 111–130, 131–147
    buying, in consumer buying decision process, 120–121, *121t*
    consumer. *See* Consumer buying, behavior associated with
Behavior buying, business. *See* Organizational buying
Behavioral responses, 9, *9f*
Behavioral segmentation, 178–179
Belief(s), buying behavior and, 119–120
Benchmark(s), 44
Benchmarking, 18
Benefit(s), core, 212, *213f*
Berry, L.L., 49, 235, *235f*
Beta testing, 194
Biography Web, 211
Blanket contract, 144
Bonding, brand, 217
Bonoma, T.V., 76
Bose Corporation, 140
Boston Beer, 4
Boston Consulting Group (BCG) model, in strategic planning, 61–62, *61f*
Bowser ads, 32
Brand(s), 8
    defined, 216, *217t*
    new, 222, 223
Brand asset management team (BAMT), 74
Brand auditing, 223–224
Brand bonding, 217
Brand competition, 10–11
Brand decisions, 216–224, *217t, 219f, 221t*
    brand auditing, 223–224
    brand equity, 217–218
    brand identity, building of, 216–217
    brand strategy decision, 222–223
    branding vs. nonbranding, 218–220
    brand-name decision, 221–222, *221t*
    brand-sponsor decision, 220–221
    challenges in, 218–222, *219f, 221t*
    packaging, 224–225

Brand equity, 47, 217–218
Brand extensions, 222–223
Brand identity, building of, 216–217
Brand ladder, 220
Brand meaning, levels of, 216, *217t*
Brand parity, 220
Brand personality, 117
Brand strategy, 211–227
Brand strategy decision, 222–223
Brand valuation, 218
Brand-management organization of marketing department, 73–74
Brand-name strategies, *221t*
Brand-sponsor decision, 220–221
Brick-to-click companies, vs. pure click companies, 29–30
Broad environment, 11
Brown, S.W., 237
Budget(s), for marketing communications, 308–309
Business(es)
    changes in, 18–19
    new, planning of, 64–65
    older, downsizing of, 64–65
Business analysis, in new product development, 193–194
Business buying behavior, 131–147. *See* Organizational buying
Business database, 34
Business markets
    analysis of, 131–147
    purchasing/procurement process in, 141–144, *142t*
    segmentation of, 175–181, *176t, 180t*
    vs. consumer market, 132–133, *134t–135t*
Business mission, in business strategic planning, 65, *65f*
Business practices, changes in, 25–26, *26t*
Business regulation, legislation in, 105
Business strategic planning, 65–69, *65f*
    business mission in, 65, *65f*
    external environment analysis in, 65–66, *65f*
    feedback and control in, *65f*, 69
    goal formulation in, *65f*, 66
    internal environment analysis in, *65f*, 66
    program formulation in, *65f*, 67–68
    strategy formulation in, *65f*, 67
    SWOT analysis in, 65, *65f*
Business-goods market testing, 195–196
Business-to-business (B2B), 27, *28f*
Business-to-consumer (B2C), 27
Buyer behavior, 111–130
Buygrid framework, 141, *142t*
Buying, organizational. *See* Organizational buying
Buying behavior, 131–147. *See also* Organizational buying
    in consumer buying decision process, 120–121, *121t*

Buying center, 137
Buying role, in consumer buying decision process, 120
Buyphases, 141, *142t*

C

C2B. *See* Consumer-to-business (C2B)
C2C. *See* Consumer-to-consumer (C2C)
Canon, 74
Capital items, 214
CarMax, marketing management at, 266–267
Case Pilot, 81, 107–108
Catalog marketing, 325–326
Caterpillar
    attracting and retaining customers at, 44–50, *47f, 49f*
    customer value and satisfaction at, 38–41, *39f*
    defining of, 38–41, *39f*
    delivering of, 43–44, *43f*
    high-performance business at, nature of, 41–43, *42f*
    marketing management at, 37–38
    total customer satisfaction at, 40–41
Cause-related marketing, 17–18
Cellular One, 48
Channel differentiation, 206–207
Channel partners, 19
Citibank, 172
Claritas, Inc., 179
Club Med, 230–231
Co-branding, 222, 223
Coca-Cola, 159, 189
Colgate, 74
Colgate-Palmolive, 100
Commercialization, 196
    in new product development, 194–196
Communicating, in positioning, 204
Communication(s)
    integrated marketing, 19, 302–331
    marketing, integrated. *See also* Integrated marketing communications
Communication channels, 10
Communication-effect research, 318
Company adjustments, 18
Company demand, 96–97
Company responses, 18
Company sales forecast, 96–97
Company sales potential, 96
Companywide marketing orientation, in marketing process, 75–76
Competing on Value, 40
Competition, 10–11, 148–169
    cost structure in, 152
    degree of differentiation in, 151–152
    entry barriers in, 152
    exit barriers in, 152

globalization in, 153
industry concept of, 151–153
market concept of, 153, *153f*
marketing channel—related, 280–281
mobility barriers in, 152
monopolistic, 152
sellers in, number of, 151–152
vertical integration in, 152
Competitive intelligence system, 156–158
    designing of, 156–157
    selection of competitor to attack and avoid, 157–158
Competitive markets, 149–153, *149f, 150f, 153f*
    attractiveness of, 149–150, *149f, 150f*
Competitive strategies
    balancing customer and competitor orientations, 166–167
    designing of, 158–167
    market-challenger, 161–164, *162f*
    market-follower, 164–165
    market-leader, 158–161, *160f*
    market-niche, 165, *166t*
Competitor(s), 149–153, *149f, 150f, 153f*
    classes of, 157–158
    costs, price, and offers of, in price setting, 250
    identification of, 151
    selection of, for avoiding and attacking, 157–158
Competitor analysis, 154–156, *154f, 155t*
    objectives in, 154–155
    reaction patterns in, 155–156
    strategies in, 154, *154f*
    strengths in, 155, *155t*
    weaknesses in, 155, *155t*
Competitor-centered company, 165–166
Complex buying behavior, 120
Concentration, defined, 317
Concept development for new products, *191f*, 192, *192f*
Concept testing for new products, *191f*, 192–193
Conflict, marketing channel—related, 280–281
Conformance quality, product differentiation on, 205
Connectivity, 24
Consumer adoption process, 197–198, *197f*
    factors influencing, 197–198, *197f*
    stages in, 197
Consumer behavior. *See* Consumer buying, behavior associated with
Consumer buying
    behavior associated with, 112–120
        attitudes, 119–120
        beliefs, 119–120
        cultural factors, 113, *114t*
        learning, 119
        personal factors, 115–117

psychological factors, 117–120
social factors, 113–115, *114t*
patterns of, 112–120
Consumer buying decision process, 120–126
alternatives in, evaluation of, 122–124, *122f*
buying behavior in, 120–121, *121t*
buying roles in, 120
information search in, 122, *122f*, 123
postpurchase behavior in, *122f*, 124–126, *126f*
problem recognition in, 122, *122f*
purchase decision in, *122f*, 124
stages of, 121–126, *122f*, *123f*, *126f*
Consumer markets
analysis of, 111–130
segmentation of, 175–181, *176t*, *180t*
vs. business market, 132–133, *134t–135t*
Consumer-goods market testing, 195
Consumer-to-business (C2B), 28
Consumer-to-consumer (C2C), 27–28
Containerization, 299
Continuity, defined, 317
Contractual sales force, 334
Controlled test marketing, 195
Convenience goods, 214
Conventional marketing channel, 278
Cooper, R.G., 190
Cooperation, marketing channel—related, 280–281
Core benefit, 212, *213f*
Core competency, 42
Core values, 178
persistence of, 106
Corporate culture, 43
Corporate retailing, 287, *287t*
Corporate strategic planning, 59–65, *61f*, *63f*
Corporate-divisional organization of marketing department, 75
Cost(s)
average, 248
fixed, 248
total, 248
types of, 248–249
variable, 248
Cost estimation, in price setting, 248–250, *249f*
Cost inflation, 261
Costing, target, 250
Covisint, marketing management at, 131–132
CPA. *See* Customer profitability analysis (CPA)
CPS. *See* Critical path scheduling (CPS)
Creative marketer, 14
Creativity, in marketing process, 76
Credit, availability of, 102–103
Critical path scheduling (CPS), 196

CRM. *See* Customer relationship management (CRM)
Cultural factors
in consumer buying, 113, *114t*
effects on organizational buying, *138f*, 140–141
Cultural values, secondary, shifts through time, 106
Culture(s)
corporate, 43
defined, 113
marketing across, 141
organizational, 42–43
Current demand, estimation of, 97–98
Customer(s)
attracting of, 44–50, *47f*, *49f*
lost, 45
winning back, 48
profitable, 51
satisfying of, 237–238
Customer bonds, forming of, 49–50
Customer churn, 45
Customer communities, 27
Customer complaints, satisfying of, 237
Customer concept, 16–17, *17f*
Customer databases, 19
in customer relationship marketing, 34
Customer equity, 47
Customer lifetime value, 19, 45
Customer mailing list, 34
Customer management organizations, 74
Customer needs, 14
Customer perceived value, 38–40, *39f*
Customer profitability, 50–52, *52f*
Customer profitability analysis (CPA), 51
Customer relationship management (CRM), 44
Customer relationship marketing (CRM), 19, 33–35, *34t*, 47–49, *47f*, *49f*
customer databases in, 34
data warehouses in, 34–35
datamining in, 34–35
Customer retention, 44–50, *47f*, *49f*
need for, 45–46
Customer satisfaction, 37–56
at Caterpillar, delivering of, 43–44, *43f*
defining of, 38–41, *39f*
gauging of, 125
Customer service, trends in, 240–241
Customer share, 19
Customer value
at Caterpillar, delivering of, 43–44, *43f*
defining of, 38–41, *39f*
Customer value analysis, 157
Customer value hierarchy, 212
Customer value triad, 8
Customer-centered company, 166
Customer-development process, 47, *47f*

Customer-driven engineering, 193
Customerization, 25
Customer-performance scorecard, 79
Customization, 25

D

DaimlerChrysler, 139
Data warehouses, in customer relationship marketing, 34–35
Database(s)
business, 34
customer, 19
in customer relationship marketing, 34
Database marketing, 34
Datamining, 34–35
Debt, 102–103
Decline stage of product life cycle, *199f*, 201–202
Dell computer, 40–41
Dell, M., 41
Demand, in price setting, 247–248
Demand chain planning, 295
Demand measurement, 95–96, *95f*
Deming prize, 52
Deming, W.E., 52
Demographic environment, 100–102
educational groups in, 101
ethnic markets in, 101
geographical shifts in population in, 101–102
household patterns in, 101
population age mix in, 100–102
shift from mass market to micromarkets in, 102
worldwide population growth in, 100
Demographic segmentation, 175–177, 176t
Dexter Corporation, 12
Diesel, 158
Differentiation
channel, 206–207
defined, 204
image, 207
management of, 234
personnel, 206
product, 204–205
services, 206
tools in, 204–207, *205t*
Digitalization, 24
Direct mail, 325, *326t*
Direct marketing, 323–328, *326t*
benefits of, 324
catalog marketing, 325–326
channels for, 325–328, *326t*
described, 323–324
direct mail, 325, *326t*
direct-response television marketing, 327

Direct marketing, (cont.)
  E-marketing, 327–328
  face-to-face selling, 325
  growth of, 324
  integrated, 324
  kiosk marketing, 327
  telemarketing, 326–327
Direct product profitability (DPP), in retailing, 288
Direct sales force, 334
Direct-response television marketing, 327
Discovery Group, 92
Discrimination, 119
Discriminatory pricing, 257–259
Disintermediation, 24–25
Dissatisfier(s), defined, 118
Dissociative groups, 113
Dissonance-reducing buying behavior, 120
Distortion, selective, 118
Distribution channels, 10
Diversity marketing, 113
Division strategic planning, 59–65, 61f, 63f
DoCoMo, defined, 23
DPP. See Direct product profitability (DPP)
Drive, defined, 119
Drucker, P., 6, 59–60, 69
Dual branding, 223
Due(s), defined, 119
DuPont, 74, 76, 79, 253
Durability, product differentiation on, 205
Dutch auctions, 254

E

Eastman Kodak, 153
EBay, marketing management at, 1–2
E-business, 26, 28f, 30
E-commerce, 18, 26
Economic circumstances, buying behavior and, 116
Economic environment, 102–103
Economy, new, 2–3. See also Marketing practices, changes in
  major drivers of, 24–25
  vs. old economy, 26t
EDLP. See Everyday low pricing (EDLP)
Edmund's, 7
Educational groups, in demographic environment, 101
Efficiency control, in marketing process, 79
El-Ansary, 268
E-marketing, 26, 327–328
Emotional appeals, 306
Employee(s), satisfying of, 237–238
Energy costs, increased, 103
English auctions, 254
Entrepreneurial marketing, 4

Entry barriers, in competition, 152
Environment
  broad, 11
  demographic, 100–102. See also Demographic environment
  marketing, 11
  natural, 103
  task, 11
Environmental factors, effects on organizational buying, 138–139, 138f
Environmental threat, 66
E-purchasing, 26
Equity
  brand, 47, 217–218
  customer, 47
  relationship, 47
  value, 47
Ericsson, 158
Essence, 179
Ethical issues
  in market target selection, 184–185
  marketing channel—related, 281–282
Ethnic markets, in demographic environment, 101
E*TRADE, marketing management at, 228–229
European Quality Award, 52
Everyday low pricing (EDLP), 253
Exchange, 8
Exclusive dealing, 281
Expected product, 212, 213f
External environment analysis, in business strategic planning, 65–66, 65f
External marketing, 15

F

Face-to-face selling, 325
Fad, defined, 99
Family, buying behavior and, 114–115
Family of orientation, 114–115
Feedback and control, in business strategic planning, 65f, 69
Fisher, R., 344
Fixed costs, 248
Flexible market offering, 172
Flighting, defined, 317
Ford, 132
Ford, H., 171
Forecasting, defined, 98
Forecasting and demand measurement, 94–98, 95f, 98t
  company demand in, 96–97
  economic environment in, 102–103
  estimating current demand in, 97–98
  estimating future demand in, 98, 98t
  markets to measure in, 94–95
  natural environment in, 103
  political-legal environment in, 104–105

sales forecast in, 96–97
  secondary cultural values through time, 106
  social-cultural environment in, 105–106
  technological environment in, 103–104
Form competition, 10–11
Freud(s) S., 117, 118
Functional hubs, 143
Functional organization of marketing department, 73
Functional quality, 232
Funtime film, 215

G

Gain-and-risk sharing pricing, 256
Gap, 220
Gates, B., 43
General Electric (GE), 139–140
General Electric (GE) model, in strategic planning, 62–63, 63f
General Foods, 79
General Motors (GM), 13, 73–74, 140
General need description, 142, 142t
General Services Administration, 135
Generic composition, 10–11
Gen-Xers, 101
Geoclustering, 179–180
Geographic organization of marketing department, 73
Geographic segmentation, 175
Geographical pricing, 257
Geographical shifts in population, in demographic environment, 101–102
Geographical-expansion strategy, 158
G&F Industries, 140
Global organization of marketing department, 75
Globalization, in competition, 153
Goal formulation, in business strategic planning, 65f, 66
Godin, S., 327
Going-rate pricing, 253–254
Goods, types of, 214
Government(s), changing role of, 103
Government market, 133, 135
Gronroos, C., 232
Group pricing, 255
Growth stage of product life cycle, 199f, 200
Guerilla warfare, described, 163

H

Habitual buying behavior, 120–121
Hallmark, marketing management at, 170–171

Harley-Davidson, 4
Harvard, 43
Henderson, B., 155
Herzberg, F., 117, 118
Hewlett-Packard, 143–144
High standards, 236
High-low pricing, 253
High-performance business
    at Caterpillar, 41–43, *42f*
    organization of, 42–43, *42f*
    organizational culture of, 42–43, *42f*
    processes in, 41–42, *42f*
    resources in, 42, *42f*
    stakeholders in, 41, *42f*
High-performance companies, 41, *42f*
Hitachi Data Systems, 88
Holding, R., 165
Horizontal marketing system, 279
Horn Group, 230
Household patterns, in demographic
    environment, 101

I

IBM, 220
Idea generation for new products, 191,
    191f
Idea screening for new products,
    191–192, *191f*
ILS. *See* Integrated logistics systems (ILS)
Image differentiation, 207
Income distribution, 102
Individual factors, effects on organiza-
    tional buying, *138f*, 140
Individual marketing, 173
Industry, defined, 151
Industry competition, 10–11
Industry convergence, 25
Infomediaries, 27
Information Resources, Inc., 89
Informative advertising, 312
Innovation, unlimited opportunities for,
    104
Innovation diffusion process, 197
Inseparability, of services, 230
Institutional market, 133
Intangibility, of services, 229–230
Integrated direct marketing, 324
Integrated logistics systems (ILS), 295
Integrated marketing, 15
Integrated marketing communications,
    19, 302–331. *See also* Marketing com-
    munications
    advertising campaign for, developing
        and managing, 312–318, *312f,*
        316t, 318f. See also Advertising
    described, 311
    designing and managing of, 302–331
    direct marketing in, 323–328, *326t*
    public relations in, 322–323

sales promotion in, 318–321, *320t*
Intel, marketing management at, 244–245
Interactive marketing, 232
Internal environment analysis, in business
    strategic planning, *65f*, 66
Internal marketing, 15, 16, 232
Internal record system, 87
Internet domains
    business-to-business (B2B), 27, *28f*
    business-to-consumer (B2C), 27
    consumer-to-business (C2B), 28
    consumer-to-consumer (C2C), 27–28
    pure click vs. brick-to-click compa-
        nies, 29–30
Interpersonal factors, effects on organiza-
    tional buying, *138f*, 140
Interstitial(s), 32
Intrepreneurial marketing, 4
Introduction stage of product life cycle,
    199f, 200
Inventory, in marketing logistics, 297–298,
    298f

J

Jaworski, B.J., 153
John Deere, 220
Johnson & Johnson, 79
Just-in-time (JIT) production, 140

K

Keller, K., 223–224
Kimberly-Clark's Kleenex, 222
Kinko's, 102
Kiosk marketing, 327
Kleinschmidt, E.J., 190
Knox, S., 40
Knoxville News—Sentinel, 144
Koch, J., 4
Kodak, 25, 215
Komatsu, vs. Caterpillar, 38–41, *39f*
Ko-operative Wijnbouwers Vereniging,
    119
Kraft, 172
Krispy Kreme, 73–74
Krugman, H.E., 314

L

Labeling, 225
Labonte, C., 140
Laddering, 117–118
Lanning, M., 40
Lauterborn, R., 11
Learning, buying behavior and, 119
Legal issues, marketing channel—related,
    281–282

Legislation, in buiness regulation, 105
Lemon, K.A., 47
Levi Strauss, 158
Levitt, T., 14, 60–61, 164
Life stage, as factor in buying behavior,
    115–116
Lifestyle, buying behavior and,
    116–117
Line extensions, 222
Line featuring, 216
Line filling, 216
Line modernization, 216
Line pruning, 216
Line stretching, 215
Little, A.D., 155
L.L. Bean, 46
Local marketing, 172
Lycos(s) T., 14

M

Macroenvironment
    demographic forces in, 100–102
    trends and forces in, 99–107
Madique, M.A., 190
Maier, F., Jr., 89
Maklan, S., 40
Malcolm Baldrige National Quality
    Award, 52, 143
Mall of America, marketing management
    at, 284–285
March of Dimes, 314
Market(s)
    available, 94
    business, vs. consumer market,
        132–133, *134t–135t*
    consumer
        analysis of, 111–130
        vs. business market, 132–133,
            134t–135t
    defined, 94
    demands of
    government, 133, 135
    institutional, 133
    measurement of, 94–95
    needs of, 7–8
    penetrated, 95
    potential, 94
    served, 94–95
    target, 6, *7f*, 94–95
        in retailing, 288
        selection of, 170–187
        in wholesaling, 293
Market channel members, evaluation of,
    276
Market demand, 95
Market demand function, 95
Market makers, 27
Market management organization, 74
Market minimum, 95

Market offering, 6
  components of, 212, *212f*
Market opportunity analysis (MOA), 66
Market potential, 96
  area, 97–98
  total, 97
Market segment, described, 171
Market segmentation
  of business markets, bases for,
      180–181, *180t*
  described, 171–172
  effective, 174–175
  individual marketing, 173
  local marketing, 172
  niche marketing, 172
  patterns of, 173–174, *173f*
  process of, 174, *174t*
  segmenting consumer and business
      markets, 175–181, *176t, 180t*
  use of, 171–175, *173f, 174t*
Market segments, 6
  evaluation of, 181–184, *183f*
  identification of, 170–187
  selection of, 181–184, *183f*
Market target(s), ethical choice of,
    184–185
Market targeting strategies, 181–185,
    183f
  multiple segments, 184
  supersegments, 184
Market-challenger strategies, 161–164,
    162f
Marketer(s)
  adjustments of, 19
  anticipative, 14
  creative, 14
  decisions made by, 5
  and prospects, 7
  responses of, 19
  responsive, 14
Market-follower strategies, 164–165
Marketing
  adaption to new economy, 23–36
  catalog, 325–326
  cause-related, 17–18
  changes in, 18–19
  concepts of, 6
    core, 6–11, *7f, 9f, 12f*
  customer relationship, 19, 33–35, *34t,*
    47–49, *47f, 49f. See also* Customer
    relationship marketing (CRM)
  database, 34
  defined, 6
  direct, 323–328, *326t. See also* Direct
    marketing
  diversity, 113
  entrepreneurial, 4
  external, 15
  individual, 173
  integrated, 15

  interactive, 232
  internal, 15, 16, 232
  intrepreneurial, 4
  local, 172
  mass, 171
  niche, 172
  permission, 327
  relationship, 9–10, 344
    levels of, 49, 49f
  scope of, 5–6
  segment, 171–172
  target, 19
  tools for, 6
  for twenty-first century, defining of,
      1–22
Marketing across cultures, 141
Marketing audit, 80
Marketing channel(s)
  alternatives for, 273–274
    evaluation of, 274–275, *274f*
  analyzing customers' desired service
      output levels in, 272
  arrangement of, modifying of,
      276–278, *278f*
  competition associated with,
      280–281
  conflict associated with, 280–281
  constraints for, 272–273
  conventional, 278
  cooperation associated with, 280–281
  design decisions for, 271–275, *274f*
  dynamics of, 278–282
  ethical issues related, 281–282
  flows of, 269–270, *270f*
  functions of, 269–270, *270f*
  legal issues related to, 281–282
  levels of, 270–271, *271f*
  management decisions for, 275–278,
      278f
  objectives of, 272–273
  service sector, 271
  work performed by, 268–271,
      269f–271f
Marketing channel members
  motivating of, 276
  selection of, 275
  training of, 275
Marketing channel system
  defined, 267
  designing and managing of, 266–283
Marketing channels, 10
Marketing communications. *See also*
    Integrated marketing communications
  budget for, 308–309
  channels for, 307–308
  communication objectives in, 304–305
  developing effective, 303–311, *304t,*
    305f, 310f
  effectiveness of, evaluation of, 318,
    318f

  integrated, 302–331. *See also*
      Integrated marketing communica-
      tions
  managing process of, 311
  marketing communications mix in,
      309–311, *310f*
  message in, designing of, 305–307
  results of, measurement of, 311
  target audience identification in,
      303–304
Marketing concept, 13–14
Marketing decision support system
    (MDSS), 94
Marketing department, organization of,
    72–75
Marketing environment, 11
Marketing implementation, in marketing
    process, 76
Marketing information systems (MISs),
    86–94, *88t, 89f*
  Case Pilot, 107–108
  described, 86–87
  internal record system, 87
  marketing intelligence system, 87–88,
    88t
  marketing research, 89–94, *89f, 93t*
  MDSS, 94
Marketing intelligence system, 87–88,
    88t
Marketing logistics, 294–299, *298f*
  decisions in, 296–299, *298f*
  described, 294
  inventory in, 297–298, *298f*
  lessons learned from, 299
  objectives of, 295–296
  order processing in, 296–297
  transportation in, 298–299
  warehousing in, 297
Marketing management
  at Arts & Entertainment (A&E)
      network, 211–212
  at CarMax, 266–267
  at Caterpillar, 37–38
  at Covisint, 131–132
  described, 12
  at eBay, 1–2
  at E*TRADE, 228–229
  at Hallmark, 170–171
  at Intel, 244–245
  at Proctor & Gamble, 148–149
  at Red Bull, 188–189
  at Starbucks, 57–84
  at Tesco, 85–110
  at Tiffany, 332–333
  at Whirlpool, 111–130
  at Yahoo!, 302–333
Marketing mix, 11, *12f*
Marketing network, 10
Marketing offers, differentiated,
    249–250

Marketing opportunity, 66
Marketing practices, changes in
    customer relationship marketing—
        related, 33–35, *34t*
    E-business—related, 26–30, *28f*
    Web site—related, 30–33
Marketing process, 69–72, *69f*, *71f*
    annual-plan control in, 77–79, *78f*
    companywide marketing orientation
        in, 75–76
    control in, 76–77, *77t*
    creativity in organization in, 76
    described, 69
    efficiency control in, 79
    evaluation of, 76–77, *77t*
    management of, 72–80, *77t*, *78f*
    marketing department organization
        in, 72–75
    marketing implementation in, 76
    product planning in, 71–72
    profitability control in, 79
    steps in, 69–71, *71f*
    strategic control in, 80
    value-delivery sequence in, *69f*, 69–70
Marketing program, 11, *12f*
Marketing public relations (MPR),
    322
    decisions in, 322–323, *323t*
    defined, 322
Marketing research, 89–94, *89f*, *93t*
    contact methods in, 92–94, *93t*
    data sources in, 90
    defined, 89
    research approaches to, 90–91
    research instruments in, 91–92
    sampling plan in, 92
    steps in, 90
Marketing research process, 89, *89f*
Marketing strategies, for service firms,
    231–239, *232f*, *233f*, *235f*. *See also*
    Service firms, marketing strategies for
Marketing strategy development, 193
Marketing systems
    horizontal, 279
    multichannel, 279–280
    vertical, 278–279
Marketing tasks, 4
Market-leader strategies, 158–161, *160f*
Market-management/customer-
    management organization of
    marketing department, 74
Market-niche strategies, 165, *166t*
Market-oriented strategic planning, 58
Market-penetration strategy, 158
Marketplace, 7
    company orientations toward, 12–18,
        17f
Marketspace, 7
Markup pricing, 250–251
Markup-buildup method, 97

Marriott Hotel, 215
Maslow, A., 117, 118
Mass marketing, 171
MasterCard, 234
Materials and parts, 214
Maturity stage of product life cycle, *199f*,
    201
Maximum market share, 246
Maytag, 246
McDonald's, 8, 73, 158
MCI, 87
M-commerce, 24
MDSS. *See* Marketing decision support
    system (MDSS)
Membership groups, 113
Message(s), in marketing communications,
    designing of, 305–307
Metamarket, 7, 121
Metamediaries, 121
Microenvironment actors, 65–66
Microenvironment forces, 65–66
Micromarket(s), mass market to, in
    demographic environment, 102
Microsite(s), 32
Microsoft, 43, 328
Miller, H., 99
MISs. *See* Marketing information systems
    (MISs)
Mission statements, 60
Missionary sales force, 136
Mitsubishi, 132
MOA. *See* Market opportunity analysis
    (MOA)
Mobility barriers, in competition, 152
Modified rebuy, 136
Monitoring systems, 236–237
Monopolistic competition, 152
Monster.com, 3
Moral appeals, 306
Motivation, buying behavior and,
    117–118
Motive(s), defined, 117
Motorola, 60, 69, 158
MPR. *See* Marketing public relations
    (MPR)
Multiattribute segmentation, 179–180
Multibrands, 222, 223
Multichannel marketing systems,
    279–280

N

NAICS. *See* North American Industry
    Classification System (NAICS)
Natural environment, 103
NEC, 215
Negotiation strategy, 344
Network(s), 9–10
    marketing, 10

New brands, 222, 223
New economy. *See* Economy, new
New product(s)
    commercialization of, 194–196
    failure of, 190
    life cycle of
        critique of concept of, 202
        marketing through, 198–202, *199f*,
            199t
        stages in, *199f*, 200–202
    management of, 190–194, *191f*, *192f*
    success of, 190
    types of, 189–190
New product development
    business analysis in, 193–194
    challenges in, 189–190
    commercialization in, 194–196
    concept development in, *191f*, 192,
        192f
    concept testing in, *191t*, 192–193
    idea generation in, 191, *191f*
    idea screening in, 191–192, *191f*
    management of, 194–196
    market testing in, 195–196
    marketing strategy development in,
        193
    positioning and differentiation strat-
        egy in, 202–207, *205t*
    stages in, 190–194, *191f*, *192f*
New York Daily News, 144
New-market segment strategy, 158
Newsweek, 317
New-task buying, 136
Niche, defined, 172
Niche marketing, 172
Nike, 42
Nippon Telephone and Telegraph (NTT)
    DoCoMo (NTT DoCoMo), marketing
    management at, 23–24
Nokia, 69, 158
North American Industry Classification
    System (NAICS), 97
NTT DoCoMo. *See also* Nippon
    Telephone and Telegraph (NTT)
    DoCoMo
    marketing management at, 23–24

O

Occupation, buying behavior and, 116
Offering, 8
Old Spice, 224
Oligopoly, defined, 151–152
Oliver, R.W., 314
One-level marketing channel, 270, *271f*
Opinion leader, 114
Order processing, in marketing logistics,
    296–297
Order-routine specification, 144

Organization
  of high-performance business, 42–43, *42f*
  of marketing department, 72–75
Organizational buying
  case study of, 145
  cultural factors in, *138f*, 140–141
  described, 132–137, *134t–135t*
  environmental factors in, 138–139, *138f*
  individual factors in, *138f*, 140
  influences on, 138–141, *138f*
  interpersonal factors in, *138f*, 140
  organizational factors in, *138f*, 139–140
  process of, participants in, 137–141, *138f*
  purchasing/procurement process in, 141–144, *142t*
  situations of, 136–137
Organizational buying behavior, case study of, 145
Organizational culture, 42–43
Organizational factors, effects on organizational buying, *138f*, 139–140
Organizational markets
  case study of, 145
  specialized, 133, 135
Outsourcing, 18
Overdemand, 262
Overhead, 248

P

Package, defined, 224
Packaging, 224–225
Packard, D., 15
Pampers Parenting Institute, 220
Parasuraman, A., 49, 235, *235f*
Parker, 88
Partial cost recovery, 247
Partner relationship management (PRM), 44
Penetrated market, 95
Perceived-value pricing, 253
Perception, buying behavior and, 118
Performance quality, product differentiation on, 205
Performance review, 144
Perishability, of services, 230–231, *231t*
Permission marketing, 327
Personal factors, buying behavior and, 115–117
Personal selling, principles of, 341–344, *341f, 342f*
Personality, buying behavior and, 117
Personnel differentiation, 206
Persuasive advertising, 312–313
Place decision

  in retailing, 289–290, *289f*
  in wholesaling, 294
Political–legal environment, 104–105
Popcorn, F., 99
Population, age mix in, in demographic environment, 100–102
Population growth, worldwide, in demographic environment, 100
Porter, M., 43, 149
Positioning, defined, 202
Positioning strategies
  communication in, 204
  differentiation in, 204
  ideas to promote in, 203–204
  views of, 202–203
Postsale service strategy, 240
Potential market, 94
Potential product, 213, *213f*
Preference segments, 173
Presale service strategy, 239–240
Price
  adapting of, 256–260, *258t, 259t*
  final, 255–256
  reference, 255
  value-in-use, 253
Price allowances, 257, *258t*
Price changes
  competitors', responding to, 262–263
  reactions to, 262
Price cuts, initiation of, 260–261
Price decision
  in retailing, 289
  in wholesaling, 293
Price discounts, 257, *258t*
Price elasticity of demand, 248
Price increases, initiation of, 261–262
Price sensitivity, 247
Pricing, 244–265
  adapting price in, 256–260, *258t, 259t*
  anticipatory, 261
  auction-type, 254–255
  changes in
    initiation of, 260–263, *261t*
    responding to, 260–263, *261t*
  competitors' costs, prices, and offers and, 250
  cost estimation in, 248–250, *249f*
  demand and, 247–248
  discriminatory, 257–259
  everyday low, 253
  final price and, 255–256
  gain-and-risk sharing, 256
  geographical, 257
  going-rate, 253–254
  group, 255
  high-low, 253
  impact on other parties, 256
  influence of other marketing-mix elements in, 256
  markup, 250–251

  method of, 250–255, *251f, 252f*
  objectives in, 245–247
  perceived-value, 253
  product-mix, 259–260
  promotional, 257, *259t*
  psychological, 255
  setting price in, 245–256, *246f, 249f, 251f, 252f*
  target-return, 251–253, *252f*
  value, 253
Pricing policies, 256
Prime contractors, 136–137
PRIZM, 179
PRM. *See* Partner relationship management (PRM)
Process(es), in high-performance business, 41–42, *42f*
Procter & Gamble, 89
Proctor & Gamble, 3, 220
  marketing management at, 148–149
Product(s), 8
  augmented, 213, *213f*
  basic, 212, *213f*
  classifications of, 213–214
  defined, 212
  expected, 212, *213f*
  potential, 213, *213f*
  types of, evaluation continuum for, *233f*
Product assortment, 214–215
  in retailing, 288
  in wholesaling, 293
Product concept, 13, 192
Product development
  new. *See* New product development
  through life cycle, 188–210
Product differentiation, 204–205
Product idea, 192
Product levels, 212–213, *213f*
Product mix, 214–215
Product planning, 71–72
Product procurement, in retailing, 288
Product services, in wholesaling, 293
Product specification, 142, *142t*
Product strategy, 211–227
Product support services, management of, 239–241
Product value analysis, 142
Production, accumulated, 249, *249f*
Production concept, 12–13
Productivity, management of, 238–239
Product-line analysis, 216
Product-line decisions, 215–216
Product-line length, 215–216
Product-management organization of marketing department, 73–74
Product-management/market-management organization of marketing department, 74–75
Product-mix pricing, 259–260
Product-quality leaders, 246

Profitability, 15–16
Profitability control, in marketing process, 79
Profitable customer, 51
Program formulation, in business strategic planning, 65f, 67–68
Promotion decision
in retailing, 289
in wholesaling, 293
Promotional pricing, 257, 259t
Proposal solicitation, 142t, 143
Prospect(s), defined, 7
Prosumer(s), 25
Prudential, 234
Psychographic segmentation, 177–178
Psychographics, 116–117
Psychological factors, buying behavior and, 117–120
Psychological pricing, 255
Public relations, 322–323
marketing in, 322
Pulsing, defined, 317
Purchasing/procurement process, in organizational buying, 141–144, 142t
general need description in, 142, 142t
order-routine specification in, 144
performance review in, 144
problem recognition in, 141–142, 142t
product specification in, 142, 142t
proposal solicitation in, 142t, 143
supplier search in, 142t, 143
supplier selection in, 142t, 143–144
Pure click companies, vs. brick-to-click companies, 29–30
Putten, J.V., 50

Q

Quality
defined, 53
functional, 232
Quality function deployment (QFD), 194

R

Radical Marketing, 4
Raleigh Bicycles, 326–327
Rapid prototyping, 192–193
Rational appeals, 305–306
Raw materials, shortage of, 103.
Rayport, J.F., 153
R&D budgets, varying, 104
Rebuy
modified, 136
straight, 136
Red Bull, marketing management at, 188–189
Red Wolf beer, 165

Reengineering, 18
Reference groups, buying behavior and, 113
Reference price, 255
Reinforcement advertising, 313
Reintermediation, 24–25
Relationship(s), 9–10
Relationship equity, 47
Relationship marketing, 9–10, 344
levels of, 49, 49f
Reliability, product differentiation on, 205
Reminder advertising, 313
Repairability, product differentiation on, 205
Response(s), behavioral, 9, 9f
Responsive marketer, 14
Retailers
marketing decisions of, 287, 287t
types of, 285–287, 286t, 287t
Retailing, 284–301
corporate, 287, 287t
described, 285
marketing decisions of retailers and, 287–290, 289t
target market in, 288
trends in, 290
Retention, selective, 118
Revenue and profit model, 32–33
Rogers, E.M., 197
Role(s), buying behavior and, 115
Rural Industrial, 179
Rust, R.T., 314
Rust, T., 47

S

Safeway, 237–239
Sales budget, 96
Sales force, 337–341, 337f
compensation for, 336–337
contractual, 334
designing of, 333–337, 334f
direct, 334
evaluating sales representatives for, 337f, 340–341
motivating sales representatives for, 337f, 339–340
negotiation by, 343–344
objectives of, 333–334
personal selling principles of, 341–344, 341f, 342f
professionalism of, 342–343, 342f
recruiting and selecting sales representatives for, 337–338, 337f
relationship marketing by, 344
size of, 336
strategy for, 333–334
structure of, 334–335, 335t

supervising sales representatives for, 337f, 338–339
training sales representatives for, 337f, 338
Sales forecast, 96–97
Sales promotion, 318–321, 320t–321t
decisions in, 319–321, 320t–321t
defined, 318
purpose of, 319
tools in, 320t–321t
Sales quota, 96
San Diego Zoo, 42
Satisfaction
customer, 37–56. *See also* Customer satisfaction
defined, 40
Satisfier(s), defined, 118
Savings, 102–103
Schultz, H., 57
Schwab, C., 232
SCM. *See* Supply chain management (SCM)
Sealed-bid auctions, 255
Search qualities, 233
Secondary groups, 113
Segment marketing, 171–172
Segmentation, 6, 7f
Selective attention, 118
Selective distortion, 118
Selective retention, 118
Self-concept, buying behavior and, 117
Selling concept, 13
Served market, 94–95
Service(s)
characteristics of, 229–231, 231t
defined, 229
designing and management of, 228–243
inseparability of, 230
intangibility of, 229–230
marketing implications of, 229–231, 231t
nature of, 229–231, 231t
perishability of, 230–231, 231t
product support, management of, 239–241
variability of, 230
Service encounter, elements in, 232f
Service firms, marketing strategies for, 231–239, 232f, 233f, 235f
managing differentiation, 234
managing productivity, 238–239
managing service quality, 234–238, 235f
types of, 233f
Service mix, categories of, 229
Service quality, management of, 234–238, 235f
Service recovery, marketing skills for, 238

Service sector marketing channel, 271
Services atmosphere, in retailing, 288–289
Services differentiation, 206
Shopping goods, 214
Simulated test marketing, 195
Skin-So-Soft, 126
Social classes, 113, *114t*
Social-cultural environment, 105–106
Societal marketing concept, 17–18
Sony, 14
Southwest Airlines, 16
Special-interest groups, growth of, 105
Specialty goods, 214
Stakeholder(s), in high-performance business, 41, *42f*
Stakeholder-performance scorecard, 79
Stallkamp, T., 139
Starbucks
    historical background of, 57–58
    marketing management at, 57–84
Status(es), buying behavior and, 115
Stern, 268
Stockless purchase plans, 144
Store atmosphere, in retailing, 288–289
Straight rebuy, 136
Strategic business units (SBUs), establishment of, 60–61
Strategic concept, 236
Strategic control, in marketing process, 80
Strategic group, 67
    defined, 154
Strategic marketing plan, 58–59
Strategic planning
    Boston Consulting Group model of, 61–62, *61f*
    business, 65–69, *65f. See also* Business strategic planning
    Case Pilot in, 81
    corporate, 59–65, *61f, 63f*
    division, 59–65, *61f, 63f*
    General Electric model of, 62–63, *63f*
    key areas in, 58–59, *59f*
    market-oriented, 58
Strategy formulation, in business strategic planning, *65f*, 67
Subculture(s), 113
    existence of, 106
Supervalu, 295
Supplier search, *142t*, 143
Supplier selection, *142t*, 143–144
Supplier-partnership, 18
Supplies and business services, 214
Supply chain, 10, 44
Supply chain management (SCM), 294
SWOT analysis, in business strategic planning, 65, *65f*
Systems buying, 136–137
Systems selling, 136–137

T

Taco Bell, 313
Tactical marketing plan, 58–59
Target audience, in marketing communications, 303–304
Target costing, 250
Target market, 6, *7f*, 14, 94–95
    selection of, 170–187
    in wholesaling, 293
Target marketing, 19
Target-return pricing, 251–253, *252f*
Task environment, 11
Tax, S.S., 237
Technical quality, 232
Technological change
    accelerating pace of, 104
    increased regulation of, 104
Technological environment, 103–104
Telemarketing, 326–327
Tesco, marketing management at, 85–110
Test markets, 195
Tiffany, marketing management at, 332–333
Top-management commitment, 236
Total, 100
Total costs, 248
Total customer cost, 38
Total customer satisfaction, at Caterpillar, 40–41
Total customer value, 38
Total market potential, 97
Total quality management, implementation of, 52–53
Transaction(s), 8–9
Transfer, 9
Transportation, in marketing logistics, 298–299
Treacy, M., 203
Trend, defined, 99
Turnkey solution, 136–137
Twedt, D.W., 314
Two-level marketing channel, 270, *271f*

U

United Parcel Service (UPS), 236–237
Unsought goods, 214
UPS. *See* United Parcel Service (UPS)
Ury, W., 344
U.S. Steel, 10

V

Value(s)
    core, 178
        persistence of, 106

customer
    defining of, 38–41, *39f*
    hierarchy of, 212
    customer lifetime, 19
    customer perceived, 38–40, *39f*
    and satisfaction, 8
    total customer, 38
Value chain, 43–44, *43f*
Value delivery network, 44
Value disciplines, 203
Value equity, 47
Value networks
    defined, 267
    designing and managing of, 266–283
Value pricing, 253
Value proposition, 40
Value-delivery process, views of, 69–70, *70f*
Value-delivery system, 40
Value-in-use price, 253
Variability of services, 230
Variable costs, 248
Vertical hubs, 143
Vertical integration, in competition, 152
Vertical marketing systems, 278–279
Visa, 234

W

Wal-Mart, 42, 87
Wangvicha, S., 188
Warehouse(s), data, in customer relationship marketing, 34–35
Warehousing, in marketing logistics, 297
Warrington, S., 172
Web sites, 30–33
    building revenue and profit model on, 32–33
    designing of, 30–31
        content factors in, 30–31
        context factors in, 30
        feedback in, 31
    placing ads and promotion online for, 31–32
Welch, J.F., Jr., 52
Whirlpool, marketing management at, 111–130
Wholesaling, 290–294
    described, 290–291
    growth of, 292–293, *292t*
    marketing decisions related to, 293–294
    place decision in, 294
    price decision in, 293
    product assortment in, 293
    product services in, 293
    promotion decision in, 293
    target market in, 293
    trends in, 294
    types of, 292–293, *292t*

Wiersema, F., 203
William Wrigley Jr. Company, 268

X

Xerox, 41–42, 74, 143
Xerox Multinational Supplier Quality
    Survey, 143

Y

Yahoo!, marketing management at, 302–333

Z

Zaltman Metaphoric Elicitation
    Technique (ZMET), 91

Zeithaml, V.A., 47, 235, *235f*
Zemke, R., 46
Zero-level marketing channel, 270, *271f*
Zirger, B.J., 190
ZMET. *See* Zaltman Metaphoric
    Elicitation Technique (ZMET)